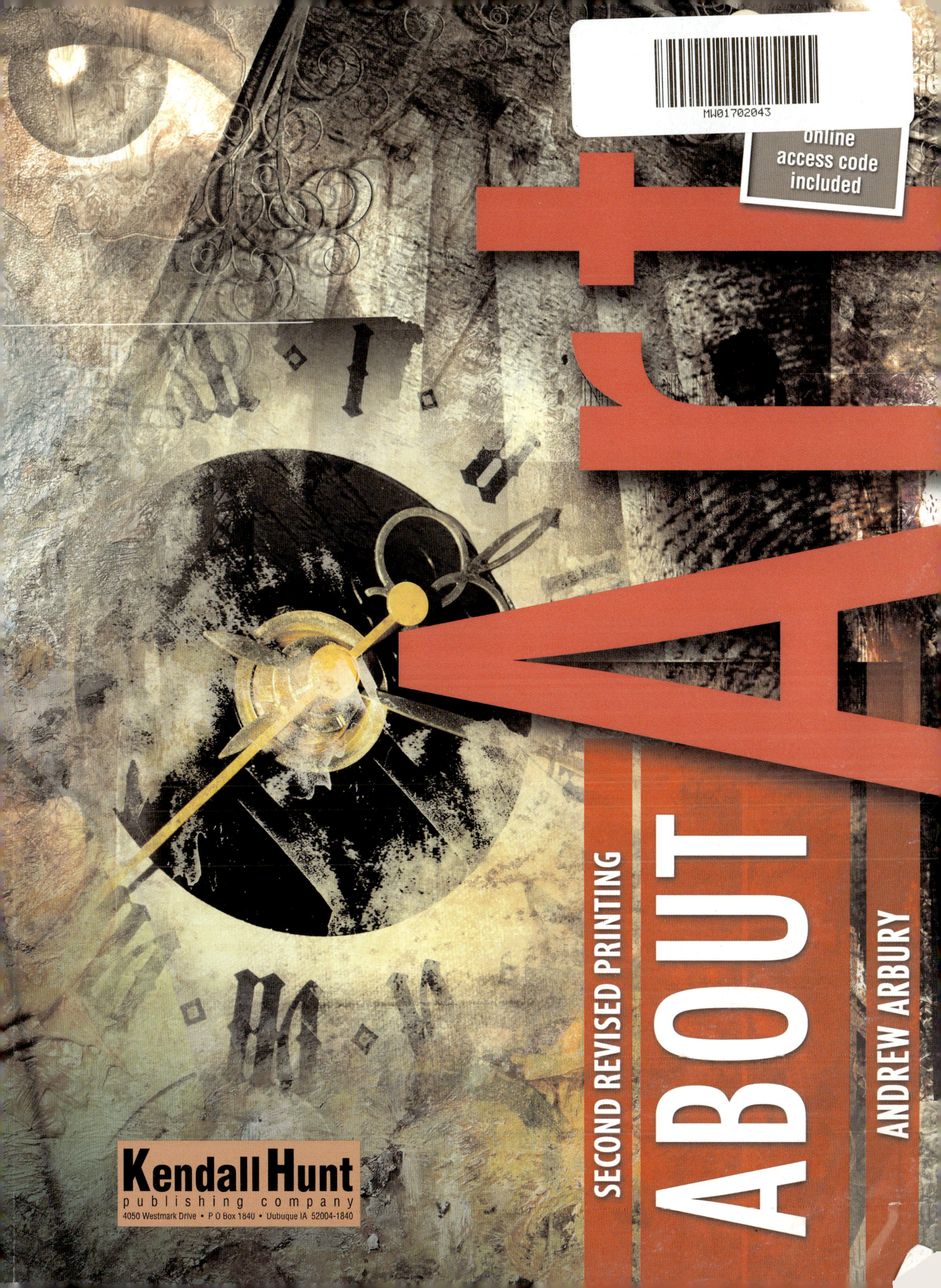

SECOND REVISED PRINTING

ABOUT Art

ANDREW ARBURY

online access code included

Kendall Hunt
publishing company
4050 Westmark Drive • P O Box 1840 • Dubuque IA 52004-1840

Kendall Hunt
publishing company

www.kendallhunt.com
Send all inquiries to:
4050 Westmark Drive
Dubuque, IA 52004-1840

Revised Printing: 2009, 2011

ISBN 978-0-7575-8721-4

Printed in the United States of America
10 9 8 7 6 5 4 3

Contents

Preface

There are many excellent art appreciation textbooks available, but most of them are more than 500 pages and they contain too much material to cover effectively in one semester. Furthermore, many students who take art appreciation are not art or art history majors. They take the course as part of their general education requirements, and many of them find the amount of detail in an art appreciation book overwhelming. To better serve these students, I decided to write a textbook that was much more succinct. My intention is to give just the essentials in a streamlined text that is more manageable for students (and hopefully kinder to their budgets). I have tried to focus on those works of art that are part of our cultural literacy—works that often appear in advertising and other media either as they are or altered as spoofs. Because of this and because of limitations of time, space, and budget, the book deals primarily with western art. This bias, however, reflects the art history curriculum in my department where we use the western art version of the art history textbook. Additionally, the earlier eras of art history are emphasized because students seem to be less familiar with them, and in later periods painting is given more attention than other art forms.

I would like to thank all the people at Kendall-Hunt who participated in this project, especially Curtis Ross and Michelle Bahr. I greatly appreciate their patience with me. I also want to thank Elizabeth Roberts, Sarah Bradford, Ryan Schnier, Stacy Beyer, and Katie Pritchard. I offer special thanks to my good friend, Jennifer Spoon, who devoted a good deal of her time to scanning my slides, adjusting the images, and proofreading text. I am eternally grateful for her assistance.

Andrew Arbury

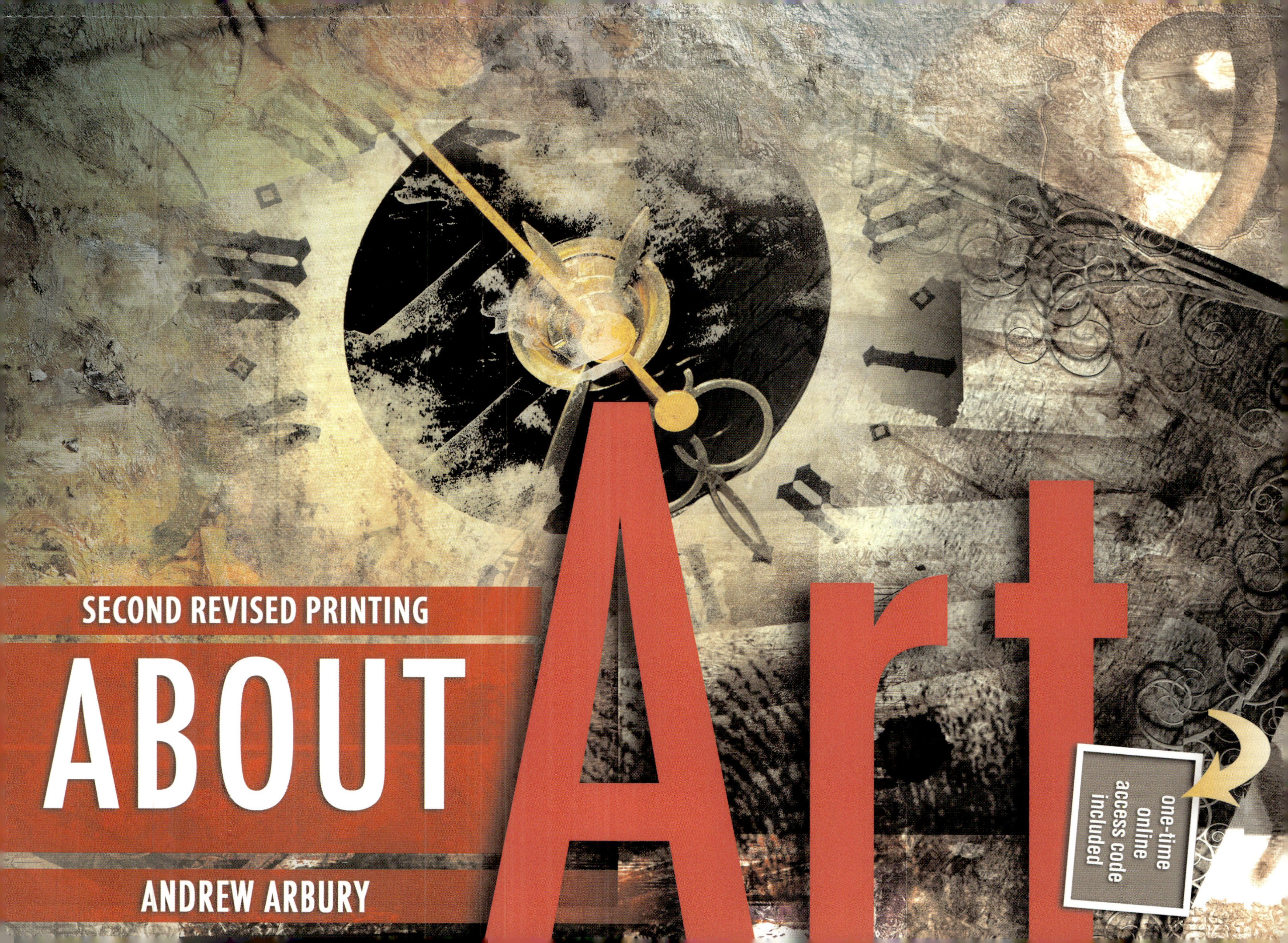
SECOND REVISED PRINTING
ABOUT Art
ANDREW ARBURY
one-time online access code included

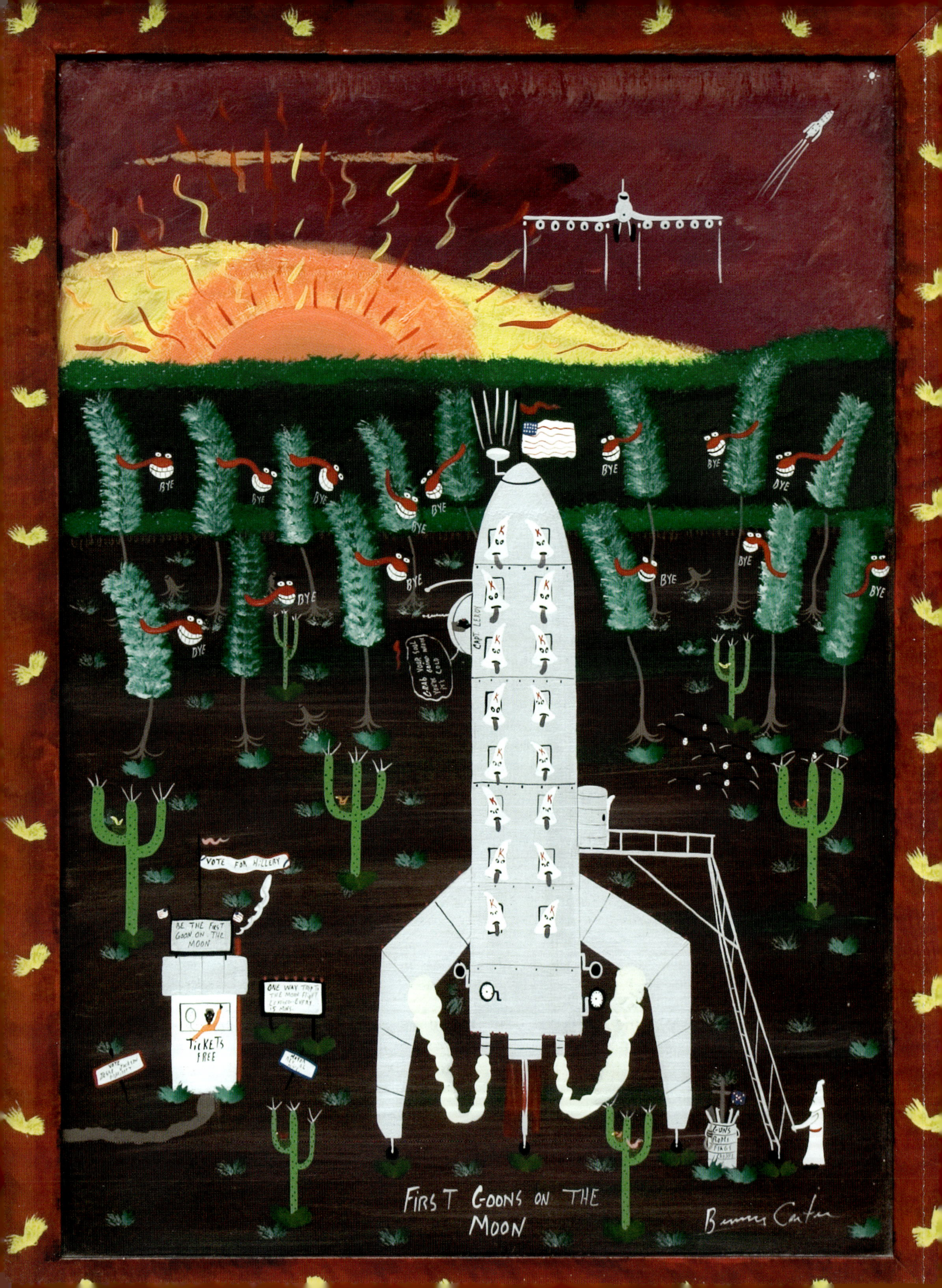
BYE
VOTE FOR HILLERY
BE THE FIRST GOON ON THE MOON
TICKETS FREE
ONE WAY TRIP TO THE MOON FLIGHT LEAVING EVERY 15 MINS.
CAPT. LEROY
FIRST GOONS ON THE MOON
Bunny Carter

1

This is the quintessential question asked at the beginning of most art appreciation textbooks. Intuitively, we may know what art is, but we can't exactly define it. Defining art is difficult because what art is to some people is not art to others. Cultural differences as well as differing individual conceptions within cultures can create varying definitions. Historical perspective also influences the definition of art. Before the **Renaissance**, artists were in the same category as shoemakers, carpenters and other craftsmen. Painting, sculpture and architecture were technical arts. People learned them by following certain rules just as with shoemaking and carpentry. There was no difference between craft and what we would now consider fine art. The concept of the fine arts is relatively new; it only came about in the sixteenth century with the founding of the first art academies in Renaissance Italy.

WHAT IS ART?

Some societies don't have a concept of "art" or even have a word for it. For example, the creator of an African mask would probably view the mask as something utilitarian or ritualistic, something necessary or desired as part of his culture. Western cultures, however, have come to admire non-Western objects and incorporate them into their concept of art. In fact, they have done so to the extent that many such non-Western objects are now produced not for their original cultural purpose, but to feed the demand of art collectors and the tourist trade. Ivory hip masks from Africa such as the one in figure 1.2 date back to the sixteenth century. They depicted the queen mother (iyoba), and the Benin king (oba) wore them as a belt ornament on the left hip to honor the queen mother's position and power in Benin society. This mask, however, dates to the twentieth century, and it is doubtful that it was made for the same purpose. It was probably made for sale to Western buyers. Does this make it any less an object of art? We can still appreciate it for its fine carving and beauty. Yet it does not have the high quality of the earlier pieces. Its carving is shallower and less detailed; nevertheless, any lessening of its value as art may only be monetary.

How then do we define art? Most would agree that Leonardo Da Vinci's *Mona Lisa* (fig. 1.3) is a work of art, but what about a drawing by a young child or a **graffiti** painting on a wall or an overpass? The boundaries of art are not fixed but always changing and expanding. Some say that art is whatever the artist says is art. This is increasingly true as we progress into the twenty-first century. **One thing can be said though: A work of art does not have to be beautiful or realistic.** Art can also be ugly or abstract. How an individual perceives a work

fig. 1.1 Benny Carter, *Goons on the Moon,* c. 2000. Acrylic on board, 30 in. × 24 in. Private collection.

depends upon the person, the culture, and the historical time period, as well as upon the quality of the work itself. And in many cases people may not appreciate a work of art simply because they do not understand it.

If we have trouble defining art, we can take comfort in the fact that even those intimately associated with the art world often have the same problem. Noted art historian E. H. Gombrich, said:

> There really is no such thing as Art. There are only artists. Once these were men who took coloured earth and roughed out the forms of a bison on the wall of a cave; today some buy their paints, and design posters . . . and do many other things. There is no harm in calling all these activities art as long as we keep in mind that such a word may mean very different things in different times and places, and as long as we realize that Art with a capital A has no existence. (Gombrich, *Story of Art,* 1995, 15)

Even artists themselves are sometimes at a loss to explain art. The famed artist Georgia O'Keeffe said in a letter to a friend: "What is Art—anyway? When I think about how hopelessly unable I am to answer that question I cannot [help] feeling like a farce." (*www.constable.net/arthistory/glo-okeeffe.html*)

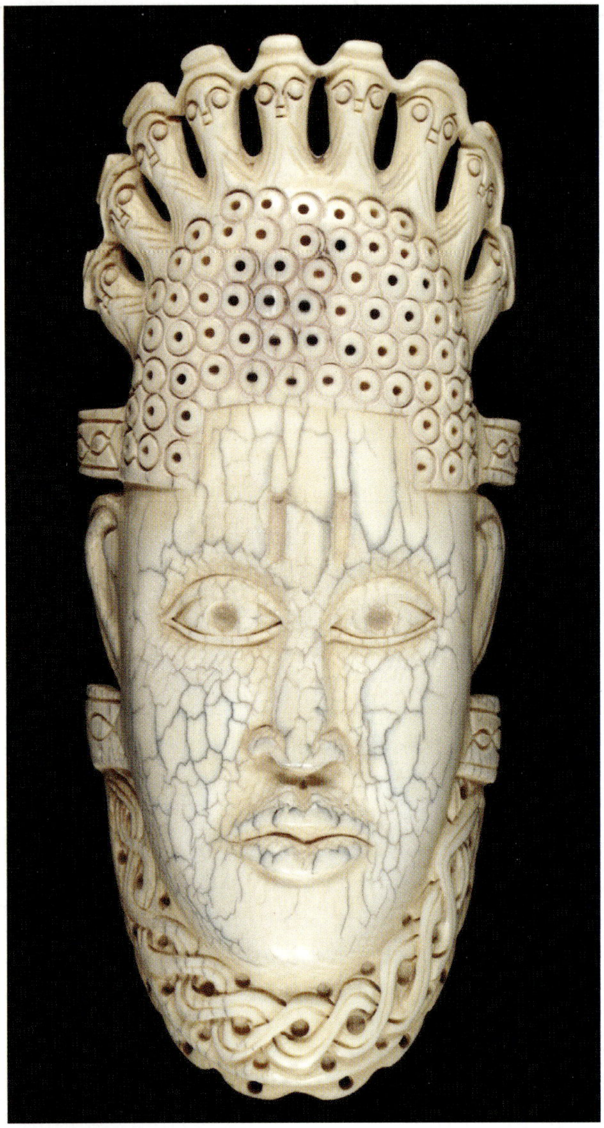

fig. 1.2 African Hip Mask, c. mid 20th century. Ivory, 9 in. high. Private collection.

THE VISUAL ARTS

One reason to gain a greater understanding of art is that art is all around us. We not only see it in museums or in our houses and places of work, or in public spaces, we see it on television, in magazines and newspapers, on billboards, at the cinema and on the Internet. Art pervades our lives whether we realize it or not. Traditionally, painting, drawing, printmaking, sculpture and architecture inspired the intellect, and so people considered them *fine art. Applied art* or *craft* had a utilitarian function. People viewed industrial design, graphic design, fashion design, interior design and the decorative arts (ornamental or functional works made of glass, wood, ceramic, metal and textiles) as applied arts. Then there is outsider or folk art—art created by artists with no formal artistic training (see box). To some there remain clear distinctions among fine art, applied art and **outsider art**. Today, however, the term *visual arts* encompasses all art forms and is thus more egalitarian. With the wide range of materials and techniques employed by artists of the twenty-first century, the term *fine arts* seems passé. Although this textbook emphasizes painting, sculpture and architecture, it also considers an exquisitely wrought piece of jewelry or an impressive ceramic vessel as an equally valid work of art.

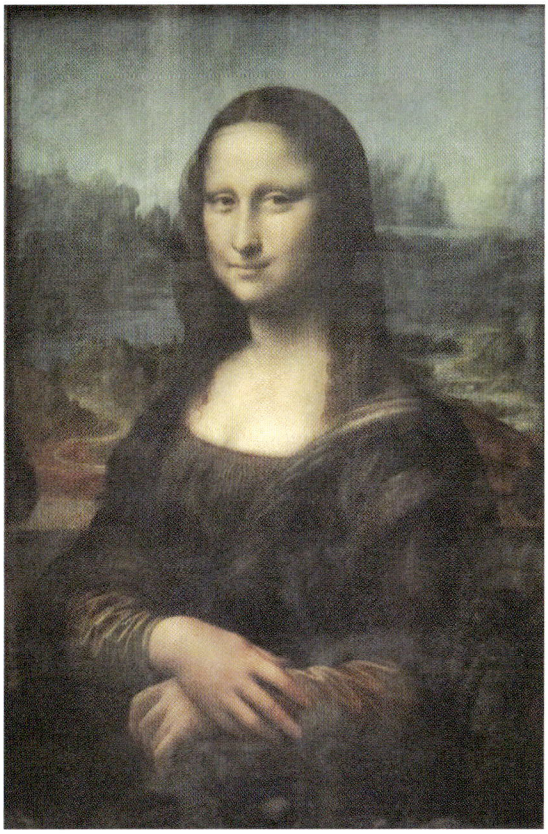

fig. 1.3 Leonardo da Vinci, *The Mona Lisa,* c. 1505. Oil on wood panel, 30 × 21 in. Louvre Museum, Paris.

ART AND BEAUTY

We frequently associate art with beauty, yet many works of art considered great are not beautiful in the traditional sense. Pablo Picasso's *Guernica* (fig. 1.4) shows the brutality of civil war and the death of innocent people. It does not show physical beauty; instead, its beauty lies in the revelation of the horrors of war. Sandro Botticelli's *Birth of Venus* (fig. 1.5) is one of the most famous paintings in Western art, and its Venus exemplifies an ideal physical beauty that harks back to ancient Greek art. Yet this is a beauty defined by Western culture. A non-Western tribal culture that sees a beautiful face as tattooed or vividly painted (fig. 1.6) might not have the same positive response to the Venus.

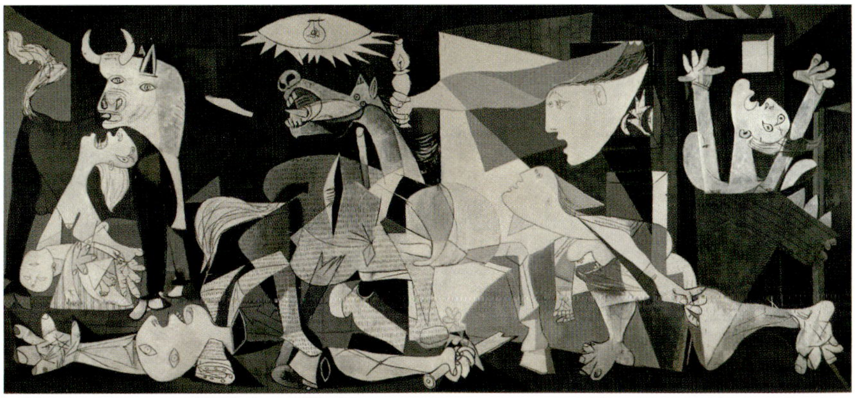

fig. 1.4 Pablo Picasso, *Guernica,* 1937. Oil on canvas, 11 ft. 5 in. × 25 ft. 5 in. Museo Nacional Centro de Arte Reina Sofia, Madrid.

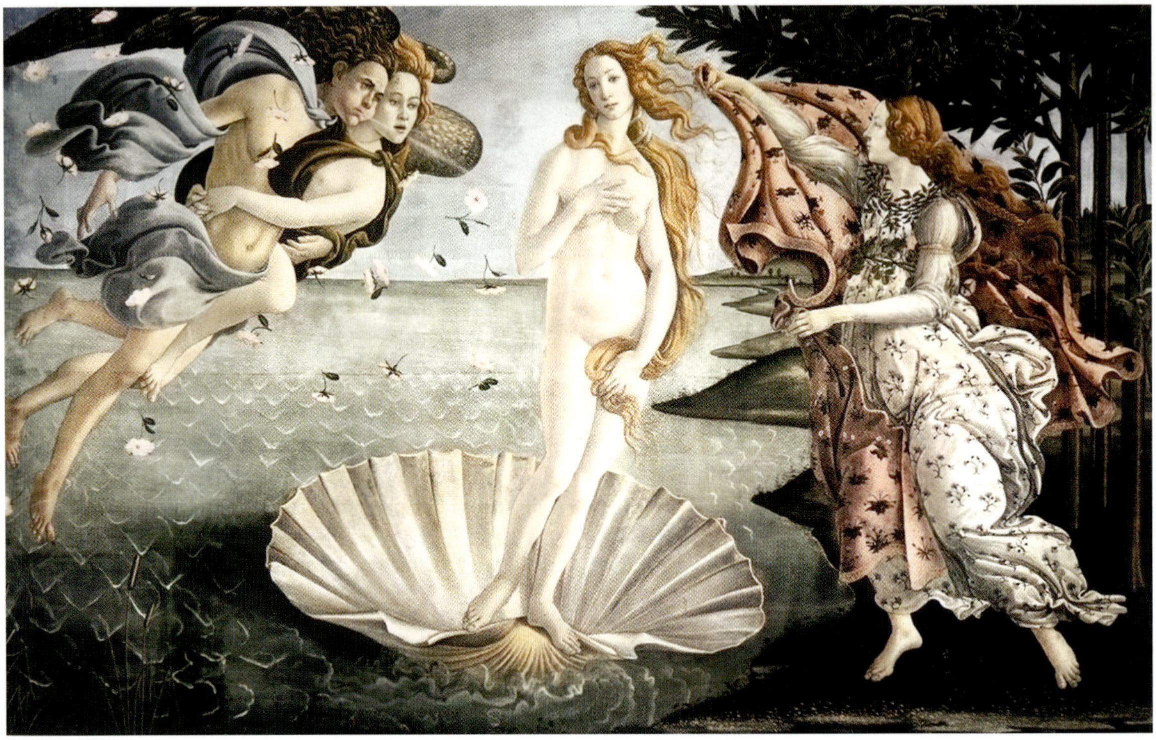

© Corel, Inc.

fig. 1.5 Sandro Botticelli, *Birth of Venus,* c. 1484–1486. Tempera on canvas, 5 ft. 9 in. × 9 ft. 2 in. Galleria degli Uffizi, Florence.

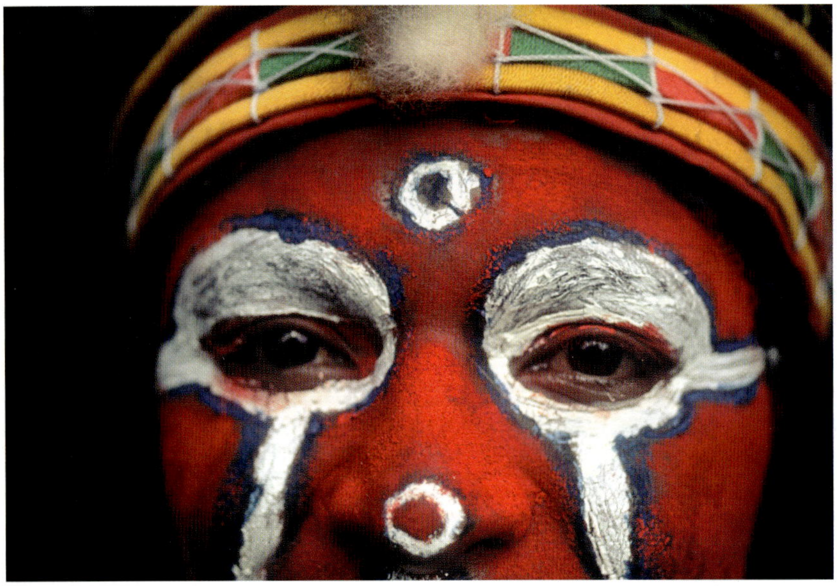

© Bill Bachman/The Image Works

fig. 1.6 Huli Wigmen female from Papua New Guinea with painted face.

Outsider Art

Outsider art is the current preferred term for art made by people who are self-taught artists living on the fringes of society. The term originally referred to artists completely outside the mainstream of society, such as those in prisons or mental hospitals who created their art not to sell, but for themselves. But now there is a lively market for outsider art, and many are actively collecting it. With this change, outsider artists are not necessarily as marginalized as before. Other terms used for this type of art are folk art, naïve art, primitive art, marginal art, vernacular art and art brut (French for 'raw art'). Critics note subtle differences among these terms, but those differences are becoming blurred.

The art of outsider artist Benny Carter ranges from painted signage to more formal works loaded with political and social overtones. *Goons on the Moon* (fig. 1.1) is Carter's scathing take on the Ku Klux Klan and its racist attitudes. Carter proposes sending all members of the Klan to the moon on a rocket ship, thus alleviating society of their hate. Other topics dealt with in Benny Carter's art are religious freedom, the aftermath of Hurricane Katrina and the horrors of 9/11.

ART AND DECORATION

With beauty in mind, artists often create art to adorn. Paintings hang on walls, carpets cover the floors, sculptures are strategically placed to enhance the aesthetics of a space and jewelry adorns the body. They may also have a practical purpose. Renaissance tapestries that hung on the walls also helped keep out the cold, and carpets could have the same purpose, but the point is they were decorative as well as functional.

ART AND DOCUMENTATION

Artists create some art to record an event or the appearance of something or someone, especially before the invention of photography. Portraits are perhaps the best example. We have a desire to be remembered, and what better way to help insure that than to have a portrait made. Perhaps the most famous portrait in Western art is Leonardo's *Mona Lisa* (fig. 1.3). From sculptures of Egyptian pharaohs to photographs of today's leaders, portraits are an enduring art form. Art can also document historical events. Theodore Gericault's *Raft of the Medusa* (fig. 1.7) documents the

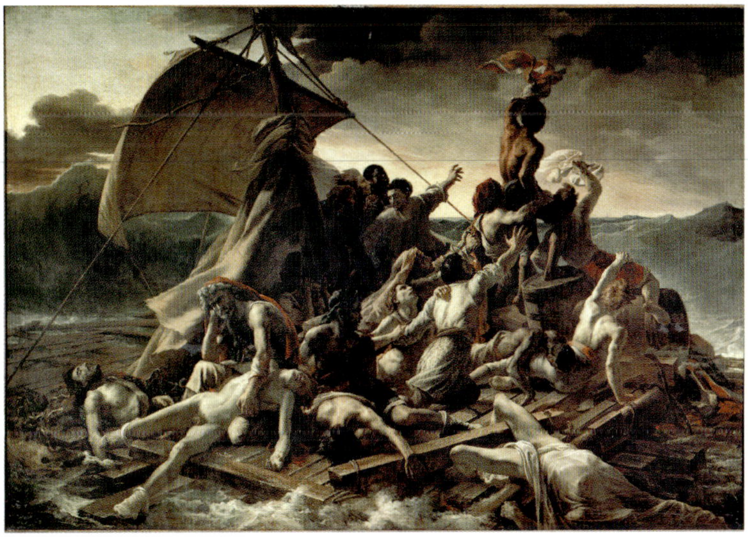

fig. 1.7 Théodore Géricault, *Raft of the Medusa,* 1818–1819. Oil on canvas, 16 ft. 1 in. × 25 ft. 6 in. Louvre, Paris.

horrors of abandonment at sea. There are many visual depictions of battles and other historical events throughout history.

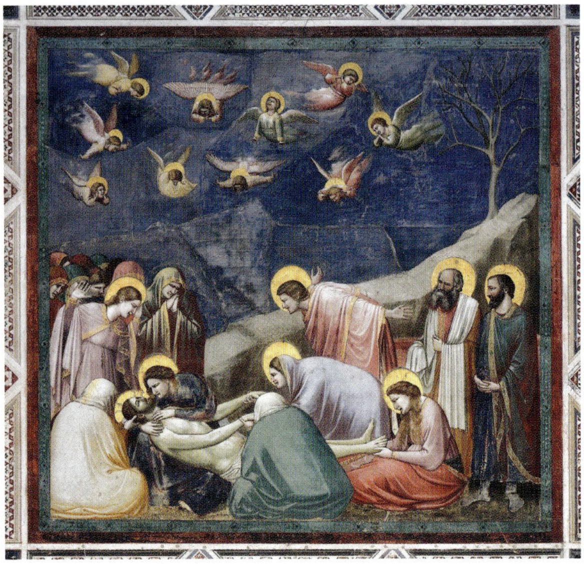

Alinari Archives/The Image Works

fig. 1.8 Giotto, *The Lamentation,* c. 1305. Fresco, 6 ft. 7 in. × 6 ft. 7 in. Arena Chapel, Padua, Italy.

ART AND RELIGION

Much art created throughout history relates to religion. In fact, until modern times most art had some religious aspect to it. Churches, temples and mosques are obvious examples, as are the many religious paintings and sculptures created in Christian Europe since the third or fourth centuries when the Church became a major patron of the arts. (Islam forbids the depiction of the human figure so its art tends to depict nature or calligraphy.) Giotto's fresco showing the dead Christ mourned by family, friends and angels is just one of many powerful religious images (fig 1.8).

ART AND POLITICS

Throughout history artists have created art for political purposes to advance a particular cause. Jacques Louis David's *Death of Marat* (fig.1.9) shows a supporter of the French Revolution dead in his bath after a political foe murdered him. By immortalizing Marat and portraying him as a martyr, David created one of the most poignant political statements of all time. Entire movements in art have sometimes been individual and group expressions of political commentary.

ART AS SELF EXPRESSION

Sometimes the artist creates art simply because he or she wants or needs expression. Works created for personal fulfillment or catharsis are sometimes not meant for public consumption and may only become known when the artist dies and they appear among the personal effects. Vincent Van Gogh's self portrait

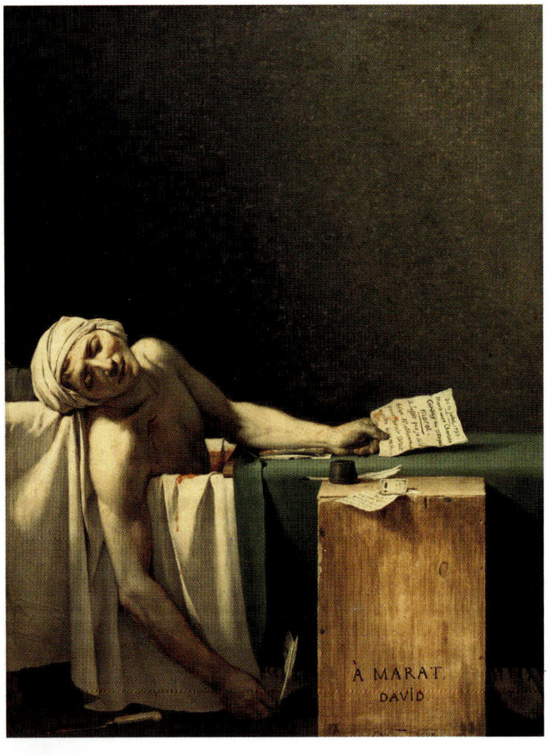

Muses Royaux des Beaux-Arts de Belgique, Brussels, Belgium/The Bridgeman Art Library

fig. 1.9 Jacques-Louis David, *Death of Marat,* 1793. Oil on canvas, 5 ft. 5 in. × 4 ft. 2.5 in. Musées Royaux des Beaux-Art de Belgique, Brussels.

(fig. 1.10), done after his self mutilation, is a case in point. Van Gogh, with an intense piercing look in his eyes, pointedly shows the bandaged side of his head, thus emphasizing what he did to his ear.

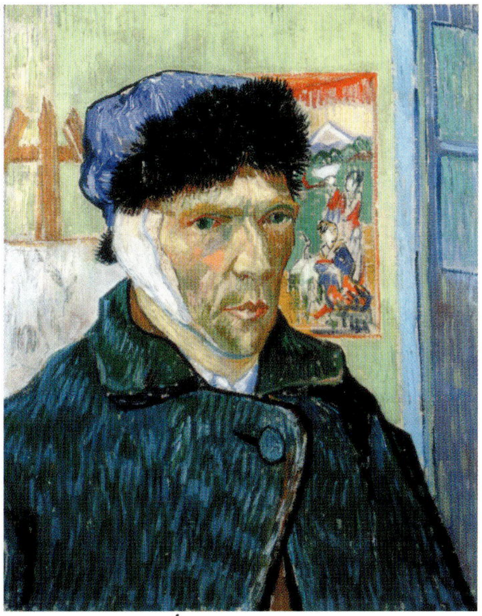

fig. 1.10 Vincent Van Gogh, *Self Portrait with Bandaged Ear,* 1889. Oil on canvas. Courtauld Institute, London.

ART AND IDEA

Artists have often created art to express an idea or a concept and to make us think. This is particularly true of modern art. Duchamp's *Fountain* (fig. 1.11) is nothing more than a urinal turned ninety degrees with an artist's signature and date added. By altering an already existing object, a urinal no less, and submitting it to an art exhibition for display, Duchamp provokes us to question the boundaries of art.

These concepts of art are by no means exhaustive, and they are certainly not exclusive. There is much overlapping. A seventeenth-century Dutch still life painting could document a family's prosperity as well as adorn their home. And Leonardo's *Mona Lisa* (fig. 1.3) is self expression as well as documentation of a woman's appearance because, even though it presumably was a commission, Leonardo never parted with it and even took it with him to France where he spent his last years.

THE CONTENT OF ART

We can classify the subject matter of most paintings, prints and sculpture throughout history into several broad categories: landscape, still life, portraiture, religion, mythology, history, genre, allegory and non-representational. Examples of all these types are found from ancient times to today.

Landscape. Perhaps the most familiar subject in art is the landscape. If someone has a painting or a reproduction hanging on the living room wall, it is often a landscape. A landscape

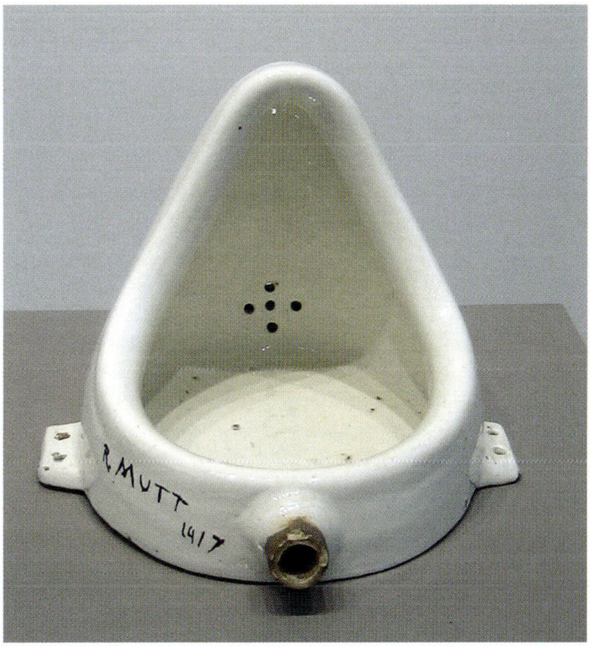

fig. 1.11 Marcel Duchamp, *Fountain* (urinal), second version, 1950 (original version, 1917). Readymade, 24 in. high. Philadelphia Museum of Art, Philadelphia.

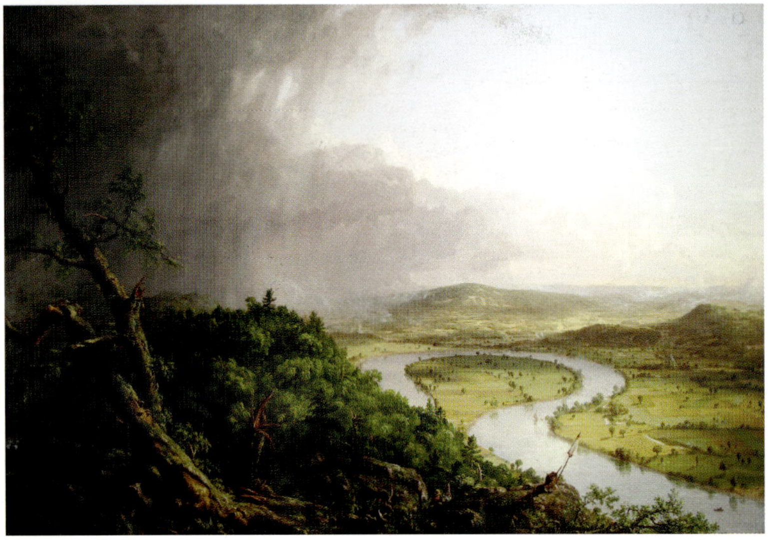

fig. 1.12 Thomas Cole, *The Oxbow,* 1836. Oil on canvas, 4 ft. 3.5 in. × 6 ft. 4 in. Metropolitan Museum of Art, New York.

is a view of a specific place, whether real or imagined, and it often conveys a pastoral or majestic beauty. One example is *The Oxbow* by Thomas Cole (fig. 1.12). If the view shows a city, then we refer to the scene as a cityscape. Landscape painting goes back to antiquity. The Romans painted them on walls not only for decoration, but also to make the room appear larger by creating the illusion of looking outside at a beautiful scene, not at a confining wall (see figs. 11.4 and 11.5). We have the same concept today in our homes. Many living rooms have a large window that frames a view of the outside for us to look at—such windows are even called 'picture' windows.

Still Life. Probably the second most familiar subject to many people is the still life, a depiction of inanimate objects. Art students paint and draw countless still lifes in their classes. From an artist's point of view, still lifes are inexpensive and easy to set up and rearrange, and the objects do not tire the way a model does. There are examples of still life painting from antiquity, and still life elements exist in paintings from the Medieval and

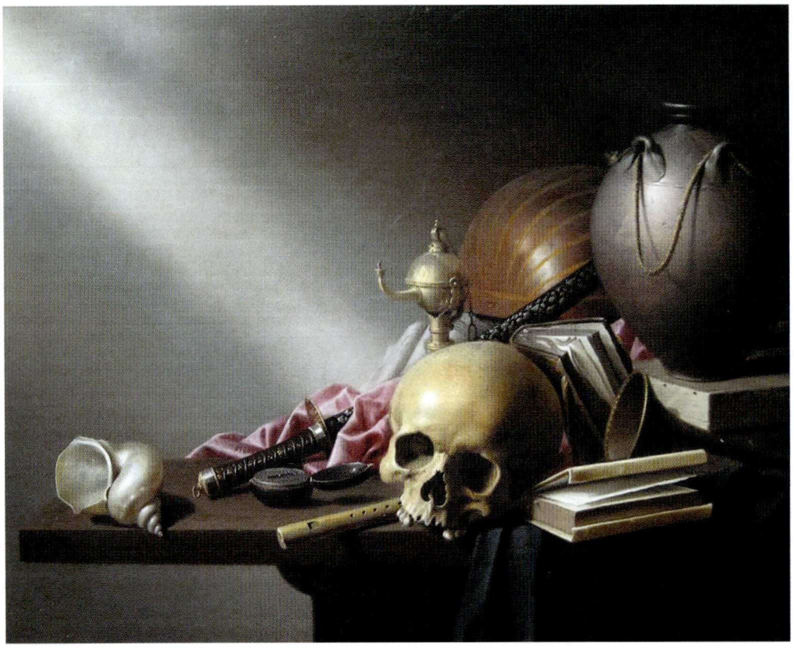

fig. 1.13 Harmen Steenwyck, *An Allegory of the Vanities of Human Life,* c. 1640. Oil on oak, 15.4 in. × 20 in. National Gallery of Art, London. The human skull is an obvious symbol of death. The sword and the shell represent wealth because they were rare objects. The timepiece and lamp that has just gone out refer to the transience and frailty of human life.

Renaissance periods, but the genre didn't become popular until the seventeenth century. Dutch artists in particular produced many still lifes of luscious fruits, exotic foods and fine silver and glassware, which served to demonstrate the wealth of the patrons. In fact there was such a demand for still life painting in The Netherlands that painters began to specialize in specific types, such as flower pieces or breakfast pieces. One type, **vanitas** (Latin for "emptiness") depicted the traditional elements such as flowers and food beginning to wilt or rot accompanied by objects indicating the passage of time such as an hourglass or a skull (fig. 1.13). As such, vanitas paintings symbolized the transitory nature of life and the certainty of death.

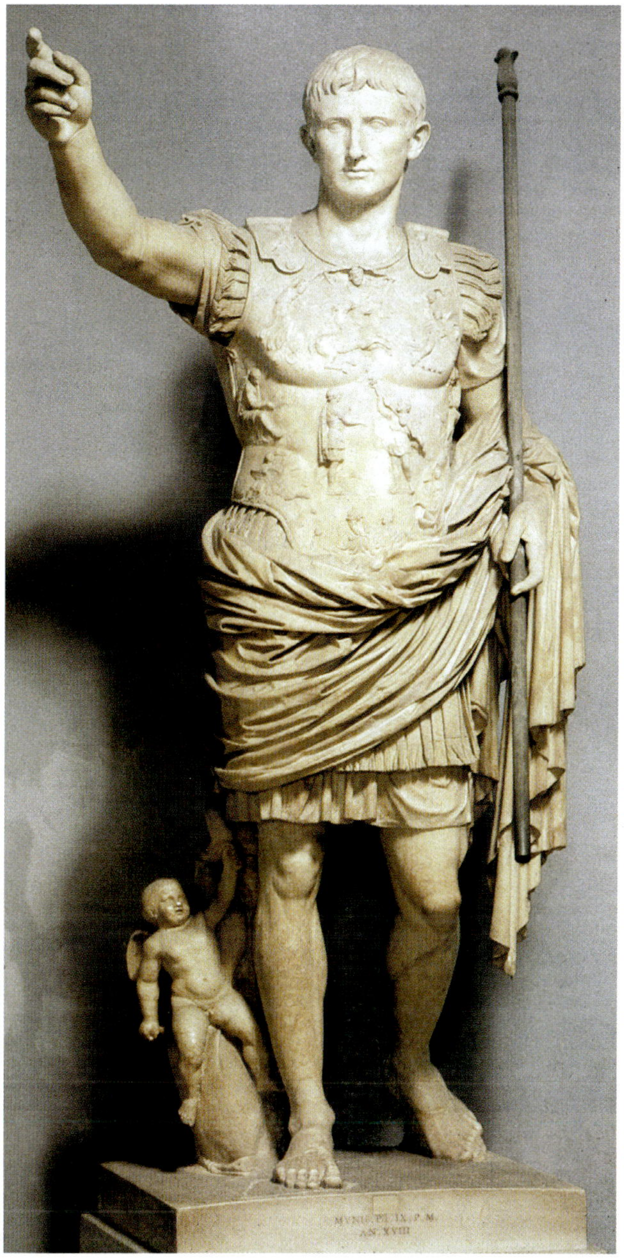

fig. 1.14 Augustus of Primaporta, early 1st century CE copy of a bronze original, c. 20 BCE. Marble, 6 ft. 8 in. high. Musei Vaticani, Rome.

Portraiture. Although portraits of people of all walks of life have become commonplace with the advent of inexpensive photography, they have a distinguished history. Since antiquity portraiture has enabled rulers to visually extend their power over their subjects and to immortalize themselves for future generations (fig. 1.14). Portraits on coins became popular in Hellenistic times during the reign of Alexander the Great in the fourth century BCE. It is a tradition that remains to this day on many modern currencies. For the wealthy, portraits were a way to promote themselves and to express their importance. Portraiture was particularly important to the ancient Romans who had a special room in the home for the display of sculptural ancestor portraits, usually death masks. In modern times, with the availability of photography, portraits abound in our homes, photo albums and computers.

Religion. Religion has existed as a prolific subject matter in many cultures. Humans in most cultures have attempted to portray their gods whether they take human or animal form. In Christian Europe it was the prevailing subject from early Christian times through the seventeenth century. Episodes from the life of Christ dominate (see box entitled, "Scenes from the Life of Christ," pages 167-169), but stories from the Bible and the martyrdoms of saints were also popular. The Church was the major patron of countless artists and accounts for numerous works with a religious subject.

Mythology. Mythology is really just an earlier culture's religion. Greek and Roman mythology are the most familiar to us today. Because so few ancient paintings remain, the stories of the ancient gods survive principally in sculpture and also in literature. Never fully forgotten, Renaissance Europe revived the ancient myths. Some of the largest and grandest paintings in Christian Europe depicted "pagan" scenes, such as the *Birth of Venus* (fig. 1.5).

History. Art has depicted historical events since ancient times. Many works portray military battles such as a sculptural relief showing a battle led by the pharaoh in ancient Egypt or a mosaic illustrating the climatic point in the battle between the armies of Alexander the Great and the Persian king, Darius. Such scenes not only document the historical event, but they also glorify the victorious ruler. Many people in the Renaissance and in later periods considered history painting one of the most noble forms of art. A good example is Francisco Goya's *Third of May,* 1808 (fig.1.15), which relates an incident in the French occupation of Spain in the early nineteenth century.

Genre. Genre scenes depict ordinary events in ordinary lives. Recreational scenes exist in ancient Egyptian tombs and in Medieval manuscripts, but genre scenes were not a common subject matter until the Renaissance. Genre painting became more popular, especially in The Netherlands in the Baroque period, but often these scenes had an underlying moral meaning. It wasn't until the eighteenth century, with the advent of a rising middle class, that people showed a greater interest in pure genre scenes. They were usually small in scale as they were meant for display in private homes. Sometimes these paintings appear to do nothing more than record an everyday event, such as Winslow Homer's *Snap the Whip* (fig. 1.16), which shows rural school children at play in the late nineteenth century. Other times,

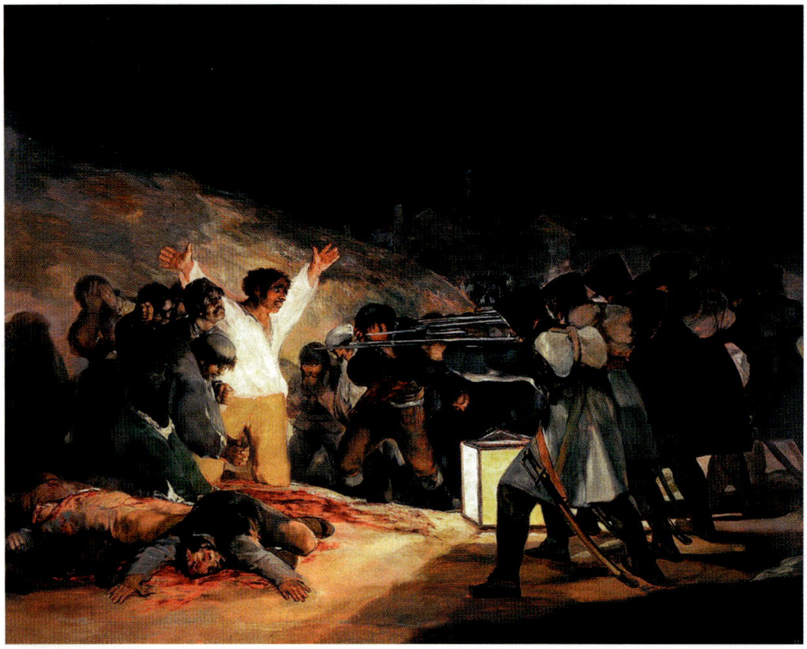

fig. 1.15 Francisco Goya, *Third of May,* 1808, 1814. Oil on canvas, 8 ft. 9 in. × 13 ft. 4 in. Museo del Prado, Madrid.

Kitsch

We need to say a word about kitsch because it is so pervasive in our society. Critics commonly define kitsch as art that is derivative or sentimental. The common criticism is that it is formulaic and lacks creativity and originality. Examples abound in our culture: Paintings of dogs playing poker, the doe-eyed children of Margaret Keane (*www.margaretkeane.com*), the "Paintings of Light" by Thomas Kinkade (*www.thomaskinkade.com*) and images of Elvis on velvet are a few examples. The Velvet Store (*www.thevelvetstore.com*), where one can purchase *Velvet Elvis in White Jumpsuit,* notes that "This piece has it all, white jumpsuit, mic, and guitar!" Many would not consider these works art, certainly not fine art. Yet they are enormously popular. Both Keane and Kinkade are financially successful artists because many people buy their art. In fact, Kinkade's works may be the most collected in the United States with retail outlets in or near furniture stores all over the country. Some critics have praised Kinkade's work for its life-affirming message and undertones of Christian values. As for The Velvet Store, at one point it had to tell its customers that they weren't taking any more custom orders because they were so backed up.

Today the line between kitsch and fine art blurs ever more as contemporary artists like Jeff Koons, whose work major museums collect, incorporate kitsch concepts into their art. (Koons' life-size gilded ceramic statue of Michael Jackson cuddling his pet Chimpanzee, Bubbles, sold for $5,600,000 at auction.) Also, many now consider retro cool traditional kitsch items from earlier decades, such as pink flamingos and garden gnomes for the yard.

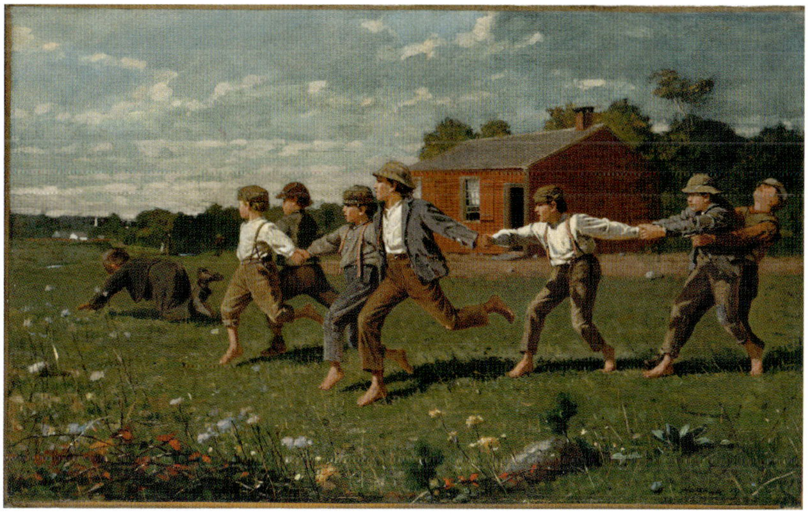

fig. 1.16 Winslow Homer, *Snap the Whip,* 1872. Oil on canvas, 12 in. × 20 in. Metropolitan Museum of Art, New York.

The Metropolitan Museum of Art/Art Resource, NY

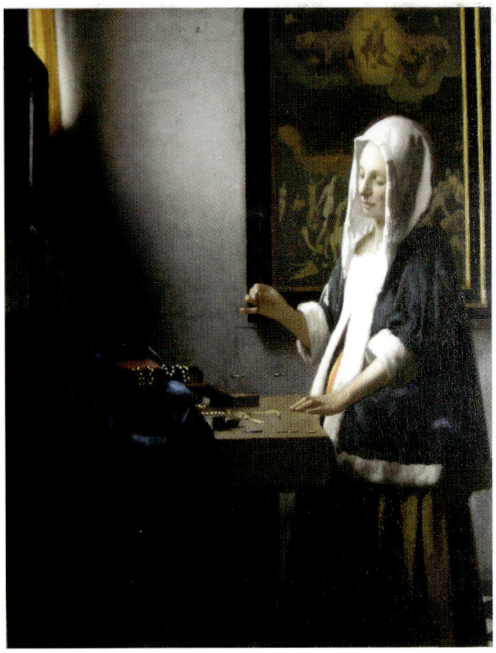

fig. 1.17 Jan Vermeer, *Woman Holding a Balance,* c. 1664. Oil on canvas, 16 in. × 14 in. National Gallery of Art, Washington, D.C.

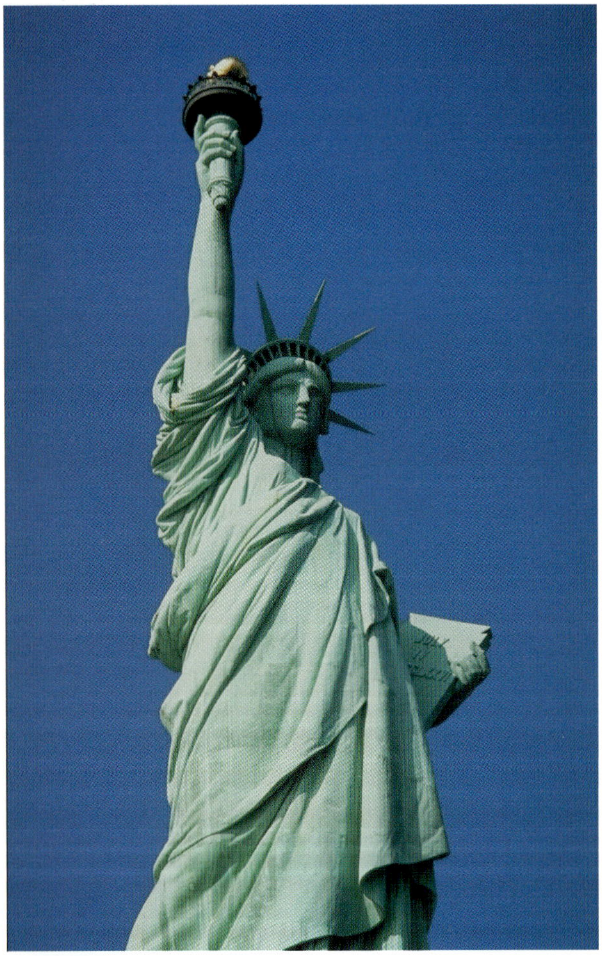

fig. 1.18 Frederic Auguste Bartholdi, *Statue of Liberty,* 1876–1884. Copper plate on a steel and wrought-iron framework, 151 ft. high. Liberty Island, New York.

there is moral content behind the scene, such as in a painting by the seventeenth-century Dutch artist, Jan Vermeer (fig. 1.17). A woman holds a scale or a balance at a table with her open jewelry box. It is a quiet, private scene. She is about to weigh her pearls and gold jewelry, but behind her on the wall is a painting of Christ and the Last Judgment wherein human souls are in the balance. Now we see that Vermeer's scene of an ordinary event—a woman with her jewelry—also refers to something more: eternal judgment.

Allegory. The *Statue of Liberty* (fig. 1.18) is not a portrait of a specific lady but a representation of a concept, in this case liberty. Lady Liberty is a **personification** of our ideal of liberty for all people. Such allegorical figures abound in the history of art. Human figures bearing various attributes have represented many of our positive human concepts, such as liberty, truth and wisdom, as well as negative ones such as greed, sin and death. Female figures representing justice go back to the Middle Ages, and we can still see the blindfolded figure of justice holding a sword and a scale in some courtrooms today. Artists can allegorize entire scenes as well. As we have already seen, we can view the still life by Dutch painter Harmen Steenwyck (fig. 1.13) not only as an excellent depiction of various objects, but it can also be seen as an allegory of the transitory nature of life. All physical things decay and cease to exist.

Nonrepresentational. Commonly referred to as abstract art, nonrepresentational (or **nonobjective**) art has no apparent subject matter. It does not represent figures or objects. Non-representational is a better term to use than abstract because a lot of art is abstract, but it still bears some relation to physical reality. Willem de Kooning's *Woman I* (fig. 1.19) is clearly abstract, but it is also clearly a human figure, whereas Jackson Pollock's *Autumn Rhythm* (fig. 1.20) is totally nonrepresentational. We cannot discern any object or a figure in it.

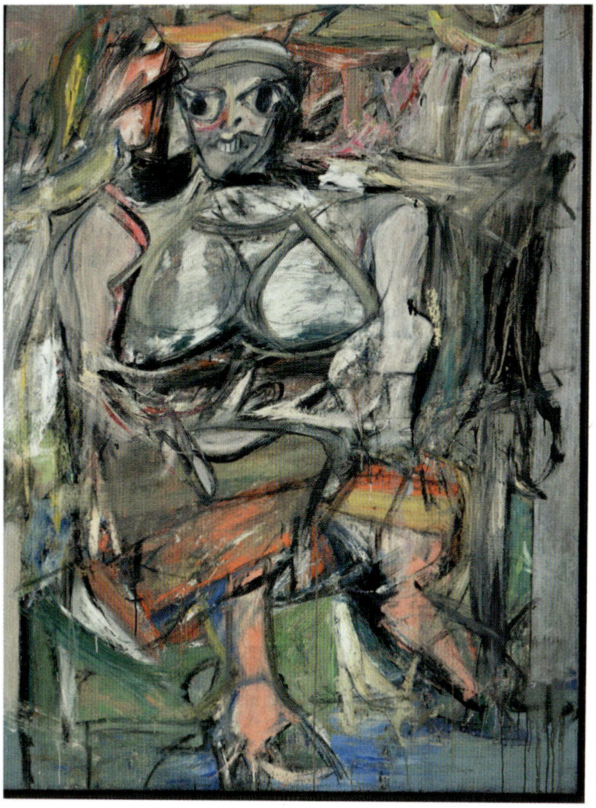

fig. 1.19 Willem de Kooning, *Woman I,* 1950–1952. Oil on canvas, 6 ft. 4 in. × 58 in. Museum of Modern Art, New York.

THE STYLE OF ART

Style refers to the way a work of art looks. That look is dependent upon the media and the techniques used to make the work of art. Style changes with different cultures, different historical periods and with different movements within the same period. Individual artists can further refine style within a culture, period or movement. We can easily recognize the difference between a figure in an ancient Egyptian painting and a figure in a Cubist painting because of their unique historical styles. Likewise, we can tell the difference between a painting by Leonardo da Vinci and one by Raphael (both from the Renaissance period) because of their individual styles.

THE MEANING OF ART: ICONOGRAPHY

Iconography is the interpretation of images. Scenes portrayed in art can often have a deeper meaning. That is, they may represent something more than meets the eye. We have already seen this in Vermeer's *Woman Holding a Balance* (fig. 1.17) and in Steenwyck's still life (fig. 1.13). Another example

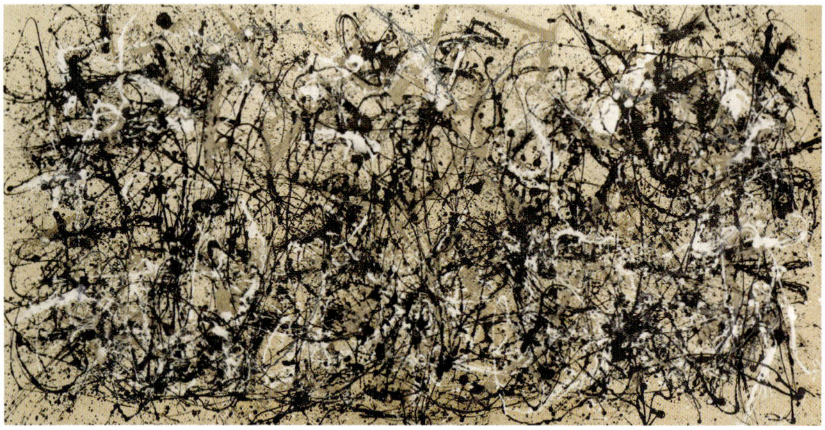

fig. 1.20 Jackson Pollock, *Autumn Rhythm,* 1950. Enamel on canvas, 105 in. × 207 in. Metropolitan Museum of Art, New York.

is Rembrandt's print entitled *The Three Trees* (fig. 1.21). We can view this as a skillfully executed landscape depicting three trees on a hill, but we can also see it in the context of the Christian religion. The three trees are situated on a hill just as the three crosses at Christ's crucifixion (for him and the two thieves) were situated on a hill called Golgotha (or Calvary). The crosses, of course, were made from the wood of trees. At the left, the forces of nature coming from the heavens above suggest a divine presence. At the same time the storm portends the death of Christ. We see hope, however, in the stream that flows below the hill as it recalls the river of life mentioned in the Book of Revelation. This print is a good example of the various levels of appreciation for art. We can view *The Three Trees* as a pleasing landscape, as a work of printmaking virtuosity and as a symbol of the essential sacrifice in the Christian faith.

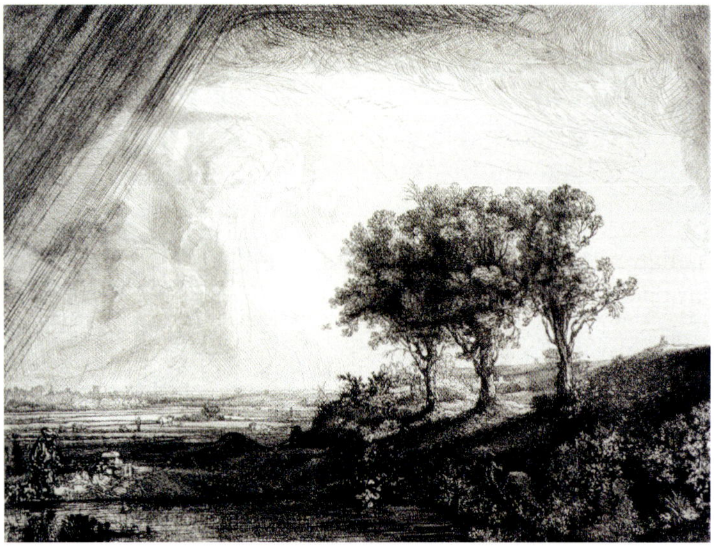

fig. 1.21 Rembrandt, *The Three Trees,* c. 1639. Etching with drypoint and engraving, 8.375 in. × 11.125 in.

THE VALUE OF ART

Art has different kinds of value. There is material value, based on what the work of art is made of. King Tut's gold coffin or a Fabergé egg studded with diamonds, rubies, and pearls is valuable because of the value of its materials. Assessed value is determined by people's opinions. The *Mona Lisa* is composed of just paint on a wood panel, yet it is priceless. Despite its lack of valuable materials, it is worth far more than a Fabergé egg because of how we assess it. Leonardo da Vinci was a genius who painted few works. The assessed value of a work can change, especially after the death of the artist. Van Gogh had trouble selling his works in his lifetime, but by the late 20th century his paintings were selling at auction for as much as 80 million dollars. Personal value is determined by the collector. A child's drawing may be worth more to someone than an expensive painting in a gallery simply because of the relationship between the child and the collector (fig. 1.22)

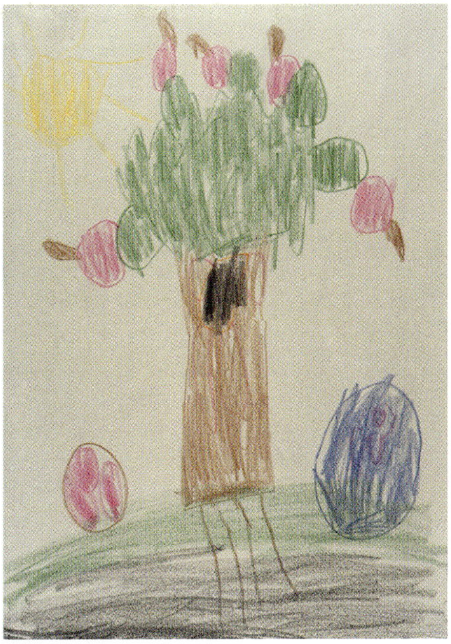

fig. 1.22 Chelsea Arbury (age 4), *Tree,* 1995. Crayon on paper.

So back to the initial question, what is art? In simple terms, art is something created by someone to communicate something. Depending upon our sensibilities, we may find a work beautiful or ugly, uplifting or disturbing. Art can take many forms: Painting, drawing, sculpture and architecture are the main traditional forms, but there are many others, and artists are continually creating new techniques and media. To understand a work of art, we generally want to know *why* and *how* the artist created it. This book will attempt to answer these questions. By briefly examining the visual elements of art that we should consider when looking at a work of art, as well as the basic history of art (which encompasses the religion, politics and social values of each historical period), we can better understand art and how it fits into its historical context. With greater comprehension comes a greater appreciation of art, and even if you don't like a certain work of art, you can appreciate it if you understand something about it.

SUMMARY

- It is not easy to define art. Different people and different cultures have different concepts of art. In the simplest terms, art is something someone creates to express something.
- The purposes of art include decoration, religion and ritual, documentation, self-expression, politics and propaganda and the conveyance of an idea or concept.
- The categories of subject matter in art, especially in painting and drawing, include landscape, still life, portraiture, religion, mythology, history, genre, allegory and nonrepresentational imagery.
- The style of a work of art is the way it looks depending on how it was made. We can discern the style of an individual artist, culture, period and artistic movement.
- The meaning of a work of art can be nothing more than a reproduction of some visual aspect of the world or of the artist's imagination, or the

work of art can have a deeper underlying meaning that goes beyond what you initially see.

- The value of a work of art is determined by its materials or by how people assess it, or a combination of both. The value of art can change over time, and a seemingly worthless work that would fetch nothing at auction might be valuable to a single person.
- To fully appreciate a work of art, you have to attempt to understand it by seeking answers to these questions: What are its formal artistic qualities? For whom was it made? Why was it made? How was it made? And what is its physical, historical and social context?

PRONUNCIATION GUIDE

Bartholdi (bar-**thal**-dee)
Botticelli (bot-tih-**chel**-ee)
David, Jacques-Louis (dah-**veed, zhahk**-loo-**ee**)
Duchamp, Marcel (doo-shaw, mar-**sel**)
Fabergé (fab-er-**zhey**)
Genre (**zhahn**-ruh)
Géricault, Théodore (zhair-ee-**koh**, tey-oh-**dore**)
Giotto (**jot**-toh or joht-toh)
Goya (**goy**-uh)
Guernica (**gwair**-nih-kuh)
Iconography (aye-kuh-**nog**-ruh-fee)
Leonardo da Vinci (lay-oh-**nar**-doh dah **vin**-chee)
Picasso, Pablo (pih-**kah**-so, pahb-loh)
Pollock, Jackson (**pah**-luck)
Rembrandt van Rijn (**rem**-brandt van **rine**)
Steenwyck (**steen**-wick)
Van Gogh (van **go**)
Vermeer, Jan (vur-**meer**, yahn)

GLOSSARY

Allegory. A story or image that refers to something else through symbolic imagery.

Graffiti. Markings or images (often spray painted) on a wall or other surface in public places.

Genre scene. A depiction of everyday life.

Iconography. The analytic study of the symbolic, often religious meaning of objects, persons, or events depicted in works of art.

Kitsch. Art that is overly sentimental and commercial.

Memento mori. A phrase or image, such as a skull, that is a reminder of death.

Nonobjective art. See Nonrepresentional art.

Nonrepresentational. Totally abstract.

Outsider art. Art created by self-taught artists living outside the mainstream of society.

Personification. An abstract idea or concept represented by a human figure.

Renaissance. The period of history that began in Italy around 1400 and lasted through the sixteenth century. It was characterized by a renewed interest in Classical antiquity.

Style. A typical manner of artistic expression that is characteristic of an individual or group of individuals, geographical region, or era; the way an artwork looks.

Tapestry. A design woven into a thick fabric with colored yarns.

Vanitas. A painting whose subject matter deals with the vanity, fragility, and transience of human life. Typical objects in a vanitas painting are skulls, timepieces, musical instruments, and wilting flowers. The term derives from Ecclesiastes 1:2 ("Vanity of vanities . . .").

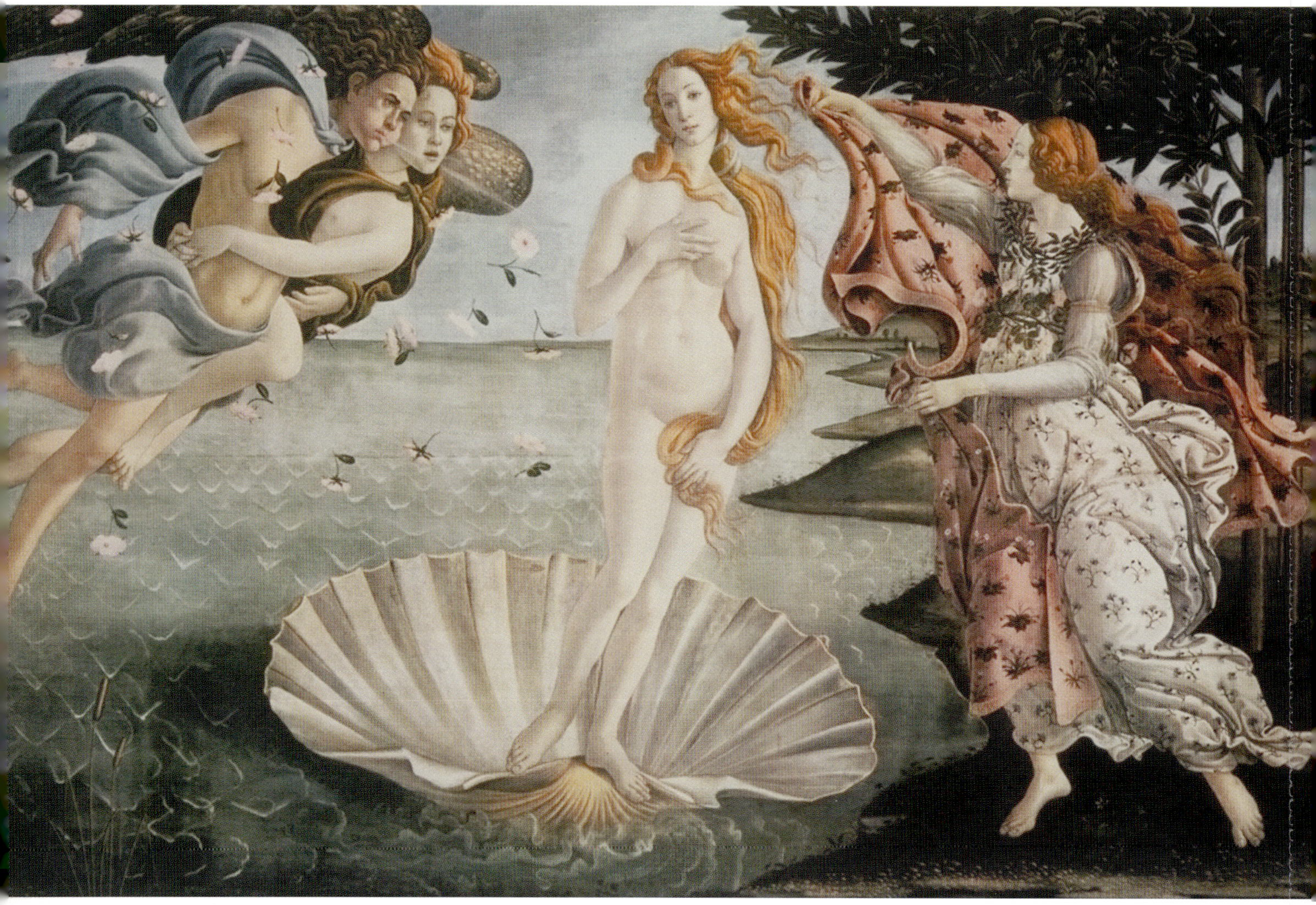

fig. 2.1 Botticelli, *The Birth of Venus.*

2

You need to understand various components of art in order to more fully understand and appreciate a painting, a sculpture, a building or other art form. For example, in Botticelli's famous painting, *The Birth of Venus* (fig. 2.1), light illuminates the scene allowing us to see the lines that define the shape of Venus' body, the color of her golden hair, the smooth texture of her skin, the movement of the figures toward her and the distant space behind her. The artist carefully composed the scene to give the viewer a comprehensible and satisfying experience. In fact, Botticelli was so successful at employing the elements and principles of art in a skillful manner that he created a masterpiece. Below is a brief discussion that identifies the basic components of the visual arts.

THE ELEMENTS AND PRINCIPLES OF ART

LINE

Lines define much of what we perceive in this world. Lines are everywhere. When we observe the edge of something we see it as a line. In nature lines tend to be curvilinear, like a bending branch or the edge of a pond. In the world made by humans lines are usually straight, like a telephone pole or the edge of a building, Of course there are exceptions. Natural mineral crystals have straight edges, and many buildings, especially newer ones like the Guggenheim Museum in Bilbao, have curvilinear edges (fig. 2.2). Botticelli was a master of line. He used lines to outline figures and forms, giving them definition. He even went so far as to define the waves of the sea with lines.

There are many kinds of lines, and they can suggest many different things, including direction, movement, emotion, shape, space and texture (fig. 2.3). They can be thick or thin, straight or curvilinear. Horizontal lines imply stability whereas diagonal lines suggest movement; jagged

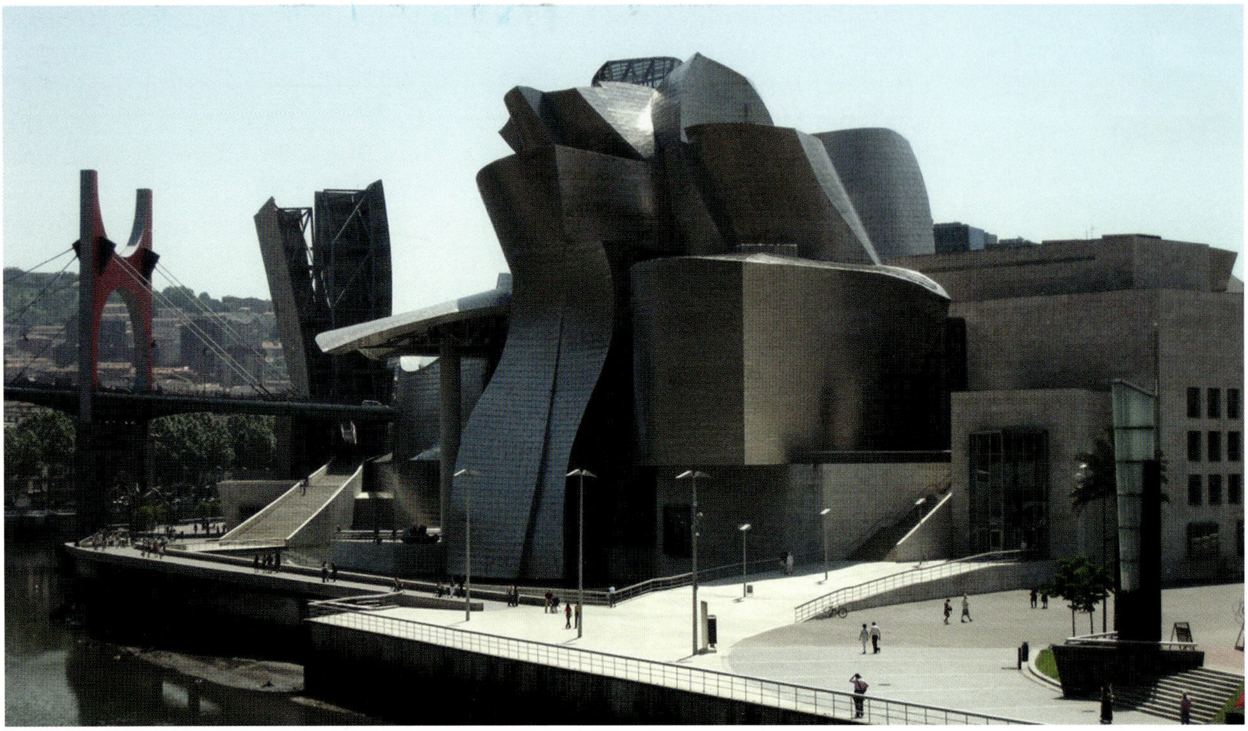

fig. 2.2 Frank Gehry, Guggenheim Museum Bilbao, 1993–1997, Bilbao, Spain.

lines can indicate aggression whereas straight lines might imply passiveness and curvy lines sensuousness. The characteristics of line also come into play. A really bold and thick jagged line would imply a greater amount of aggression. You can actually draw lines or you can imply them fig. (2.4).

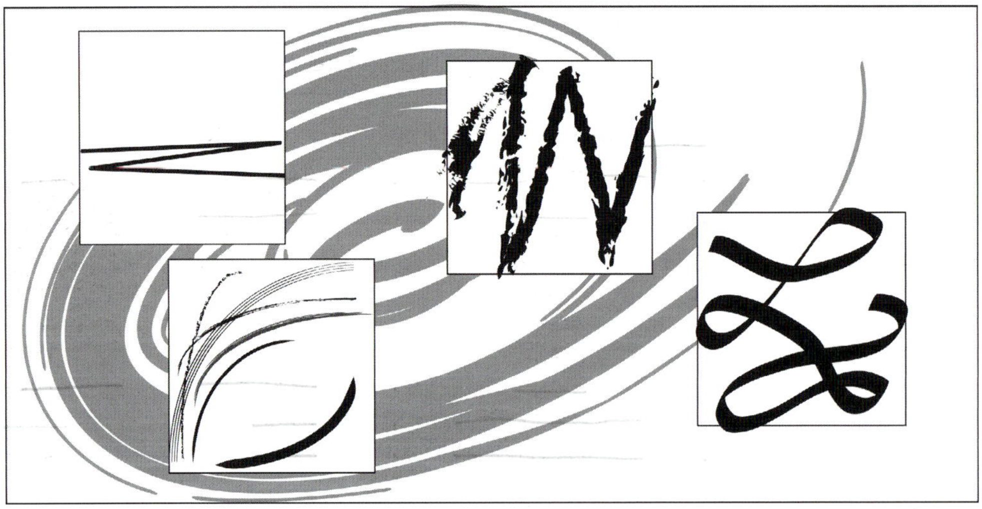

fig. 2.3 Types of lines.

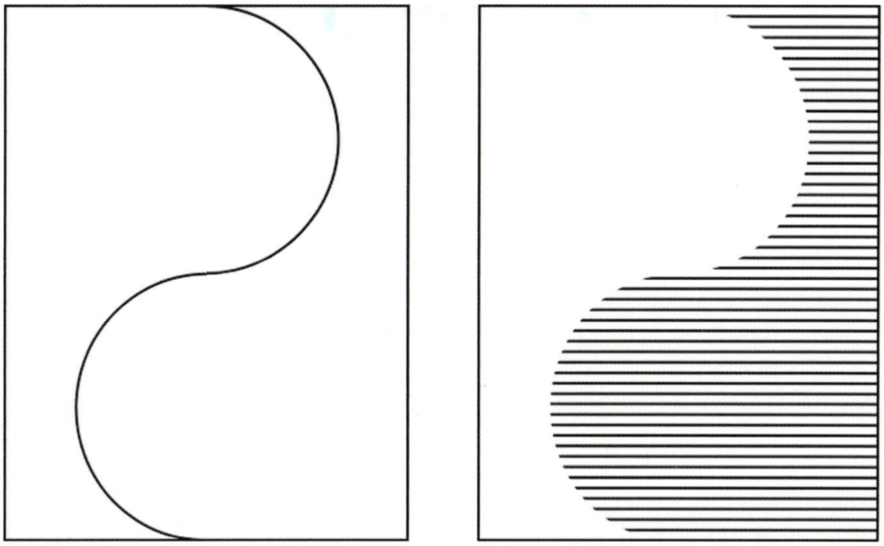

fig. 2.4 Actual and implied line.

The *Birth of Venus* illustrates some of these kinds of lines. The outline of Venus's body defines her form, the v-shaped lines in the sea suggest the gentle motion of the waves and the outline of the shore suggests a recession into space.

SHAPE

Shape is the area defined by lines (actual or **implied**). Shapes can be geometric (such as a circle, triangle or square) with precise outlines or organic with irregular outlines. As with lines, most geometric shapes are made by humans whereas most shapes found in nature are organic. (Again, there are exceptions: For example, snowflakes are geometric.) In the *Birth of Venus* an implied triangle shape forms as a result of the diagonal line of the two allegorical wind figures to the left of Venus and the diagonal line of the cloak on her right. They meet at Venus's head, which forms the apex of the triangle.

Shapes can be positive or negative depending upon the background and our perception of them. For instance, the so-called Rubin Vase (fig. 2.5 left) illustrates a black vase against a white background, but the white background suggests its own shape, that of two faces in profile defined by the outer edges of the vase.

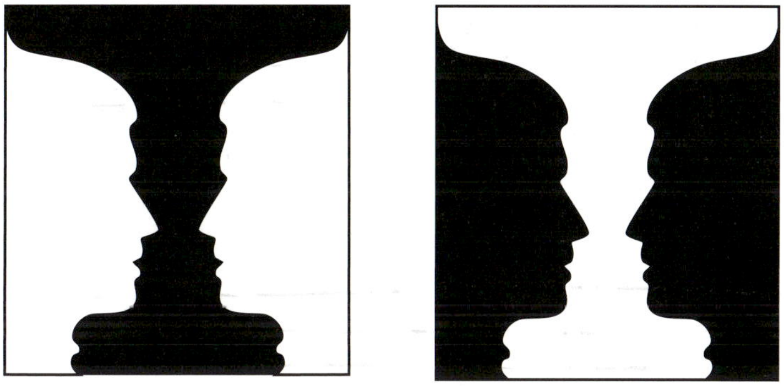

fig. 2.5 Rubin Vase.

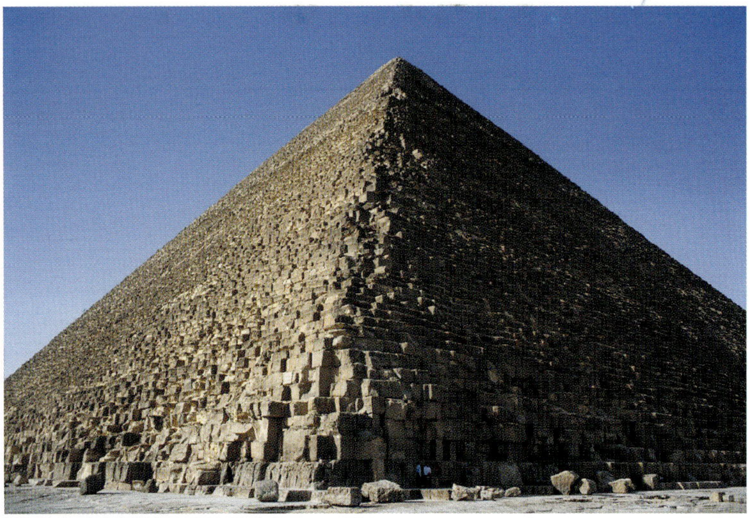

fig. 2.6 Great Pyramid at Giza, Egypt.

The vase is the positive shape, and the faces are negative shapes. The other image shows two profiles in black, with the white background suggesting a vase. This is called figure ground reversal. Artists should be aware of how the shapes they create can produce negative shapes and how the viewer might perceive them. In the *Birth of Venus,* the negative areas among the windblown locks of Venus' hair and in the collar of the cloak mimic the little bays of the undulating coastline.

MASS

Mass refers to the bulk of a three-dimensional area such as a sculpture or a building. Whereas a triangle is a two-dimensional shape that has no mass, its three-dimensional counterpart, a pyramid, does. Mass can be a significant aspect of the work. The monumental mass of the Great Pyramid (fig. 2.6) in Egypt is its most imposing quality. Mass does not have to be solid. The Louvre Pyramid in Paris (fig. 2.7) is a shell that encloses a space, yet it is perceived as a mass from the outside.

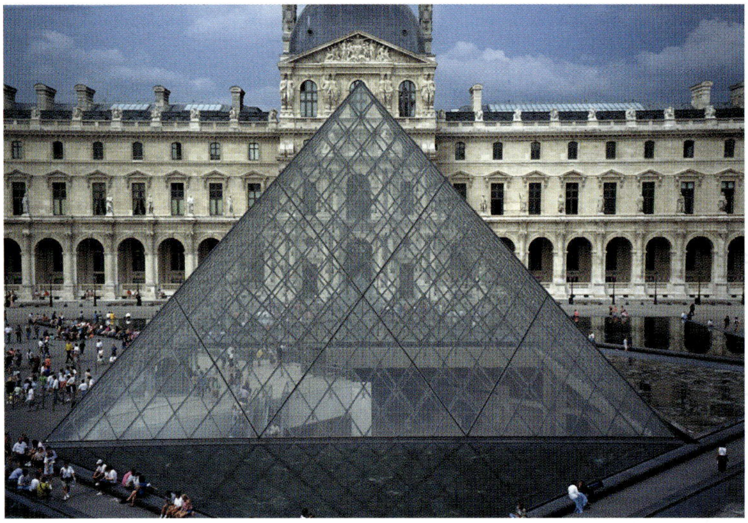

fig. 2.7 Louvre Pyramid, Paris.

The artist must suggest mass in two-dimensional art. In the *Birth of Venus,* the transition between light and shaded areas on the drapery creates the illusion of mass in the figure with the cloak. This makes her dress appear three-dimensional and suggests the bulk of her body beneath.

Space is the area that envelops something—it is everything around an object or a person. Space is of primary importance in buildings. The space enclosed by the Louvre Pyramid is the dramatic entrance to one of the great art museums of the world. The soaring interior space of a Gothic cathedral is what gives the church its spiritual quality (fig. 2.8).

In two-dimensional works such as paintings and drawings, various pictorial means indicate space. The diagrams in figure 2.9 demonstrate various methods of suggesting depth on a flat surface that involve overlapping, diminishing size, vertical placement or a combination of the three. Diego Velázquez' painting showing a princess and her attendants illustrates these spatial techniques (fig. 2.10). The dog has the lowest placement in the picture, and we perceive him as being closest to us. The dog is the first of several figures that overlap each other in turn so that we read each successive figure as being further back in space. The dog is in front of the small boy who is in front of the dwarf who is in front of the girl who is in front of the two adults behind her. Each figure further back in space also has a slightly higher vertical placement on the canvas surface. And the man in the doorway at the back of the room appears much smaller to indicate his greater distance from the others.

An artist can emphasize the illusion of space in a scene or not. Velázquez chose to show a pronounced recession into space in his painting. It is just the opposite in David's painting of the *Death of Marat* (fig. 2.11) where the flat background contains nothing to detract from the figure of Marat.

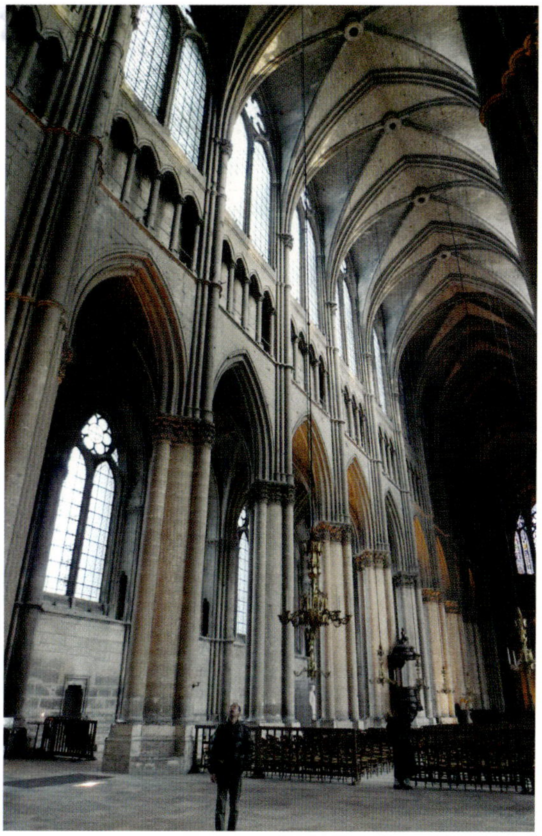

fig. 2.8 Interior of Reims Cathedral, France.

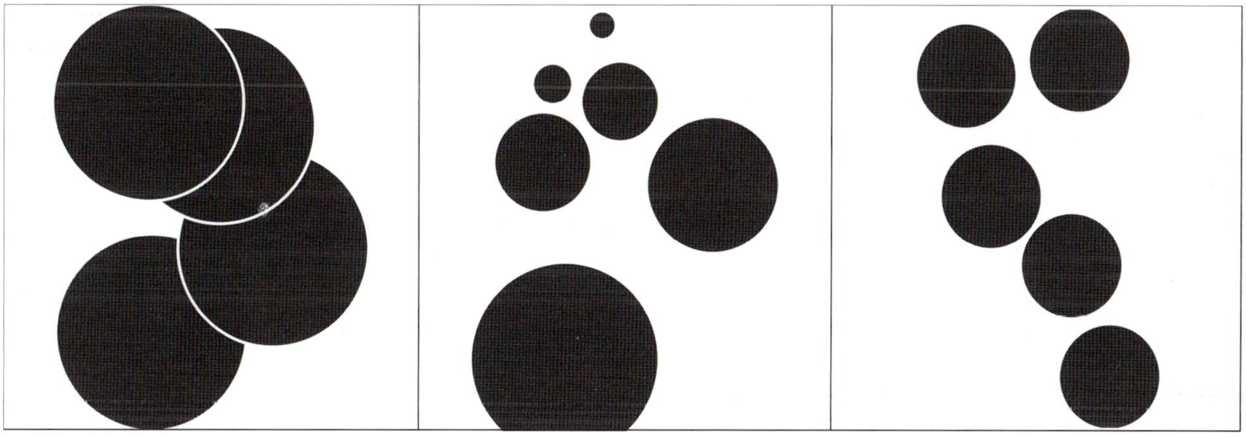

fig. 2.9 Ways to indicate spatial depth.

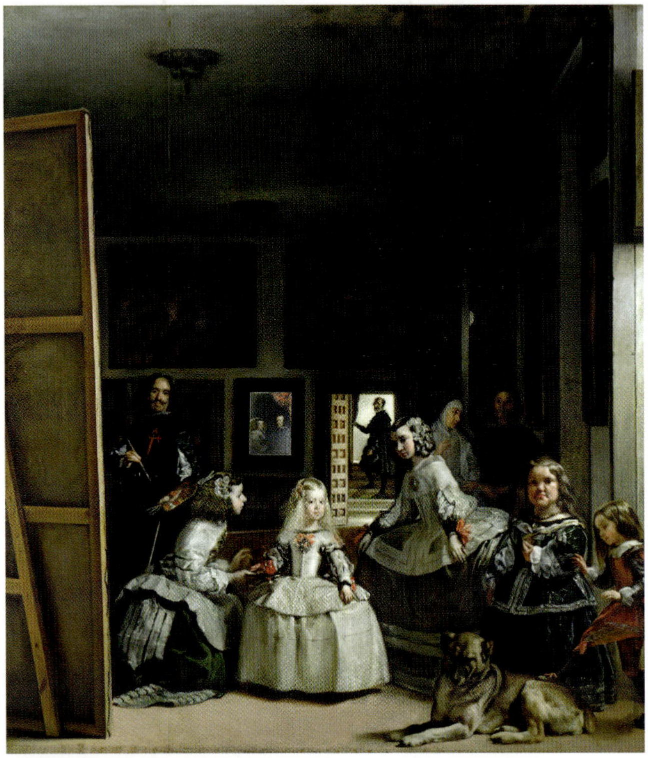

Las Meninas or The Family of Philip IV, c.1656 (oil on canvas) by Diego Rodriguez de Silva y Velazquez (1599–1660) Prado, Madrid, Spain/ Giraudon/ The Bridgeman Art Library

fig. 2.10 Diego Velázquez, *Las Meninas* (The Maids of Honor).

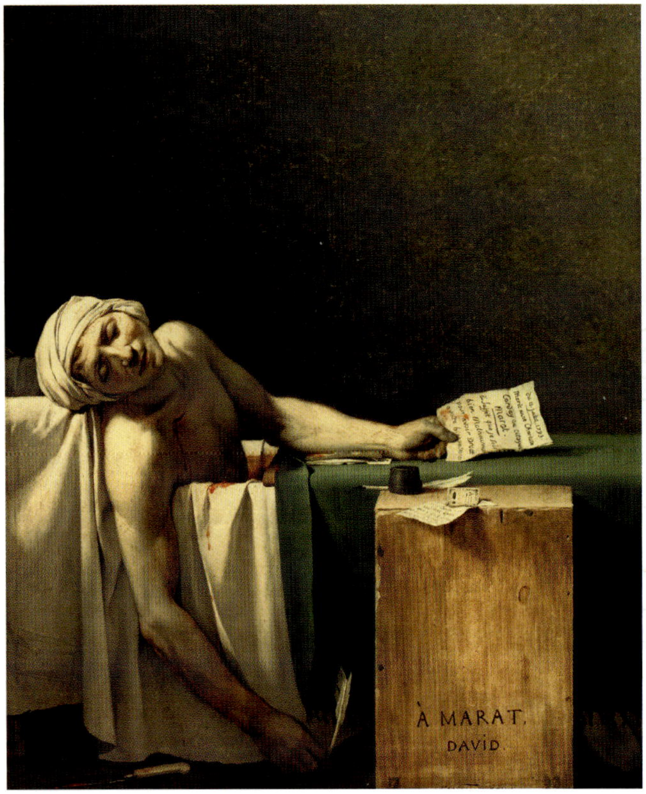

The Death of Marat, 1793 (oil on canvas) by Jacques Louis David (1748–1825) Musees Royaux des Beaux-Arts de Belgique, Brussels, Belgium/ The Bridgeman Art Library

fig. 2.11 Jacques-Louis David, *Death of Marat.*

Linear and atmospheric **perspective** are two additional techniques used to give the illusion of depth on a flat surface, such as a painting or a drawing. **Linear perspective** is based on the way we see. Objects appear smaller in the distance, and perceived parallel lines (like railroad tracks or the edges of a sidewalk) appear to converge in the distance. For example, when you look down empty train tracks the two rails appear to come together on the horizon (where the land and the sky meet). The tracks appear to converge at a point called the **vanishing point** (fig. 2.12).

With one-point linear perspective receding parallel lines in reality appear to meet at a single vanishing point. If you want to show the corner of a building (or other rectangular object) as closer to the viewer than the sides of the building, then two sets of receding parallel lines must appear to converge at two different vanishing points. This is called two-point perspective (fig. 2.13 bottom). There can be as many vanishing points as needed. In Raphael's *School of Athens* (fig. 2.14) the main vanishing point is between the two central figures, Plato and Aristotle. The implied lines of the floor pattern below and the vault coffers above also converge at that point. The block of marble in the foreground, however, is shown from its corner so it has two vanishing points (one of which is outside the picture).

Another kind of perspective is **isometric perspective** where parallel lines do not converge (fig. 2.15). This perspective system is traditional in Asian art, and architects prefer it because it does not distort, and they can make accurate measurements from architectural drawings. Because the lines remain parallel one can perceive the cube in figure 2.15 in two different ways. It can look as though we are viewing the cube from above or from below.

Atmospheric perspective (sometimes called aerial perspective) mimics how things appear bluish and less distinct in the distance because of the moisture and dust in

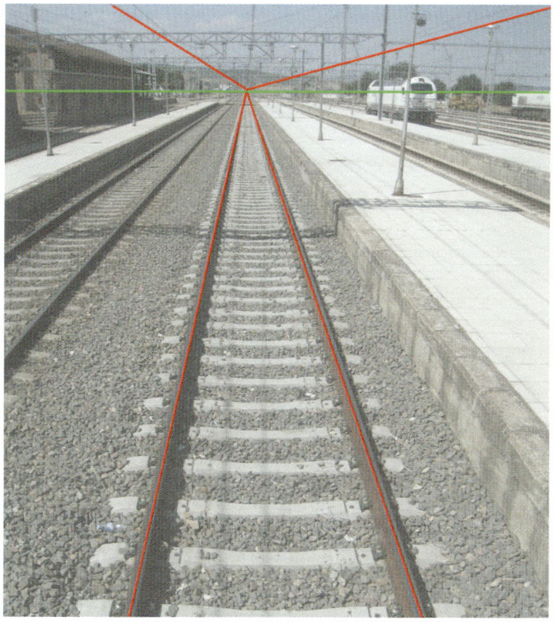

fig. 2.12 Train tracks and linear perspective.

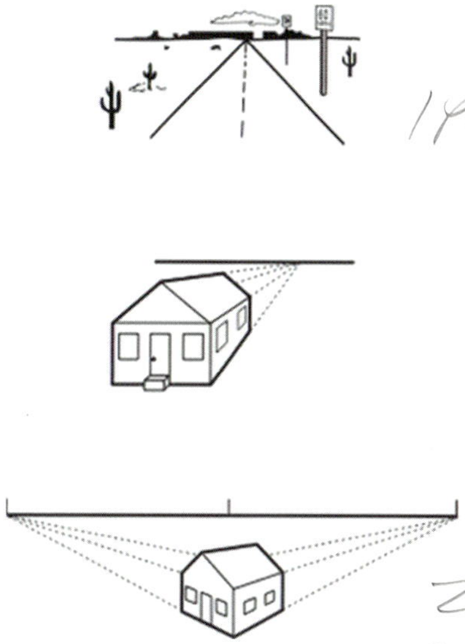

fig. 2.13 Linear perspective.

the air. The Blue Ridge Mountains in the southeast United States are so named because they appear blue from afar (fig. 2.16). A good example of atmospheric perspective in painting is the mountainous landscape in the background of the *Mona Lisa* by Leonardo da Vinci (fig. 2.17).

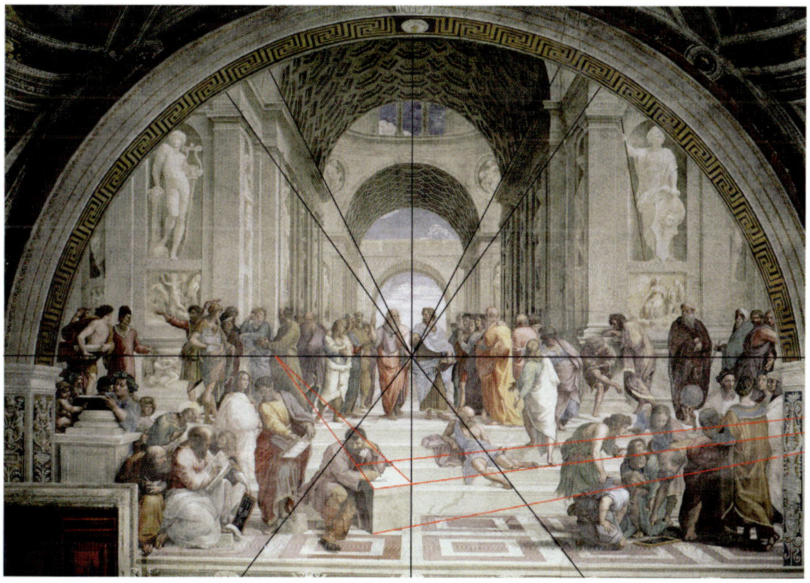

fig. 2.14 Raphael, *The School of Athens* with perspective lines, horizon line and vanishing points. See also fig. 15.16.

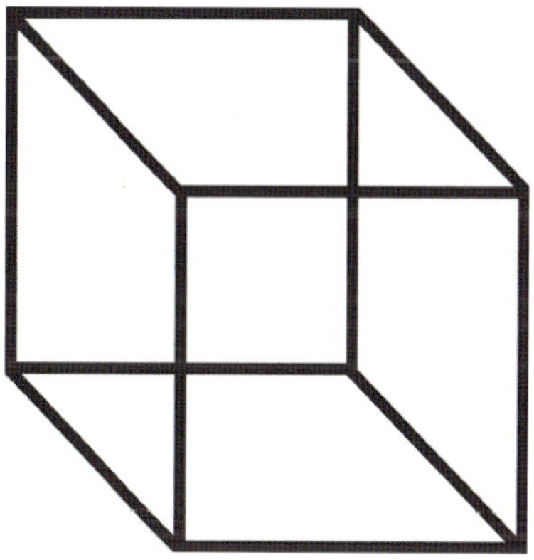

fig. 2.15 Isometric perspective (Necker cube).

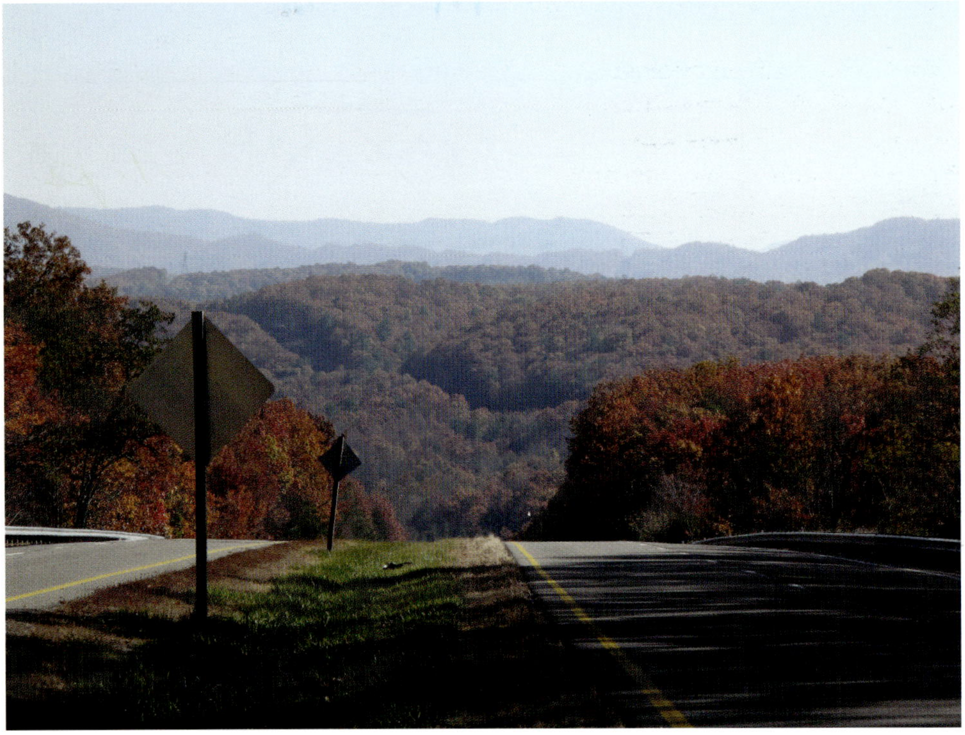

fig. 2.16 Blue Ridge Mountains.

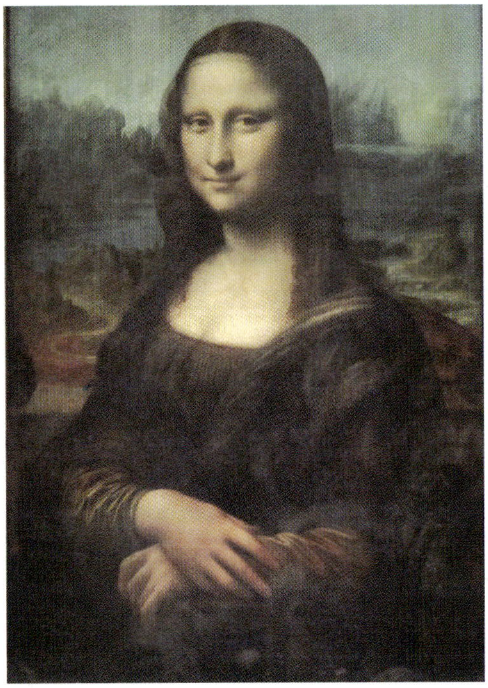

fig. 2.17 Leonardo da Vinci, *Mona Lisa.*

LIGHT AND VALUE

Light allows us to see things, and the way they are lit can greatly alter our perception of them. A statue illuminated from above will look different if lit from below. Children use this phenomenon when they light their faces from below with a flashlight in the dark to create an eerie effect. The lightness or darkness of a surface is its value. **Value** ranges from white to black with various shades of gray in between (fig. 2.18 top row). The surrounding background can affect the perception of value. In figure 2.19 the gray circle has the same value in each square—it only looks lighter or darker in contrast to the value of the square background.

Chiaroscuro (Italian for "light dark") is the use of gradations of light and shade to create the illusion of three-dimensional form. Figure 2.20 shows a sphere with such gradations. Without the changes in value, the sphere would simply be a colored circle. The face of Mona Lisa is a good example of chiaroscuro in painting.

COLOR

Color can suggest various moods and psychological states. There are two kinds of color: transmitted color and reflected color (fig. 2.21). Various wavelengths compose light, and each wavelength corresponds to a particular color or hue. Violet, for instance, is a shorter wavelength than red. The colors that compose white light are red, orange, yellow, green, blue and violet. One can see the colors of the visible spectrum when white light passes through a prism. In nature, one sees the same effect when sunlight passes through moisture to create a rainbow.

The colors we see most are reflected colors. A red ball appears red because it reflects the red wavelength of white light (and absorbs the other wavelengths). If an object reflects all wavelengths it appears white. If it absorbs all wavelengths it appears black. Color has three aspects: hue, value and saturation (fig. 2.18). **Hue** refers to the specific wavelength that gives a color its name. We use hue interchangeably with color. **Value** is the relative lightness or darkness of a color depending on whether we add white or black **pigments**. If we add white to a color, it creates a **tint**. Adding white to red produces pink. If we add black to a color, it creates a **shade** of that color. Adding black to red makes maroon. **Saturation** (also called intensity) is the purity of a color. A color is pure if it is at its highest saturation. Adding another color to red will reduce its saturation and make it duller.

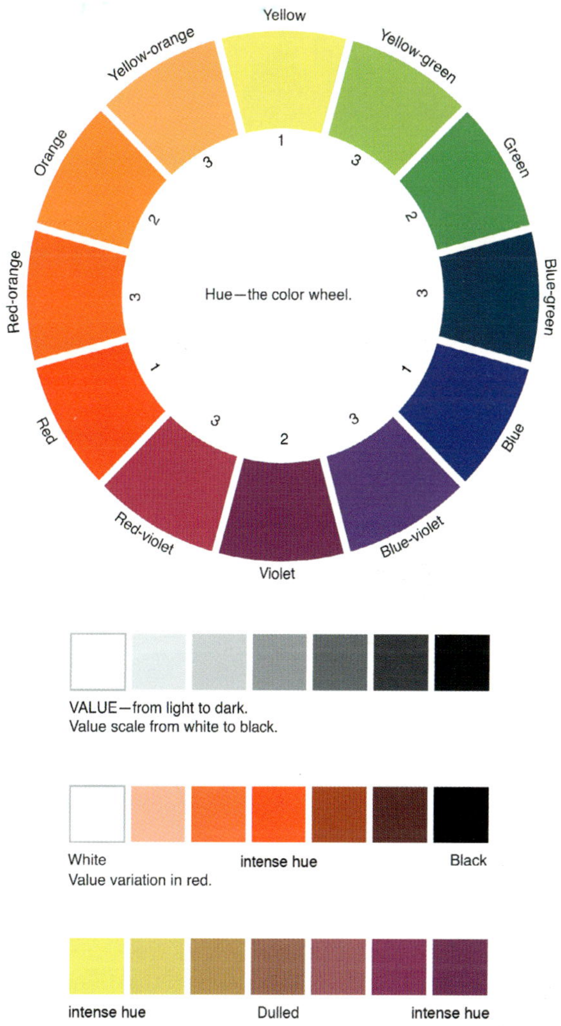

fig. 2.18 Color wheel of hues, value, and intensity (saturation).

When we mix different colored pigments the resulting mixture is darker because more wavelengths are being absorbed. If we mix all the colors (or even just the three pigment primary colors of red, blue and yellow) the resulting mixture is nearly black (fig. 2.21 top). This is a **subtractive**

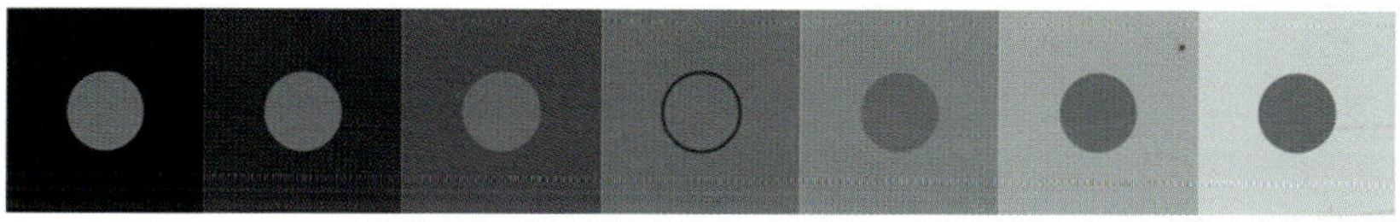

fig. 2.19 Value scale with a uniform middle gray.

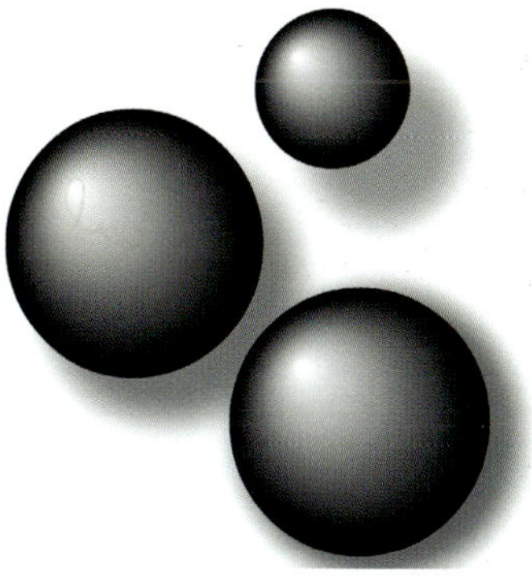

fig. 2.20 Illuminated spheres with cast shadows.

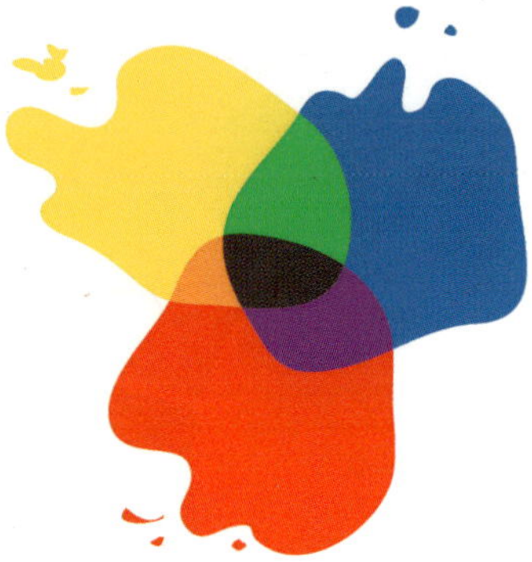

Pigment primaries: Subtractive color mixture. (Reflected color)

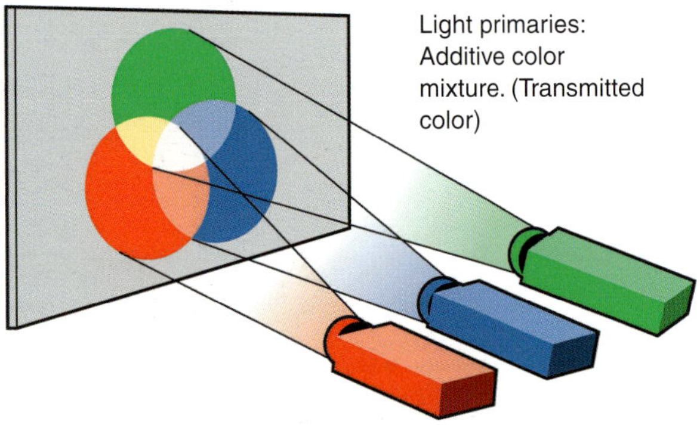

Light primaries: Additive color mixture. (Transmitted color)

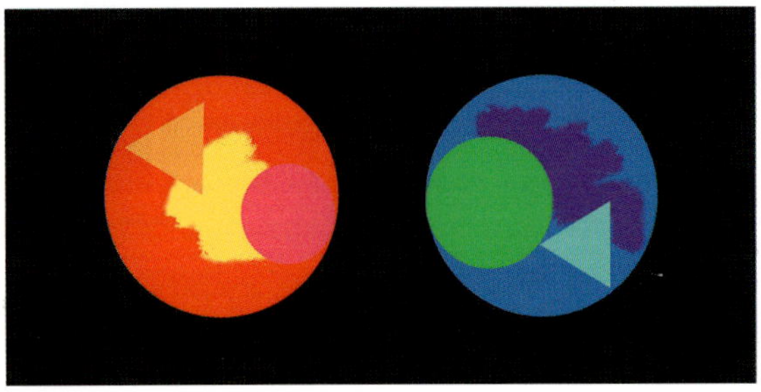

Warm/cool colors.

fig. 2.21 Reflected (pigment) and transmitted (light) color.

process because less and less light is reflected as we mix more colors together. Conversely, if we combine all the color wavelengths of transmitted light (or even just the three primary light colors of red, blue and green), they form white light (fig. 2.21 middle). This is an **additive** process.

The color wheel (fig. 2.18 top) shows the relationships among pigment colors. **Primary colors** are hues that we cannot make by mixing other colors together. The pigment primaries are red, blue and yellow. (The light primaries are red, blue and green.) Various mixtures of the primary colors produce the other colors. Red-orange colors are considered **warm colors**, while blue-green colors are considered **cool colors**. In a composition warm colors tend to advance while cool colors tend to recede (fig. 2.21 bottom). **Complementary** colors are opposite each other on the color wheel. Blue and orange are complementary colors as are red and green. When placed next to each other complementary colors intensify each other. The pale greens of the foliage intensify the pink dress of the woman in Fragonard's *The Swing* (fig. 2.22).

TEXTURE

Texture is the tactile quality of a surface or the representation of it. Textures can be real as in gestural artist Paul Fret's work (fig. 2.23), or they can be simulated such as the fur-trimmed garment on Mr. Arnolfini in Van Eyck's double portrait (fig. 2.24). In the former, the actual surface is highly textured with paint. In the latter, the actual surface of the painting is smooth, but the illusion of fur is very real.

An artist uses the above visual elements to create **form**, but he or she must organize the forms into a **composition**, and there are certain basic principles of design that help do this successfully. The basic design principles are movement, unity and variety, balance, emphasis, contrast, scale and proportion, and repetition and rhythm.

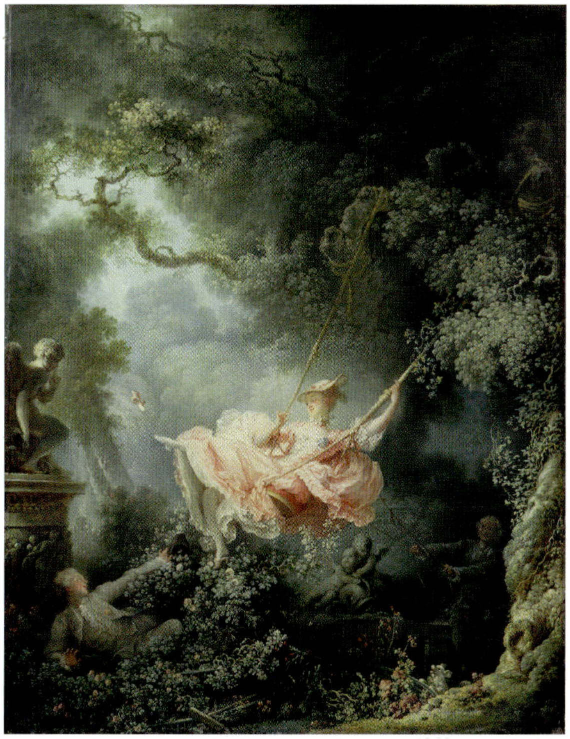

fig. 2.22 Jean-Honoré Fragonard, *The Swing.*

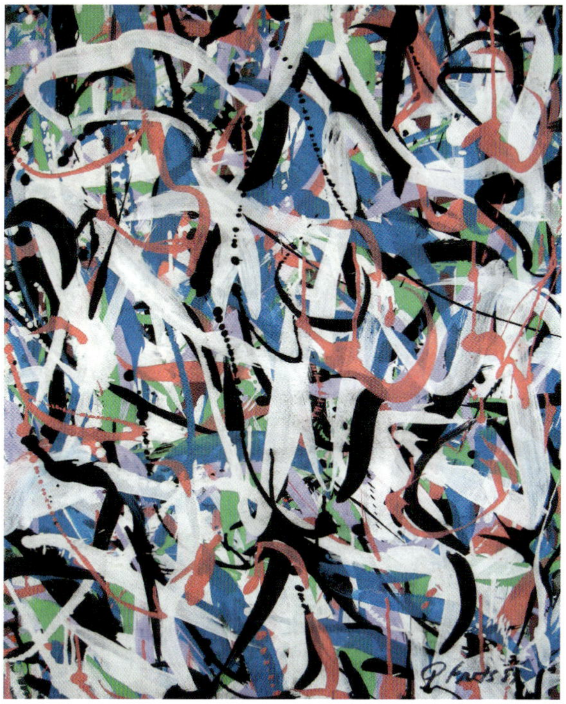

fig. 2.23 Paul Frets, *Reflections.*

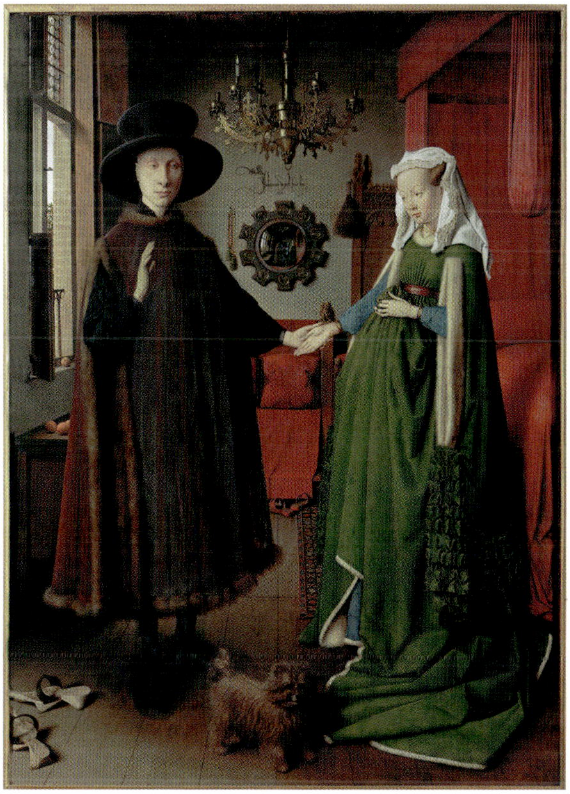

fig. 2.24 Jan van Eyck, *Arnolfini Double Portrait.*

MOVEMENT

Movement can be action (such as a battle scene) or the path our eyes take as they look at a work of art. In Francisco Goya's execution scene (fig. 2.25) our eye is led to the poor fellow about to be shot by the direction of the pointed rifles and by the illumination from the lantern.

UNITY

Unity (or harmony) is the appearance of completeness and consistency. It shows that the various parts of the composition belong together. **Variety** complements unity by adding diversity so that the composition doesn't become boring. In Goya's painting the scene is unified by strong visual connections between the two opposing groups: the soldiers and the condemned. The pointing rifles, the group of people in the middle ground between the two foreground groups and the light transmitted from the lantern by the soldiers to the man about to be shot all serve to unify the composition. Goya adds variety with

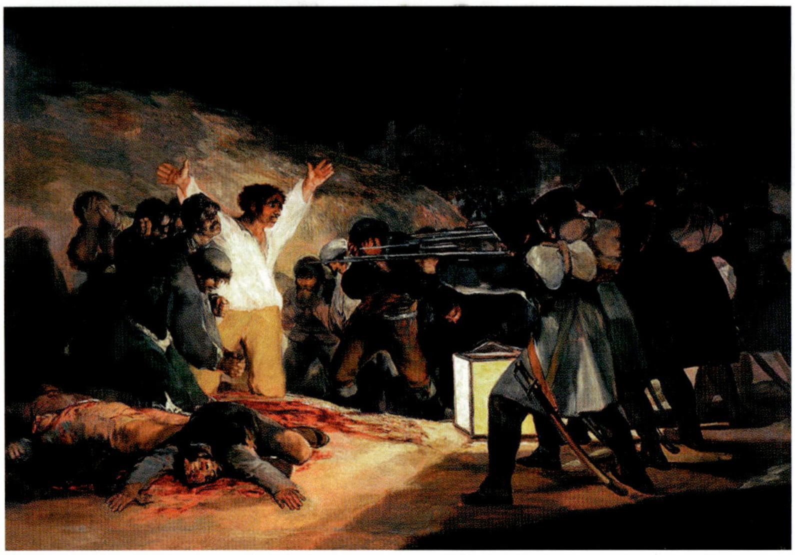

fig. 2.25 Francisco Goya, *The Third of May, 1808.*

the two groups, which oppose each other in type (executioners versus those about to be executed) and in posture (erect soldiers versus crumpling victims).

BALANCE

Balance is arranging the parts of the composition so that no one part becomes overpowering. There is symmetrical balance and asymmetrical balance. Goya's *Third of May, 1808,* is an example of symmetrical balance. The group of soldiers on the right and the victims on the left balance each other out. We can say the same of Botticelli's *Birth of Venus* (fig. 2.1). Venus is in the center, and the wind figures on one side balance the figure with the cloak on the other. Most traditional architecture is balanced because of its **symmetry**. If you were to divide Thomas Jefferson's Monticello in half (fig. 2.26), each half would be the mirror image of the other.

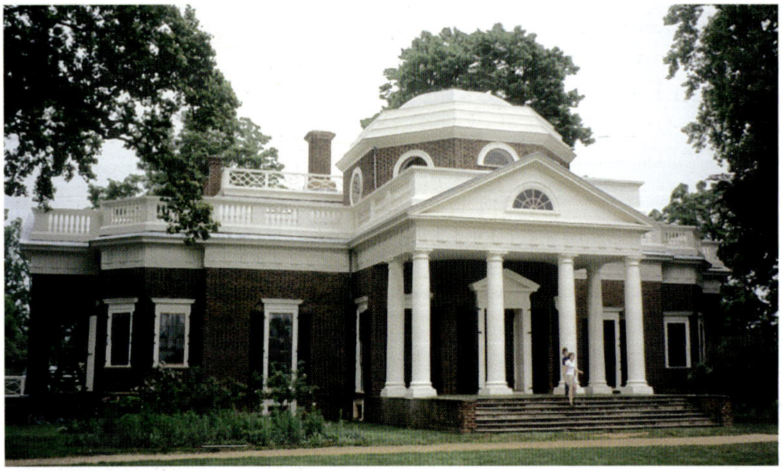

fig. 2.26 Thomas Jefferson, Monticello.

Giotto's *Lamentation* (fig. 2.27) demonstrates asymmetrical balance. The main focus of the scene is Christ cradled by his mother, not in the center but at the lower left. Normally, this lack of symmetry might cause an unbalanced composition, but Giotto offsets this by placing a substantial group of people on the right side of the scene as well as a wall of rock that extends upward to the opposite part of the composition.

EMPHASIS

Emphasis draws our attention to a particular place. If that place is specific it is a **focal point**. In Giotto's *Lamentation,* the focal point is Christ and Mary. They are emphasized by all the other figures who look or gesture toward them. Even the rock slopes down toward them. (These two compositional devices also help unify the composition and provide directional movement.)

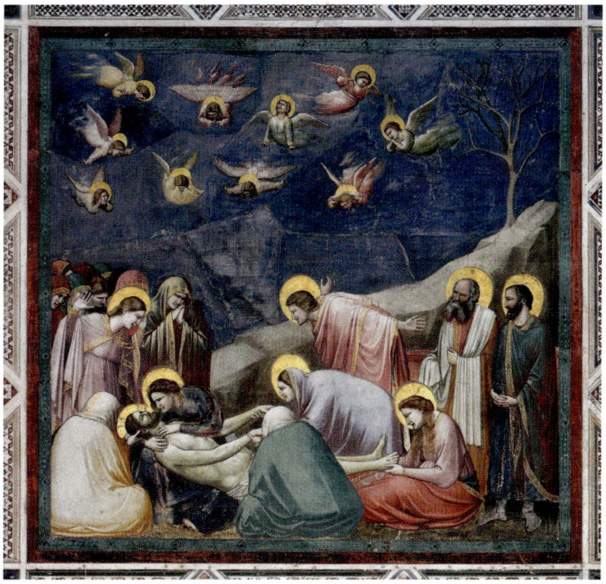

fig. 2.27 Giotto, *Lamentation.*

CONTRAST

Contrast is the use of dissimilar elements and often provides dramatic effect. In *The Third of May, 1808,* the victims about to be shot are different in their poses and emotions from the soldiers about to execute them. In Caravaggio's *Conversion of St. Paul* (fig. 2.28), the strong contrast of the background darkness with the illuminated saint in the foreground creates a dramatic effect.

SCALE AND PROPORTION

Scale refers to the sizes of related objects. A toy poodle is small in scale compared to a St. Bernard. **Proportion** refers to the size of the parts of an object in relation to the whole object. When Pinocchio lied his nose grew out of proportion to the rest of his body. Michelangelo's *David,* at seventeen feet, is large in scale compared to human beings (fig. 2.29). The size of his head and his hands is large and slightly out of proportion to the rest of his body. This is probably because people would be looking up at the figure from below, and Michelangelo took that point of view into account when he carved it. Also, David was a youth when he killed Goliath and a teenager's head and hands often grow larger before the rest of his body.

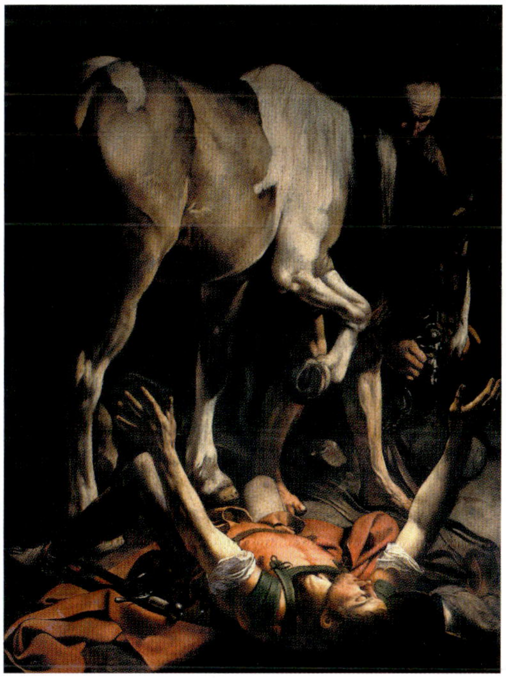

fig. 2.28 Caravaggio, *Conversion of St. Paul.*

REPETITION AND RHYTHM

Repetition and rhythm help unify a composition. The repetition of soldiers' bodies in Goya's *Third of May, 1808* gives them a mechanical quality suggesting a merciless killing machine. The ancient Greek artist Exekias used a series of curves to unify his scene of Dionysus in a sailboat (fig. 2.30), painted on the inside of drinking cup. The curve of the bottom of the boat

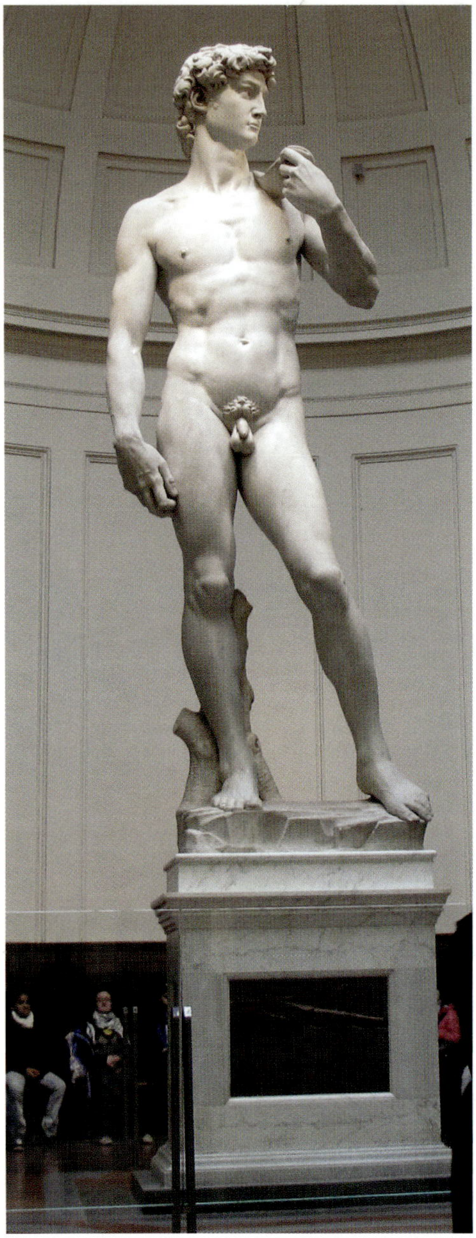

fig. 2.29 Michelangelo, *David.*

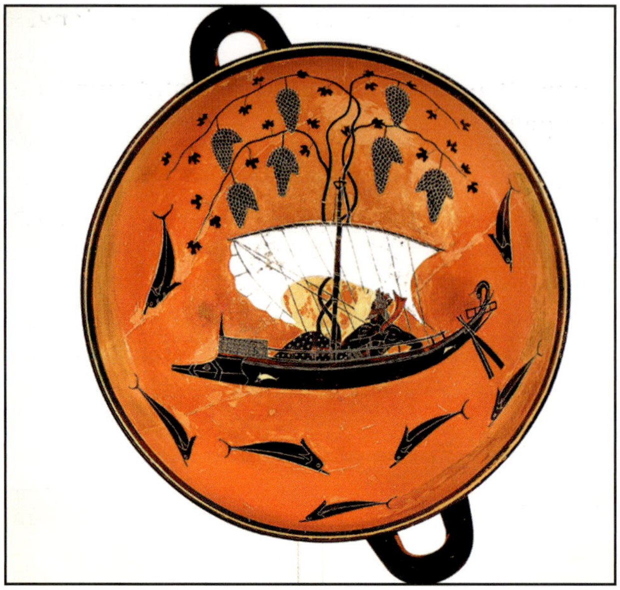

fig. 2.30 Exekias, *Dionysos in a Sailboat.*

mimics the curve of the circular cup rim as do the curves of the dolphins' bodies, the curve of the sail and the curved way the grape vines cascade down around the sail.

When we see a work of art in a museum its composition usually seems natural and evident, but artists may go through many versions before they can consider the work finished. (Sometimes an artist keeps making adjustments and never finishes the work.) Producing a unified, balanced composition with all the elements in their proper places and working together is often a painstaking task. Keep that in mind the next time you visit a museum or a gallery.

SUMMARY

The basic visual components of art are: Line, Shape, Mass, Space, Light and Value, Color, Texture, Movement, Unity and Variety, Balance, Emphasis, Contrast, Scale and Proportion, and Repetition and Rhythm.

Line. Lines can be thick or thin, straight or curvilinear, and they can suggest many different things including direction, movement, emotion, shape, space, and texture. Lines can be actual or implied.

Shape. Shape is the area defined by lines. They can be geometric (usually human made) or organic (as in nature). Shapes can be positive or negative depending upon the background and our perception of them.

Mass. Mass is the bulk of a three-dimensional area such as a sculpture or building. It can be imposing, such as the mass of the Great Pyramid in Egypt. It does not have to be solid (for example the glass pyramidal entrance to the Louvre).

Space. Space is the area that envelops something—it is everything around an object or person. It is of primary importance in buildings, such as the interior of a cathedral. In two-dimensional art, such as painting, **perspective** gives the illusion of space. **Linear perspective** gives the illusion of depth by depicting distant objects as smaller. **Atmospheric perspective** shows distant objects as less defined and bluish.

Light and Value. The way objects are lit can alter our perception of them. The lightness or darkness of a surface is its value. Value ranges from white to black with various shades of gray in between. **Chiaroscuro** (Italian for "light dark") is the use of gradations of light and shade to create the illusion of three-dimensional form.

Color. Color can suggest various moods and psychological states. There are two kinds of color: transmitted color and reflected color. The colors we see most are reflected colors. A red ball appears red because it reflects the red wavelength of white light (and absorbs the other wavelengths).

Texture. Texture is the tactile quality of a surface or the representation of it. Textures can be real or they can be simulated.

Movement. Movement can be action (such as a battle scene) or the path our eyes take as they look at an artwork.

Unity and Variety. Unity (or harmony) is the appearance of completeness and consistency—that the various parts of the composition belong together. Variety complements unity by adding diversity so that the composition doesn't become boring.

Balance. Balance is arranging the parts of the composition so that no one part becomes overpowering. Balance can be symmetrical or asymmetrical.

Emphasis. Emphasis draws our attention to a particular place.

Contrast. Contrast is the use of dissimilar elements and often provides dramatic effect.

Scale and Proportion. Scale refers to the sizes of related objects. Proportion refers to the size of the parts of an object as related to the whole object.

Repetition and Rhythm. Rhythm is the effect of repeating forms, colors, or other elements in a composition. Repetition and rhythm help unify a composition.

PRONUNCIATION GUIDE

Botticelli (bah-tih-**chel**-ee)
Caravaggio (car-ah-**vah**-jyoh)
Chiaroscuro (kee-ar-oh-**skoor**-oh)
David, Jacques-Louis (dah-**veed**, **zhahk**-loo-**ee**)
Dionysos (dye-uh-**nigh**-sus)
Exekias (eh-**zee**-kee-us)
Fragonard, Jean-Honoré (**fra**-goh-nar, zhon-oh-no-**ray**)
Gehry (**gair**-ee)
Giotto (**jot**-toh or joht-toh)
Giza (**gee**-zah)
Goya (**goy**-uh)
Leonardo da Vinci (lay-oh-**nar**-doh dah **vin**-chee)
Louvre (Loovre)
Michelangelo Buonarroti (my-kul-**an**-juh-loh, bwan-nah-**roh**-tee)
Monticello (mon-tih-**chel**-oh)
Orthogonal (or-**thog**-uh-nal)
Raphael (rahf-eye–**el**)
Reims (reems)
Van Eyck, Jan (van **ike**, yahn)
Velázquez (veh-**lahs**-kez)

GLOSSARY

Additive process. 1) In color, when the various colors of the visible light spectrum are added together the result is white light. 2) In sculpture, the creation of a form by construction, assemblage, or modeling.

Atmospheric perspective. See Perspective.

Balance. Forms to achieve equilibrium or harmony.

Chiaroscuro. The gradations of light and dark in a painting or drawing used to create the illusion of three-dimensional form. Also called modeling.

Complementary colors. Pairs of colors that are opposite each other on the color wheel (see fig. 2.18), such as red and green or blue and orange.

Composition. The way an artist organizes the visual elements in a work of art.

Contour line. A line that defines the outer shape of an object.

Contrast. An abrupt change, such as that caused by juxtaposed light and dark areas.

Cool color. A color such as blue or green that appears to be cool in temperature and to recede in space when contrasted with warm colors such as red and yellow.

Figure-ground relationship. The relationship between the main figure or subject and the rest of the composition or background.

Figure-ground reversal. A shift in the viewer's perception causing the figure and the background to switch back and forth so that what was the figure becomes the background and what was the background becomes the figure. (See the Rubin Vase, fig. 2.5)

Focal point. The place in a composition that is the center of visual attention.

Foreshortening. The illusion of figures or objects extending back from the picture plane by diminishing the size of their parts.

Form. The shape and mass of an object or figure.

Hue. Color.

Implied line. A line that is completed in the mind of the viewer.

Intensity. See Saturation.

Linear. A style of art in which lines are used to depict figures and forms with precise outlines.

Linear perspective. See Perspective.

Local Color. An object's actual color in white light. (See also Optical color.)

Mass. The bulk of a three-dimensional object, or the implied bulk of an object on a two dimensional surface.

Medium. 1) A material used to create a work of art. 2) In painting, a liquid added to pigment so that it can be applied to the support.

Optical color. The perceived color of an object, which varies according to atmospheric and other light conditions. (See also Local color.)

Orthogonals. Perceived lines that converge at the vanishing point in scientific perspective.

Perspective. A method of showing depth on a two-dimensional surface. In scientific perspective (also called linear perspective), real or implied parallel lines (orthogonals) converge at one or more vanishing points to give the illusion of recession into space. Objects intended to be further away from the viewer are shown smaller. In atmospheric perspective (also called aerial perspective) forms in the distance are shown less distinct and bluish in color.

Pigment. A powdered material used to give color to inks and paints.

Primary colors. Colors that cannot be created from a mixture of other colors and from which all other colors are made. With pigments, they are red, blue, and yellow.

Proportion. The relation of parts to the whole with regard to size. Compare Scale.

Rhythm. The effect created by repeating forms, colors, or other elements in a composition.

Saturation. The degree of purity of a color. Also called intensity.

Scale. The relative size of an object compared to other objects. Compare Proportion.

Scientific perspective. See Perspective.

Shade. A color modified by the addition of another color, usually black, resulting in a hue of lower value. For instance, the addition of black to red produces maroon. Compare Tint.

Shape. In a two-dimensional work, an area defined by a border.

Subtractive process. 1) With color, when the various pigment colors are added together the result is a darker and duller color. The more colors added together, the closer to black the resulting color becomes. 2) In sculpture, the carving process in which material is taken away to form the image. Compare Additive process.

Symmetry. When two halves of a composition are aesthetically balanced in terms of size, shape, color, and/or the placement of forms.

Texture. The visual (implied) or tactile (actual) surface quality of a form or object.

Tint. A color modified by the addition of another color, usually white, resulting in a hue of higher value. For instance, the addition of white to red produces pink. Compare Shade.

Unity. The oneness or wholeness of a work of art.

Value contrast. The degrees of difference between shades of gray.

Value. The degree of lightness (high value) or darkness (low value) in a color.

Vanishing point. In scientific or linear perspective, the point on the horizon line where parallel lines appear to converge.

Volume. The mass or bulk of a three-dimensional object, or the amount of space it contains.

Warm color. A color such yellow or orange that appears to be warm in temperature and to advance in space when contrasted with cool colors such as blue or green.

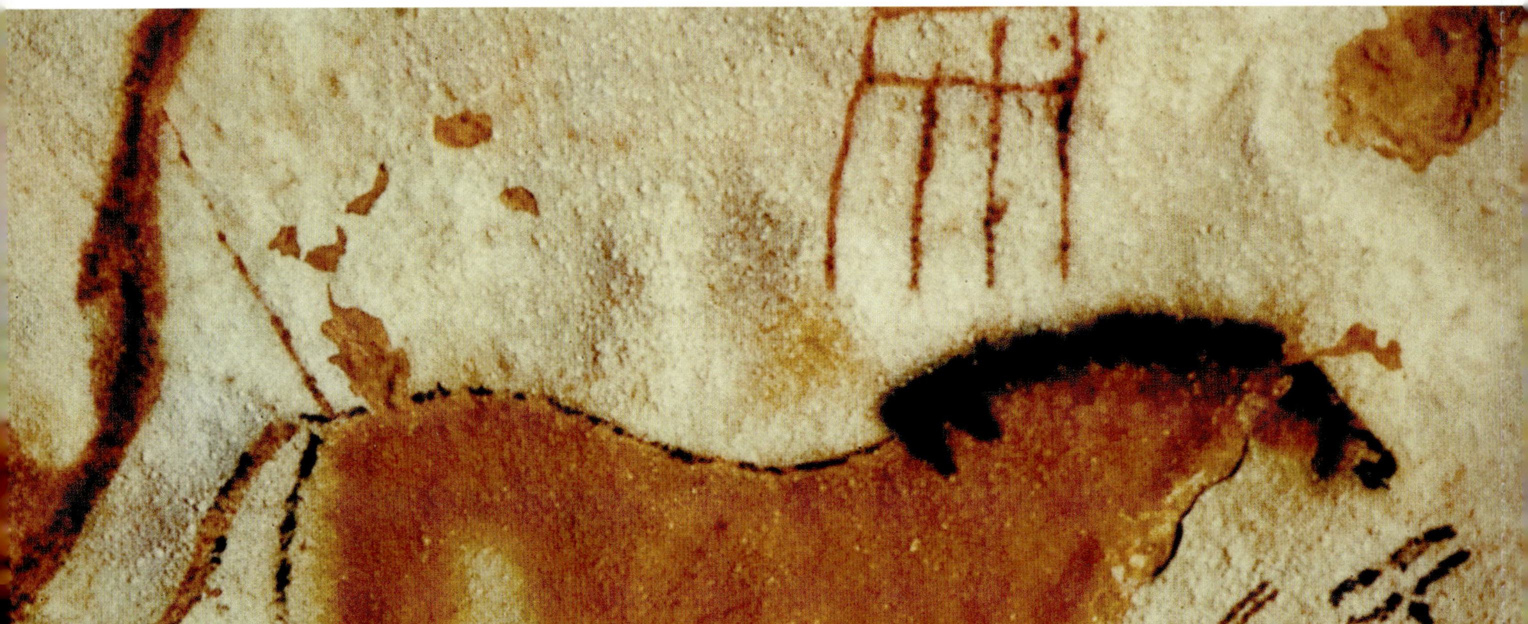

fig. 3.1 So-called Chinese Horse from Lascaux cave, France, c. 15,000–13,000 BCE. Pigment on limestone rock, 5 ft. 6 in. long. The nickname, Chinese Horse, came about because it resembles the Chinese style of art.
© Corel, Inc.

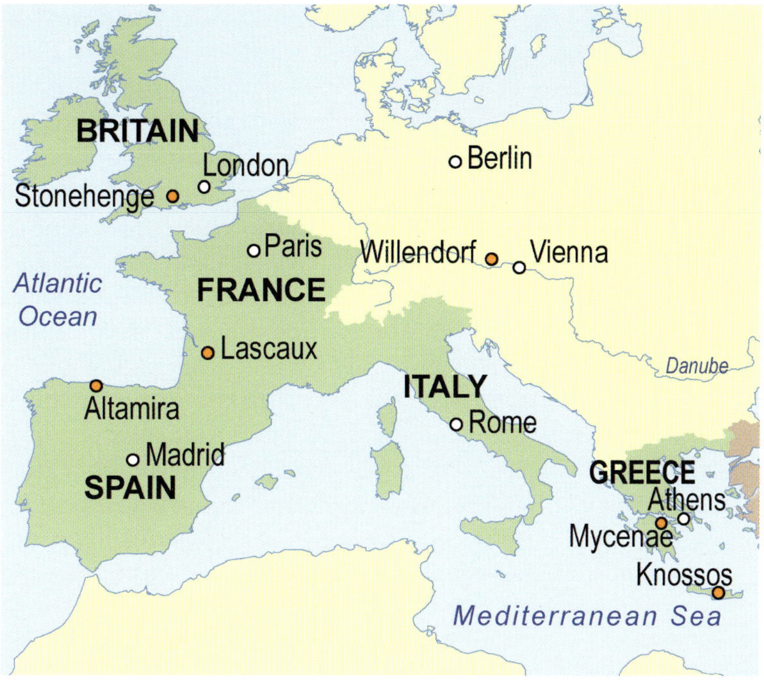

Map of Europe showing prehistoric sites.

3 PREHISTORIC ART

When did humans begin creating art? No one knows for sure, but we have examples going back nearly 40,000 years. The first indications that prehistoric humans created images came in 1879 when the young daughter of an amateur archaeologist discovered late Paleolithic paintings in a cave on the family property in Altamira, Spain. Although the archaeologist thought they were prehistoric, the scientific community scoffed at his claims. The paintings were too "good" and too well preserved to date back 12,000 years or more. They assumed the paintings had to be a hoax. But in the early twentieth century others discovered paintings partially obscured by stalactites in other caves, proving that they were indeed thousands of years old.

Most of the images represent animals. Bison, horses (fig. 3.1), deer, ibexes and aurochs (an extinct type of cattle) are most common, but researchers have also found images of seals, jellyfish and auks. What is amazing is the **naturalistic** quality of the depictions. Black pigment outlined the animals' contours, often taking advantage of a contour or a projection on the cave wall to give a more naturalistic effect. The "artists" then added color **pigments** of red and yellow ochre, hematite and manganese oxide. They applied them with chunks of raw pigment, with fingers or sticks, or by blowing ground pigment through a reed or a hollowed-out bone or even by spitting chewed pigment onto the wall surface. Despite these somewhat primitive application techniques, they used **foreshortening**, overlapping and **modeling** to give a naturalistic three-dimensional effect. Clearly the creators of these images wanted them as realistic as possible. Apart from tracings of hands, there are few representations of humans, and those that exist tend to be schematic rather than natural. The earliest known cave paintings (Chauvet cave in France) date to around 32,000 BCE.

Scientists are still debating the exact purpose of these paintings, and we may never know for certain, but they are not "art" in the modern sense of the word. They were not done to decorate living areas because some of the paintings were found in hard-to-access areas that would not have had humans occupying them. Theories abound. Was there a magical purpose to these images? Were they done to ensure a good hunt? Did these prehistoric people think that if you captured the animal in an image you would be better able to capture it in the wild? (And perhaps the more realistic the image the more powerful the magic?) Some of the images found were in areas where the inhabitants might have performed rituals related to the hunt. Chips in the stone on some images indicate that hunters might have thrown spears at them. Or were they made to ensure the health of the herds since they depended on these animals for food, clothing and fuel? There is one painting of a horse that seems pregnant (fig. 3.1). Fertility would have been important to maintain the population. Were they related to some sort of primitive religion? Artists did not create all the images in a cave at the same time; it appears there were successive generations of artists, yet they did not destroy earlier images.

Prehistoric Periods

Prehistoric art divides into three periods that roughly span the years from 40,000–2000 BCE: Upper Paleolithic (later years of the Old Stone Age), Mesolithic (Middle Stone Age) and Neolithic (New Stone Age). These names derive from the Greek:

Lithos = Stone
Paleo = Old
Meso = Middle
Neo = New

Fertility may be the purpose behind small sculptures representing the female human body, such as the famous **Venus of Willendorf** (fig. 3.2), named after the place in Austria where researchers discovered it in 1908. Early archaeologists referred to these female figures as Venuses, after the Roman goddess of beauty, because they thought they represented a prehistoric idea of beauty. The artists greatly emphasized the breasts, abdomen, hips, thighs and vulva. In a time before agriculture, access to plentiful food would have been limited and an image of a well-fed person could have been a talismanic defense against hunger. The fact that these figures are females and that the artists accentuated their female attributes leads us to think that they may also have served as fertility figures for successful reproduction of the species or possibly for the fertility of the earth as well. They could also be images of success or representations of a mother goddess.

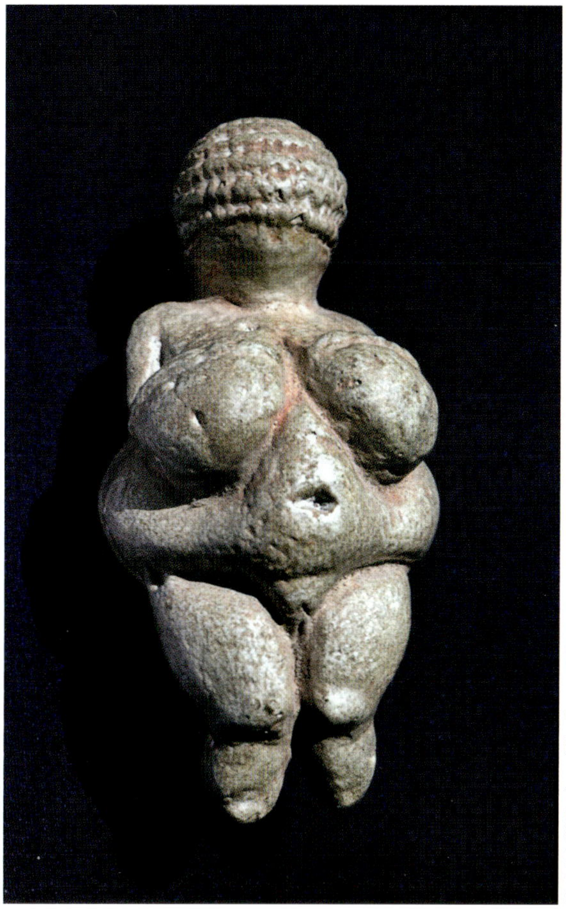

fig. 3.2 Nude Woman (Venus of Willendorf) from Willendorf, Austria, c. 25,000 BCE. Limestone, 4.25 in. high. Naturhistorisches Museum, Vienna.

That brings us to ask, when did religion begin? Many have assumed that early humans did not possess a belief in supernatural beings, but there are indications that this may not be so. Ritual burial of the dead with grave goods implies a belief in some sort of transcendence to another realm. The earliest such burial known occurred over 100,000 years ago, long before the cave paintings and Venus figures. In fact, some scientists suggest that humans are genetically hardwired for religion and that there may be a gene that gives us a predisposition to religious revelation. In any event, viewing upper Paleolithic art in the context of early religious beliefs may not be farfetched. At the other end of the spectrum, figures like the Venus of Willendorf might be nothing more than pornographic fetishes. What the Venus of Willendorf is *not* is a portrait. Its creator did not delineate the face at all; in fact, there really isn't a face with the braided hair taking up most of the head. Like the cave paintings, we may never know the true meaning of the Venus of Willendorf and similar figures, but we can appreciate their aesthetic qualities nonetheless.

Stonehenge. One of the enduring artifacts of the Neolithic period is Stonehenge, situated on a plain in southern England (fig. 3.3). A henge is a circle of **megaliths** (from the Greek for "large stones"), found mostly in Britain. Stonehenge is one of the largest and most impressive of the henges despite its numerous fallen stones. It has a complex history spanning centuries. It began as a simple mound with a ring of holes and a ditch around it.

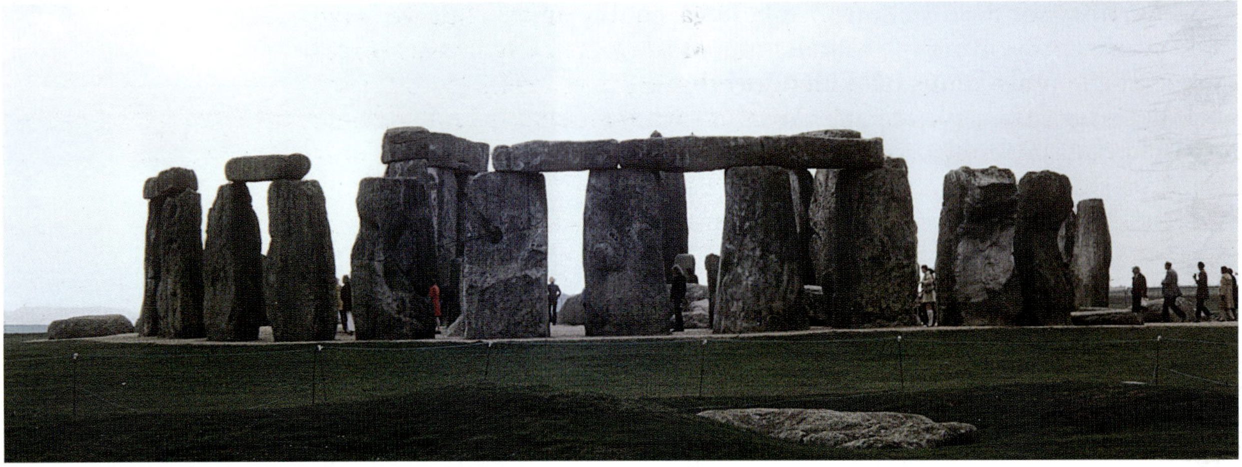

fig. 3.3 Stonehenge, Salisbury Plain, England, c. 2700–1600 BCE. Diameter of circle is 97 ft. The largest stones are 24 ft. tall.

Some of the holes contained human skeletons. Later the inhabitants erected a wooden structure on the mound. In its final stage it came to consist of two rings of stone that enclose a horseshoe-shaped arrangement. Sarsen trilithons in a **post-and-lintel construction** compose the outer ring and horseshoe arrangement. (Sarsen is a type of sandstone, and trilithon refers to a structure made of three stones.) The largest of these stones weighs some fifty tons. Outside the henge to the east is a "heel stone" that marks the rising sun on the summer solstice if one is standing in the center of the henge.

How did the prehistoric Britons move such large stones over long distances and then erect them? Why did they build it? There is no definitive answer to either question. Many humans with the possible help of oxen probably dragged the stones to the site on wooden sleds or log rollers. Theories exist that they dug deep holes and then many men using ropes and wood braces pulled the large stones upright into place. In the Middle Ages people thought the magician Merlin had magically transported Stonehenge from Ireland where giants had built it with stones from Africa. Later on people incorrectly associated it with the Celtic Druids (priests), but they came long after Stonehenge had been built. Although its purpose could have changed over the centuries, in its final incarnation it seems to be a sophisticated astronomical observatory and solar calendar used in a religious or ceremonial context.

SUMMARY

The prehistoric art is divided into three basic periods that span the years from around 40,000–2,000 BCE: Paleolithic, Mesolithic, and Neolithic. The Neolithic persisted longer is some parts of the world than others. For instance, historic Egyptian culture arose around 3,500 BCE, but at that same time Northern Europe was still in the Neolithic age.

We do not know when humans began creating art, but we have examples as far back as 50,000 years ago. Most of the early images represent animals, often depicted in a naturalistic style. Prehistoric artists used minerals ground to a powder as pigments and reeds, sticks, fingers, and other natural implements to apply the pigments to the cave wall surface. Sometimes the pigments were blown or even spit onto the walls. The purpose of these animal paintings is not known. They might have been done to ensure the fertility and health of the herds or to guarantee a successful hunt.

Prehistoric artists also created small stone sculptures of female figures, such as the so-called Venus of Willendorf. Such figures could also relate to fertility since the female aspects are emphasized.

The Neolithic age saw the creation of monumental architectural structures such as Stonehenge in England, which evolved over many centuries from about 2700–1600 BCE. The exact purpose of this structure has long been debated. Theories include an astronomical observatory and solar calendar. Based on recent finds, the most current theory is that it was a healing center. It is possible is served a variety of purposes over the centuries.

PRONUNCIATION GUIDE

Lascaux (lass-**koh**)
Willendorf (**vil**-en-dorf)

GLOSSARY

Foreshortening. The illusion of figures or objects extending back from the picture plane by diminishing the size of their parts.

Megalith. A large stone used in prehistoric monuments.

Modeling. 1) The use of hatching or chiaroscuro to create the illusion of three-dimensional form on a two-dimensional surface. 2) Shaping a form in a pliable material such as clay or plaster.

Naturalism. A style of art that attempts to depict things as they actually appear in nature.

Pigment. A powdered material used to give color to inks and paints.

Post-and-lintel construction. A building technique in which two vertical elements (posts) support a horizontal element (lintel).

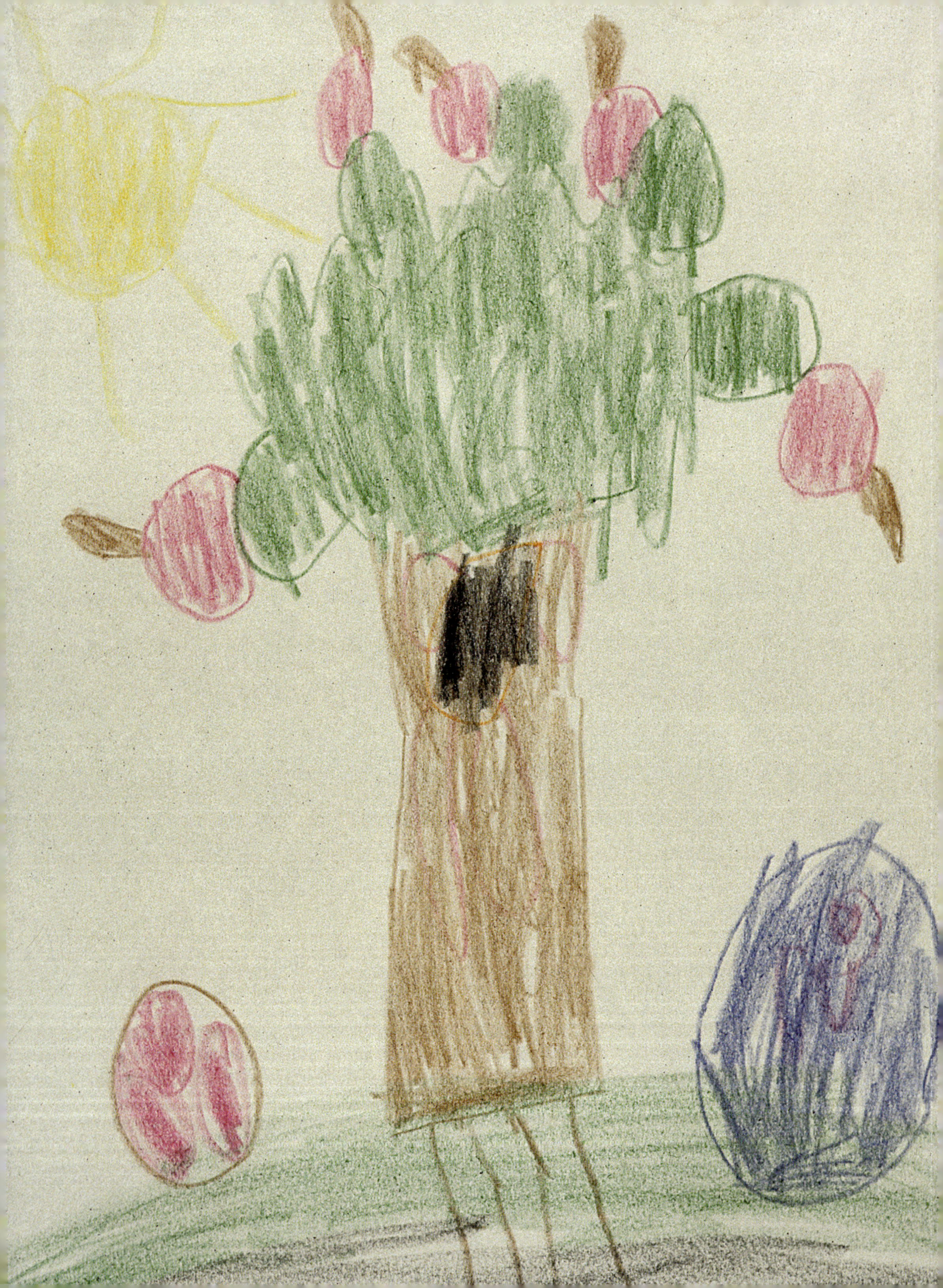

4

Drawing is the basis for most other kinds of art. Works of art such as paintings, sculpture and architecture usually begin as preparatory drawings that the artist uses to work out ideas. The artist can solve problems of composition or fine tune details with large or small sketches. Surviving preliminary drawings have greatly increased our knowledge about major works of art and the individual artist's creative process. To be sure, drawings can also be works of art in their own right. Many painters or sculptors have created beautifully finished drawings intended as such and not in preparation for a painting or a sculpture. We call an artist who draws a draftsman (or draughtsman). Drawing is the first art form most people experience. As soon as children are able to hold a crayon or a pencil they begin to draw (fig. 4.1). It is almost as though the desire to make pictures is part of our human makeup. Sadly, many of us cease to draw after childhood.

DRAWING

Drawings can take many forms. **Finished drawings** are those in which the artist has usually spent considerable time making the drawing. They can have fine detail and sophisticated modeling to give the illusion of three-dimensional forms. Michelangelo and Leonardo da Vinci are known for their masterful drawings. Doodles are just the opposite. **Doodles** are informal drawings often done in a classroom or during a long telephone conversation where the person's attention is directed elsewhere. **Sketches** are quickly executed drawings done to get an idea or an image down on paper. Courtroom artists make sketches because they do not have time to make finished drawings, and their subjects are in constant motion. A **gesture drawing** is a quick sketch of a live model. The artist has the benefit of a still subject, but the model does not hold the pose long enough for the artist to make a finished drawing. **Cartoons** are full-size drawings often done in preparation for a fresco painting or a tapestry. Today we usually associate the word cartoon with a humorous drawing or a series of drawings (comic strips) that tell a story. Drawing could even include making designs in a fogged up bathroom mirror.

Line is the basis of drawing, and the way we combine lines produces the illusion of three-dimensional form. Simple **contour lines** can suggest form. Adolf Dehn's *Sleeping Girl* is a good example (fig. 4.2). Hatching is a technique used to create shading effects with closely spaced parallel lines that darken the value of an area (fig 4.3). Pamela Lawson uses hatching and **cross-hatching** in her drawing, *I See Bones*

fig. 4.1 Child's drawing. Wax crayon.

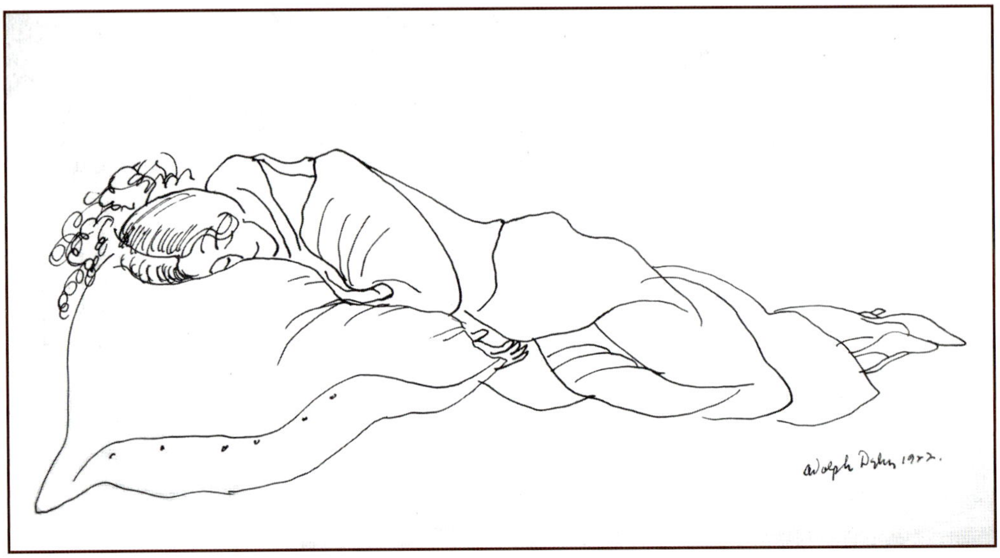

fig. 4.2 Adolf Dehn, Sleeping Girl, 1922. Pen and ink on paper. Radford University Art Museum, Radford, Virginia.

(fig. 4.4), to give form to her surrealistic figure. Ed LeShock's *Portrait of K.B.* (fig. 4.5) employs hatching to achieve a range of values. **Stippling**, the close placement of small dots together, is another method of simulating form. The artist can also achieve **modeling** by using the side of a pencil to gradually blend the values. He or she can achieve highlighting by using the whiteness of the paper itself. Ber Bevan's *Forest* (fig. 4.6) illustrates both these techniques, especially in the tree in the left foreground.

An artist chooses from an incredible range of drawing techniques and mediums to create a seemingly infinite variety of drawing types. Furthermore, the kinds of drawing tools and the type of paper used can dramatically affect the nature of the drawing. Drawing tools include pencil, pen and brush, among others. There is further variety within each tool type. For example, in the pen category there are quill pens, ballpoint pens, roller ball pens and felt-tip pens, just to name a few. There is yet more variety within each pen type. Felt tip pens come in many thicknesses and colors, each with its own characteristics.

Drawing mediums can be dry or liquid. Dry mediums include pencil, colored pencil, charcoal, pastel and Conté crayon. An advantage

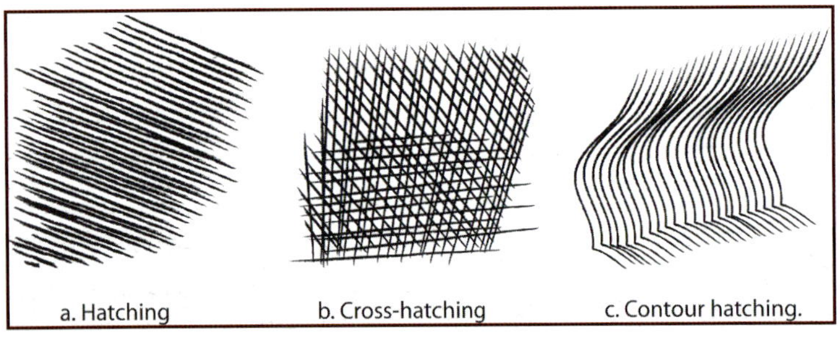

fig. 4.3 Hatching techniques.

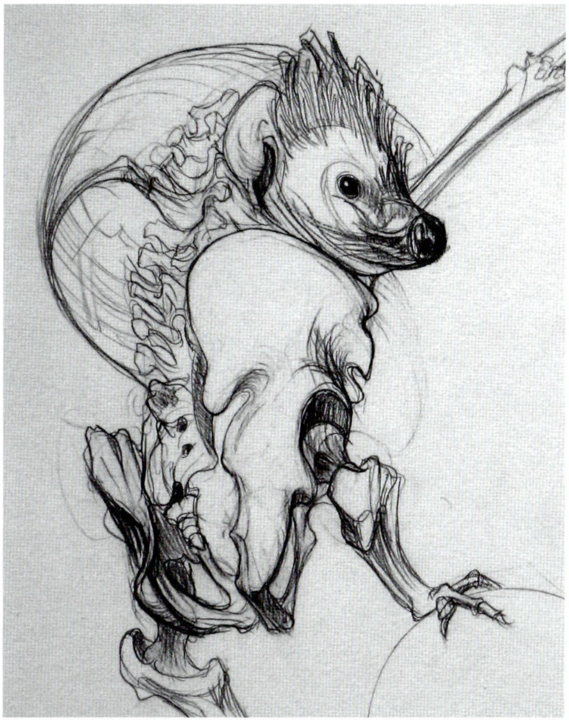

fig. 4.4 Pamela Lawson, *I See Bones,* 2001. Charcoal pencil on paper.

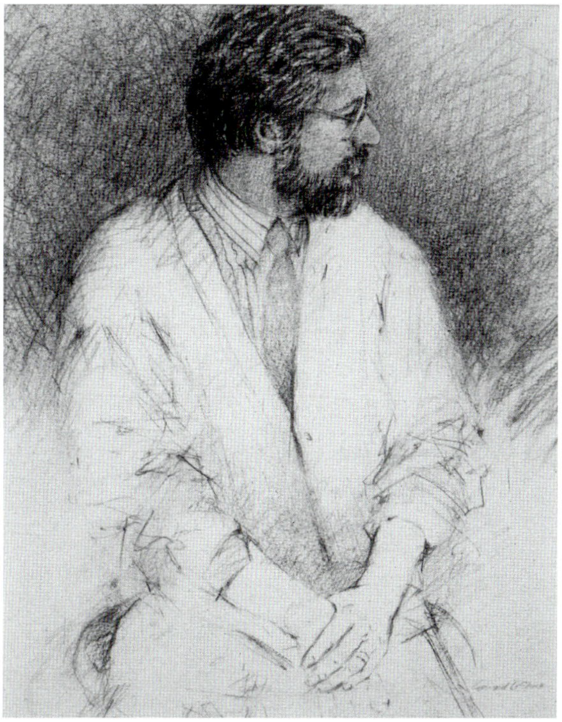

fig. 4.5 Ed LeShock, *Portrait of K.B.,* 1996. Charcoal on paper.

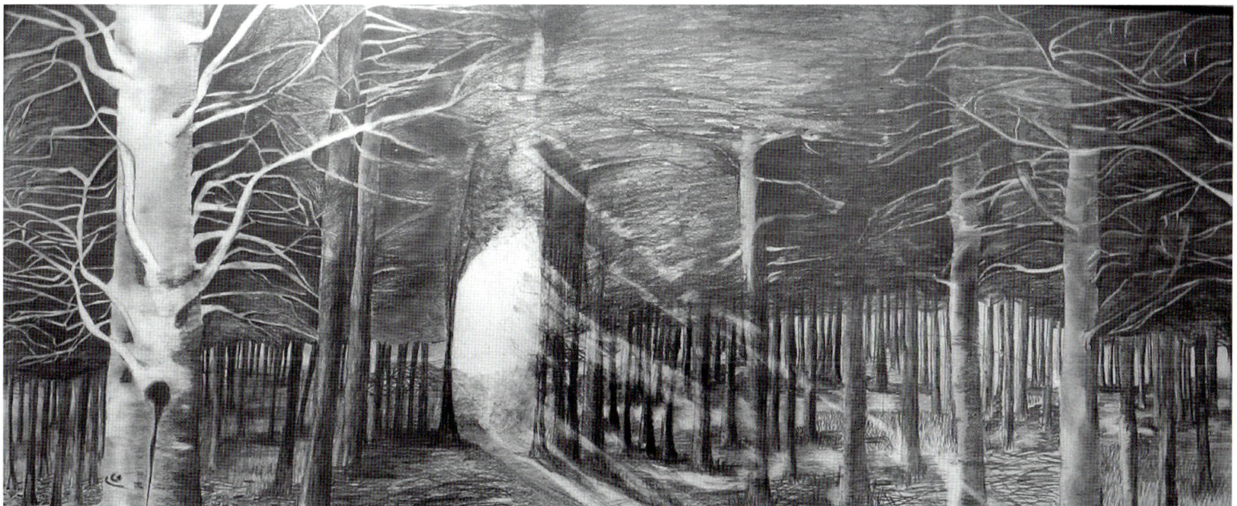

fig. 4.6 Ber Bevan, *Forest,* 1989. Pencil on paper.

with **pencil** is the fact that you can easily make changes and corrections by erasing the undesired portion and redrawing. The quality of lines produced by pencils depends on the hardness of the graphite, the texture of the paper and the pressure applied when drawing. The artist can make different kinds of marks depending upon whether he or she uses the tip or the side of the pencil point. *Forest* by Ber Bevan (fig. 4.6) illustrates this as well as the tonal range from light gray to near black that is possible with the pencil medium. Pencil is a fairly new medium in the history of art. Prior to the seventeenth century artists used **silverpoint**, which is a method of drawing using a stylus made of silver to produce fine, but faint lines.

Charcoal, used by prehistoric peoples on cave walls, is perhaps the oldest drawing medium. Like pencil, charcoal allows a fairly wide tonal range, but it smears easily. To avoid this problem, artists often spray finished charcoal drawings with a varnish fixative to help bind the charcoal to the paper. In *Portrait* of G.D. by Ed LeShock (fig. 4.7), the artist uses charcoal to show a wide range of tone.

Pastels are sticks of powdered pigment held together with a **binder**. They became popular in the eighteenth century. Soft pastels, the most common type, have a higher proportion of pigment to binder than do

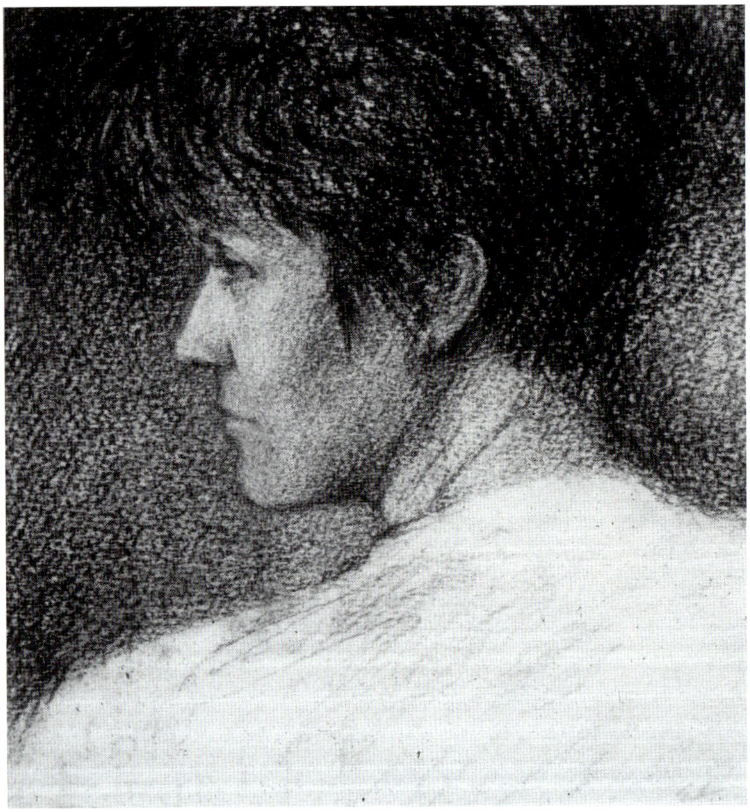

fig. 4.7 Charcoal on paper, Ed LeShock, *Portrait of G.D.*, 1997.

hard pastels. This gives them more intense colors that are easily blended, but as with charcoal, the artist must fix the drawings or they will smudge. Jan Knipe's *Japanese Flowers* (fig. 4.8) illustrates how pastels are pure in color but do not permit fine detail. **Conté crayon** is a semi-hard **chalk** composed of compressed powdered graphite with a clay binder. Conté crayons are waxier and firmer than soft pastels, so they produce less dust and are easier to control. Nicolas-Jacques Conté invented them in 1795 in response to the shortage of graphite during the Napoleonic Wars. **Wax crayons** are yet another dry drawing medium especially favored by children (fig. 4.1).

Liquid drawing mediums include the various forms of ink, either black or colored. Traditional **ink** drawings are made with ink and a quill-like pen. Adolf Dehn's *Sleeping Girl* (fig. 4.2) is a good example of a contour pen-and-ink drawing. With an economy of line he has suggested a complete female form. **Washes** are ink thinned with water, usually applied with brushes. **Felt-tip markers** come in varying values of gray and colors, and you can thin and blend them with a solvent.

Artists introduced a new drawing technique in the late twentieth century: **digital drawing** using a computer. Various software programs allow the artist to simulate almost any medium by drawing with a mouse or a stylus and a computer tablet. Digital drawings are viewed on a monitor or printed by any of several means, inkjet and laser ink printers being the most common.

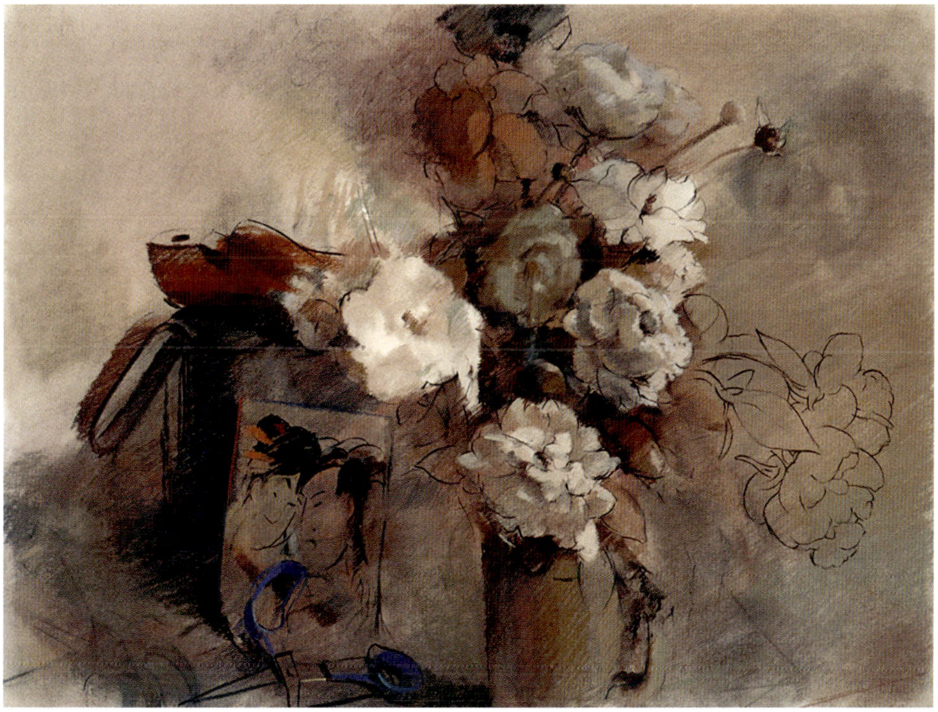

fig. 4.8 Jan Knipe, *Japanese Flowers,* 1999. Pastel on paper.

SUMMARY

Drawing is the basis for most art. Most works of art and architecture start off as a drawing or series of drawings to work out ideas. **Sketches** are quickly executed drawings, **doodles** are informal drawings, **gestural drawings** are quick sketches of a live model, **cartoons** are full-size preparatory drawings for a fresco or tapestry design, and **finished drawings** are more fully worked. Finished drawings can also be works of art in themselves.

Line is the basis of drawing. The way lines are drawn and combined can create many effects, including the illusion of three dimensionality. **Shading** effects are created by **hatching** techniques that use closely spaced lines.

There are many drawing mediums, including **pencil**, **charcoal**, **pastel**, **conté crayon**, **wax crayon**, **ink washes**, and felt-tip markers. Drawings can also be made digitally using a computer. Each of these mediums has its own characteristics.

PRONUNCIATION GUIDE

Caricature (**care**-ih-kuh-cher)
Chiaroscuro (kee-ar-oh-**skoor**-oh)
Dehn, Adolf (dane)
Pastel (pa-**stel**)

GLOSSARY

Binder. A substance that that holds pigments together and allows them to adhere to the support.

Caricature. A picture or description, often humorous, that distorts or exaggerates certain characteristics.

Cartoon. A full-size drawing often done in preparation for a fresco painting or a tapestry.

Chalk. A type of soft limestone that can be pulverized and formed into sticks for drawing.

Charcoal. A black carbon substance produced by partially burning organic material (such as wood) that can be used a drawing tool.

Chiaroscuro. The gradations of light and dark in a painting or drawing used to create the illusion of three-dimensional form. Also called modeling.

Conté crayon. A crayon made of graphite and clay used for drawing.

Contour line. A line that defines the outer shape of an object.

Cross-hatching. Intersecting sets of closely spaced parallel lines that create modeling and the illusion of three-dimensional form on a two-dimensional surface.

Doodle. An informal drawing (n.), or to make informal drawings (v.).

Drawing. The art of moving an implement that leaves a mark across a surface, such as paper. Drawings are typically made with pencil, charcoal, pen & ink, etc., and include the finished drawing, cartoon, sketch, and doodle.

Gestural drawing. A quick sketch of a live model.

Hatching. Closely spaced fine lines that create the effect of shading or modeling.

Modeling. 1) The use of hatching or chiaroscuro to create the illusion of three-dimensional form on a two-dimensional surface. 2) Shaping a form in a pliable material such as clay or plaster.

Pastel. 1) A drawing stick or crayon made of dry pigments, chalk, and gum. 2) A drawing made with pastels.

Pencil. A drawing implement made of a rod of graphite encased in wood.

Pigment. A powdered material used to give color to inks and paints.

Shading. A gradual change from light to dark on a surface.

Silverpoint. A method of drawing using a stylus made of silver to produce fine, but faint lines.

Sketch. A quickly executed drawing done to get an idea or an image down on paper.

Stippling. The use of closely spaced dots to create a form.

Wash. A thin, watery layer of paint, especially watercolor.

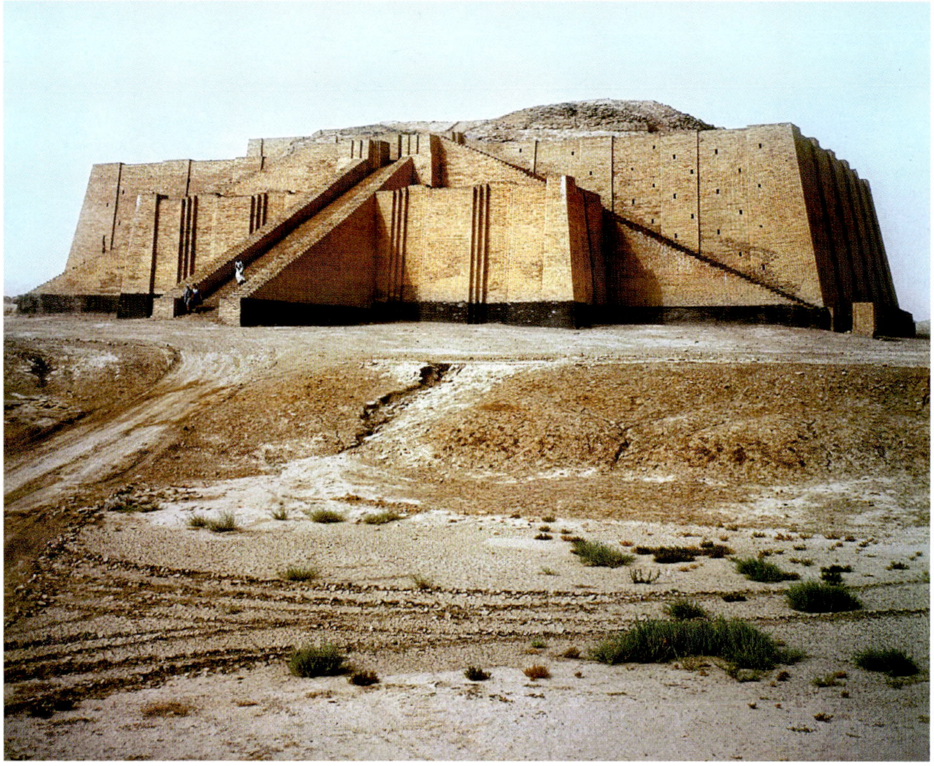

fig. 5.1 Ziggurat at Ur (modern Tell Muqayyar)
Iraq, c. 2100 BCE.

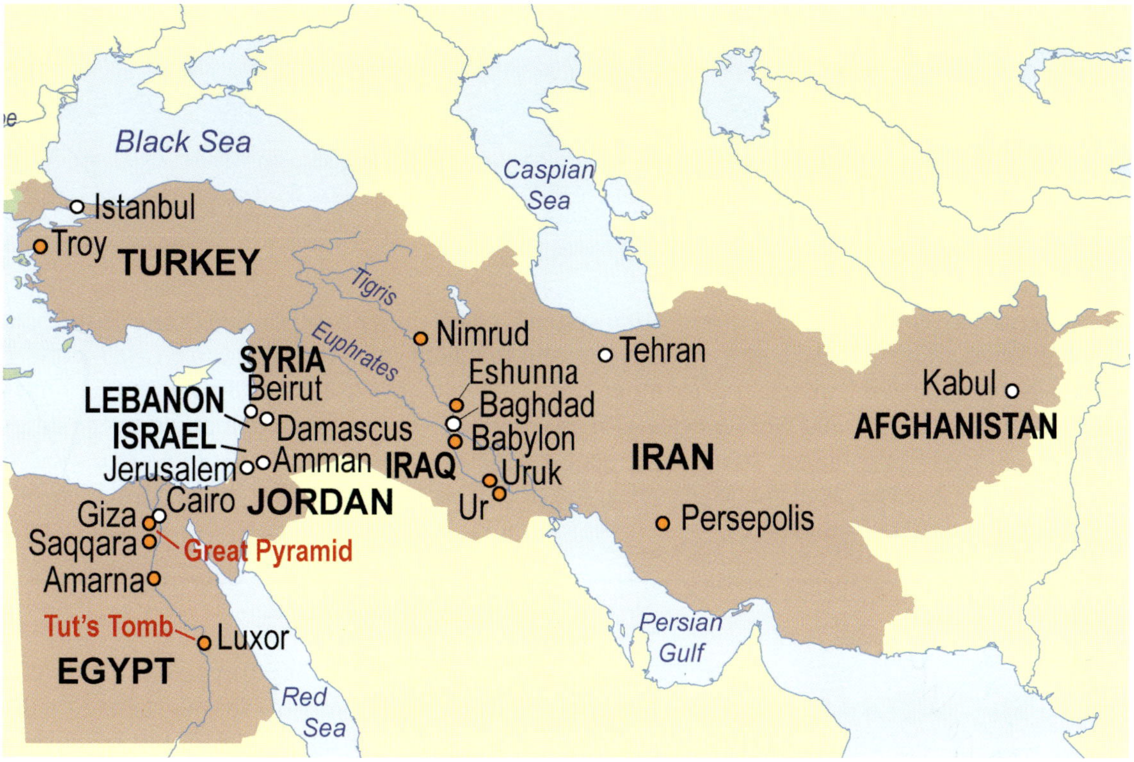

Map of the Ancient Near East.

5 ANCIENT NEAR EAST

SUMER

Western civilization began around 5500 years ago in Mesopotamia in the fertile area between the Tigris and Euphrates rivers in what is now Iraq. In fact the name derives from the Greek word for "between the rivers." The Sumerians developed the first known system of writing (see box). They also organized city-states, codes of law and royal tomb burials rich with artifacts. Their culture was followed by those of the Babylonians and the Assyrians.

The first great civilization of Mesopotamia was that of Sumer, which emerged in the fourth millennium BCE. Sumer was not a unified country; it consisted of independent city-states, with the city of Ur one of the most important. The Bible even mentions Ur—it was the birthplace of Abraham. A god "owned" each Sumerian city-state—the city's rulers were merely the god's representatives on earth. A Sumerian city was designed around a

Writing

The Sumerians invented one of the first writing systems, called **cuneiform**. Writing is one of the hallmarks of a civilization because only then can you begin to record your history and to create literature. Writing systems, however, generally have more prosaic beginnings—usually dealing with economics. Much of the earliest surviving writing deals with inventories of farm animals and other commodities. As society shifted from nomadic to agrarian, people began to settle in permanent communities. As trade and barter became more important so did the need to keep track of everything. Hence, writing developed as a matter of necessity.

temple complex dedicated to the city's god. The most visible structure of the complex was a **ziggurat**, a large, high platform that supported a temple. In many ways the ziggurat recalls an Egyptian pyramid, but because stone was not readily available to the Sumerians, they made ziggurats of mud brick. This means that they have not survived as well as the stone pyramids.

The best example is the ziggurat at Ur because of its partial restoration (fig. 5.1). Composed of three platforms, this was one of the largest and grandest ziggurats built. The base alone rises 50 feet and is 205 × 141 feet at its perimeter. It has three large stairways that lead to a gateway at the top of the base. From there a single pathway led to the top where the temple once stood. Later Mesopotamian societies built even higher ziggurats. Archaeologists think the one in Babylon may have been nearly 300 feet in height and that it may have given rise to the story of the Tower of Babel in the Bible.

Some of the best examples of Sumerian art remained unknown until the excavation of the royal tombs at Ur in the 1920s, the same decade as the discovery of King Tut's tomb in Egypt. Excavations at other sites also revealed interesting artifacts. Figure 5.2 shows a small statue from a temple. This is one of a number of statuettes found at the site ranging in height from a few inches to two and a half feet. Carved of alabaster (a type of gypsum), they have inlays of shell and black limestone. The style of this votive figure, which may honor the vegetation god Abu, is quite different from Egyptian figures. It has a markedly cylindrical quality. Wearing a skirt-like fringed garment and sporting a long beard, he holds a cup used for religious rites in his clasped hands. This was just one of many votive figures, both male and female, found in the temple where they substituted for human

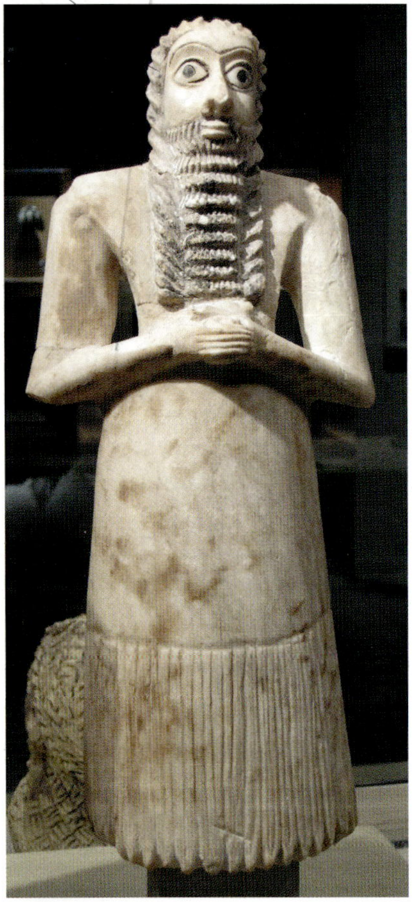

fig. 5.2 Statuette from the "Square Temple" at Eshnunna (modern Tell Asmar), Iraq, c. 2700 BCE. Alabaster, shell, black limestone, bitumen, 11.5 in. high. Metropolitan Museum of Art, New York.

worshippers. Their overly large, wide-open eyes may indicate constant alertness as they offer continual prayers to their god—something an actual person could not do. Despite the stylization of the beard and the continuous eyebrow, this figure displays a palpable intensity of religious devotion with an ever attentive attitude of prayer.

BABYLON

After several other cultures came to dominate Mesopotamia (notably the Akkadians, the Guti and the Elamites), in the early second millennium the city of Babylon came to the fore. Its greatest ruler was Hammurabi who is famous for establishing one of the earliest recorded codes of laws (see box). Literally set down in stone, it is inscribed on a large **stele** with a relief sculpture of Hammurabi before the god Shamash (fig. 5.3) above it. Hammurabi stands before a seated Shamash who wears a crown composed of four tiers of bull's horns and who holds a staff and a ring in his right

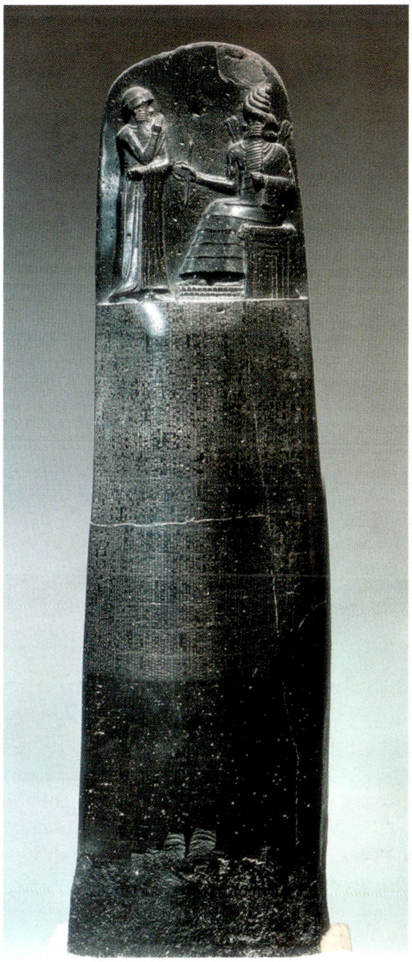

fig. 5.3a Stele with the Law Code of Hammurabi, c. 1780 BCE. Basalt, 7 ft. 4 in. total height. Louvre Museum, Paris.

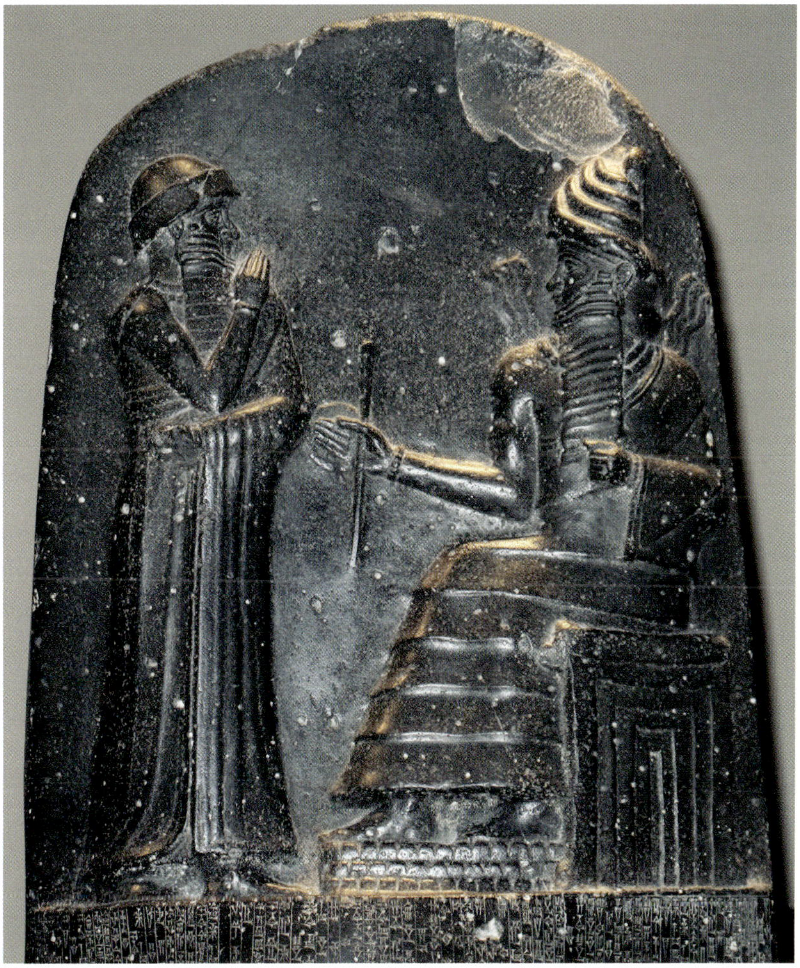

fig. 5.3b Detail.

Law Code of Hammurabi

Although the Law Code of Hammurabi standardized the laws of the land, it could be harsh as well as biased against the lower classes. The 282 laws inscribed on the stele covered many facets of Babylonian daily life. Here are a few of them:

- If a man puts out the eye of another man, his eye shall be put out.
- If a man knock out the teeth of his equal, his teeth shall be knocked out. [These two laws may be the origin of the "eye for eye, tooth for tooth" phrase in the Bible.]
- If a freed man strike the body of another freed man, he shall pay ten shekels in money.
- If the slave of a freed man strike the body of a freed man, his ear shall be cut off.
- If a man's wife is caught in bed with another man, both will be tied up and thrown in the water.
- If any one is committing a robbery and is caught, then he shall be put to death.
- If any one brings an accusation of any crime before the elders, and does not prove what he has charged, he shall, if it be a capital offense charged, be put to death.

hand. These are symbols of his power and authority. Shamash's larger size (if he were to stand up he would tower over Hammurabi) and the fact that he sits on a throne with his feet on a **stylized** mountain further emphasize his importance. There are also divine flames emanating from his shoulders. Stylistically, the projecting parts of the figures have the same cylindrical quality as the votive worshipper of a thousand years earlier (fig. 5.2). Like human representation in other ancient cultures, the figures appear in a combination of frontal and profile views. Shamash's head and crown are in profile, but his torso is frontal. As a lesser being than the god, Hammurabi's depiction is allowed a bit more **naturalism**. Still seen in both profile and frontally, his torso turns a little so that we see his right shoulder.

ASSYRIA

The Assyrians originated in what is now northern Iraq and became known as a ruthless people as they conquered neighbor after neighbor with little mercy. The height of their culture was about 900–600 BCE, and by that time they controlled a huge swath of the ancient Near East. The Assyrian rulers built large palace complexes comprised of courtyards, a ziggurat, reception halls, royal apartments and other quarters. Guarding the gates to these citadels were large stone monsters called **lamassu**. They had the form of winged, human-headed bulls or lions and they were huge—some were over thirteen feet tall. The two lamassu in figs. 5.4 and 5.5 illustrate each type. Note the lion paws of the lamassu in fig. 5.4 and the bull hooves in fig. 5.5. Everyone entering the palace would have to pass by these imposing monstrous creatures. Keep in mind that this was in a superstitious era long before the realistic horror movies and video games of modern times. These creatures could well strike fear into those who had to pass by them. The

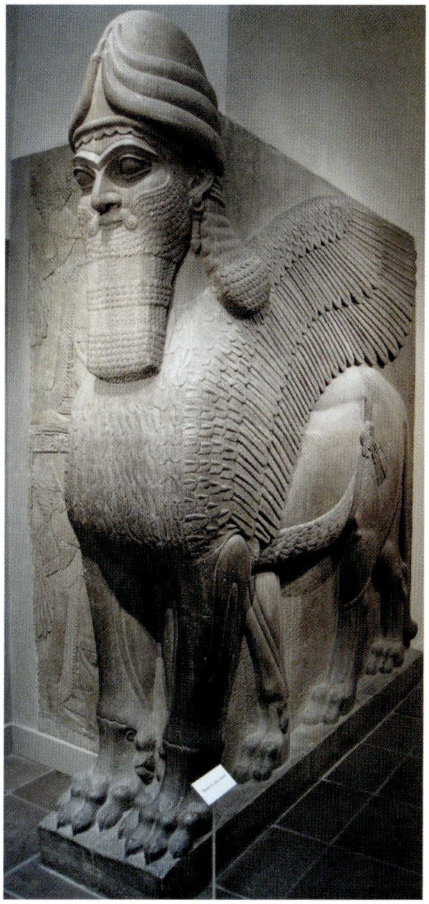
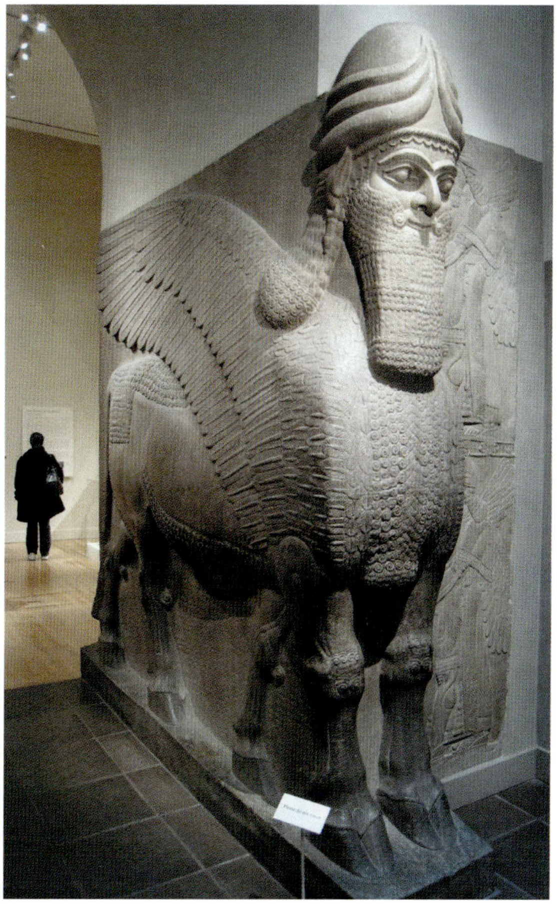

figs. 5.4 and 5.5 Lamassu from the Palace of Ashurnasirpal II at Nimrud, Iraq, ninth century BCE. Alabaster, 10 ft. 3.5 in. high. Metropolitan Museum of Art, New York.

lamassu are technically relief sculptures because they are attached to the wall, but they are very deep relief, and they have an interesting composition. If you look carefully you will see that each has five legs instead of four. This is so that the creature will look correct from the front as one approaches the gate and from the side as one passes through the gate. Had the artist not repeated the far front leg in the side view, it would have looked as though the lamassu had only three legs from the side, which would have greatly diminished its daunting sense of power.

NEO BABYLONIA

The Babylon in the Bible with its famed ruler, Nebuchadnezzar, is from a much later period than Hammurabi's Babylon. To distinguish the two, the later phase in Babylon's history (sixth century BCE) is called Neo Babylonian. This Babylon was home to the famous hanging gardens of Babylon, one of the seven wonders of the ancient world. They, unfortunately, do not survive, but restoration has taken place on part of the gates and walls surrounding the city. One of the famous Ishtar gates, excavated by Germans, is now in a museum in Berlin, but a reconstruction of another exists in Iraq (fig. 5.6). Composed of blue-glazed mud brick with molded reliefs, it features a large

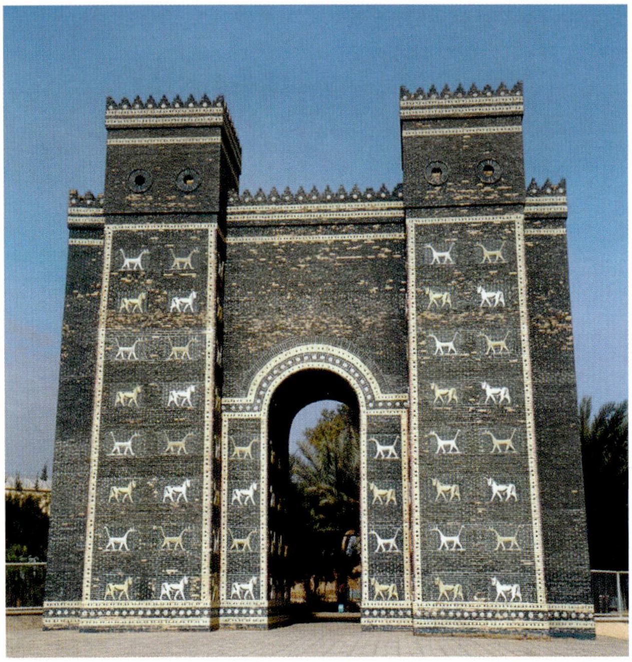

© Topham/The Image Works

fig. 5.6 Ishtar Gate (reconstruction), Babylon, Iraq, c. 575 BCE.

arch flanked by crenellated towers. The reliefs depict the dragon of the god Marduk and the bull of the god Adad. The walls that enclosed the processional way leading to the gate featured the lion sacred to the goddess Ishtar (fig. 5.7). Like the gateway in the Assyrian citadel, this also made a strong impression on passersby.

SUMMARY

Western civilization began around 3500 BCE in the area that is now Iraq. Ancient Near Eastern history comprises many cultures including Sumerian, Babylonian, Assyrian, and Neo-Babylonian. The Sumerians were the first to develop writing. They built large religious structures called ziggurats, which had the appearance of a stepped pyramid. It

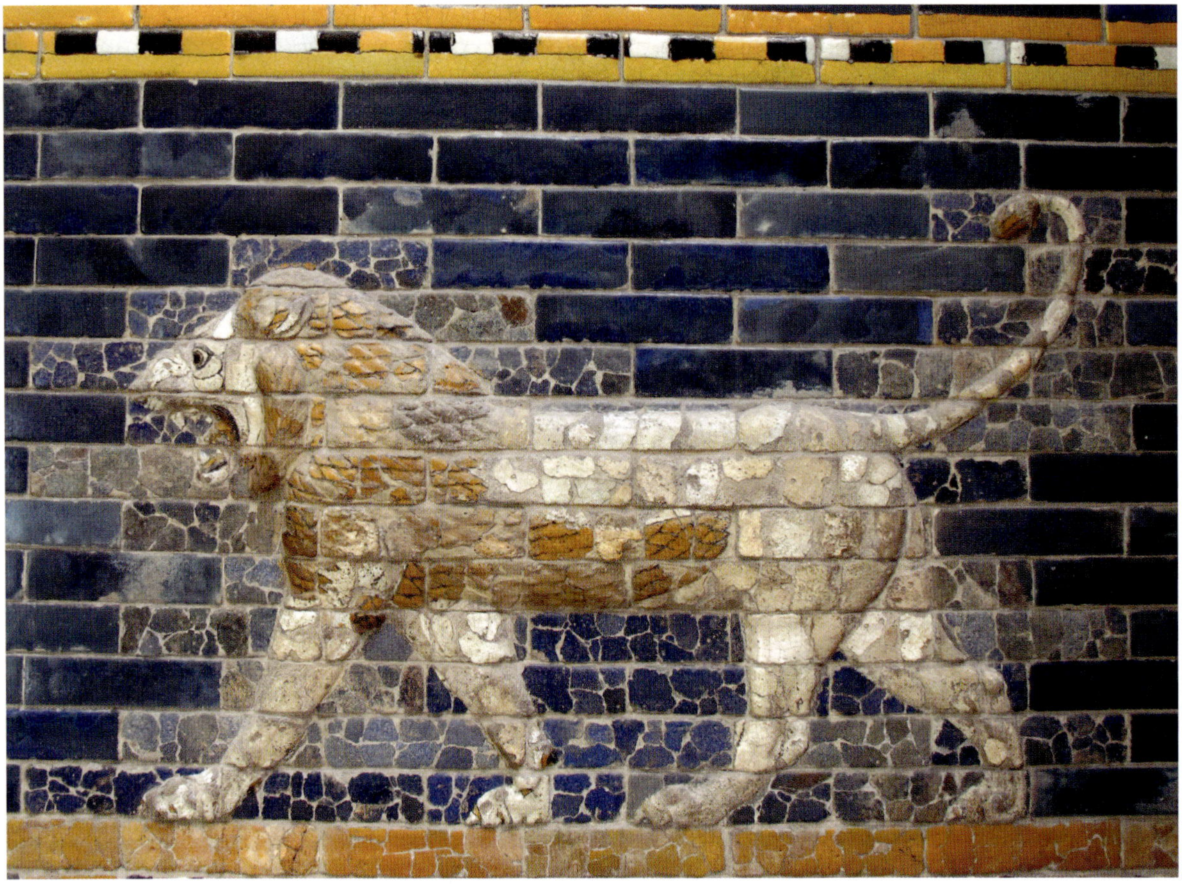

fig. 5.7 Striding lion from the wall of the processional way in Babylon, Iraq, c. 575 BCE. Glazed brick, 42 in. high. Pergamon Museum, Berlin.

was probably a ziggurat that gave rise to the story of the Tower of Babel in the Bible.

Babylon became a dominant force in the area around 1800 BCE. Its most famous ruler was Hammurabi who is noted for his law code, which he had carved in stone on a large stele that shows him standing before the god Shamash. Shamash, being of greater importance, is depicted larger than Hammurabi.

The height of Assyrian culture was 900–600 BCE, and the Assyrian rulers had a reputation for being ruthless. They built vast palace complexes that evoked the power of the king. Guarding many entrances were large sculptures of lamassu, mythological winged creatures that were part human and part lion or bull. These animals impressed in a frightful way all those who had to pass by them.

Babylon once again rose to power in the sixth century BCE. We refer to the period as Neo-Babylonian to distinguish it from the earlier Babylonian period. This is the Babylon referred to in the Bible and its most famous ruler was Nebuchadnezzar. The famous Hanging Gardens of Babylon, one of the Seven Wonders of the Ancient World, were there. The Ishtar Gate and other remnants of glazed brick walls indicate the city's magnificence.

PRONUNCIATION GUIDE

Assyrian (uh-**seer**-ee-un)
Cuneiform (**kyoo**-nih-form or kyoo-**nee**-uh-form)
Hammurabi (hah-moo-**rah**-bee)
Hierarchical (high-uh-**rahr**-kih-kuhl)
Hieratic (high-uh-**rat**-ik)
Lamassu (la-**mah**-soo)
Mesopotamia (mes-uh-puh-**tay**-mee-uh)
Nebuchadnezzar (neh-boo-kahd-**nez**-zar)
Stele (**stee**-lee)
Sumer (**soo**-mer)
Ur (er)
Ziggurat (**zig**-uh-rat)

GLOSSARY

Cuneiform. A system of writing consisting of wedge-shaped characters that was used in ancient Mesopotamia.

Hierarchical or hieratic scale. Depicting more important figures larger than less important ones.

Lamassu. In ancient Assyrian art, a hybrid creature with a human head and the winged body of a lion or bull.

Naturalism. A style of art that attempts to depict things as they actually appear in nature.

Stele. An inscribed vertical stone slab that marks something such as a grave.

Stylized. When the depiction of a figure or form departs from optical reality to conform to artistic conventions or to emphasize certain characteristics.

Ziggurat. A rectangular religious structure in ancient Mesopotamia composed of several stacked platforms of diminishing sizes.

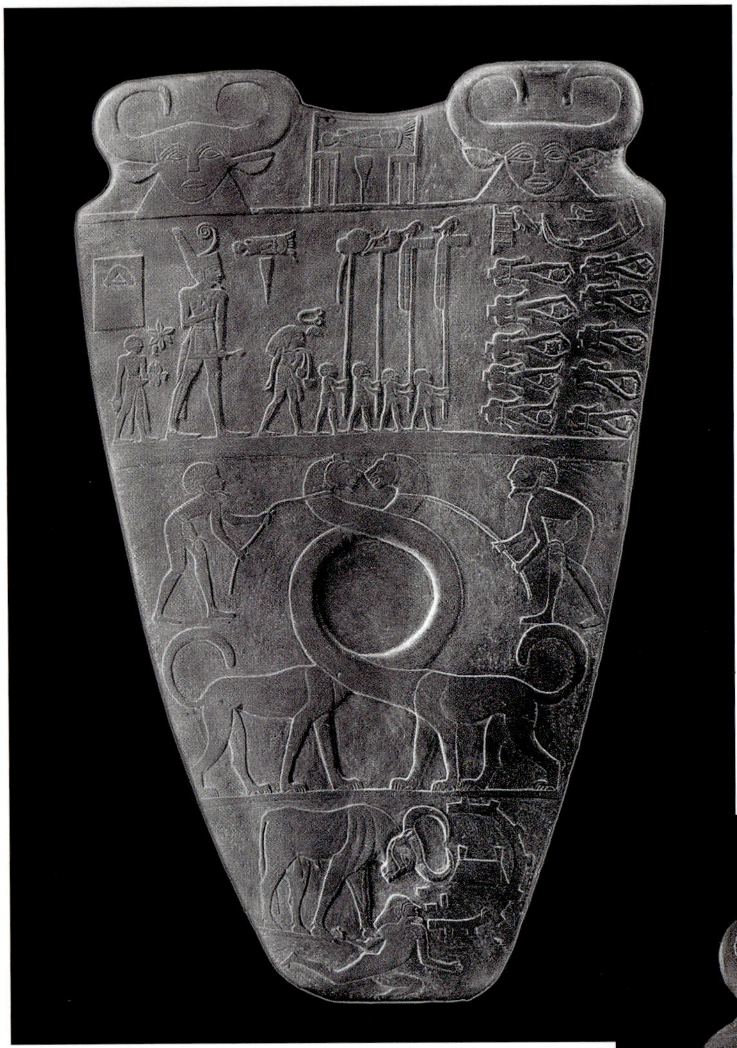

A. Palette of Narmer
B King Narmer
C Old Kingdom

twisted perspective

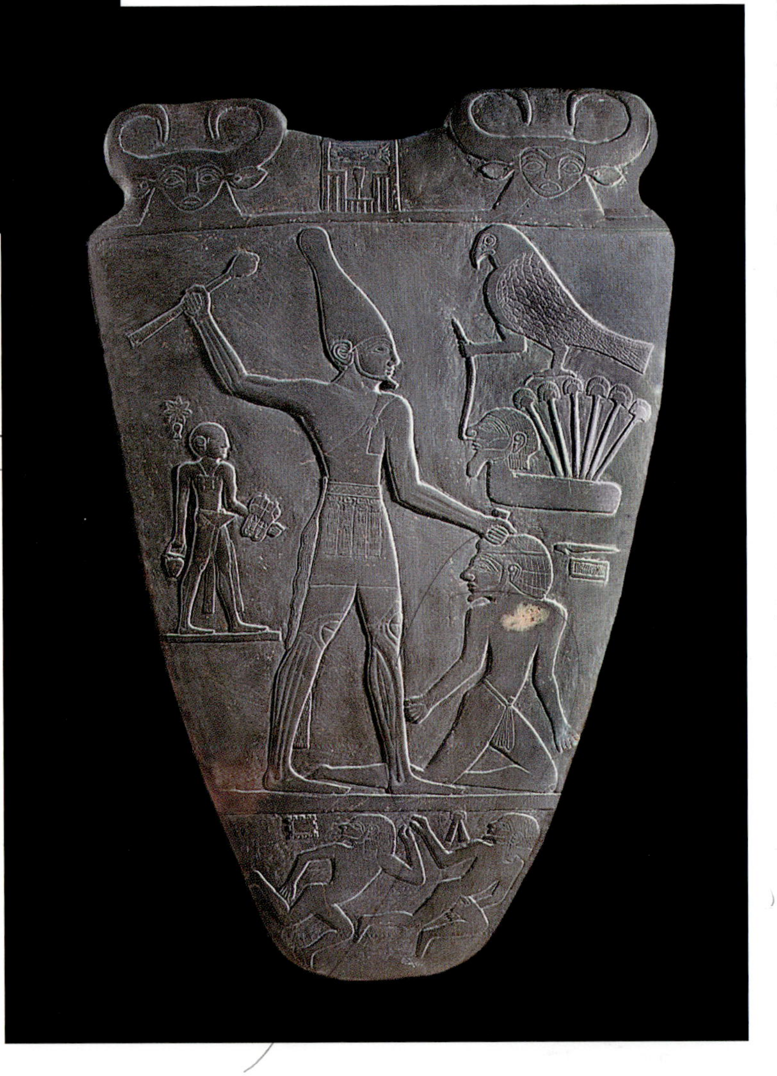

fig. 6.1 Palette of Narmer (left top image: front view; right bottom image: back view), c. 3000 BCE. Slate, 25 in. high. British Museum, London.
© Werner Foreman/Topham/The Image Works

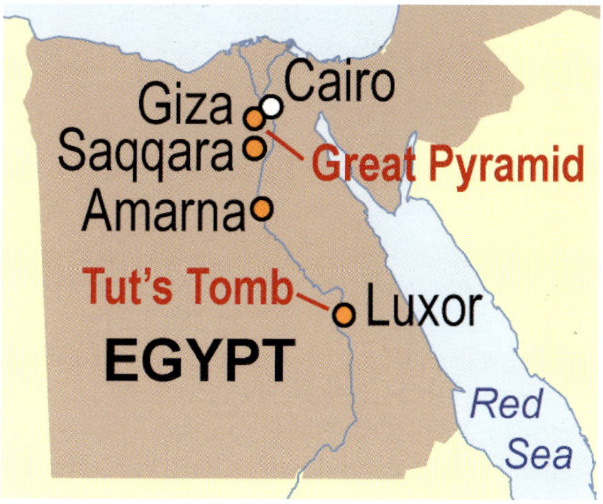

Map of Ancient Egypt.

6 ANCIENT EGYPTIAN ART

Ancient Egyptian society began along the banks of the Nile River in the fourth millennium BCE. The Nile was the lifeblood of ancient Egypt. It provided water, fertile soil with its annual flooding and a means of transport. The Egyptians developed one of the first writing systems (see "Egyptian Hieroglyphs" box) and a political system of ruling pharaohs considered divine. Thirty-two dynasties of pharaohs ended with the suicide of the last pharaoh, Cleopatra in 30 BCE. The more than 3,000 years of Egyptian history divide into various periods with the Old Kingdom (c. 2600–2100 BCE) and the New Kingdom (c. 1550–1070 BCE) producing the best known works of art and architecture. One of the earliest and most important works, however, comes from the Early Dynastic period, which preceded the Old Kingdom.

The Palette of Narmer (fig. 6.1) is a ceremonial makeup palette decorated with relief carving. This object not only illustrates the conventional Egyptian figure style, it also records an important historic event: the unification of Upper (southern) and Lower (northern) Egypt by King Menes, identified with Narmer. The front side has three registers. At the top is a hieroglyph of Narmer's name flanked by cow heads representing the goddess Hathor who protects Narmer. Below that we see Narmer (the largest figure) wearing the crown of Lower

Egyptian Hieroglyphs

Hieroglyph is a Greek word meaning "sacred carving." Developed in the later fourth millennium BCE, hieroglyphs are one of the oldest forms of writing. The Egyptians used this system for over 3,000 years, until the late fourth century AD. After that, the ability to read them was lost until the nineteenth century. In 1799 explorers found a stone inscription at Rosetta, Egypt, with a text in Egyptian hieroglyphics and classical Greek. With the help of the Greek translation and earlier work by Thomas Young in England, Jean-Francois Champollion, a French linguist, succeeded in translating the hieroglyphic text on the Rosetta Stone in 1824. The reason hieroglyphs were so difficult to translate was because a hieroglyph could represent one of three things: a phonetic sound, a word or a concept, or a symbol that would help clarify the meaning of the word. Once Champollion had solved the mystery of hieroglyphs, scholars could translate thousands of hieroglyphic texts and learn much about ancient Egyptian culture.

Egypt and a tunic with a bull's tail attached. Behind him is his sandal bearer. That Narmer is barefoot indicates a sacred act. In front of him men carry standards, and beyond them are ten dead enemy bodies with their decapitated heads tucked between their legs. The middle register shows two feline creatures with elongated necks that intertwine to form a circular depression where the makeup would have gone if this were an actual cosmetic palette. The bottom register depicts a powerful bull, representing Narmer, knocking down a citadel with another fallen warrior below.

On the back side, Narmer, with the same tunic and bull's tail but now wearing the crown of Upper Egypt, wields a club to slay a fallen enemy. As on the front, a man behind him carries his sandals. To the right we see the falcon god Horus, associated with the pharaoh, holding a tether to the head of a man from whose back sprout **papyrus** plants, another symbol of Lower Egypt. This then is a more symbolic representation of the conquering of Lower Egypt by Narmer. Below the king are two fallen enemies.

The figure of Narmer on both sides illustrates the early establishment of the conventional Egyptian figure style. He is depicted in a twisted perspective. His head and legs are in profile, whereas his eye and torso appear frontally. This type of view shows as much of the figure as possible and enhances the pharaoh's importance, as does his larger size. Note that on the front side the torsos of the standard bearers and the men tethering the felines appear in a more realistic profile view.

OLD KINGDOM

The Pyramids at Giza. The Old Kingdom pyramids at Giza, just across the Nile River from Cairo, are one of the greatest human achievements. Commissioned as impressive, impregnable tombs by three successive pharaohs, Khufu (Cheops), Khafre (Chephren) and Menkaure (Mycerinus), they still stand after 4,500 years. In fact, the Great Pyramid, that of Khufu, is the only one of the Seven Wonders of the ancient world (see "The Seven Wonders" box) that survives (fig. 6.2). It was built c. 2500 BCE and is the largest and oldest. Composed of roughly 2.3 million blocks of limestone (with an average weight of 2.5 tons each), it is 775 feet long on each side and covers some 13 acres. Its original height was 480 feet (the top 30 feet are now missing). It is the most massive structure ever built, and it remained the tallest structure ever built for nearly 4,000 years. Originally, polished white limestone slabs sheathed it that would have glistened in the sunlight (see fig. 6.3). An earthquake loosened these outer casing stones in 1301, and people removed many and used them as building material in Cairo. Although mostly solid, the pyramid contains numerous passages and chambers (fig. 6.4). The pharaoh's tomb chamber lies in the middle of the pyramid, accessed via a

A. great pyramids of Giza

B. various pharos (old Kingdom

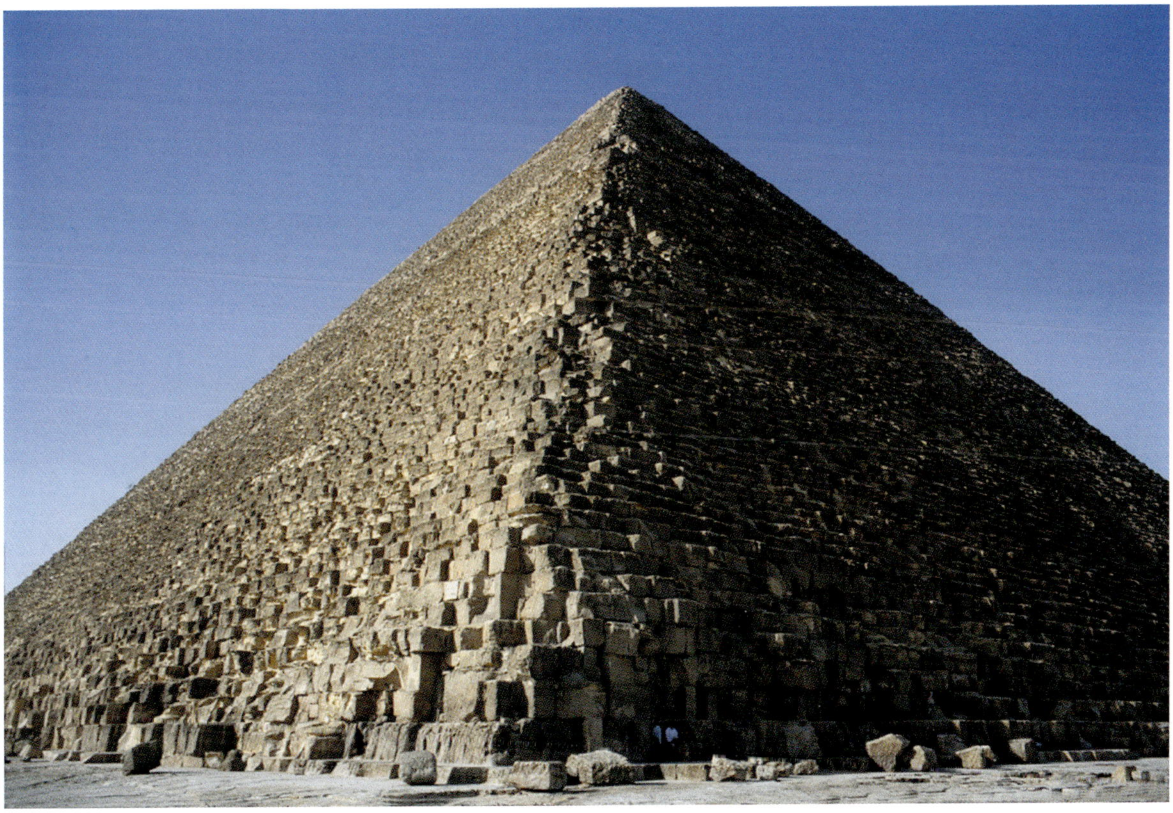

fig. 6.2 Pyramid of Khufu, c. 2500 BCE. Limestone, 450 ft. tall. Giza.

> Solid mass w/ a few rooms inside

> most robbed by grave robbers.

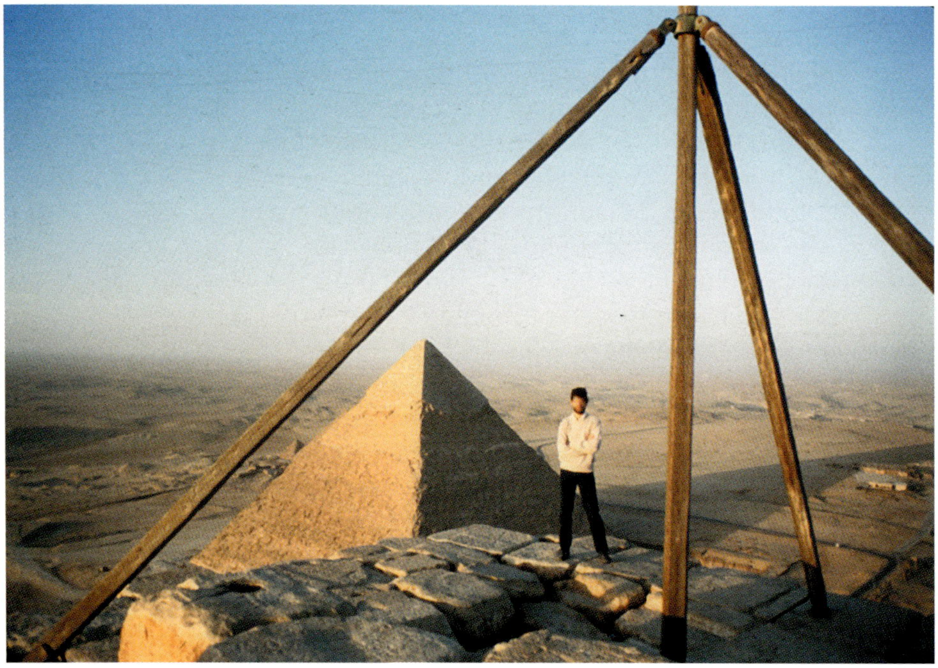

fig. 6.3 Top of the Pyramid of Khufu with wooden scaffolding to indicate the missing top portion. You can see the Pyramid of Khafre in the distance—it still has some of its limestone casing intact at the top.

grand passageway. After the burial, workers lowered massive stone slabs to block the entrance to the chamber and sealed the exterior entrance to the pyramid itself as well. Nevertheless, thieves were able to break in and plunder the tomb so that nothing remains of what must have been a spectacular burial treasure.

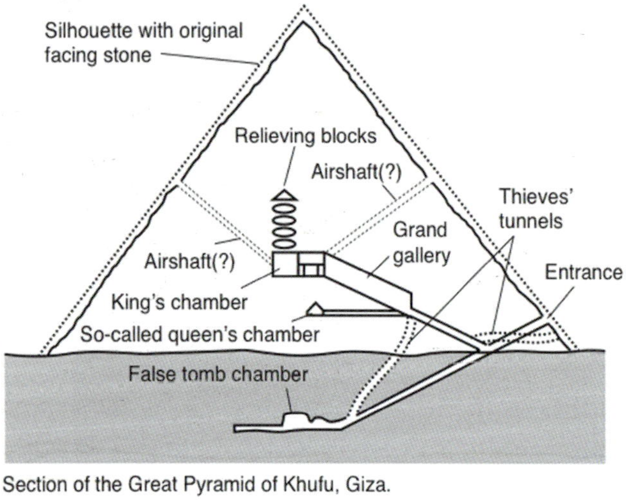

fig. 6.4 Section of the Great Pyramid of Khufu, Giza.

Much controversy exists as to exactly how pyramids such as Khufu's were built, but the engineering skill and craftsmanship were unparalleled. Researchers no longer think that slaves built them but rather paid laborers housed in a vast worker city near the site. They hauled large blocks of stone to the site on wooden rollers or sleds and positioned them to the proper height using a series of ramps. They then put them in place with ropes, pulleys and levers. They used no mortar, and the joints between the blocks of the outer casing were so fine that they were scarcely visible. Because they were so expensive and labor intensive to build as well as such obvious targets for tomb robbers, later pharaohs built tombs that were more modest and well hidden.

The Seven Wonders of the Ancient World

By tradition the seven wonders were:

1. The Great Pyramid of Khufu (Egypt), c. 2500 BCE.
2. The Hanging Gardens of Babylon (Iraq), 7th century BCE.
3. The Temple of Artemis at Ephesus (Turkey), 6th century BCE.
4. The Statue of Zeus at Olympia (Greece), 5th century BCE.
5. The Mausoleum at Halicarnassus (Turkey), 4th century BCE.
6. The Colossus of Rhodes (Greece), 3rd century BCE.
7. The Pharos (Lighthouse) at Alexandria (Egypt), 3rd century BCE.

Lion torso wide shoulders small @ waist upside down triangle

A Menkaure & his queen
B Menkaure
C old Kingdom

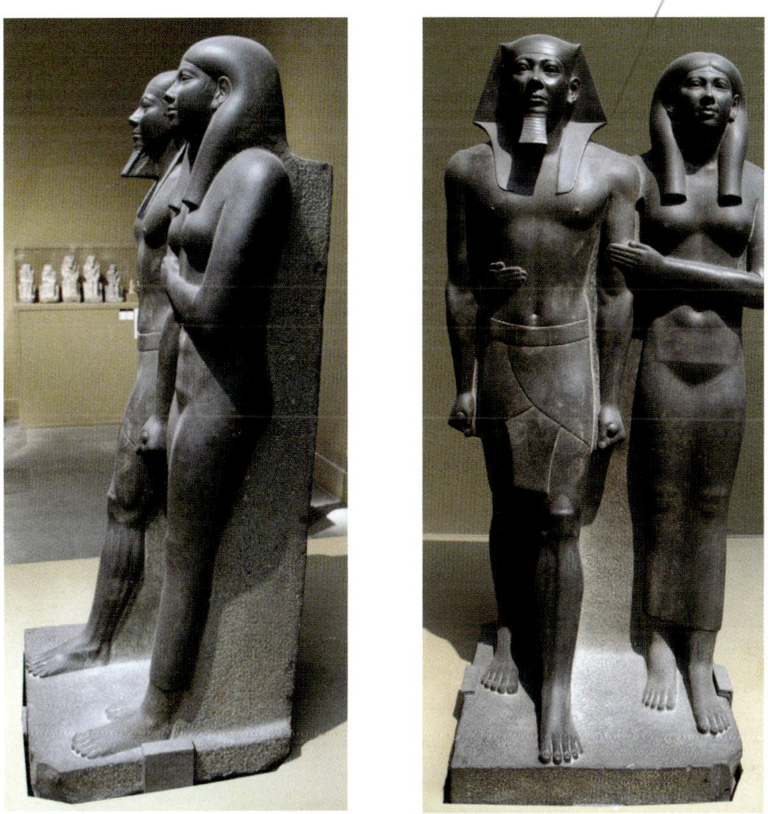

fig. 6.5 Menkaure and his Queen, c. 2500 BCE. Graywacke (a type of hard sandstone), 56 in. high. Museum of Fine Arts Boston.

woman's body type not very different than man. — no curves woman woman taller.

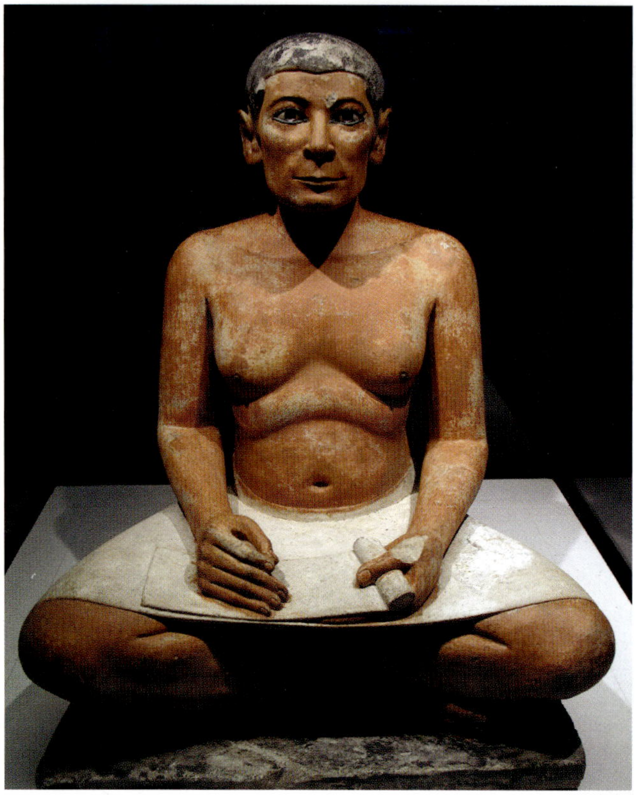

fig. 6.6 Seated Scribe, c. 2500 BCE. Painted limestone, 21 in. high. Louvre, Paris.

Menkaure. The statue of Menkaure, builder of the smallest pyramid at Giza, with his queen (fig. 6.5), is a good example of Old Kingdom sculpture in the round and the conventions of Egyptian figure style. Because the figures attach to the back slab and are not fully carved from behind, one might consider this sculpture extremely **high relief**. Menkaure stands erect in a conventional pose with arms close to his side and one leg forward. His body is well-formed, but rigid, and it shows certain unrealistic features such as his sharp-edged shins. There are no open spaces, and there is even a wedge of stone left behind his advanced leg to keep it connected to the slab of stone behind. This is because the artist made the figure as a repository for the pharaoh's ka, or life force, and it therefore needed to be as permanent and unbreakable as possible.

Seated Scribe. A statue of a seated scribe (fig. 6.6) clearly indicates that Egyptian artists had the ability to portray the human figure more realistically. As someone of lower social standing, the scribe appears in a more relaxed and naturalistic manner. Although still somewhat rigid, he does not have the idealized face and torso of the pharaoh in figure 6.5. Instead, his face is more individualized, and his chest and belly show some middle-aged flab. The fact that the artist painted the statue and gave it inlaid eyes adds to the **realism**.

NEW KINGDOM

Egypt reached the height of its power, size and prosperity during the New Kingdom, which began after the expulsion of the Hyksos (see Hyksos box). Some of the best known pharaohs ruled during the New Kingdom: Hatshepsut, a rare female pharaoh; Ramses II, one of the most powerful and longest reigning pharaohs; Akhenaten, a radical pharaoh; and Tutankhamen, the only pharaoh whose burial chamber was found intact.

Akhenaten and the Amarna Style. Egyptian culture and art changed radically in the New Kingdom under the reign of the pharaoh Akhenaten. In the fourteenth century BCE Akhenaten abolished all the

Egyptian gods save the sun god, Aten, who became the sole god in Egyptian religion. Akhenaten made another radical change to accompany his institution of a monotheistic religion. He moved the capital to a new site at Tel el-Amarna where he built a new city. The style of art also changed. Royal figures became less rigid and more fluid with curving lines and swelling forms. With his elongated face and full lips, distended belly and swelling hips, Akhenaten (fig. 6.7) appears somewhat effeminate—he is clearly not as **idealized** or heroic looking as Menkaure (fig. 6.5). Whether the artist was recording how the pharaoh actually looked or reacting to the conventional figure style remains a question.

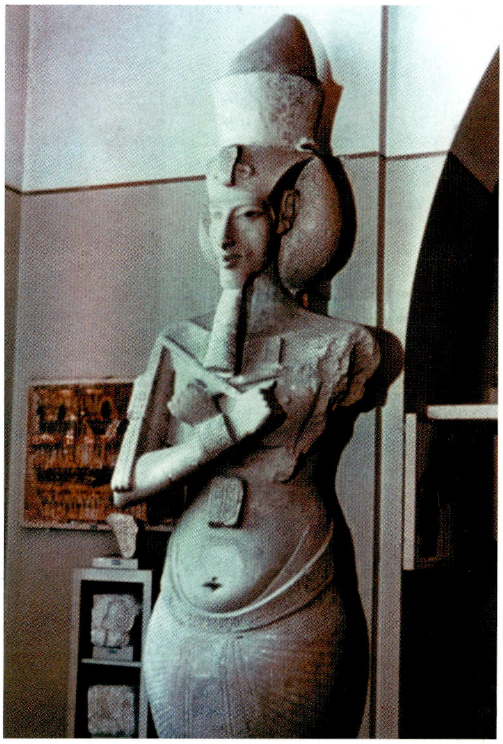

fig. 6.7 Akhenaten, c. 1350 BCE. Sandstone, 13 ft. high. Egyptian Museum, Cairo.

Nefertiti. The famous bust of Akhenaten's wife, Nefertiti (fig. 6.8), maintains the curvilinear quality seen in her husband's statue, but she remains an object of natural beauty with her fine features, swan-like neck and carefully applied make-up. Timeless, she could easily be a glamorous fashion model of today.

When Akhenaten died his radical monotheistic religion died with him and his new capital abandoned. The priests quickly reinstated the pantheon of Egyptian gods and returned to the old ways. It took a little longer, however, for the more naturalistic Amarna style to fade away.

Mask of Tutankhamen. Perhaps the most famous pharaoh is Tutankhamen. This is not because he was the most important—in fact, he was a minor pharaoh—but because explorers found his burial chamber undisturbed. Plunderers robbed the known tombs of all other pharaohs in antiquity. Tutankhamen was a child king. He ascended the

Hyksos

The Hyksos people came from the Near East and invaded northern Egypt in the seventeenth century BCE. With their superior weaponry and the horse-drawn chariots (which they introduced into Egypt), they gained control over much of the country and ruled for more than a century.

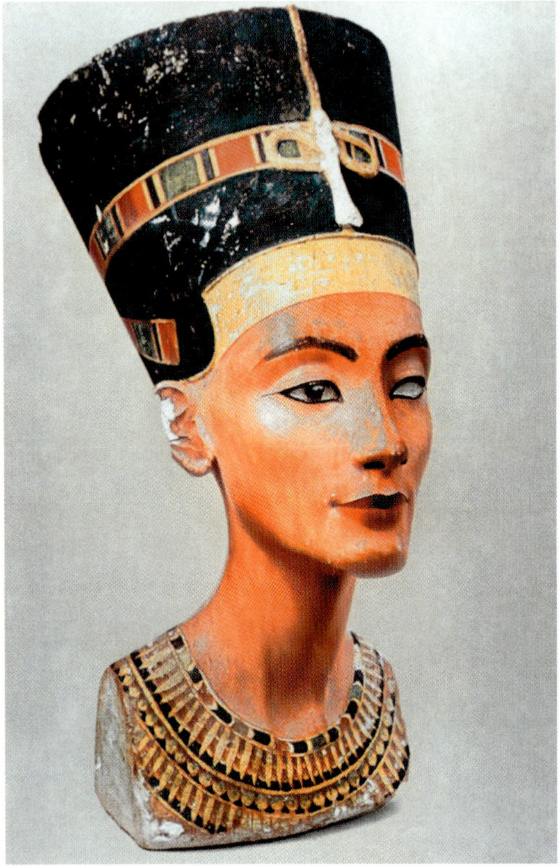

fig. 6.8 Bust of Queen Nefertiti, c. 1350 BCE. Painted limestone, 20 in. high. Ägyptisches Museum, Berlin.

throne at age nine and died at age eighteen. The discovery of his tomb in 1922 by Howard Carter was one of the great archaeological finds of the twentieth century (see King Tut's Tomb box). Although small and cramped, hundreds of precious objects filled Tut's tomb. One of the more spectacular finds is the mask placed over the head of Tut's mummy (fig. 6.9). Made of gold and inlaid with glass and semi-precious materials, it shows Tut as Osiris, god of death and resurrection. Many thought the gods of Egypt had hair of gold and lapis lazuli (a semi-precious blue stone), and the headcloth Tut wears refers to this. The cobra and vulture on the headcloth represent two goddesses and indicate sovereignty over Lower and Upper Egypt respectively. The plaited beard imitates the ceremonial beards that the pharaohs wore in real life. Although many of objects from the tomb exhibit figures that still reflect the more naturalistic Amarna style, the mask is more conventional in style, which recalls Old Kingdom art.

Mummies

The Egyptians believed that the ka, or life force, needed the body to survive so they developed methods for preserving the bodies of pharaohs and other important people after death. The earliest **mummification** in the Pre-dynastic era occurred naturally. Buried in shallow pits in the desert sands, the body dried out and mummified on its own. By the time of the New Kingdom, a sophisticated process had evolved that took seventy days. The embalmers removed the internal organs (stomach, liver, intestines and lungs) from the body cavity, mummified them separately and placed them into stone jars buried with the pharaoh. They discarded the brain, which they thought of no importance, after pulling it out in pieces through the nose with a hook. They left the kidneys, associated with emotion, and the heart, considered the seat of wisdom and needed for final judgment in the afterlife, in the body. They then packed the pharaoh's body in natron, a naturally occurring salt, for about forty days to dehydrate and preserve it. After that they cleaned it, anointed it with oils and wrapped it in linen bandages. Magic amulets to protect the mummy were placed at strategic points in the bandaging.

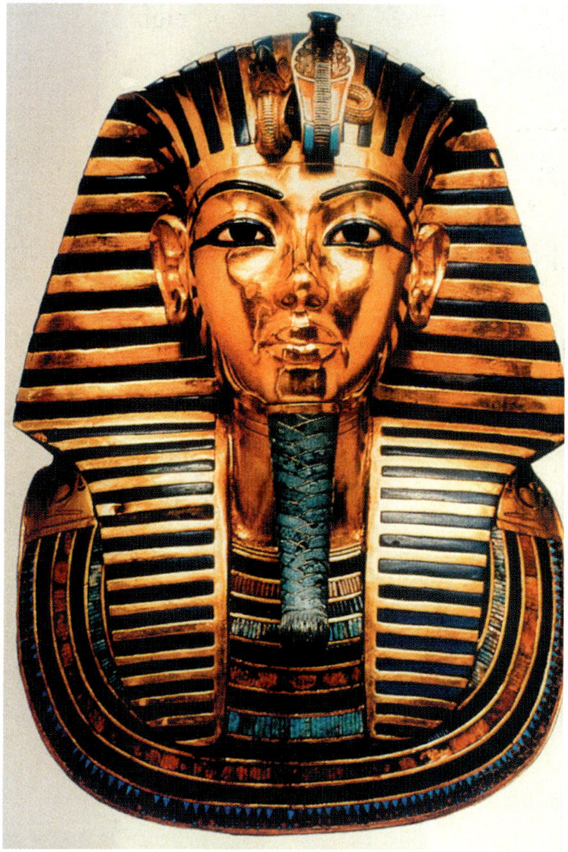

A. Tutankhamen
B. unknown
C New Kingdom

fig. 6.9 Funeral Mask of Tutankhamen, c. 1323 BCE. Gold inlaid with colored glass, lapis lazuli, faience, carnelian, green feldspar, quartz and obsidian. Egyptian Museum, Cairo.

King Tut's Tomb

Howard Carter searched for Tut's tomb for years with the financial backing of the English Lord Carnarvon. The tomb was difficult to locate because Ramses VI had built a later and larger tomb over it. Finally in 1922 Carter's workers uncovered the first step of a stairway leading down into the sand. After excavating to reach the entrance, they realized that thieves had broken into the tomb in ancient times. They had gained access to the entry passageway and the front room of the tomb but did not succeed in breaching the actual burial chamber, which Carter found undisturbed. The mummy, wrapped in linen bandages with amulets and other jewelry, remained well protected. It lay within three nested coffins placed in a stone **sarcophagus** covered by four wooden shrines, one inside the other. The innermost coffin was solid gold and weighed several hundred pounds. The splendor and richness of this burial for a minor pharaoh leads us to wonder what treasures would have been found in the tomb of a major pharaoh such as Khufu or Ramses II had thieves not robbed their tombs. Carter was one of the first to carefully document an excavation in great detail. Despite the tomb's small size, it took ten years to complete the excavation.

SUMMARY

Ancient Egyptian culture is divided into various kingdoms and dynasties. The most famous Egyptian art comes from the Old Kingdom (c. 2600–2100 BCE) and the New Kingdom (c. 1550–1070 BCE). *The Palette of Narmer*, however, comes from the Early Dynastic Period, which preceded the Old Kingdom. This carving has all the stylistic hallmarks of the typical figure in Egyptian art. The Great Pyramid (c. 2500 BCE) is one of three Old Kingdom pyramids at Giza, near Cairo, and is one of the most massive structures built by humans. It is the only one of the Seven Wonders of the Ancient World to survive.

Human figures are depicted more naturalistically if they are of lesser social standing. Comparing an image of a pharaoh such as Menkaure with the seated scribe clearly illustrates this. A brief stylistic change occurred with the reign of the Pharaoh Akhenaten, who abolished all the Egyptian gods except for the sun god Aten. During Akhenaten's reign figures became less rigid with curves and swelling forms. The most famous pharaoh, Tutankhamen, was one of the least important rulers politically, but the discovery of his tomb sparked a sensation in 1922 because it is the only pharaoh's tomb to be found intact.

PRONUNCIATION GUIDE

Akhenaten (ah-ken-**ah**-ten)
Bas relief (bah-rih-**leef**)
Giza (**gee**-zah [hard 'g' as in gun])
Hierarchical (high-uh-**rahr**-kih-kuhl)
Hieratic (high-uh-**rat**-ik)
Hieroglyphics (high-roh-**glif**-iks or high-er-uh-**glif**-iks)
Hyksos (**hick**-sohs)
Khufu (**koo**-foo)
Menes (**mee**-neez)
Menkaure (men-**cow**-ray)
Nefertiti (nef-er-**tee**-tee)
Papyrus (puh-**pie**-ruhs)
Sarcophagus (sar-**koff**-uh-gus)
Tutankhamen (toot-ahng-**kah**-muhn)

GLOSSARY

Bas relief. In sculpture, low relief in which the forms project only slightly from the background plane.

Hierarchical or hieratic scale. Depicting more important figures larger than less important ones.

Hieroglyphic. A system of writing in ancient Egypt that used images of objects as characters.

High relief. Sculpture in which the figures project prominently from the background to which they are attached.

Idealism. The representation of figures and forms that conforms to a concept of perfection rather than to reality.

Mummification. The process of preserving the body, usually by means of desiccation.

Naturalism. A style of art that attempts to depict things as they actually appear in nature.

Papyrus. A type of paper in the ancient world made from the reeds of the papyrus plant.

Realism. Portraying objects as they actually are.

Relief sculpture. Sculpture whose figures are only partially carved out so that they are still attached to the background. Relief sculpture can be high relief, low (bas) relief, or sunken relief where the figures are carved into the surface of the stone or other material.

Sarcophagus. Literally, "consumer of flesh," it is a large coffin (usually stone), often decorated with relief sculpture.

Stylized. When the depiction of a figure or form departs from optical reality to conform to artistic conventions or to emphasize certain characteristics.

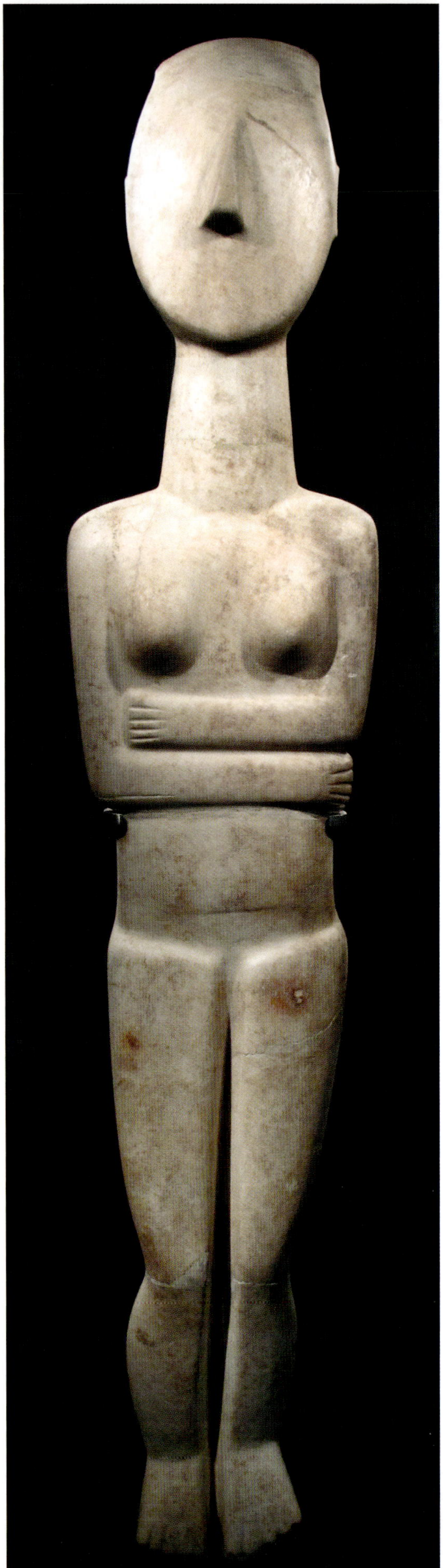

fig. 7.1 Cycladic Idol, c. 2500 BCE. Marble, approximately 4.5 ft. tall. N.P. Goulandris. Foundation—Museum of Cycladic Art, Athens.

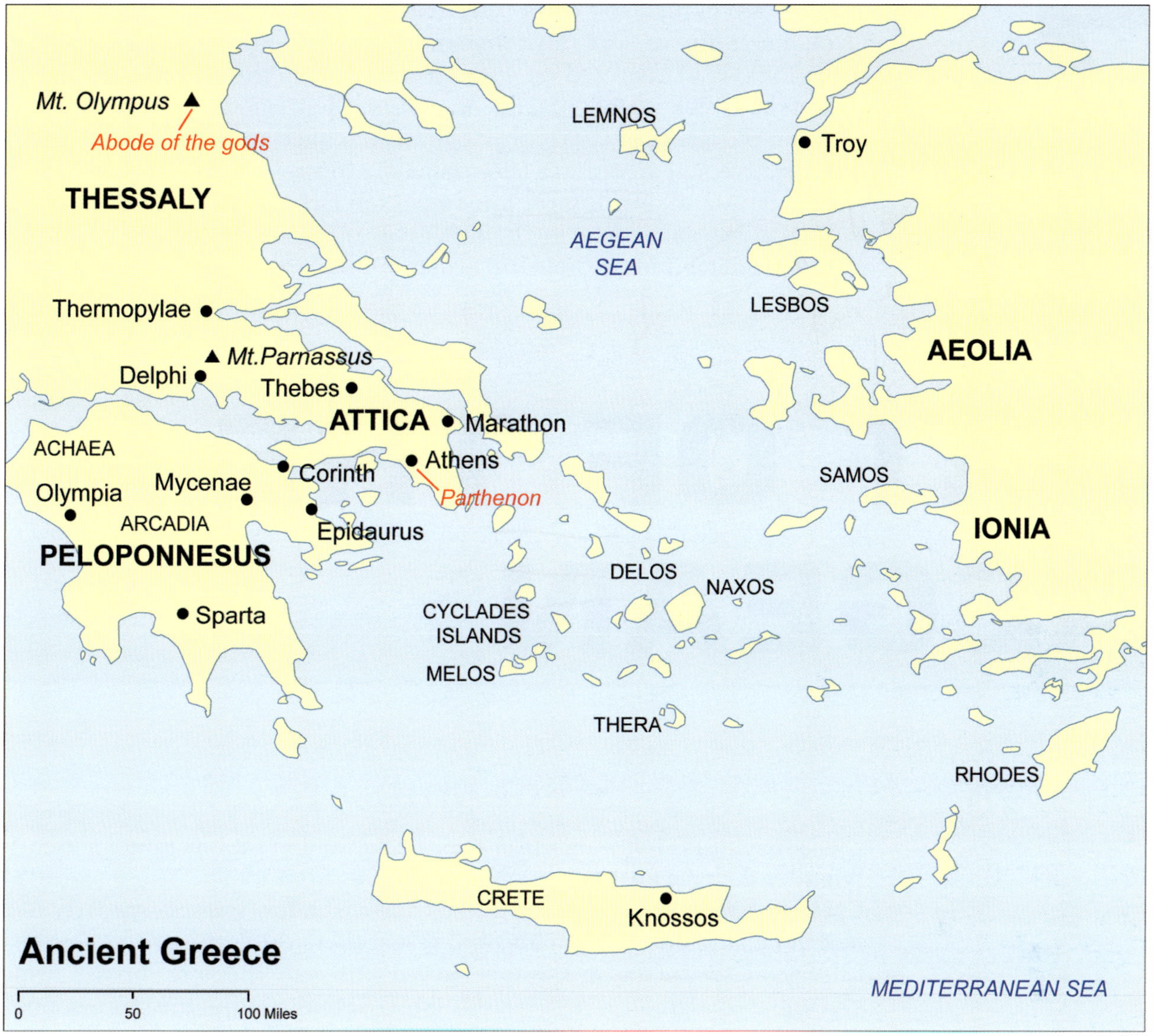

Map of the Ancient Greece with Cyclades Islands and Crete.

7

Aegean art comprises three cultures in the eastern Mediterranean: Cycladic, Minoan and Mycenaean. Cycladic culture (flourished c. 2800–2000 BCE) centered on a group of islands in the Aegean Sea southeast of the Greek mainland. Minoan culture (flourished c. 2000–1400 BCE) arose on the island of Crete, although its influence spread to the Cyclades Islands. Mycenaean culture (flourished c. 1600–1100 BCE) began on the Greek mainland, but it later encompassed Crete. The Aegean cultures existed at the same time as the kingdoms of ancient Egypt, and the cultural influences among them are evident in the art they produced.

ART OF THE AEGEAN

CYCLADIC ART

Cycladic culture left no written records so we don't know much about it. What we do have are numerous stone figures from tombs. These so-called **Cycladic idols** (fig. 7.1) vary in size from just a few inches to nearly five feet in height. Most are female, and researchers think they represent fertility goddesses. They are simply carved with only the nose, breast, arms and pubic triangle shown. A vertical line descending from the groin defines the legs. With their simple geometric form they appear oddly modern. Pigment traces found on them indicate that the artists painted on the eyes and other details. Although museums display these figures upright, they are thin with toes pointed down and they cannot stand on their own. Most were found in prone positions in graves.

Archaeologists also found a few male figures, which tend to represent musicians. A man playing a double reed pipe (fig. 7.2) displays the same simplified geometric form as the female in figure 7.1, although he is more fully three dimensional and able to stand because of the small flat base. Again, we are not sure of the exact purpose of figures such as these, but they were found in a funerary context.

MINOAN ART

Palace of Minos at Knossos. In 1900 a British archaeologist, Arthur Evans, began excavating the site of a great civilization on the island of Crete in the Mediterranean Sea. He called this civilization Minoan after the fabled King Minos in Greek mythology. The Minoans developed a highly sophisticated society that manifested itself in skillful art and advanced architecture. The palace complex that Evans excavated is at Knossos, which is near the sea and just south of the island's modern day capital of Heraklion. Although explorers later discovered other palace sites in Crete, Knossos is the largest, and it appears it was the most important. Covering approximately six acres, its plan is a maze of hundreds of rooms arranged around a large central courtyard. Among the rooms identified are living quarters, a throne room, reception areas, shrines, workshops and storage rooms. The myth of the Minotaur and the labyrinth may have arisen from the complex layout of the palace (see "The Myth of the Minotaur" box). It was an architectural wonder for its time with multistory structures, a plumbing system and a stone and wood construction that was resistant to earthquakes (see "The Great Eruption" box). The palace did not have defensive walls so evidently the Minoans did not fear attacks from outsiders.

Evans reconstructed parts of the palace (see "Reconstructions" box). Figure 7.3 shows a partially restored portico with the typical Minoan-style column that tapers downward. The back wall had a relief painting of a charging bull, part of which is reconstructed. The bull played a significant role in Minoan culture, and much Minoan art features it. Researchers also found other paintings with bulls, and stylized bull horns adorned parts of the palace. The palace houses the oldest throne in Europe (fig. 7.4). Flanking the stone chair are vibrant depictions of **griffins** (restored), a hybrid creature with the body of a lion and the head of an eagle. We know little of Minoan

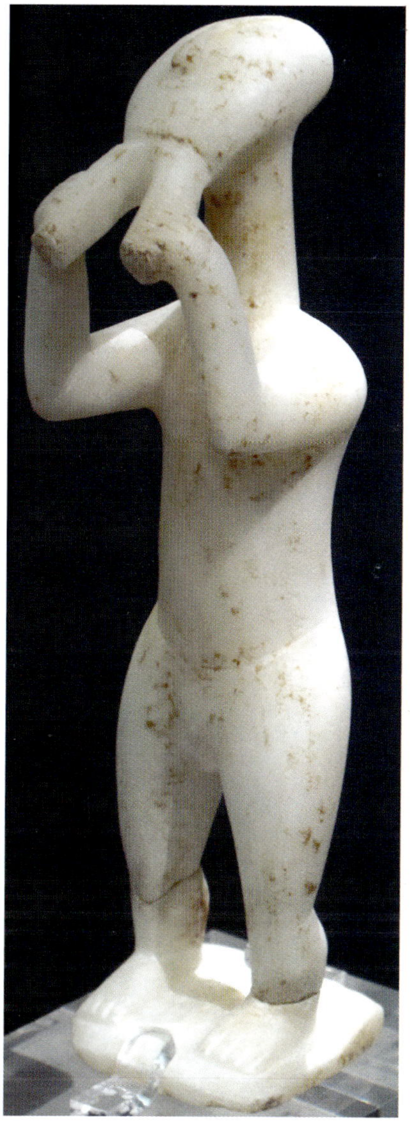

fig. 7.2 Musician, c. 2500 BCE. Marble. National Archaeology Museum, Athens. Museum, Cairo.

The Myth of the Minotaur

King Minos was supposed to sacrifice a bull to the god Poseidon, but the bull was so magnificent that he decided to keep it instead. An offended Poseidon punished Minos by making the queen, Pasiphae, lust after the bull. So strong was her sexual desire for the bull that she commissioned Daedalus, the court inventor, to create a cow costume for her so that she could attract the bull. The result of this bestial union was the Minotaur, a creature that was part human and part bull. He was fed seven youths and seven maidens from Athens each year and kept in a **labyrinth** (designed by Daedalus) to prevent his escape. The Athenian prince Theseus decided to put an end to this grisly practice. With the help of the king's daughter, Ariadne, he slew the Minotaur.

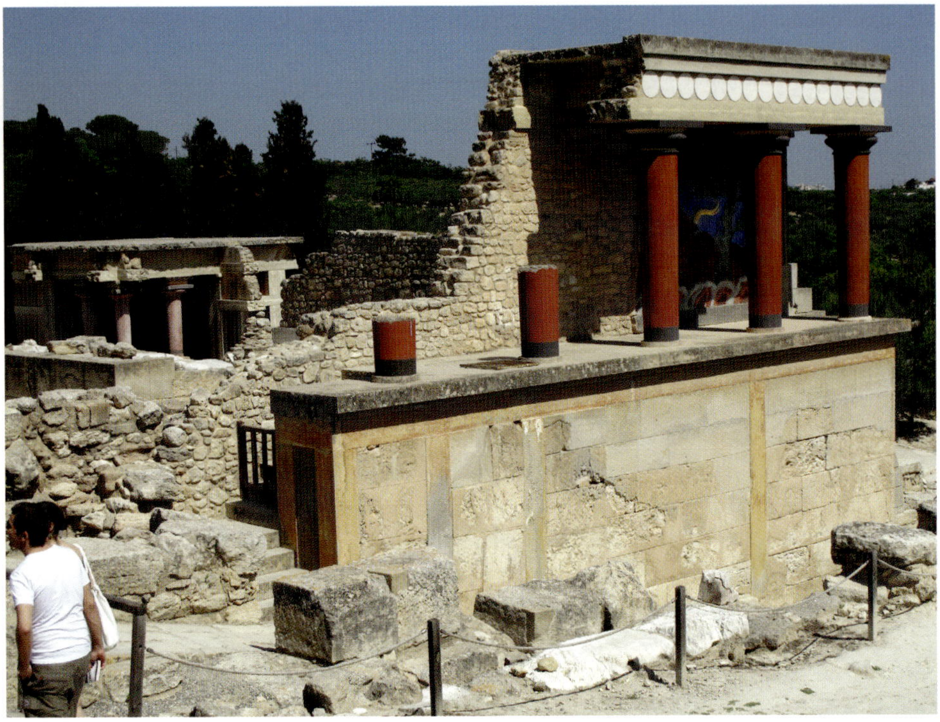

fig. 7.3 Partially reconstructed portion of the Palace of Minos at Knossos, Crete.

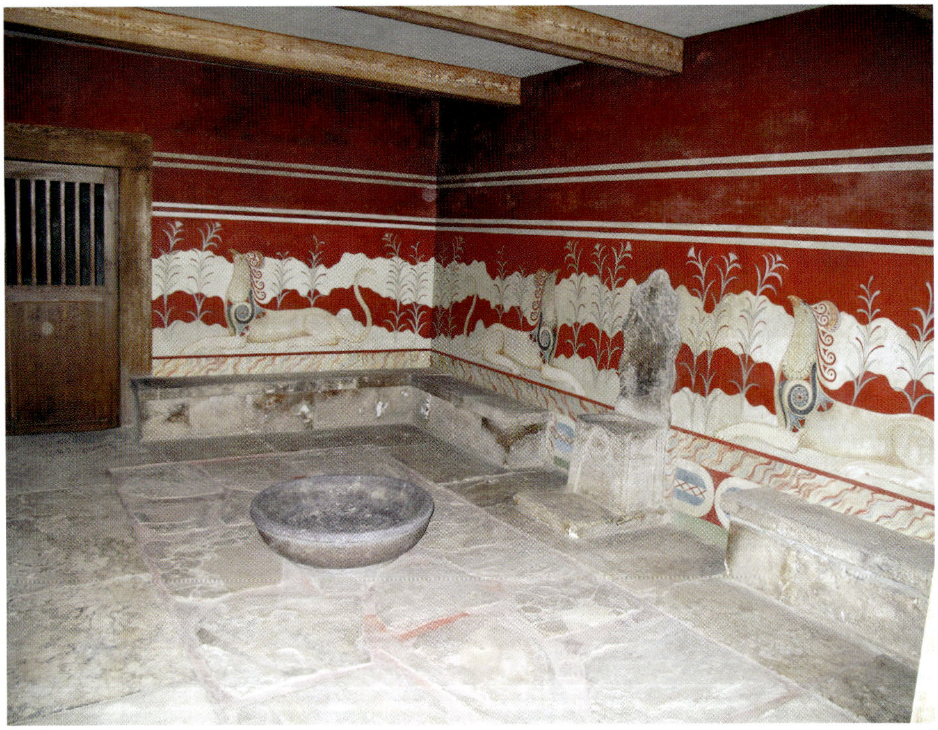

fig. 7.4 So-called throne room of the Palace of Minos at Knossos, Crete.

The Great Eruption

Historians once thought that the volcanic eruption that blew away most of the island of Santorini (Thera) was what caused the decline of Minoan civilization after 1400 BCE. But more recent investigations of ice cores from Greenland and tree rings (dendrochronology) indicate that the eruption occurred around 1632 BCE, several hundred years before the demise of the Minoans. There was a great destruction of the Minoan palaces around 1700 BCE, but the Minoans recovered from this and rebuilt the palaces. The destruction of Thera, however, certainly would have had repercussions on Crete. Being only eighty miles away from Thera, Crete would have suffered earthquakes and tsunami. The wooden beams strategically placed in the stone structure of the Minoan palaces, however, allowed some flexibility and made the walls more resistant to quakes. Another result of this great volcanic eruption may be the origin of the myth of Atlantis sinking into the sea.

rulers and religion. Although the palace has rooms now assigned to the king and queen, we do not actually know if Minoan society had such rulers. The society may have used its palaces more as administrative centers than as royal palaces in the modern sense. A priest-king or a priestess may in fact have used this throne during ritual ceremonies.

Being surrounded by water, the Minoans became great seafarers. The sea was crucial to their successful economy and way of life, and their art

Reconstructions

Reconstructing an ancient building or site is often controversial, especially if sufficient evidence is lacking as to the original appearance. Evans based his reconstruction on buildings depicted in Minoan paintings and clay models. Today some archaeologists fault Evans for being over zealous or fanciful with some of the details. For example, some think the restored columns (fig. 7.3) taper a bit too much. Or, some now think that the dolphin fresco in the Queen's **megaron** (fig. 7.5) may have originally been on the floor, not on the wall. Opinions on reconstructing ancient sites vary. Some think we should leave excavated ruins as we found them even if only foundations remain. The contrasting view holds that it is more educational and certainly more interesting to reconstruct as much as possible. A sensible middle ground is to reconstruct certain parts and buildings where feasible. The Palace of Minos is only partially restored, but it gives the visitor a much better idea of what the original complex may have looked like (even if Evans erred in places) than if only the foundations were visible. The general public seems to prefer more reconstruction rather than less—the Palace at Knossos receives far more visitors than the other less reconstructed Minoan palace sites.

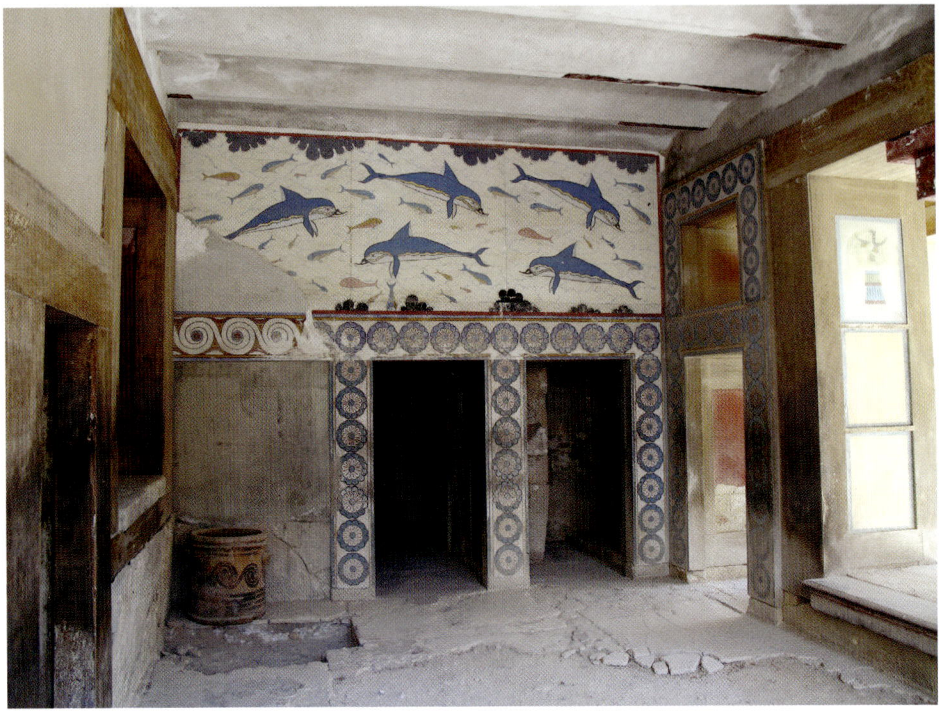

fig. 7.5 So-called Queen's Megaron of the Palace of Minos at Knossos, Crete. The dolphin fresco may have originally been on the floor.

reflects this—marine motifs are common. A fresco depicting dolphins and other sea creatures adorns one of the upper walls in the queen's bedroom (fig. 7.5). The realistic and energized dolphins are quite different from the more static images found in the art of other ancient cultures. This fresco, along with all the others seen at Knossos, is a reconstruction; researchers transferred what is left of the originals to the Archaeological Museum in Heraklion.

The Octopus Vase. The Octopus Vase (fig. 7.6) is one of many found decorated with this creature. It clearly shows the Minoans' love of sea motifs along with a refined melding of image and form. The octopus is fairly realistic—the vase even shows the suction cups on its arms. The rounded form of the vase enhances the illusion of the octopus floating in water; likewise the way the octopus' arms wrap around the vase emphasizes its three dimensional form. With its large staring eyes, the octopus gives us a sense of liveliness and animation that is rare in ancient art. Note that the artist fills all the empty spaces between the arms with other marine motifs such as seaweed and anemones.

Bee Pendant. We find the Minoan love of animal imagery on a small scale as well (fig. 7.7). A gold pendant consisting of two bees or wasps with a granulated honeycomb between them illustrates the great skill of Minoan goldsmiths. This artist uses **granulation** (tiny spheres of gold) with the same kind of realism seen in the Octopus Vase to define the bees' eyes and abdomens as well as the honeycomb.

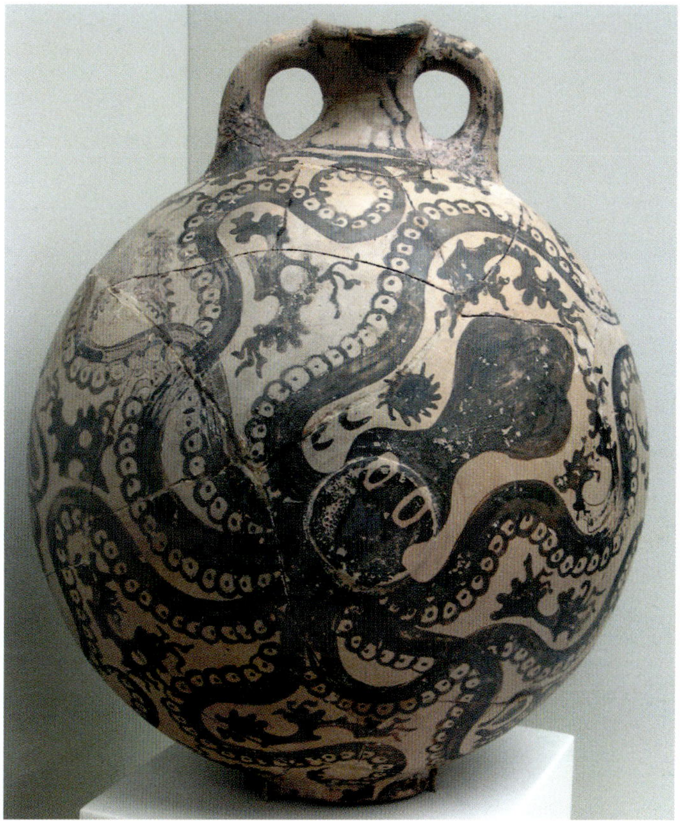

fig. 7.6 Octopus Vase, c. 1500 BCE. Ceramic, 11 in. high. Archaeological Museum, Heraklion.

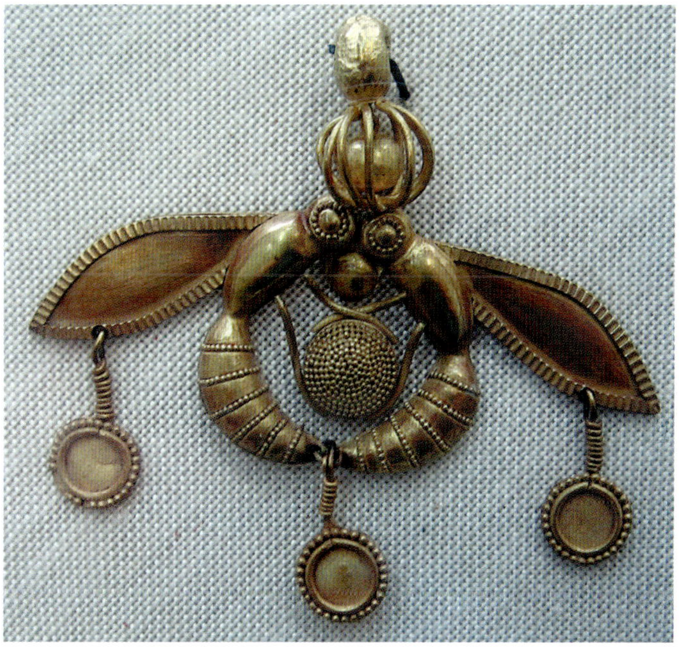

fig. 7.7 Bee pendant, c. 1600 BCE. Gold, 1.8 in. high. Archaeological Museum, Heraklion, Crete.

MYCENAEAN ART

Mycenaean culture takes its name from the **citadel at Mycenae** on the Peloponnesus on the Greek mainland. As there were a number of Minoan palaces on Crete, there were various Mycenaean citadels in Greece. Mycenae was the largest and most important. Unlike Minoan palaces, which were open and airy, the Mycenaean citadels were heavily fortified with high thick walls and bastions, indicating a constant threat of warfare. The Mycenaeans were the subject of Homer's epics, *The Iliad* and *The Odyssey.* Just as Arthur Evans proved that the myth of the Minotaur had its origins in reality, another amateur archaeologist, Heinrich Schliemann, proved that the mythical Trojan War also had its source in reality when he discovered the ruins of ancient Troy in western Turkey. After excavating Troy, Schliemann thought that history might actually be the basis for other parts of the Homeric epics so he began excavating at Mycenae.

The walls of the citadel are nearly forty feet thick in some places and are composed of huge stones, some weighing as much as fifty tons (see "Cyclopean Walls" box). We call walls like these called Cyclopean because the later Greeks thought that only a Cyclops (a one-eyed giant) could have lifted such gigantic stones. The most prominent extant portion of Mycenae is the Lion Gate (fig. 7.8). The Lion Gate gets its name from a large relief panel inserted into a triangular area above the gateway's massive lintel. Two lions (or lionesses) flank a tapering column that is clearly Minoan in character (see fig. 7.3). The heads of the lions, perhaps made of precious materials, have long since disappeared. A sculpture such as this has several purposes. On a symbolic level the large powerful beasts proclaim the power of the king and warn against intrusion. On a practical level, the relief, which is lighter than the massive stones surrounding it, provides the entryway with greater strength by lessening the weight upon the lintel.

Schliemann found various precious objects in grave shafts at Mycenae, including several gold death masks. He originally thought the most famous

Cyclopean Walls

In Greek mythology a **Cyclops** was a one-eyed giant. Polyphemus, blinded by Odysseus after eating some of his crew, is the most famous one. The later Greeks who saw the ruins of Mycenae did not think humans could have lifted such massive stones. Their conclusion was that only a Cyclops would have the strength to put them in place. Hence, walls such as those found at Mycenae are referred to as Cyclopean masonry. The word Cyclops derives from the Greek kuklos (circle), which is also the source of the word Cycladic.

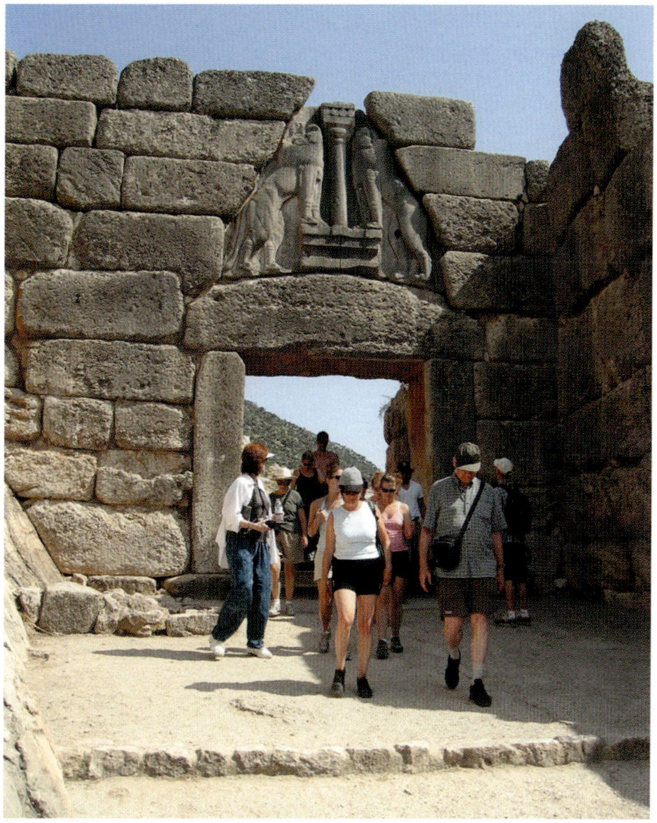

fig. 7.8 Lion Gate at Mycenae, c. 1300 BCE. The limestone sculpture is 9 ft. 6 in. high.

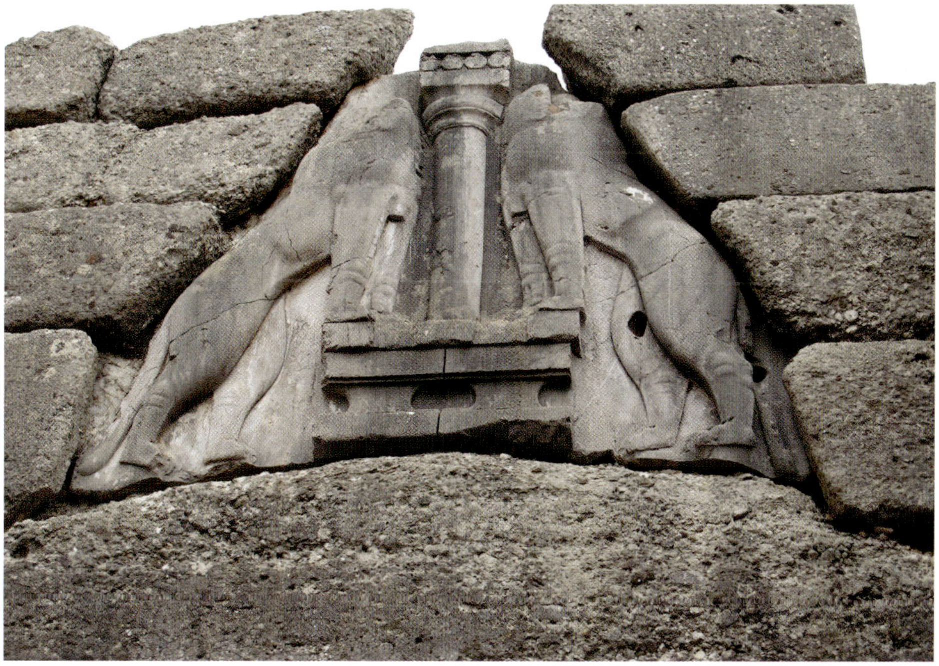

fig. 7.8b Detail.

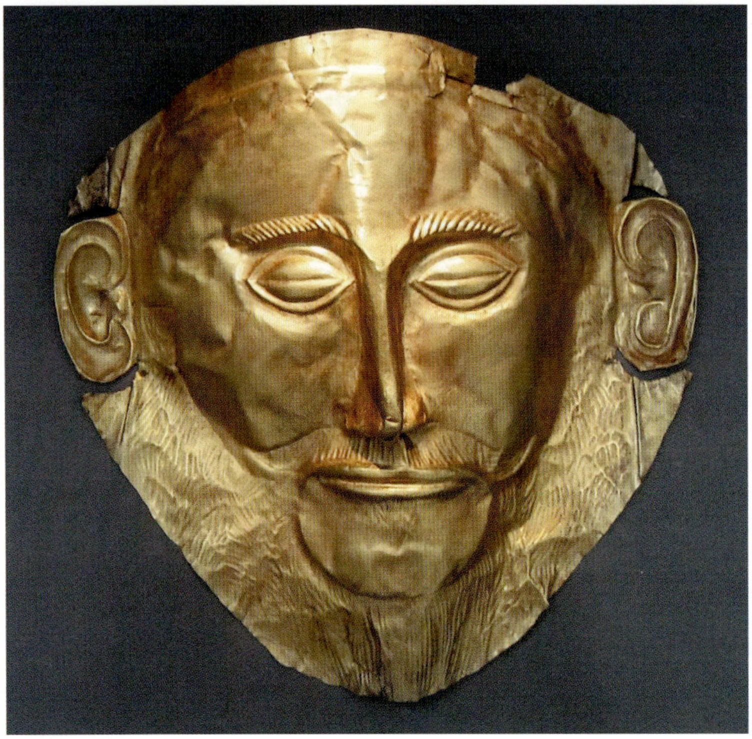

fig. 7.9 Funeral Mask from Mycenae (so-called Mask of Agamemnon), c. 1500 BCE. Gold, 12 in. high. National Archaeology Museum, Athens.

one (fig. 7.9) belonged to Agamemnon, one of the Mycenaean rulers who attacked Troy, but we now know that it is several centuries older than the time of Agamemnon. Made by hammering out the facial details from behind, the mask recalls the famous funerary mask of King Tut (fig. 6.9) and is evidence of cross cultural ties among these ancient cultures. Although not nearly as refined as Tutankhamen's mask, it clearly has the features of a specific individual, and it indicates the person's importance in Mycenaean society.

The Mycenaeans eventually overtook the Minoans and established themselves in Crete, but after 1200 BCE the Mycenaean civilization itself faded away. This led to several centuries of dark ages before the Greeks emerged.

SUMMARY

Aegean Art is comprised of three cultures: **Cycladic, Minoan**, and **Mycenaean.** Cycladic culture flourished on a group of central islands in the Aegean Sea to the east of Greece from about 2800–2000 BCE. Many stone figures (simply called Cycladic idols) remain from Cycladic culture; most were found in a funerary context, but their exact purpose is not clear.

Based on the island of Crete, Minoan culture flourished around 2000–1400 BCE. Skillful craftsmanship, accomplished art, and advanced building techniques indicate that Minoan society was sophisticated. Examples of their art and architecture come from the ruins of a large multi-story palace complex at Knossos on the island of Crete, which has been partially reconstructed. The bee pendant shows exquisite goldsmithing techniques, the Octopus Vase demonstrates a naturalistic style and a love of marine motifs, and the palace at Knossos indicates a high standard of living with such amenities as indoor plumbing.

Mycenaean society flourished on the Greek mainland in the Peloponnesus from about 1600 BCE to 1100 BCE. After 1400 BCE they also dominated Crete and displaced Minoan culture. Mycenaean architecture, as exemplified by the citadel at Mycenae, differs from Minoan architecture in its use of massive stones and defensive features. Mycenaean art is also less refined, as seen in the gold funeral mask from Mycenae.

PRONUNCIATION GUIDE

Cycladic (sih-**kla**-dik)
Cyclopean (sigh-kluh-**pee**-un)
Knossos (**nos**-ohs or kuh-**nos**-ohs)
Labyrinth (**lab**-uh-rinth)
Megaron (**meg**-uh-ron)
Minoan (mih-**noh**-uhn)
Minotaur (**min**-oh-tore)
Mycenae (my-**see**-nee or my-**see**-nigh)
Mycenaean (my-sih-**nee**-un)
Repoussé (reh-poo-**say**)

GLOSSARY

Cyclopean walls. Walls composed of large irregularly shaped blocks of stone, so called because later peoples thought only a Cyclops could have built them. They are associated with Mycenaean architecture.

Cyclops. In Greek mythology, a one-eyed giant.

Granulation. The soldering of tiny spheres of gold (or silver) to a flat gold (or silver) background.

Griffin. A mythological creature with the body of a lion and the head and wings of an eagle.

Labyrinth. A maze.

Magazine. Storeroom for food or munitions.

Megaron. The principal hall of a Mycenaean palace with a hearth in the center.

Minotaur. A creature borne by Pasiphae (wife of King Minos of Crete) that was half human and half bull.

Repousée. A metalworking technique in which a malleable metal is ornamented or shaped by hammering from the reverse side.

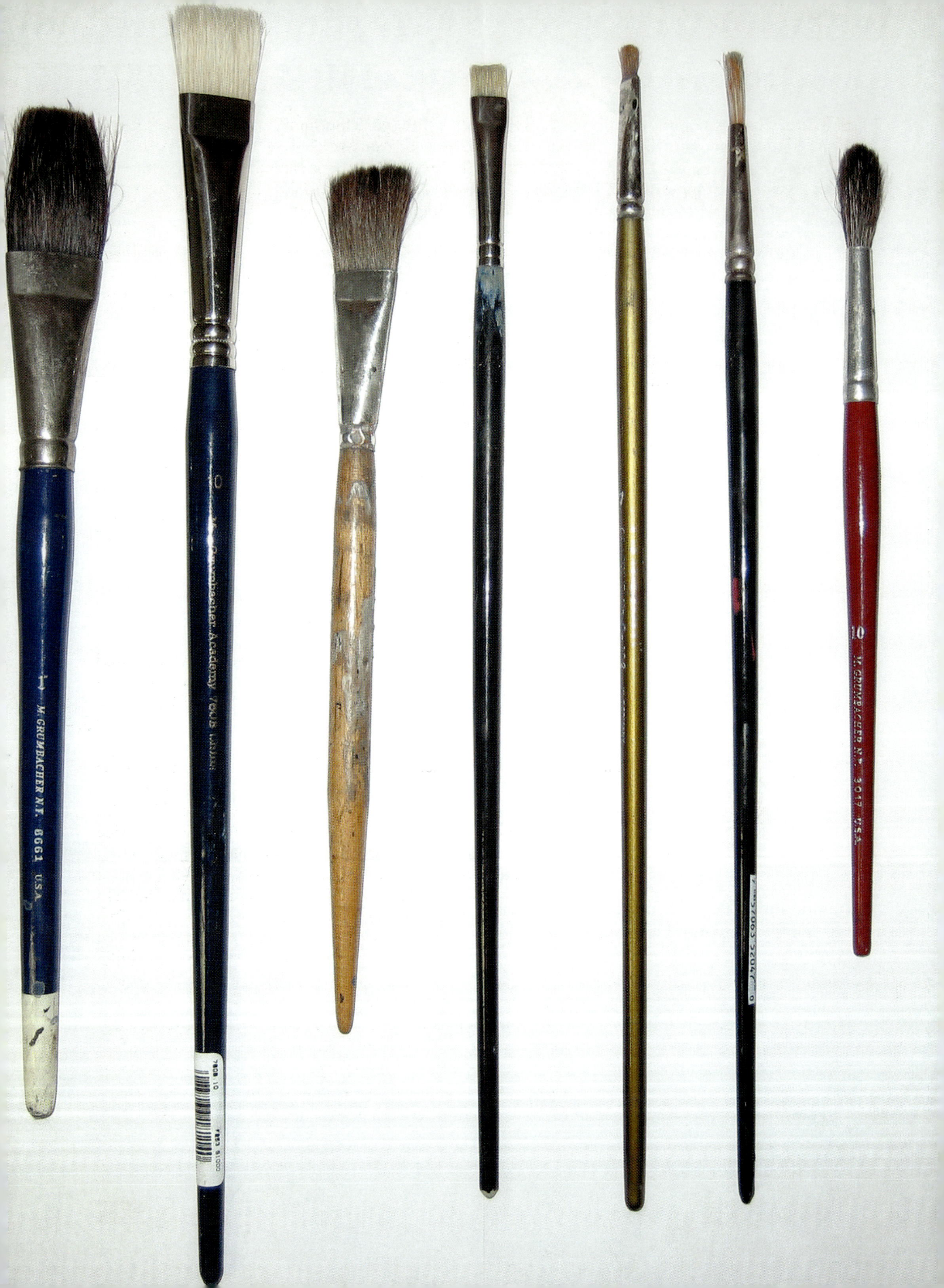
M. GRUMBACHER N.Y. 6661 U.S.A.
M. Grumbacher Academy 7608
M. GRUMBACHER N.Y. 3017 U.S.A.

8 PAINTING

Painting is probably the most popular and familiar of the visual arts in Western culture. The most recognized works of art tend to be paintings, such as Michelangelo's Sistine Ceiling, Leonardo da Vinci's *Mona Lisa* and Vincent van Gogh's *Starry Night.* Painting is the medium you are most likely to encounter in a museum, gallery or public building. Some of the earliest works created are cave paintings dating back over 30,000 years. Although sculpture and architecture are also crucial to the history of art, there is a bias toward painting, especially for the last 600 years. Accordingly, this book has many more examples of painting than other forms of art.

Painting and drawing are closely linked. In fact, in some cases it can be difficult to distinguish the two. We can consider prehistoric cave paintings and many Asian paintings drawings as much as paintings. The two forms maintain a close relationship because a painting's composition usually derives from preparatory drawings either on paper or directly on the canvas.

Paints consist of **pigment** for color and a **medium** (also called a **binder**) to hold the pigment together. The artist may add a solvent such as mineral spirits or water to make the paint thinner and easier to spread.

Pigments initially derived from plant and mineral sources and were ground by hand into powder. Today most pigments are synthetic and produced in bulk. This reduces cost and also permits a wider range of hues. The qualities of the medium directly affect how the artist applies the paint and how it will look after it dries.

Painters usually apply their paint to a flat **support**, most often canvas stretched taut over a wooden framework (called a stretcher). Many supports such as canvas are porous and absorbent so they need preparation with a sizing or a primer before receiving paint. Sizing is a mixture made with glue (or wax or clay) spread over the support to seal it. A primer is simply a first coat of paint on the support. Both provide a smooth surface to paint on. The primer is usually white or a neutral grey, but the artist can use other colors to give the finished work a warmer or cooler undertone.

Artists can apply paint with just about any tool, including their fingers. They most commonly use brushes, which come in many sizes, widths and materials, each with their own characteristics. Figure 8.1 shows some of the brushes in a typical artist's studio.

Oil paint has been a major medium in Western art since the fifteenth century. Pigments traditionally are mixed with linseed oil (made from the seeds of the flax plant). Oil has many advantages. It is easy to work, and it dries slowly, giving the artist time to blend colors and to make corrections. Oil is flexible so it is less prone to cracking, and one can even roll up oil

fig. 8.1 Paint brushes. Some of the best brushes are made of sable hair.

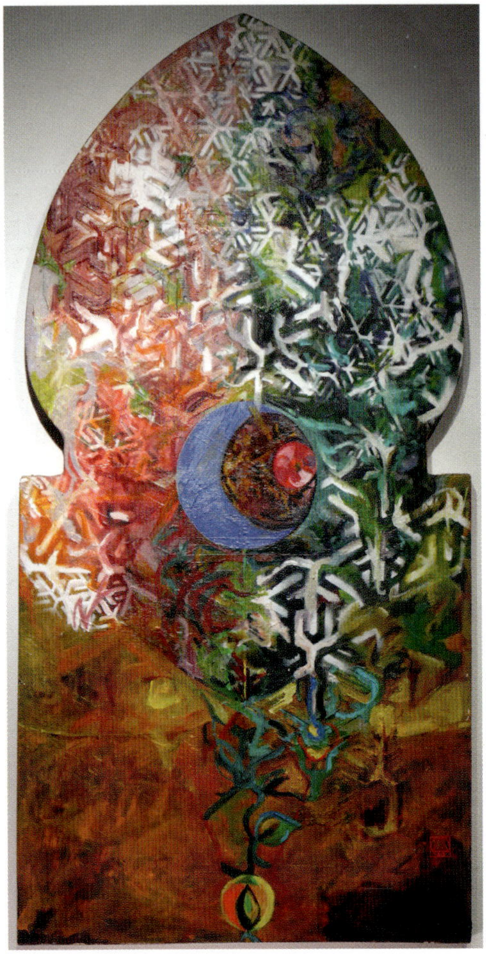

fig. 8.2 Halide Salam, *Tree of Light* from the *Trees of Existence* series, 1999. Oil and rubber on canvas. The rubber enhances the textural imagery Salam uses in her work, which is an appeal to individual consciousness through vision.

canvases for transport. Oil also maintains its shiny surface when dry. Although oil can darken over time, it is remarkably stable. The old yellow-tinted paintings you see in museums are often the result of the protective varnish coating yellowing over the centuries, not the actual paint. Contemporary artists use oil in combination with other materials to achieve new effects. Halide Salam combines rubber with oil in her *Trees of Existence* series to better express her visual metaphors (fig. 8.2)

Jan van Eyck's *Arnolfini Double Portrait* (figs. 8.3a and 8.3b) is a marvel of minute detail and texture with a luminous jewel-like surface. Van Eyck was able to distinguish various materials such as brass, fur, cloth and wood with incredible realism by building up the surface with **glazes** (thin layers of paint) and using smooth, uniform brushstrokes. In an opposing oil technique, Vincent van Gogh applied his oil paint very thickly in *Starry Night* (fig. 8.4), imparting a strong physical texture to the paint known as **impasto** (see also fig. 8.5b). Each painting's surface suits the subject matter well. Van Eyck's smooth surface permits the minute detail that is the painting's essence; Van Gogh's thick impasto expresses the emotional quality of the landscape.

Tempera is an old medium used as far back as ancient Egypt. Egg yolk is the traditional binder for tempera, although today the term also applies to poster paints, which are water based and do not contain egg yolk. Tempera dries to a smooth, matte finish. It enables the artist to achieve brilliant colors although not the deep color saturation possible with oil. Like oil, tempera permits the artist to achieve precise details, but it is unforgiving of errors, and blending is difficult because it dries quickly. Tempera is not as flexible as oil, and it cracks more easily, so wood is the usual support. Botticelli's *Birth of Venus* (fig. 8.6) illustrates tempera's qualities (although he painted it on canvas rather than wood). Botticelli achieved fine detail in the floral patterns of the garments and a sensual luminosity in the porcelain-like skin of Venus.

WATERCOLOR

Watercolor is usually a child's first experience with a paint medium. With watercolor the pigments are suspended in water mixed with **gum arabic** (a resin made from the African acacia tree). The type and texture of the paper greatly influences how the painted surface will look. Artists normally use acid-free cotton paper because it absorbs the pigment better and does not yellow with age. Smooth textured papers allow the artist more control and the ability to paint in greater detail. Often the artist

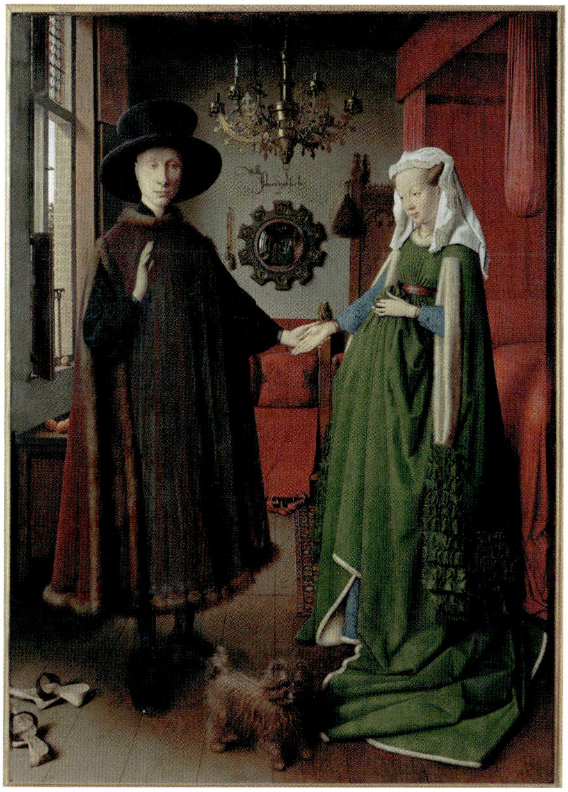

fig. 8.3a Jan van Eyck, *Arnolfini Double Portrait,* 1434. Oil on wood.

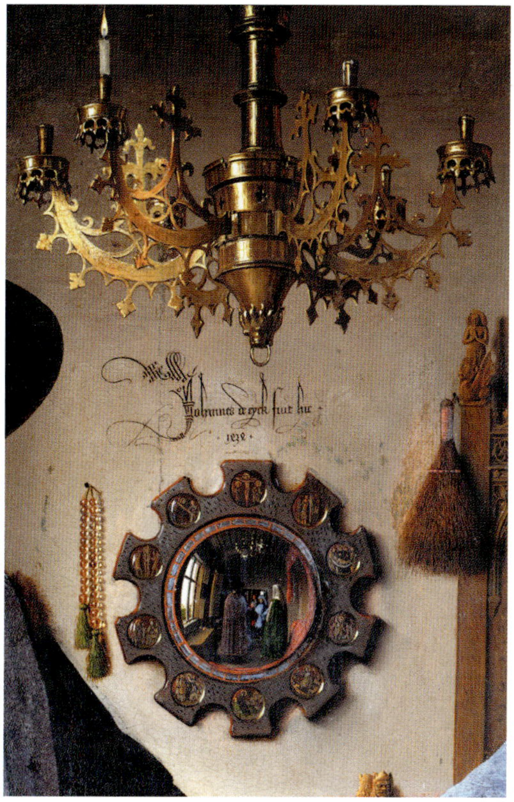

fig. 8.3b Detail.

dampens the paper before painting. This creates a challenge because the paint does not necessarily stay where it is put, and it is not easy to make changes. Thin applications of watercolor washes on white paper result in a translucent quality not possible with oil or tempera. Where highlights are desired, the artist simply lets the white paper show through. Because of its spontaneous quality, the watercolor technique lends itself to outdoor scenes, such as Zheng L. Feng's *New River Colors* (fig. 8.7), where he allows the medium to enhance the effects of light, water and atmosphere.

Gouache is a drier form of watercolor that is opaque—it has less

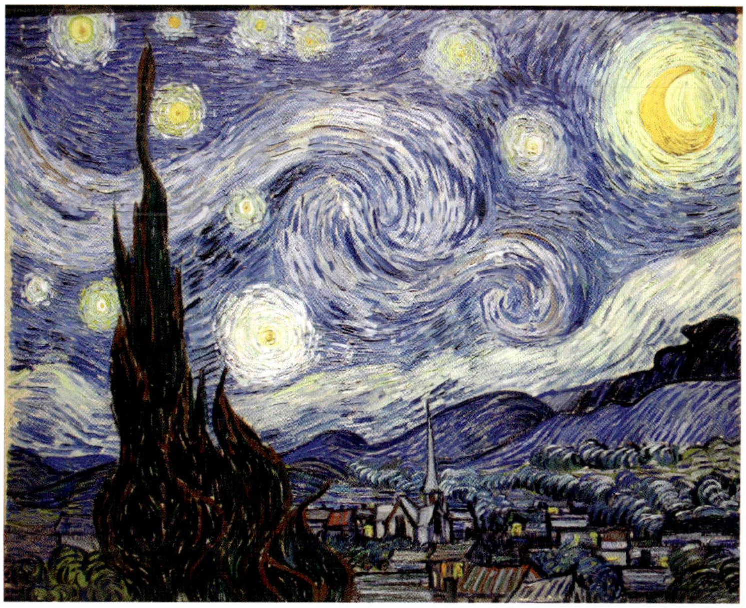

fig. 8.4 Vincent van Gogh, *Starry Night,* 1889. Oil on canvas.

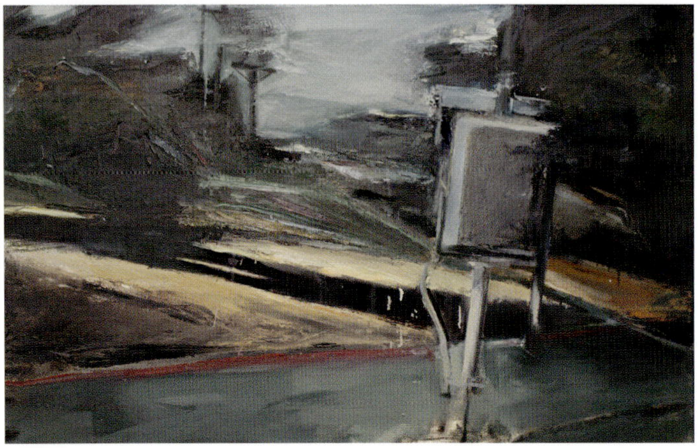

fig. 8.5a Charles Goolsby, *Switchbox,* 2002. Oil on canvas. Charles Goolsby fuses painterly brushwork and impasto textures with landscape imagery to express movement, feelings of transition and anxiety.

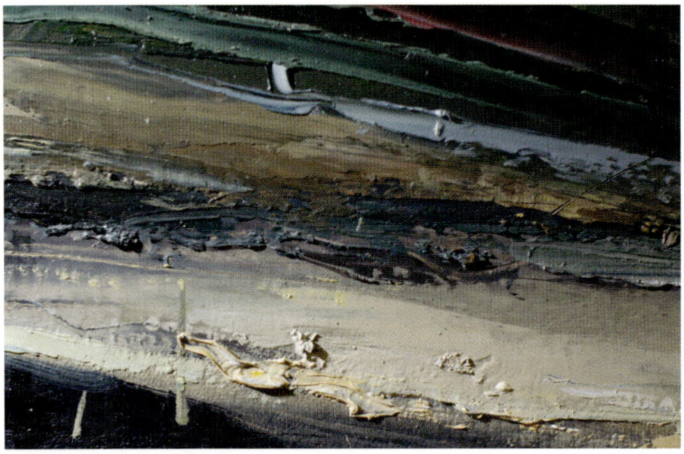

fig. 8.5b Detail of *Switchbox* showing impasto technique. *Switchbox* contrasts thicker impasto passages of paint with fluid, thinner and broader applications, emphasizing the importance of process as part of the visual statement.

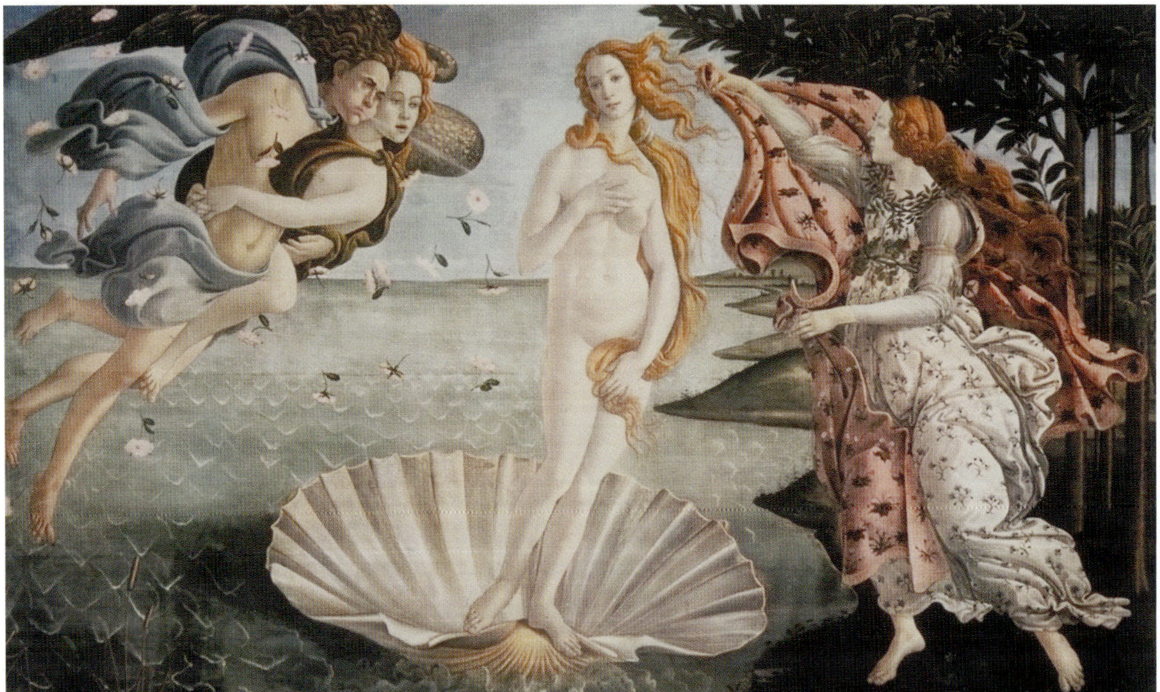

fig. 8.6 Botticelli, *Birth of Venus,* 1482. Tempera on canvas.

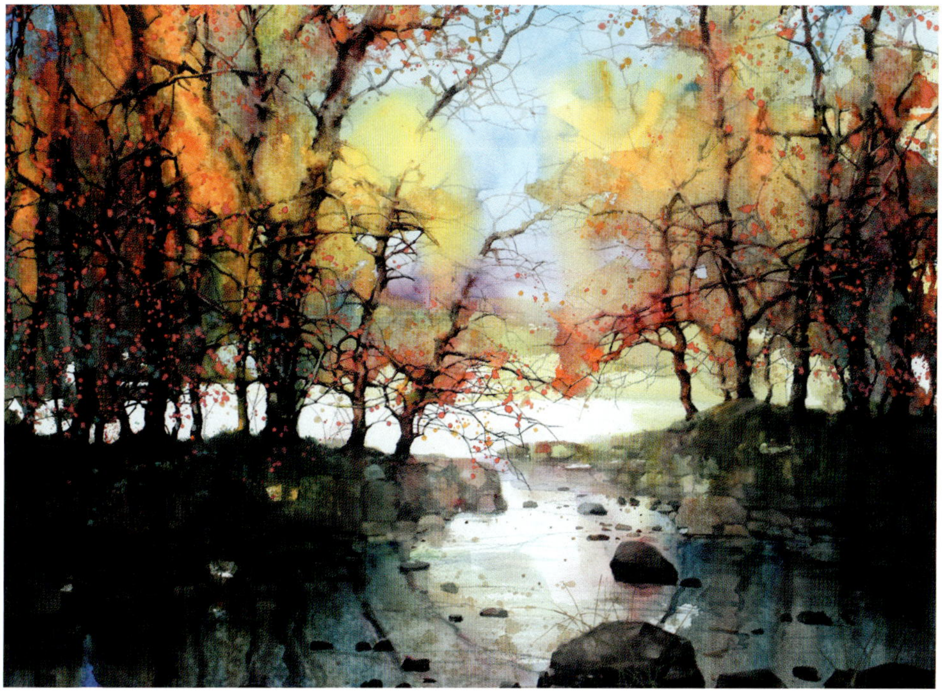

fig. 8.7 Zheng L. Feng, *New River Colors,* 2006. Watercolor on paper.

water and a small amount of chalk powder. Yumiko Ichikawa's *Imari & Pears* (fig. 8.8) illustrates how gouache allows the artist to paint in great detail.

Acrylic is a synthetic medium invented in the 1950s. The pigment is suspended in an acrylic polymer emulsion instead of in oil or egg yolk. You can dilute acrylic paints with water, yet they become water resistant when dry. Because acrylics dry rapidly, artists have the same restrictions with reworking the paint as they do with tempera, but they can apply the layers of paint much more quickly than with oil. Artists can use acrylics on a wider variety of supports, and a primer is not necessary so they can paint directly onto raw canvas if desired. The medium is quite transparent, and the colors can be intense, as seen in Benny Carter's *Goons on the Moon* (fig. 8.9 and fig. 1.1).

Fresco has a long pedigree stretching back to the Minoans of ancient Crete (c. 2000 BCE). In true fresco the pigment is mixed with water and applied to fresh wet lime-plaster. The lime in the plaster acts as a binder so a separate binder is not necessary. As the plaster dries it absorbs the pigment, which effectively becomes part of the wall. Fresco is thus a very durable medium as evidenced by the frescoed bedroom walls from a Villa near Pompeii (fig. 8.10). These

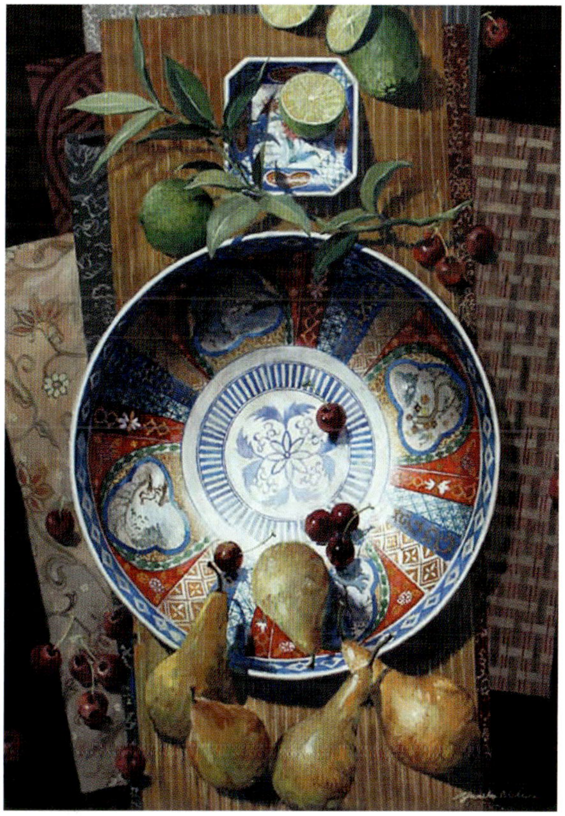

fig. 8.8 Yumiko Ichikawa, *Imari & Pears.* Gouache on paper. Imari is a type of porcelain made in Japan exported from the port city of Imari.

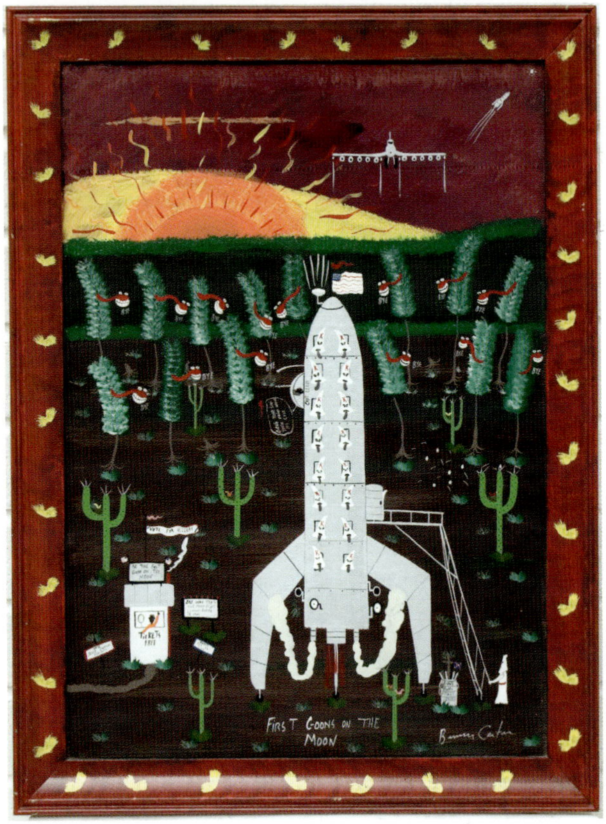

fig. 8.9 Benny Carter, *Goons on the Moon.* Acrylic on board.

walls still maintain their vivid colors after nearly 2000 years.

Artists paint wall frescos in small sections so that each section can be completed before the plaster dries. Any portion of the plaster not painted before it dries has to be chipped out and re-plastered. Careful preparation is therefore crucial, and the artist must paint quickly and carefully. For frescos like Michelangelo's Sistine Ceiling, the artist makes **cartoons** (full-scale drawings) of each section of the composition with holes pricked along the outlines of the figures and objects. He then holds the cartoon in place against the wet plaster and dusts it with charcoal, transferring a dotted line through the holes that serve as a guide. True fresco is called by its Italian name, *buon fresco. Secco fresco* is dry fresco. In the dry fresco technique the artist applies the pigment to dry plaster walls. Often this was done over a buon fresco painting to increase color intensity. Because the pigment does not bind with the wall, dry fresco needs a binder such as egg yolk, and because the pigment is on the surface of the wall rather than becoming part of the wall, it is not as durable as true fresco.

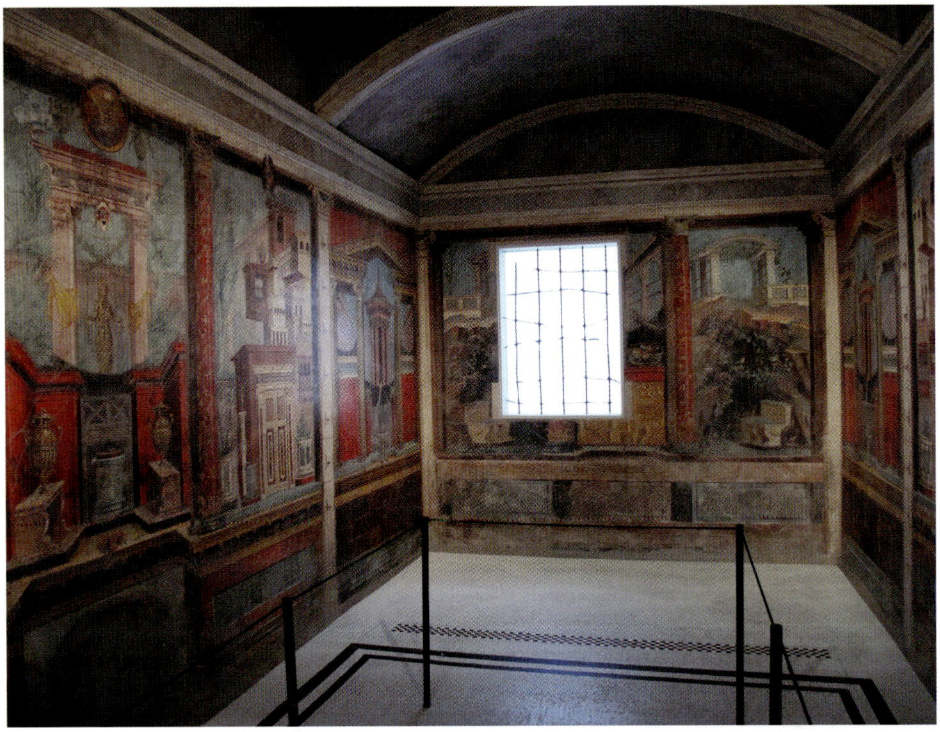

fig. 8.10 Bedroom from a Roman villa at Boscoreale (near Pompeii), first century BCE.

Encaustic is another medium used since ancient times. Pigments are suspended in hot beeswax, creating a rich paint that the artist must apply quickly before it hardens. Encaustic is very durable. A number of mummy portraits from Egypt survive in excellent condition, and numerous ancient statues retain traces of encaustic. Artists such as Jasper Johns revived the technique in the twentieth century. His *Flag* (fig. 8.11) illustrates the lush colors and highly textured surface possible with encaustic. Today working with encaustic is easier because heated tools, hot guns and heat lamps allow the artist to keep the wax softer longer.

Mosaic and stained glass are essentially two-dimensional art forms that mimic painting more closely than any other medium so we briefly describe them here. **Mosaics** are made with small cube-like pieces of stone, colored glass or other materials. The artist sets each piece (called a **tessera**) into mortar according to a preconceived design. Early mosaics first used pebbles; then artisans made tesserae by cutting marble or limestone into small cubes. These mosaics were limited to the color palette found in nature, as seen in a mosaic from ancient Rome (fig. 8.12). Ancient mosaics usually appeared on floors. In the Middle Ages mosaics moved from the floors to the walls, and the tesserae were made from colored glass or glass backed with metal foils (fig. 8.13). This provided a much wider range of richer colors. Byzantine craftsmen made gold tesserae by sandwiching gold leaf between two layers of glass, which they used for gold backgrounds and saints' halos. The uneven surfaces of the glass reflect and refract the light, creating a spiritual effect well suited for church interiors.

Stained glass traditionally refers to the windows made of colored glass in churches and other buildings, especially churches from the Gothic period. Adding metallic oxides to molten glass resulted in brilliant colors.

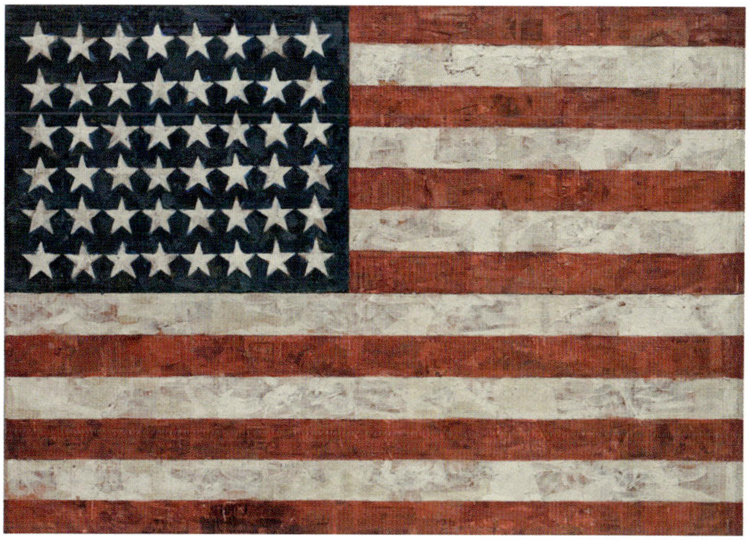

fig. 8.11 Jasper Johns, *Flag*, 1954. Encaustic on canvas.

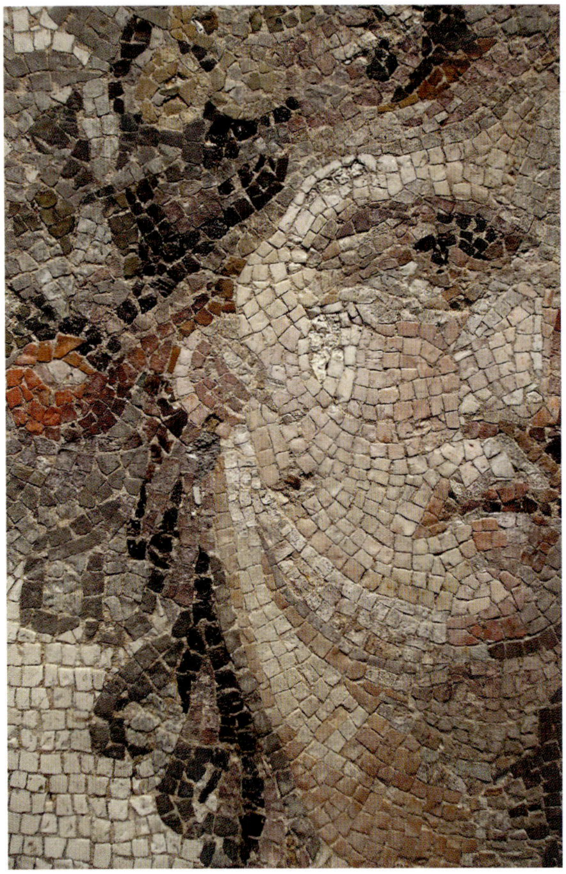

fig. 8.12 Detail of Roman mosaic, second century AD. Metropolitan Museum of Art, New York.

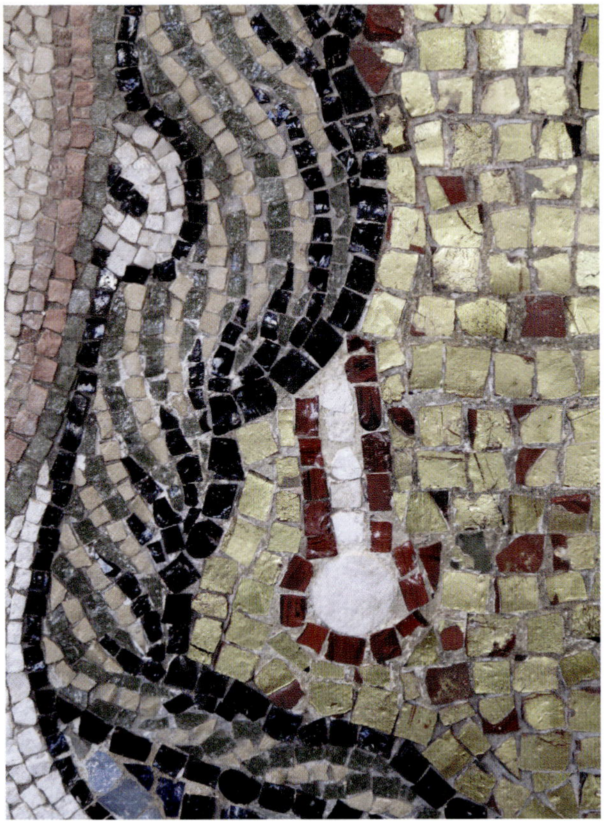

fig. 8.13 Byzantine Mosaic detail, 12th century. St. Peter's, Rome.

After cooling, artisans cut the colored pieces of glass into the shapes required by the design. Strips of lead with the same shape held each piece in place. For large windows, horizontal iron bars helped support the weight of the glass. They added details such as facial features, hair and drapery folds with a special paint developed for glass. Figure 8.14 shows these characteristics. The appearance of stained glass windows changes throughout the day depending on the position of the sun and whether or not there is cloud cover.

Mixed media refers to works of art that combine various mediums. They can be two-dimensional, three-dimensional or a combination of the two and often the media chosen is crucial to fully understanding the work. Richard Bay's *The Perils of Pleasure* (fig. 8.15) includes actual bottle caps as part of the frame to convey a hidden message to the viewer.

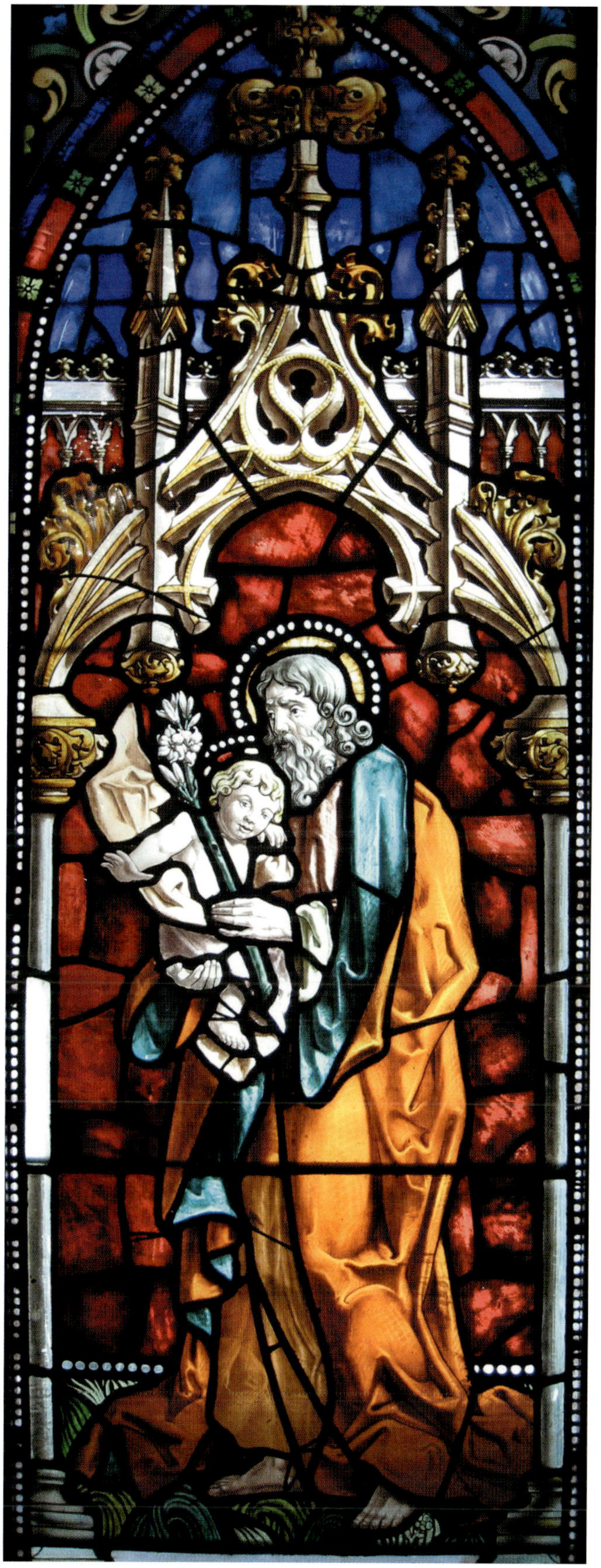

fig. 8.14 Stained glass window showing Joseph and the infant Jesus. San Gerónimo, Madrid.

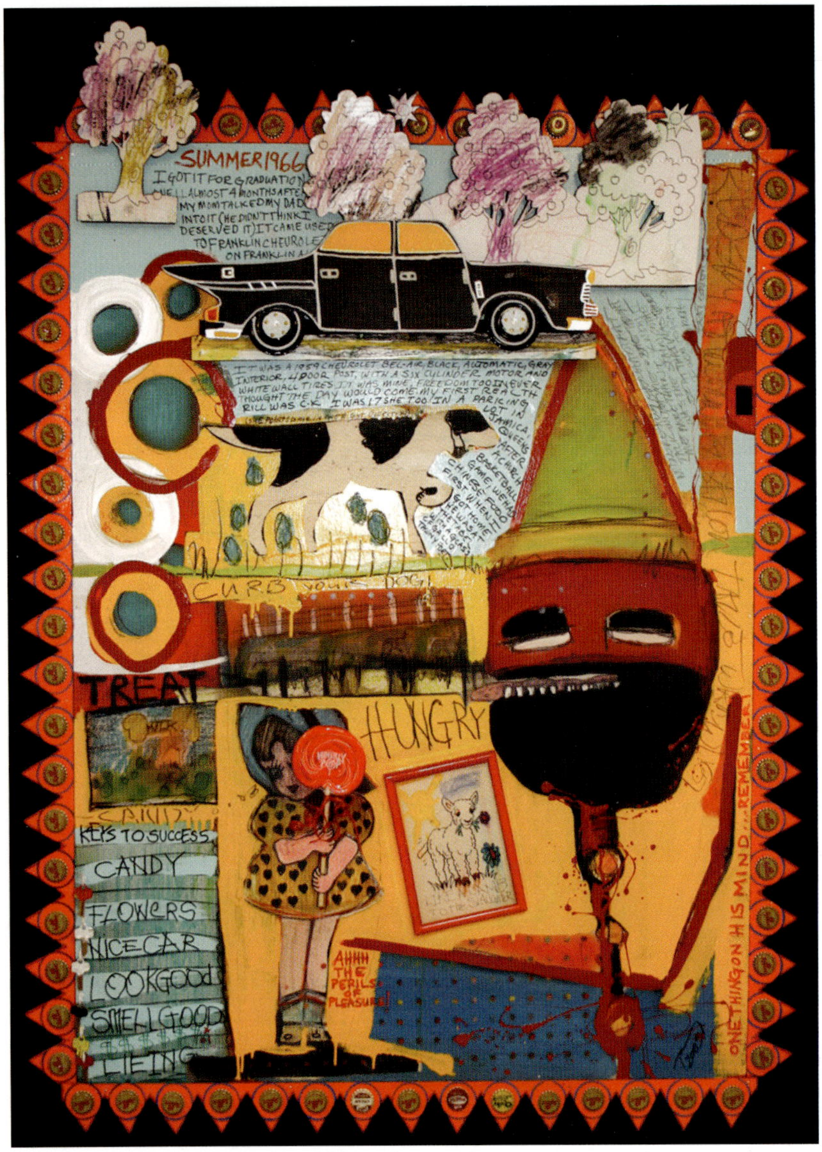

fig. 8.15 Richard J. Bay, *The Perils of Pleasure,* 2007. Mixed media construction, 63 in. × 37 in. × 6 in. Bay's pictorial narration documents the artist's earliest introduction to dating. It includes tongue and cheek metaphors concerning social mores and timely insights into the dating ritual.

SUMMARY

Painting is probably the most familiar of the visual arts in Western culture, and one of the oldest going back to prehistoric times with cave paintings. Paint consists of a **pigment** for color and a **medium or binder** to hold the pigment together. Pigments initially derived from plant and mineral sources that were ground into a powder; today most pigments are synthetic.

There are various kinds of painting mediums. With **oil paint**, pigments are mixed with linseed or other oil that will slowly dry. **Tempera paint** uses egg yolk or **casein** as the binder. It is not as flexible as oil. With **watercolor**, the pigments are suspended in water mixed with **gum** arabic (the sap from an African tree). **Gouache** is a form of watercolor with chalk powder and less water; it is therefore not as translucent.

PRONUNCIATION GUIDE

Boscoreale (bos-kor-ee-**ah**-lay)
Botticelli (bah-tih-**chel**-ee)
Buon fresco (bwon **fres**-ko)
Casein (**kay**-seen)
Gouache (gwash)
Pompeii (pom-**pay**)
Tesserae (**tes**-uh-rye or **tes**-uh-ree)
Van Eyck, Jan (van **ike**, yahn)
Van Gogh (van **go**)

GLOSSARY

Acrylic paint. A durable and water soluble paint made by combining pigments with a synthetic resin medium.

Binder. A substance that that holds pigments together and allows them to adhere to the support.

Cartoon. A full-size drawing often done in preparation for a fresco painting or a tapestry.

Casein. A protein-based substance derived from milk. Used as a binder for tempera paint.

Encaustic. A painting medium in which the pigment is mixed with molten wax and applied to the surface while hot.

Fresco. A painting on plaster. With true fresco (buon fresco) the paint is applied while the plaster is still wet and it chemically binds with the plaster. With dry fresco (fresco secco), the paint is applied to plaster that has already dried.

Gesso. A plaster mixture applied to a support or canvas and used as a surface for painting.

Glaze. A thin layer of translucent paint

Gouache. A type of watercolor that is opaque rather than transparent because pigment has been added.

Ground. A coating applied to a canvas or printmaking plate to prepare it for painting or etching.

Gum. A sticky substance found in many plants that is used to bind pigments.

Gum Arabic. A specific gum from the African acacia plant.

Impasto. A thick application of paint on the canvas or other support.

Medium. 1) A material used to create a work of art. 2) In painting, a liquid added to pigment so that it can be applied to the support.

Mixed media. The combination of two or more media in a work of art.

Mosaic. A decoration composed of small pieces of colored glass, stone or other material.

Oil paint. A slow drying and flexible paint made by mixing pigments with an oil medium.

Panel painting. Painting on a wooden panel.

Pigment. A powdered material used to give color to inks and paints.

Stained glass. Windows made of pieces of colored glass held in place with lead strips.

Support. The two-dimensional surface on which an artist works, such as canvas, paper, a panel of wood, or a wall.

Tempera. A type of paint in which the binding medium is egg yolk or casein.

Tesserae. Small cubes of stone, glass, etc., used in mosaic work.

Vehicle. A liquid such as water or oil used to mix pigments for painting.

Watercolor. A painting medium in which the pigments are suspended in a solution of water and gum Arabic.

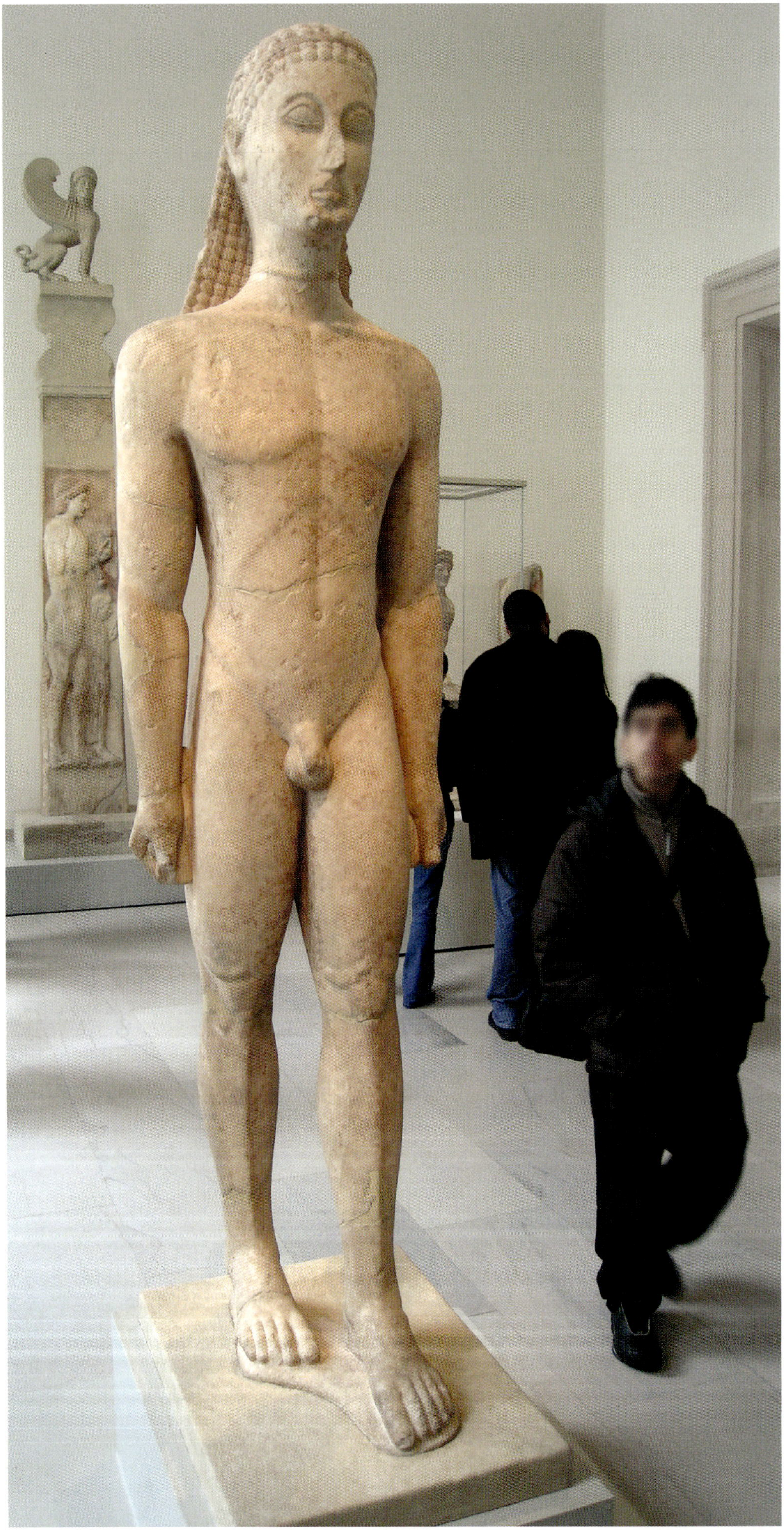

fig. 9.1 Kouros figure, c. 600 BCE. Marble, 6 ft. 4 in. high. Metropolitan Museum of Art, New York.

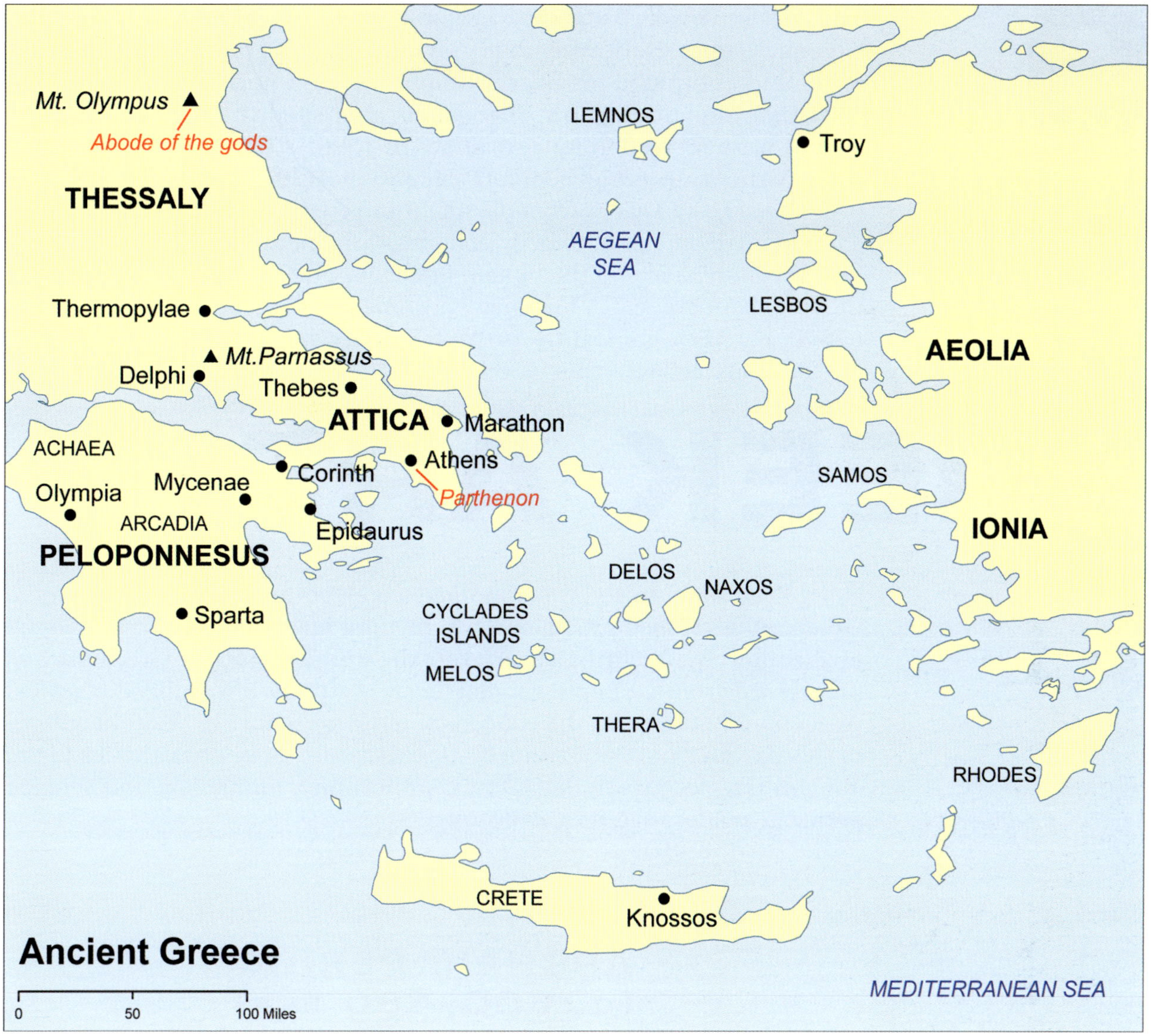

Map of Ancient Greece.

9

The ancient Greeks dated their beginnings to 776 BCE, the year of the first Olympic Games. Held every four years, the Games grew in size and popularity and continued for over a thousand years until 393 CE when the Christian Roman emperor Theodosius abolished them. (The Olympic Games were revived in modern times in 1896.) The Games were a time when participants set all conflicts aside so the athletes from city states all over Greece could get to Olympia safely and compete in peace. The idea of a sound mind and a sound body epitomizes the nature of the Greeks. They held the individual and the human intellect in high esteem and developed the first democracy. (Unfortunately, women and slaves could not participate in it.) They constantly strove for perfection, and the development of Greek art reflects this. Unlike Egyptian art, which (except for the

GREEK ART

short-lived Amarna style) maintained a conventional style for millennia, Greek art developed prodigiously in the first few hundred years of Greek civilization. By the fifth century BCE, the human figure in Greek art had progressed from a simple geometric style to one of idealized classical perfection that remains the concept of physical beauty in Western culture to this day. In fact, we owe much more than our sense of aesthetics to the ancient Greeks. Greek democracy, philosophy, humanism and science permeate modern Western civilization.

ARCHAIC PERIOD (c. 600–480 BCE)

Kouros Figure (fig. 9.1). **Kouros** (plural, kouroi) means "male youth" and is a term used for a commemorative statue of an important man. Kouroi could be votive offerings in a temple or a sanctuary or grave markers in a cemetery. This Kouros clearly shows the influence of Egyptian sculpture (compare to Menkaure in fig. 6.5). It has the same erect standing pose with one leg forward and arms at the sides with clenched fists, but there are significant differences. Although the Greek kouros is more **stylized** than its Egyptian counterparts and thus less naturalistic overall, it is a true **free-standing** figure completely liberated from the block of stone from which the artist carved it. The figure is also nude, something we do not see in Egyptian art. We see the stylization in the patterned hair, hard-edged eyebrows and overlarge, bulging eyes—all typical traits of Archaic kouroi. Furthermore, the sculptor did not accurately define the musculature, and the ears are too large and positioned too high. Unlike the Egyptians, the Greeks were not concerned with permanence in their figural sculptures because they did not have the same concept of the afterlife. Instead, they wanted to portray the human body and its movement as naturally as possible.

Peplos Kore (fig. 9.2). **Kore** (plural, korai) means "maiden" and is the term used for female figures. They likely had a commemorative purpose as well or could represent a goddess. Like her male counterpart, she has the same erect pose, stylized hair and bulging eyes. Her slight smile is typical of Archaic figures, and historians refer to it as the "archaic smile," although it is probably more of a stylistic convention than an actual smile. Unlike the kouros figure, this kore had one arm extended (now lost) and probably offered something in her hand. She is also clothed. (The female nude does not appear in Greek art until the fourth century BCE.) The simple woolen garment she wears is a **peplos**, hence the name of the sculpture. Traces of paint on her lips, eyes, hair and clothing indicate ancient Greek artists painted their statues. In most cases the paint has worn away over the centuries, but explorers found this statue inside a wall where it was protected. Furthermore, the paint was encaustic (pigment in a wax medium), which is very durable.

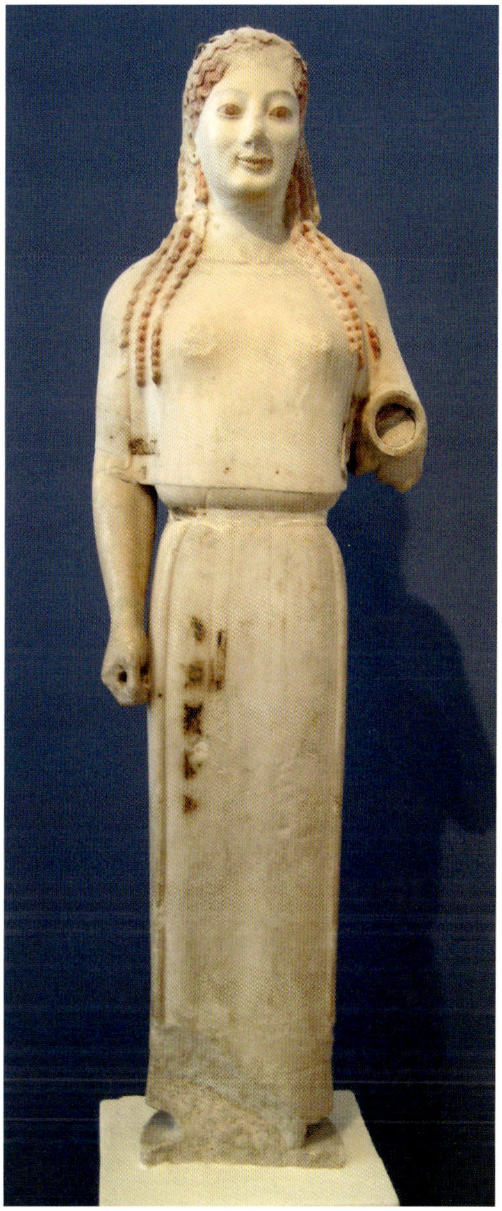

fig. 9.2 Kore figure (Peplos Kore), c. 530 BCE. Marble, 48 in. high. Acropolis Museum, Athens.

Drinking Cup (fig. 9.4). Written records attest to the skill of Greek painters, many of whom became famous (see "Greek Artists" box), but very little painting survives with the exception of painted **ceramics**. The Greeks produced a wide variety of vases (fig. 9.3), each suited to a specific function. The **kylix** was a large cup used for drinking wine, usually decorated on both the outside and interior. The artist painted this one in the black figure style (see "Black and Red Figure Style" box). Exekias was a skilled and famous vase painter, and a number of his works survive. Figure 9.4 shows the kylix from above so you are looking at what you would see after drinking the wine. The scene, appropriately for a wine cup, depicts the wine god Dionysus reclining in a ship. One day while in mortal form, pirates abducted him. When they refused to release him he revealed his divinity and made grape vines sprout from the mast. The terrified pirates jumped into the sea where Dionysus turned them into dolphins. Exekias has superbly married the composition to a circular format. The vines with their bunches of grapes cascade above the sail in a curved manner that follows the curved rim of the cup. The keel of the ship and the curved arrangement of the dolphins (whose backs are also curved) also mimic the shape of the circular cup.

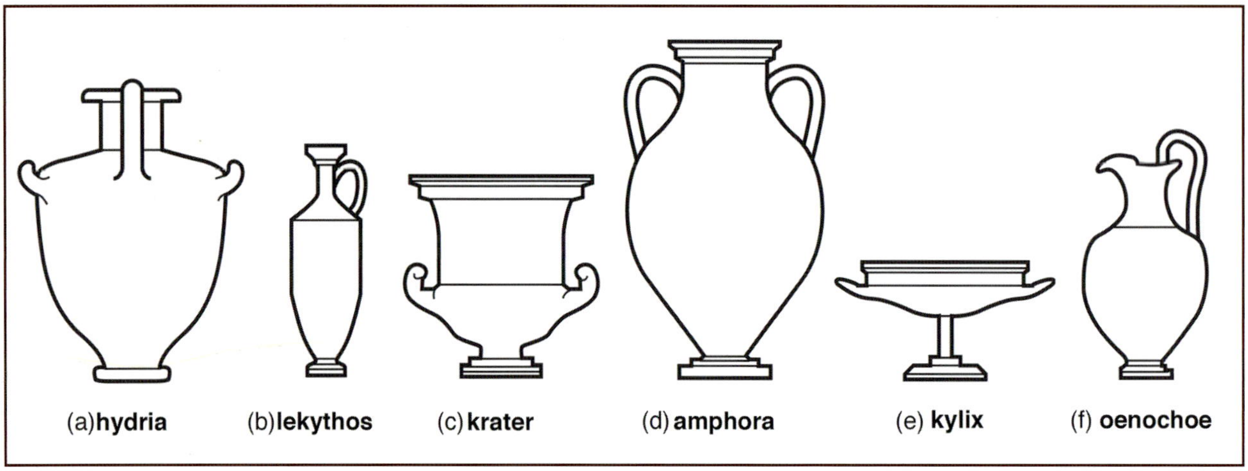

fig. 9.3 Greek vases. A few of the basic vase types are the (a) the **hydria** for water (with three handles—two for carrying and one for pouring); (b) the lekythos for pouring oil; (c) the **krater** for mixing wine and water (the Greeks diluted their wine); (d) the **amphora** for storing liquids such as wine, oil, and honey; (e) the kylix, a drinking cup; and (f) the oenochoe for pouring wine.

CLASSICAL PERIOD (c. 480–400 BCE)

The Classical period of Greek art is dated to the defeat of the invading Persians in 480 BCE at the Battle of Salamis (an island just off the coast from Athens). Greek sculptors perfected the human figure to a classical ideal of beauty and proportion, while Greek architects did the same with temples. The concept of the classical ideal remains viable in Western culture to this day. We can trace our sense of physical beauty, seen in advertising, fashion, television and the cinema, as well as the architectural style of many traditional banks, libraries and government buildings, back to Classical Greece. Athens became the most powerful of the Greek city states with Pericles as its brilliant leader. It was Pericles' idea to rebuild the Athenian Acropolis

Greek Artists

With their emphasis on the individual, the Greeks were the first to elevate their artists to a higher level. Artists often signed their work and became highly esteemed. Zeuxis (fifth century BCE) and Apelles (fourth century BCE) are two artists whose renown endures to this day despite the fact that no works by either painter remain. The recognition of artists is something we take for granted today, but most ancient cultures considered artists anonymous craftsmen. The Greeks changed this just as they changed how they depicted the human figure in art.

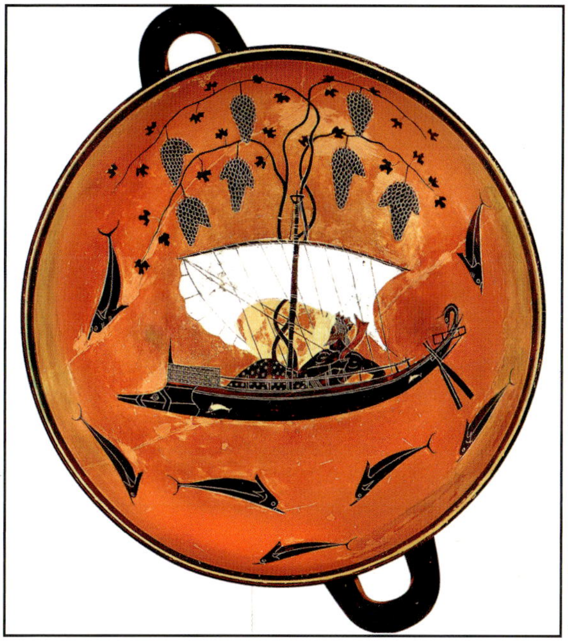

fig. 9.4 Exekias. Drinking cup (kylix) showing Dionysus in a sailboat, c. 530 BCE. Terracotta (black figure style), 12 in. diameter. Antikensammlungen und Glyptothek, Munich.

after its destruction by the Persians, which resulted in one of the most beautiful and harmonious architectural ensembles of all time.

Parthenon. Dedicated to Athens' patron goddess, Athena, this temple is one of the most influential buildings in Western architecture (fig.9.5). Its builders created it in just sixteen years, using marble blocks without the use of mortar, and it contains many interesting refinements. Although vertical and horizontal elements compose the structure, they are not all

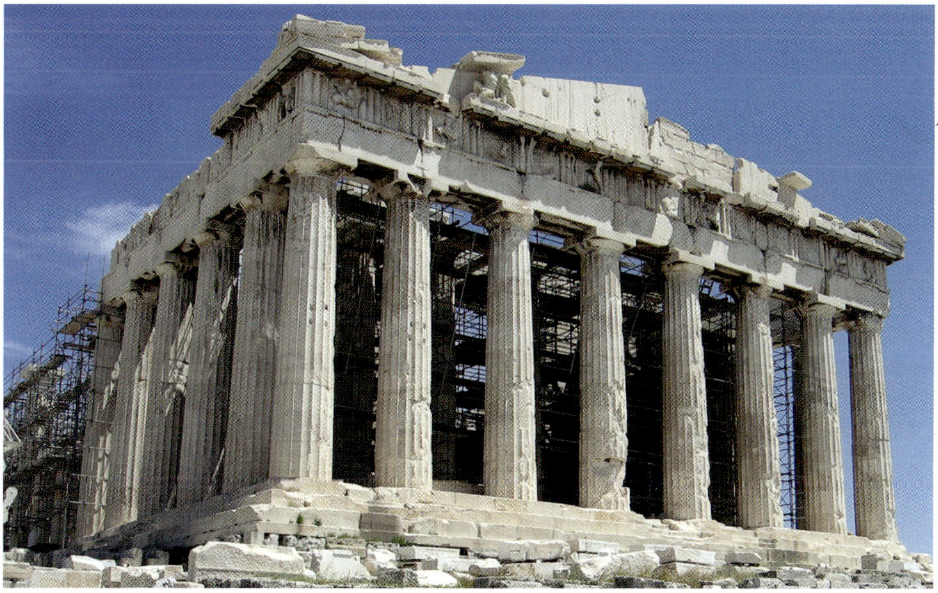

fig. 9.5 Iktinos and Kallicrates, The Parthenon, 448-432 BCE. Acropolis, Athens.

Black and Red Figure Style

Exekias painted his kylix in the black figure style, so called because the figures are in black. He achieved this using a three-stage **firing** process. He painted the scene on the cup using a slip, a mixture of clay and water. Then he fired the cup in a kiln with oxygen allowed in. This turned both the cup and the painted design red as they absorbed the oxygen. In the second firing he eliminated the oxygen. This turned everything black, and he raised the temperature to a sufficient point to vitrify the slip into a glass-like consistency. In the third firing he reintroduced oxygen. The non-painted parts of the cup turned red again as they reabsorbed the oxygen, but the slip remained black because it was now impermeable. He could then scratch out such details as Dionysus' hair, the prow of the ship or the individual grapes on the black portions. Sometimes he added paint, such as for the white sail, but this tended to flake away eventually because it was less permanent.

By the late sixth century BCE, the red figure style became popular. Artists used the same three-stage firing technique, but they applied the slip to all parts of the vessel except the figures and other parts of the scene. They added details using slip applied with a small syringe or brush. The red figure style allowed for more naturalistic figures in both appearance and the illusion of movement so it quickly supplanted the black figure style.

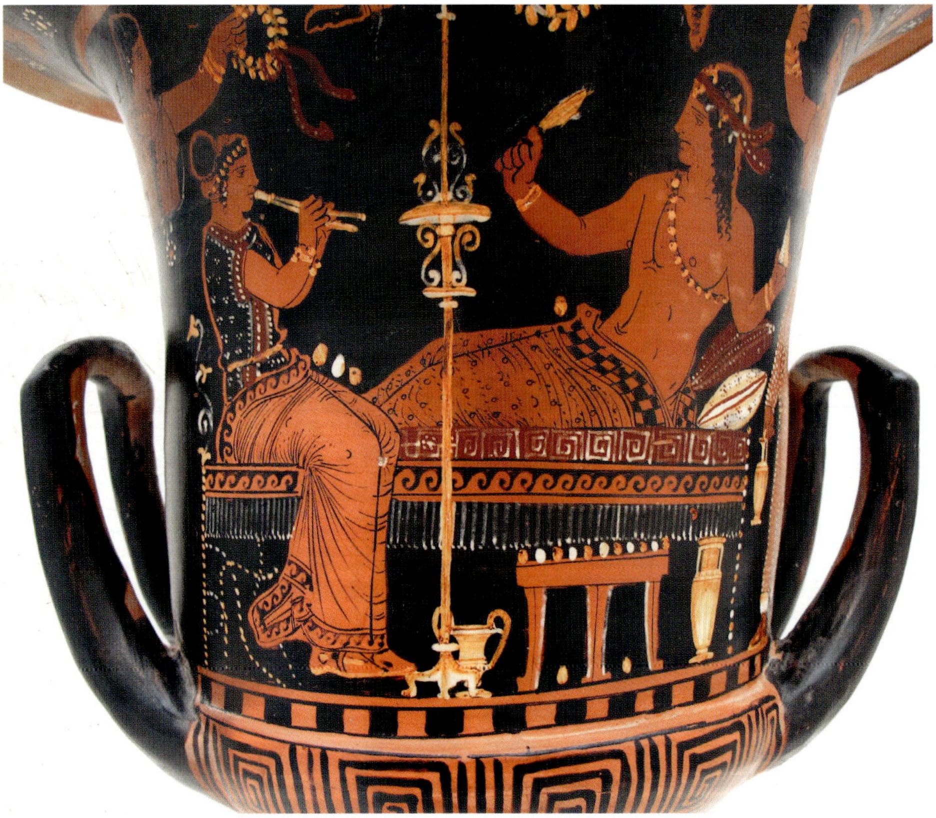

Red figure style Greek Vase

straight. The temple floor (**stylobate**) is slightly convex, and the **columns** exhibit **entasis**; that is, they bulge a bit in the center. Furthermore, the columns tilt inward and are more closely spaced at the corners. The corner columns are also wider in diameter than the other columns. We do not fully understand the reasons for these deviations, which could be practical or aesthetic. For example, the convex floor might help with drainage or it could correct an optical illusion that the floor would appear to sag in the middle if it were perfectly flat. Whatever the reasons, the swelling forms give the building an organic, living quality that is unique in ancient architecture.

Inside the temple within a two-story **colonnade** stood a huge **chryselephantine** (gold and ivory) statue of Athena created by the great sculptor Phidias, who oversaw all the sculptural decoration of the Parthenon. (Phidias also made the equally huge seated statue of Zeus at Olympia, one of the seven wonders of the ancient world.) Although the original statue disappeared in the fifth century CE, a life-size reconstruction exists in Nashville, Tennessee (fig. 9.6). Approximately forty feet tall, Athena holds a shield in her left hand and a six-foot Nike (the winged female personification of Victory) in the other, referring to the victory over the Persians.

While basically a Doric temple, the Parthenon has Ionic elements as well (see "Architectural Orders" box). The exterior colonnade and the triglyph and metope **frieze** are Doric, but the continuous inner frieze around the outside of the walls within the colonnade is Ionic. The Greeks may have done this for political reasons to appease the Ionian Greeks because Pericles used funds collected from all the Greek city states (originally intended for other purposes) to rebuild the Acropolis.

Although it was later transformed into a church and then a mosque, the Parthenon remained in relatively good shape until 1687 when the Turks, who ruled Greece at the time and were at war with the Venetians, used it as a munitions depot. The Venetians scored a direct hit with one of their rockets, and the ensuing explosion destroyed the interior. In the early nineteenth century, Lord Elgin took much of the Parthenon's remaining sculpture to England (see "Elgin Marbles and the Restitution of Art" box). The Parthenon is currently undergoing an extensive restoration that began in 1975.

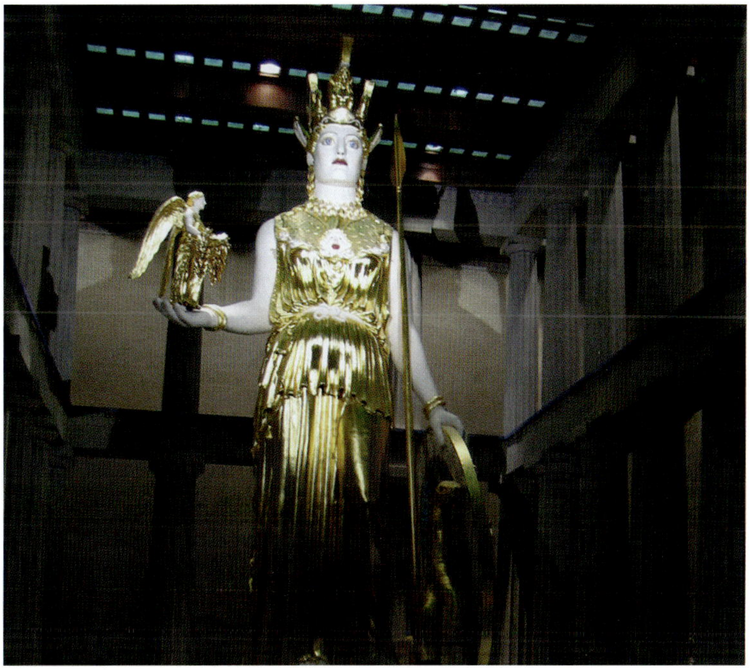

fig. 9.6 Interior of the Parthenon in Nashville, TN (1921–1931), showing a reconstruction of the statue of Athena (made by Alan LeQuire, 1982–1990).

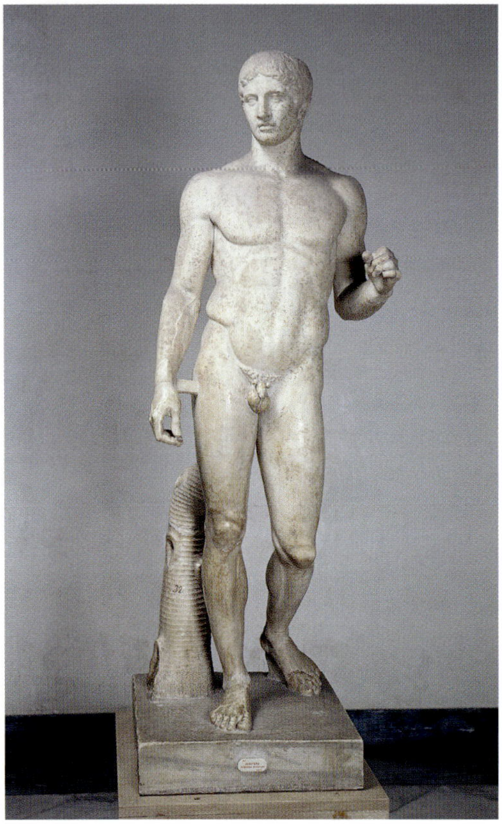

fig. 9.7 Polykleitos, *Doryphoros* (*Spear Bearer*), c. 450 BCE. Marble, Roman copy of bronze original.

Doryphoros. Compared to the figures from the Archaic period, the Doryphoros (*Spear Bearer*) by Polykleitos (fig. 9.7) indicates how quickly Greek artists developed the ideal human form. Compared to the stiff and rigid kouros (fig. 9.1), the Doryphoros is relaxed and natural. This is because Polykleitos employs the recently discovered concept of **contrapposto**, or weight shift, and a canon of proportion. The figure's straight right leg bears the weight; the left leg is relaxed and bent at the knee. The bent leg causes one hip to be slightly higher than the other. This is exactly how people stand naturally, and once the Greeks realized this, they could portray the human figure much more realistically.

Although the *Doryphoros* appears very natural, Polykleitos carefully calculated the figure's composition. The weight-bearing left arm that originally held the spear is opposite the right weight-bearing leg, and the relaxed right arm is opposite the relaxed left leg. On the other hand, both straight limbs are on one side and both bent limbs are on the other. This provides a harmonious balance of opposing and like features.

The original statue by Polykleitos was bronze, but it no longer survives (see "Bronze Statues" box). It was a famous work, however, and people have made many copies. Figure 9.7 shows a Roman copy in stone.

HELLENISTIC PERIOD (c. 323–30 BCE)

Contrapposto or "weight shifted"

The Hellenistic period begins with the death of Alexander the Great in 323 BCE and ends with the deaths of Anthony and Cleopatra in 30 BCE. Alexander conquered vast territories in his short life and created a huge empire that included Greece, Egypt, the Near East, Persia and parts of India. Upon his death his generals divided the lands among them; they established their own dynasties and spread Greek culture. Likewise, these foreign cultures influenced the Greeks as well. Hellenism was a great melding of cultures, and it produced a rich variety of art.

Aphrodite of Melos (Venus de Milo). We often see one of the most famous Hellenistic sculptures, the *Aphrodite of Melos* (fig. 9.8), in advertising. Her image is also the source for such modern works as Salvador Dali's *Venus de Milo with Drawers* or Jim Dine's three pastiches of the sculpture on the Avenue of the Americas in New York City. The figure continues the ideals of the Classical period with her emotionless face, ideal body and contrapposto stance, but the pose is more exaggerated, and her torso is nude.

Architectural Orders

There are three Greek architectural orders: Doric, Ionic and Corinthian. The easiest way to identify them is by their column **capitals**. The oldest and most masculine is the **Doric order**. Its column shaft has sharp-edged flutes (vertical grooves), and a flat bowl-like capital tops it. The columns have no bases. The frieze above is composed of **metopes** (blank areas usually filled with relief sculptures) and triglyphs, which look like three vertical bars. (The design of the triglyphs may derive from the ends of wooden beams used in early Greek temples before they began using stone.)

The **Ionic order** originated in Ionia (now the western coast of Turkey). It is more feminine and elegant than the Doric. The capital of an Ionic column is a scroll or **volute**. The column shaft's flutes have flat edges, and the shaft rests on a base. The frieze above was continuous, which allowed more freedom with sculptural programs.

The **Corinthian order** is the most elaborate with fancy leaf-like capitals that imitate the acanthus plant. Like the Ionic order, the frieze is continuous, and the columns have bases. The Corinthian order was more common in the Hellenistic and Roman periods.

All three orders had pitched roofs with a triangular pediment at the front and rear filled with large relief sculpture.

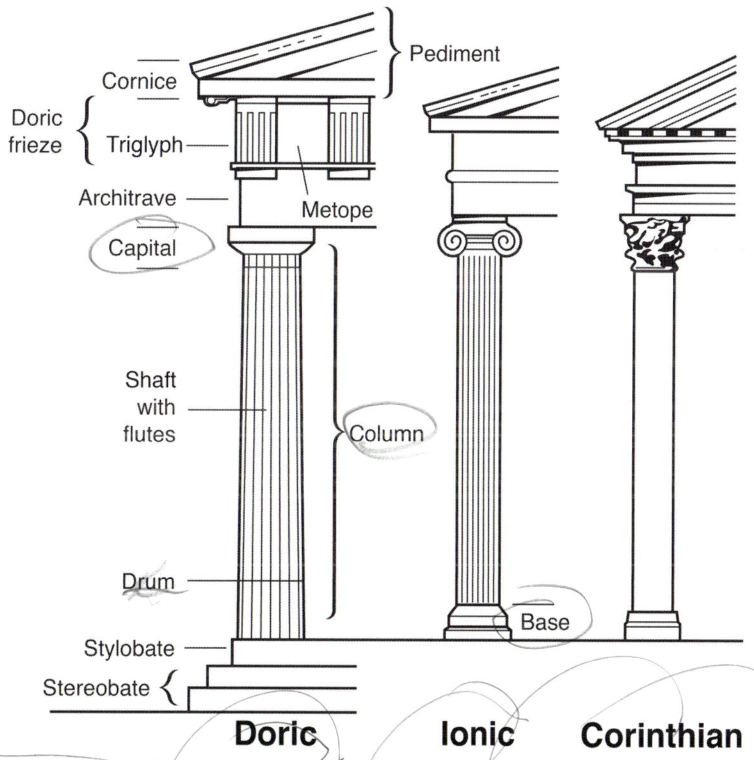

Elgin Marbles and the Restitution of Art

Many of the famous sculptures from the Parthenon are currently in the British Museum in London, sold to the museum by Lord Elgin in the early nineteenth century. Now Greece wants them back, and a longstanding legal debate exists as to where the Parthenon sculptures should reside. From the British point of view, Elgin saved some of the marbles, which probably would not have survived into the twentieth century if he had not removed them to safety. From the Greek point of view, the sculptures are part of the Parthenon and should be repatriated to Greece where the new Acropolis Museum can house them very near the Parthenon.

Repatriation of ancient art is now a hot topic in the museum world. Countries with a rich classical heritage such as Italy and Greece claim that some of their national treasures from archaeological sites or ancient shipwrecks were either stolen or acquired by dubious means. The Metropolitan Museum of Art in New York and the Getty Museum in Malibu have negotiated the return or long-term loans of some of their most prestigious pieces that do not have pristine provenances. A complicating circumstance with the Elgin marbles is the fact that Lord Elgin was given permission by the Turks (who controlled Greece at the time) to remove the sculptures from the Parthenon.

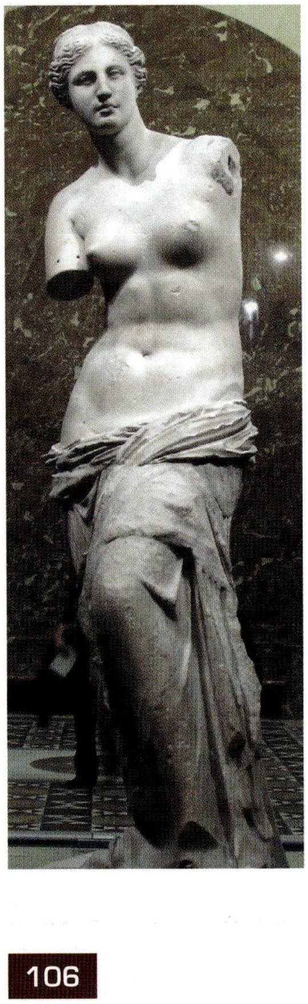

Old Market Woman (fig. 9.9). Unlike the *Aphrodite of Melos,* the *Old Market Woman* clearly departs from the Classical ideal. It never would have occurred to a fifth century sculptor to create such an image, but Hellenistic artists depicted a wide range of human emotions and ages. With disheveled clothing, sagging breasts and a well-worn face, the poor woman carries foodstuffs and a basket of chicks to market. Her hunched pose is a perversion of the classical contrapposto stance.

Laocoön. The sculptors explored human emotion in *Laocoön and His Sons* (fig. 9.10a). Laocoön was a Trojan priest who warned the Trojans against accepting the large wooden horse offered by the Greeks as a gift. The goddess Athena, who supported the Greeks, sent sea serpents to kill Laocoön and his sons. The three figures writhe in torment as the giant serpents attack them. The face of Laocoön is particularly anguished with his open mouth, furrowed brow, deeply set eyes and unruly hair (fig. 9.10b). His open mouth and deeply set eyes catch more shadow and thereby increase the dramatic effect.

As realistic as this work appears, there are some incongruities that illustrate the dichotomy that can exist in Hellenistic art. First, the sculpture

fig. 9.8 *Aphrodite of Melos* (*Venus de Milo*), c. 150 BCE. Marble, 6 ft. 7 in. high. Louvre, Paris.

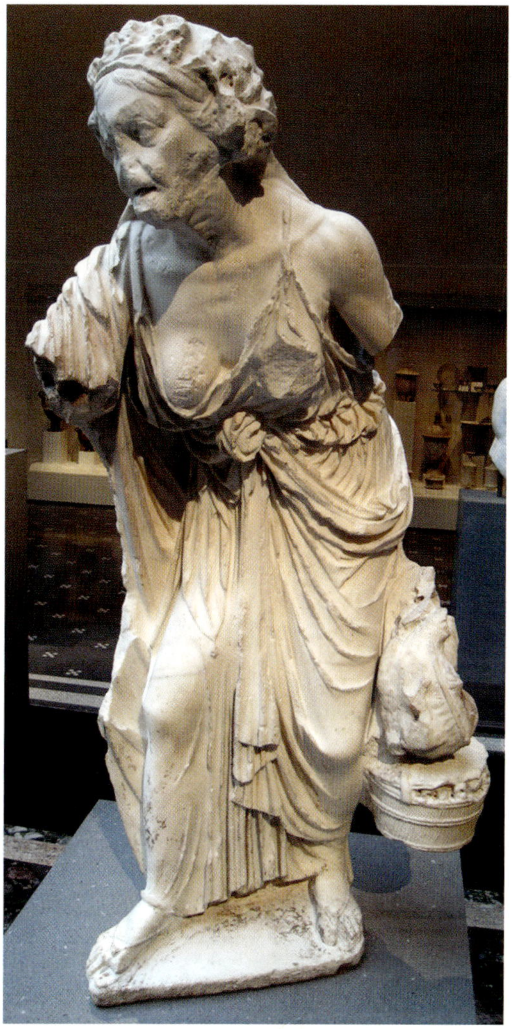

fig. 9.9 *Old Market Woman*, c. 100 BCE. Marble, 4 ft. high. Metropolitan Museum of Art, New York.

Bronze Statues

It is said that 90 percent of all Greek statues were made of bronze, yet 99 percent of what survives is made of stone (usually marble). This is because bronze was a valuable material, and people eventually melted down most ancient statues so they could use the bronze for more practical things, especially weaponry. Those bronze statues that survive became buried or were lost in shipwrecks and then found in modern times. The Greeks made larger bronze sculptures using the **lost wax technique**, which the chapter on sculpture discusses (fig. 10.7). The Romans, who conquered Greece in 146 BCE, became enamored of Greek sculptures and had many of the more famous bronzes copied in stone. You can usually tell a Roman copy because marble does not have the tensile strength of bronze and therefore requires extra support. That support often takes the form of a tree trunk, such as the one behind the right leg of the Doryphoros in figure 9.7.

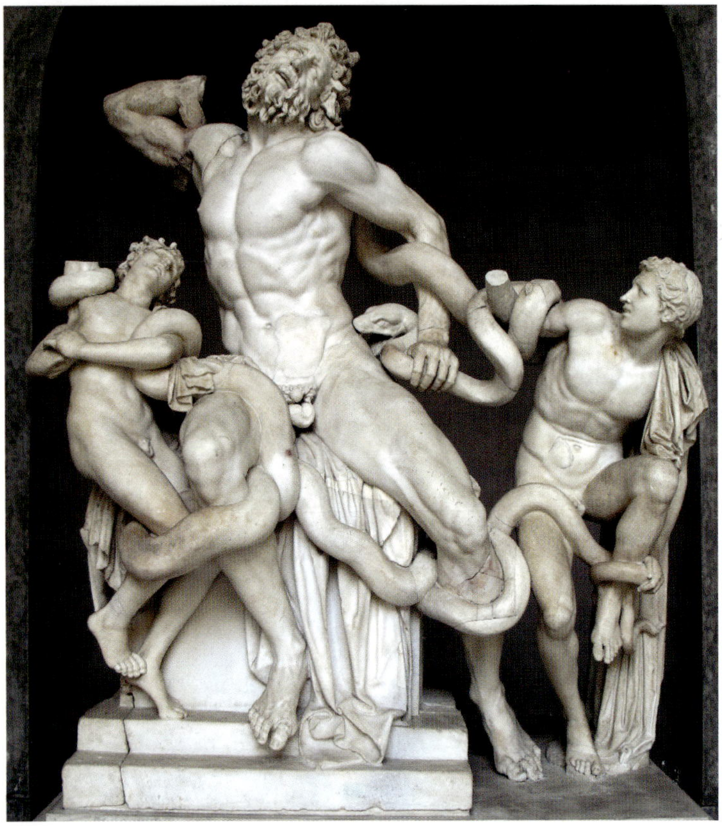

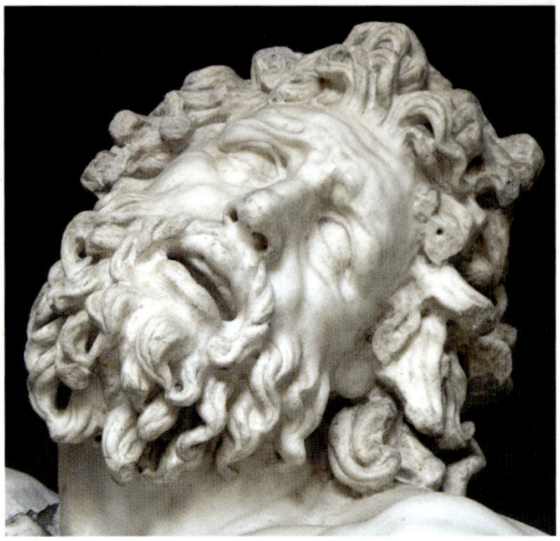

fig. 9.10b Detail.

fig. 9.10a *Laocoön and His Sons,* late 1st century BCE or early 1st century CE. Marble, 7 ft. 10 in. high. Vatican Museums, Rome.

is more or less in a single plane. The three figures should be thrashing about in all directions in their attempt to rid themselves of the deadly serpents. Second, although Laocoön has the face of a middle-aged man, his muscular and idealized torso is clearly that of a younger man. And the two sons look more like miniature adults than children.

SUMMARY

The ancient Greeks began their recorded history with the first Olympic Games in 776 BCE. Greek art is divided into several major periods: Archaic, Classical, and Hellenistic.

Archaic (c. 600–480 BCE). This period shows the development of the human figure. The early male figure (Kouros) is derived from earlier Egyptian statues, but the Kouros figures are nude and there is a progression from highly stylized features to more naturalistic features. The clothed female figure (Kore) shows a similar development.

Greek painting survives in pottery decoration. There were two types of figure painting—the **black figure technique** in which the figures were shown in black against the natural red-orange color of the ceramic vessel, and the **red figure technique** in which the color scheme is reversed. The Greeks made many different kinds of ceramic vessels, each with its own specific purpose.

Classical Period (c. 480–400 BCE). After defeating the Persians at the Battle of Salamis off the coast near Athens, Greek art entered a new phase. The human figure reaches a state of ideal perfection as seen in the *Doryphoros* (Spear Bearer) by Polykleitos. This statue exhibits contrapposto (**weight shift**), which gives the spear bearer a natural pose. This work was enormously influential for later artists.

In architecture, the Parthenon (a temple dedicated to the goddess Athena) is one of the best surviving examples of Classical building style and technique. This hallmark structure is one of the most important in Western architecture.

Hellenistic (323–30 BCE). Another phase of Greek art begins with the death of Alexander the Great. During the Hellenistic period the calm restraint of the Classical era gives way to a wider variety of subjects and emotions. The *Laocoön*, who is killed with his two sons by giant serpents, is a good example of melodrama not seen in earlier periods. Likewise, the depiction of figures only in their idealistic prime gives way to realistic images of young and old people, such as the *Old Market Woman*.

CLASSICAL MYTHOLOGY

Gods are listed by their Greek name with their Roman equivalent in parentheses. Attributes are in *italics*.

Achilles: Greek hero in Trojan War. Son of Peleus (King of Phthia) and the nereid Thetis.

Aeneas: Trojan prince who escaped to Italy and became legendary ancestor of the Romans. Son of Anchises and Aphrodite.

Agamemnon: legendary king of Argos during the Trojan War. Son of Atreus. Married to Clytemnestra. Murdered by Clytemnestra.

Ajax: Greek hero in Trojan War.

Amazons: mythical race of warrior-women.

Aphrodite (Venus): goddess of love. *Cupid, golden apple*

Apollo: god of arts, reason, inspiration. *Lyre, crown of laurel leaves*

Ares (Mars): god of war. *Armor*

Argonauts: heroes who helped Jason in his quest for the Golden Fleece on the ship, Argos.

Ariadne: daughter of king Minos who helped Theseus kill the Minotaur. Abandoned by Theseus on the island of Naxos, but then married Dionysos.

Artemis (Diana): goddess of the hunt. *Dogs, stags, moon*

Athena (Minerva): goddess of war, wisdom, and arts and crafts. *Armor*

Bacchus: see Dionysos.

Caduceus: magic staff entwined by two snakes and topped by wings that was carried by Hermes.

Centaurs: creatures that are half human, half horse.

Ceres: see Demeter.

Cupid: see Eros.

Cyclops: a one-eyed giant.

Daedalus: mythical craftsman and inventor.

Demeter (Ceres): goddess of grain and agriculture. *Cornucopia*

Dionysos (Bacchus): god of wine. *Crown of grape leaves, thyrsus*

Eos (Aurora): goddess of the dawn.

Erinyes: the three Furies (Alecto, Tisiphone, Megaera)

Eros (Cupid): god of love and son of Aphrodite. *Bow and arrow*

Europa: daughter of the King of Tyre who was abducted by Zeus (in the form of a bull). One of her three sons was Minos.

Ge or Gaia: earth goddess, mother of the Titans.

Gorgons: three hideous sisters, including Medusa.

Hades (Pluto): god of underworld. *3-headed dog*

Hector: Trojan hero in Trojan War.

Helen of Troy: Queen of Sparta abducted by Paris.

Hephaistos (Vulcan): blacksmith of the gods, husband of Venus. *Forge, anvil*

Hera (Juno): chief goddess, wife of Jupiter. *Peacock*

Herakles (Hercules): hero of great strength, son of Jupiter. *Club, lion's skin*

Hermes (Mercury): messenger god. *Caduceus, winged helmet*

Homer: 8th-century BC Greek poet who wrote the *Odyssey* and the *Iliad*.

Iris: female messenger of the gods. *Rainbow*.

Jason: Argonaut who sought the Golden Fleece.

Jupiter: see Zeus

Laocoön: Trojan priest who warned of Trojan horse and was killed by sea serpents.

Maenad: an ecstatic female follower of Dionysos.

Medea: sorceress wife of Jason who murdered her children.

Medusa: see Gorgon.

Meleager: Hunted a wild boar.

Minerva: see Athena.

Minos: King of Crete who built the labyrinth for the Minotaur.

Minotaur: monster that was half man, half bull; conceived from the union of Pasiphae (wife of Minos) and a bull.

Moirai (Parcae): the three Fates (Atropos, Clotho, and Lachesis).

Narcissus: a youth who fell in love with his own reflection.

Nepture: see Poseidon.

Nike: winged goddess of victory.

Odysseus (Ulysses): Greek hero in Trojan War.

Oedipus: Prince of Thebes who solved the riddle of the Sphinx, then unknowingly murdered his father and married his mother.

Pan: a satyr (half goat, half man); protector of shepherds.

Paris: Trojan hero in Trojan War.

Pasiphae: wife of King Minos. Poseidon caused her to lust for a bull, and she gave birth to the Minotaur.

Pegasus: winged horse that sprang from the blood of Medusa.

Persephone (Proserpina): goddess of fertility and queen of the underworld.

Perseus: hero who killed Medusa.

Poseidon (Neptune): god of the sea. *Trident*

Theseus: hero who killed the Minotaur.

Ulysses: see Odysseus.

Venus: see Aphrodite.

Vulcan: see Hephaistos.

Zeus (Jupiter): ruler of the gods. *Thunderbolt, eagle*

PRONUNCIATION GUIDE

Amphora (**am**-fer-uh)
Apelles (uh-**pel**-eez)
Archaic (ar-**kay**-ik)
Architrave (**ar**-kih-trave)

Caryatid (care-ee-**at**-id)
Chryselephantine (kris-el-uh-**fan**-tin)
Contrapposto (kohn-trah-**pah**-stoh)
Dionysos (dye-uh-**nigh**-sus)
Doryphoros (doe-**rif**-or-os)
Elgin (**el**-gin [the 'g' is hard like in gun] or **el**-jin)
Entasis (**en**-tuh-sis)
Exekias (eh-**zee**-kee-us)
Hydria (**high**-dree-uh)
Ionic (eye-**on**-ik)
Iktinos (ik-**tie**-nohs)
Kallicrates (kuh-**lik**-rah-teez)
Kore (**kor**-ey)
Kouros (**koor**-os)
Krater (**kray**-ter)
Laocoön (lay-**ahk**-oh-on)
Lekythos (**lek**-uh-thos)
Metope (**met**-uh-pee)
Oenochoe (ee-**nok**-oh-ee)
Parthenon (**par**-thuh-non)
Perikles (**pear**-ih-kleez)
Polykleitos (polly-**klayh**-tus)
Zeuxis (**zook**-is)

GLOSSARY

Allegory. A story or image that refers to something else through symbolic imagery.

Amazons. Mythical race of warrior-women.

Amphora. A large vase for the transport and storage of liquids.

Archaic period. The period of ancient Greek art (c. 600–480 BC) before the Classical period.

Architrave (also called an epistyle). In classical architecture, the lower portion of the entablature that rests on the columns and supports the frieze.

Black figure technique. A vase painting technique in which the painted figures end up black against a red background after a three-stage firing process.

Bronze. A metal alloy of copper and tin.

Capital. The topmost part of a column.

Caryatid. A column in the form of a female figure.

Casting. Making a sculpture by pouring molten material into a mold that has an impression of the sculpture.

Cella. The sanctuary of a classical temple containing the cult statue of the god.

Ceramics. Objects formed out of clay and then hardened by being baked (fired) in a very hot oven (kiln).

Chryselephantine. Made of gold and ivory.

Classical period. The period in ancient Greece from around 480 to 400 BCE.

Colonnade. A row of columns supporting a roof or arcade.

Column. A cylindrical supporting element in architecture that usually consists of a base (sometimes omitted), shaft, and capital. Stone columns can be monolithic (made of a single piece of stone) or composed of drums.

Contrapposto. The natural stance of the human body in which one leg is relaxed while the other bears most of the weight, causing one hip to be slightly higher than the other.

Corinthian order. One of the orders of Greek architecture where the capitals of the columns have the form of acanthus leaves. It is more ornate than the Doric or Ionic orders.

Cornice. The uppermost part of the entablature that frames the pediment.

Doric order. One of the orders in Greek architecture characterized by columns with sharp-edged fluting, no bases, and simple bowl-like capitals; and a frieze consisting of triglyphs and metopes.

Drum. One of the cylindrical blocks of stone that are used to build a column.

Entablature. The portion of a Greek architectural order above the column capital. The entablature consists of and architrave, frieze, and cornice.

Entasis. Slight swelling in the shaft of Classical columns.

Façade. The front of a building.

Firing. Baking a clay object in a very hot oven (kiln).

Freestanding sculpture. Sculpture that is carved fully in the round and not attached to a wall or slab.

Frieze. The portion of the entablature between the architrave and the cornice. It often contains relief sculpture.

Gorgons. Three hideous monster sisters, including Medusa.

Gymnasium. In ancient Greece, a building complex with facilities for athletics, intellectual education, and socializing.

Hellenistic. The period in the ancient world between the death of Alexander the Great in 323 BCE and the death of Cleopatra in 30 BCE.

Hydria. A vessel for water.

Idealism. The representation of figures and forms that conforms to a concept of perfection rather than to reality.

Ionic order. One of the orders in Greek architecture characterized by columns with flat-edged fluting, bases, and capitals in the shape of scrolls or volutes; and a continuous frieze.

Kore. Greek for "maiden." A sculpture of a clothed female figure in Archaic Greek art.

Kouros. Greek for "male youth." A sculpture of a nude male figure in Archaic Greek art.

Krater. A large open vessel used for mixing wine with water.

Kylix. A type of drinking cup.

Lost wax technique (cire-perdue). A method of casting bronze (and other materials) in which a mold is made around an image modeled in wax. The wax is then melted out and replaced with bronze.

Meander pattern. A zigzag key-like pattern.

Metope. An architectural element consisting of a square area, often filled with relief sculpture, between two triglyphs on a Doric frieze.

Modeling. Shaping a form in a pliable material such as clay or plaster.

Oinochoe. A wine pitcher or jug with a curved handle.

Palaistra. In ancient Greece, a complex of rooms around a court, used for educational or athletic (especially boxing or wrestling) purposes; often attached to a gymnasium.

Peplos. A one-piece mantle worn by women in ancient Greece.

Red figure technique. A vase painting technique in which the painted background ends up black after a three-stage firing process leaving the figures in the natural reddish color of the pottery.

Slip. A mixture of fine clay, water and sometimes pigment used to decorate pottery.

Stylized. When the depiction of a figure or form departs from optical reality to conform to artistic conventions or to emphasize certain characteristics.

Stylobate. The top step of the platform of a Greek temple. It supports the columns.

Volute. A scroll-like architectural element typically found on Ionic capitals.

Weight shift. See Contrapposto.

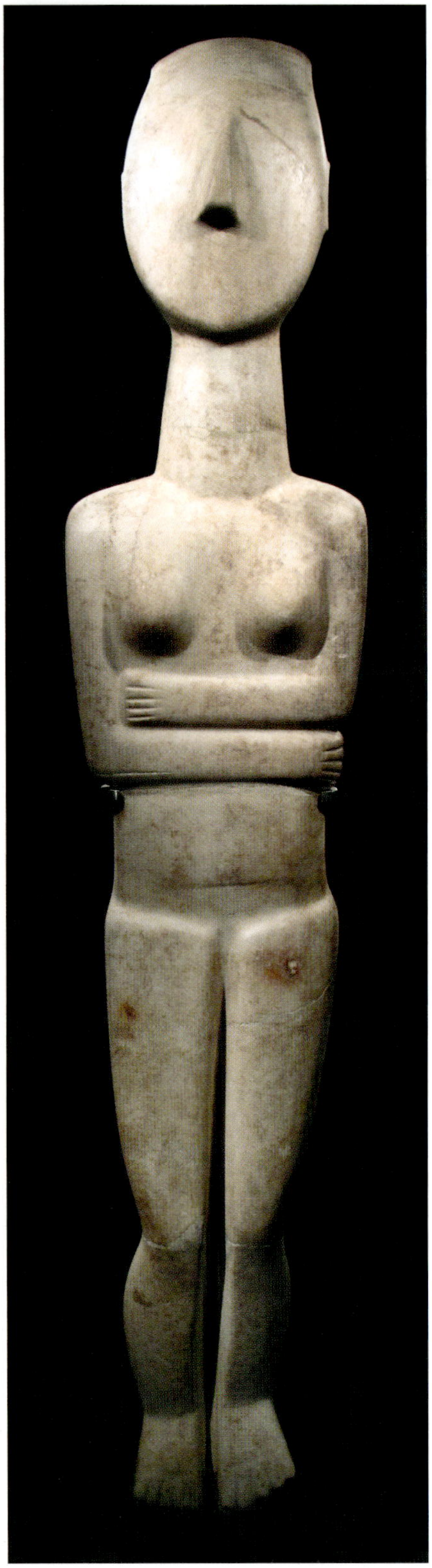
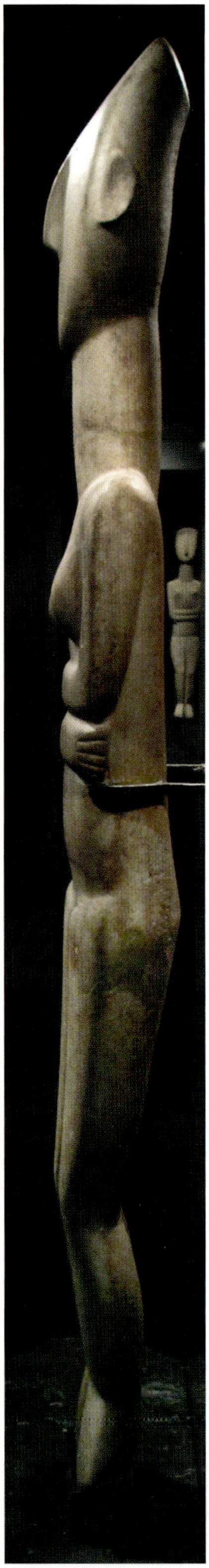

10 SCULPTURE

Sculpture is three-dimensional art with a strong tactile component—the viewer often has a desire to touch the work. There are two basic kinds of sculpture: freestanding and relief.

Freestanding sculpture is sculpture in the round. You can walk around it and see it from many different points of view. This makes free-standing sculpture more difficult to fully appreciate in a photograph than a painting because you see only one viewpoint. The view from the front of a marble sculpture of a male figure from the Aegean islands (fig. 10.1 left) is the principle view and the one traditionally shown in photographs, but the side view (fig. 10.1 right) shows just how thin this sculpture is, something you probably could not ascertain from the single frontal view.

Relief sculpture can be either low relief (also called **bas-relief**) or high relief, but it is not fully carved in the round. It remains attached to the material from which it is made. In low-relief sculpture the forms project from the surface only slightly. The Palette of Narmer (fig. 6.1) and the carving in figure 10.2a from ancient Egypt are good examples of low-relief sculpture. The artist has carved away the stone slab to leave shallow figures that project just enough to easily see and read. In high-relief sculpture, more of the form projects and is much more three dimensional. The sculpture showing an Egyptian pharaoh with his queen illustrates high relief (fig. 10.3). The two figures are still attached to the back slab of stone, but they are almost fully carved. Another type of relief sculpture is sunken relief (fig. 10.2b), where the figures are carved into the material so that the background projects.

SCULPTURE METHODS AND MATERIALS

There are four basic sculptural methods: modeling, carving, casting and assemblage. Sculptors use many different materials, but the most traditional are clay, wood, stone and metal.

Modeling in two dimensional art refers to shading to produce the illusion of three-dimensional form. In sculpture, modeling refers to manipulating a material to produce an actual three-dimensional form. The artist works and shapes a pliable material such as clay or plaster by hand to produce a form. Most of us modeled in Play-Doh® as children. One can easily model small objects in one piece without extra support, but larger objects, such as the terracotta sarcophagus from ancient Italy (fig. 10.4) were modeled around an armature (a rigid interior support) or made in sections and then put together.

Carving is the cutting away of material to arrive at a final form. Michelangelo's *David* is a famous example (fig. 10.5). Michelangelo felt he

fig. 10.1 *Left:* Cycladic Idol, front view, c. 2500 BCE. Marble. *Right:* Side view.

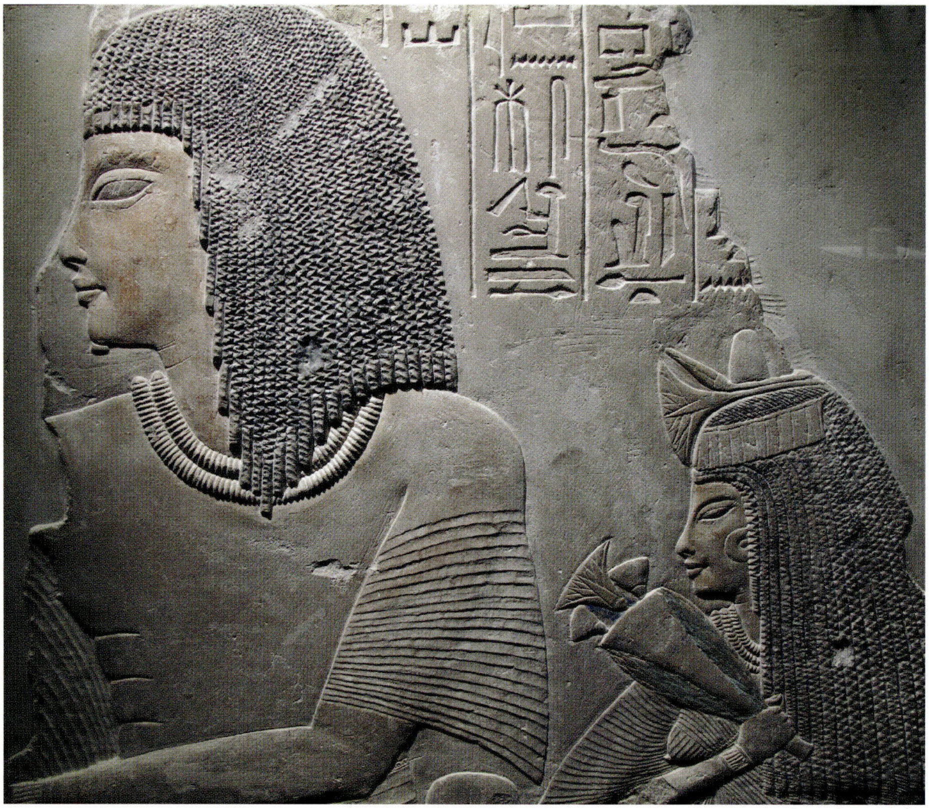

fig. 10.2a Bas relief, Egyptian.

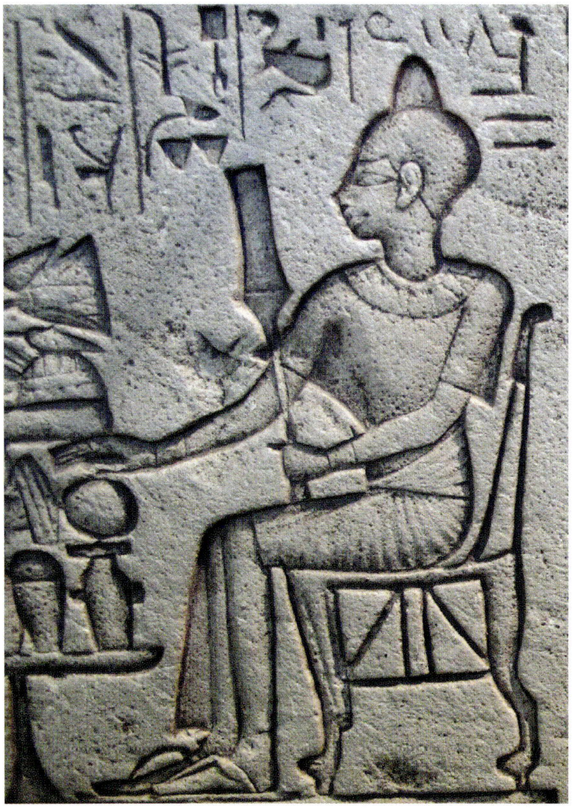

was releasing a form when he carved. If he thought he could not successfully do so, he would abandon the figure. A number of unfinished works by Michelangelo remain as reliefs because he never fully liberated the figures from the stone. Carving is considered more difficult than modeling because it is impossible to correct errors. If the artist removes too much of the material, the original intended figure is lost. This means sculptors must carefully plan the work ahead of time and know the characteristics of their chosen material. The ability to visualize the finished work from every angle while viewing a block of stone or wood is crucial.

Every carving material has its own positive and negative qualities. Wood is relatively easy to carve, but it can burn or degrade with exposure to weather. Since ancient times many sculptors have preferred marble. It is relatively soft so that one can carve it with a chisel and polish it to a lustrous finish. The ancient Greeks and Romans

fig. 10.2b Sunken relief, Egyptian.

produced thousands of marble sculptures, many of them intended for outdoor display. The problem in modern times is that because marble is a softer stone, it is highly susceptible to air pollutants and acid rain. The female figures on the Acropolis in Athens, Greece, became so badly worn in the twentieth century that they had to be removed before their faces disappeared completely (fig. 10.6). Other favorite carving stones such as limestone and sandstone have the same problem. Hard stones, like granite or schist, resist corrosion, but they are difficult to carve.

Casting transforms an object modeled in a soft material like clay into a harder material like **bronze**. Casting is complicated, and the process varies depending on the materials involved. In general, you make a mold of the object you want to cast. You then separate the mold into two pieces so that you can remove the original object once the mold has hardened. You then put the mold back together, creating a cavity that has the impression of the object. The next step is to make a hole at the top so that you can pour the molten material, such as bronze, into the mold. The bronze takes the form of the original object, and after it cools you can take the mold apart and remove the bronze object. After filing away any jagged edges and polishing the surface, you have a replica of your object in durable metal.

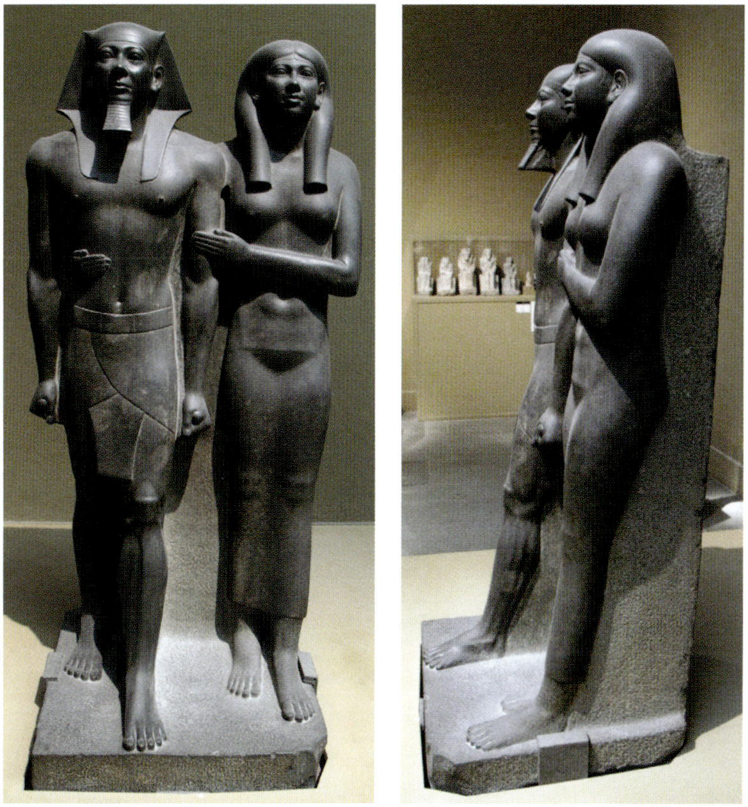

fig. 10.3 Egyptian Pharaoh with His Queen, c. 2500 BCE. Sandstone.

This process of solid casting works well with small objects, but larger objects require the hollow casting technique (or **lost-wax technique**). Attempting to make a solid bronze cast of a life-size figure would be fruitless for several reasons. The center part would cool at a significantly slower rate than the surface, causing it to crack; the cost of the bronze needed would be prohibitive, and the finished piece would weigh so much that it would be difficult to move. Hollow casting eliminates these problems.

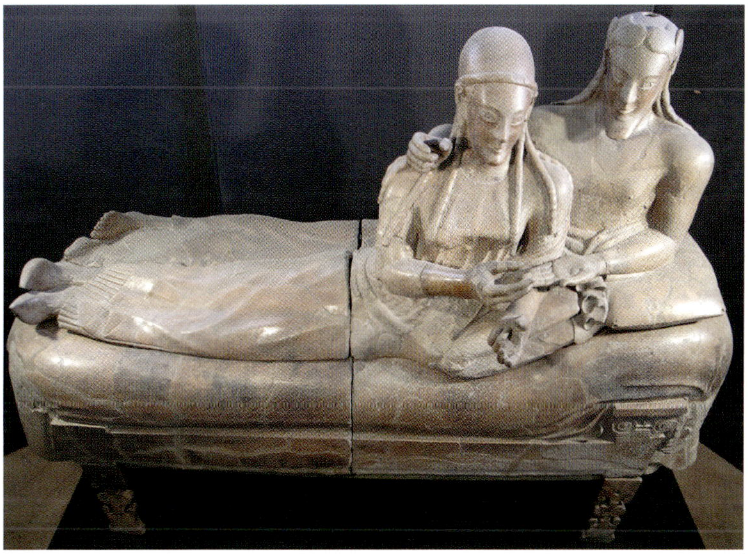

fig. 10.4 Sarcophagus from Ancient Etruria, c. 520 BCE. Terracotta.

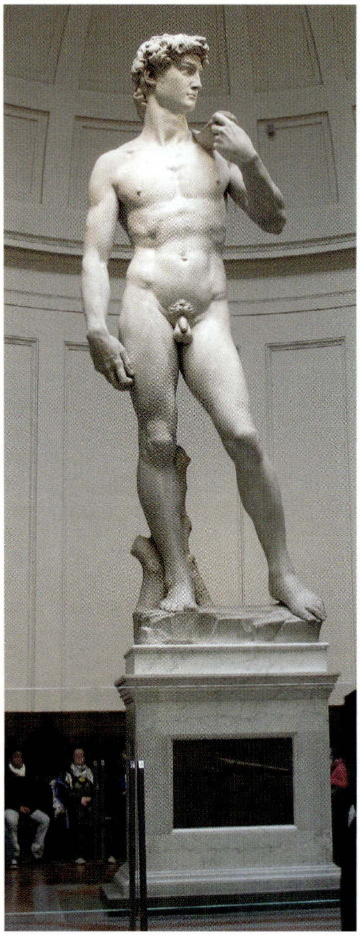

fig. 10.5 Michelangelo, *David,* 1501–1504. Marble.

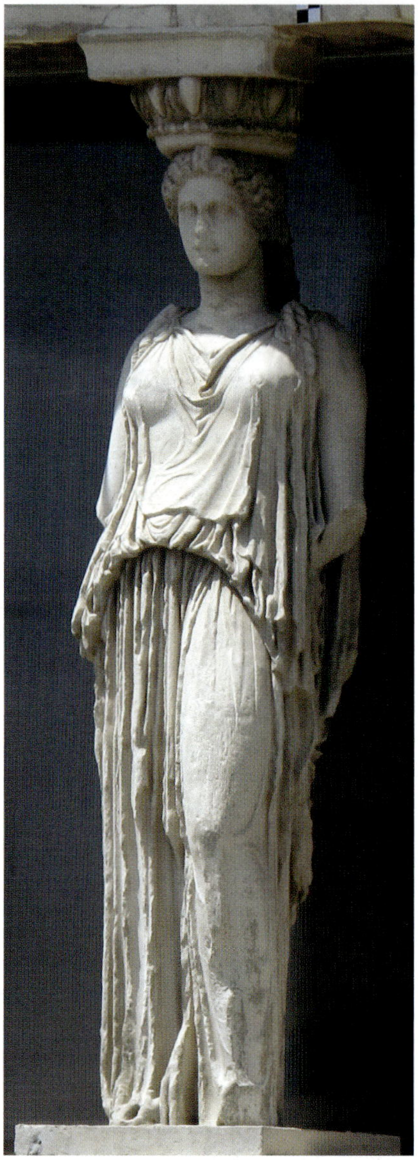

fig. 10.6 Caryatid (a column in the form of a female figure) from the Erechtheum on the Athenian acropolis, fifth century BCE. Marble. The caryatids were placed inside a museum and resin replicas put in their place on the Erechtheum.

Hollow casting is even more complex than solid casting, but the basic process is illustrated in figure 10.7. First the artist covers a clay core in the shape of the final work with a layer of wax as thick as the desired thickness of the bronze (usually ⅛ to ¼ inch). He or she then models the wax to form the features of the work of art and constructs a latticework of wax rods and metal pins around it. The ensemble is covered with a clay casing, which acts as a mold around the modeled wax. After heating, the melted wax drains out through the channels created by the rods while the pins hold the core in place. Molten bronze is then poured in to take the place of the lost wax. After cooling the artist breaks the clay mold, revealing the bronze figure. He or she cuts away the channels and pins and burnishes and polishes the piece.

Rodin's *Thinker* is an example of hollow casting in bronze (fig. 10.8). Although made of metal, it has very plastic features because the bronze was made from a modeled form. Bronze and other metals are not the only materials that one can cast. Artists also use plaster, concrete, plastic and resin, among others.

With **Assemblage** the artist creates a sculpture by putting together individual pieces or found objects. It is a method that developed in the twentieth century and now has a firm place in the history of art. Assemblages range from large welded works to small constructions of cardboard and paper in shadow boxes. Charlie Brouwer created *How Then Shall We Live* from pieces of treated wood (fig. 10.9). The separate pieces of wood are joined to mimic parts of the body and thus form a human figure. The **texture** of the wood is integral to his work and enhances it. Louise Nevelson, who assembled her sculptures from found pieces of wood, was not concerned with the wood per se or with its particular texture. She painted most of her works, like *Sky Cathedral* (fig. 10.10), a uniform black, forcing the viewer to focus on the forms rather than on the nature of the material.

Installation art uses sculptural forms and other media to modify the way a viewer experiences a particular space. Artists intend some installations to be looked at, others to be entered. And they create some installations only for a specific site and the temporary time period of the installation. Jennifer Spoon's *A River Runs Through It* (fig. 10.11), installed in the Radford University Art Museum, was a commentary on pollution. It combined objects found dumped in the New River with a video of the river itself.

Although artists often create installations in a museum or gallery setting, they can use any appropriate space. Radford University students used an entire building for a series of installations as a final tribute to the building, scheduled for

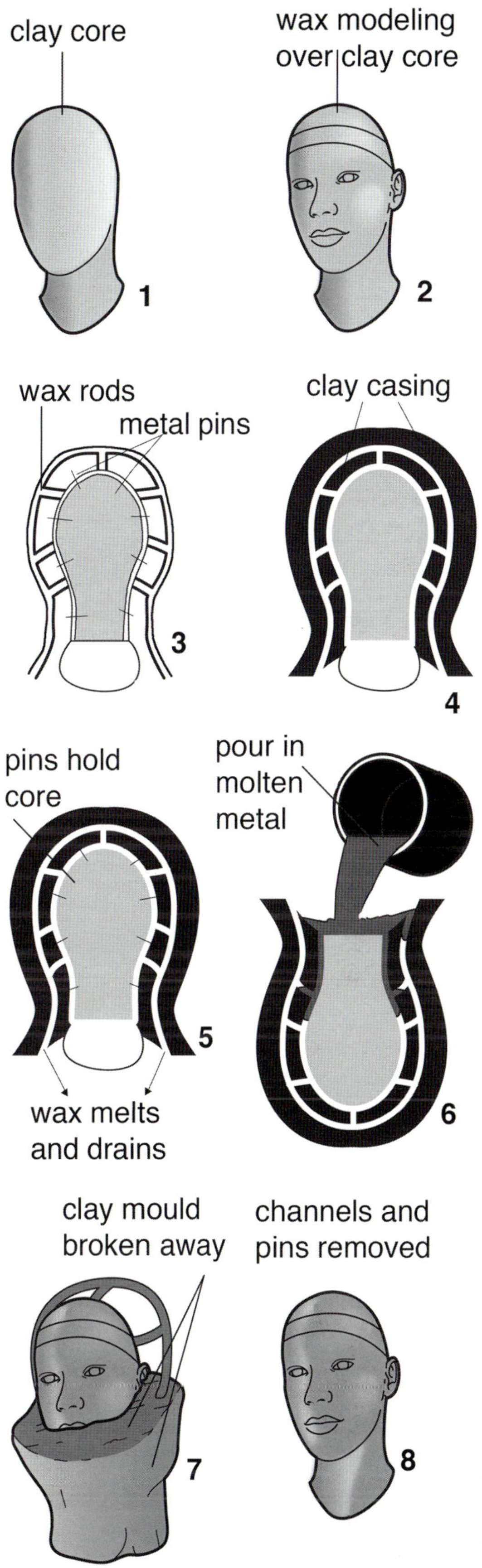

fig. 10.7 Hollow casting (Lost wax method).

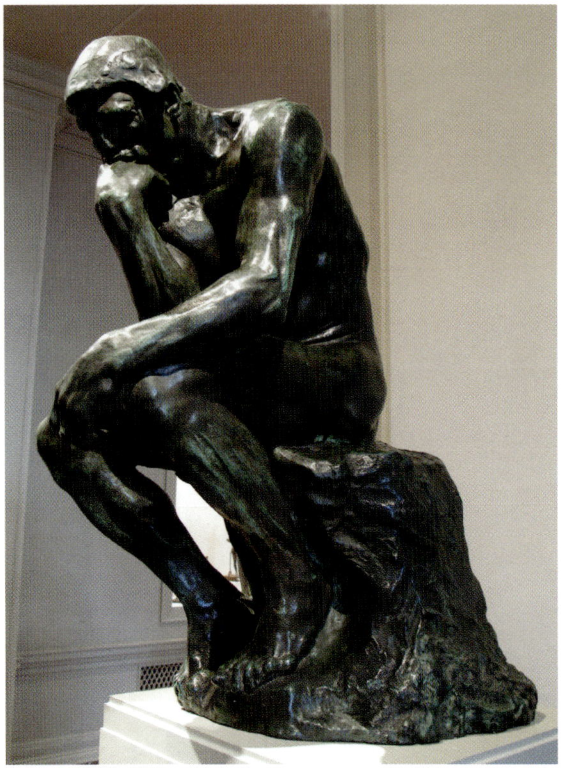

fig. 10.8 Auguste Rodin, *The Thinker.* Bronze.

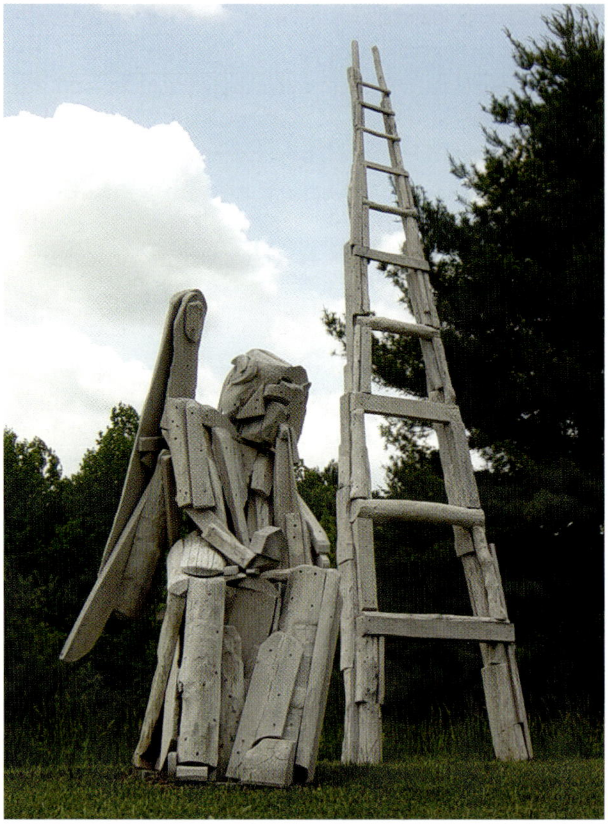

fig. 10.9 Charlie Brouwer, *How Then Shall We Live,* 2004. Locust wood, preservative stain, 13 ft. tall. This work is inspired by Albrecht Dürer's print, *Melencolia* from 1514.

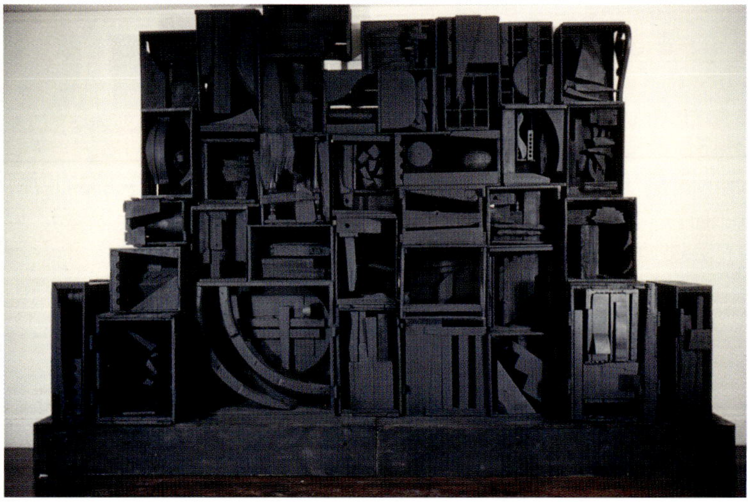

fig. 10.10 Louise Nevelson, *Sky Cathedral,* 1958. Painted wood.

demolition (figs. 10.12 and 10.13). In this case, spectators experienced individual installations in the context of an entire series at a single site.

Artists often incorporate electronic media, such as video and audio, and sometimes the installation is interactive. Ann Stoddard creates installations with delayed live video, forcing the participation of the viewer. After entering the installation space, the viewers immediately see themselves on a large video screen as they entered the installation five seconds earlier.

There are artists whose work blurs the distinction between sculpture and painting. Sculptor Charlie Brouwer and painter Jennifer Collins have combined their talents to produce **mixed media** works that incorporate both mediums. In *Before the Crossing* (fig. 10.14) the lower foreground is a projecting sculpture that merges seamlessly with the painted landscape in the background. We can consider many of Dorothy Gillespie's works either painted sculpture or sculptural painting. Her *Landscape Arrangement* (fig. 10.15) depicts painted geometric forms on copper-colored aluminum she has cut and shaped. It is a two-dimensional painting on a flat surface that she has given three-dimensional depth.

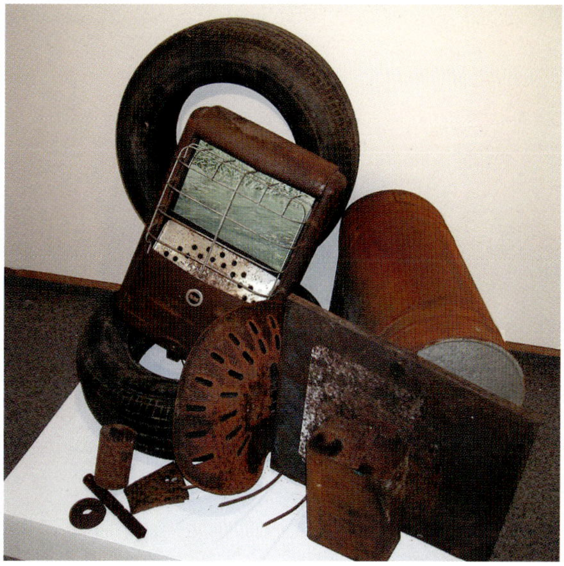

fig. 10.11 Jennifer Spoon, *A River Runs Through It,* 2002. Found objects and video.

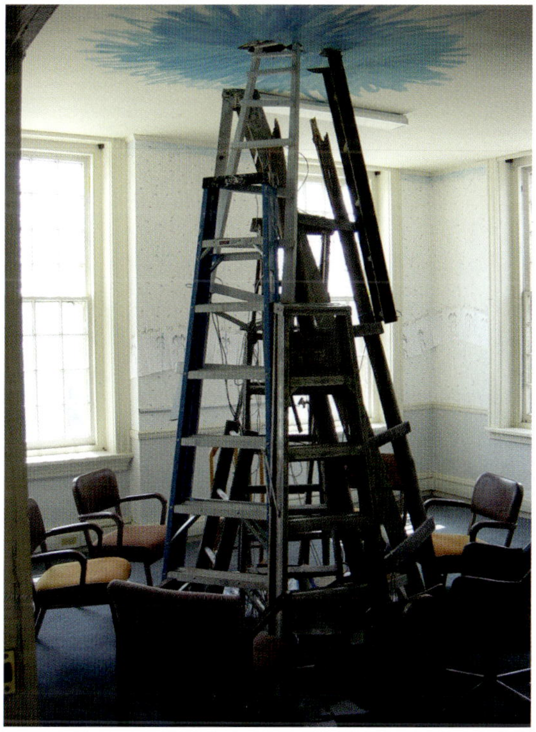

fig. 10.12 Installation at Radford University, 2006.

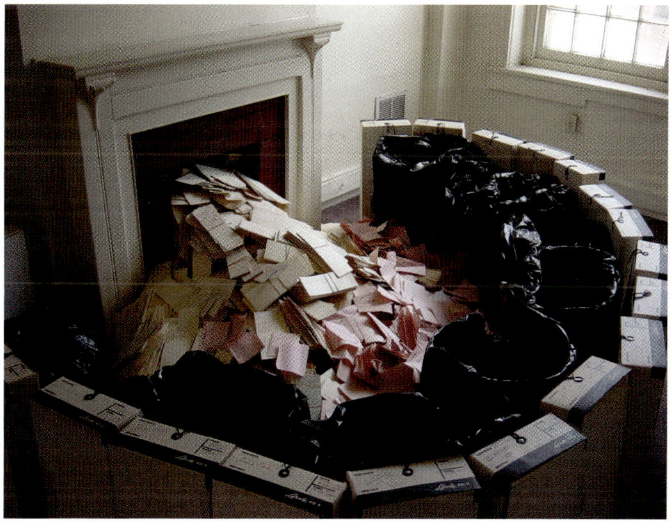

fig. 10.13 Installation at Radford University, 2006.

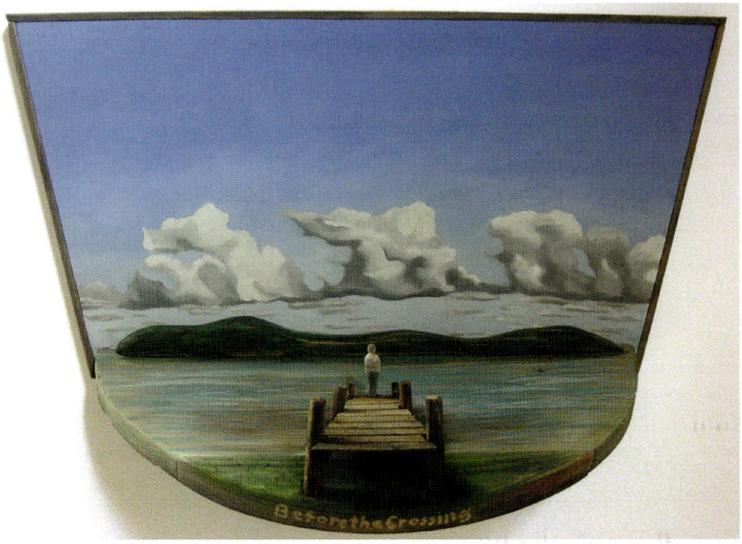

fig. 10.14 Charlie Brouwer and Jennifer Collins, *Before the Crossing,* 2004. Oil on panel, acrylic and mixed media on hemlock wood.

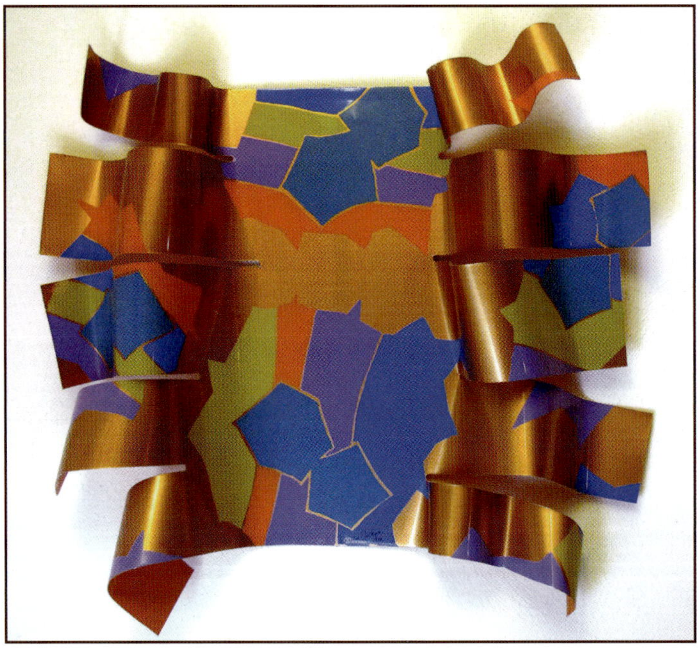

fig. 10.15 Dorothy Gillespie, *Landscape Arrangement,* 1980. Enamel on aluminum.

SUMMARY

Types of Sculpture

Freestanding sculptures are sculptures that one can walk around and view from many angles.

Relief sculpture is sculpture that emerges only partly from the material from which it is made. It can be low relief, high relief, or sunken relief.

Low relief (also called bas-relief): the forms project only slightly from the background surface.

High relief: the forms project a great deal from the background surface. Usually at least half of the most rounded parts, such as heads and legs, must emerge from the surface for the work to be considered high relief.

Sunken relief: the forms are carved into the material so that they are below the original surface.

Sculpture Methods

Modeling: The manipulation of a pliable material, such as clay or plaster, into a three-dimensional form.

Carving: The cutting away of material to arrive at the final form.

Casting: The process of replicating a form made of one material (usually a softer one like clay) into another material (usually a harder one like bronze) with the use of a mold. **Solid casting** is used for small forms. Larger objects must be **hollow cast** because of their size and weight.

Assemblage is like a three-dimensional collage. The sculpture is created by combining individual objects (sometimes found objects) into a unified whole.

Installation art uses sculptural forms and/or objects along with other media (often digital media) to change the way a viewer experiences a space. Often these works can be installed in a variety of locations; if they are meant only for a certain place, then they are called site specific installations.

PRONUNCIATION GUIDE

Bas relief (bah-rih-**leef**)
Caryatid (care-ee-**at**-id)
Cycladic (sih-**kla**-dik)
Etruscan (ih-**truss**-kun)
Michelangelo Buonarroti (my-kuhl-**an**-juh-loh, bwan-nah-**roh**-tee)
Patina (puh-**tee**-nuh)
Rodin (roh-**dan**)
Sarcophagus (sar-**koff**-uh-gus)

GLOSSARY

Additive process. In sculpture, the creation of a form by construction, assemblage, or modeling.

Assemblage. An additive sculptural process in which various materials and objects are combined.

Bas relief. In sculpture, low relief in which the forms project only slightly from the background plane.

Bronze. A metal alloy of copper and tin.

Carving. Cutting a figure or object out of a solid material such as wood or stone (as opposed to modeling).

Casting. Making a sculpture by pouring molten material into a mold that has an impression of the sculpture.

Freestanding sculpture. Sculpture that is carved fully in the round and not attached to a wall or slab.

High relief. Sculpture in which the figures project prominently from the background to which they are attached.

Installation. A work of art created for a specific gallery space or outdoor site.

Lost wax technique (cire-perdue). A method of casting bronze (and other materials) in which a mold is made around an image modeled in wax. The wax is then melted out and replaced with bronze.

Mixed media. The combination of two or more media in a work of art.

Modeling. Shaping a form in a pliable material such as clay or plaster.

Patina. A fine crust that forms on bronze and copper as a result of oxidation. It is often greenish in color.

Relief sculpture. Sculpture whose figures are only partially carved out so that they are still attached to the background. Relief sculpture can be high relief, low (bas) relief, or sunken relief where the figures are carved into the surface of the stone or other material.

Subtractive process. In sculpture, the carving process in which material is taken away to form the image. Compare Additive process.

Texture. The visual (implied) or tactile (actual) surface quality of a form or object.

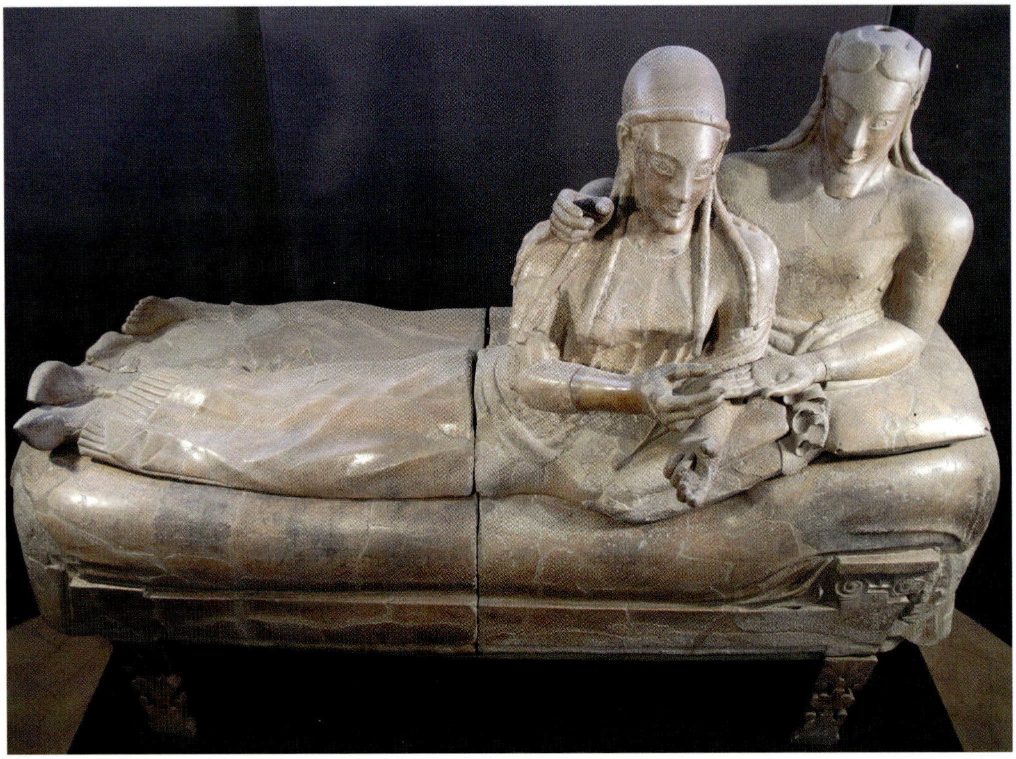

fig. 11.1 Sarcophagus from Cerveteri, c. 520 BCE. Terracotta, 6 ft. 7 in. long. Museo Nazionale de Villa Giulia, Rome.

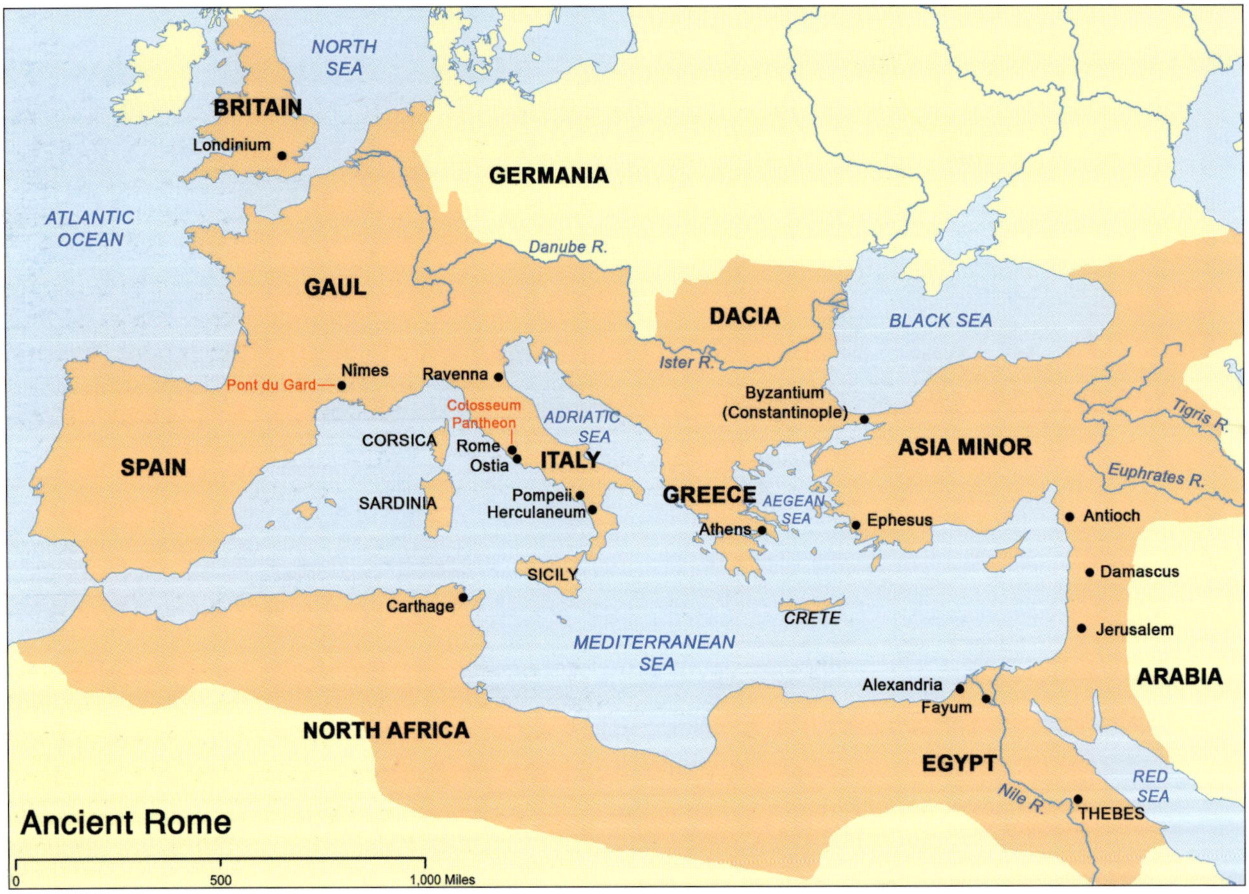

11

ETRUSCAN AND ROMAN ART

ETRUSCAN ART

The Etruscans achieved a high civilization in Italy before the Romans did. They lived in the area of Tuscany in central Italy referred to as Etruria. In fact, the name Tuscany derives from *Tusci,* the Roman word for the Etruscans. The Etruscans dominated much of Italy by the mid seventh century BCE, and they traded with the Greeks. Like ancient Greece, Etruria was a collection of city states. Unlike Greece, however, they never banded together against a common enemy, and so Rome was able to conquer them one by one. The Etruscans not only gave the Romans their land, they also imparted knowledge of building techniques and of Greek culture.

Sarcophagus from Cerveteri (fig. 11.1). The conquering Romans did not disturb the Etruscans' cemeteries, whose tomb interiors and contents have revealed much about Etruscan life. The tombs also reveal a robust trade with the ancient Greeks; we have found some of the best-preserved examples of Greek pottery in Etruscan tombs. This **sarcophagus**, originally painted with bright colors, shows an intimate couple on a dining couch. The life-size figures recall the Archaic Greek style with the stylized hair, hard-edged eyebrows and archaic smile. Yet they are livelier with their gestures and more relaxed than their Greek counterparts. This may be due in part to the clay medium, which the artist modeled rather than sculpted, but it also represents a different attitude from the Greeks as well as a different concept of the afterlife. This piece also indicates that women played a more significant role in Etruscan society than they did in Greece, which shuttered women away with few rights.

ROMAN ART

Rome's dominance in Italy began with the expulsion of the last Etruscan king from Rome and the establishment of the Roman Republic in 509 BCE. By the second century CE, Rome controlled a vast empire that stretched from Spain in the west to the Tigris River (in what is now Iraq) in the east, and from Britain in the north to Egypt in the south. It was an empire composed of many different cultures. For centuries the empire was stable and relatively peaceful because the Romans did not force the people they conquered to give up their local beliefs and customs. Furthermore, those who came under Roman rule benefited from Roman law, a good road system, aqueducts, public buildings such as baths and sports arenas and expert engineering. Rome also gave much of Europe its languages. Italian, Spanish, French, Portuguese, Catalan and Romanian are languages derived from Latin (the Romance languages), and the Catholic Church still uses a form of Latin today. Rome conquered Greece in 146 BCE and became captivated with Greek art and culture. Roman artists took thousands of Greek statues and other artwork to Italy or copied them. (Some of the few original Greek bronzes that survive came from ancient Roman shipwrecks found in modern times off the Italian coast.)

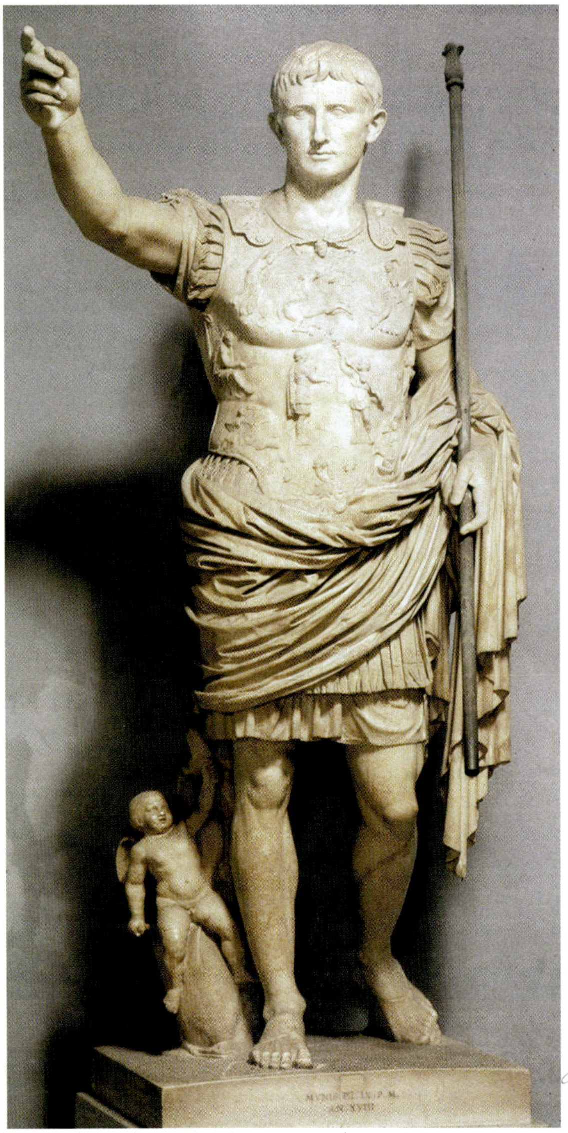

fig. 11.2 Augustus of Primaporta, c. 20 BCE. Marble, 6 ft. 8 in. high. Copy of a bronze original. Musci Vaticani, Rome.

STATUE OF AUGUSTUS OF PRIMAPORTA

The Roman Republic became an empire under Augustus, who ruled from 27 BCE to 14 CE. He came to power after defeating Mark Anthony and Cleopatra at the naval battle of Actium off the Western coast of Greece. Augustus held all the major titles: First Citizen, Consul, Commander-in-Chief, and Chief Priest. This statue (fig. 11.2) shows him in military garb addressing the troops. Roman imperial portrait sculpture had a strong propaganda component. The pose recalls the Classical Greek sculpture, *The Spear Bearer,* by Polykleitos with its **contrapposto** stance (see fig. 9.7). The relief on Augustus' cuirass (breastplate) shows a military victory, and the cupid riding a dolphin (which helps support the statue) refers to the emperor's claimed lineage from the goddess Venus. Furthermore, although idealized, the face is that of Augustus. All of these features serve to glorify the emperor.

EQUESTRIAN PORTRAIT OF MARCUS AURELIUS

Another type of sculpture developed by the Romans was the life-size bronze **equestrian portrait**. That of the emperor Marcus Aurelius (fig. 11.3) is the only one to survive and that is only because it was later mistaken to be that of Constantine, the first Christian emperor, and thus spared being melted down in the Middle Ages. The emperor sits astride his horse and gestures to the people. The fact that his body is larger than it should be in relation to the size of the horse emphasizes his commanding presence. Originally gilded, this larger-than-life sculpture shows Roman bronze-making skill at its height. This sculpture was the source for later equestrian portraits when artists revived them in the Renaissance.

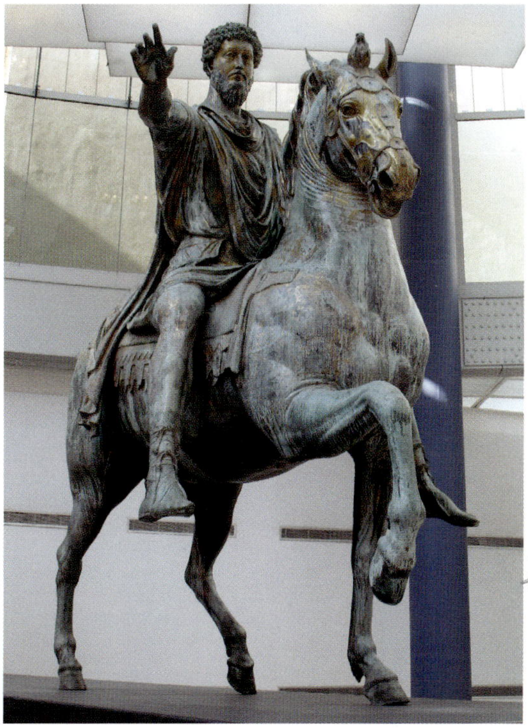

fig. 11.3 Equestrian Portrait of Marcus Aurelius, mid-2nd century CE. Bronze, 11.5 ft high. Musei Capitoline, Rome.

ROMAN PAINTING

The Romans were skilled at painting illusionistic scenes to decorate walls. A room from a villa (now in a museum) illustrates this well (fig. 11. 4). The scene visually transforms the bedroom's solid walls into an open **colonnade** with views of city buildings in the distance. This greatly lessens the claustrophobic confines of the small room. From a detail (fig. 11.5) you can see that the Romans understood linear and atmospheric perspective. Although the **perspective** is not completely consistent, we clearly see the illusion of depth as the sides of the buildings recede and become less distinct in the distance.

AQUEDUCT AT NÎMES

The Romans were expert engineers. They developed the use of the arch (derived from the Etruscans), the **vault** and concrete. This allowed them to erect structures of great size. A mainstay of Roman civilization was the **aqueduct** that brought fresh water to cities from nearby sources. One of the best preserved is the so-called Pont-du-Gard (bridge over the Gard river) in Nîmes, France (figs. 11.6 and 11.7). This structure shows the genius of Roman engineering. Once bringing thousands of gallons of water a day from some thirty miles away, it is built of large stones (some weighing two tons) without mortar. Furthermore, the Romans constructed it so that the water flowed to the city by gravity alone. Composed of three tiers of arches, it was both strong and aesthetically pleasing. In fact, people used this section of the aqueduct as a foot bridge well into the eighteenth century, more than 1700 years after it was built. The top tier of smaller arches supports the actual channel that transported the water (fig. 11.7)

COLOSSEUM

Most Roman cities had an **amphitheatre** for public entertainment. The Colosseum (named after a colossal statue of the emperor Nero that stood nearby) was the largest with a seating capacity of fifty thousand (figs. 11.8 and 11.9). In use for over five hundred years, it was the site of gladiator combats, criminal executions, man-animal contests and other public spectacles on a grand scale. When it opened in 80 CE, the Romans flooded the arena with water so that they could reenact a mock

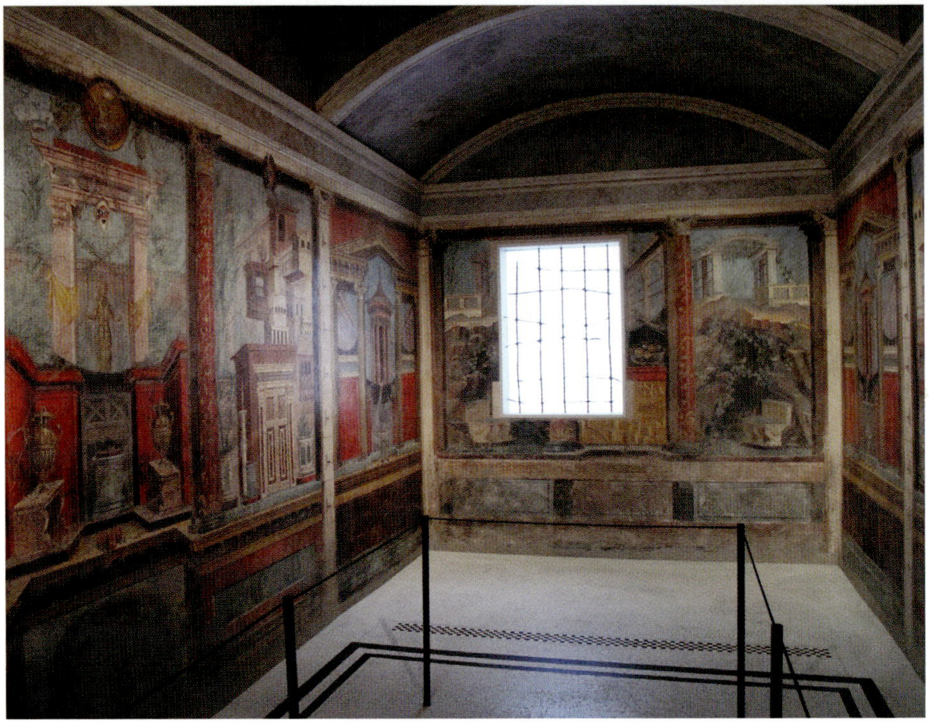

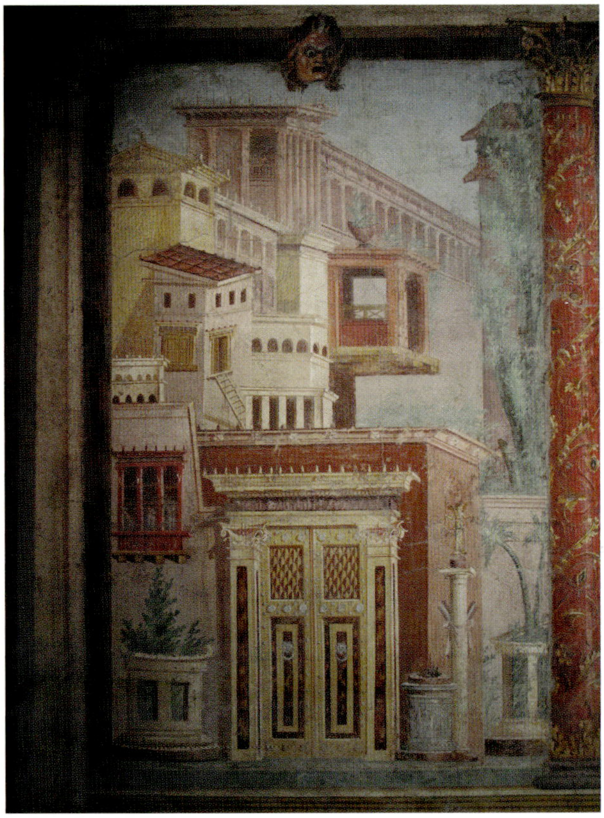

figs. 11.4 and 11.5 Bedroom from Villa in Boscoreale (near Pompeii), Italy, 1st century BCE. Fresco. Metropolitan Museum of Art, New York.

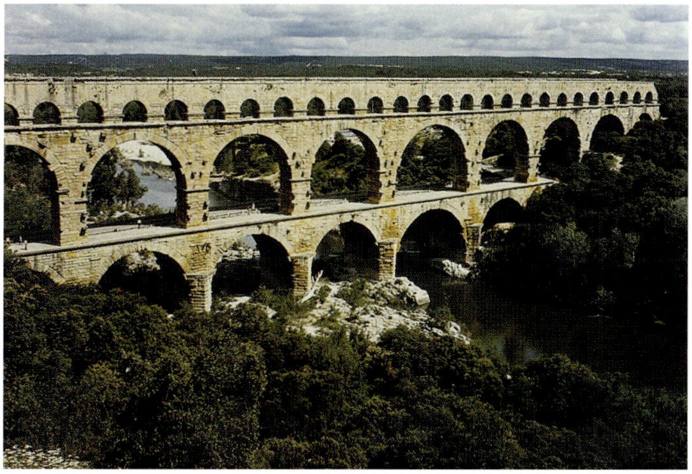

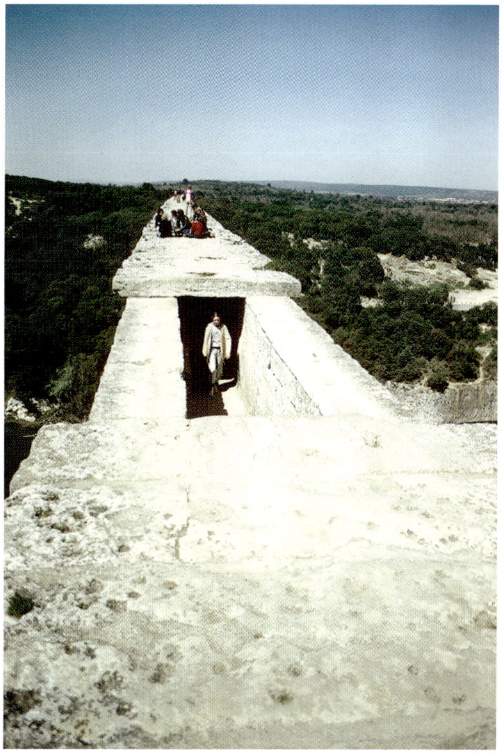

figs. 11.6 and 11.7 Pont-du-Gard, late 1st century BCE. Nîmes, France.

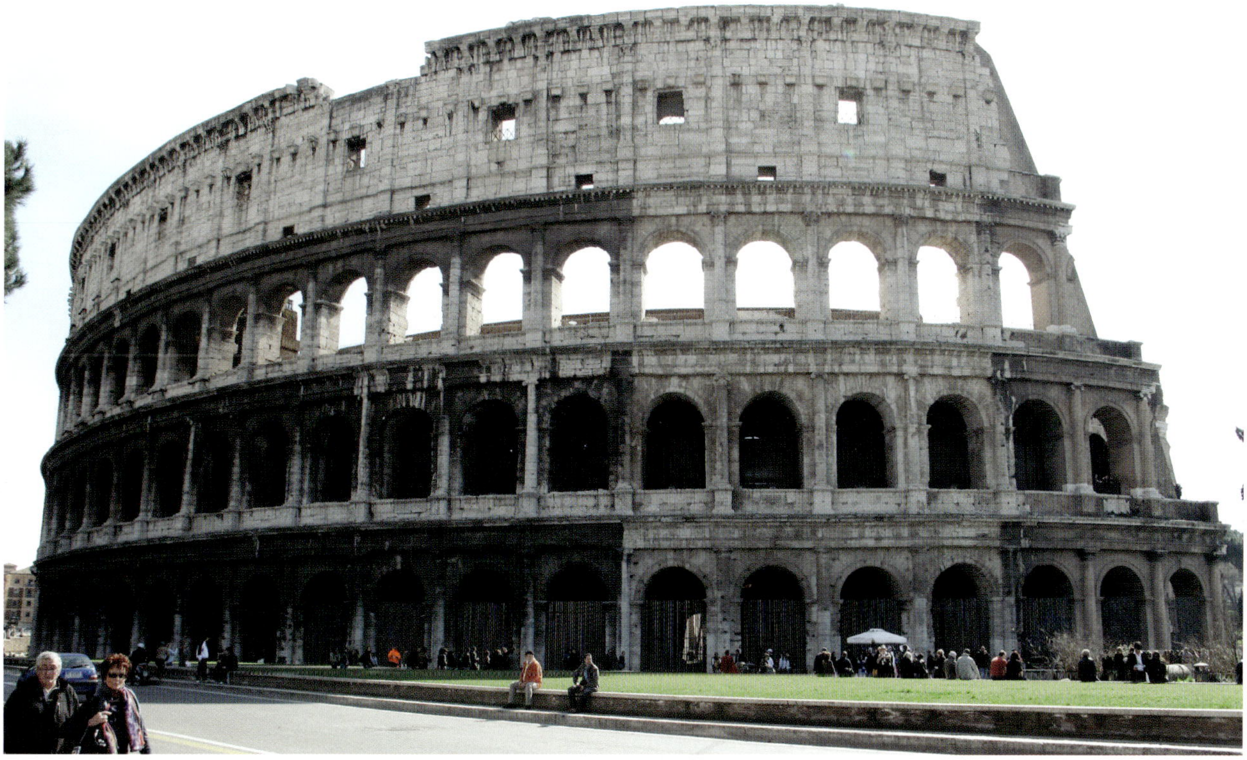

fig. 11.8a Colosseum, 80 CE. Rome.

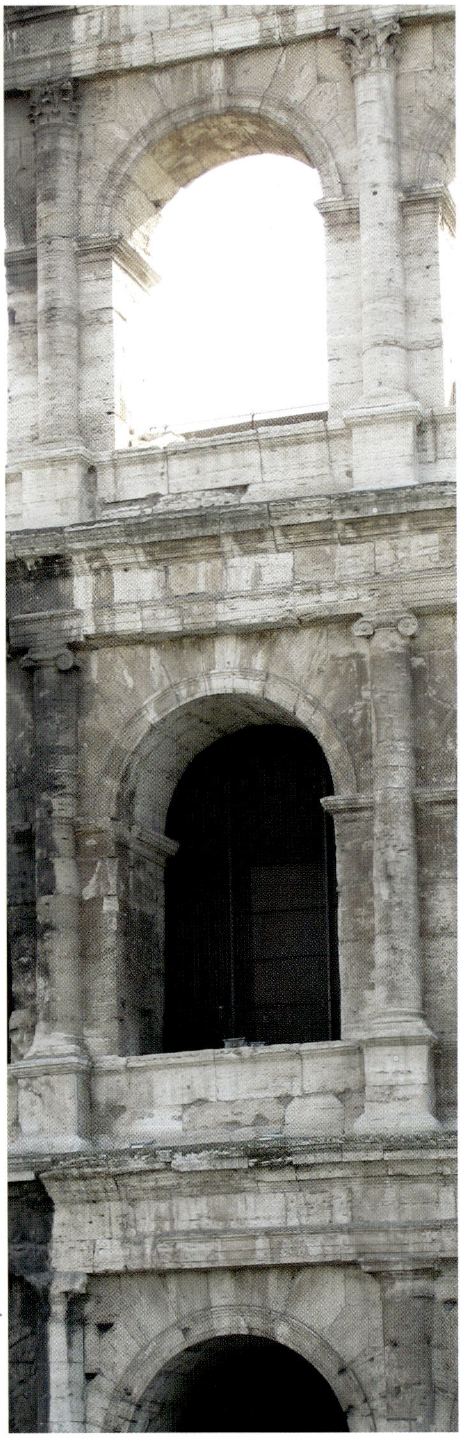

fig. 11.8b Detail.

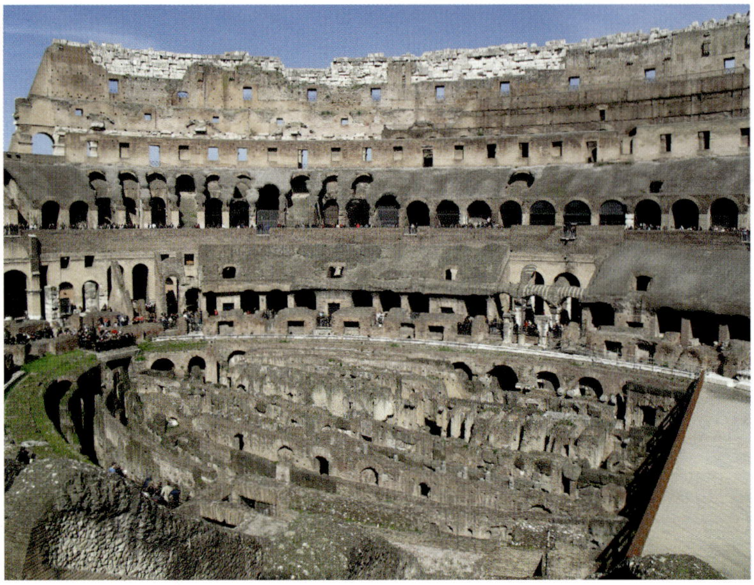

fig. 11.9 Colosseum, 80 CE. Rome.

naval battle with some three thousand participants. One single event during the reign of Trajan sacrificed eleven thousand animals. It is said that this extreme demand over the centuries wiped out the wild large animal population of North Africa where most of the animals came from.

The Colosseum is an engineering marvel. At approximately 615 feet long and 510 feet wide, it covers six acres. The oval arena (from the Latin word for sand, which Romans spread on the floor to absorb blood) is more than 40,000 square feet. The use of concrete made the Colosseum possible. A sophisticated arrangement of vaults supported the seating, and a complex of substructures below the arena provided areas for gladiators, animals and lifting machines to get them up to the arena level.

The exterior of the Colosseum displayed a façade of four tiers and has a total height of about 160 feet. The first three tiers are a series of arches flanked by imbedded **columns** of the three major orders: Tuscan (a variation of the Doric) on the first tier, Ionic on the second tier and Corinthian on the third (fig. 11.8b). Imbedded Corinthian **pilasters** articulated the fourth tier. Wooden brackets for poles stood between them to support a large awning to shade the spectators from the hot sun. Unlike the columns of a Greek temple, the columns on the Colosseum had no supporting function—they were for aesthetic purposes only.

Only a portion of the Colosseum survives because people took much of its stone and used it for other buildings during the Middle Ages and beyond, but we see its successful design of many aisles for easy seat access in today's sports stadiums.

PANTHEON

Roman engineering skill is truly evident in the Pantheon, a huge domed structure in Rome that still stands (figs. 11.10, 11.11, and 11.12). Built as a temple dedicated to the planetary gods, it is one of the most influential Roman buildings. The Pantheon is a large **dome** on a **drum** with no interior columns for support. It is 142 feet in diameter, and the top of the dome is 142 feet from the floor. Again, concrete made this domed structure possible. The Romans employed a number of techniques to ensure that the dome would be stable. They used a harder, denser type of concrete in the lower part of the dome, which had to support everything above it, while they used a lighter more porous concrete in the upper portion. At the top is a circular opening, the **oculus**, which dramatically lessens the weight of the dome at a critical area and also allows light into the interior. The inner side of the dome is coffered. These sunken squares not only add a decorative effect, but they significantly reduce the amount of concrete needed and hence the weight of the dome. Originally each **coffer** had a **bronze** rosette imitating a star, but people removed them in the seventeenth century. Also, the dome becomes thinner as it rises,

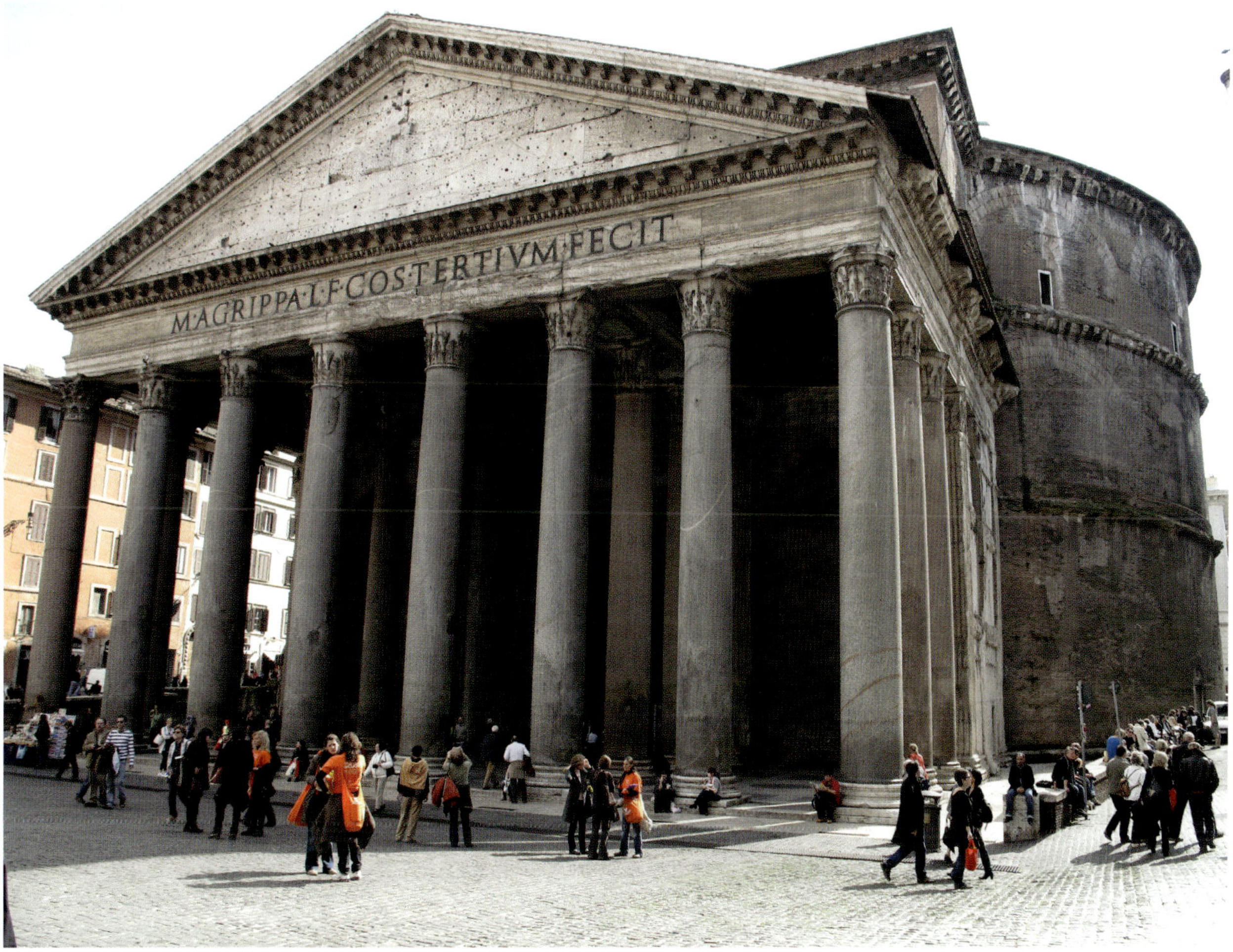

fig. 11.10 Pantheon, 118–125 CE. Rome.

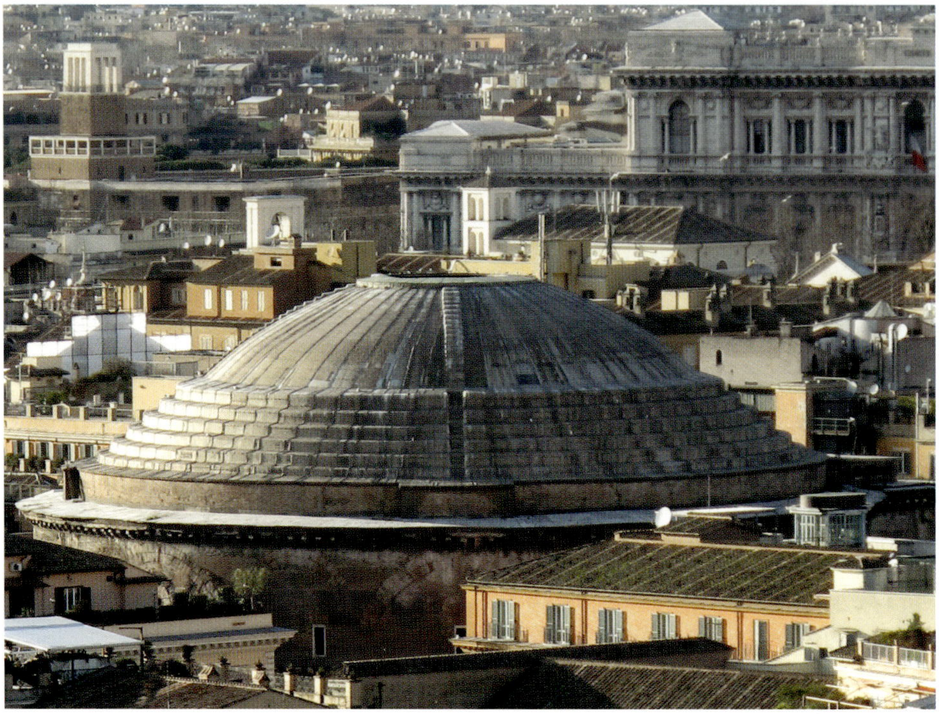

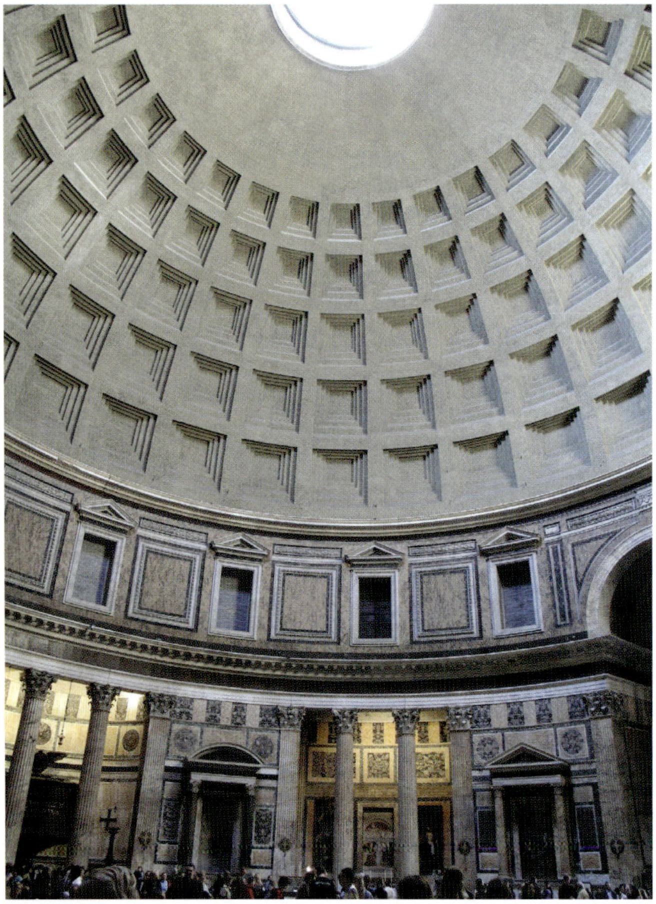

which further lessons its weight. Other methods used to ensure stability included a series of interlocking brick arches in the upper walls of the drum that helped distribute the weight of the dome evenly.

From the front, the exterior of the Pantheon mimics a Greek temple with its Corinthian columns supporting a triangular **pediment**. In Roman times a courtyard existed in front of the Pantheon that obscured the drum. The drum was made of brick without any fancy veneer because it wasn't seen as it is today. When visiting the Pantheon the bustle and noise of a big city is left behind as you enter the cool quiet interior of vast proportions. It is something to feel rather than to describe.

The Pantheon inspired many later buildings such as Thomas Jefferson's home, Monticello (fig. 17.13) in Virginia, the Rotunda at the University of Virginia in Charlottesville (fig. 11.13) or Baldwin Auditorium at Duke University in Durham, North Carolina (fig. 11.14).

figs. 11.11 and 11.12 Pantheon, 118–125 CE. Rome.

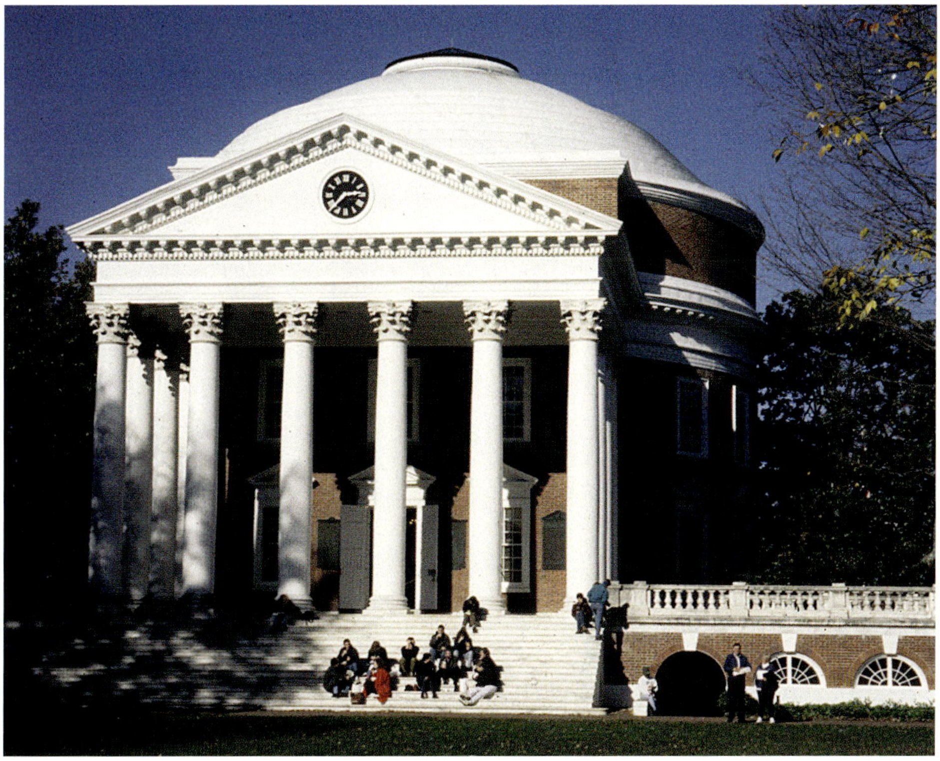

fig. 11.13

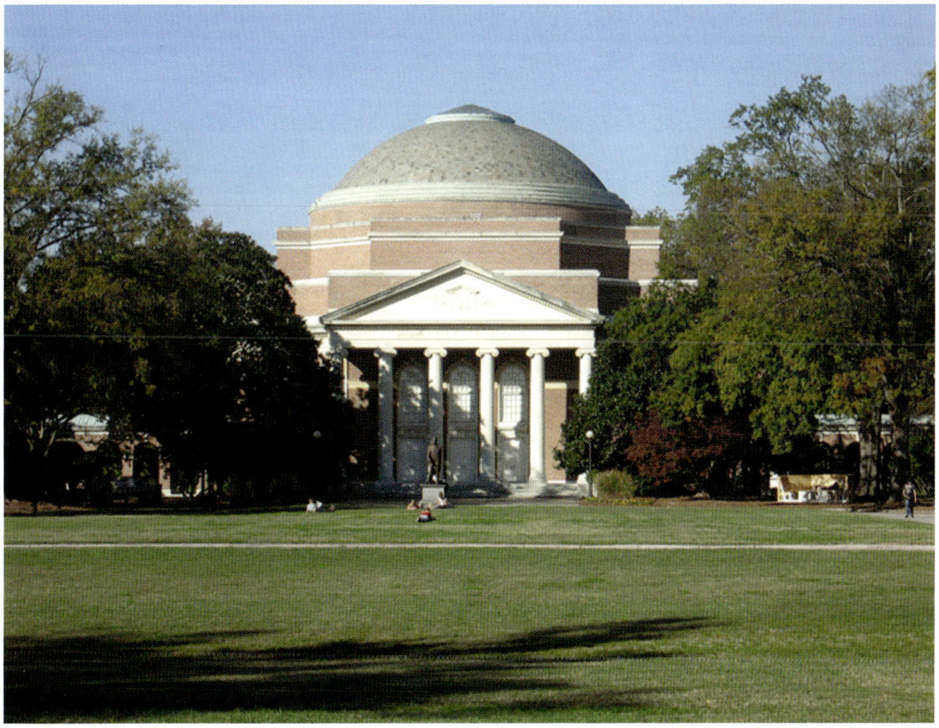

fig. 11.14 Horace Trumbauer and Julian Abele, Baldwin Auditorium, 1926–1930. Duke University, East Campus, Durham, North Carolina.

SUMMARY

Etruscan culture dominated Italy in the seventh century BCE before the rise of the Romans. Etruscan society was highly developed and produced sophisticated art. Sarcophagus figures from one of the many excavated Etruscan tombs show a style that is similar to the Greek Archaic style.

Established as a republic in 509 BCE, Rome endured for nearly a thousand years. At its greatest extent it ruled lands from Mesopotamia in the East to Spain in the West, and from North Africa in the south to the British Isles in the North. As a result, it encompassed many different cultures.

In portraiture, Roman sculptors combined a native realism with the ideal style of classical Greek art. This is particularly evident in the *Augustus of Primaporta,* a statue of the Emperor Augustus that recalls the *Spear Bearer* by Polykleitos.

Roman painting survives in the preserved ruins of Pompeii and surrounding cities. Scenes from the walls of a bedroom demonstrate both aerial perspective and an approximate linear perspective to give the illusion of depth.

Perhaps the Roman's greatest contribution was in architecture. They were great builders who perfected the use of concrete. This allowed them to roof vast areas without internal supports as seen in the Pantheon in Rome, a building that still stands and has influenced architecture ever since its construction. Roman aqueducts and amphitheatres (such as the aqueduct at Nîmes and the Colosseum in Rome) also demonstrate the sophisticated engineering skills of the Romans.

PRONUNCIATION GUIDE

Amphitheatre (**am**-fuh-thee-uh-ter)
Aqueduct (ah-kwa-duct
Boscoreale (bos-kor-ee-**ah**-lay)
Colosseum (kahl-uh-**see**-um)
Contrapposto (kohn-trah-**pah**-stoh)
Equestrian (eh-**kwes**-tree-uhn)
Etruscan (ih-**truss**-kun)
Ionic (eye-**on**-ik)
Marcus Aurelius (**mar**-kus oh-**ree**-lee-us)
Nîmes (neem)
Pompeii (pom-**pay**)
Pont du Gard (pohn-dew-**gar**)
Sarcophagus (sar-**koff**-uh-gus)

GLOSSARY

Amphitheatre. A circular or oval arena with tiered seating used for various spectacles and events. The Colosseum in Rome is an amphitheatre.

Aqueduct. A structure for transporting water from its source to a city or town.

Bronze. A metal alloy of copper and tin.

Central plan. In architecture, a building with a central space surrounded by symmetrical areas.

Coffer. A sunken panel in a ceiling or vault.

Colonnade. A row of columns supporting a roof or arcade.

Column. A cylindrical supporting element in architecture that usually consists of a base (sometimes omitted), shaft, and capital. Stone columns can be monolithic (made of a single piece of stone) or composed of drums. An engaged column is a column embedded in a wall.

Contrapposto. The natural stance of the human body in which one leg is relaxed while the other bears most of the weight, causing one hip to be slightly higher than the other.

Corinthian order. One of the orders of Greek architecture where the capitals of the columns have the form of acanthus leaves. It is more ornate than the Doric or Ionic orders.

Cornice. The uppermost part of the entablature that frames the pediment.

Dome. A roof with a hemispherical shape.

Doric order. One of the orders in Greek architecture characterized by columns with sharp-edged fluting, no bases, and simple bowl-like capitals; and a frieze consisting of triglyphs and metopes.

Drum. One of the cylindrical stones that make up the shaft of a column. Also, a circular wall that supports a dome.

Entablature. The portion of a Greek architectural order above the column capital. The entablature consists of an architrave, frieze, and cornice.

Equestrian portrait. A depiction of a person on horseback.

Ionic order. One of the orders in Greek architecture characterized by columns with flat-edged fluting, bases, and capitals in the shape of scrolls or volutes; and a continuous frieze.

Modeling. Shaping a form in a pliable material such as clay or plaster.

Oculus. A round central opening in a dome.

Order. One of the architectural systems (Doric, Ionic, and Corinthian) used by the ancient Greeks and Romans. An architectural order consists of three basic parts: a base or platform, a colonnade, and an entablature. Other orders, such as Tuscan and Composite, were later developed based on these three original orders.

Pediment. The triangular area defined by the cornice.

Perspective. A method of showing depth on a two-dimensional surface. In scientific perspective (also called linear perspective), real or implied parallel lines (orthogonals) converge at one or more vanishing points to give the illusion of recession into space. Objects intended to be further away from the viewer are shown smaller. In atmospheric perspective (also called aerial perspective) forms in the distance are shown less distinct and bluish in color.

Pilaster. A flat vertical element projecting from a wall. It usually does not have a supporting function.

Sarcophagus. Literally, "consumer of flesh," it is a large coffin (usually stone), often decorated with relief sculpture.

Vault. An arched roof or ceiling usually made of stone, brick, or concrete.

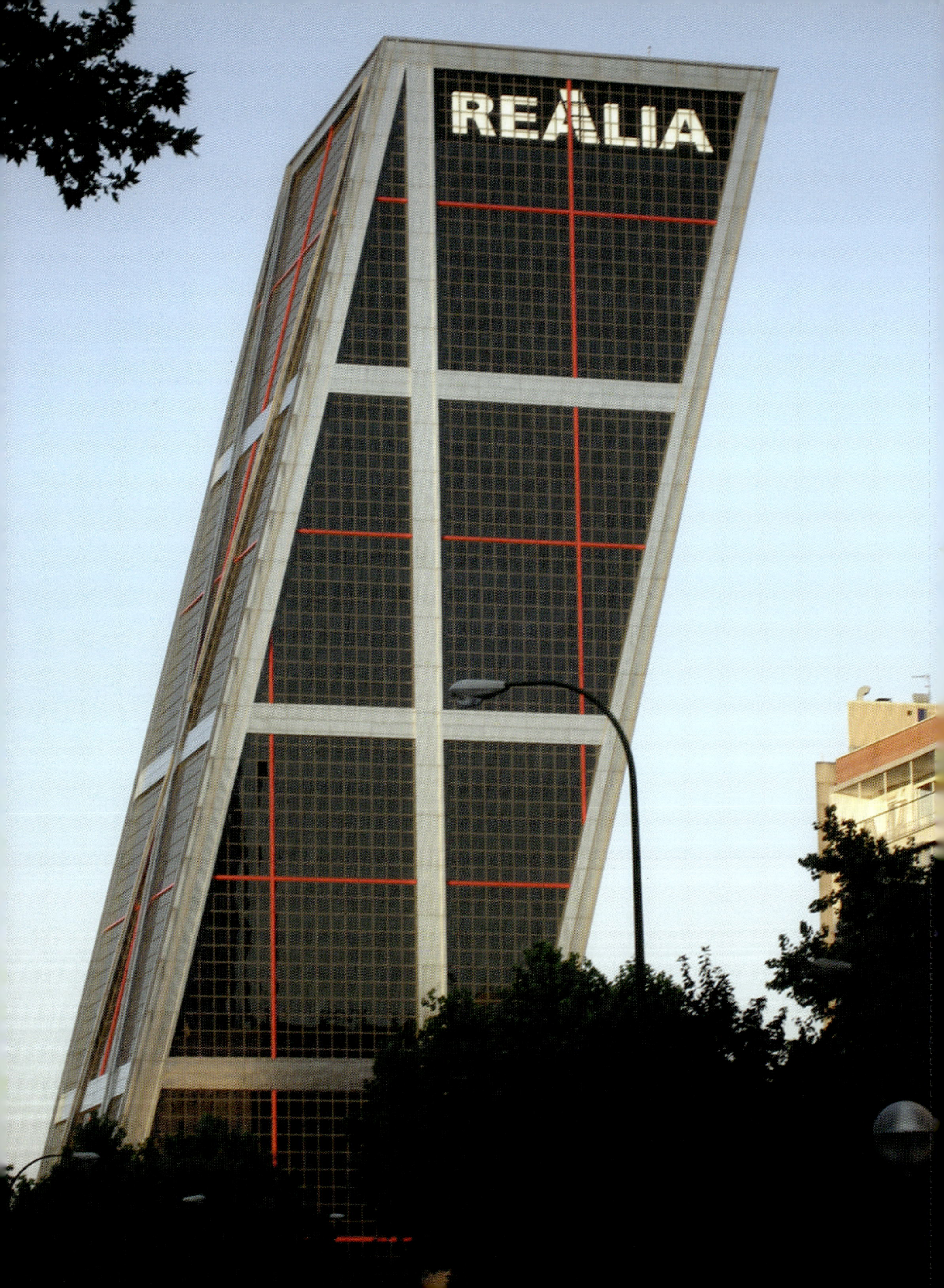
REALIA

12

Architecture refers to the design and construction of buildings. The word derives from the Greek word for "master builder." We often take architecture for granted because it is such an integral part of our lives. Architecture is everywhere, and much of it is a necessity—we need buildings to live and work in. You can live without a painting or a sculpture, but it would be difficult to live without houses, schools, government offices and other buildings. Architecture is as diverse as painting and sculpture, and it often is more closely identified with a particular culture than are other art forms. When we think of Egypt, pyramids come to mind; Greece conjures up Classical temples; we associate cathedrals with the Middle Ages, igloos with Eskimo culture and pagodas with China. This cultural identification, however, is quickly disappearing as we develop new technologies that apply anywhere and enlist foreign architects who design buildings all over the world. Buildings are unique in that they enclose a space, so we must experience them from both the outside and the inside. We have to walk through buildings to fully understand and appreciate them.

ARCHITECTURE

Architecture deals with three basic concepts: form, function and structure. The form is the appearance of the building. This aspect allows the architects the opportunity to create something original and aesthetically pleasing, and it is the first characteristic we notice when looking at a building. But the form should not conflict with the function. After all, the building's intended use was probably the reason for building it. A sleek building with low ceilings would not make sense for a museum where height is essential for moving around large works of art. The famous architectural maxim, form follows function, means the shape of a building should be based upon its purpose. Structure is paramount to a building's physical success. If the building is not soundly constructed, it becomes useless. History shows us numerous occasions when a major building collapsed because of faulty engineering.

Building materials and techniques have improved throughout history, although we would be hard pressed to duplicate some of the engineering feats of the ancients. We still don't know how they built the great pyramids or how they raised the huge stones of Stonehenge. Today, the array of traditional and high tech materials and construction methods is mind-boggling. Architects now design buildings so tall or so weirdly shaped that it seems a wonder they remain standing (fig. 12.1).

fig. 12.1 Philip Johnson and John Burgee. Europe's Gate, Madrid, Spain, 1996. This is one of two buildings that tilt toward each other.

BASIC BUILDING MATERIALS

Stone, wood and brick were among the earliest materials used for building, and they continue as a mainstay of construction today, especially in the housing industry. Most homes in the United States are still built with these materials. New materials began to appear in the nineteenth century, and they changed architecture forever. With its strength and fire-resistant qualities, **cast iron** permitted new and larger kinds of buildings and other structures. Bridges could span longer distances, factories could be bigger and safer, and people could construct buildings not possible before. One such building was the Crystal Palace designed by Joseph Paxton in 1850 for an international exposition in London (fig. 12.2). Built of iron and glass, the building was 1,850 feet long and 108 feet high, and it covered an area of nearly one million square feet. Nothing like it had ever been seen. Unfortunately, it was destroyed in 1936.

One of the culminating cast iron constructions is the Eiffel Tower in Paris (fig. 12.3) built in 1889. Perhaps more than any other structure, the Eiffel Tower epitomizes the fancifulness possible with cast iron.

Steel was introduced as a building material at the turn of the twentieth century. It led directly to the development of the skyscraper, with Louis Sullivan as the leading architect of the genre. Tall buildings became possible with steel skeletal structures and the invention of the modern elevator in the mid-nineteenth century. With skyscrapers the

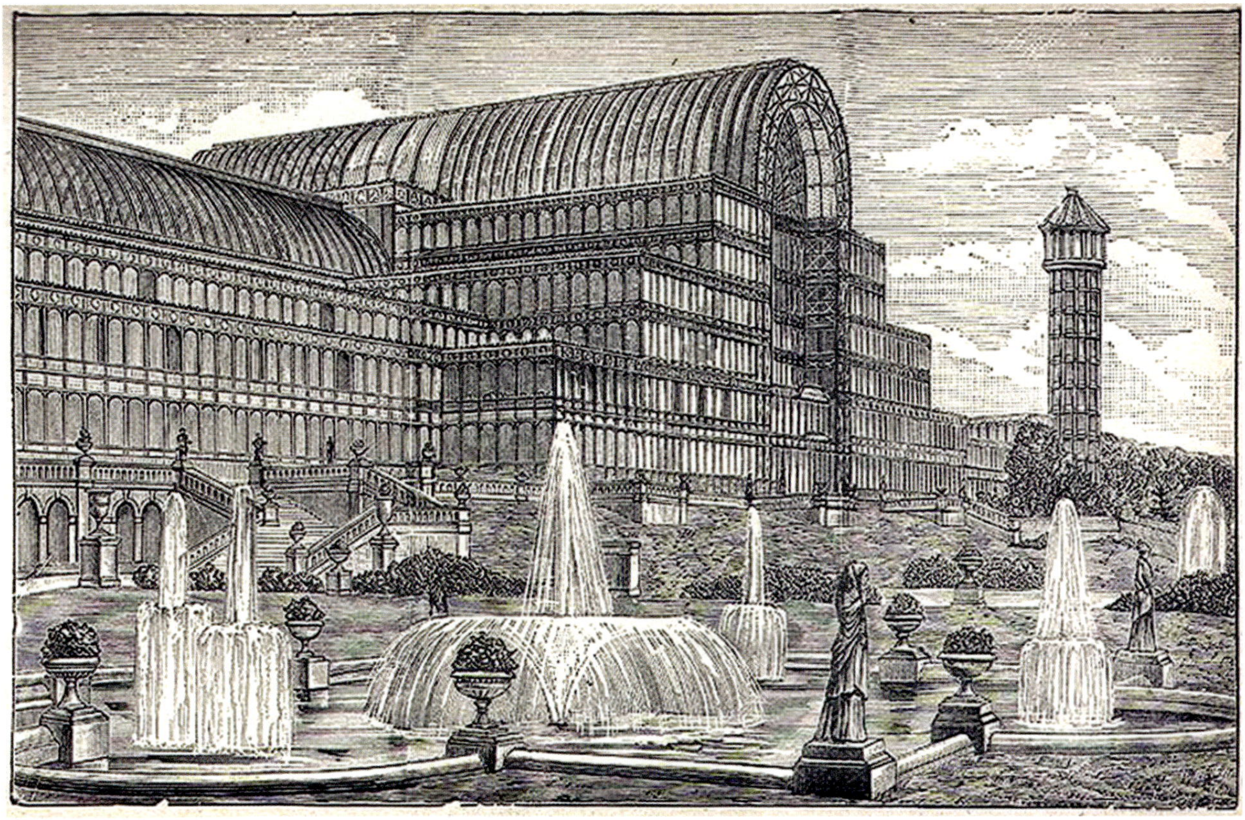

fig. 12.2 Joseph Paxton, Crystal Palace, London, 1850–1851. Cast iron and glass.

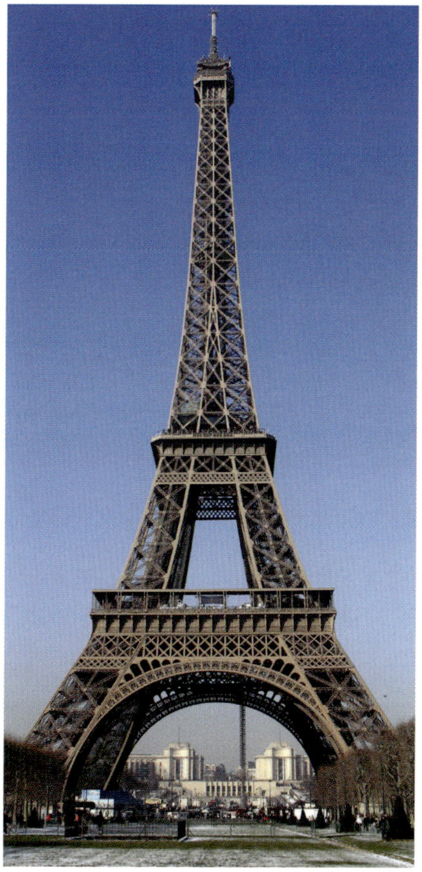

fig. 12.3a The Eiffel Tower, 1889. Paris, France.

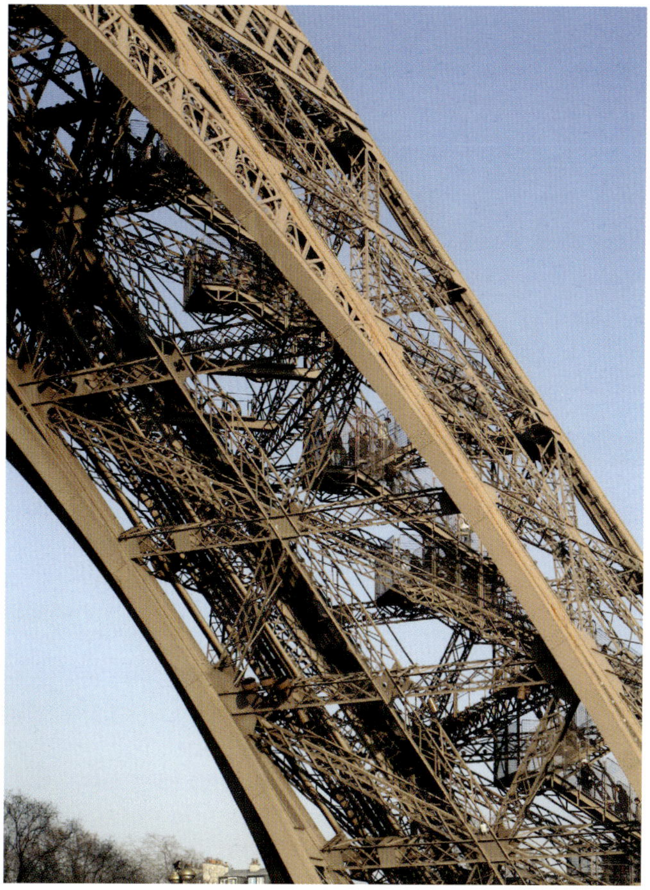

fig. 12.3b Detail of the Eiffel Tower, 1889. Paris, France.

exterior walls have no support function. They hang from the steel framework and only serve to keep out the elements and give the building a pleasing aspect.

Reinforced concrete is concrete with steel reinforcement bars (rebar) or steel mesh embedded in it. This greatly increases the tensile strength of concrete, which is fairly brittle. It was invented in the mid nineteenth century, but it did not come into common use until the twentieth. Today most concrete used in construction is reinforced.

BASIC BUILDING SYSTEMS

Post-and-lintel is the most basic architectural structure type. It consists of two vertical elements that support a cross beam. Most of the buildings we encounter still use this system. Stonehenge (fig. 12.4), the Parthenon (fig.12.5) or most of the doorways in your house or apartment use the post-and-lintel system. The strength of a post-and-lintel system is dependent upon the materials used. A longer beam is possible with wood than with stone because stone, although stronger, is heavier and brittle. Modern materials such as steel permit much longer beams, and as a result interior spaces can be more open.

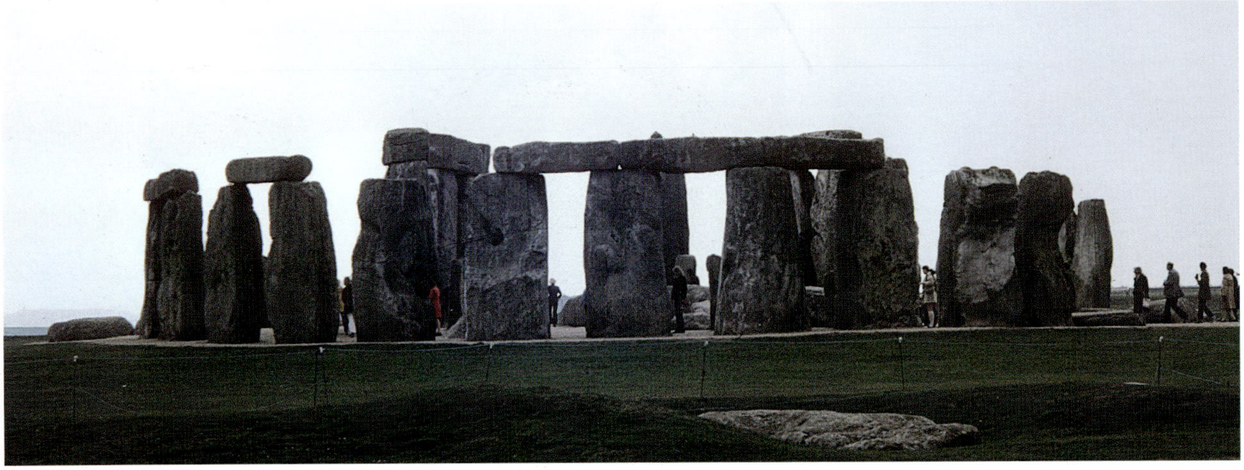

fig. 12.4 Stonehenge, c. 2700–1600 BCE. Salisbury Plain, England.

Vaulting (fig. 12.6) allows greater spans and larger spaces without interior supports. The **arch** is the basis of a vault; it is stronger than post-and-lintel because the weight on the curved top channels down to the vertical supports. The same principle applies to the **barrel vault**. The walls carry the weight of the curved ceiling. Barrel vaults have their limitations also. Because the walls are the supporting element, windows must remain small and few. Also, the taller the vault the thicker the walls need to be; thus at some point the walls would become so thick as to preclude sufficient interior space.

Groin vaulting (also called cross-vaulting) reduces these problems. A groin vault is simply the intersection of two barrel vaults, with the result that four large supporting **piers** eliminate the need for walls. All the weight of the vault channels down to these piers. This permits huge open interiors with numerous large windows. The Gothic period introduced pointed arches in cathedrals and, along with external buttressing, permitted even

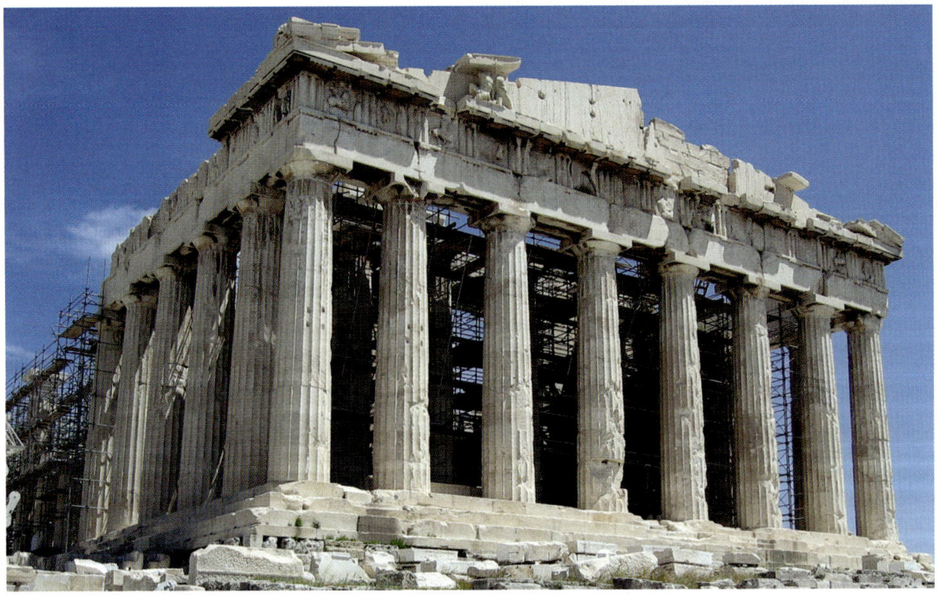

fig. 12.5 The Parthenon, fifth century BCE. Athens, Greece.

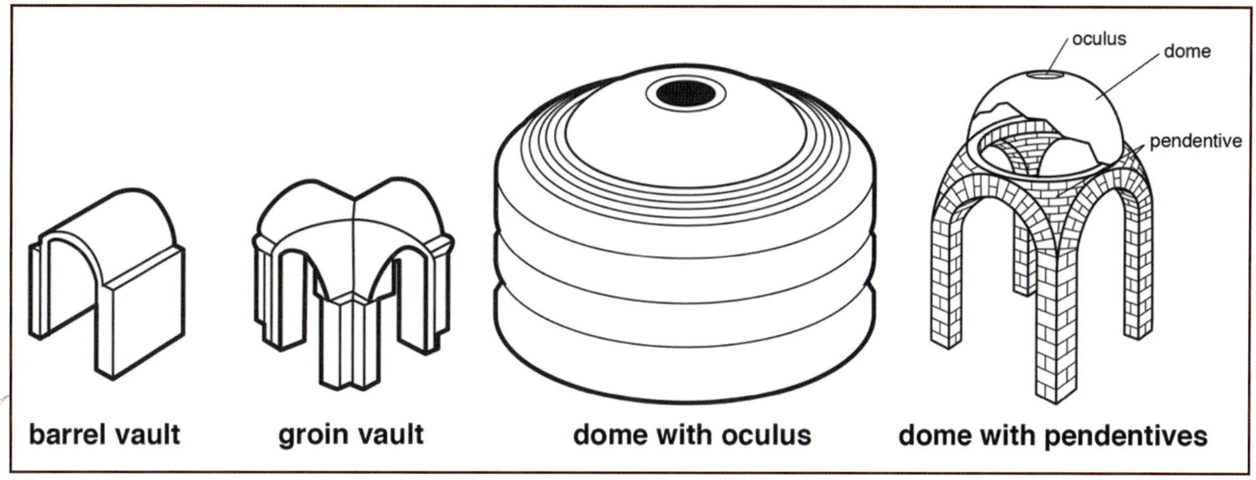

fig. 12.6 Vaulting. © Kendall Hunt Publishing Company

higher and wider naves and larger window spaces for stained glass (see figs. 13.16a and 13.16b).

Conceptually, a **dome** is an arch rotated 180 degrees on its vertical axis. Domes can rest on a cylindrical base such as in the Pantheon (figs. 11.10, 11.11, and 11.12) where the entire circular wall helps support the dome. If the area the architect wishes to cover is square, then the dome cannot rest directly on the wall. There has to be a transition from square to circle. A **dome on pendentives** achieves this. A dome on pendentives is as though you cut off the top of a groin vault and place the dome on top. The triangular areas left are the pendentives. As with the original groin vault, all the weight channels down to the four piers. A spectacular example of a dome on pendentives is the church of Hagia Sophia in Istanbul (fig. 12.7), which is now a museum. The dome is pierced by forty windows at its base making it appear to float on a ring of divine light.

Today, continuing innovations in building materials and further advances in construction techniques allow architects greater flexibility to design ever more imaginative buildings. Some of these newer materials and methods include shell structures (the Sydney Opera House, fig. 12.8) and pneumatic structures where air pressure supports a flexible roof as well as improved suspension capabilities (the Akashi-Kaikyo bridge in Japan has a

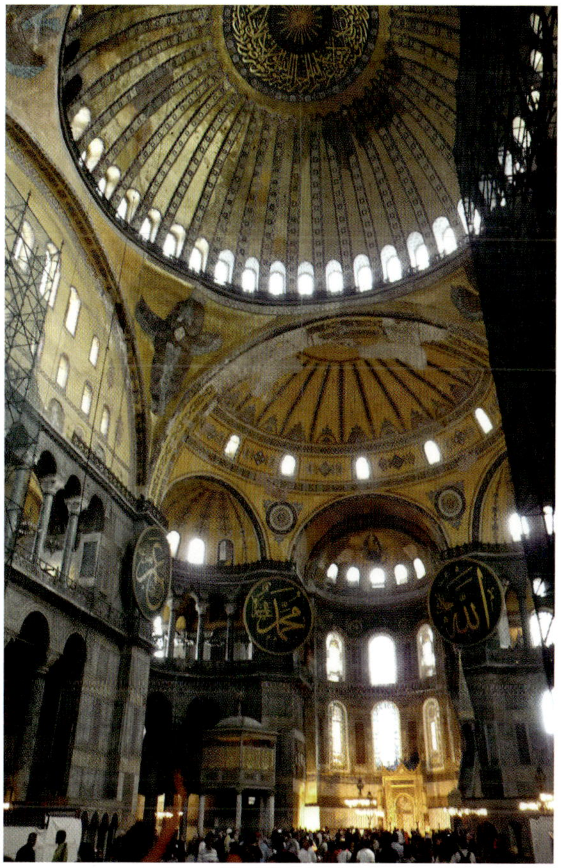

fig. 12.7a Hagia Sophia, 532–535. Istanbul, Turkey.

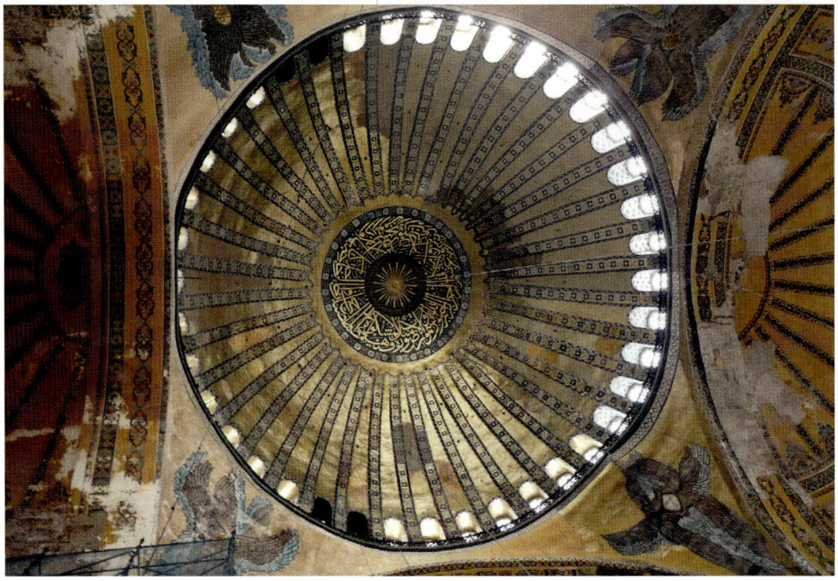

fig. 12.7b

central span of more than a mile). Perhaps the best example of how architects are freed from the technological constraints of earlier eras is the work of Frank Gehry (fig. 12.9). The Walt Disney Concert Hall with its unorthodox soaring, curved walls is a true flight of fancy made real.

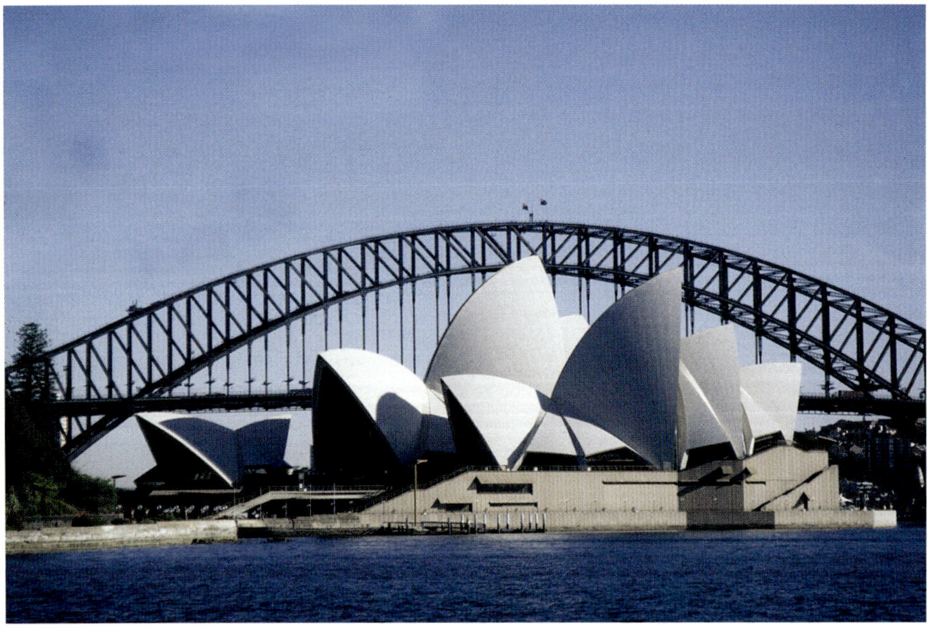

fig. 12.8 Jørn Utzon, Sydney Opera House, completed 1972. Sydney, Australia.

Architectural Diagrams

There are four basic kinds of architectural renderings to describe a building. A **ground plan** shows the floor plan of the building. It is as though the building were sliced off at ground level. It reveals the placement and thickness of walls, columns, doorways and so forth. An **elevation** shows the exterior **façade** of a building. The architect draws it from a neutral point of view without perspective distortion. A **section** is as though the building has been sliced in two vertically to reveal the interior. A **cutaway** (or **axonometric view**) shows the building from an angle in a three-dimensional format to reveal the exterior and part of the interior.

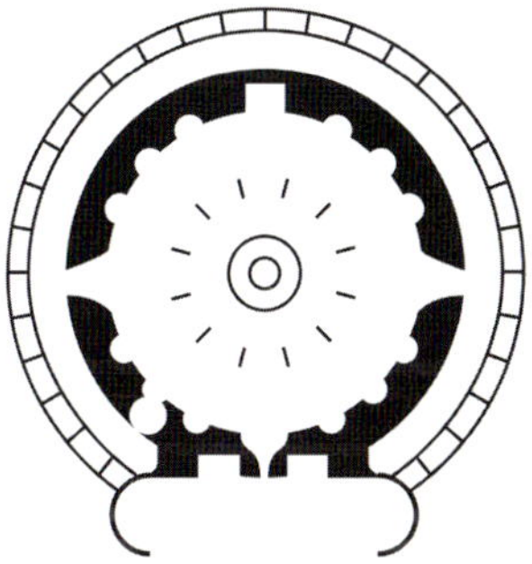

plan

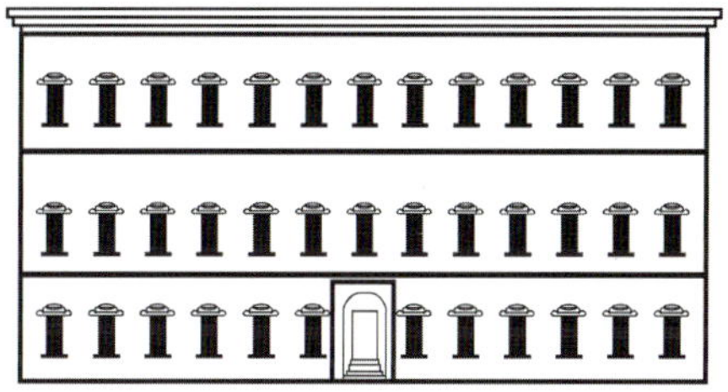

elevation

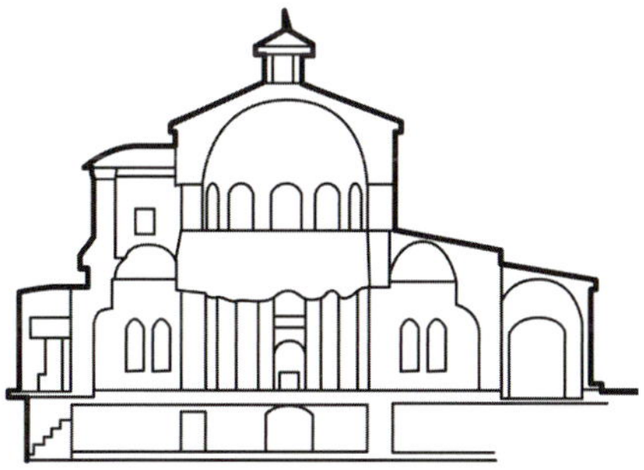

section

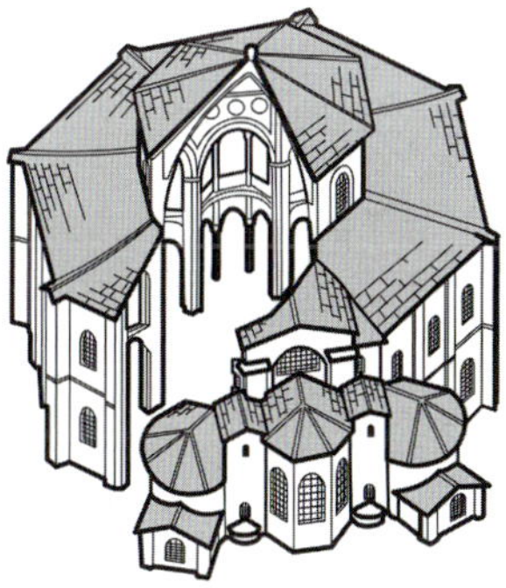

cutaway

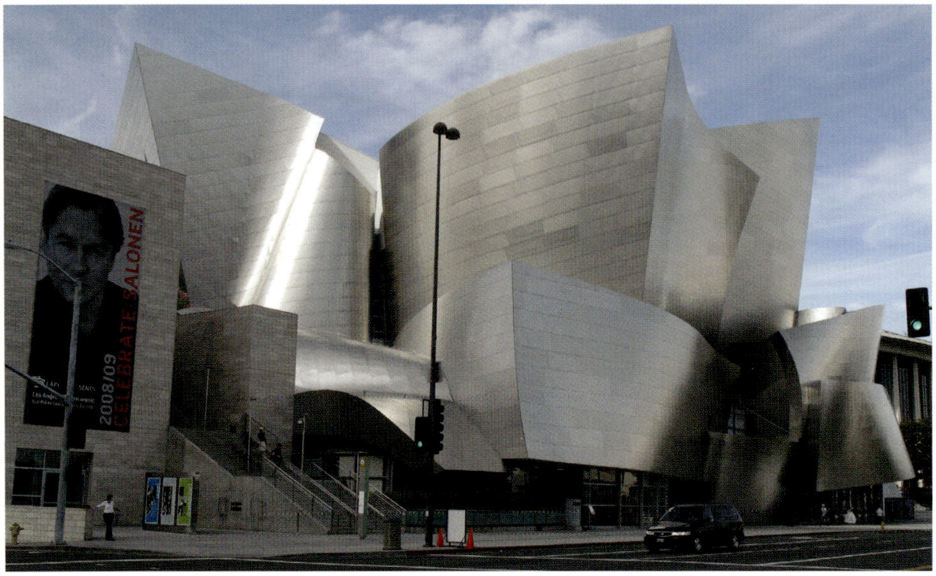

fig. 12.9a Frank Gehry, Walt Disney Concert Hall, 1987–2003. Los Angeles.

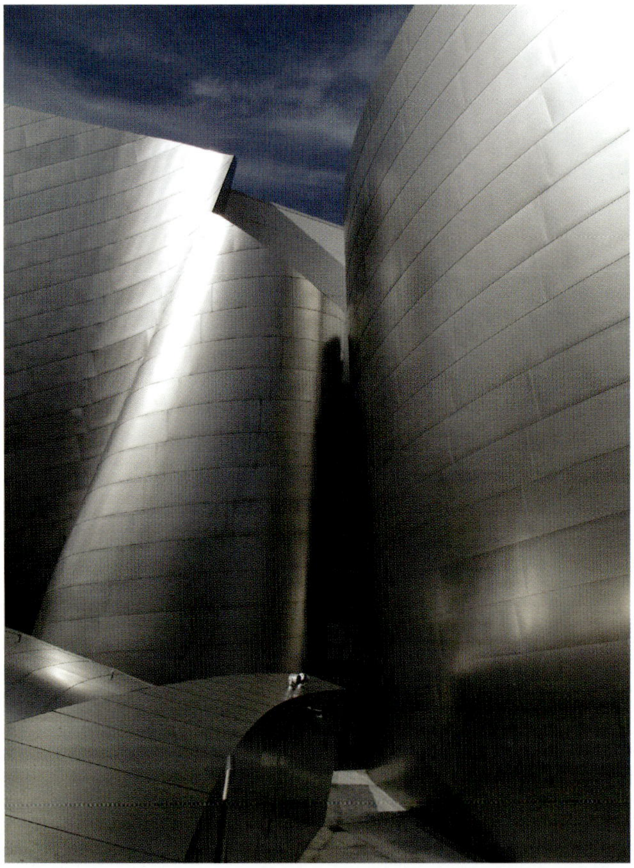

fig. 12.9b People can walk along a path on the roof of the Walt Disney Concert Hall.

PRONUNCIATION GUIDE

Axonometric (ak-suh-noh-**meh**-trik)
Façade (fuh-**sahd**)
Gehry (**gair**-ee)
Oculus (**ock**-yuh-luhs)
Parthenon (**par**-thuh-non)
Pendentive (**pen**-den-tiv)
Utzon, Joern (**oot**-zuhn, yohrn)

SUMMARY

Basic Concepts of Architecture

Form: The building's appearance; the way it looks.

Function: The building's purpose; what the building is for.

Structure: How the building is built; the way it is put together.

Form should follow function; in other words, the form of a building should not conflict with its function.

Materials

Stone, **wood** and **brick** are some of the earliest used materials in architecture.

Cast iron (19th century) allows for the construction of larger structures.

Steel (late 19th century), along with the invention of the elevator, allowed for the construction of skyscrapers.

Reinforced concrete (20th century) is concrete with imbedded steel rods or mesh for greater tensile strength.

Architectural Systems

Post-and-lintel consists of two vertical elements (posts) that support a horizontal beam (lintel) to span a space. This is a simple construction, but limited weight can be supported and the heavier the lintel, the closer the posts must be together.

Vaulting systems are based on the arch. They can span greater spaces because the weight of the vault is channeled down to the corner piers (or **drum**). The three main types of vaults are the barrel vault, the groin vault, and the dome.

Architectural Diagrams

The four main types of architectural diagrams are the ground plan, the elevation, the section, and the cutaway view.

GLOSSARY

Arch. A curved structural element that spans a space. It is built from wedge-shaped stones that are held in place at the top by a central block called the keystone.

Axonometric view. An architectural drawing that shows a cutaway view of a building from an angle in a three-dimensional format to reveal the exterior and part of the interior.

Barrel vault. A semi cylindrical roof constructed on the arch principle. It is essentially a deep arch over an oblong space.

Cantilever. An architectural element that projects out horizontally with no vertical support at the far end.

Cast iron. A hard but brittle alloy of iron and carbon produced in molds.

Central plan. In architecture, a building with a central space surrounded by symmetrical areas.

Dome. A roof with a hemispherical shape.

Drum. A circular wall that supports a dome.

Elevation. An architectural drawing that shows the exterior façade of a building.

Façade. The front of a building.

Groin vault. A vault formed by the intersection of two barrel vaults.

Ground plan. The floor plan of a building.

Longitudinal plan. An architectural plan in which the parts of the building are organized around a central axis.

Oculus. A round central opening in a dome.

Pendentive. A dome on pendentives is as though you cut off the top of a groin vault and place the dome on top. The triangular areas left are the pendentives.

Pier. In architecture, a rectangular supporting element.

Post-and-lintel construction. A building technique in which two vertical elements (posts) support a horizontal element (lintel).

Reinforced concrete. Concrete with steel reinforcement bars (rebar) or mesh imbedded in it.

Section. An architectural drawing that shows a building as though it has been sliced in two vertically to reveal the interior.

Stainless steel. Steel made rust resistant by the addition of chrome and other materials.

Steel. An alloy of mostly iron to which carbon and other elements have been added to make it stronger and less brittle.

Vault. An arched roof or ceiling usually made of stone, brick, or concrete. See also Barrel vault and Groin vault.

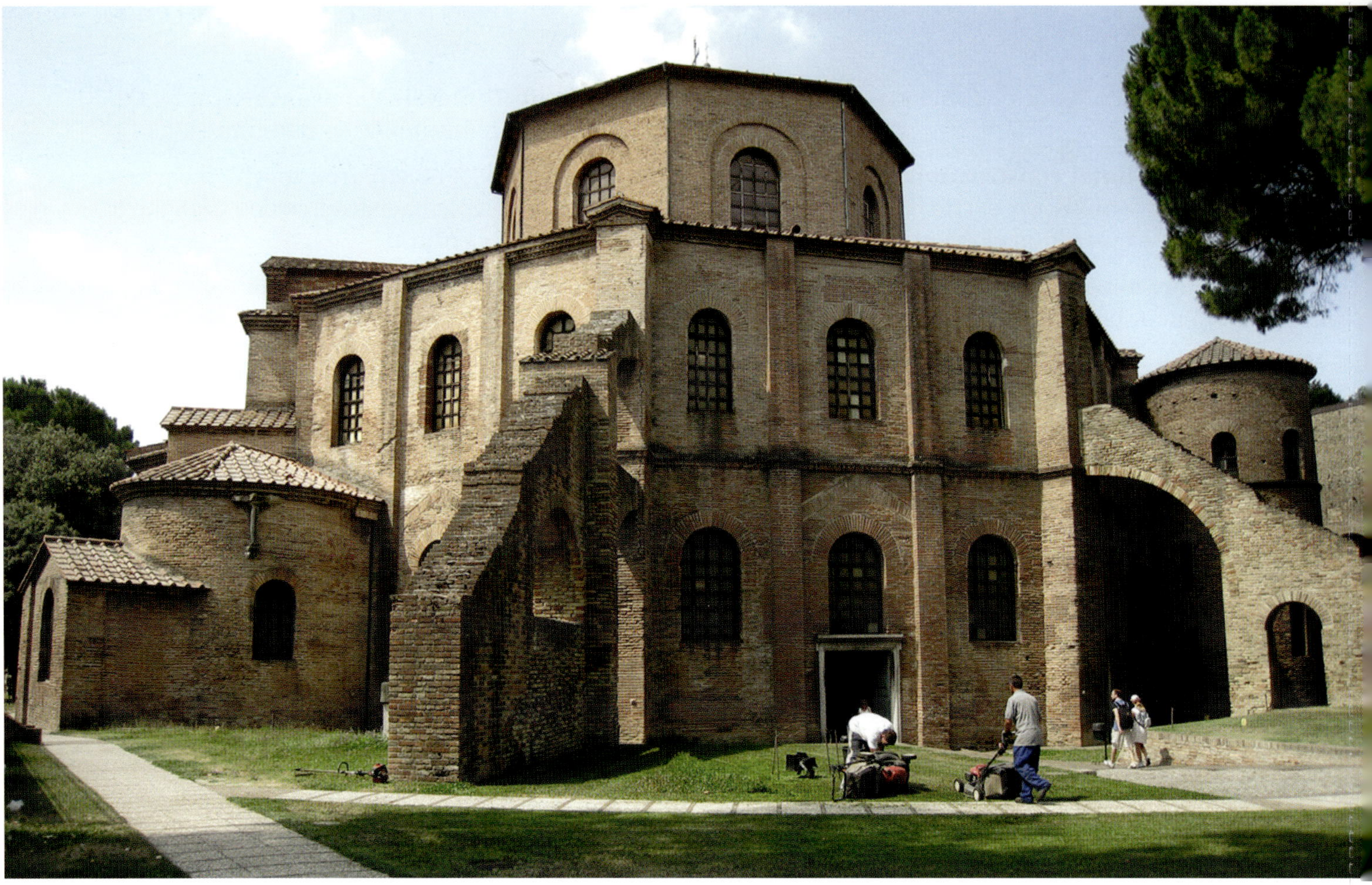

fig. 13.1 San Vitale, 526–547. Ravenna.

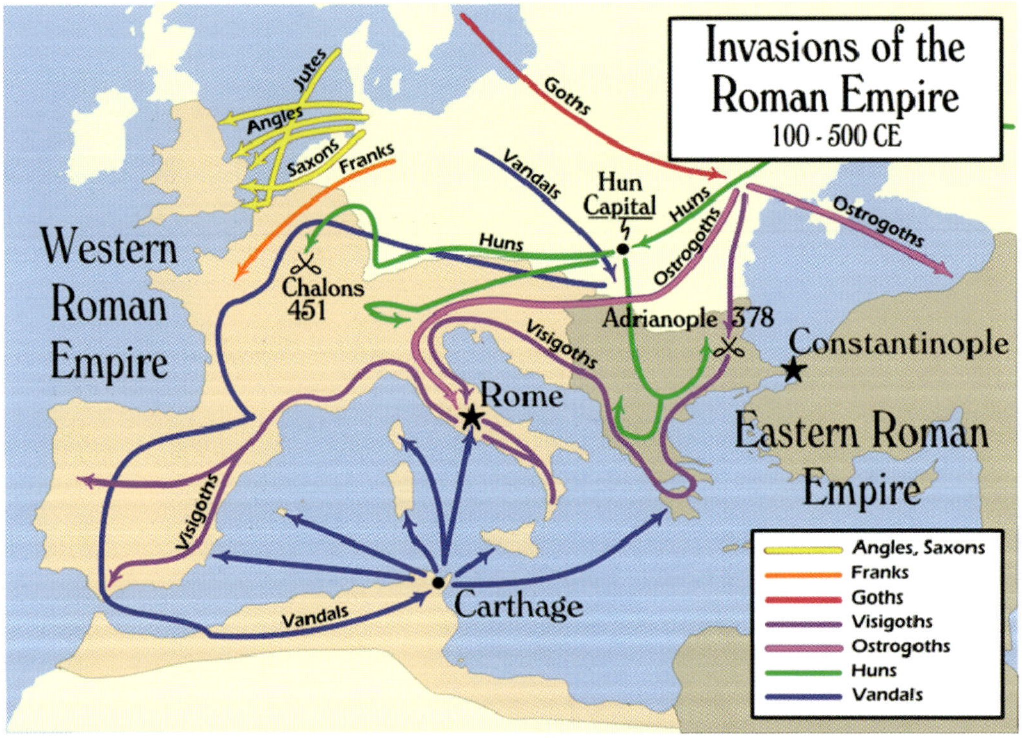

13

The Middle Ages is an outmoded term, but we still use it to refer to the period between the decline of the Roman Empire in the late fifth century and the Renaissance period, which began in Italy around 1400 AD.

BYZANTINE ART: THE AGE OF JUSTINIAN

The pagan Roman Empire quickly evolved into a Christian one in the fourth century AD. The emperor Constantine, whose mother Helen was a Christian, issued the Edict of Milan in 313 that granted full tolerance to all religions. This stopped the persecutions of the Christians, so prevalent at the end of the previous century. Before the end of the century, Christianity became the official religion of the Roman Empire. In 330 Constantine made another radical change: He transferred the capital from Rome to Byzantium in what is now Turkey. He renamed the city Constantinople after himself, a name it retained until 1930 when it changed again to Istanbul. These were profound changes that occurred in a relatively short period of time.

THE MIDDLE AGES

Before 313, early Christians worshipped in catacombs (underground burial places), protected under Roman law, or in private homes. Once their religion became legal, then Christians began building churches based on the design of Roman basilicas (**longitudinal plans**) and mausoleums (**central plans**). The Byzantine period gets its name from Byzantium, and its golden age occurred during the rule of the emperor Justinian in the sixth century. The western part of the Roman Empire suffered great losses in the fifth century with the repeated invasions of Germanic tribes from the north, such as the **Goths** and the Huns. Justinian recaptured Italy and extended the boundaries of the Byzantine Empire to its greatest extent.

One of the surviving gems from Justinian's reign is the church of San Vitale in Ravenna, Italy (figs. 13.1 and 13.2). Based on a **central plan**, the church consists of two octagons, one inside the other. Eight piers support the domed inner octagon, and the outer octagon forms an **ambulatory** around the center. The **apse** where the altar is gives the church its orientation. A **narthex** precedes the entrance, which is oddly off the central axis. Unlike many earlier Roman buildings, early churches were not concerned

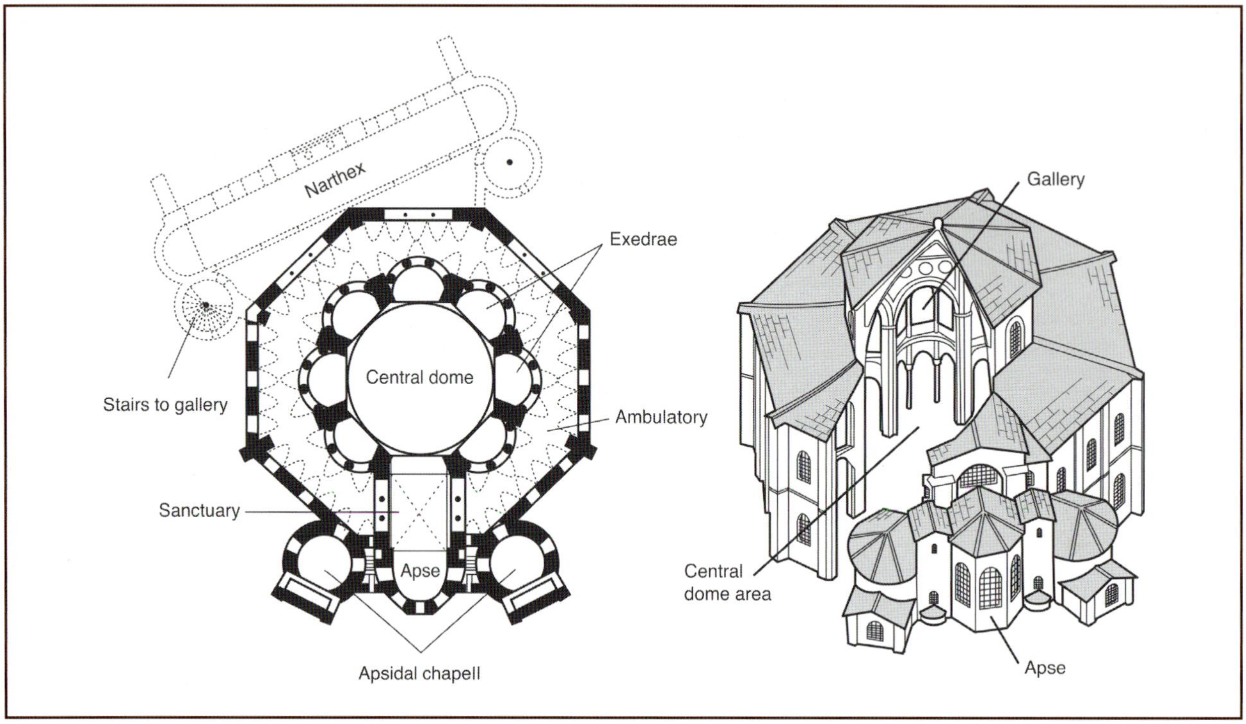

fig. 13.2 **Ground plan** and cutaway view of San Vitale.

with ostentatious exteriors. The outside of the church was usually just plain brick, as it is with San Vitale. They reserved the decoration for the sacred inner space, and San Vitale excels with beautiful marble veneers and dazzling **mosaics**.

Two large mosaics in the apse depict Justinian and his wife, Theodora, with their attendants (figs. 13.3 and 13.4). Justinian, who was head of state and also head of the church, has both a crown and a halo. Centrally positioned and wearing royal purple, twelve men flank him, alluding to the twelve **Apostles**. One figure has a label. He is Bishop Maximianus, who was instrumental in the construction of San Vitale. On the opposite wall Theodora, also crowned and dressed in purple, stands before a niche with her ladies in waiting and other attendants. Embroidered on the lower portion of her robe is a scene of the three wise men bringing gifts to the Christ child. Justinian carries a paten for the bread of the **Eucharist**, while Theodora carries a chalice for the wine.

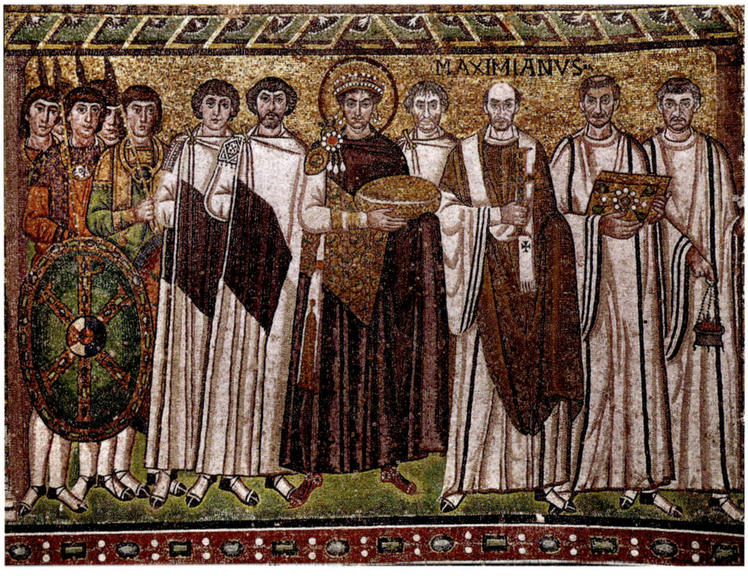

fig. 13.3 Justinian and Attendants, c. 547. Apse of San Vitale, Ravenna.

The style of these works is very different from that of the Classical period. The illusion of

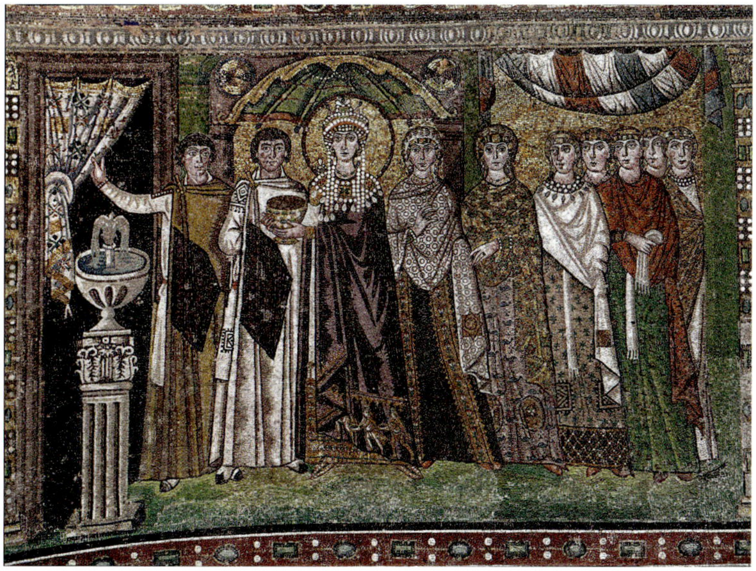

fig. 13.4a Theodora and Attendants, c. 547. Apse of San Vitale, Ravenna.

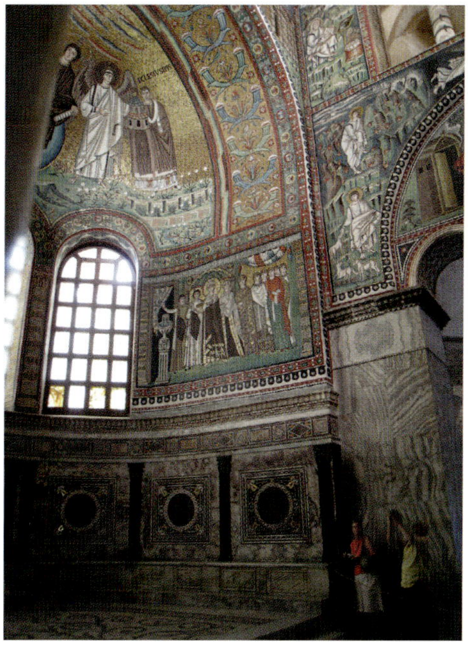

fig. 13.4b Interior of S. Vitale showing Theodora Mosaic.

physical reality is gone. Instead, the figures are flat and elongated with small heads and large eyes. Head clusters, such as that of the soldiers to the left of Justinian, stand in for full figures. We can see only two of the six bodies of the soldiers. The background is a celestial gold that denies any kind of recession into space. Indication of depth is solely by overlapping figures, and even that is ambiguous. From the waist up Justinian appears in front of everyone else, but if you look at Maximianus' feet, they

Christian Imagery

The early Christians had to create imagery and architecture for their new religion, and they did so by adapting what they knew from Roman art and architecture. Therefore, much of Christian imagery is pagan in origin. Angels have their source in the winged Nike goddess of victory. We can trace early images of Christ as a youthful beardless shepherd back to Egyptian and Greek sculptures of men with a sheep or a calf around their shoulders or to similar images of Orpheus and the god Hermes. The youthful Christ also has parallels to images of Apollo. Christ depicted as a more mature bearded man derives from images of bearded philosophers or Zeus. The Madonna and Child recall similar images of the Egyptian goddess Isis with the infant Horus. In architecture, the Christian church took its basic form from the Roman **basilica**—a civic building that had a rectangular form. Early Christian architects changed the orientation so that the entrance was at a short end rather than on a long end. Church atriums recall atriums in the houses of wealthier Christians where early Christians often met.

Theodora

Theodora was an exceptional woman. An actress (and also probably a prostitute), she was an unlikely candidate to become empress. Justinian, fifteen years her senior, fell in love with her, and they eventually wed despite her low social status. Theodora was not only beautiful but intelligent and brave. She saved the empire during a revolt in 532 when she convinced Justinian and his generals not to flee Constantinople as their ministers had advised. They didn't, and the revolt failed.

appear in front of Justinian. Likewise, the fountain in the Theodora mosaic seems both in front of and beneath the curtained doorway. The rich colors and patterns of the mosaics and their glittering quality give both scenes a jewel-like character more concerned with spirituality than with physical reality. (Watch the video clip on San Vitale on the Kendall Hunt website for this book.)

EARLY MIDDLE AGES

Society changed dramatically in Western Europe as Rome declined and various Germanic peoples overran the continent. Art changed as well. With the continuing invasions of Huns, Goths, Franks, Vandals, Saxons and other tribes (see Map, page 150), portable art replaced monumental art and architecture, especially in metalwork. A good example of this type of art is an Anglo-Saxon **cloisonné** purse lid found in a ship burial in England (fig. 13.5). In the cloisonné technique, soldering metal strips on

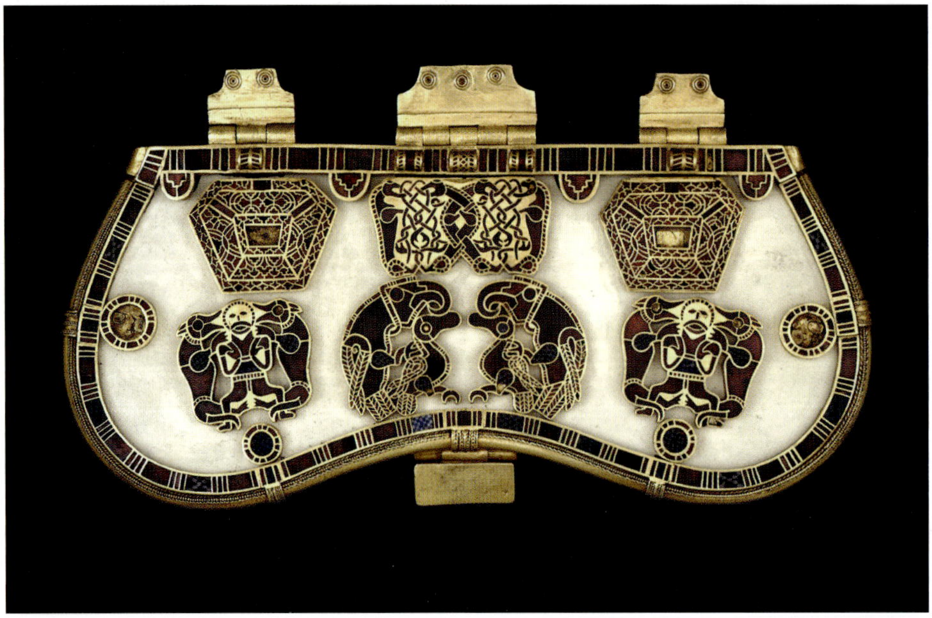

fig. 13.5 Sutton Hoo purse lid, c. 630. Gold, glass, garnets and cloisonné enamel, 8 in. wide. British Museum, London.

the edges of a metal background forms tiny compartments. The artist then fills the compartments with enamel, glass or other materials.

The symmetrical design of the Sutton Hoo purse lid depicts intricate interlacing patterns and stylized animals. At the top two hexagons with linear designs flank a central shape containing fighting beasts and interlace. Below are two mirror images, each one depicting a duck with an eagle on its back. The eagles' beaks fit neatly into the concave part of the ducks' beaks. At either end is a human figure flanked by two beasts. The sources for this type of design are early Christian interlace patterns and animal motifs that originated in Scythia and the Near East.

The animal interlace patterns found in portable art came to influence other art forms such as manuscript **illumination**. The Cross Page from the Lindisfarne Gospels is an explosion of intricate interlaces (fig. 13.6). Monks illustrated the book around 700 in a monastery located on the small island of Lindisfarne just off the northeast coast of England. Known as carpet pages because of their dense decoration, such illuminated (decorated) pages as the Cross Page illustrate the skill and patience of the monks who laboriously painted them. A seemingly infinite number of serpent-like animals devour one another in writhing patterns so complex and impenetrable that their maze-like interlacings are difficult to follow. The clearly outlined cross serves not only as a Christian symbol, but also as a stabilizing factor that constrains the animals' movements. The incredibly well-planned design done in a harmonious balance of reds, greens and blues makes this illuminated **manuscript** page one of the masterpieces of early Medieval art.

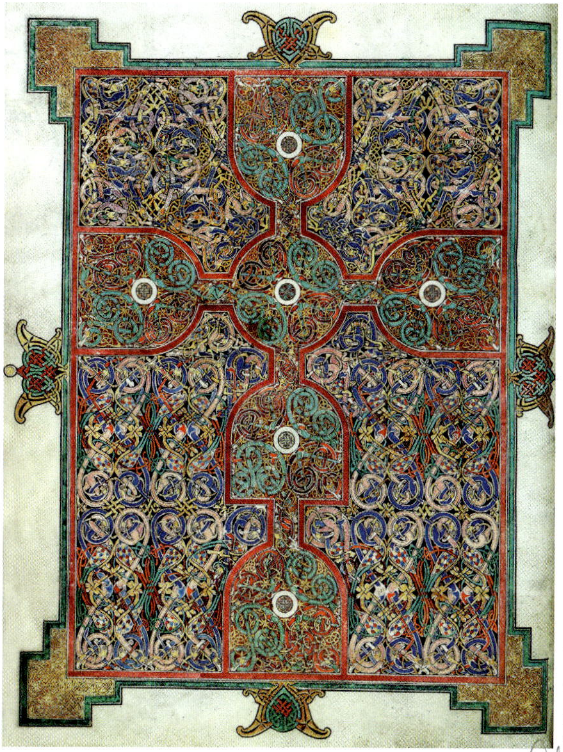

fig. 13.6 Cross Page from the Lindisfarne Gospels, c. 700. **Tempera** on **vellum**, 13.5 in × 9.5 in. British Library, London.

ISLAMIC ART

In the seventh century another cultural force began to manifest itself: Islam. After the death of Mohammed, the religion's founder, in 632, Islam quickly spread across the Middle East, North Africa and most of Spain. The Frankish king Charles Martel halted its expansion into France in 732. Islamic culture in the Middle Ages was incredibly important for the future development of Western Europe because it preserved many of the writings of the ancient Greeks (such as Aristotle) that would have been otherwise lost. Islamic cities such as Cordoba in Spain were sophisticated centers of learning and culture. At its height in the tenth century, Cordoba was probably the largest city on earth with a population of more than five hundred thousand. Islamic scientists kept the art of scientific discovery alive and developed the scientific method based on empirical observation and experimentation. They

Anglo- and Hiberno-Saxon

Anglo-Saxon refers to the people living in southern Britain from about 400–1000 AD. They were probably descendants of three Germanic tribes: the Angles, the Saxons and the Jutes. Hiberno-Saxon refers to the style of art of the British Isles in the seventh to ninth centuries. It applies especially to illustrated manuscripts, metalwork and stone crosses whose decoration contains intricate interlacing designs. Hiberno-Saxon art is also known as Insular art.

made significant advances in medicine, optics, astronomy and mathematics (an Islamic mathematician developed algebra). They also introduced paper-making to the West, a skill they obtained from the Chinese.

THE GREAT MOSQUE AT CORDOBA

Because of Islamic belief, representations of the human figure are rare in Islamic art, and sacred buildings do not depict either animals or humans. Instead, Islamic artists created geometric and floral designs. The **mosque** is the place of worship for Muslims (believers in Islam), and the mosque at Cordoba was one of the largest ever built. The prayer hall (fig. 13.7) is a vast sea of hundreds of columns taken from earlier Christian and Roman buildings. Since the columns are short (less than ten feet tall), the architect

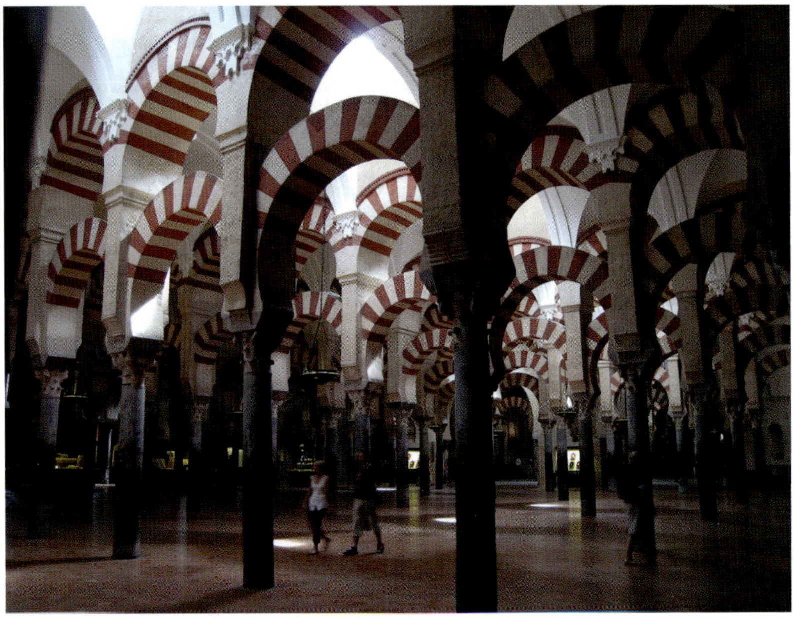

fig. 13.7 Prayer Hall of the Great Mosque at Cordoba, Spain. 8th–10th centuries.

devised a system of double red and white striped arches above them in order to have sufficient height. (The inspiration for this may have come from Roman aqueducts such as that at Nîmes (fig. 11.6).) The lower arches are horseshoe shaped, which became typical of Islamic architecture. The columns seem to go on forever, thus evoking the infinite nature of Allah. Sadly, a large cathedral was erected in the center of the prayer hall in the sixteenth century, but even that was not enough to destroy the beauty and spiritual quality of this unique mosque. (Watch the video clip on the Mosque at Cordoba on the Kendall Hunt website for this book)

ROMANESQUE ART

Romanesque (Roman-like) refers to an artistic style in the eleventh and twelfth centuries characterized by round arches and stone vaults that recalled ancient Roman architecture. When the invading barbarian tribes overrunning Europe since the decline of the Roman Empire became assimilated into Christian society, Europe became more stable, permitting an era of great church building. With Christianity firmly established, pilgrimage routes allowed people to travel to the most sacred sites in Christendom where they could express their devotion and revere relics of the saints (see "Relics" box). The preferred places of pilgrimage were Jerusalem and Rome, but they were long and difficult journeys. The more accessible third choice was Santiago de Compostela in northwestern Spain where there is a shrine to St. James that contains his bones.

Romanesque churches were made of stone, including the vaults, for several reasons. Stone reduced the threat of destruction by fire, allowed for better acoustics and made for a more imposing place to house the relics.

The church of Ste. Foy in Conques, France (fig. 13.8), is one of the pilgrimage churches along the route to Santiago. It houses the relics of Sainte Foy, a third-century virgin **martyr**. The massive **façade** is typical of Romanesque churches. A large arch frames the portal, which has two doorways beneath a semicircular **tympanum**. Like Early Christian and Byzantine churches, the exterior is still fairly plain. The exception is the sculpted tympanum, which shows the Last Judgment (figs. 13.9 and 13.10). Portal sculptures offered the opportunity to educate the largely illiterate worshippers as they entered the Church. The Last Judgment, where Christ decides who will go to heaven and who will go to hell, must have had a sobering effect on those who looked upon it.

Christ sits enthroned in the center. Above him in the top tier angels trumpet the final judgment. To his right (our left) on his level and the

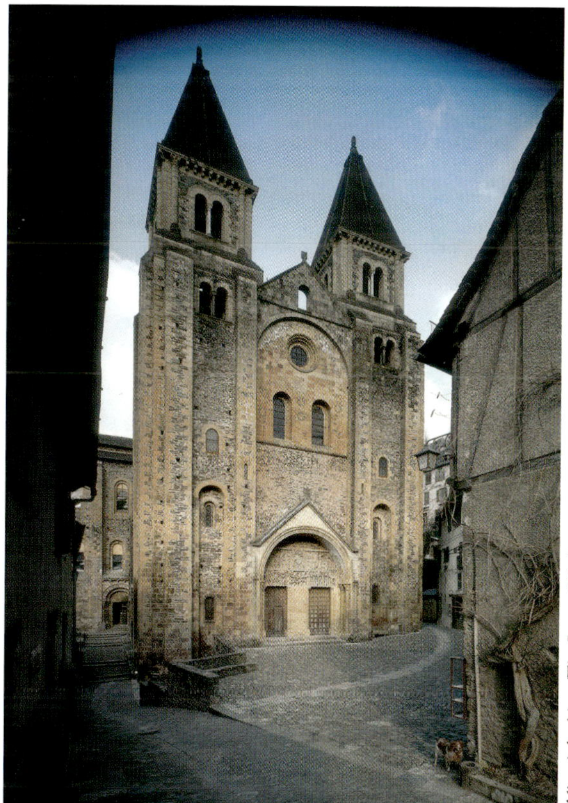

fig. 13.8 Ste. Foy, Conques, France, c. 1050–1120.

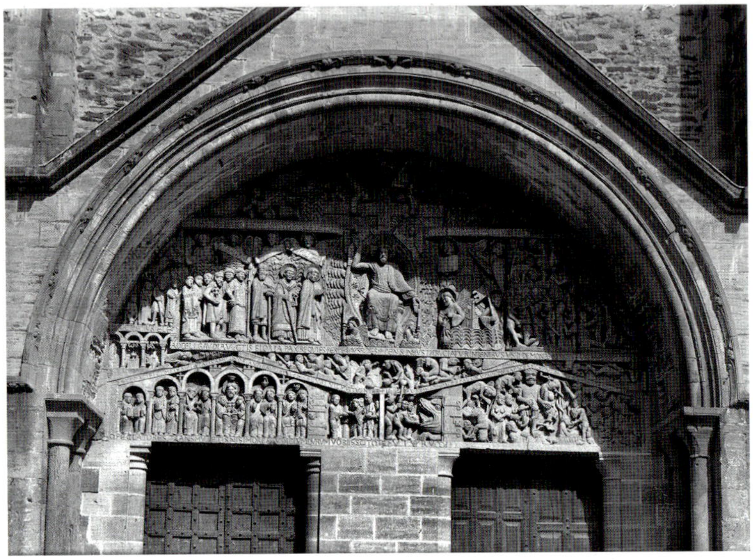

fig. 13.9 *Last Judgment,* west portal of Ste. Foy.

tier below are those who are saved and will go to heaven. Those below are neatly arranged under arches. To Christ's left are the damned who will go to hell. Directly below Christ on our left angels greet the saved; on the right demons shove the damned into the mouth of hell. At the lower right (fig. 13.10) a crowned Satan presides over the tormenting of the damned souls. It is difficult to put oneself in the mindset of someone a thousand years in the past, but the gruesome monsters and tormented souls seen in the hell portion of the tympanum probably inspired fear in a superstitious era before television, the movies and video games made such monsters commonplace.

The famous **Bayeux Tapestry** is not actually a tapestry but an **embroidery** work illustrating the Norman conquest of England in 1066 by William the Conqueror. It is called the Bayeux tapestry because it ended up in the Bayeux Cathedral in France, although we do not know if the original intention was to display it there. More than 230 feet long, it contains hundreds of figures. Women, either French or English, undoubtedly did the needlework. The portion shown in figure 13.11 depicts a battle between the troops of the doomed English King Harold and William of Normandy. The main register shows foot soldiers with shields and spears and armored cavalry falling off their horses. In the narrow band below lie dead warriors; in the band above are both real and imaginary animals often found in books of that time. The needle-workers used eight colors of wool thread to create the scenes against the natural off-white color of the linen. A running inscription in Latin relates what is happening in each portion of the tapestry. This unique work portrays an important event shortly after it occurred, and it provides historians with valuable details of weapons and costume in the late eleventh century. Thus, it is not only a work of art but also an historical document.

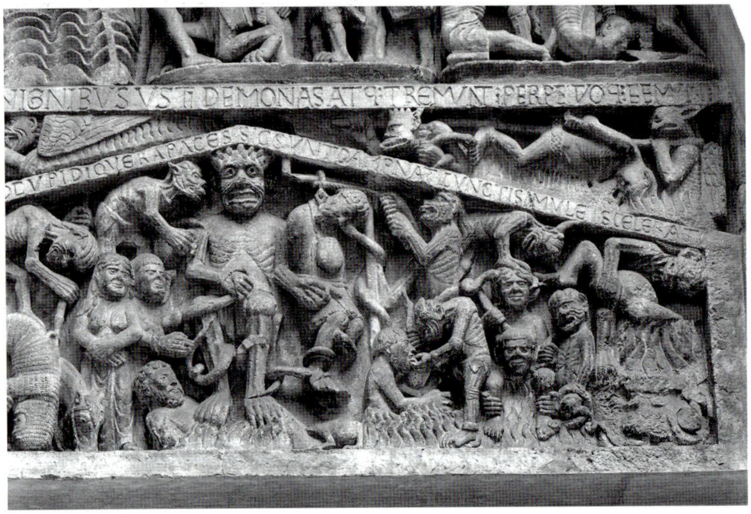

fig. 13.10 Detail of 13.8 showing hell.

The familiar Leaning Tower of Pisa (fig. 13.12a) is actually the **campanile** (bell tower) for the Pisa Cathedral and is part of a complex that also includes a separate baptistry (fig. 13.12b). Bell towers were often freestanding structures in Italy. Italian Medieval architecture remained closer to the classical style of ancient Rome because there were more Roman ruins in Italy than in northern Europe. On a tall base decorated with blind **arcades**, six tiers of arcaded galleries support a smaller eighth story that houses the bells. The delicate design harmonizes with that of the cathedral and the baptistry. The tower leans because the builders laid an insufficient foundation on unstable ground. In fact, it began to tilt while under construction, and the builders tried to compensate for this by changing the vertical axis of the upper portion, which tilts less than the lower part. But it was to no avail. Each year one side of the tower sank a little bit more, causing it to tilt more. By the end of the twentieth century it had to close to tourists because it was in imminent danger of collapse. After removing tons of soil from beneath the raised side, the tower was straightened enough to be safe for another two centuries, and it reopened to the public.

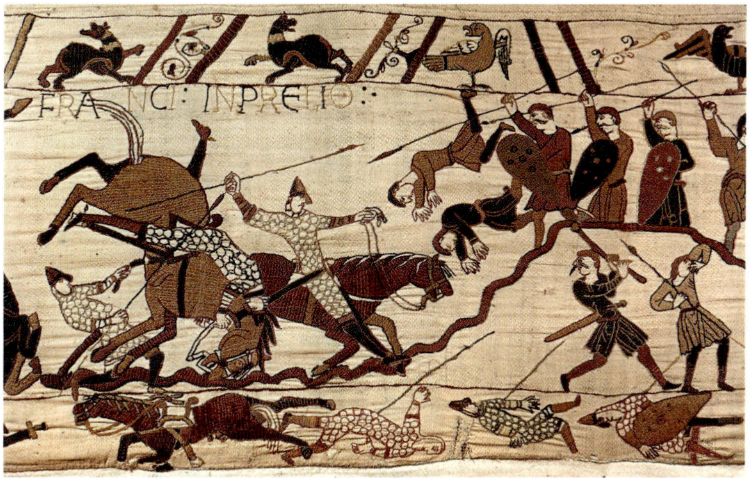

fig. 13.11 Bayeux tapestry, c. 1070–1080. Wool embroidery on linen, 20 in. high × 230 ft. long. Musée de l'Evêché, Bayeus, France.

GOTHIC ART

The Gothic style had its beginnings in the mid twelfth century and lasted until about 1500 in Northern Europe. The term "Gothic" originally had a negative connotation. The Renaissance period coined it to refer to the older architectural style of the preceding era, which people mistakenly associated with the Goths of the early Middle Ages who sacked Rome in 410. Church building became more sophisticated and daring as technology improved. Striving to reach ever-greater heights and to flood the churches with divine light, Gothic architects and masons produced some of the most spectacular structures ever built. The key to this was the development of the pointed arch, **ribbed** vaulting and the flying **buttress** (see fig. 13.13). To build higher **vaults** with traditional round arches meant having to use thicker walls to support the extra weight. Eventually the walls would become so thick that they left little room for the **nave** and aisles. Vaults with pointed arches, however, channeled the weight of the vault more directly downward to the supporting piers,

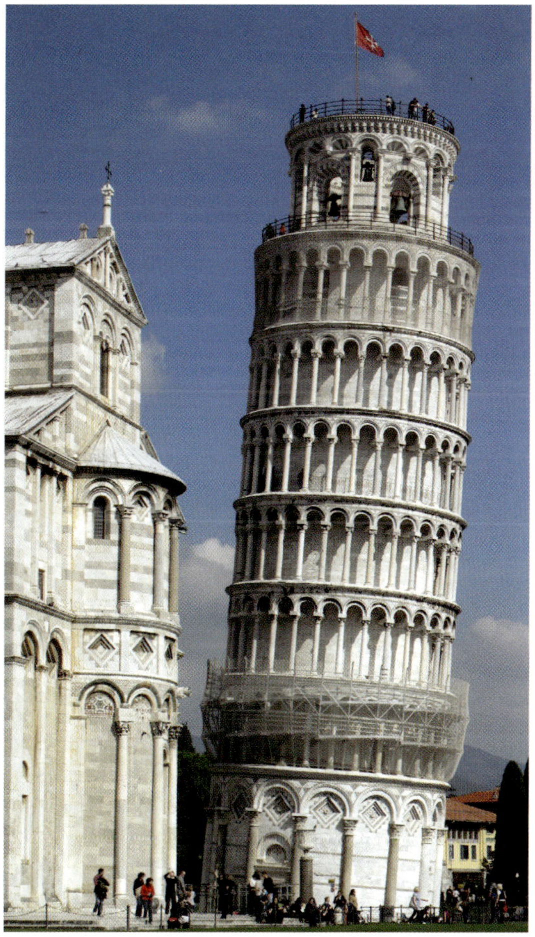

fig. 13.12a Campanile at Pisa (Leaning Tower of Pisa), begun 1174. Pisa, Italy.

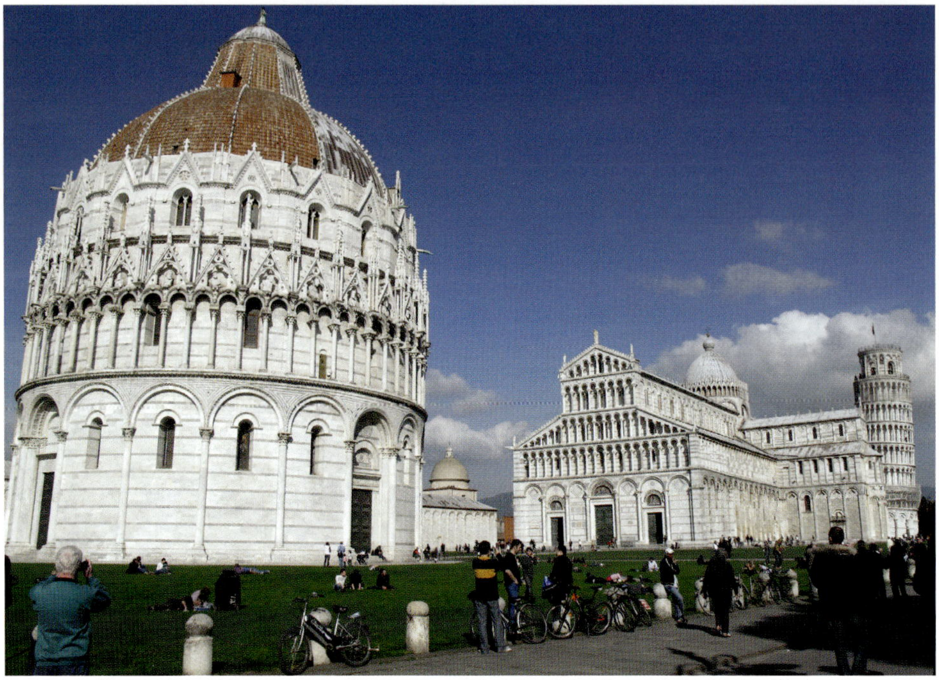

fig. 13.12b The complex at Pisa consists of the baptistry (left), the cathedral (center), and the campanile (right).

Relics

Many people believed that body parts, articles of clothing, instruments of martyrdom and other items associated with the saints had special powers to heal the body and the soul. They put them into elaborate reliquaries made of precious materials and displayed them in churches. In many cases the reliquary took the form of the body part inside, such as an arm or a head. The returning Crusaders brought many relics to Europe from Constantinople (especially in 1204 after sacking the city) and other places in the Holy Lands. Relics were important economically as well as spiritually because pilgrims, like today's tourists, spent money for food, lodging and souvenirs in the places they visited. It was important for a town to have a respectable relic that would attract pilgrims and improve the town's economy. There are even a few cases where a town stole a relic from another town so they could have a good relic. This was the case with the relics of St. Foy (Faith), stolen from the town of Agen. They are now in the church of St. Foy in Conques (fig. 13.8).

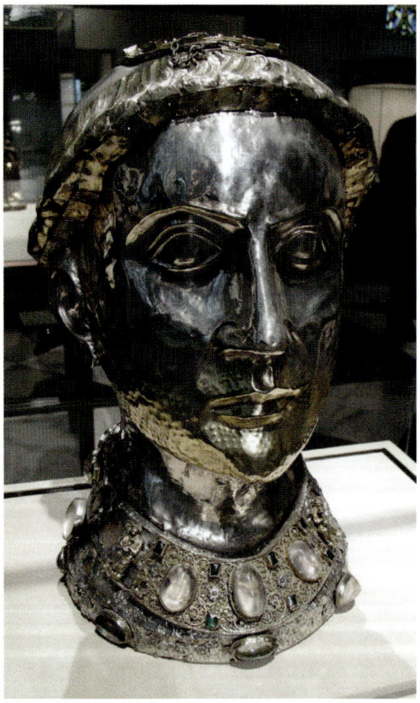

Reliquary bust of a saint, 13th century.
Metropolitan Museum of Art, New York

permitting greater heights. Ribs along the seams of the vaults also made them stronger (see fig. 13.16c). The builders introduced further support on the exterior of churches with a new type of buttress—they separated the main vertical part of the buttress from the church wall and connected it by

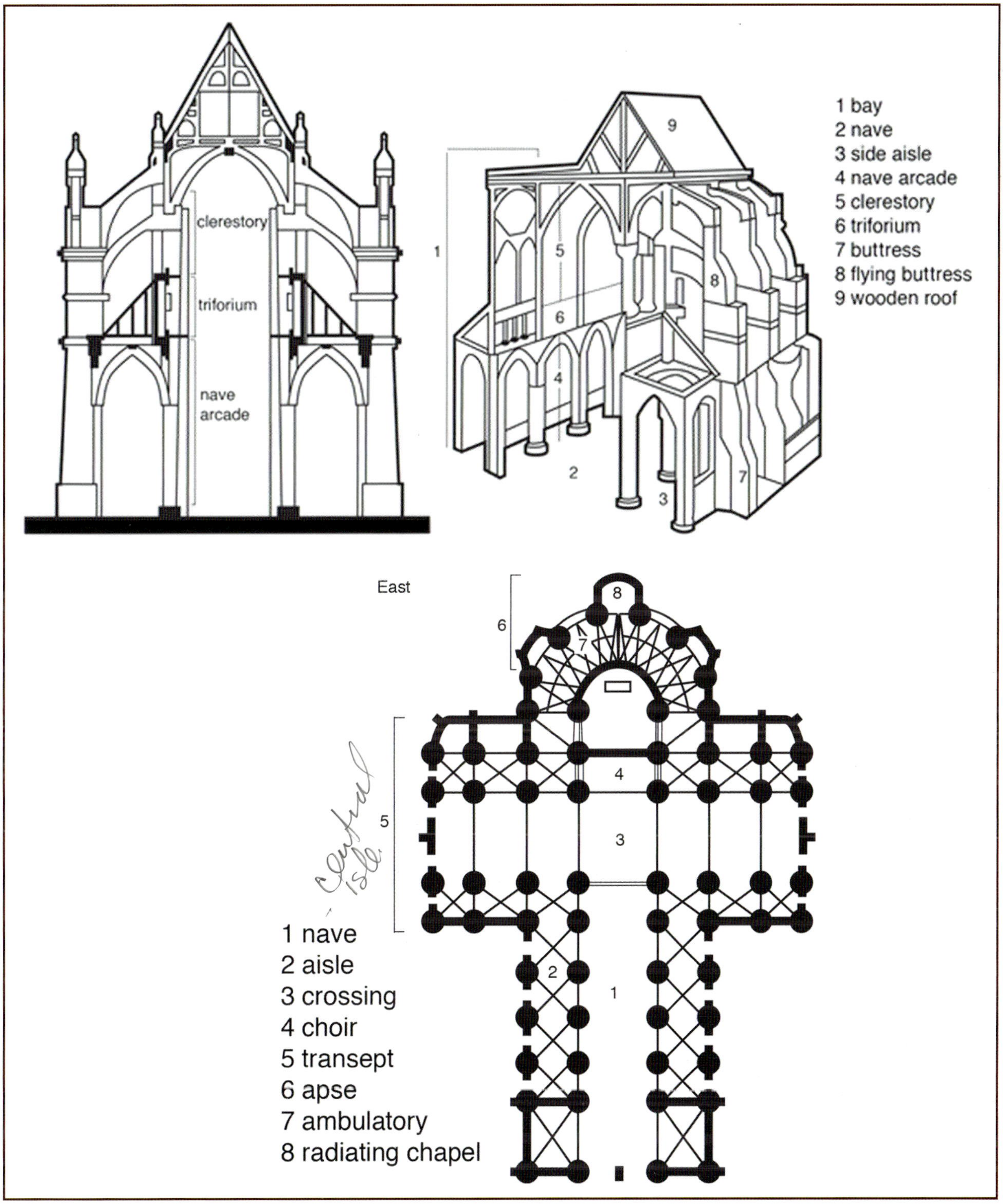

fig. 13.13 The Gothic Cathedral.

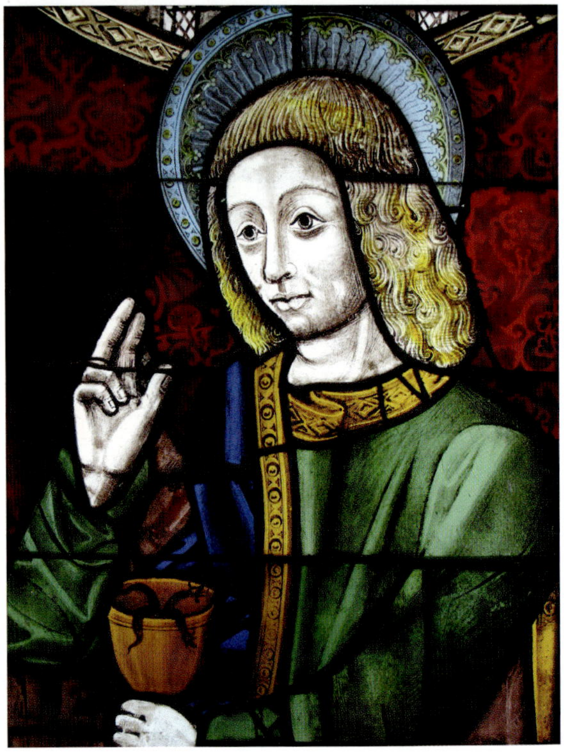

fig. 13.14 Stained and painted glass window depicting St. John the Evangelist, French, c. 1380–1410. The small pieces of colored glass are held in place by strips of lead and supported by a rigid frame.

flying buttresses. These advances meant that the walls were no longer the main load-bearing structure of the church as in the Romanesque era. They could now open walls up with large windows of **stained glass** that not only let in light, but gave the interior a spiritual quality as the colored light filtered down (see figs. 13.14 and 13.16a).

Cathedrals were places of great civic pride for the communities that erected them, and a competition developed for ever taller structures. The Cathedral at Beauvais, France, finally reached the physical limit of approximately 150 feet when the vault collapsed. (The tallest successful Gothic vault is 144 feet at Amiens Cathedral.) Cathedrals were expensive undertakings and often took many years to complete, sometime centuries. The cathedral chapter collected donations from rich and poor alike, and they might even tour church relics to raise funds. The exteriors of early Gothic churches remained relatively plain, but they soon became more elaborate with many sculptures and large circular stained glass windows (called rose windows because of their delicate tracery.)

Reims Cathedral is a good example of the High Gothic style that arose in the thirteenth century. The elaborate façade (fig. 13.15) seems to dissolve in arched openings, stained glass windows and sculptural figures. A gallery of ornate niches that contain figures of kings connects the two tall towers. Below that is a large **rose window** flanked by tall narrow openings with pointed arches that allow a view through the towers. Three portals defined by tall pinnacles filled with sculpted scenes are at ground level. Interestingly, the traditional sculpted tympanum has given way to stained glass. All three tympana above the doorways are stained glass. (Refer to fig. 13.16a to see what the large central rose window looks like from the inside.)

Four doorjamb sculptures (fig. 13.17) illustrate the *Annunciation* and the *Visitation*. The figures are nearly fully carved in the round and stand on pedestals in front of Corinthian-like columns. The Angel of the *Annunciation* is tall and elongated with a small head, and it has a slight sway to the body. Mary is more erect with simpler carving of the face and drapery. The *Visitation* depicts both Mary and Elizabeth in approximate contrapposto poses with classical-looking drapery that begins to reveal the body underneath. This recalls ancient Greek sculpture (see fig. 9.7). These three distinct figure styles indicate the involvement of three different sculptors. The sculptor of the angel maintains the current courtly Gothic figure style seen in paintings of the time, while the sculptor of the Visitation group clearly must have seen sculptures from antiquity. What is new here is the communication among the characters. The figures in both groups turn and gesture toward each other. (Watch the video clip on Reims Cathedral on the Kendall Hunt website for this book.)

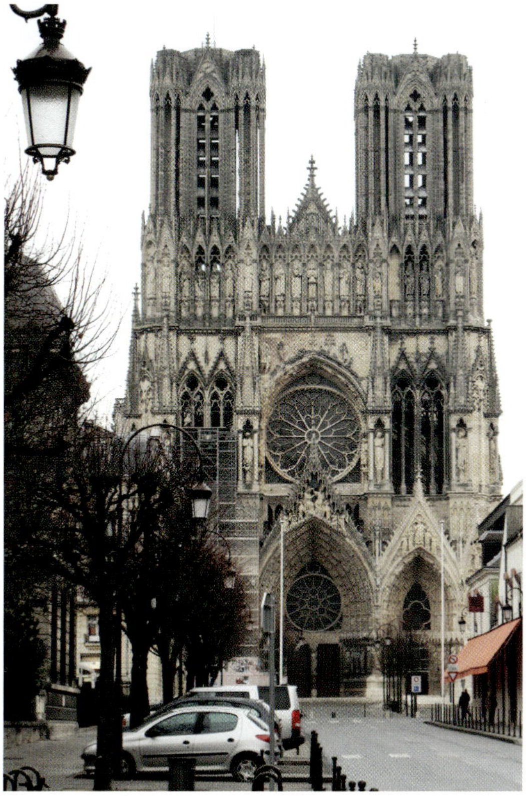

fig. 13.15a Reims Cathedral, Reims, France: Façade c. 1211–1290.

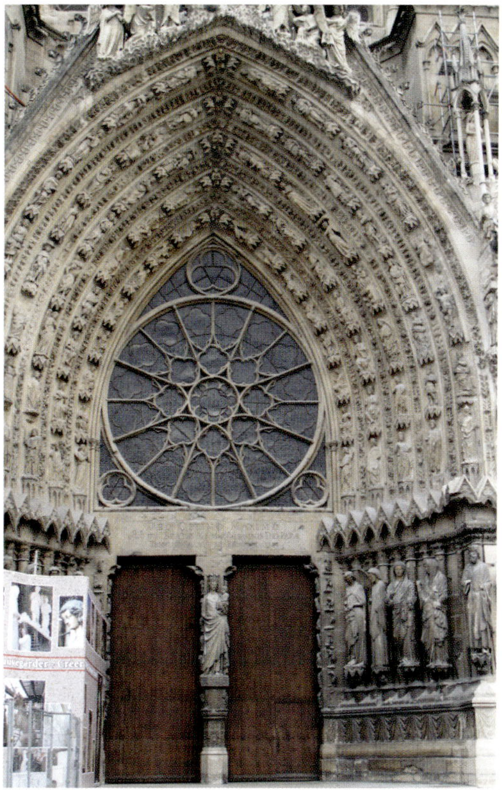

fig. 13.15b Central Portal of Reims Cathedral with rose window. The Annunciation and Visitation figures are on the right doorjamb.

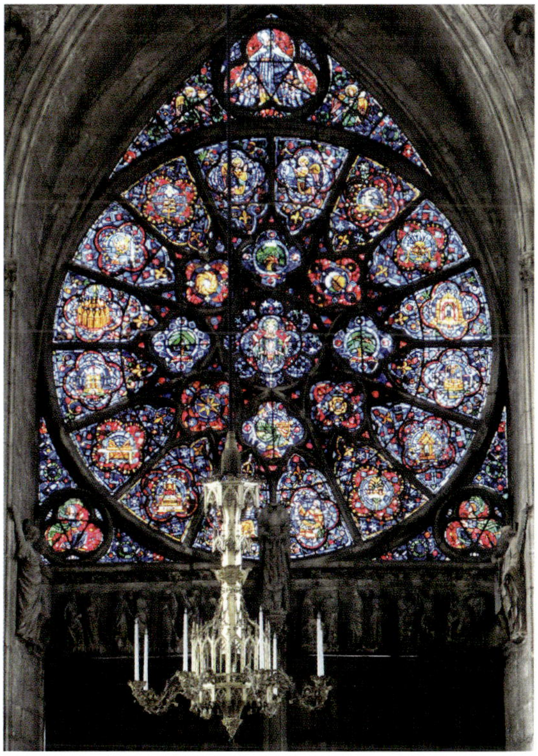

fig. 13.16a Rose window of the central portal seen from the inside.

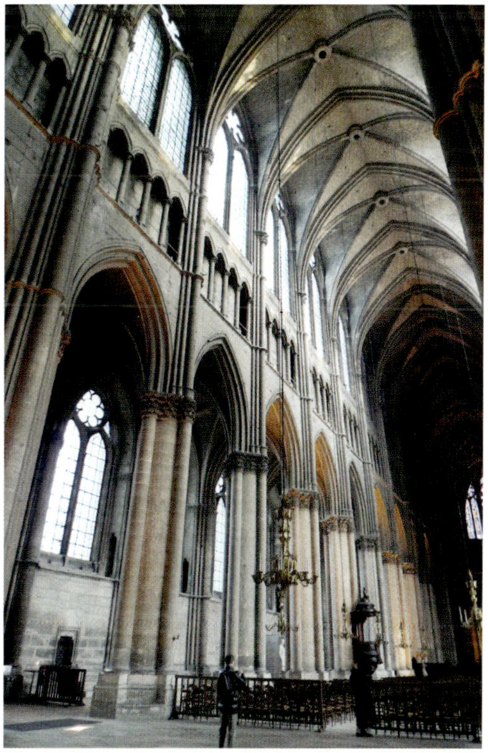

fig. 13.16b Nave of Reims Cathedral

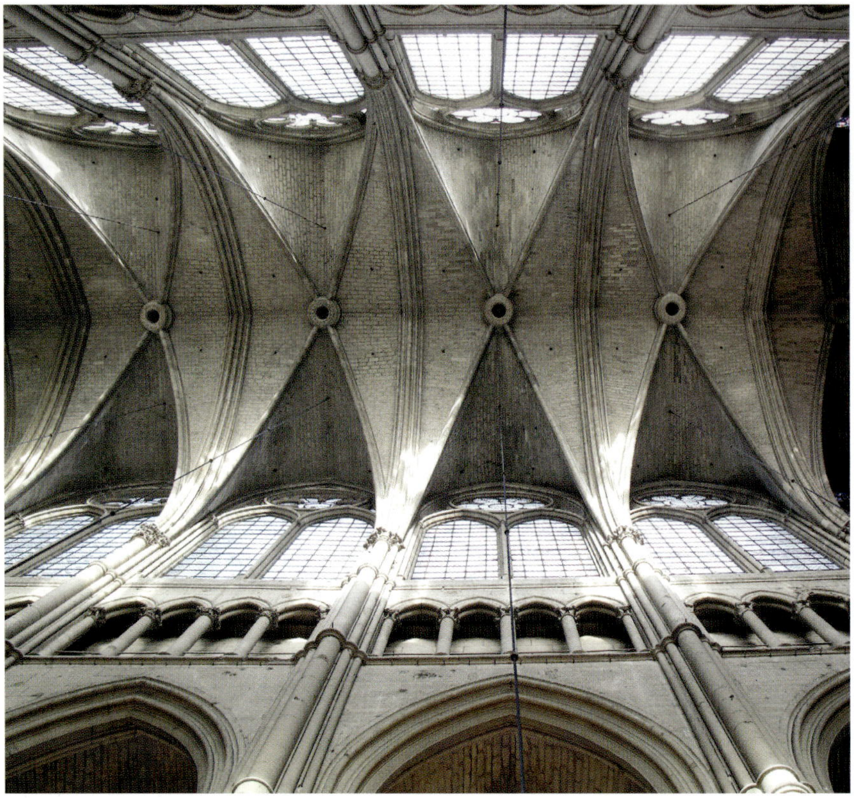

fig. 13.16c Nave vault of Reims Cathedral showing ribbed groin vaults.

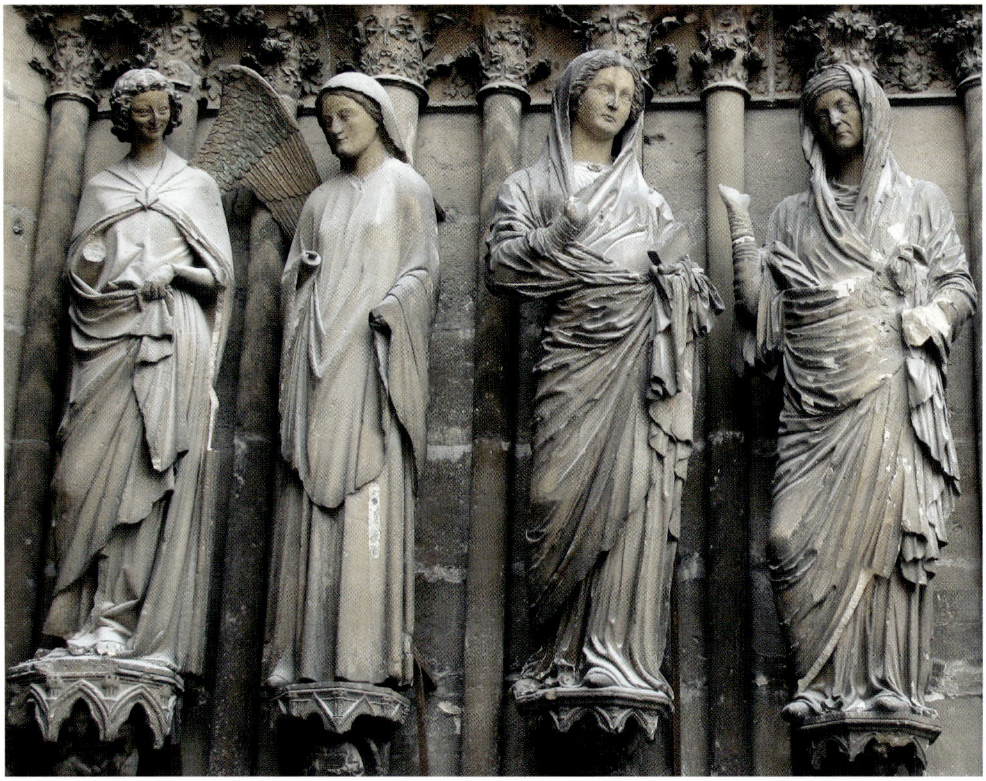

figs. 13.17 Reims: Exterior sculpture: *Annunciation* and *Visitation* from the doorjambs of Reims Cathedral. In the Annunciation, the angel Gabriel tells Mary that she will bear Christ. In the Visitation, a pregnant Mary visits her cousin Elizabeth, who is pregnant with John the Baptist, Jesus' second cousin and playmate, c. 1225–1255.

CHRISTIAN RELIGION

Attributes are in *italics*.

Abraham: founder of the Hebrew people and the first of the great Hebrew patriarchs; lived in the 18th century BCE.

St. Anne: mother of the Virgin Mary.

Apostles: Twelve disciples of Christ: Peter (*keys, upside down cross, cock*), Andrew (*X-shaped cross*), John (*chalice with snake, eagle, book*), Matthew (*angel, axe, book*), Thomas (*set-square, ruler, girdle, spear or dagger*), Bartholomew (*knife, his skin*), James the Greater (*scallop shell, sword, staff*), James the Less (*fuller's club, hatter's bow*), Simon (*saw, cross)*, Philip (*cross*), Thaddeus [Jude] (*club, halberd or lance*), and Judas (*bag of silver coins, dark profile*)

St. Catherine: early Christian saint from Alexandria. *Spiked wheel*

St. Cecilia: patron saint of music. *Organ*

Christ: see Jesus.

Constantine: 4th-century Roman emperor who legalized Christianity.

David: 10th-century BCE shepherd boy who killed Goliath and later became the second king of the Israel. *Harp, crown*

Deësis: Christ enthroned between the Virgin Mary and John the Baptist.

Dormition: the death (or sleep) of the Virgin.

Ecce Homo = Latin for "Behold the Man."

Elizabeth: cousin of the Virgin Mary and mother of John the Baptist.

Evangelists, Four: Authors of the Gospels: Matthew (*book, angel, axe*), Mark, (*book, winged lion*), Luke (*book, winged ox; patron saint of painters*), and John (*book, eagle, chalice with snake*).

St. Francis: 13th-century founder of Franciscan Order. *Stigmata (the wounds of Christ)*

Gabriel: archangel who announced to Mary that she would bear the son of God.

Goliath: Philistine giant warrior who threatened the Israelites.

Holofernes: Assyrian general who laid siege to the Jewish town of Bethulia. He was killed by Judith.

Iconostasis: a screen bearing icons; it separates the sanctuary from the nave.

IC XC: first and last letters of Jesus (Ihcuc) and Christ (Xpictoc) in Greek.

IHS or IHC: first three letters of Jesus's name in Greek (Ihsus or Ihcuc).

INRI: The first letters of the four Latin words Jesus Nazarenus Rex Judaeorum (Jesus of Nazareth King of the Jews)

Isaac: son of Abraham and father of Jacob.

Jacob: son of Isaac and father of Joseph.

St. James: one of the 12 apostles, and brother of John the Evangelist. In the Middle Ages legends arose that he traveled to Spain to spread the word of Christ. *Sword, broad-brimmed hat, scallop shell*

St. Jerome: translator of Bible into Latin. *Lion, cardinal's hat*

Jesus (Jesus of Nazareth, Jesus Christ): Central figure in Christianity. Considered by Christians to be the son of God and the Virgin Mary who provides humankind with salvation. *Halo with inscribed cross*

St. John the Baptist: last of Old Testament prophets. *Tunic of animal skins, honeycomb, lamb* ("Ecce Agnus Dei" = Behold the Lamb of God)

John the Evangelist: youngest of the 12 apostles and one of the four evangelists. In art he is often depicted at the Crucifixion with Mary.

Joseph (1): son of Jacob; sold into slavery.

Joseph (2): husband of the Virgin Mary and step father of Jesus. *Carpenter's tools, flowering rod*

Judith: Jewish heroine who slew the Assyrian general, **Holofernes**, by decapitating him with his own sword.

Martyr: one who suffers death for his or her faith.

Mary Magdalene: traditionally a repentant sinner who washes Christ's feet with her tears. Recently, it has been proposed she was a female apostle. *Jar, skull*

Moses: 13th-century BCE leader and lawgiver who led the Jews out of Egyptian captivity and founded the Israelite nation. He received the Ten Commandments from God. *Rod or wand, tablets*

Pantocrator: "Ruler of All;" Christ as Ruler and Judge.

St. Paul: apostle, but not one of the original twelve. He was a 1st-century Jewish tentmaker named Saul who was converted to Christianity and then began using his Roman name. *Sword*

Sacrament: a Christian rite conferring grace. The seven sacraments are Baptism, Confession, Confirmation, Eucharist [Mass], Holy Orders, Matrimony, and Extreme Unction.

Sins, Seven Deadly: Lust, Gluttony, Envy, Anger, Sloth, Pride, Greed [Avarice].

Theodosius: Byzantine emperor who abolished the Olympic Games and other pagan ceremonies in 393 CE

Virtues: The **Theological Virtues** are Faith, Hope, and Charity. The **Cardinal Virtues** are Justice, Fortitude [Strength], Temperance, and Prudence.

GIOTTO

The innovative Italian painter Giotto di Bondone (c. 1267–1337) led the way from the Gothic style to the Renaissance. Because we are accustomed today to super realistic paintings and photography, Giotto's works may seem a bit primitive to us, but in his day his paintings were a revelation. He left behind the stylization of Byzantine art and created paintings with natural backgrounds; more rational space; fuller bodied, better-proportioned figures; and more realistic drapery. Many of his works also show human emotion.

Giotto was commissioned to decorate the Arena Chapel in Padua with a series of **frescoes** depicting the life of Christ. In the *Lamentation* (figs. 13.18 and 13.19) we see Mary cradling her dead son in her arms (just as she did when he was a baby) after his removal from the cross. A more naturalistic blue background replaces the gold background of the Byzantine style. The figures appear to have real weight to them, and two of them appear with their backs to us, a novelty at the time. We see grief clearly indicated in the faces of Mary, the other mourners and the angels above, some of whom pull their hair or wring their hands in despair. Although the space is shallow because the sloping rock behind the figures limits it, the overlapping figures and the **foreshortening** of the angels' bodies above clearly indicate depth. The use of light and shade also adds to the illusion of three-dimensionality. Giotto was one of the first artists since antiquity to really observe nature and to attempt to produce an optically faithful representation of it.

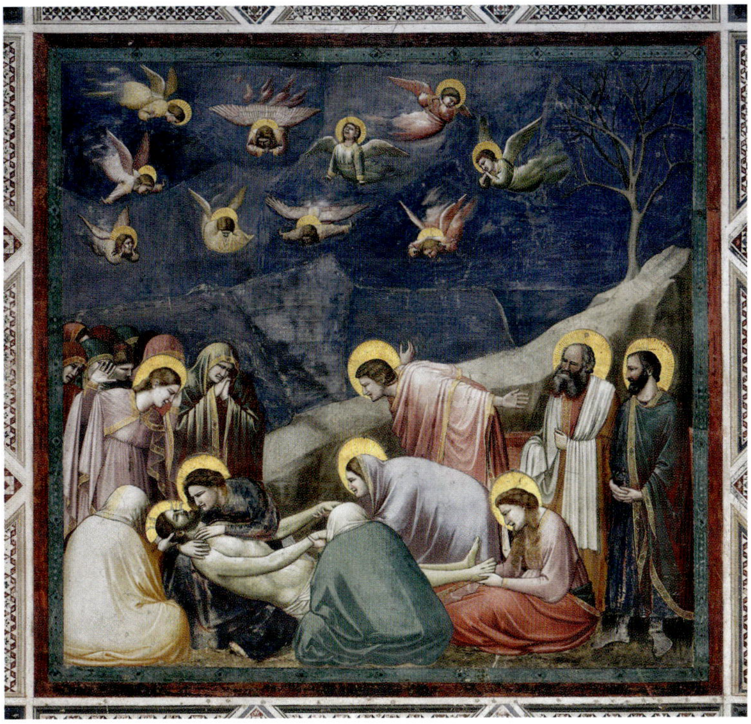

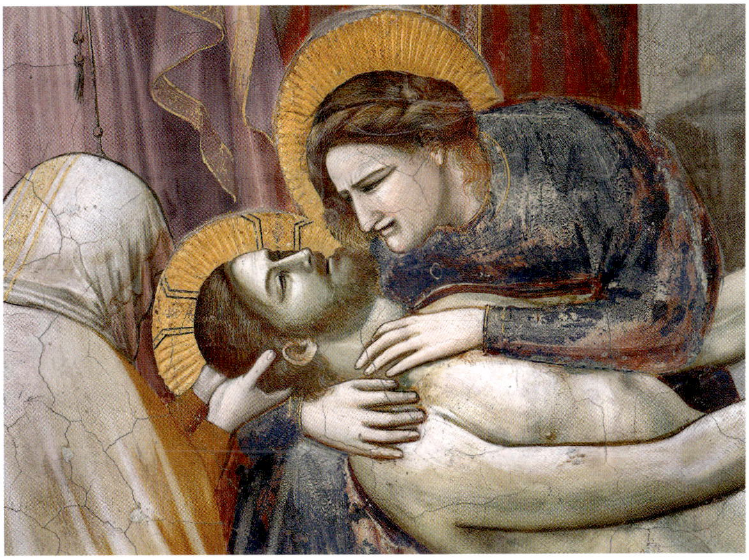

figs. 13.18 and 13.19 Giotto, *Lamentation* from the Arena Chapel in Padua, Italy, c. 1305.

The composition is well designed for the greatest dramatic impact. Everything leads our eye to the focal point of Christ's and Mary's haloed heads. John the **Evangelist** leans toward Christ with his arms outstretched. All the figures look at Christ, and the rock (with its symbolic dead tree) slopes down to him. Giotto's breakthroughs were enormously influential in the development of the later Renaissance style.

SCENES FROM THE LIFE OF CHRIST

EARLY LIFE (scenes of Jesus' incarnation and childhood).

Annunciation: The archangel Gabriel comes to Mary and tells her she will bear the son of God.

Visitation: Mary, pregnant with Jesus, visits her cousin Elizabeth, who is pregnant with John the Baptist.

Nativity: The Holy Family (Mary, Joseph, and the infant Christ) are shown in a stable or cave in Bethlehem.

Annunciation to the Shepherds and the Adoration of the Shepherds: Angels announce the birth of Christ to shepherds in the fields who then go to Bethlehem to adore him.

The Adoration of the Magi: Three wise men from the East follow a star to Bethlehem where they present the baby Jesus with gifts of gold, frankincense, and myrrh. (Frankincense and myrrh are fragrant gum resins from trees.) The magi were later named as Caspar (the oldest), Balthazar (a middle-aged black man), and Melchior (the youngest).

The Circumcision: A priest circumcises the eight-day-old Christ and gives him the name Jesus.

Presentation in the Temple: When Jesus is forty days old, Mary and Joseph bring the baby to the Temple in Jerusalem and present him to the high priest.

Flight into Egypt: The Holy Family leaves Bethlehem to escape the massacre of male infants ordered by King Herod. Mary and Jesus are shown on a donkey as they flee to Egypt.

Christ among the Elders: Twelve-year-old Jesus discusses issues with Jewish scholars in the temple in Jerusalem.

PUBLIC MINISTRY (scenes of Jesus' teachings and miracles)

Marriage at Cana: As his first miracle, Christ turns water into wine at a wedding feast.

The Cleansing of the Temple: Christ angrily evicts the money changers from the temple.

The Baptism: Christ is baptized by his cousin, John the Baptist, in the Jordan River.

The Miraculous Draft of Fishes: Jesus causes a great many fish to be caught by Peter in the Lake of Gennesaret (the Sea of Galilee).

Christ Walking on the Water: Jesus walks on the water toward a boat with the apostles during a storm in the Sea of Galilee.

The Calling of Levi (Matthew): Christ calls upon the tax collector Levi to follow him.

The Raising of Lazarus: Jesus brings his friend Lazarus back to life after he had been dead for four days.

The Transfiguration: Christ reveals his divinity on Mt. Tabor to Peter, James, and John.

The Tribute Money: When asked to pay the temple tax, Jesus asks Peter to catch a fish, which has the necessary coin in its mouth.

THE PASSION (scenes related to Christ's death and resurrection)

Entry into Jerusalem: Jesus rides a donkey into Jerusalem on Palm Sunday.

The Last Supper: At a Passover dinner Jesus reveals his impending death to his disciples.

Jesus Washing the Apostles' Feet: After the Last Supper, Jesus washes the apostles' feet.

Christ in the Garden of Gethsemane (The Agony in the Garden): In a garden on the Mount of Olives, Jesus agonizes over his fear of death.

Christ before Pilate: Christ is questioned by Pontias Pilate, the Roman governor of Judea, who charges him with treason.

The Flagellation (The Scourging): Christ is whipped by Roman soldiers.

The Mocking of Christ and Ecce Homo: Roman soldiers dress Christ in a royal robe and a crown of thorns and mock him as the King of the Jews. Afterwards he is shown to the people (*Ecce Homo,* which means Behold the Man).

Bearing the Cross: Christ is forced to carry the instrument of his death to the place of his execution.

The Crucifixion: Christ is nailed to a cross and left to die on a hill called Golgotha.

The Descent from the Cross (The Deposition): Christ's followers, including Joseph of Arimathea and Nicodemus, remove him from the cross.

The Lamentation (Pietà): Christ's followers mourn him. If Mary is shown alone holding her dead son in her lap, it is called the pietà.

The Entombment: Christ is laid to rest in a stone tomb.

The Resurrection: Christ rises from his tomb three days after his death while the Roman guards sleep.

Noli me tangere (Do not touch me): After his resurrection, Christ appears to Mary Magdalene and tells her not to touch him when she reaches toward him.

Supper at Emmaus: After his resurrection, Christ shares a meal with two disciples, who at first do not realize who he is.

The Doubting Thomas (The Incredulity of Thomas): After his resurrection, Christ tells Thomas, who doubts it is Christ, to examine the wound on his side as proof.

The Ascension: Forty days after his resurrection, Christ ascends to heaven.

SUMMARY

The **Middle Ages** refers to the period between the fall of the Roman Empire in the fifth century and the advent of the Renaissance around 1400. Christianity replaced the panoply of Roman gods. This process began with the Emperor Constantine in the early fourth century.

Byzantine Period: In 330 Constantine moved the capital from Rome to Byzantium in what is now Turkey. (He renamed the city Constantinople after himself; today it is called Istanbul.) In the west Rome fell in 476, but the eastern Byzantine empire thrived and persisted until it fell to the Turks in 1453. The realistic illusionism of the Greco-Roman period disappears in the Byzantine era. Figures become elongated, drapery folds become linear, and there is little recession into space. Often figures are shown against a flat gold background, as seen in the mosaic of Emperor Justinian and his attendants in the church of San Vitale.

Early Middle Ages: In the West, Germanic tribes overrun Roman Europe. Art becomes portable because people are on the move. Stylized animals in interlacing patterns become popular decoration, as seen in the purse lid from Sutton Hoo and the cross page from the Lindisfarne Gospels.

Islamic Art: Islam begins its great rise in the seventh century and Islamic culture soon dominates the Middle East, North Africa, and Spain. Because of religious restrictions, the human figure is rarely seen in Islamic art; instead Islamic artists concentrate on calligraphy and plant forms. Cordoba, Spain, becomes the greatest city in Europe and is home to a great mosque, which still stands.

Romanesque Art: By 1100 Europe is coalescing into the countries that are familiar to us today. Monumental church building is re-established. Large churches made of stone have intricately carved scenes over the entrances. The round arches found in many of these buildings recall ancient Roman architecture. Sculpted figures become larger, but are still stylized. The famous Leaning Tower of Pisa (actually a bell tower for the Pisa cathedral) is from this era.

Gothic Art: The Gothic period begins around 1150 in France and lasts until about 1500 in many parts of Europe. Churches become taller and display more elaborate sculptural carving. The incredible height of these churches is made possible by the use of flying buttresses, which help distribute the weight of the vaults away from the walls of the church. This allows the walls to be pierced with large windows filled with stained glass. Sculpted figures become larger and more lifelike, as seen in the figures on the exterior of Reims cathedral in France.

In painting, the Italian artist Giotto makes a great leap forward. He is the first artist to leave the Byzantine style behind and begin to portray human figures in a more natural way. The people in his paintings have real bulk, show emotion, and inhabit a more rational and naturalistic space, as seen his *Lamentation*.

PRONUNCIATION GUIDE

Bayeux (bay-**yoo** or bay-**yer**)
Byzantine (**biz**-uhn-teen)
Campanile (com-pah-**nee**-lay)
Cloisonné (kloy-za-**nay** or klwa-zo-**nay**)
Façade (fuh-**sahd**)
Giotto (**jot**-toh or joht-toh)
Hierarchical (high-uh-**rahr**-kih-kuhl)
Hieratic (high-uh-**rat**-ik)
Mihrab (**mee**-rahb)
Mosque (mosk)
Pendentive (pen-**den**-tiv)
Reims (reems)
Reliquary (**rel**-ih-kwair-ee)
San Vitale (sahn vih-**tah**-lee)
Tesserae (**tes**-uh-rye or **tes**-uh-ree)
Triptych (**trip**-tik)
Zeus (zoos)

GLOSSARY

Ambulatory. In a church, a continuation of the side aisles that becomes a passageway around the apse.

Apostles. The twelve disciples of Christ (attributes in parentheses): Peter (keys, upside down cross, cock), Andrew (X-shaped cross), John (chalice with snake, eagle, book), Matthew (angel, axe, book), Thomas (set-square, ruler, girdle, spear or dagger), Bartholomew (knife, his skin), James the Greater (scallop shell, sword, staff), James the Less (fuller's club, hatter's bow), Simon (saw, cross), Philip (cross), Thaddeus [Jude] (club, halberd or lance), and Judas (bag of silver coins, dark profile)

Apse. A semicircular projection of a building, especially in a church.

Arcade. A series of arches on columns or piers.

Barrel vault. A semi cylindrical roof constructed on the arch principle. It is essentially a deep arch over an oblong space

Basilica. A Roman hall of justice, later an early Christian church.

Buttress. A mass of masonry against the wall of a building to help support a vault. In Gothic cathedrals, flying buttresses are external supports that counteract the forces of the vault above the level of the aisles.

Byzantine. The period from the time of the Roman emperor Constantine who moved the capital from Rome to Byzantium (now Istanbul) in the fourth century to 1453, when the Turks conquered the city.

Campanile. A church bell tower that is a separate structure.

Central plan. In architecture, a building with a central space surrounded by symmetrical areas.

Cloisonné. A metalwork technique wherein small compartments (made by soldering metal strips on the edges of a metal background) are filled with enamel or glass.

Dome. A roof with a hemispherical shape.

Embroidery. The art of sewing colored threads (needlework) onto fabric to form a design or composition.

Eucharist. The sacrament of Holy Communion to commemorate the Last Supper, or the bread and wine used for the sacrament.

Evangelists, The Four. Authors of the Gospels: Matthew, Mark, Luke, and John. They are often accompanied by their symbols: Angel (Matthew), lion (Mark), ox (Luke), and eagle (John). Luke is the patron saint of painters.

Façade. The front of a building.

Foreshortening. The illusion of figures or objects extending back from the picture plane by diminishing the size of their parts.

Fresco. A painting on plaster. With true fresco (*buon fresco*) the paint is applied while the plaster is still wet and it chemically binds with the plaster. With dry fresco (*fresco secco*), the paint is applied to plaster that has already dried.

Gild. To apply thin sheets of gold leaf to a surface.

Gothic. An art historical period from about 1150 to 1500 in Europe (to 1400 in Italy). In architecture, it is characterized by pointed arches.

Goths. Germanic tribe that settled north of the Black Sea in the 3d century. They split into the Visigoths and the Ostrogoths; the latter conquered Italy in the 5th century. The term Gothic derives from their name.

Groin vault. A vault formed by the intersection of two barrel vaults.

Ground plan. The floor plan of a building.

Hierarchical or hieratic scale. Depicting more important figures larger than less important ones.

IHS or IHC. First 3 letters of Christ's name in Greek (Ihsus or Ihcuc).

Illumination. See Manuscript.

INRI. Latin initials for *Jesus Nazarenus Rex Judaeorum* (Jesus of Nazareth King of the Jews).

Jamb. In architecture, a vertical element on either side of a doorway.

Kufic. Relating to or being an angular form of the Arabic alphabet used by early Muslims to record the Qur'an.

Latin cross plan. An architectural plan in the form of a cross that has one arm longer than the other three.

Lintel. The upper horizontal portion of a doorway or opening.

Longitudinal plan. An architectural plan in which the parts of the building are organized around a central axis.

Manuscript. A handwritten book made in the Middle Ages or Renaissance. If it has illustrations, it is called an illuminated manuscript.

Martyr. Someone who dies for their faith.

Middle Ages. The period in western history from the fall of the Roman empire in the late 5th century to the Renaissance in the 15th century.

Mosaic. A decoration composed of small pieces of colored glass, stone or other material.

Mosque. A place of prayer in the Islamic religion. The word derives from the Arabic for "place of prostration."

Narthex. The lobby or entrance area to a church.

Nave. The central aisle of a church that leads to the altar.

Parchment. Treated animal skin prepared as a surface for painting or writing.

Pendentive. A dome on pendentives is as though you cut off the top of a groin vault and place the dome on top. The triangular areas left are the pendentives.

Pigment. A powdered material used to give color to inks and paints.

Pilaster. A flat vertical element projecting from a wall. It usually does not have a supporting function.

Relic. A body part, article of clothing, a piece of an instrument of martyrdom or other item associated with a saint. They are often thought to have special powers to heal the body and the soul.

Rib. In architecture, a structural element that helps support a groin vault.

Romanesque. An artistic style of the Middle Ages that preceded the Gothic style. In architecture it was characterized by round arches and barrel vaults.

Rose window. A large circular window decorated with stained glass in a petal-like pattern.

Stained glass. Windows made of pieces of colored glass held in place with lead strips.

Stylized. When the depiction of a figure or form departs from optical reality to conform to artistic conventions or to emphasize certain characteristics.

Tapestry. A design woven into a thick fabric with colored yarns.

Tempera. A type of paint in which the binding medium is egg yolk or casein.

Tesserae. Small cubes of stone, glass, etc., used in mosaic work.

Transept. The "arm" of a church that intersects the nave at a right angle.

Triptych. A panel painting in three sections. Often the two outer sections (wings) are smaller and hinged so that they can close over the larger central panel.

Tympanum. The semicircular area or lunette over the doorway of a church, defined by an arch above and a lintel below. It often contains sculpture.

Vault. An arched roof or ceiling usually made of stone, brick, or concrete. See also Barrel vault and Groin vault.

Vellum. A high quality parchment made from calfskin, kidskin, or lambskin.

NOTES

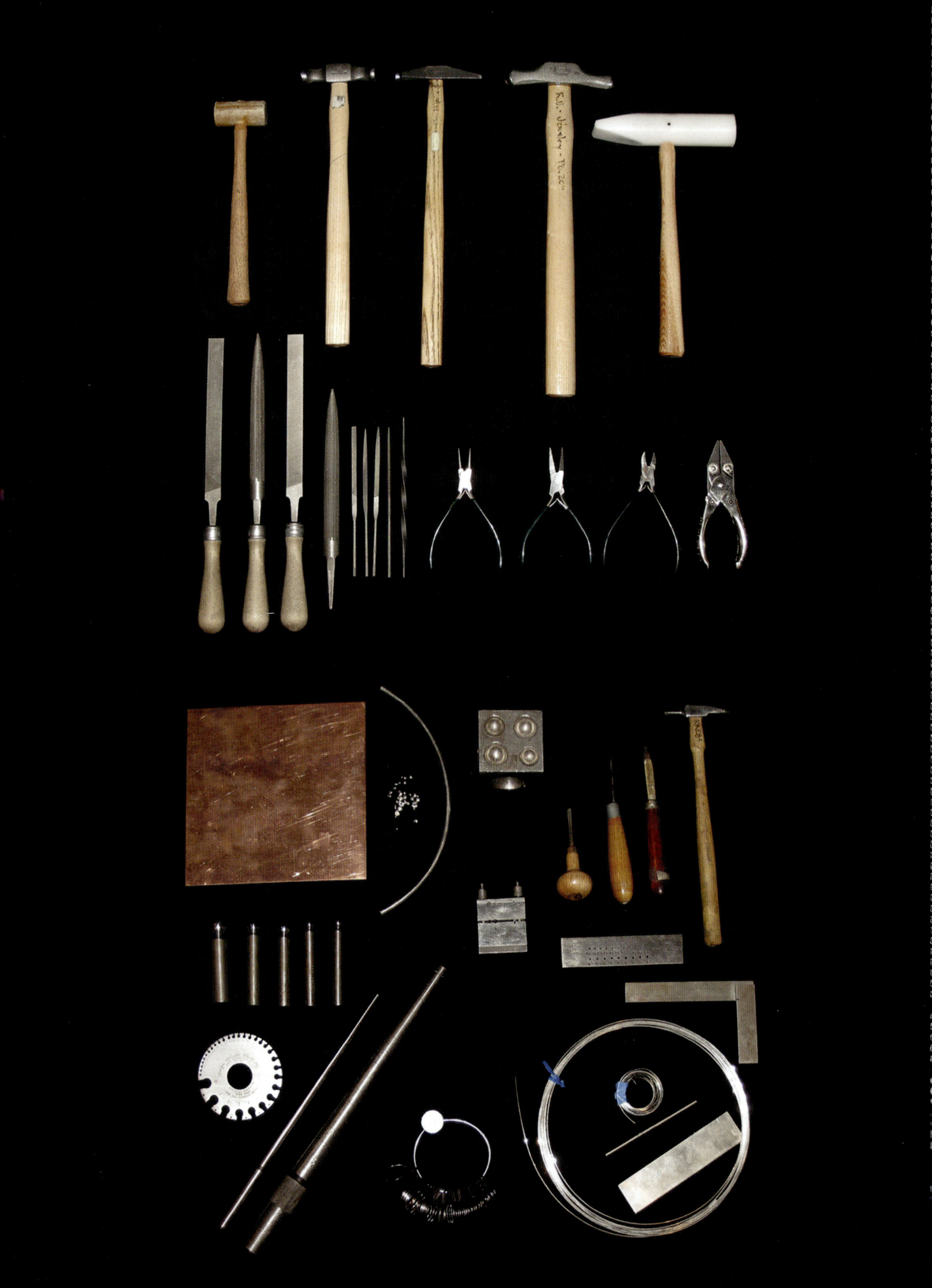

14

A battle has raged for centuries in the West between craft and art. Many people still consider crafts such as ceramics, jewelry and glass lesser arts than the fine arts of painting and sculpture because they often have a practical use and are often less expensive. Whereas the purpose of a painting or sculpture is display and contemplation, jewelers mean for a piece of jewelry to be worn, and potters intend for a ceramic bowl to be used in some manner. Many consider crafts merely decorative. This was not always the case. In ancient Greece vase painters were highly regarded, and in many non-Western cultures there is no difference between craft and art. There are many people in the West as well who put craft on an equal footing with the traditional fine arts. Artist Dorothy Gillespie displays her jewelry collection on the walls of her home along with her collection of prints. When she wants to wear a piece, she simply takes it off the wall and puts it on. Today, the distinction between high craft and art blurs ever more as artists create sophisticated and unique works in traditional craft media. Many of these pieces no longer have a functional use; instead their purpose is display and contemplation—and their prices rival those of the traditional fine arts.

FINE APPLIED ARTS

JEWELRY AND METALSMITHING

The majority of artists working in metal make jewelry. Humans have adorned themselves since prehistoric times with jewelry, and our fascination with it and desire for it have never waned. Travel to any place that caters to tourists and you may well find more jewelry stores than any other kind of store. The earliest jewelry consisted of strung beads and shells; in fact, a Neanderthal shell pendant dating from c.50,000 BCE may be the oldest piece of art we have. Once humans learned to extract and refine metal ores, gold and silver jewelry appeared. Setting precious and semi-precious stones into metal followed soon after.

Artists use various techniques and a variety of tools (fig. 14.1) to create jewelry and other works in metal, including casting, cutting, sawing, punching, hammering and filing. If an artist incorporates gemstones into a piece, they can be smooth and polished or cut using a faceting machine. Debra Hill Santos solid cast the band portion of her large ring entitled *Blue Anvil* (fig. 14.2) using the **lost wax technique**.

fig. 14.1 Jewelry and metalsmithing tools.

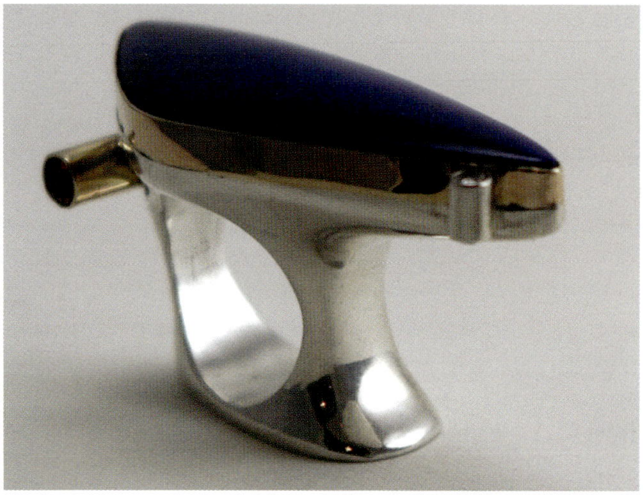

fig. 14.2 Debra Hill Santos, *Blue Anvil* (ring), 2006. Sterling silver and 14K gold structural ring featuring **lapis lazuli** accented with diamond, sapphire and synthetic padparadscha sapphires. Collection of the artist.

She polished the large stone using a tumbler, a machine that tumbles stones with a fine abrasive material, and then set it into the silver band.

Painter and sculptor Dorothy Gillespie (see page 121) also makes jewelry, which she calls portable sculpture. Her pendant (fig. 14.3) recalls her painted sculptures (see fig. 10.15), but instead of enamel paint on a large piece of aluminum the pendant is baked enamel on silver with a handmade silver link chain.

Some of the ancient techniques that survive today in jewelry and other metalwork are filigree, granulation and niello. With **filigree**, the artist intertwines and interlaces thin wires of silver or gold into delicate patterns, as seen in a silver cup from the Byzantine period (fig. 14.4). The intricate yet delicate complex patterns of silver wire are a testament to the silversmith's masterful skill.

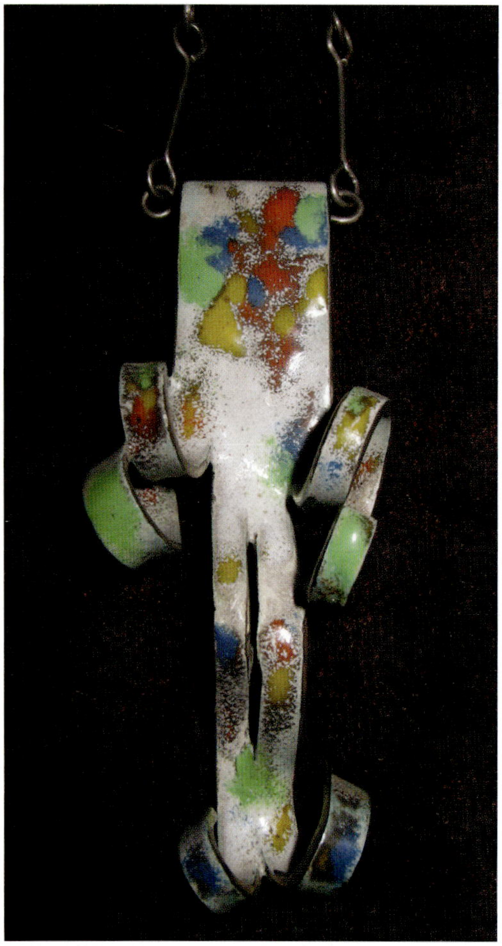

fig. 14.3 Dorothy Gillespie, Pendant, 2002. Baked enamel on silver, 3 in. × 1 in. Private collection.

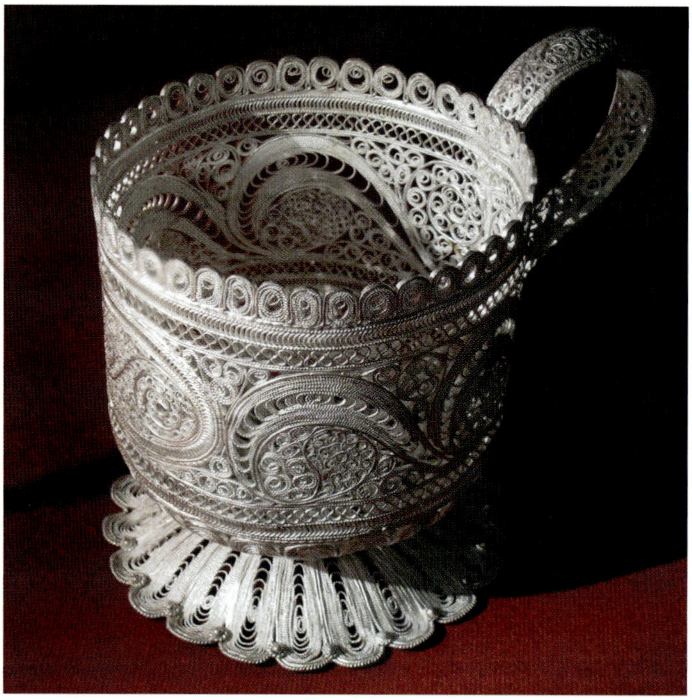

fig. 14.4 Cup, Byzantine. Silver filigree. Silver Museum, Ioannina, Greece.

Granulation is the soldering of tiny spheres of gold to a flat gold background. In the Minoan bee pendant (fig. 14.5), granulation forms the outlines of the bees' eyes and the dangling medallions, and it defines the segments of their bodies and the honeycomb between them. **Niello** is a process that darkens certain areas of silver objects, as seen in a bracelet from the Byzantine period (fig. 14.6). The contrast between the polished silver relief work and the dark niello inlay adds contrast and depth to the piece.

Alison Pack employs a variety of techniques and materials in her metalwork, which uses overt and subtle feminine forms. *L'il Birthday Girl* (fig. 14.7) is a pink-frosted birthday cake in the shape of a female form. Largely composed of painted copper, it also incorporates two kinds of silver. She cut and hand formed each piece and then soldered them together. The bottom border of the "girl cake" is twisted silver wire that doubles as a typical cake frosting trimming as well as the hem of the dress. The curvilinear shapes and patterns emphasize the feminine quality of the piece. (Watch the video clip on the Kendall Hunt Website for this book.)

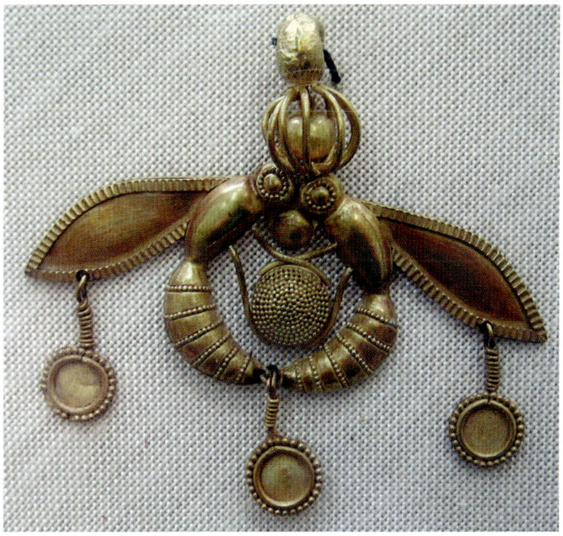

fig. 14.5 Bee pendant, c. 1600 BCE. Gold, 1.8 in. high. Archaeological Museum, Heraklion, Crete.

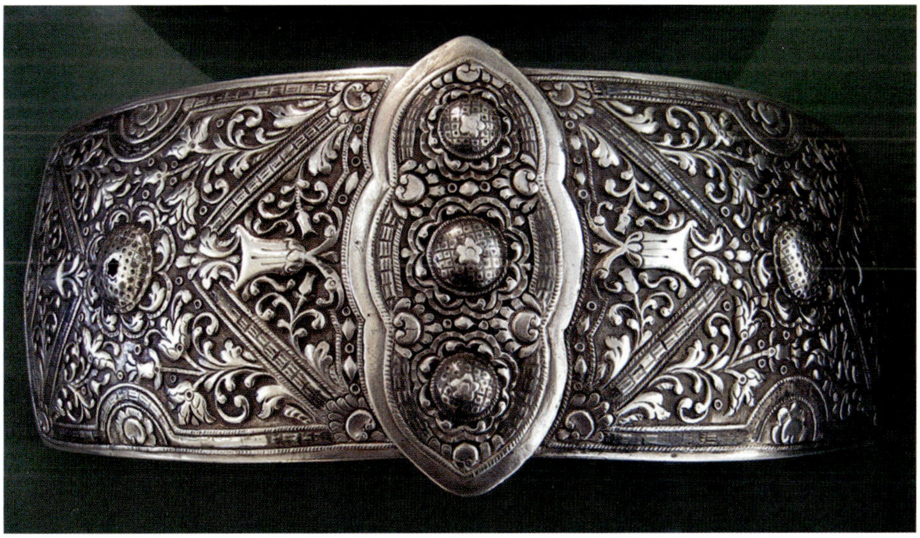

fig. 14.6 Bracelet, Byzantine. Silver with niello. Silver Museum, Ioannina, Greece.

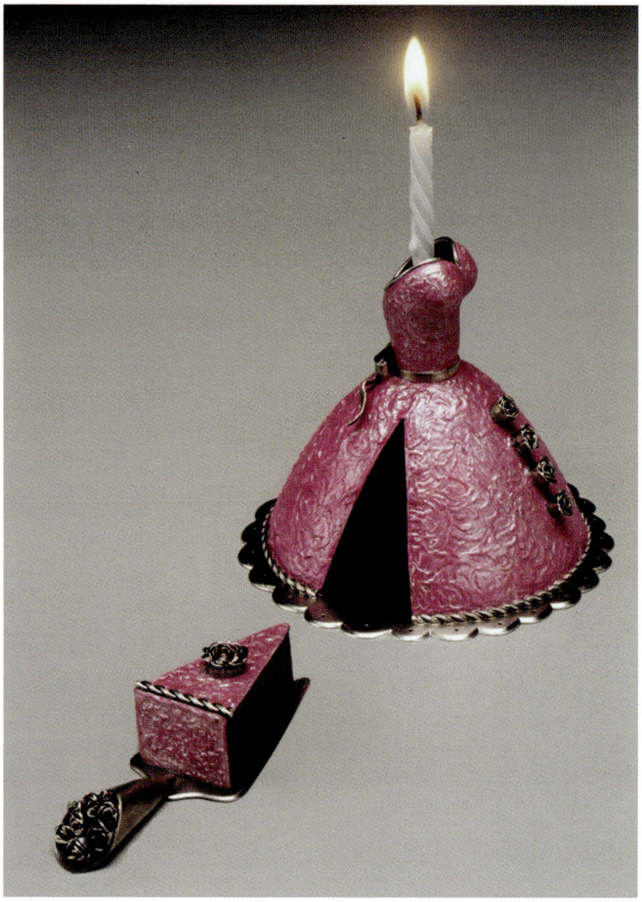

fig. 14.7 Alison Pack, *L'il Birthday Girl,* 2004. Copper, sterling silver, fine silver, acrylic paint and colored pencil, 5 in. tall.

CERAMICS

Ceramics refers to objects made of clay heated to a high temperature to harden them (firing). The word comes from the Greek word, *kerameikos,* which means "potter's clay." The term now includes "ceramics" made of materials that contain no clay. We cannot overstate the importance of **pottery** in human civilization. Pottery vessels not only provided their makers with useful (and often beautiful) objects, but discarded broken pieces of pottery (called potsherds or potshards) have proved invaluable to archaeologists. **Potsherds** (especially those with decoration) have taught us much about earlier cultures and have been crucial in helping to establish historical chronologies.

Before making a ceramic piece you have to rid the clay of air pockets. The artist does this by wedging the clay by hand (watch the video clip on the Kendall-Hunt Website for this book) or by letting a machine called a pugmill do it. Once the artist has de-aired the clay, he can form the object by hand with coils, slabs or balls of clay. He or she can then stick pieces of clay together with a mixture of clay and water called a slurry. The artist uses his hands alone to do much of the forming, but there are specialized tools that make the process easier (fig. 14.8).

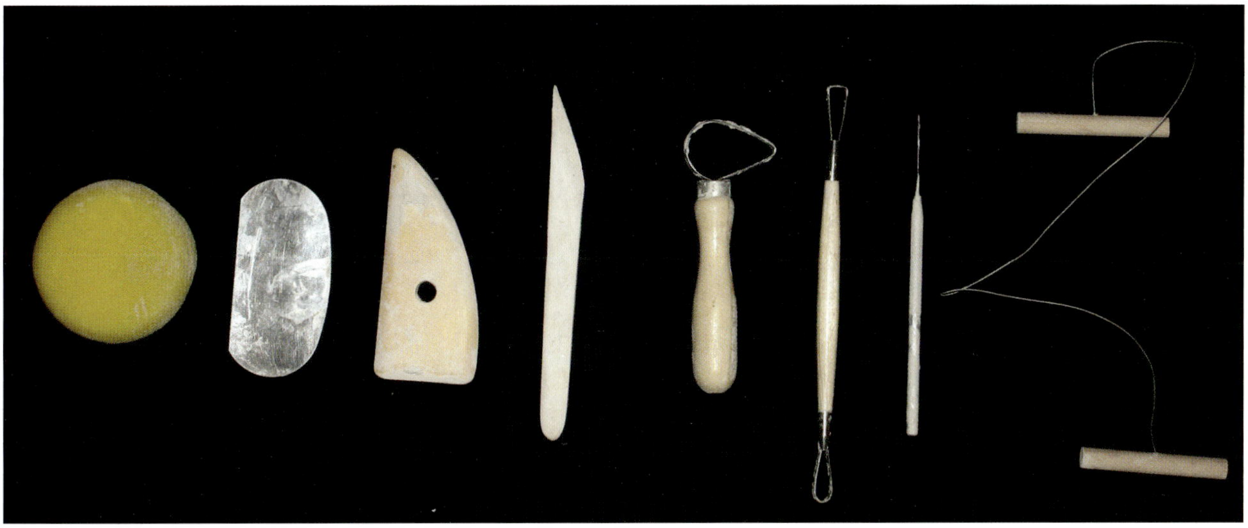

fig. 14.8 Ceramist tools.

Artists can also form clay using a potter's wheel in a process called throwing, invented in the Ancient Near East around 6,000 years ago. Modern potter's wheels are electric. The artist puts a ball of clay in the center of a turntable (the wheel), which rotates at various speeds. As the wheel rapidly turns, the artist presses, squeezes and pulls the clay into the desired form, often with the aid of ceramist tools (fig. 14.9). A wet sponge is one of the more useful tools. A skilled potter can "throw" a pot quite quickly (see the Website video clip). Forms produced on the potter's wheel are symmetrical, but the artist can modify them further by hand manipulation and by adding handles, lids, spouts and so forth.

After the artist forms the clay piece, it must dry completely; otherwise it will explode when fired. Most pieces are **bisque fired** and then glazed before being fired again. The glaze provides surface decoration and complements the form. Drew Dodson's *Striped Vase* (fig. 14.10) uses a metallic **glaze** applied in hard-edged strips to stress the vase's verticality and also to emphasize and contrast with the curvature of the body. Because glazes harden to a glass-like consistency when subjected to intense heat, they also have a practical function of making the vessel impervious to water. The **firing** process takes place in a **kiln** (fig. 14.11), which can attain the high temperatures required (anywhere from 1,000 to 1,400 degrees Celsius, depending on the kind of clay). Firings can take many hours or even days. The artist achieves various surface effects by controlling the amount of oxygen during the firing process and the length of the firing as well as by other techniques. The artist attains the crackled carbonized surface of Raku ware, for instance, by removing the pottery from the kiln while they are still hot and then smothering them in ashes or woodchips.

fig. 14.9 Throwing a vase on a potter's wheel.

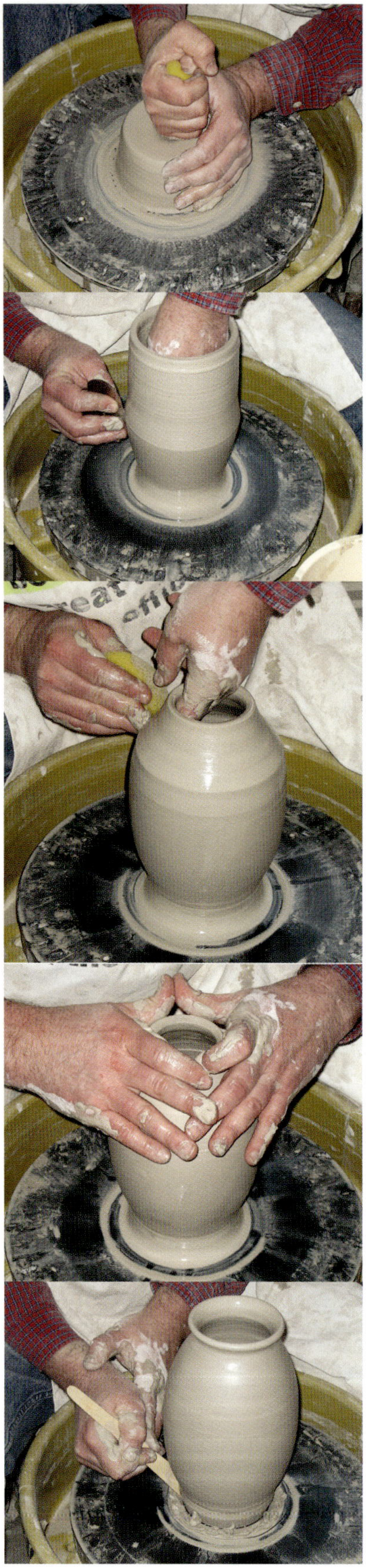

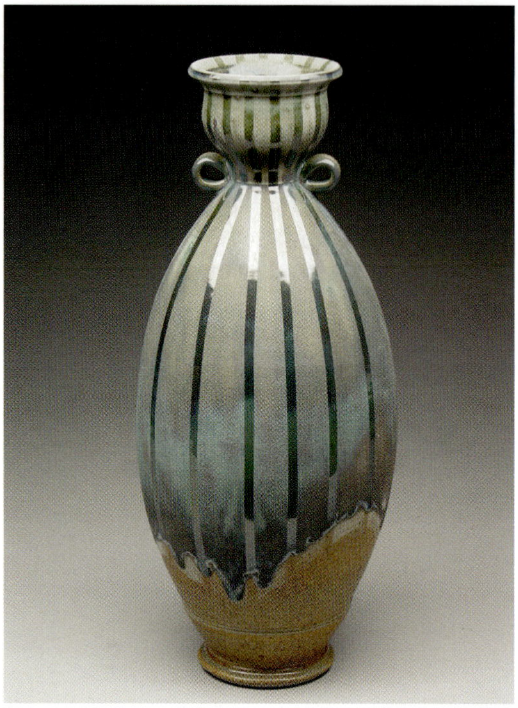

fig. 14.10 Drew Dodson, *Striped Vase,* 2008. Ceramic, 22 in. high.

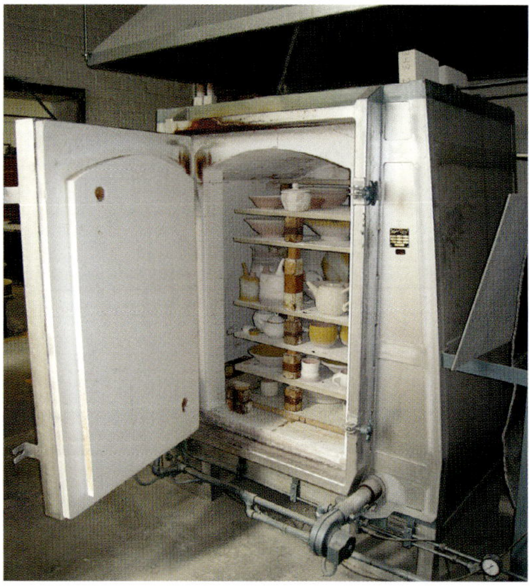

fig. 14.11 A gas kiln loaded with pottery.

GLASS

Glass is one of the most fascinating substances on earth. Its transparency, along with its reflective and refractive qualities, gives it a jewel-like appearance that is naturally appealing. The ancient Egyptians learned how to make glass, and people have treasured it ever since. Glass has been used for such vessels as goblets and perfume bottles as well as for jewelry. Artisans used colored glass set in lead to make the majestic **stained glass** windows of the Middle Ages (fig. 14.12). With increasing technical skill, artists create incredible forms and achieve spectacular effects with glass. Individuals and major museums now avidly collect glass, and there are museums dedicated solely to glass, such as the Corning Museum of Glass in Corning, New York.

Artists can blow, cast and shape molten glass by various methods to create almost any form desired. Because glass is actually a supercool liquid in its solid state, it does not crystallize when it cools, leaving it totally transparent. It takes sophisticated equipment and great skill to successfully work with molten glass on a large scale. The glass artist must work quickly before the glass cools too much and must have the strength to handle this heavy material. Artists who create large works of glass usually need assistants.

Josh Simpson creates miniature planets in spheres of glass at his studio in Massachusetts (fig. 14.13). They range in size from just an inch or two in diameter and weighing a few ounces to several feet and weighing hundreds of pounds. Each one is unique with the varying shapes and colors of its imbedded forms that beckon the viewer to peer into the tiny world and explore it in all its minute detail. You can view Simpson's working process on his Website (www.joshsimpson.com). Perhaps

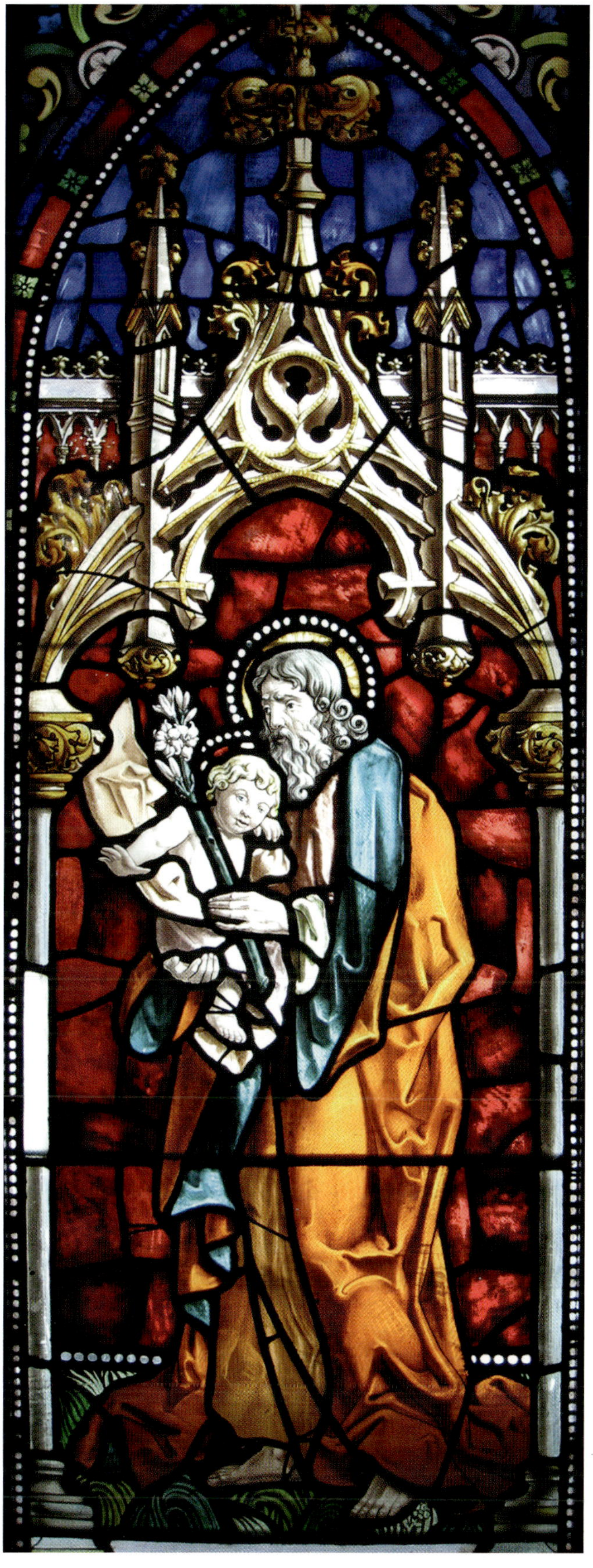

fig. 14.12 Stained glass window showing Joseph and the infant Jesus. San Gerónimo, Madrid.

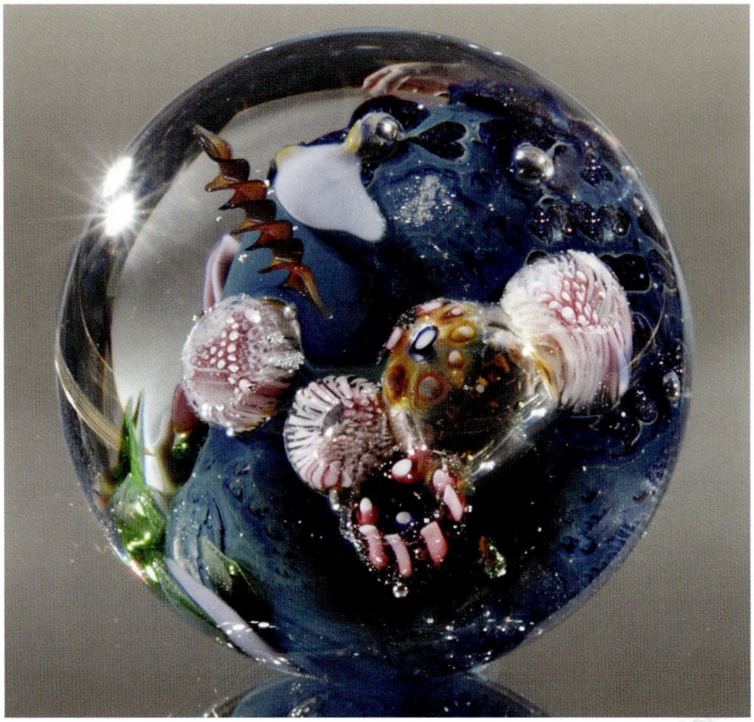

fig. 14.13 Josh Simpson, *Universe,* 2007. Glass, 1.5 in. diameter. Private Collection.

the most well known glass artist today is Dale Chihuly, who has created huge, complex installations of glass both inside in large buildings and outside in garden settings (www.dalechihuly.com).

FIBER

Weaving, needlework, basketry, patterned textiles, handmade paper and yarn paintings are but some of the vast array of fiber arts. Fibers can be natural—grasses, bark, wool, cotton and flax—or synthetic—acrylic, plastic and wire. Historically pieces made of fibers were as common as ceramics, but fewer examples survive since the materials were more perishable. We find beautifully dyed and intricately woven textiles (many in fragments) from Egyptian tombs and later **Coptic** weaving. **Weaving** exists in many variations, but it basically consists of a ***warp*** or threads stretched taut and intertwined with a ***weft*** of perpendicular threads.

Baskets and other examples of off-loom weaving have been made since prehistoric times using local grasses, reeds, twigs and bark. Contemporary artists use wire, plastic and recycled paper for a nearly endless variety of **coiled**, plaited, twined and sewn works (fig. 14.14).

Fabrics woven on looms clothed the body, draped the sleeping area and covered the floors and walls. Huge densely woven tapestries depicting scenes copied from artists' designs hung on the walls of

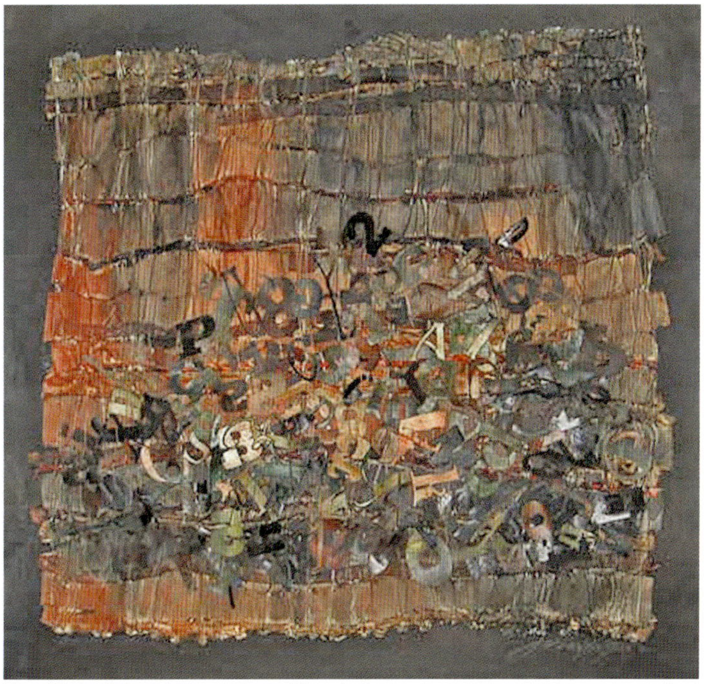

fig. 14.14 Jennifer Spoon, *Woven Messages.* Woven paper weft and cotton warp with cut paper letters and *kakishibu* (fermented persimmon juice for waterproofing). Private collection.

palaces and monasteries, providing warmth and decoration to cold stone chambers. Woven fabrics can be works of art in themselves or they can form the substrate for pattern printing, dyeing or needlework. The so-called *Bayeux* ***Tapestry*** (fig. 14.15) is an example of early needlework (wool **embroidery**) on woven linen (see page 158). A later example of needlework is the richly embroidered vestment using silk and gold thread (fig. 14.16).

Quilting, a form of needlework practiced throughout history, enjoys a particularly rich history in North America (fig. 14.17). Pioneers created quilts, recycling scarce fabrics by sewing pieces together into such traditional patterns as "log cabin" or "double wedding ring" or the more random "crazy quilt." Contemporary African-American quilts with their spontaneous abstract designs have elevated the craft to an art. After the quilter finishes the piecework, she sews the "front" onto a padded backing. This "quilting" can follow the design of the piecework or create another embossed pattern for more visual texture.

Hand papermaking uses fibers cooked and beaten into a pulp. Fiber artists today commonly use such plant fibers as cotton, flax, hemp and the inner bark of the paper mulberry, but early European and American papermakers used rags, which they recycled into pulp. The pulp is mixed into a vat of water and a framed screen is used to "pull a sheet," which the artist then ***couches*** (from the French for "to lie down") onto a felt blanket or board and allows to dry. (See the papermaking video on the Kendall-Hunt Website.) Paper forms the substrate

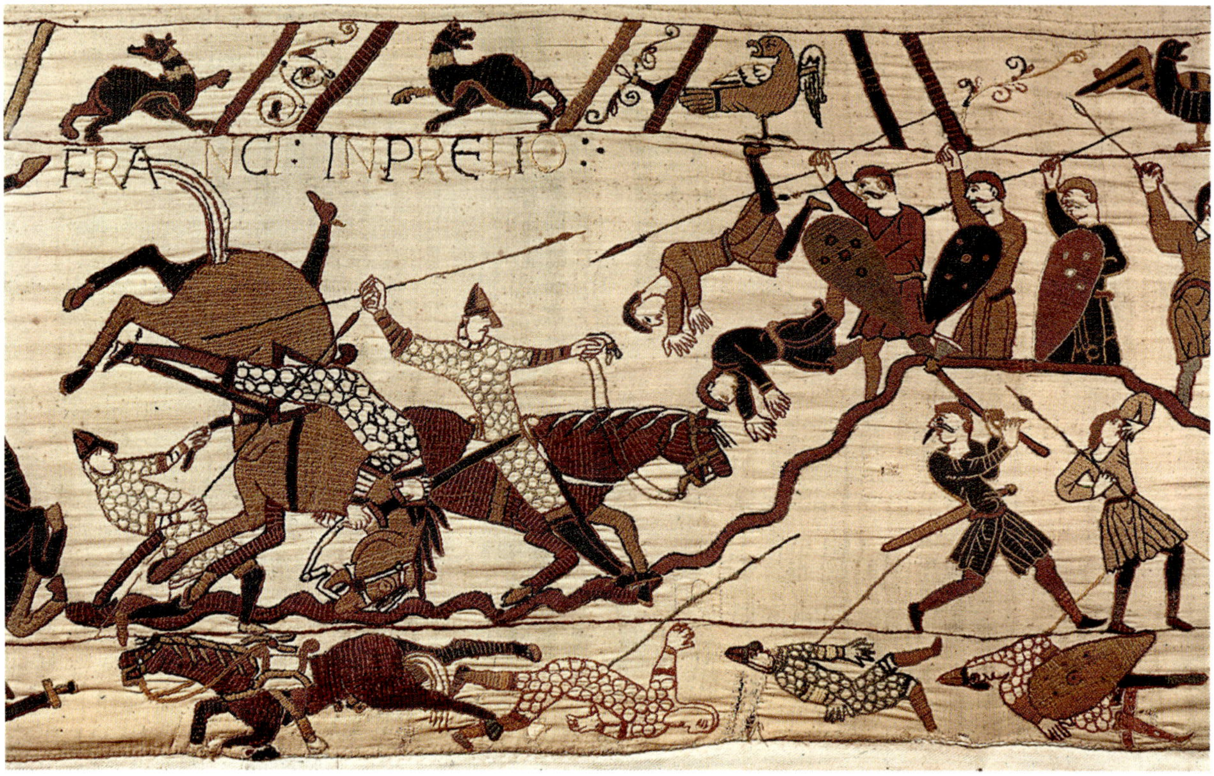

fig. 14.15 Bayeux tapestry, c. 1070–1080. Wool embroidery on linen, 20 in. high × 230 ft. long. Musée de l'Evêché, Bayeux, France.

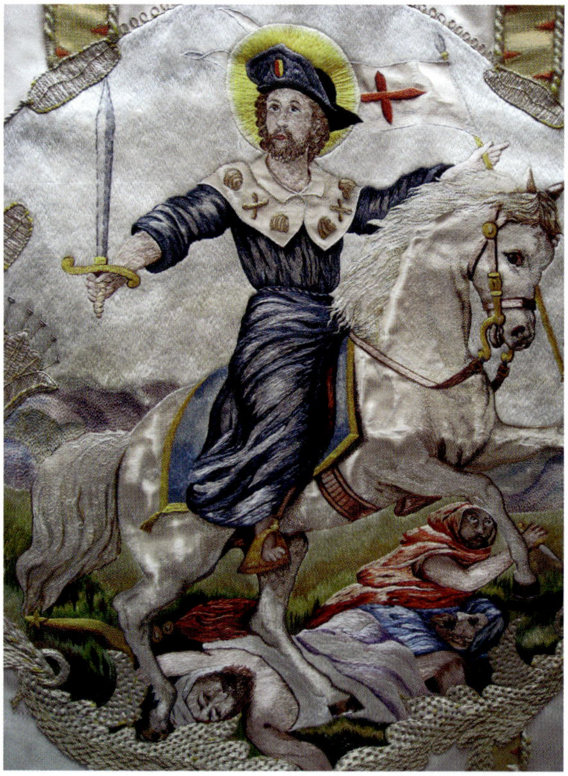

fig. 14.16 *St. James,* detail of a bishop's vestment, 18th century. Silk and gold thread embroidery. Cathedral Museum, Baeza, Spain. The scene depicts Santiago Matamoros (St. James, Moor killer) and refers to one of the many battles between Christians and Moors during the Christian reconquest of Muslim Spain, which took several hundred years to accomplish. The last Muslim stronghold was reclaimed in 1492.

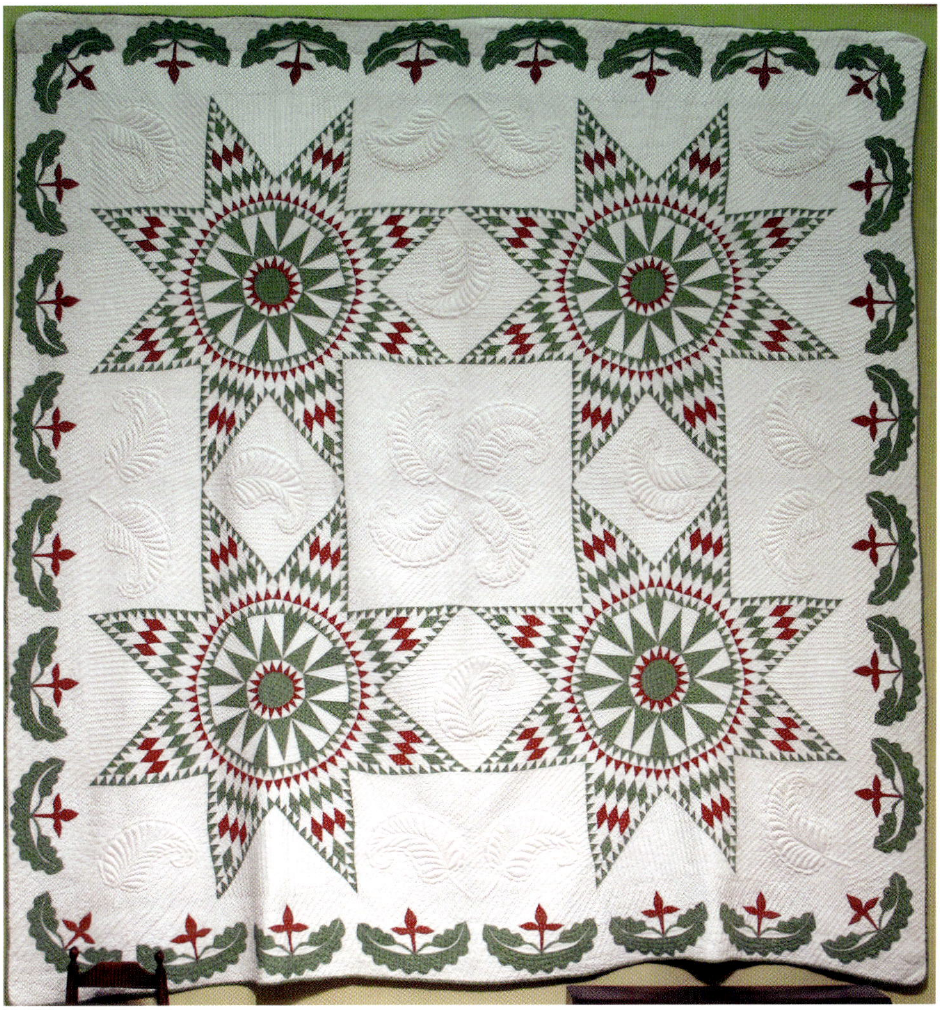

fig. 14.17a Sarah means (1826–1924), Quilt, American, c.1850.

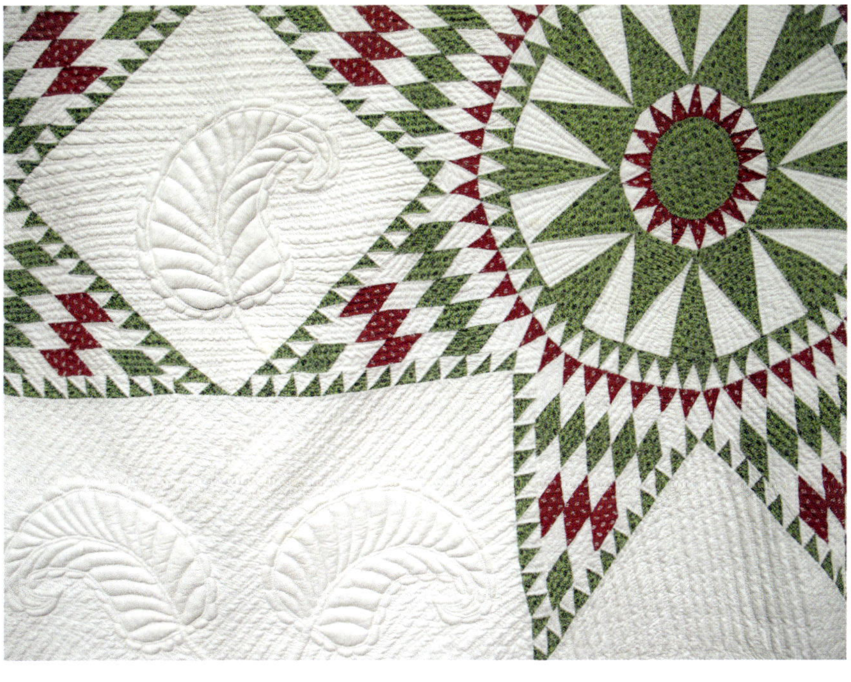

fig. 14.17b Detail.

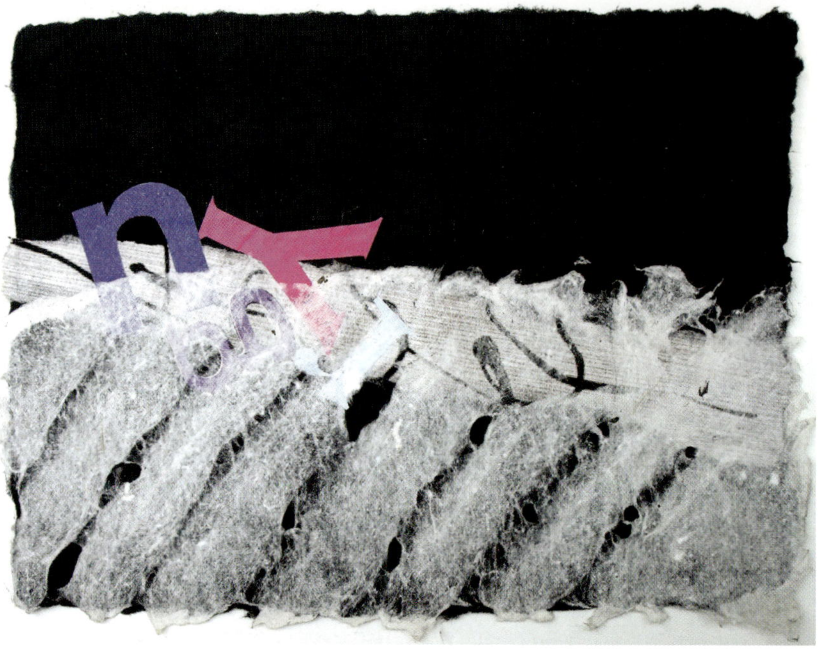

fig. 14.18 Jennifer Spoon, *Lingua Franca,* 2007. Handmade paper laminated with collage.

of many art forms or it can be an art in itself. The availability of relatively inexpensive paper considerably influenced scholars and artists. First invented in China, paper was introduced to Europe through Islamic Spain and rapidly replaced animal skins or parchment and vellum as a popular medium for printmakers, calligraphers and artists working in water media.

Contemporary hand papermakers paint in colored pulp, laminate layers of wet sheets of paper and draw, paint and print on a wide variety of weights and textures of handmade paper. Paper pulp can be cast, sprayed or formed into sculpture. *Lingua Franca* by Jennifer Spoon uses collage laminated in different colors of pulp (14.18).

Yarn paintings are one of the more unusual arts made with fibers. The Huichol Indians from the mountains of central Mexico make "paintings" using yarn dyed with intense colors (fig. 14.19). The artist coats a plywood panel with a layer of beeswax and then imbeds strings of yarn into the wax with his thumbnail to form the images. The designs depict tales of the deities (often in animal form) and shamans from the Huichols' native religion with highly stylized figures and symbols such as jaguars, peyote buttons and radiating suns. The yarn paintings are in essence religious documents, and the Huichols do not create them for decorative purposes, though collectors prize them for their detailed and brilliantly colored designs.

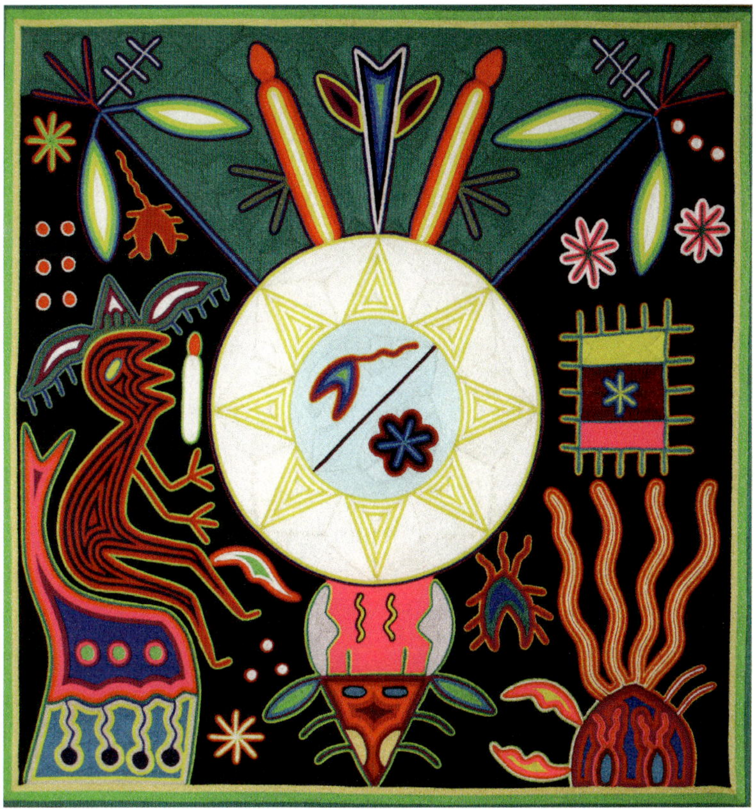

fig. 14.19 Huichol yarn painting, c. 1996. Colored yarn and wax on wood, 24 in. × 24 in. Private Collection. The Radford University Art Museum has a significant collection of Huichol yarn paintings made before the art form became commercialized. Small Huichol yarn paintings are now produced in large quantities for the tourist trade. They do not have the quality or the original religious significance of earlier works.

SUMMARY

Fine Applied Arts refer to functional pieces that transcend their utilitarian purpose. This term includes jewelry and metalsmithing, ceramics, glass, and fiber, among others.

Metalsmithing techniques include filigree, granulation, and niello. **Patinas** provide aesthetically pleasing finishes on bronze and copper. For a video clip about making the piece in figure 14.7, visit the Kendall Hunt website for this textbook using your login.

Ceramics can be hand built or thrown on a potter's wheel. When formed and dried, the work is bisque fired in a kiln, and then glazed and fired again. For a video clip showing a vase being thrown visit the Kendall Hunt website for this textbook using your login.

Glass can be blown, cast and shaped when in its molten state.

For a video clip of glass blowing, visit: http://www.handblownglass.net/Hand-Blown-Glass-Video

Fiber arts include weaving, needlework (including quilting), basketry, handmade paper, and yarn paintings.

PRONUNCIATION GUIDE

Byzantine (**biz**-uhn-teen)
Couch (kooch)
Cire perdue (**seer** per-**doo**)
Huichol (**wee**-chole)
Niello (nee-**el**-oh)
Patina (puh-**tee**-nuh)
Repoussé (reh-poo-**say**)

GLOSSARY

Bisque firing. In ceramics, a first firing that hardens the vessel.

Ceramics. Objects formed out of clay and then hardened by being baked (fired) in a very hot oven (kiln).

Coiling. A method of ceramic construction in which long ropelike pieces of clay are wound in a spiral formation, and then smoothed, to form the vessel.

Coptic. Pertaining to Egyptian Christian culture, especially in the 5th–8th centuries.

Couch. In papermaking, to transfer (a sheet of pulp) from the wire mesh or screen to a felt blanket or board.

Embroidery. The art of sewing colored threads (needlework) onto fabric to form a design or composition.

Filigree. Thin wires of silver or gold intertwined and interlaced.

Firing. Baking a clay object in a very hot oven (kiln).

Glass. A transparent or translucent hard, brittle material made by fusing sand with soda and lime at a high temperature and then cooling it rapidly.

Glaze. In ceramics, a thin liquid mixture applied to pottery that when fired forms a glassy surface.

Granulation. The soldering of tiny spheres of gold (or silver) to a flat gold (or silver) background.

Kiln. An oven used to bake ceramics at very hot temperatures.

Lapis lazuli. A semi-precious blue stone found mostly in Afghanistan. The polished stones are used in jewelry. It was ground to form the blue pigment known as ultramarine.

Lost wax technique (cire-perdue). A method of casting bronze (and other materials) in which a mold is made around an image modeled in wax. The wax is then melted out and replaced with bronze.

Modeling. Shaping a form in a pliable material such as clay or plaster.

Niello. A process that darkens certain areas of silver objects.

Patina. A fine crust that forms on bronze and copper as a result of oxidation. It is often greenish in color.

Porcelain. A fine translucent ceramic made from white clay that is fired at a high temperature.

Potsherd (Potshard). A broken piece of pottery.

Pottery. Bowls, dishes, cups, etc., made of clay that have been hardened by heat.

Repousée. A metalworking technique in which a malleable metal is ornamented or shaped by hammering from the reverse side.

Stained glass. Windows made of pieces of colored glass held in place with lead strips.

Tapestry. A design woven into a thick fabric with colored yarns.

Warp. The vertical threads of a loom or woven cloth.

Weaving. A way of making fabrics by interlacing horizontal and vertical threads or fibers.

Weft. The horizontal threads of a loom or woven cloth. Also called woof.

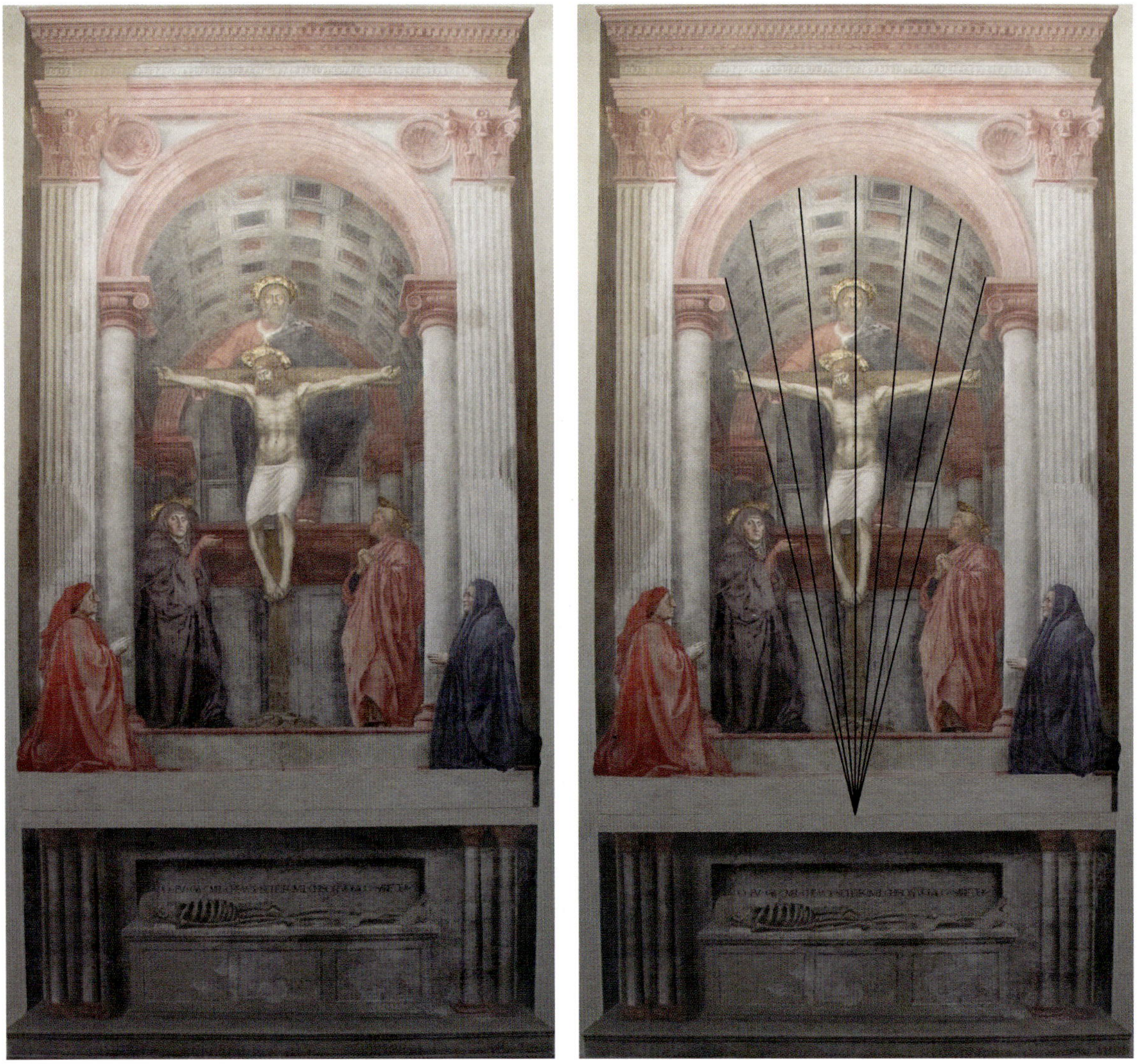

fig. 15.1 Masaccio, *Holy Trinity,* c. 1425. Fresco, 21 ft. 9 in. × 9 ft. 4 in. S. Maria Novella, Florence.

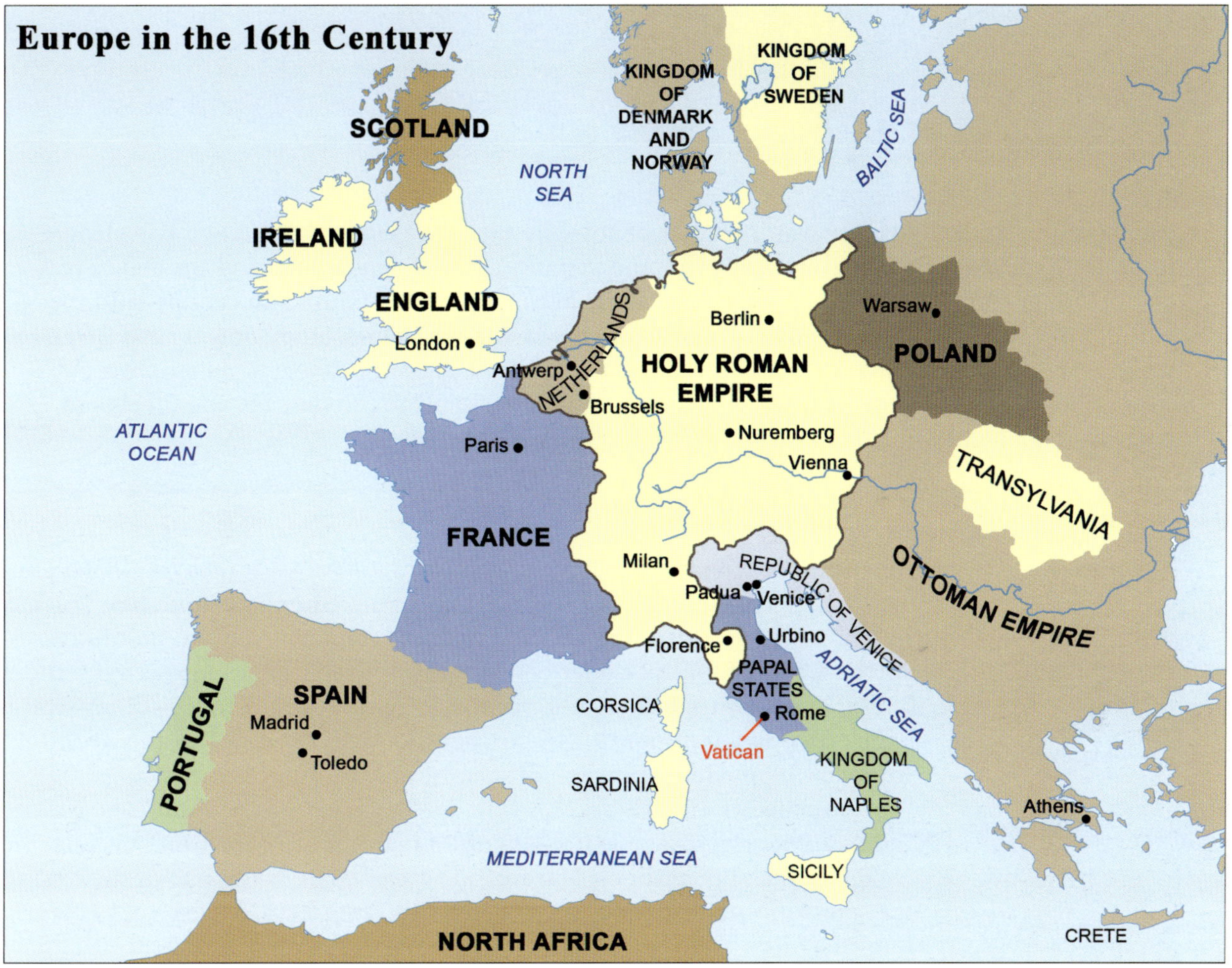

15

THE EARLY RENAISSANCE IN FIFTEENTH CENTURY ITALY

Renaissance is a French word that means rebirth, and it refers to the revival of Classical antiquity in Western Europe in the fifteenth and sixteenth centuries. The promotion of Humanistic ideas (see "Humanism" box) by literary figures such as the fourteenth-century Italian poet Petrarch led to a profound interest in the ancient world. Artists rediscovered the **realism** and **idealism** of ancient Greek and Roman art, and with new scientific advances, they were able to surpass the achievements of

RENAISSANCE & MANNERIST ART

Humanism

Humanism in the Renaissance was a secular philosophy that stressed education and knowledge (especially knowledge of Classical antiquity), the importance of the individual and the ability for self-determination (free will) and civic duty. It arose in Florence in the fourteenth century with the writings of the poet Petrarch (1304–1374). Humanist scholars revived the study of Latin and Greek and translated the surviving works of Socrates, Plato, Aristotle and other ancient philosophers and writers. Humanism was largely secular, although attempts were made to correlate the ancient philosophies to Christianity.

the ancient artists. Two significant advances were the use of oil on canvas (rather than tempera on panel) and true **linear perspective** (rather than the inconsistent perspective of the ancients). The oil medium provided a greater range of richer colors with smooth transitions between them allowing artists to create more realistic textures and three-dimensional forms. The development of linear perspective, credited to the architect Brunelleschi, made the illusion of space and depth more convincing.

Masaccio (1401–1428) was one of the early geniuses of the Renaissance. (Masaccio is a nickname meaning "Sloppy Tom" because he neglected his appearance.) Masaccio is credited as being one of the first to use **scientific perspective** in painting. *His Holy Trinity* (fig. 15.1) clearly demonstrates this. Just behind an arched opening a crucified Christ appears in a coffered barrel-vaulted room. Above his halo is a white dove symbolizing the Holy Spirit, and behind him on a ledge stands God the Father who supports the arms of the cross. Flanking Christ are the Virgin Mary and John the Evangelist. In front of the arch (and therefore outside the sacred space of the crucifixion) kneel the donors who commissioned the painting. Below, a painted crypt (that conceals an actual crypt) displays a skeleton and a Latin phrase that translates as "I was once what you are. You will be what I am." This warning is a ***memento mori***, or a reminder of death.

The **vanishing point** is situated below the foot of the cross at eye-level, which creates a dramatic perspective view. The composition is a stable pyramid defined by the head of God the Father at the top and the donors at the bottom. People of the time much admired the illusion of space in this work, and Masaccio, despite his early death at age twenty-seven, greatly influenced later artists. The *Holy Trinity* is a good example of the basic principles of Renaissance composition: **symmetry**, **balance**, harmony, **unity** and stability.

The *Birth of Venus* (fig. 15.2) by **Sandro Botticelli** (1445–1510) is one of the icons of Western art. According to myth, Venus, who was born fully grown when the severed testicles of Uranus fell into the sea, arrives at her sacred island of Cythera on a scallop shell. Flanking her are the wind

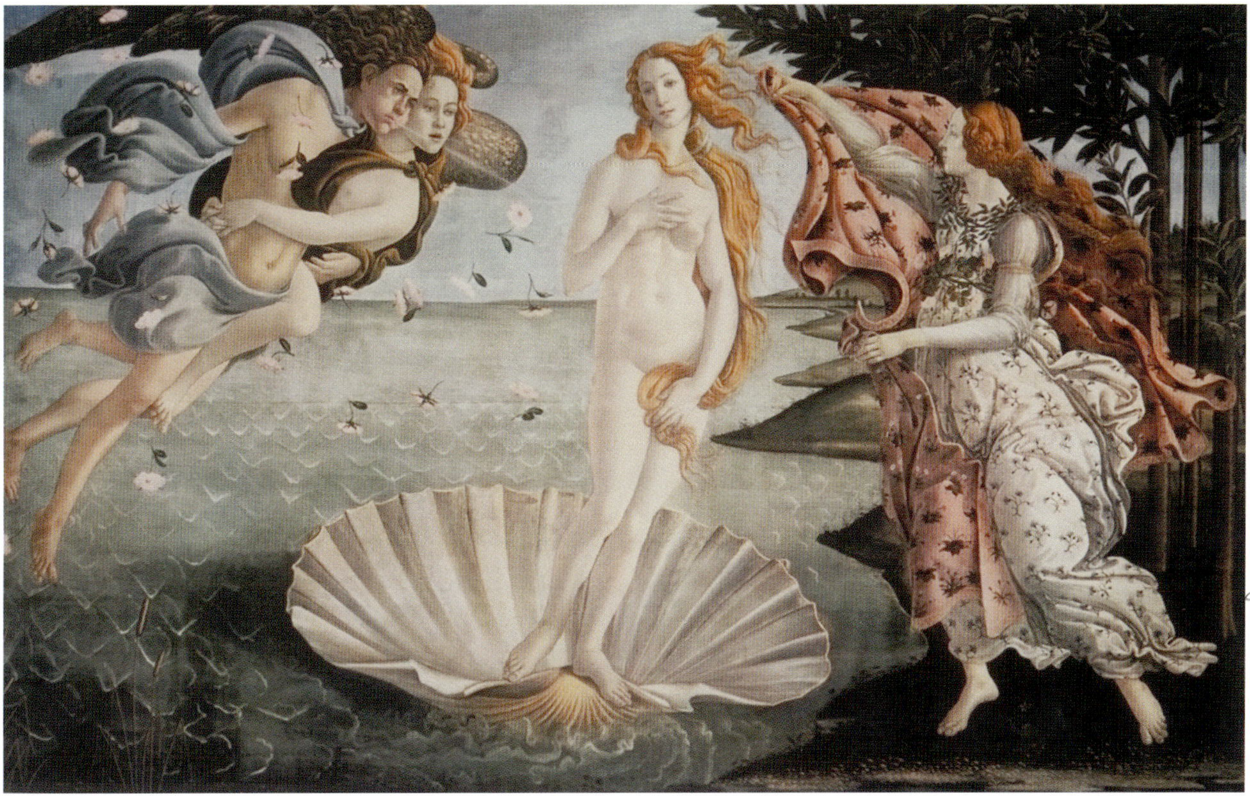

© Corel, Inc.

fig. 15.2 Sandro Botticelli (1445–1510), *The Birth of Venus*, c. 1482. Tempera on canvas, approx. 5 ft. 8 in. × 9 ft., Galleria degli Uffizi, Florence. Botticelli means "Little Barrel," a nickname derived from his older brother.

gods who blew her to land and an attendant ready to clothe her. The artist modeled Venus after a famous ancient statue of the goddess in the Medici collection. Although Venus' body shows **modeling**, it is the linear quality of the work that Botticelli is known for. People often **spoof** this work, as we can see in a mural from Venice Beach showing a hip "Venus" on rollerblades and in a jewelry display in a shop window in Athens, Greece (figs. 15.3 and 15.4).

Donatello (1386–1466) was the leading sculptor in the early Renaissance. His *David* (fig. 15.5) is the first life-size nude sculpture since antiquity. Donatello was probably inspired by studying fragments of ancient statues that wealthy collectors, like the Medici family, had acquired. We see a contemplative David with an exaggerated classical contrapposto stance with his left foot on the head of Goliath. With an introspective look, he holds the stone from the slingshot that killed Goliath in his left hand and the sword that decapitated him in his right. The highly polished surface emphasizes the erotic aspect of David's adolescent body, effeminate pose and foppish hat. The long wing that sprouts from Goliath's helmet and rises up David's leg to his groin area enhances the eroticism.

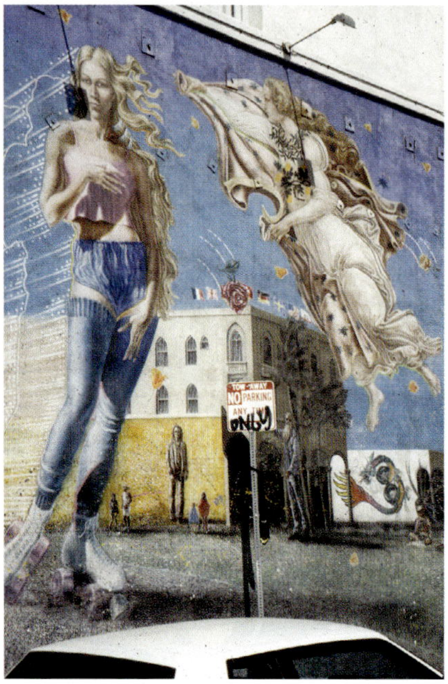

fig. 15.3 Rip Cronk. Wall mural in Venice Beach, California.

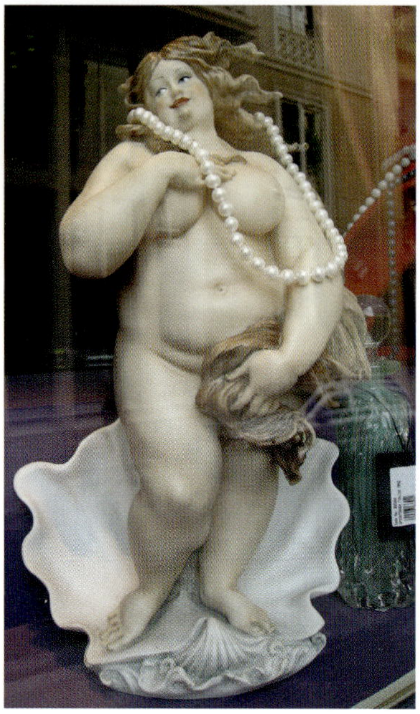

fig. 15.4 Jewelry display in Athens, Greece.

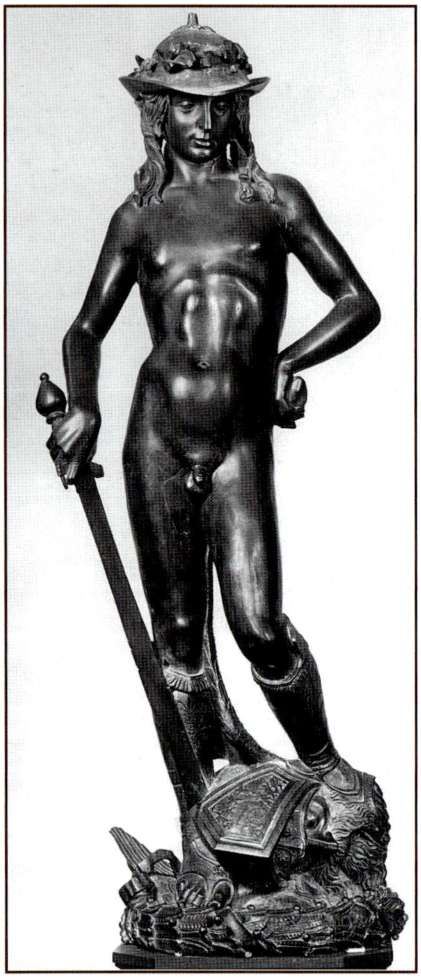

fig. 15.5 Donatello, *David,* c. 1440. **Bronze,** 5 ft. 2 in. high. Museo Nazionale del Bargello, Florence.

Filippo Brunelleschi (1377–1446) began his career as a sculptor and later invented scientific perspective, but we know him best as an architect. He devised an innovative solution for the unfinished **dome** of the Gothic cathedral of Florence (figs. 15.6 and 15.7). Because he had seen the Pantheon in Rome, Brunelleschi knew it was possible to span a large space with a dome, but the cathedral walls were not strong enough to support a concrete dome, and the octagonal space was too wide and too high for traditional wooden scaffolding. So Brunelleschi designed a dome made of two light shells around a skeleton of twenty-four ribs connected to each other by regularly spaced ties. (The eight main ribs are visible on the exterior.) He made the sides of the dome steep for greater stability and also so that scaffolding was unnecessary until a certain height. Then he invented a new type of scaffolding that the **drum** supported (rather than the floor far below). He topped the dome with a heavy **lantern** that helped anchor it and let light into the interior. Many later architects used this ingenious double-shelled design, including Michelangelo (the dome of St. Peter's Basilica in Rome) and Christopher Wren (the dome of St. Paul's in London).

The Ducal Palace at Urbino. Federico da Montefeltro, Duke of Urbino, invited the best writers, philosophers and artists to his court. His new palace was a showcase for the new

Symbolism

The pagan gods and the Christian saints all had their attributes. For example, Zeus has his thunderbolt and eagle, Hercules his club and Venus the golden apple Paris awarded her. Among the saints, St. Peter has the keys to heaven and David has his sling; the four **Evangelists** have their corresponding animals (an eagle for St. John, an angel for St. Matthew, a lion for St. Mark and an ox for St. Luke). These attributes made it easy for people to identify the figures even if they were illiterate.

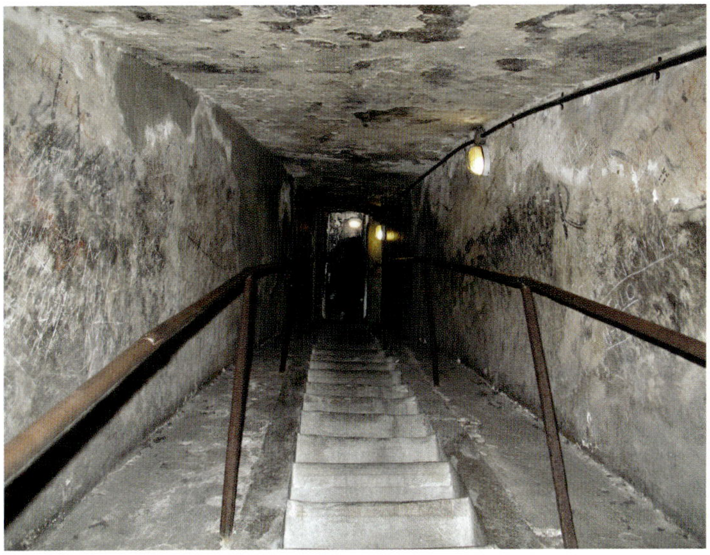

fig. 15.6b Between the two shells of the Florence Cathedral dome.

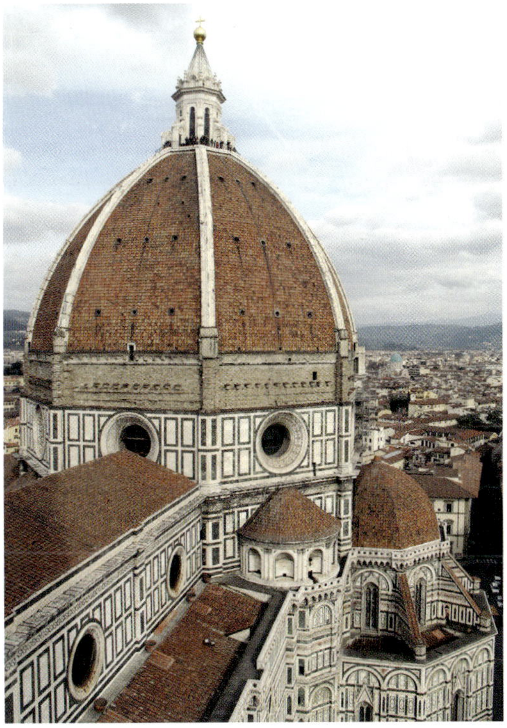

fig. 15.6a Filippo Brunelleschi, *Dome of the Florence Cathedral,* c. 1420–1436.

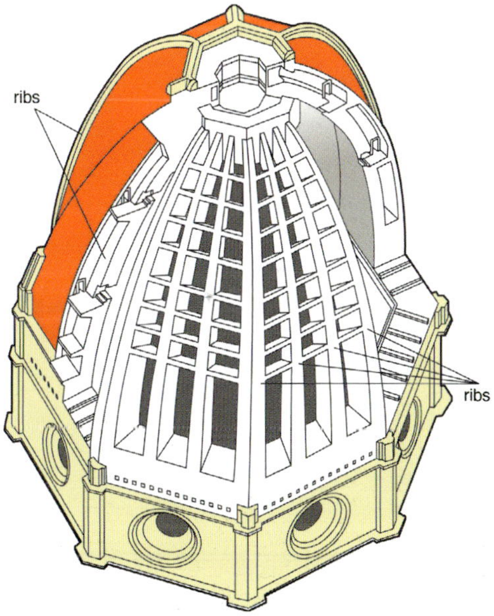

fig. 15.7 Cutaway view of the Florence Cathedral dome.

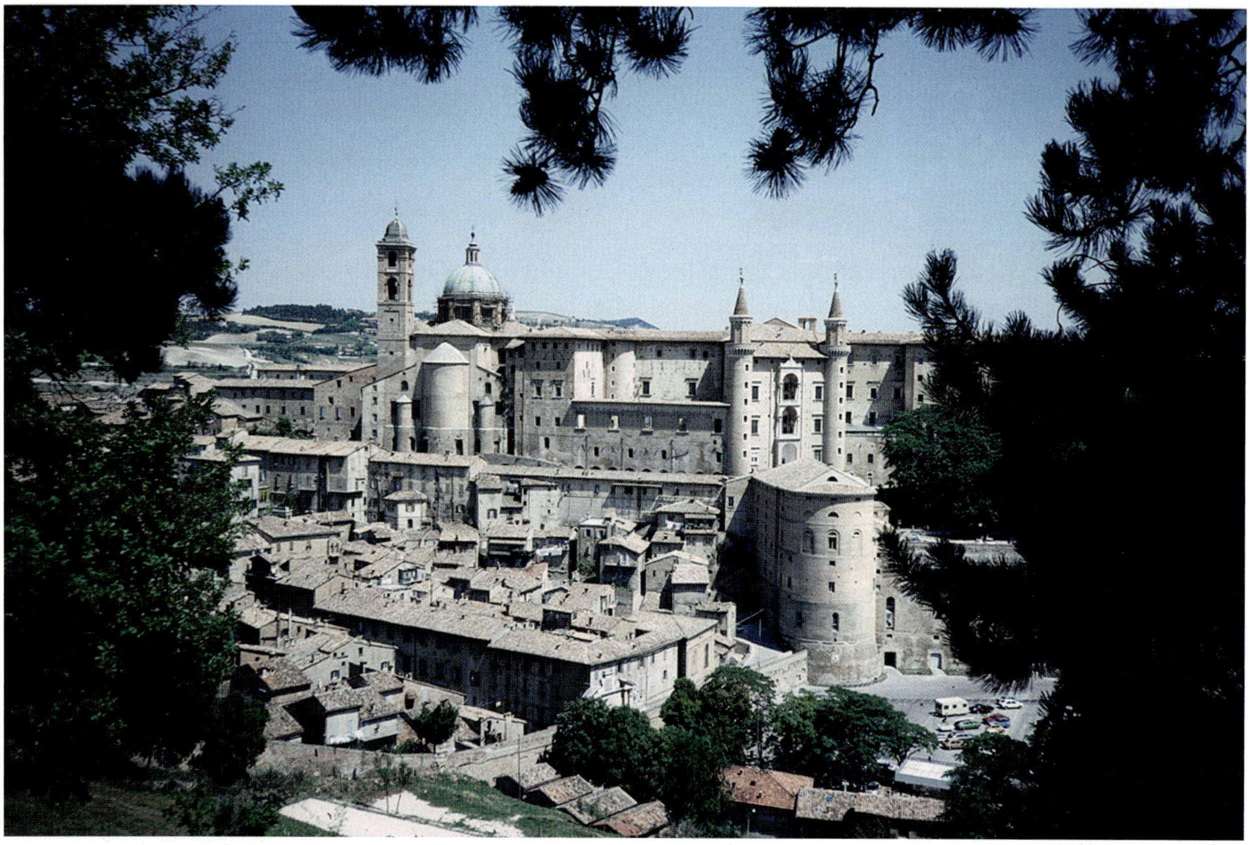

fig. 15.8 Ducal Palace at Urbino, Italy, begun 1450. The Duke left the palace unfinished when his beloved wife died in 1472 at the age of twenty-six after the birth of her ninth child.

Renaissance ideas (fig. 15.8). Many consider the courtyard, designed by **Luciano Laurana** (c. 1425–1479), one of the most perfect Renaissance designs (fig. 15.9). The graceful **arcade** avoids a sense of weakness at the corners by substituting piers with attached columns in place of single freestanding columns. This also avoids the awkwardness of having two arches spring from a single column. The shorter second story is proportional to the first and has Corinthian pilasters to mirror the columns directly below them without detracting from them. (The two small upper stories are not part of the original design.) The palace's window design (fig. 15.10) has nothing to do with the delicate Gothic tracery of the preceding period. The windows are robust and strongly evoke the architecture of classical antiquity.

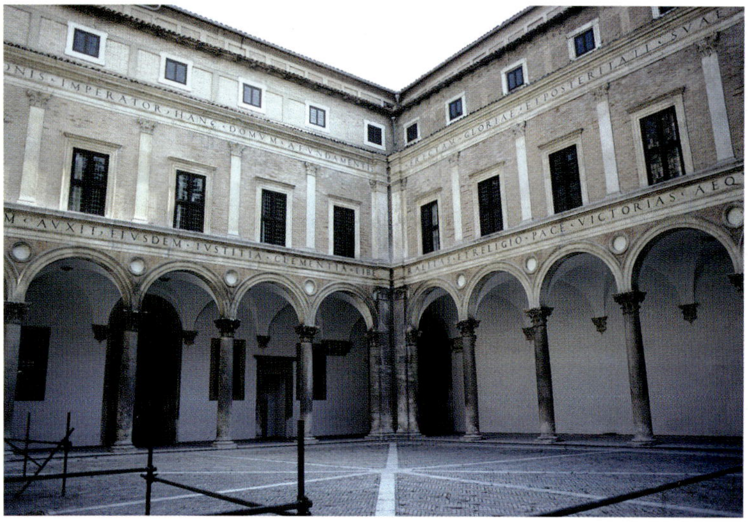

fig. 15.9 Luciano Laurana, Courtyard of the Ducal Palace at Urbino, c. 1467–1472.

THE HIGH RENAISSANCE IN ITALY

The Renaissance reached its greatest heights in the first quarter of the sixteenth century with artists such as Leonardo da Vinci (1452–1519), Michelangelo (1475–1564) and Raphael (1483–1520) achieving international renown. During this time Florence declined as the artistic center of Italy, replaced by Rome.

Leonardo da Vinci (1452–1519) was one of the great geniuses of all time—a true Renaissance man. He was an architect, scientist, military engineer and musician, as well as a painter. He painted few pictures, however, probably because his curiosity and wide-ranging interests distracted him, and he left many projects unfinished. Two of the most famous paintings in the world (and two of the most spoofed) are Leonardo's *Last Supper* and the *Mona Lisa*. He painted the *Last Supper* (fig. 15.11) for the dining room of a convent. The painting is a model of the Renaissance style with its balanced and symmetrical composition. The twelve **Apostles** are arranged in groups of three with Christ in the center. Leonardo has chosen to

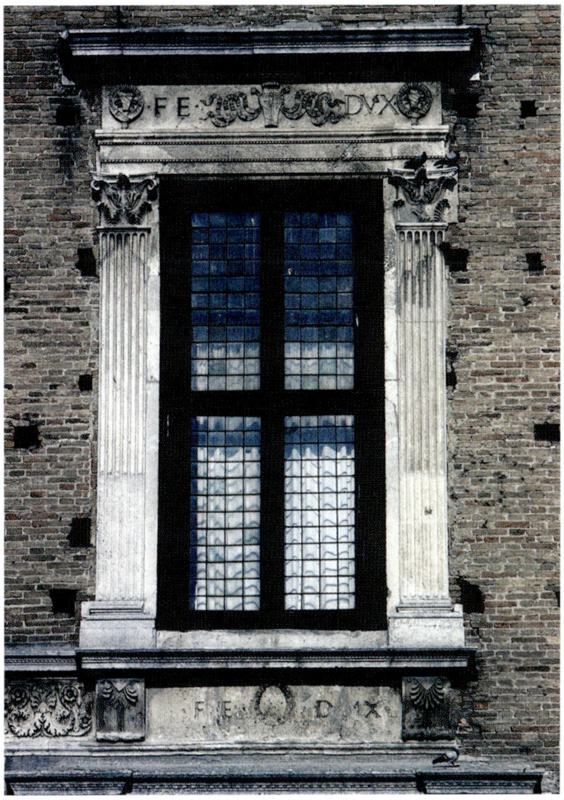

fig. 15.10 Window of the Ducal Palace at Urbino.

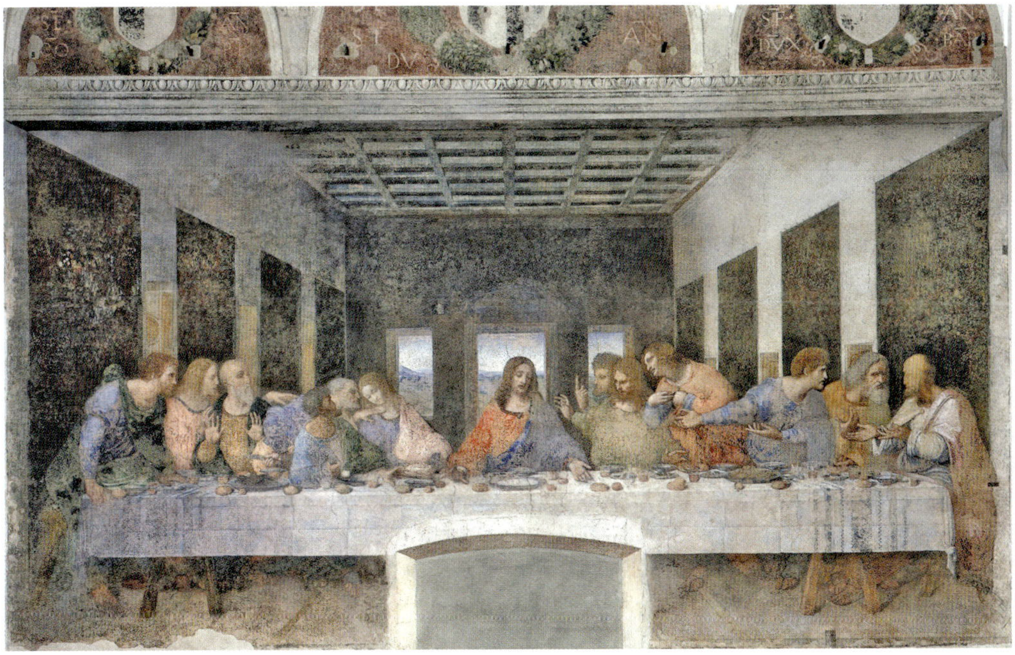

fig. 15.11 Leonardo da Vinci, *The Last Supper*, c. 1495–1498. Oil and tempera on plaster, 13 ft. 9 in. × 29 ft. 10 in. Santa Maria delle Grazie, Milan. Although recently restored, the painting does not survive in good condition. Leonardo attempted a new technique that combined tempera with oil, but it was a failure. The paint began to peel soon after the work was completed.

portray the dramatic moment when Christ announces that one of them will betray him. The Apostles react with astonishment in a variety of poses and emotional expressions. Christ remains unaffected—a stable point in the center of the composition and the focal point of the **perspective**. Judas, usually isolated on the other side of the table, sits with the first group to Christ's right. He is identifiable by the dark outline of his head and the bag of silver coins he clutches. In keeping with the naturalism of the Renaissance, there are no halos; the curved pediment over the window behind Christ acts as a symbolic halo.

The *Mona Lisa* (fig.15.12) has spawned much speculation about the sitter's identity and mysterious smile over the centuries. One scholar even proposed that it was a self portrait of Leonardo in drag. We now know it is a portrait of Lisa del Giocondo, the wife of a wealthy Florentine silk merchant. (The painting has always been called "La Gioconda" in Italian.) The painting has fascinated people for centuries, and it was obviously something Leonardo treasured because he never parted with it. The lady sits on an open loggia with a strange and mysterious landscape in the background. Leonardo effectively unites the figure and the landscape with subtle devices. For example, the winding road in the left background picks up the pleats of her right sleeve, and the line of the swath of drapery over her left shoulder continues in the aqueduct in the distance. Perhaps Leonardo's most distinct stylistic feature is the delicate modeling and the hazy, misty atmosphere (called ***sfumato***) that softens outlines and creates a dreamy effect.

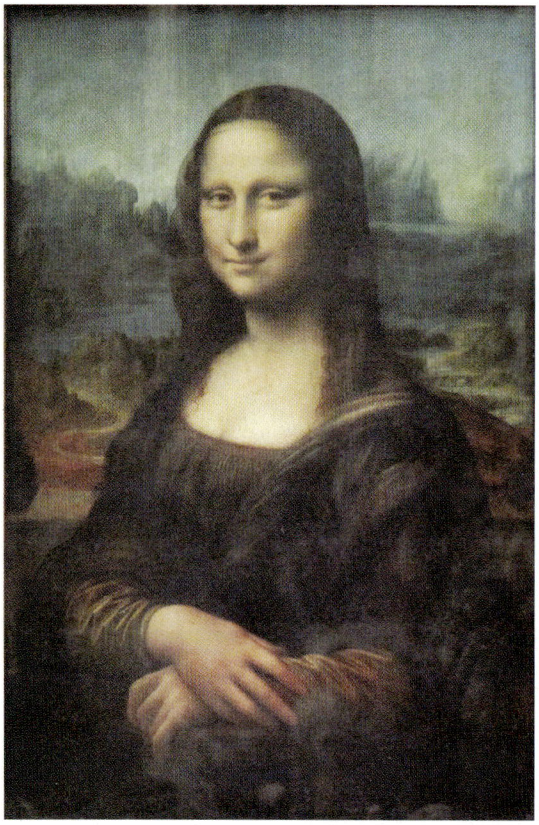

fig. 15.12 Leonardo da Vinci, *Mona Lisa,* c. 1505. Oil on wood, 2 ft. 6 in. × 1 ft. 9 in. Louvre, Paris. This painting was with Leonardo's possessions in France where he died (which is why it is in the Louvre in Paris today and not in an Italian museum). Unlike the profile portraits of the previous century, Leonardo portrays Mona Lisa in a three-quarter half-length pose—the kind still used today for many portraits whether painted or photographed.

Michelangelo Buonarroti (1475–1564) was multi-talented like Leonardo, being a painter, architect, writer and sculptor. His most famous sculpture is his *David* (fig. 15.13), which differs significantly from Donatello's *David* (fig. 15.5). Michelangelo shows his over life-size David before killing Goliath. With the sling over his shoulder he contemplates how he will accomplish the deed. A furrowed brow and tense neck muscles belie his concentration. The nude, muscular (and masculine) figure with its **contrapposto** stance evokes Classical sculpture, which Michelangelo had studied, and its huge size demonstrates Michelangelo's tremendous **carving** skill.

In 1508 Pope Julius II cajoled Michelangelo into painting the 5,800 square feet of the Sistine Chapel ceiling (fig. 15.14). He completed the project, with great physical discomfort, in just four years. It is a tour de force and with its twentieth-century restoration, we can now view it again in all its original glory. The main panels of the ceiling relate principal events in the Old Testament from the creation of the universe to the Flood and the Drunkenness of Noah. Most of the lateral figures are the ancestors of Christ or prophets and pagan **sibyls** who foretold his coming. The most reproduced portion is the Creation of Adam (fig. 15.15) where God extends his hand to touch that of Adam and give him the spark of life. Enveloped in God's cloak are a number of figures, two of whom may be the as yet unborn Virgin Mary and the Christ child. God's dynamic gesture contrasts with Adam's languid and limp pose. Like all of Michelangelo's figures, whether in sculpture or painting, these figures are muscular, monumental and imposing.

Raphael Sanzio (1483–1520) was primarily a painter. Where Leonardo was aloof and Michelangelo brooding, Raphael was affable, outgoing and very popular among the ladies. And unlike Leonardo's paintings with their dark, mysterious background landscapes, Raphael's paintings are filled with sun and light. His monumental *School of Athens* (fig. 15.16), painted for a room in the Vatican palace, is the epitome of Classical balance and harmony. It shows ancient Greek philosophers and scientists gathered together in a large ensemble in a fantastic architectural setting that may refer to the new St. Peter's basilica, then under construction. Raphael also honors a few of his contemporaries by using their features for some of the figures. The focal point of the painting is the two central figures: Plato, who gestures toward the heavens and has the features of Leonardo da Vinci, and Aristotle who gestures more towards the earth. The rest of the figures group to the right or left depending on whether their concern is with the spiritual (Plato's side) or with nature and human affairs (Aristotle's side). On the left Pythagoras writes; the brooding philosopher Heraclitus in the front is a portrait of Michelangelo; sprawled on the steps is Diogenes who scoured Athens in search of an honest man; and at the right Euclid, a portrait of the architect Bramante, draws on a board while Zoroaster holds a globe. Raphael's own portrait is at the far right looking out at the viewer. The scene exemplifies the reconciliation of two different modes of ancient thought and suggests the reconciliation of Classical paganism and Christianity.

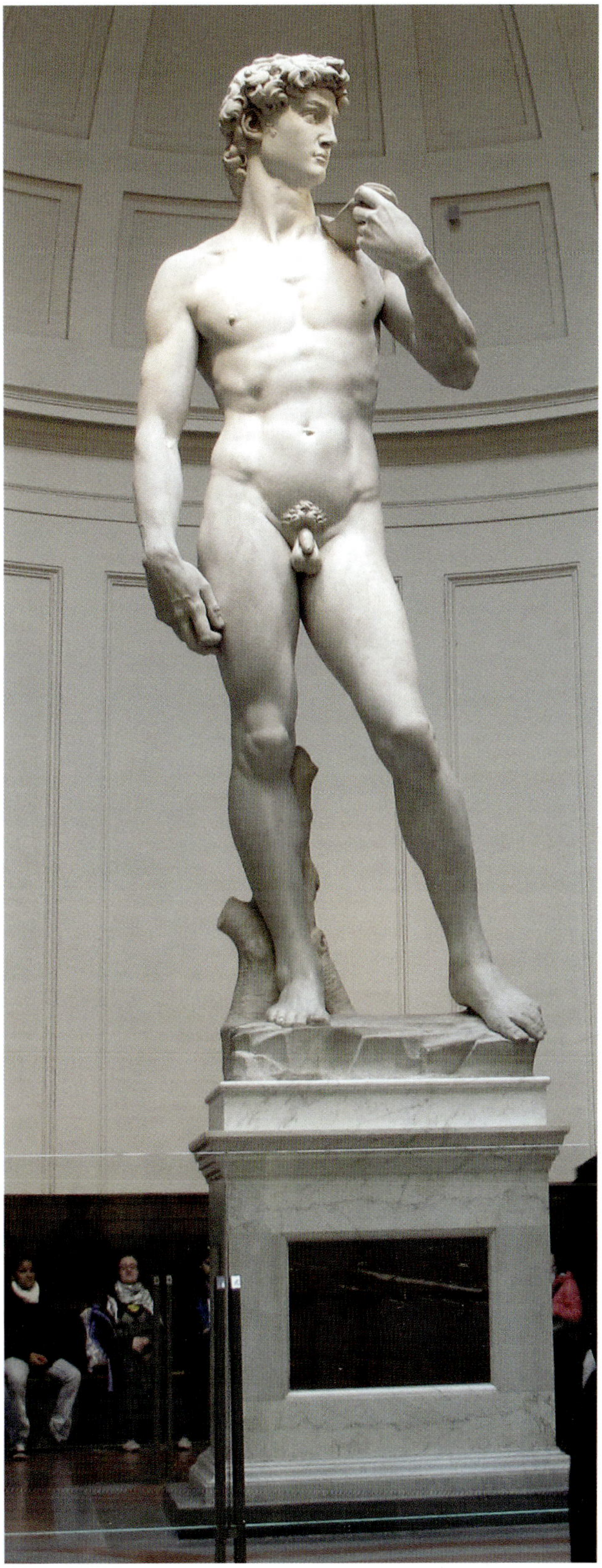

fig. 15.13 Michelangelo, *David,* 1501–1504. Marble, 17 ft. high. Galleria dell'Accademia, Florence.

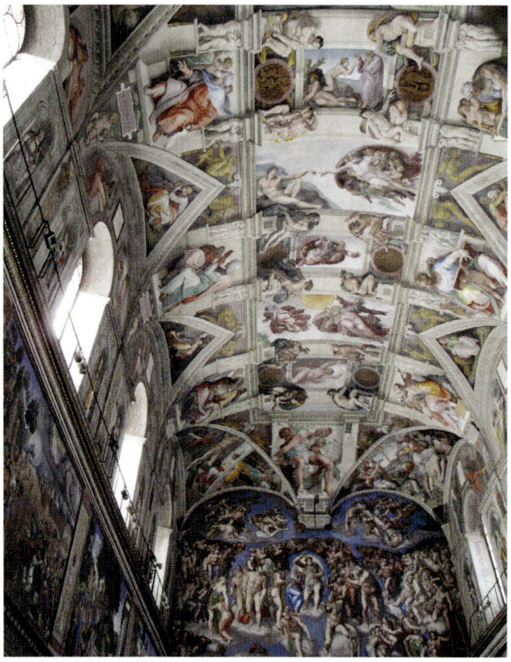

fig. 15.14 Michelangelo, *Sistine Ceiling,* 1508–1512. Sistine Chapel, Vatican City, Rome.

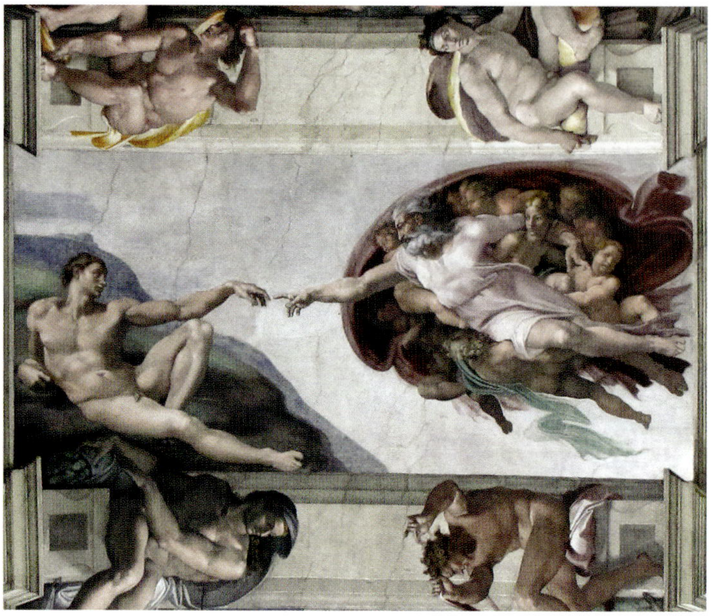

fig. 15.15 Michelangelo, *God Creating Adam,* Sistine Ceiling.

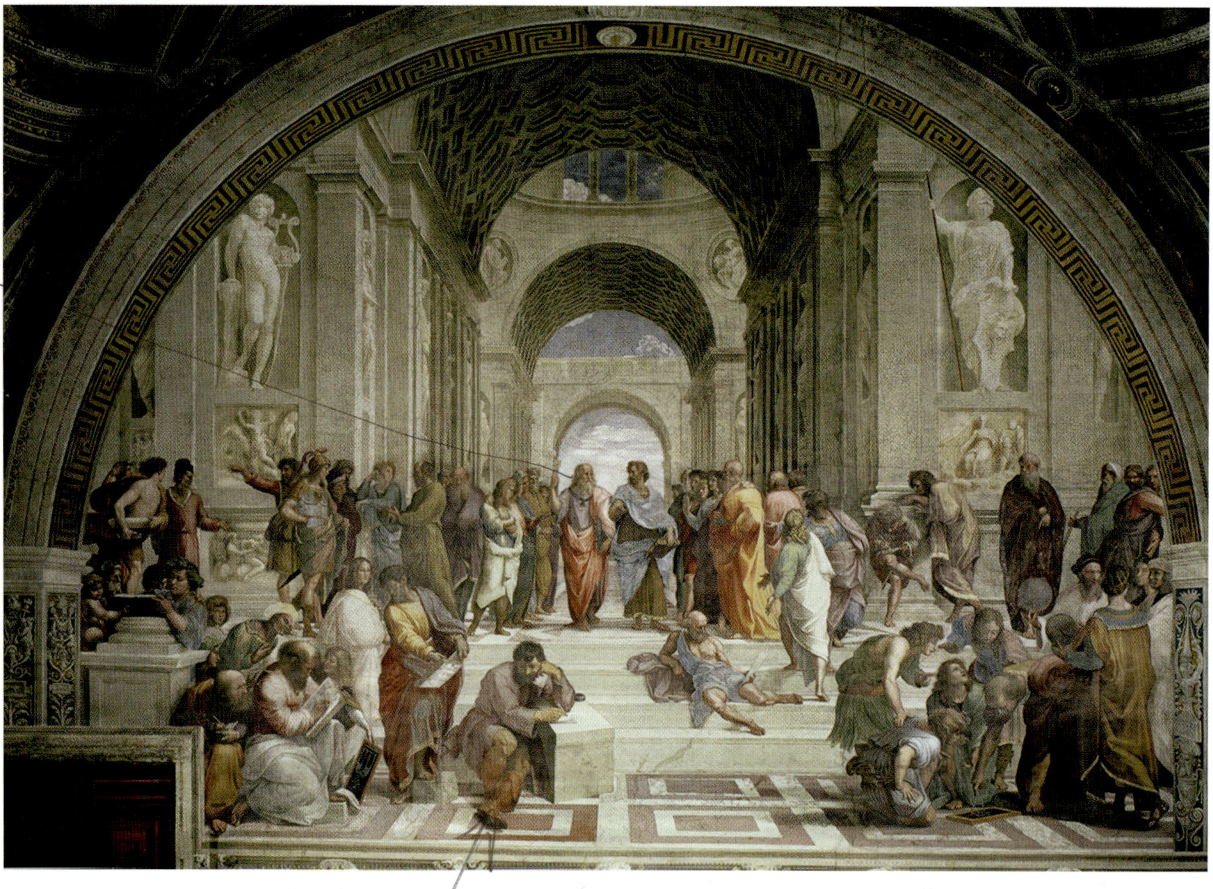

fig. 15.16 Raphael, *The School of Athens,* 1509–1511. **Fresco**, 19 ft. × 27 ft. Stanza delle Segnatura, Vatican Palace, Rome, Italy.

Titian (c. 1490–1576) had a warm rich palette typical of painters from Venice. We know him for his sensuous nudes, such as the *Venus of Urbino* (fig. 15.17). Titian continues the type of reclining female nude known from antiquity. We do not know the identity of the sitter, but she was probably someone's mistress. She lounges languidly on a couch while two servants in the background take clothes out of a trunk. With her left hand somewhat modestly placed, she stares unabashedly at the viewer. The roses in her right hand and the myrtle bush in the window are associated with Venus, while the sleeping dog at her feet symbolizes both fidelity and erotic desire.

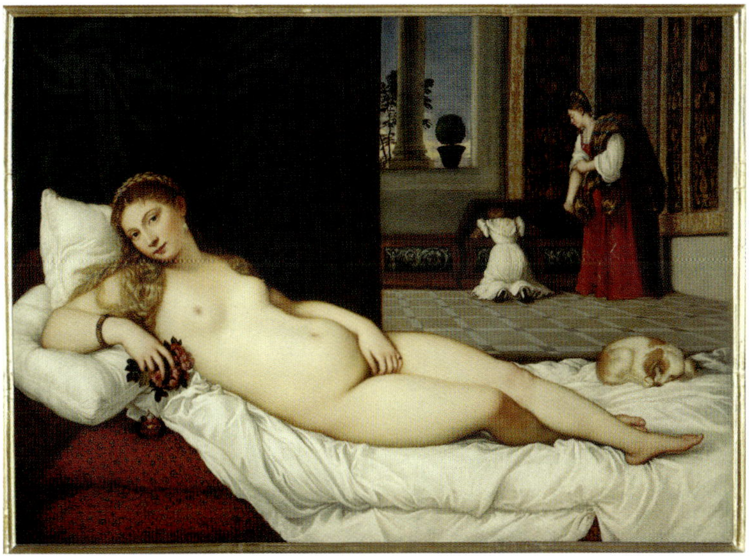

fig. 15.17 Titian, *Venus of Urbino*, c. 1538.
Oil on canvas, 3 ft. 1 in. × 5 ft. 5 in. Galleria degli Uffizi, Florence.

THE RENAISSANCE IN NORTHERN EUROPE

The Renaissance came later in the north. The **Gothic** style persisted until 1500 or so in many areas long after the advent of the Renaissance in Italy. Where Italian artists concerned themselves with the underlying anatomical structure of the figures they depicted, northern artists were more concerned with realistic surface detail. Northern artists used oil before the technique was adopted in Italy, and it allowed them to achieve jewel-like precision. One of the best early northern Renaissance painters was **Jan van Eyck** (c. 1390–1441), and his most famous work is the double portrait of Giovanni Arnolfini and his wife, Giovanna Cenami (fig. 15.18). Traditionally thought to be a wedding portrait, the couple stands in a well-appointed bedroom with a fancy bed, a brass chandelier and a framed mirror. Van Eyck painted everything from the fur-trimmed garments to the wood grain of the floorboards to the reflections in the mirror in minute detail. Like many fifteenth-century northern works, the painting is full of hidden symbolism. Mr. Arnolfini stands in his stocking feet (and her red shoes are at the back of the room) indicating that the bedroom is also a sacred space. (Compare this with the King Narmer Palette in figure 6.1.) The round mirror, which reflects the entire scene, symbolizes the all-seeing eye of God. Its frame contains miniature round paintings illustrating scenes from the Passion of Christ. Reflected in the mirror are two figures who witness the event (see fig. 15.18b). They stand in front of the couple in the same approximate place as the viewer. The single lit candle in the chandelier recalls the marriage candle and may also refer to Christ's presence. To the right of the mirror atop the bedpost finial is a small, carved statue of St. Margaret, the patron saint of childbirth; the whiskbroom hanging from it represents domesticity. The oranges on the chest beneath the window may symbolize fertility whereas the dog represents fidelity.

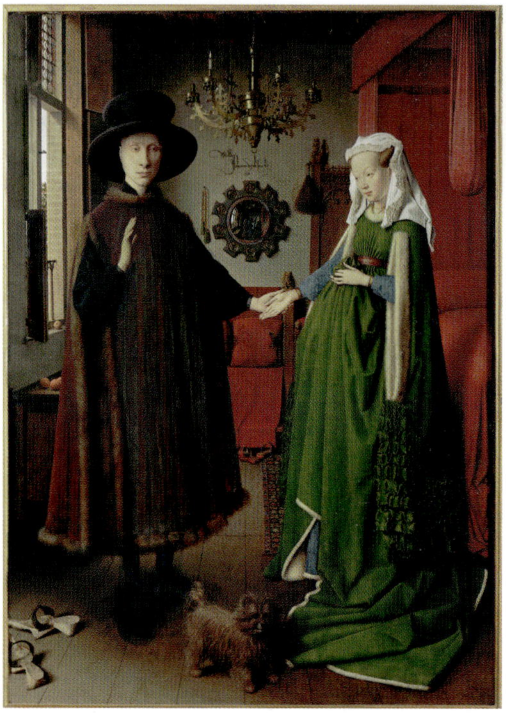

fig. 15.18a Jan van Eyck, *Arnolfini Double Portrait,* 1434. Oil on wood, 2 ft. 9 in. × 30.5 in. National Gallery, London.

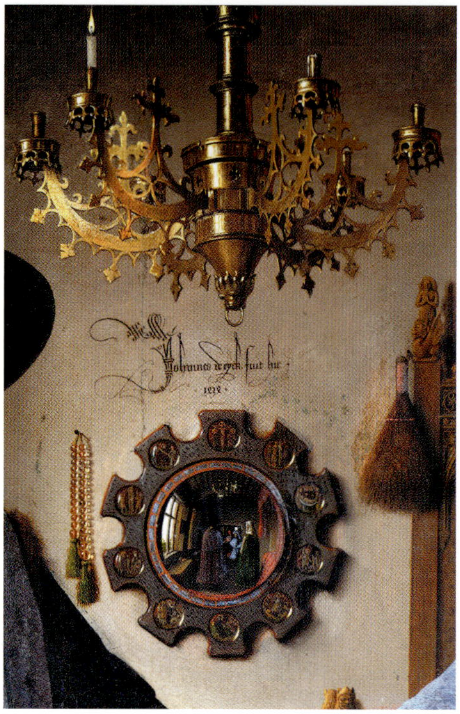

fig. 15.18b

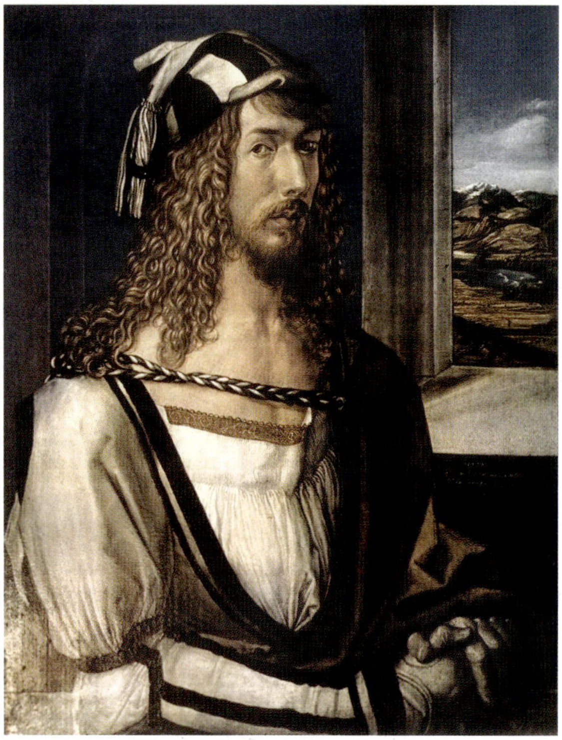

fig. 15.19 Albrecht Dürer, *Self-Portrait,* 1498. Oil on panel, 20.5 in. × 16 in. Prado, Madrid.

The painting is signed and dated above the mirror with a Latin inscription that reads "Johannes de eyck fuit hic 1434" (Jan van Eyck was here 1434), implying that he is one of the two witnesses seen in the mirror. The rich oil colors, intricate detail and complex symbolism make this portrait one of the stellar paintings of the northern Renaissance.

Albrecht Dürer (1471–1528) was a leading northern painter in the following century. Born in Germany, he traveled to Italy as young man and studied Italian Renaissance art firsthand. The pose and distant landscape in his *Self-Portrait* (fig. 15.19) indicate the influence of Leonardo. Like van Eyck, Dürer pays attention to detail, carefully delineating every hair of his curly locks. Dressed as a gentleman with white leather gloves, there is a certain air of superiority in the portrait. A renowned printmaker as well, his engravings and woodcuts also display a skilled linear quality and fine detail. Dürer's work was an important transition from the lingering late Gothic to the Renaissance style in the north.

One of the strangest paintings of the northern Renaissance is the so-called *Garden of Earthly Delights* (fig. 15.20) by the Netherlandish painter

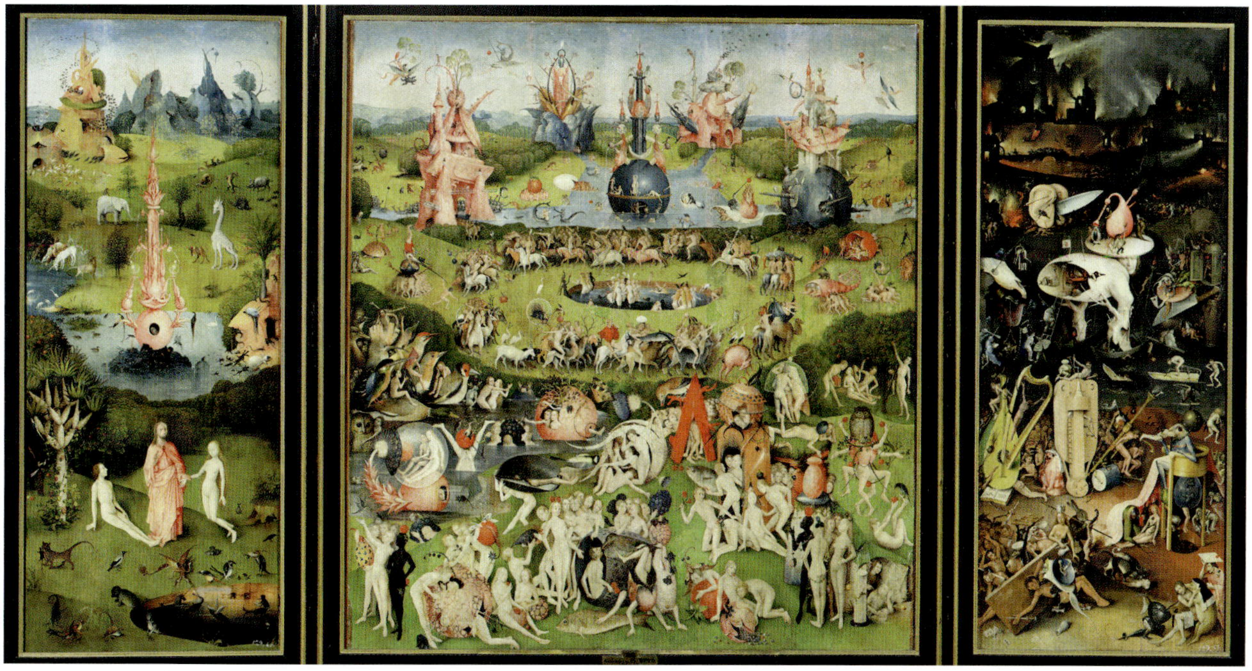

fig. 15.20 Hieronymus Bosch, *Garden of Earthly Delights,* c. 1505. Oil on wood, central panel 7 ft. 2 in. × 6 ft. 5 in., each wing 7 ft. 2 in. × 3 ft. 2 in. Prado, Madrid.

Hieronymus Bosch (c. 1450–1516). The work is a **triptych** with a large central panel and two wings that can swing shut over the central panel. The left wing shows God with Adam and Eve in a bizarre garden full of odd creatures and structures. A weird fountain stands in a pool in the middle ground. Its spherical base has an opening with an owl perched in it. Death is evident. At the lower left a cat carries off a dead rat and in the distant background at the upper right a monkey is about to strike a dog that has killed and is eating another animal. The central panel displays an equally odd fountain above. Below are hundreds of figures cavorting in strange, sexual ways. They are small in comparison to the animals and fruits in the scene. The right panel shows Hell with a fiery scene in the distance and demonic monsters tormenting people in the foreground. At the lower right an enthroned bird-like demon wearing a kettle on his head eats a man (who has swallows emerging from his rear) while he excretes two other people into a black pit into which someone vomits while another relieves himself of gold coins (fig. 15.21). This is just one of a myriad of strange scenes among the three panels. The overall meaning of this complex and confusing work is unclear, although art historians have

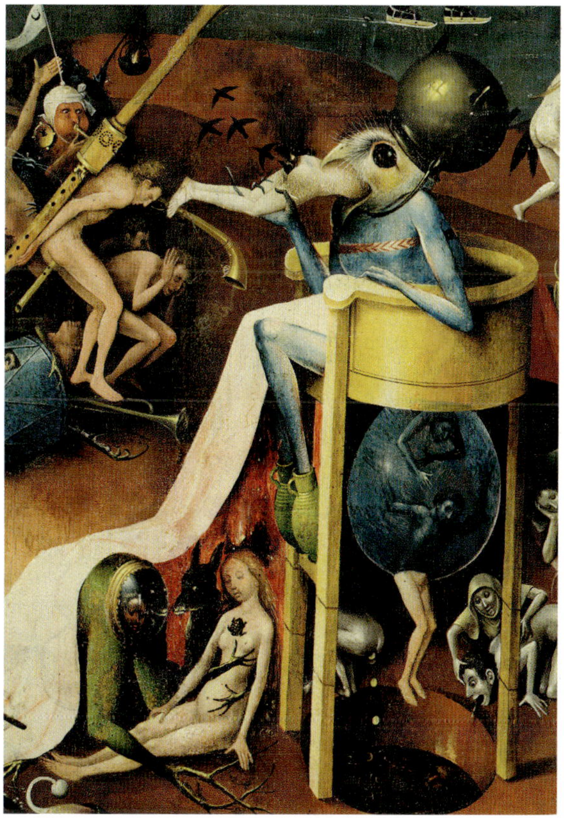

fig. 15.21 Hieronymus Bosch, *Garden of Earthly Delights,* detail of Hell panel.

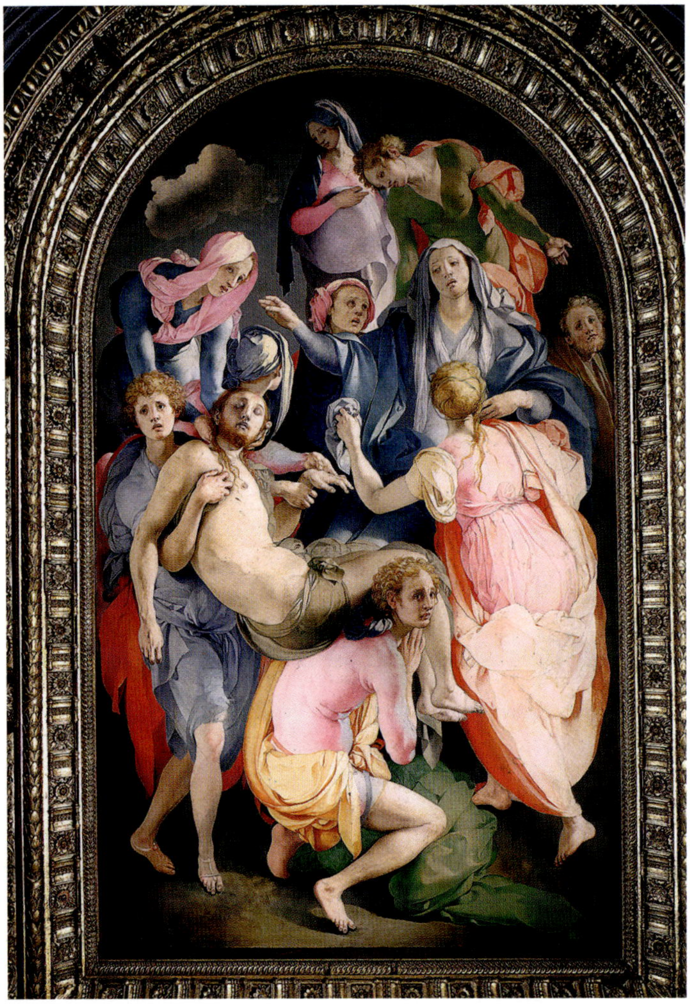

fig. 15.22 Jacopo da Pontormo, *The Entombment of Christ,* 1524–1528. Oil on wood, 10 ft. 3 in. × 6 ft. 4 in. Capponi Chapel, Santa Felicità, Florence.

proposed many interpretations. We cannot see it as a perversion or critical attack on Christianity, however, because King Philip II of Spain, a devout Catholic, purchased it. It may show the traditional Christian progression from Paradise to Hell as a result of human sin.

MANNERISM

Once artists had reached the perfection of the High Renaissance, many of them sought other directions. The human body, which figures prominently in **Mannerist** works, becomes elongated and exaggerated. The basic tenets of the Renaissance style, such as **balance** and **symmetry**, are abandoned, and the subject matter often becomes obscure.

The *Entombment of Christ* (fig. 15.22) by **Jacopo da Pontormo** (1494–1557) illustrates a traditional Christian scene in a very different manner. Figures pushed to the edges of the frame cramp the composition. The bold primary colors of the Renaissance have become iridescent pastels, and the clothing is so tight fitting on some of the figures that it suggests an erotic quality. Two figures bear Christ, who Mary no longer cradles (as seen in Giotto's *Lamentation,* fig. 13.19). Christ's body is elongated, and his small head is oddly positioned directly in front of another head behind him, making it look like a second head sprouts from his own. The kneeling figure is bent at mid torso (rather than at his waist) in a physically impossible manner. Both figures are on their toes, something they would probably be unable to do while bearing the weight of Christ's body. Space and the placement of certain individuals are ambiguous. The figures at the back seem somehow elevated above the foreground figures with no apparent explanation for their positions. Even the title causes confusion because the figures are not actually placing Christ in the tomb.

Bronzino (1503–1572), a pupil of Pontormo, illustrates a lascivious scene with his *Venus, Cupid, Folly and Time* (fig. 15.23). Cupid, with his rear prominently positioned, fondles his mother's breast while kissing her on the lips. Venus holds the golden apple in her left hand and Cupid's arrow in her right. A putto representing Folly is about to pelt them with flowers. Behind him Time, with an hourglass on his shoulder, pulls back a blue curtain to reveal the incestuous scene. The female behind Folly in the shadows

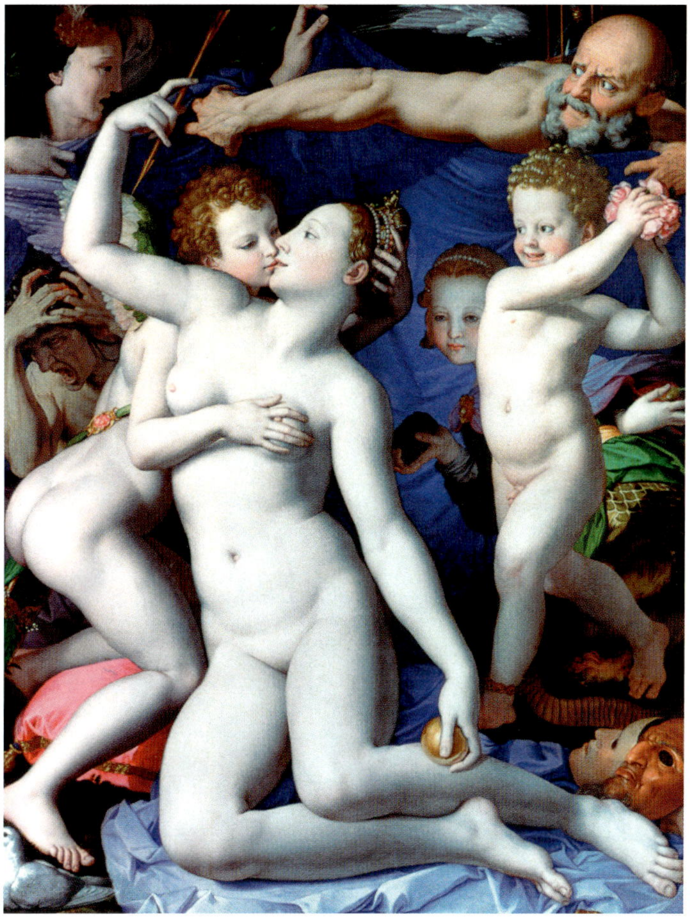

fig. 15.23 Bronzino, *Venus, Cupid, Folly and Time,* c. 1546. Oil on wood, 5 ft. 1 in. × 4 ft. 8 in. National Gallery, London.

may be Fraud. Her hands are reversed, and she has a scaly body with a serpent-like tail. And the figure pulling her hair at the left behind Cupid may be Envy. Again, the artist pushed the figures up against the edges of the composition. The elegant positioning of Venus and Cupid's fingers are typical of Mannerist art, especially in the hand of Cupid with the third and fourth fingers close together. The colors are rich, but cool and metallic. The overall meaning of the painting is obscure, and it may be personal since the Grand Duke of Tuscany commissioned it as a gift for the king of France.

The Spanish painter **El Greco** (1541–1614) is in a category by himself. Born in Crete and trained in Italy, he spent most of his career in Toledo, Spain, producing portraits and spiritual religious paintings. His masterpiece is a huge painting depicting the burial of Count Orgaz (fig. 15.24). He divided his composition into two realms: the earthly and the heavenly. Spanish Grandees look on as two church officials lay the body of the Count to rest. The celestial scene above shows a host of heavenly figures, including Christ, St. Peter and angels. El Greco gives each realm its own style. The figures in the lower terrestrial portion are more realistic with natural proportions. Those in the upper heavenly region are more elongated and ethereal. The two worlds are bridged by the upward glances of some of the Grandees and the acolyte and also by the angel who carries the count's soul to heaven where the Virgin and St. John the Baptist will intercede on his behalf for his eternal salvation.

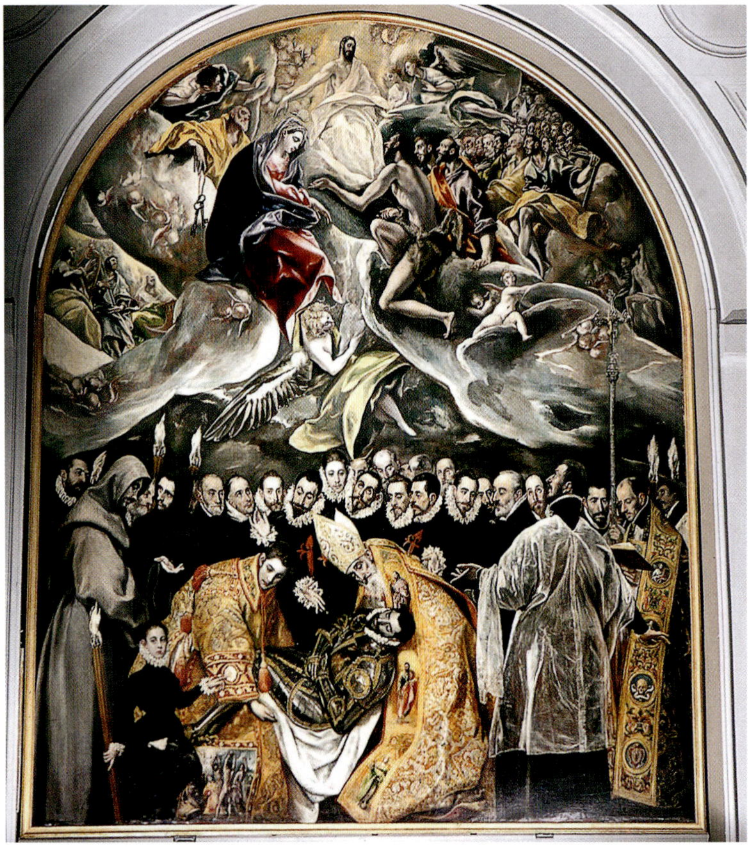

fig. 15.24 El Greco, *Burial of Count Orgaz,* 1586. Oil on canvas, 16 ft. × 12 ft. Santo Tomé, Toledo.

SUMMARY

Renaissance

1. Renaissance is French for "rebirth."
   a. Revival of architectural styles from classical antiquity
   b. Artists rediscover realism and idealism of ancient Greek and Roman art
   c. Rise of Humanism (secular philosophy stressing the importance of the individual)
   d. Characteristic compositional traits are balance, symmetry, harmony, unity, and stability
2. Renaissance began around 1400 in Italy and lasted until the late 16th century.
3. Major artists in Italy:
   a. Masaccio (*Holy Trinity,* c. 1425)
   b. Botticelli (*Birth of Venus,* c. 1482)
   c. Donatello (*David,* c. 1440)
   d. Brunelleschi (*Dome of Florence Cathedral,* c. 1420–36)

   e. Laurana (*Courtyard of the Ducal Palace at Urbino,* c. 1467–1472)
   f. Leonardo da Vinci (*Last Supper,* c. 1495 and *Mona Lisa,* c. 1505)
   g. Michelangelo (*David,* 1501–04 and *Sistine Ceiling,* 1508–12)
   h. Raphael (*School of Athens,* 1508–11)
   i. Titian (*Venus of Urbino,* c. 1538)
4. Major artists in Northern Europe:
   a. Jan van Eyck (*Arnolfini Double Portrait*)
   b. Dürer (*Self-Portrait,* 1498)
   c. Bosch (*Garden of Earthly Delights,* c. 1505)

Mannerism

1. Figures become elongated and exaggerated, and are often pushed to the edges of the composition.
2. Balance, symmetry and clarity of the Renaissance often ignored.
3. Primary colors of Renaissance give way to secondary colors.
4. Subject matter is sometimes obscure.
5. Major artists:
   a. Pontormo (*Entombment of Christ,* 1524–28)
   b. Bronzino (*Venus, Cupid, Folly and Time,* c. 1546)
   c. El Greco (*Burial of Count Orgaz,* 1586)

PRONUNCIATION GUIDE

Bosch, Hieronymus (bosh, hir-**own**-uh-mus)
Botticelli (bah-tih-**chel**-ee)
Bronzino (bron-**zee**-no)
Brunelleschi, Filippo (broon–el-**les**-kee, fih-**lee**-po)
Chiaroscuro (kee-ar-oh-**skoor**-oh)
Contrapposto (kohn-trah-**pah**-stoh)
Donatello (don-ah-**tell**-oh)
Dürer, Albrecht (**dur**-er, awl-brecht)
Iconography (eye-kuh-**nog**-ruh-fee)
Leonardo da Vinci (lay-oh-**nar**-doh dah **vin**-chee
Masaccio (ma-**sah**-chee-oh)
Medici (**med**-ih-chee)
Michelangelo Buonarroti (my-kuhl-**an**-juh-loh, bwan-nah-**roh**-tee)
Pontormo, Jacopo da (pon-**tore**-moh, **yah**-kopo da)
Raphael (rahf-eye–**el**)
Renaissance (**ren**-uh-sahnce)
Sfumato (sfoo-**mah**-toh)
Titian (**tish**-uhn)
Triptych (**trip**-tik)
Van Eyck, Jan (van **ike**, yahn)

GLOSSARY

Allegory. A story or image that refers to something else through symbolic imagery.

Apostles. The twelve disciples of Christ (attributes are in parentheses): Peter (keys, upside down cross, cock), Andrew (X-shaped cross), John (chalice with snake, eagle, book), Matthew (angel, axe, book), Thomas (set-square, ruler, girdle, spear or dagger), Bartholomew (knife, his skin), James the Greater (scallop shell, sword, staff), James the Less (fuller's club, hatter's bow), Simon (saw, cross), Philip (cross), Thaddeus [Jude] (club, halberd or lance), and Judas (bag of silver coins, dark profile).

Arcade. A series of arches on columns or piers.

Atmospheric perspective. See Perspective.

Balance. Arranging forms to achieve equilibrium or harmony.

Bronze. A metal alloy of copper and tin.

Carving. Cutting a figure or object out of a solid material such as wood or stone (as opposed to modeling).

Chiaroscuro. The gradations of light and dark in a painting or drawing used to create the illusion of three-dimensional form. Also called modeling.

Colonnade. A row of columns supporting a roof or arcade.

Contrapposto. The natural stance of the human body in which one leg is relaxed while the other bears most of the weight, causing one hip to be slightly higher than the other.

Dome. A roof with a hemispherical shape.

Drum. A circular or polygonal wall that supports a dome.

Eucharist. The sacrament of Holy Communion to commemorate the Last Supper, or the bread and wine used for the sacrament.

Evangelists, The Four. Authors of the Gospels: Matthew, Mark, Luke, and John. They are often accompanied by their symbols: Angel (Matthew), lion (Mark), ox (Luke), and eagle (John). Luke is the patron saint of painters.

Fresco. A painting on plaster. With true fresco (buon fresco) the paint is applied while the plaster is still wet and it chemically binds with the plaster. With dry fresco (fresco secco), the paint is applied to plaster that has already dried.

Gothic. An art historical period from about 1150 to 1500 in Europe (to 1400 in Italy). In architecture, it is characterized by pointed arches.

Humanism. A secular philosophy in the Renaissance that stressed education and knowledge (especially knowledge of Classical antiquity), the importance of the individual and the ability for self-determination (free will), and civic duty. It emphasized humankind as the standard by which all things are measured.

Iconography. The analytic study of the symbolic, often religious meaning of objects, persons, or events depicted in works of arts.

Idealism. The representation of figures and forms that conforms to a concept of perfection rather than to reality.

Lantern. A structure crowning a dome that lets in light.

Linear perspective. See Perspective.

Mannerism. A style of art in the sixteenth century characterized by elongated forms, cramped compositions, and vivid colors.

Memento mori. A phrase or image, such as a skull, that is a reminder of death.

Modeling. 1) The use of hatching or chiaroscuro to create the illusion of three-dimensional form on a two-dimensional surface. 2) Shaping a form in a pliable material such as clay or plaster.

Perspective. A method of showing depth on a two-dimensional surface. In scientific perspective (also called linear perspective), real or implied parallel lines (orthogonals) converge at one or more vanishing points to give the illusion of recession into space. Objects intended to be further away from the viewer are shown smaller. In atmospheric perspective (also called aerial perspective) forms in the distance are shown less distinct and bluish in color.

Realism. Portraying objects as they actually are.

Renaissance. The period of history that began in Italy around 1400 and lasted through the sixteenth century. It was characterized by a renewed interest in Classical antiquity.

Scientific perspective. See Perspective.

Sfumato. Literally, "vanished in smoke," it refers to the smoky, hazy atmosphere that softens outlines, typical of the paintings by Leonardo da Vinci.

Sibyl. In ancient times a woman who foresaw the future.

Spoof. A humorous imitation of something, such as a work of art.

Symmetry. When two halves of a composition are aesthetically balanced in terms of size, shape, color, and/or the placement of forms.

Triptych. A panel painting in three sections. Often the two outer sections (wings) are smaller and hinged so that they can close over the larger central panel.

Unity. The oneness or wholeness of a work of art.

Vanishing point. In scientific or linear perspective, the point on the horizon line where parallel lines appear to converge.

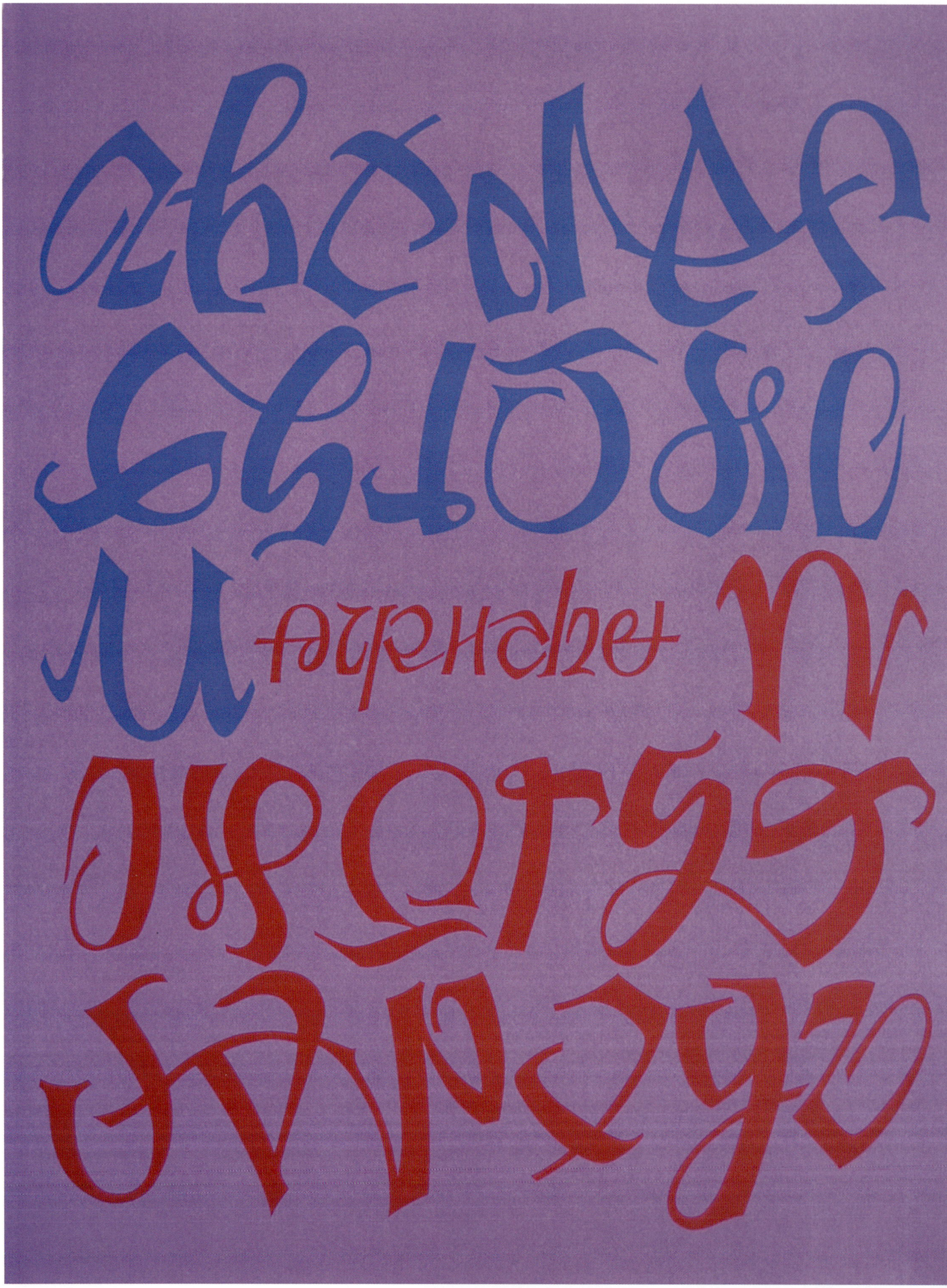
alphabet

16 PRINTMAKING

Printmaking produces multiple impressions of a single image on paper (or sometimes other materials). **Prints** can be original compositions or they can reproduce works of art in other media. Technologically speaking, printmaking is an obsolete technique. Photomechanical processes, and now digital methods, are able to reproduce almost any image mechanically or electronically without the need for a printmaker. Printmaking survives in the art world, however, because of its inherent beauty and unique qualities unobtainable in other media.

Printmaking revolutionized art in the Renaissance because it made art available to many more people than previously. Prior to its invention, only the wealthy could afford to buy art. Prints also spread knowledge of art because artists made prints of famous works of art. Not only did people in general become more familiar with art, but artists themselves benefited because they could obtain images of works by contemporary artists in other countries. Rembrandt, one of the most skilled printmakers of all time, never travelled outside of the Netherlands, yet he was familiar with current artistic trends because of prints. Prints greatly affected the spread of artistic styles from the Renaissance on.

To make a print copy of a painting, the artist first makes a drawing of it. Then, depending on the type of print, he reproduces the composition again on wood, metal, stone or some other material using the drawing as a guide. Then he makes multiples of those images using one of numerous print processes. Artists make prints in editions, labelling each print so that you know how large the edition is and what the number of each print is. For example, if you buy a print that says 27/250, it implies your print was the 27th print made out of a total of 250 prints (although prints are often numbered out of sequence). The plate becomes slightly more worn with each print pulled so that the last print of a large edition is not quite as crisp as the first print pulled. While working on a print the artist can pull an example to see how the image is progressing. This is called an **artist's proof** (AP).

Prints such as engravings and etchings produce a mirror image of the original work. To avoid this, the artist has to create the design in reverse so that it will print with the same orientation as the original work.

PRINT TECHNIQUES

There are many kinds of prints, each with their own characteristics. The four basic types are relief, intaglio, planographic, and stencil (fig. 16.1).

fig. 16.11 Noel Lawson, *Palindrome Alphabet,* 1985. Silkscreen. A palindrome is a word or a phrase that is the same whether read left to right or right to left, such as "radar" or "never odd or even." In this case, the image remains the same if turned upside down. Turn this book upside down and look at this work again to see the palindrome effect.

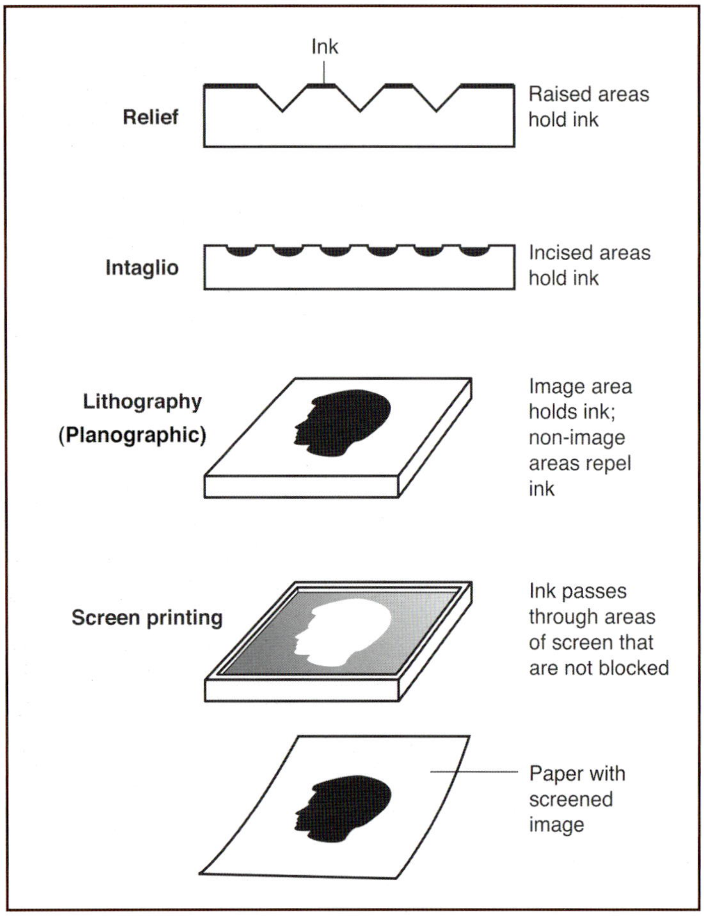

fig. 16.1 Printmaking processes.

Relief

With relief, the artist cuts away all parts of the surface he does not want to print with sharp carving tools, leaving the design in raised relief. When he inks the surface, only the design will take the ink because he has cut away the other portions. (It is the same principle as a muddy shoe print on the floor or an image made with a rubber stamp.) The artist places paper (often dampened to take the ink better) over the inked design, applies pressure and the ink is tranferred to the paper creating the print. Relief techniques include woodcut, wood engraving, and linocut.

Woodcut. Woodcut is the earliest printmaking technique. Developed in China, it was probably first used to print patterns on fabric. It wasn't until around 1400 that woodcuts printed on paper appeared in Europe. The artist first draws the design on a wood block (or on paper and then transfers it to the block) and uses sharp carving tools to cut away the unwanted parts. Usually he uses a softer wood, cut along the grain, to facilitate carving. Fine detail and shading are not possible with woodcuts because of the nature of wood. Color prints are possible, however, but discrete areas must be inked or separate blocks carved for each color. With multiple blocks the artist has to carefully align (register) paper for each color so that the final image is not blurred. The Japanese produced beautiful color woodcuts beginning in the seventeenth century. *The Great Wave* by Hokusai (fig. 16.2) shows the sophistication attained by Japanese artists. Unusually detailed for a woodcut, the scenes illustrate a huge wave threatening three small boats of fisherman. Hokusai contrasts the swelling motion of the sea with Mt. Fuji in the distance. This image began as a watercolor by the artist.

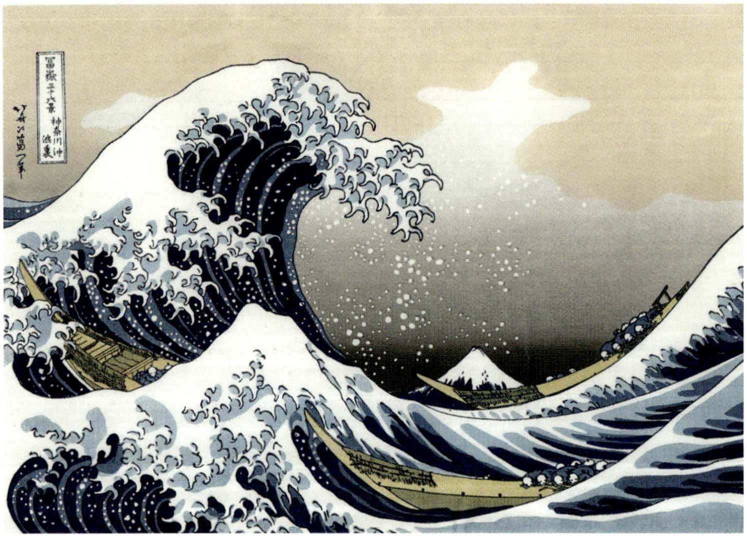

fig. 16.2 Hokusai, *The Great Wave*, c. 1830. Color woodblock print.

Craftsmen specializing in woodcut carving then duplicated the design in wood. They needed many blocks to produce all the colors and tones in this scene.

Wood Engraving. Wood engraving is the same technique as woodcut except that artists use harder woods and do the carving on the end grain (instead of with the grain on the side). This technique, developed in the late eighteenth century, permitted much more detail (fig. 16.3). Another advantage to wood engraving is that artists can make many more prints from the block before it deteriorates because of its hardness.

Linocuts. Linocuts use linoleum as the relief surface. Developed at the beginning of the twentieth century, linocuts are easier to carve because the rubbery surface of linoleum is softer than wood, and there is no grain to worry about. Because linoleum is a soft material, it degrades more quickly, allows less detail, and permits fewer prints than with woodcut and wood engraving. Pam Lawson's *Black Hand* (fig. 16.4) illustrates the bold dramatic qualities possible with a linocut.

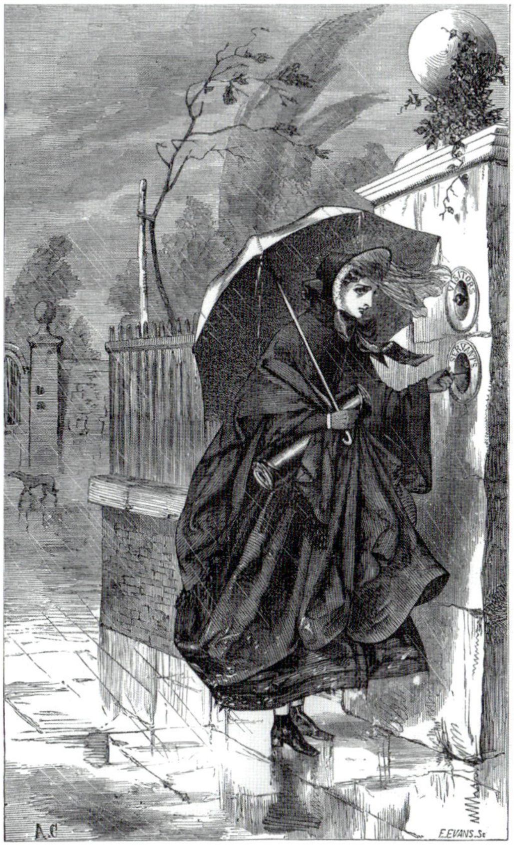

fig. 16.3 Adelaide Claxton, *The Daily Governess,* 1862. Wood engraving.

INTAGLIO

Intaglio is the reverse of relief. The surface does not print, but rather the portions taken away do. Intaglio comes from an Italian word meaning "to cut into." Artists make intaglio prints with metal plates, traditionally copper because of its softer nature, although today they use many other metals such as steel and zinc. They carve the design with sharp metal tools or etch it with acid. They then ink the plate and wipe the surface clean. This leaves the ink only in the grooved lines of the design. Damp paper is placed over the plate and pressure is applied by running the plate through a printing press. The pressure forces the paper into the inked grooves, which take the ink. The pressure also results in an impression of the plate (a plate mark) on the paper. Intaglio includes engraving, drypoint, etching, aquatint, and mezzotint.

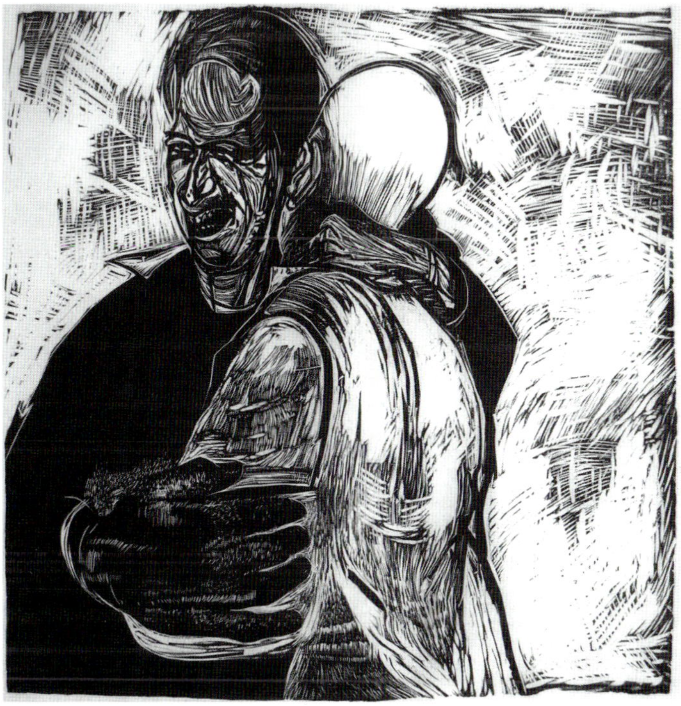

fig. 16.4 Pam Lawson, *Black Hand,* 2007. Linocut.

Engraving. Engraving evolved in the early fifteenth century. The artist creates it by cutting into the surface of the plate with an engraving tool called a **burin** (also called a **graver**) (fig.16.5). Typically the tip is V-shaped, but burin tips come in different shapes to produce different kinds

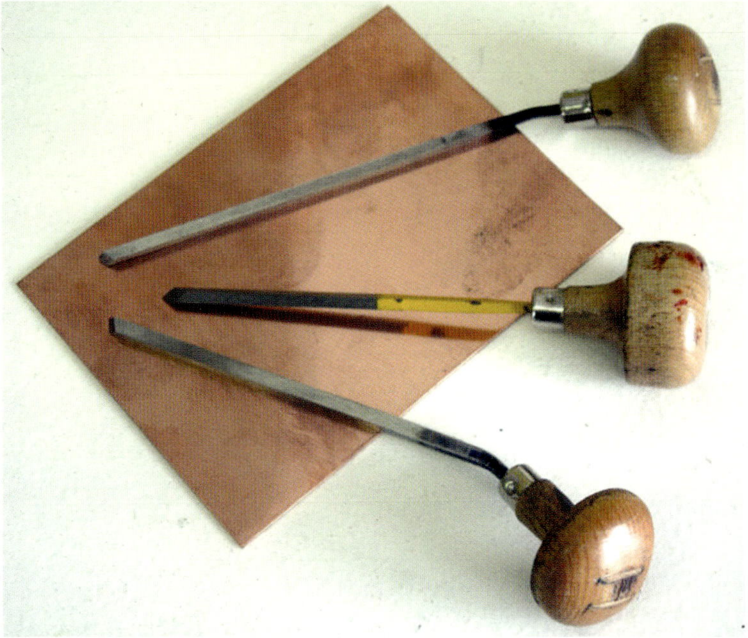

fig. 16.5 Engraving tools.

of lines. It is a difficult process because the artist has to push the burin through metal and scrape away any rough edges. A good example of engraving is our paper money. The portraits of George Washington ($1 bill), Thomas Jefferson ($2 bill) (fig. 16.6) and Abraham Lincoln ($5 dollar bill) illustrate the fineness of detail possible with engraving. Take a dollar bill out of your wallet and look closely at the portrait of George Washington. **Engraving** achieves subtle modeling solely through the use of line in the form of contour and cross hatching.

Drypoint. Drypoint is a variant of engraving developed in the sixteenth century. The artist scratches the image into the metal using a metal tool with a sharp tip, which leaves rough edges (a burr) on the sides of the groove. The **burr** produces a soft slightly blurred effect when inked and printed. Fewer prints can be pulled from a drypoint plate because the burr wears down fairly quickly.

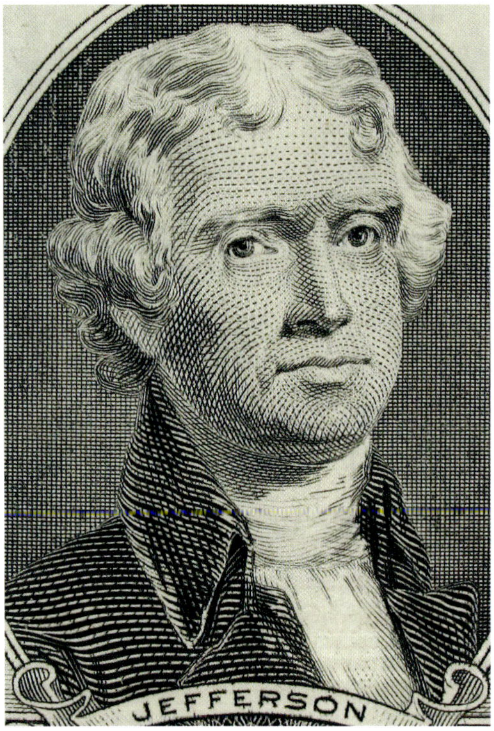

fig. 16.6 Detail of a $2 bill.

Mezzotint. Mezzotint is another variant of engraving developed in the seventeenth century. First the artist uses a special tool with tiny metal teeth to roughen the plate finely and evenly all over. He then makes the image by scraping or burnishing smooth the roughened surface where he wants it to print lighter. This technique allows greater control of tonal values because the roughened surface takes a lot of ink, resulting in deeper tones, and because the scraping and burnishing process permits fine gradations in tone. *What is this my son Tom?* (fig. 16.7) illustrates the fine gradations of tone possible in the drapery folds in the foreground and in the foliage in the background.

Etching. The etching technique was invented in the early sixteenth century as decorative treatment for armor that then was applied to printmaking. With etchings, acid does the hard work for the artist. The artist covers a metal plate with a waxy substance called a ground. Then he or she draws the design in the ground using an etching needle. Wherever a line is drawn the ground is scraped away and the metal is exposed. Once the composition is complete, the artist places the plate in an acid bath. The acid eats or bites into the metal where exposed while the untouched ground areas protect the rest of the plate from the acid. The stronger the acid and the longer the artist leaves the plate in the acid bath, the deeper the etched lines will become and the more ink they will take, resulting in thicker darker lines. After the acid bath, the artist rinses the plate, removing the ground. He then prints it in the same manner as an engraving.

Etching is a much less demanding process for the artist because drawing in wax is obviously easier than drawing in metal. Etching allows more freedom of expression, detail, and variety of line quality than engraving. Harold Little's *Bus Stop* (fig. 16.8) displays a complexity of fine lines and tonal values that would be difficult to reproduce with the engraving technique.

Aquatint. Aquatint is a variant of etching invented in the eighteenth century. It uses an acid-resistant powdered resin as the ground, which the artist heats to melt the resin. When placed in an acid bath, the acid eats away at the miniscule spaces between the resin particles producing a finely bitten surface to take the ink. The result is subtly shaded areas of light and dark. Artists usually combine aquatint with other techniques such as drypoint.

Artists often use several intaglio techniques in a single print. For example, Rembrandt used drypoint and engraving as well in his etching of *The Three Trees* (fig. 16.9).

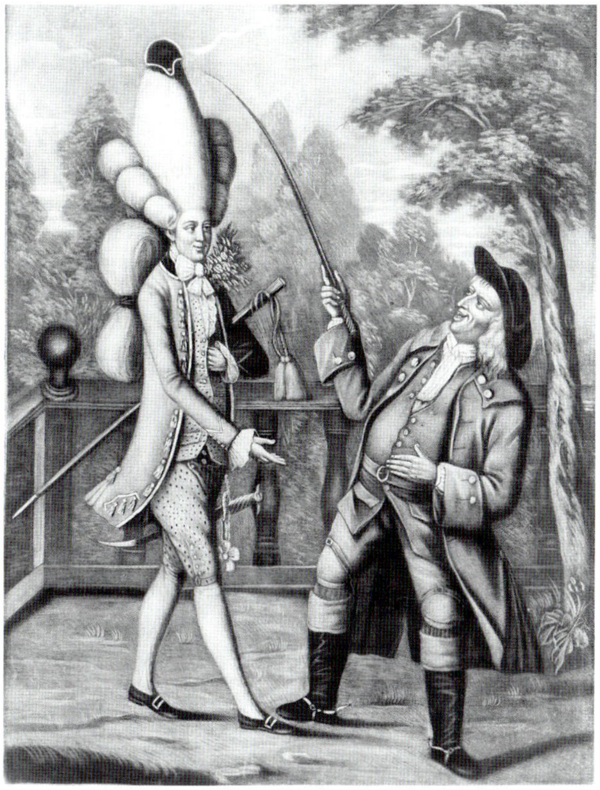

fig. 16.7 R. Sayer & J. Bennett (publishers), *What is this my son Tom?* 1774. Mezzotint. This is a satirical comment on the exaggerated hairstyles that became popular in the late eighteenth century.

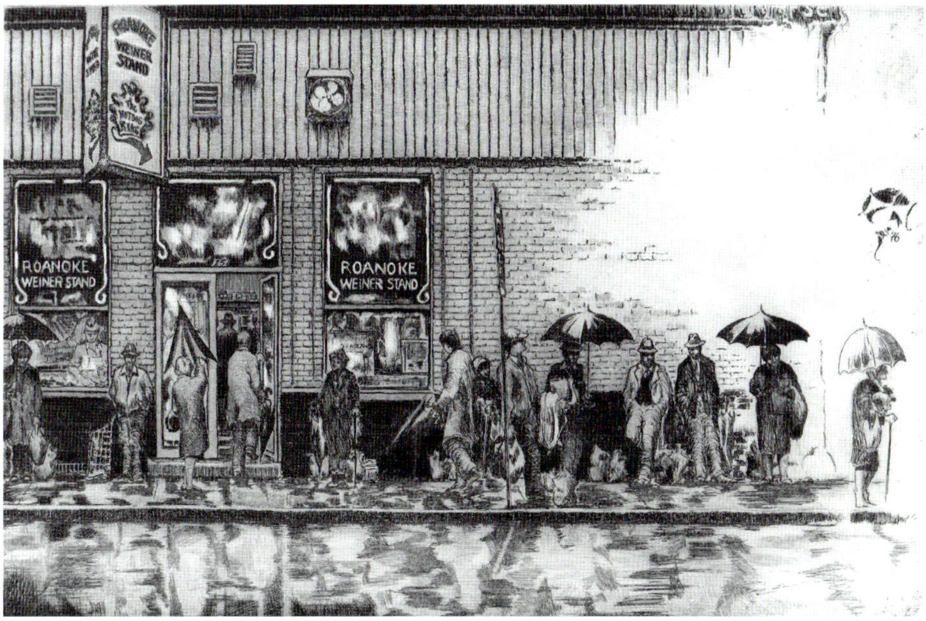

fig. 16.8 Harold Little, *Bus Stop on Campbell Avenue: Roanoke City Market*, 1976. Etching.

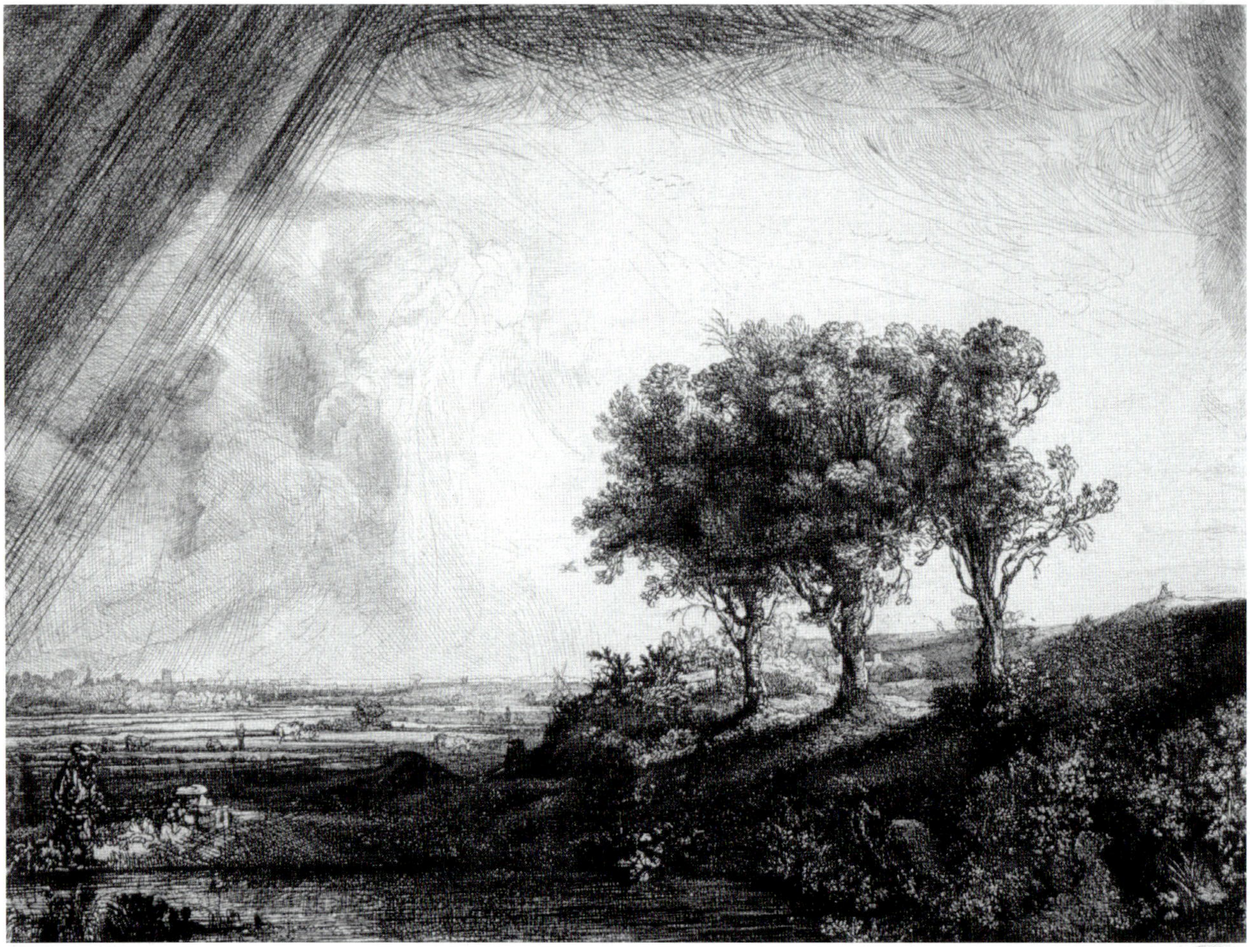

fig. 16.9 Rembrandt, *Three Trees,* c. 1639. Etching with drypoint and engraving.

Planographic

Planographic refers to printing from a flat surface rather than a raised surface (relief) or an incised surface (intaglio). Planographic techniques include lithography, offset lithography, and various digital processes.

Lithography. Invented in 1798, lithography is a technique based on the natural repulsion of oil and water. The artist draws an image with a waxy medium (such as litho crayons or litho pencils) on a limestone slab (or on another material that mimics the fine porous quality of limestone). He or she then applies acid to fix the image onto the surface, followed by gum arabic (which is water soluble) to seal the surface not covered by the image. The stone is wetted, but the water does not stick to the image because of its greasy nature. The stone is then inked, but since water repels the oil in the ink, only the drawn image takes the ink. A sheet of paper is placed on the stone and then run through a press to transfer the image from the stone to the paper. Lithography soon became a popular printing technique because it was quick and easy. Printers made posters, such as Toulouse-Lautrec's *La Goulue* (fig. 16.10) in large quantities to advertise products and events. The lithographic process permits yet more freedom and spontaneity than relief and intaglio.

Offset Lithography. In offset lithography the inked image is transferred (or offset) from a plate to a flexible blanket (a rubber-coated fabric wrapped around a cylinder) and then printed on paper so that the image is not reversed. It has the further advantage of producing high quality prints more quickly, and the plate lasts longer because there is no direct contact between it and the paper.

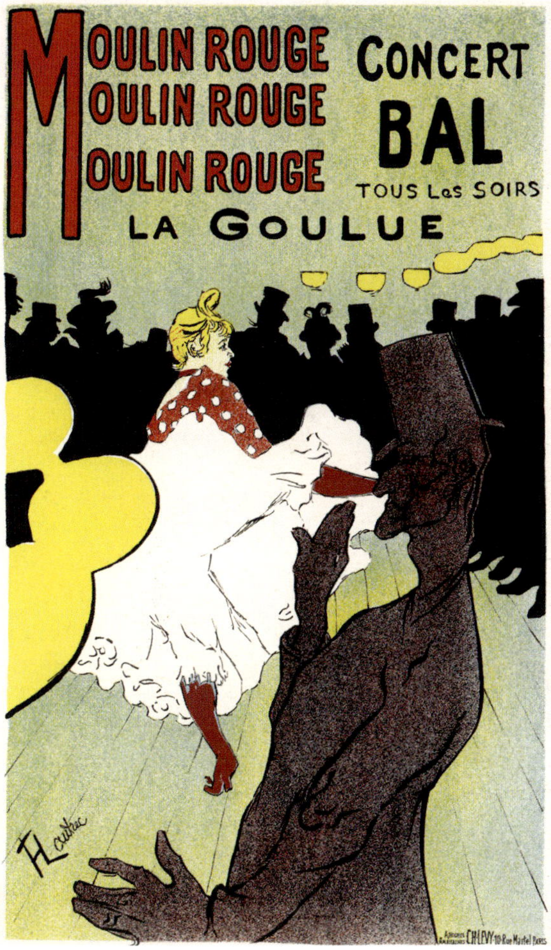

fig. 16.10 Henri de Toulouse-Lautrec, *La Goulue at the Moulin Rouge Concert Bal,* 1891. Lithograph.

© Mary Evans Picture Library/The Image Works

Stencils

Stencils are text or images cut out of a material to create a negative form. In art, **screenprinting** (also called **silkscreening** or **serigraphy**) is based on this process. It is both an artistic process used by artists and a commercial process used by firms to print images on T-shirts, CDs, ceramics, and the like. The artist creates an image in stencil form and adheres it to a screen—a piece of fabric (originally silk, but now usually synthetic) stretched over a frame. The artist places the screen on top of the material to receive the image (usually paper) and pushes colored ink through the screen with a squeegee. The ink transfers to the paper where the openings in the stencil are, producing a positive image of the design on the paper. A separate stencil and screen are necessary for each color. Nowadays artists often use a photographic stencil created by coating the screen with a light-sensitive emulsion. Those parts of the emulsion not exposed to light wash away leaving a negative stencil of the image.

Screenprinting is especially good for creating images that have large areas of solid color. Because a screenprint is a direct transfer from stencil to paper, the image is not reversed as it is in the other printmaking processes. The solid and uniformly colored letters in Noel Lawson's *Alphabet Palindrome* (fig. 16.11, page 210) are well suited to the screenprint process.

Digital printing involves creating an image on a computer using various software programs and then printing it on a high-quality inkjet or laserjet printer. This eliminates the need to have a plate, stone, or screen as with the other processes described above. With the extremely high resolution now possible with printers, digital printing has revolutionized the art of printmaking. **Giclée** is a digital method popular with artists and commercial galleries. It is a fine art print made from a digital source using an inkjet printer. The name comes from the French word for nozzle (as in the nozzle of an ink jet printer). They first appeared on the market in the early 1990s. Many artists have their traditional paintings and other two-dimensional works digitally photographed and then reproduced with the Giclée method. These prints are not original works of art; they are faithful high-quality reproductions, and galleries offer them to customers as a less expensive alternative to original works of art.

SUMMARY

Printmaking developed in the early Renaissance in Europe. It radically changed art because, with its reasonable cost and multiple copies, it spread artistic styles across the continent allowing artists to see art that they normally could not have seen otherwise.

Print Techniques

1. **Relief** (areas of the block are cut away)
   a. Woodcut (the oldest kind of print—developed in China).
   b. Wood engraving—uses the end grain of the wood allowing greater detail.
   c. Linocut—made using linoleum, which is easy to cut.
2. **Intaglio** (lines are engraved or etched into a metal plate)
   a. Engraving (lines are incised in the plate using a burin).
   b. Drypoint (the image is scratched into the plate, leaving rough edges).
   c. Mezzotint (a rocker with metal teeth is used to roughen the plate first).
   d. Etching (lines are scratched in a soft resin and are eaten into the plate with acid).
   e. Aquatint (an acid resistant powdered resin is used as ground).
3. **Planographic** (printing from a smooth surface)
   a. Lithography (uses the principle of oil and water not mixing).
   b. Offset lithography.
4. **Stencil**
   a. Screenprinting (silkscreen or serigraphy).
5. **Digital printing** (using a computer and inkjet or laser printer)
   a. Giclée.

Videos

Intaglio printmaking:
http://www.youtube.com/watch?v=SNKn4PORGBI

Color woodblock printing:
http://www.youtube.com/watch?v=dliF74ojOho&feature=related

Lithography:
http://www.youtube.com/watch?v=JHw5_1Hopsc

Offset lithography:
http://www.youtube.com/watch?v=ClbQL_Oso40

Silkscreen printing:
http://www.youtube.com/watch?v=wogKeYH2wEE&feature=related

Giclée:
http://www.youtube.com/watch?v=2LmtQti5QgE&feature=related

PRONUNCIATION GUIDE

Giclée (jee-**clay** OR zhee-**clay**)
Gravure (gruh-**vyoor**)
Intaglio (in-**tah**-lyoh)
Lithography (lih-**thog**-ruh-fee)

Rembrandt van Rijn (**rem**-brandt van **rine**)
Renaissance (**ren**-uh-sahnce)
Serigraphy (sih-**rig**-ruh-fee)
Toulouse-Lautrec, Henri de (too-**loos**-loh-**trek**, on-**ree** de)
Tusche (toosh)

GLOSSARY

Aquatint An intaglio printmaking process that uses powdered particles of resin to give the print a granular appearance.

Artist's proof. In printmaking, a trial print that the artist uses to see the progress of his/her work.

Burin. A sharp cutting tool used by engravers.

Burr. In the drypoint printmaking process, the ridge of metal that results from the engraving tool being pulled across the printing plate.

Drypoint. An intaglio printmaking process in which the burin is pulled back across the surface of the printing plate leaving a burr.

Engraving. 1) The process of incising an image on a hard surface, such as a copper plate. 2) A print made by this process.

Etching. 1) A printmaking process in which the image is etched, or eaten into the metal plate by acid. 2) A print made by this process.

Giclée. A fine art print made from a digital source using a high quality inkjet printer.

Graver. A cutting tool used by engravers.

Ground A coating applied to a canvas or printmaking plate to prepare it for painting or etching.

Intaglio. Any of several printmaking processes in which lines are incised into the printing plate. Engraving, drypoint, etching, aquatint, and mezzotint are all intaglio processes.

Linocut. A form of relief printmaking in which the design is carved in a block of linoleum. The resulting print is also called a linocut.

Lithograph. A print made from the lithography process in which involves drawing the image with a greasy material on a polished stone.

Mezzotint. A type of print in which the plate is pitted with a special tool.

Offset lithography. A printing process where an inked image is transferred from a plate to a rubber-coated fabric (the blanket) wrapped around a cylinder and then printed on paper. (The term offset refers to the fact that the image isn't printed directly from the plate.)

Planographic printing. Any method of printing from a flat surface, such as lithography.

Print. A work of art made by one of the printmaking processes such as engraving or etching. A print can also be a photograph made from a negative.

Proof. See Artist's proof.

Relief printing. Any printmaking process wherein any area of the plate not to be printed is carved away leaving the projecting areas to form the image.

Screenprinting. A printmaking process where paint or ink is forced through the open areas of a stencil that has been applied to a fine mesh fabric, such as silk, stretched taut on a frame. Also called silkscreen printing or serigraphy.

Serigraphy. See Screenprinting.

Silkscreen. A print made by the silkscreen process. See Screenprinting.

Tusche. A greasy material used for drawing on a lithography stone.

Wood engraving. 1) A relief printmaking process in which fine lines are carved into a wood block. 2) A print made by this process.

Woodcut. 1) A relief printmaking process in which a wood block is carved so that those parts not intended to print are cut away, leaving the design raised. 2) A print made by this process.

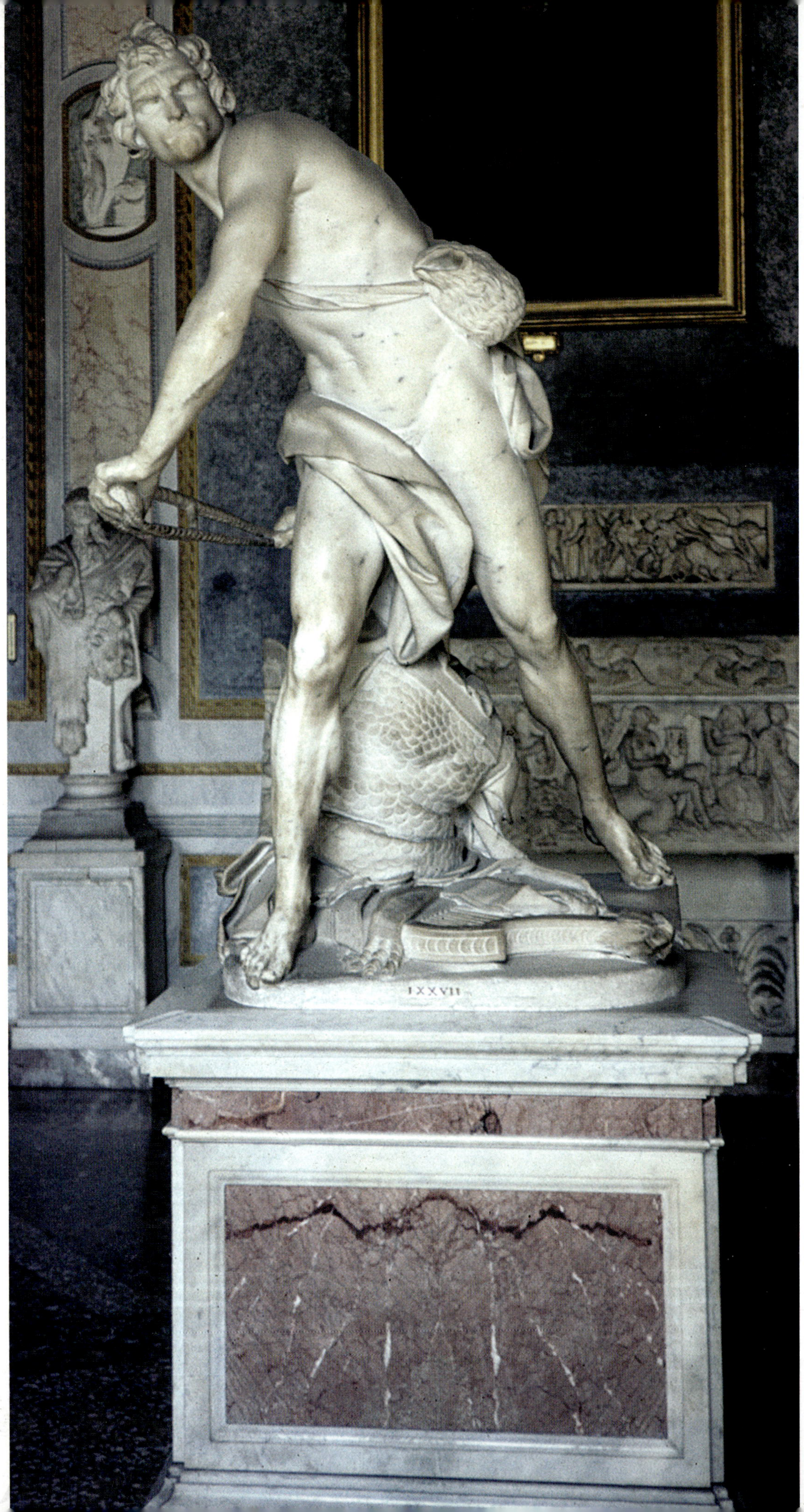

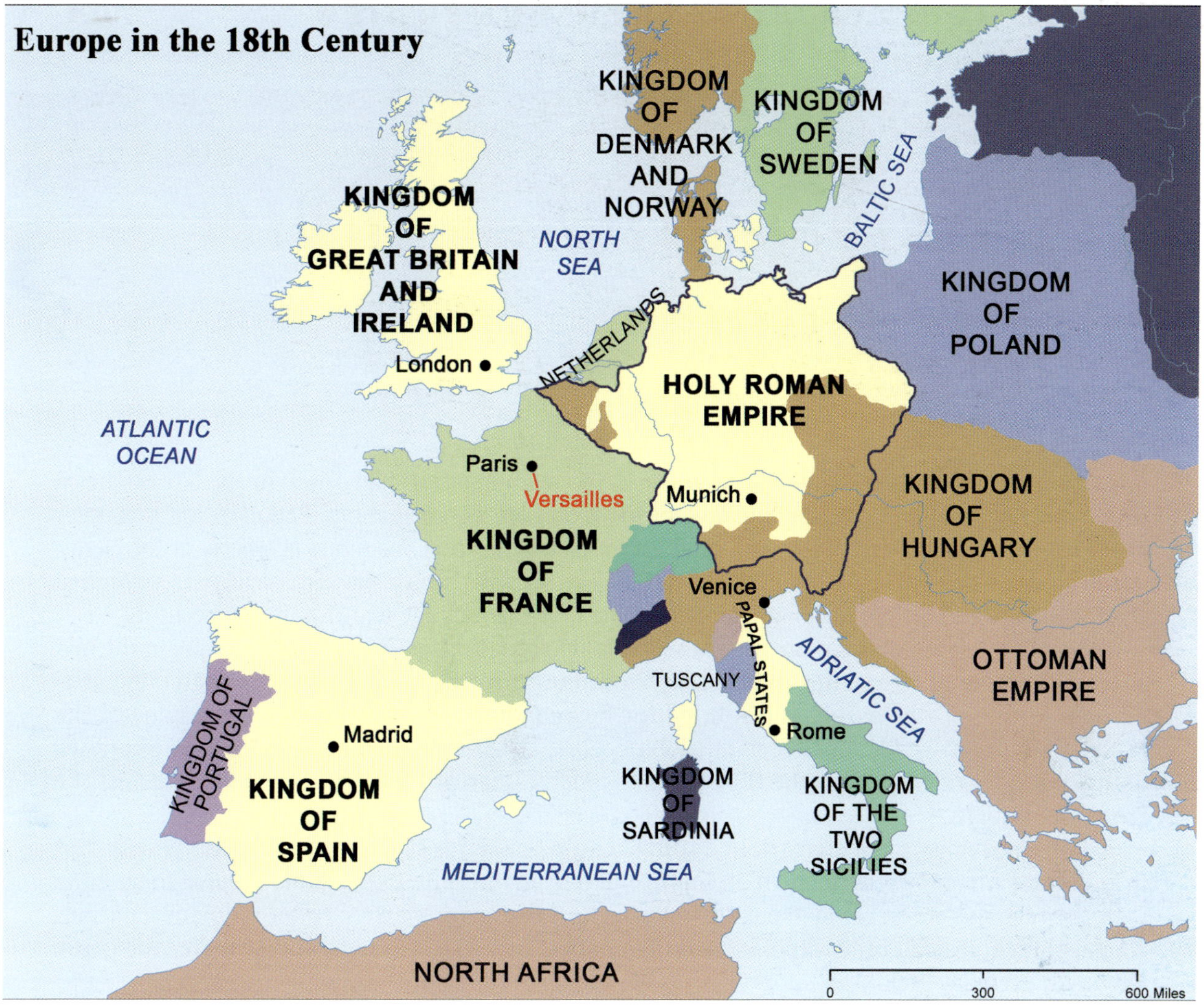

17

BAROQUE ART

Baroque refers to the art of the seventeenth century. There is no single Baroque style; it is a multiplicity of national and regional variations ranging from energetic melodrama to classical calm. In general, however, Baroque painting and sculpture are dynamic, emotional and theatrical.

ART OF THE 17TH AND 18TH CENTURIES

fig. 17.1 Gian Lorenzo Bernini, *David*, 1623. Marble, life-size. Galleria Borghese, Rome.

The Reformation, Counter Reformation, and Art

A reaction to the corruption and abuses in the Catholic Church that had arisen in the late medieval period, the Reformation led to the founding of the Protestant denominations. Begun by Martin Luther in 1517 to return Christianity to its roots and improve the education and moral character of the clergy, its spread was aided by the recent invention of the printing press, which allowed the Bible to be printed in local languages. Much of northern Europe became Protestant by the mid-seventeenth century.

Reacting to the Reformation, the Catholic Church initiated the Counter Reformation in the mid sixteenth century to reform the Church, keep Protestant theology at bay, and attempt to bring people back into the Catholic fold. It instituted the Roman Inquisition to root out heresy, allowed the Jesuits to undertake educational and missionary work, and tried to improve the training of priests. Catholic secular rulers such as the Holy Roman Emperor Charles V took military action against the Protestant nations.

Both movements affected art. In Catholic Europe religious scenes continued to flourish, but they became more immediate in an attempt to better instruct the faithful and involve them more with the religious scene being depicted. In Protestant Europe there were fewer religious paintings commissioned; instead other types increased in importance such as landscape, still life, and genre (scenes of everyday life).

Baroque artists rejected the artifice of the Mannerists and preferred the direct study of nature. Under the influence of the Catholic Counter-Reformation, religious painting sought to involve the viewer more directly by appealing to the emotions. Rome was still the center of European art at the beginning of the Baroque period, but by the end of the century that honor had passed to Paris where it remained until World War II.

As a sculptor, painter and architect, **Gian Lorenzo Bernini** (1598–1680) was one of the geniuses of the Baroque. His sculpted *David* (fig. 17.1) provides a striking contrast to the earlier Davids by Donatello (fig. 15.5) and Michelangelo (fig. 15.13). Where Donatello's *David* calmly reflects after killing Goliath and Michelangelo's *David* contemplates the act, Bernini's *David* is about to sling the stone. Bernini portrays the most climactic moment—David has pulled the sling back and in the next instant he will release it with all his strength. David's twisted pose with its dominant diagonals implies action, and his furrowed brow and pursed lips add to the emotional impact. Although this sculpture has a principal viewing point like the two Renaissance Davids, it also has interesting and diverse views from a variety of angles. The calm staid aspect of the Renaissance style here explodes into theatrical and dynamic movement.

In painting, **Michelangelo Merisi da Caravaggio** (1571–1610) was the master of the early Baroque. One of the most influential artists of all time, his new style quickly spread all over Europe. Caravaggio placed his protagonists close to the picture plane and against a dark background. He also did not idealize his subjects. He shows saints as they really were with dirty feet and all. This made the scenes he painted more immediate and allowed the viewer to feel as though he or she was witnessing the event.

His *Conversion of St. Paul* (fig. 17.2) shows all these qualities. A Roman Pharisee, Saul (Paul's name before his conversion) became a Christian when a divine blinding light struck him and he heard the voice of Christ speaking to him. Like Bernini, Caravaggio shows the most dramatic moment—Paul in the act of conversion after the force of his vision caused him to fall from his horse. Paul's body forms a diagonal with his head at the edge of the picture plane so that he appears to spill out into our space, drawing us into the scene. Caravaggio's dramatic lighting—strong contrasts of light and dark to achieve a theatrical effect—was one of his most important contributions and one of the most widely imitated. Saul's servant quietly attends the horse, oblivious to his master's divine revelation.

Contemporaries criticized Caravaggio as being vulgar for showing saints as common people and for what they considered uncouth details (such as the large rear end of the horse that is nearly in the viewer's face). But this is precisely why his work was popular and influential.

Artemisia Gentileschi (1593–c.1652) was one such artist who fell under Caravaggio's influence. Trained by her painter father (as were most woman painters before the nineteenth century), Artemisia is one of the outstanding female painters in the history of Western art. *Judith Slaying Holofernes* (fig. 17.3) is her most powerful work.

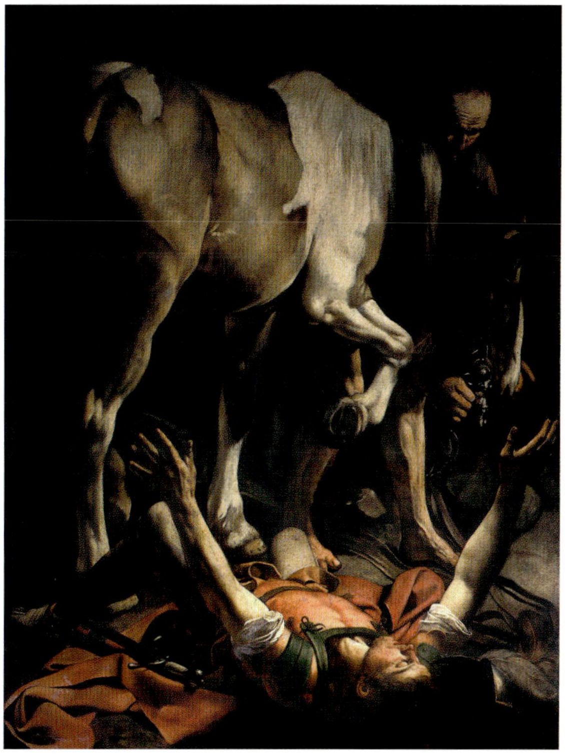

fig. 17.2 Caravaggio, *Conversion of St. Paul,* 1601. Oil on canvas, 7 ft. 6 in. × 5 ft. 9 in. Cerasi Chapel, Santa Maria del Popolo, Rome.

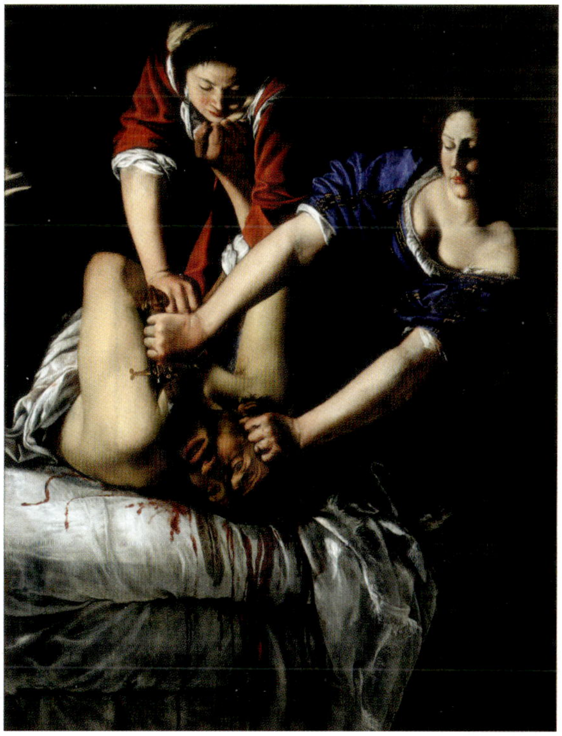

fig. 17.3 Artemisia Gentileschi, *Judith Slaying Holofernes,* c. 1614–1620. Oil on canvas, 6 ft. 6 in. × 5 ft. 4 in. Galleria degli Uffizi, Florence. Artemisia painted this subject several times, and an unfortunate event in her life may have been the reason. Another artist raped her, but when it went to trial Artemisia was tortured with thumbscrews to determine if her accusations were true. That unpleasant experience could well have led to her preference for depicting female heroines punishing evil men.

The Assyrian general Holofernes was about to destroy Judah so Judith, pretending to be a traitor to her people and offering to spend the night with him, got him drunk and then cut off his head with his own sword. Once again the painting depicts the most dramatic moment. While Judith's maidservant holds Holofernes down, Judith draws the sword through his neck. Blood spurts forth and dribbles down the bed sheets. Holofernes awakes from his stupor just in time to realize he is being decapitated. Judith pulls back, indicating her distaste for having to do this necessary deed. The Caravaggesque lighting heightens the drama, as does the placement of the figures in the foreground.

Peter Paul Rubens (1577–1640) was another artist whose early work shows the influence of Caravaggio. But his study of the works of Titian proved more important for him. The Flemish artist soon developed into one of Europe's most preeminent (and wealthy) painters. He traveled widely to complete foreign commissions and as a diplomat for the rulers of Flanders. The demand for his works was so great that he formed a large workshop of assistants, each one with his own specialty (such as animals, foliage, drapery or still life elements). This permitted Rubens to produce a tremendous amount of work. It also causes us to wonder how much of his own hand is in each painting. One of his more popular themes was the great hunting scene. The huge painting *Wolf and Fox Hunt* (fig. 17.4)

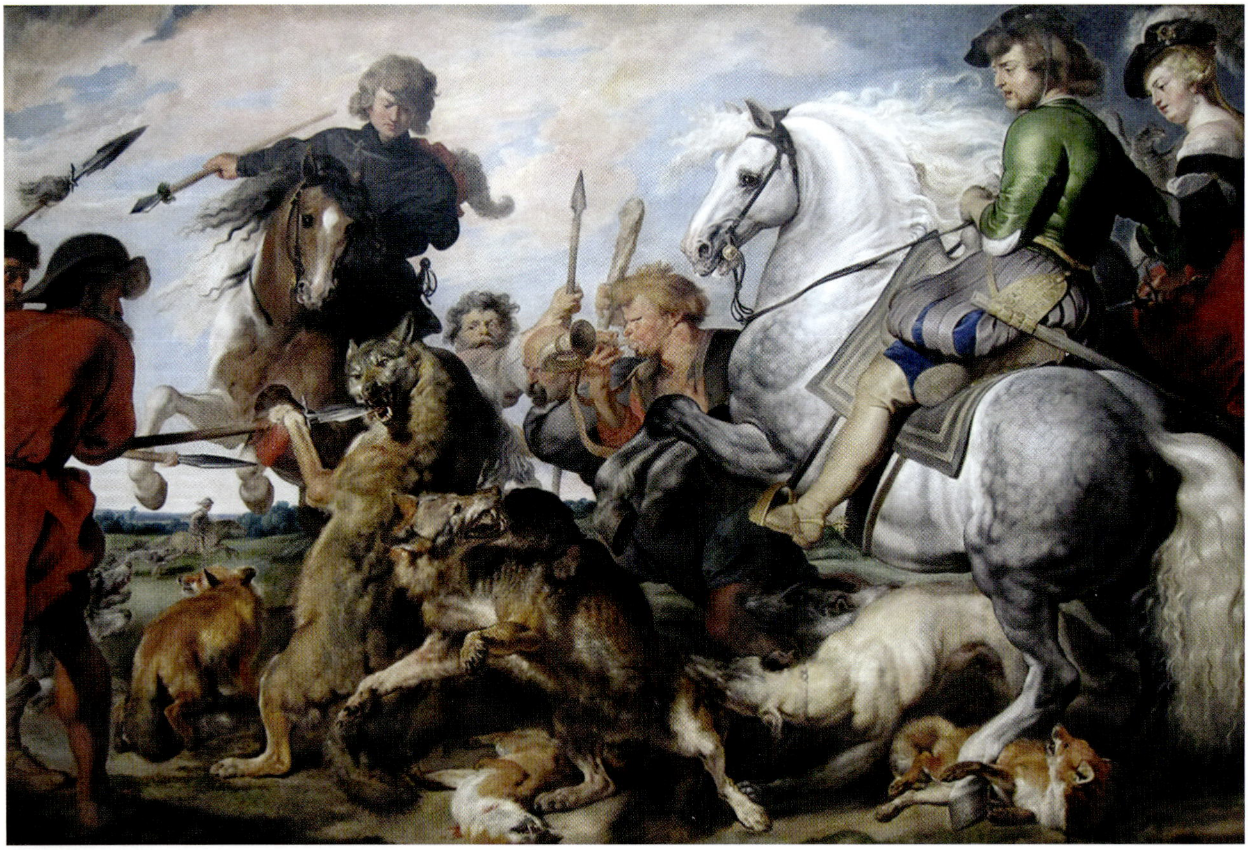

fig. 17.4 Peter Paul Rubens, *Wolf and Fox Hunt*, 1615–1621. Oil on canvas, 8 ft. 1 in. × 12 ft. 4 in. Metropolitan Museum of Art, New York.

shows a fierce battle between man and beast. Riders on horseback approach as men on foot threaten the wolves with lances. The hunters' hounds viciously attack the center wolf, which tries to bite back. Beneath him one of the three foxes is already dead, while a horse is trampling another to the right. The scene is like a stage set with the action up close to the picture plane. The rich colors and the sensuous pink flesh of the woman rider at the far right show his debt to Titian. A work such as this is the epitome of the dynamic and theatrical Baroque style.

Just to the north of Flanders in the Netherlands, **Rembrandt van Rijn** (1606–1669) developed a very different Baroque style. A master of portraiture, Rembrandt was able to penetrate the souls of his sitters and reveal their inner selves. He painted a number of self-portraits over the course of his lifetime that document his changing physical and mental state as he progressed through life's trials and tribulations. The self-portrait in figure 17.5 shows the artist at the height of his career. Wealthy and still relatively young, Rembrandt exudes an air of privilege and confidence. His popularity later waned, and he plunged into bankruptcy, dying in poverty. In addition to his vast output of paintings, Rembrandt was also one of the best printmakers of his time (see fig. 1.21).

fig. 17.5 Rembrandt van Rijn, *Self Portrait,* 1640. Oil on canvas, 3 ft. 4 in. × 2 ft. 7.5 in. National Gallery, London.

Spain produced one of the best painters of the century, yet he was not widely known outside his country until centuries later. **Diego Velázquez** (1599–1660) was the court painter to King Philip IV, and, like Rembrandt, he had a gift for portraiture. His masterpiece is *Las Meninas* (fig. 17.6). The scene depicts Velázquez working on an unseen painting. The king's young daughter stands in the center looking at the viewer. Two ladies-in-waiting (the *meninas*) and two dwarfs attend her while two chaperones converse in the background. The mirror on the back wall reflects an image of the king and queen. The painting is a tour de force of composition and meaning, even though the subject of the painting within the painting remains a mystery. Is Velázquez painting the king and queen whose daughter has come to visit them? No such portrait exists nor is there any record of one. Or is the artist painting the princess while her parents have stopped by to check on the progress of the portrait? It is not clear. Like Jan van Eyck's Arnolfini portrait (fig. 15.18), which was in the Spanish king's possession at the time so Velázquez would have known it, we stand where the reflected royal couple would be standing, giving us a sense of intimacy. We may never fully understand the narrative, but we can certainly appreciate Velázquez' talent.

One of the most inventive architects of the Baroque (and a rival of Bernini) was **Francesco Borromini** (1599–1667). His little church in Rome, nicknamed S. Carlino, is a gem of innovation (fig. 17.7). Borromini ingeniously fit the church into an unusually small plot of land. Unlike the rectilinear

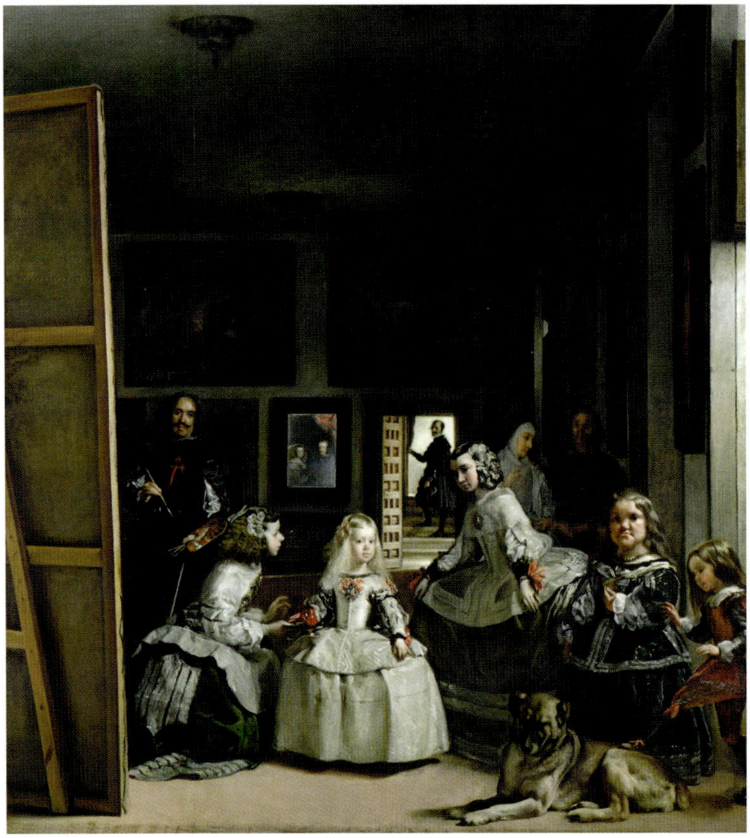

Credit: Las Meninas or The Family of Philip IV, c. 1656 (oil on canvas) by Diego Rodriguez de Silva y Velazquez (1599–1660) Prado, Madrid, Spain/Giraudon/ The Bridgeman Art Library.

fig. 17.6 Diego Velásquez, *Las Meninas,* 1656. Oil on canvas, 10 ft. 5 in. × 9 ft. Prado, Madrid. Scholars have proposed many interpretations for Las Meninas. Spain, unlike Italy, did not view painting as a liberal art but as a craft, so it taxed painters accordingly. Velázquez was probably trying to raise his status as a painter by showing his intellectual abilities (as well as his technical skill) and by placing himself in the company of his royal patrons.

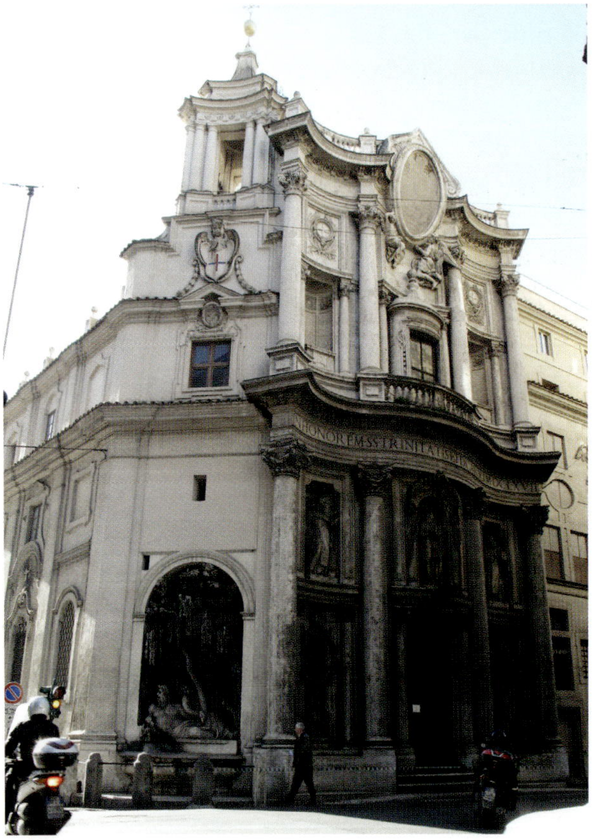

fig. 17.7a Borromini, *San Carlo alle Quattro Fontane,* Rome, 1638–1641. The church was named after the four fountains at the corners of the street. One of them is visible in the corner of the church.

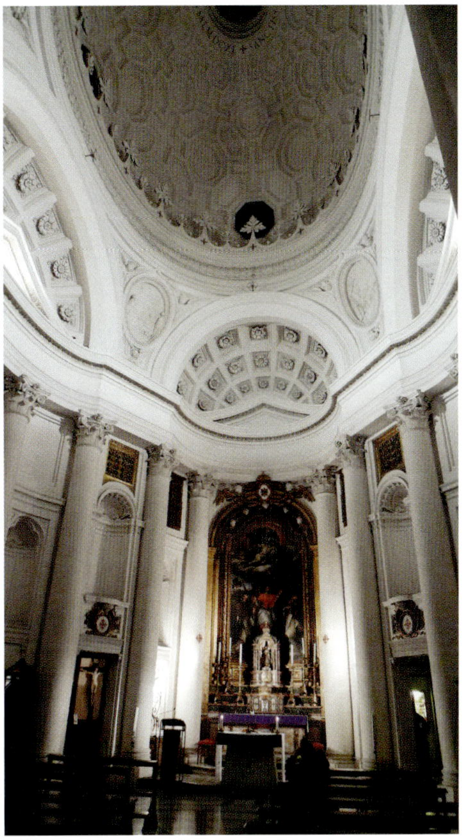

fig. 17.7b Interior.

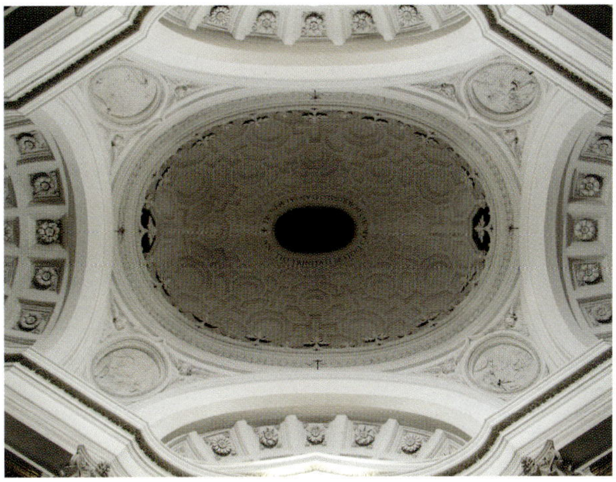

fig. 17.7c Borromini, *San Carlo alle Quattro Fontane,* interior.

facades of Renaissance architecture, the façade of this church undulates with concave and convex curves, giving the building a dynamic elastic quality. The play of concave versus convex extends to the tower and lantern above. The vertical emphasis of the central bay with the statue above it continues in the projecting niche and oval medallion with its pointed arch on the second story. A radical break from Renaissance architecture, this church made Borromini's reputation, and his fame spread well beyond Italy.

The grandest architectural undertaking in France in the seventeenth century was the palace at Versailles just outside Paris. Even though nearly a quarter mile in length, the vast garden behind dwarfs it. The largest and most spectacular room in the palace is the Hall of Mirrors (fig. 17.8). The gallery has seventeen huge arched mirrors along its 240-foot length that reflect the gardens outside, giving the illusion of an even larger hall. The mirrors also bring in more light with their reflective surfaces. With parquet floors, crystal chandeliers, marble pilasters with gilt capitals and large ceiling paintings in gilded frames, the hall displays an ornate opulence typical of the Baroque. It was even more opulent before Louis XIV had to melt down the silver furniture to pay for his many wars.

The palace of Versailles continued to evolve in the eighteenth century, and its owners further developed the gardens. Far from the palace Marie Antoinette had a hamlet built where she and her ladies-and-waiting could go and pretend to be peasants (fig. 17.9). She was in

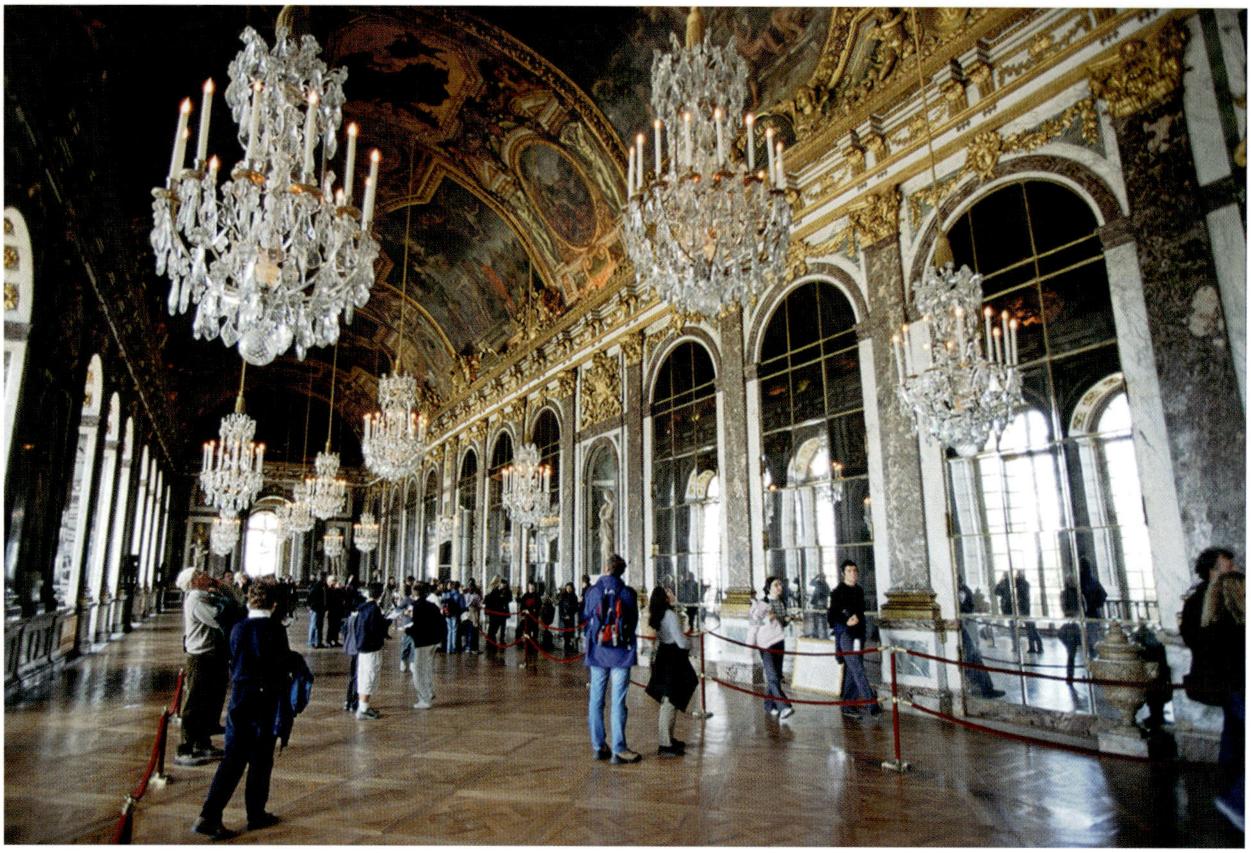

fig. 17.8 Jules Hardouin-Mansart and Charles Lebrun, Hall of Mirrors at the Palace of Versailles, c. 1680.

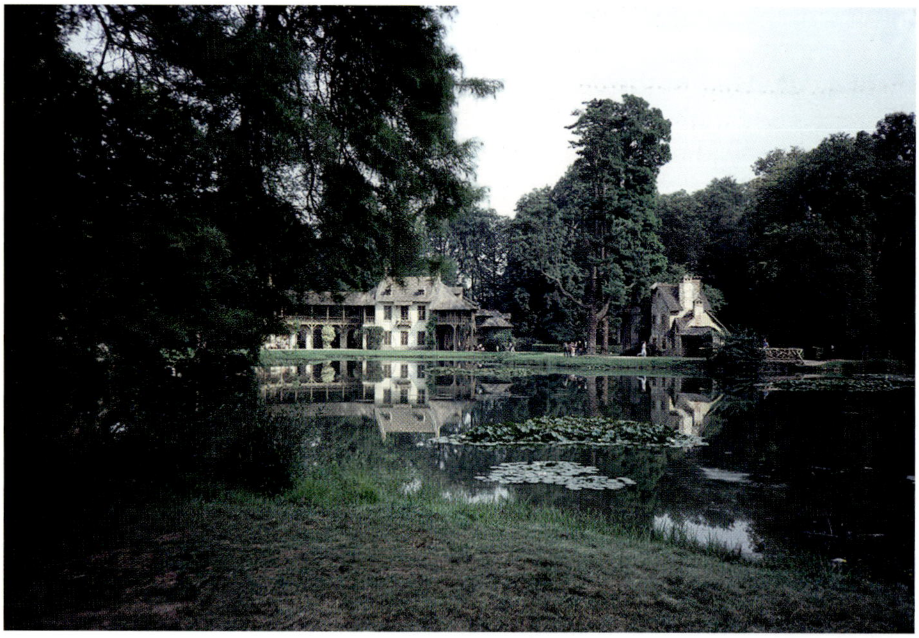

fig. 17.9 The Hamlet on the grounds of Versailles, 18th century.

the hamlet when word came that real peasants were marching on Versailles as the French Revolution began.

ROCOCO

By the early eighteenth century, life at Versailles was becoming oppressive. When Louis XIV finally died in 1715, the court flocked back to Paris and set up households in much smaller, yet still elegant houses called hôtels. There they held spirited gatherings, called salons, of prominent people in the arts and politics whose wit and repartee were the fashion of the day. Wealthy, well-educated women hosted many of these salons. With this societal transition came a more intimate and playful style in the arts called Rococo. Figures are graceful and elegant and often depicted in garden settings idling away the hours. Robust primary colors give way to soft pastels, and heavy masculine forms are transformed into curvilinear decorations.

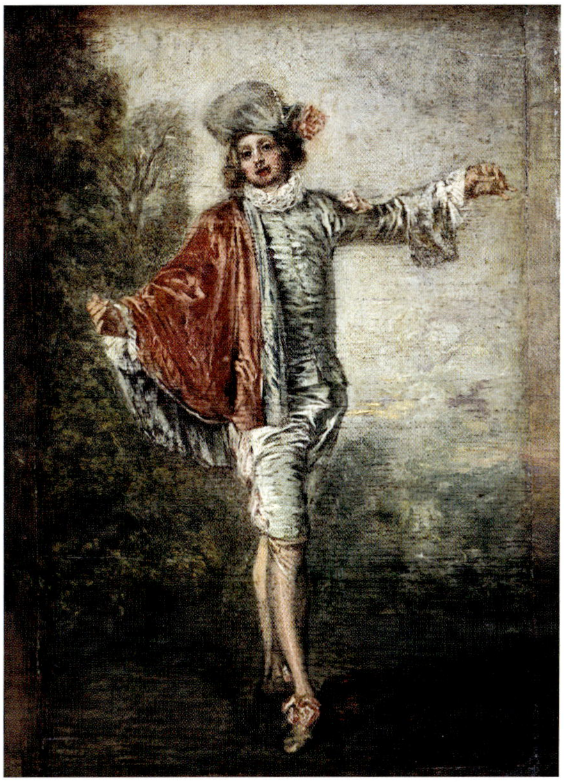

fig. 17.10 Antoine Watteau, *L'Indifferent,* c. 1716. Oil on canvas, 10 in. × 7 in. Louvre, Paris.

Antoine Watteau (1684–1721) was an early proponent of the new Rococo style, and his painting, *L'Indifferent* (*The Indifferent One*), is a perfect example. (fig. 17.10). Beautifully dressed in shimmering pastel-colored silks, the young man gracefully and delicately dances a minuet. His effeminate appearance and carefree attitude are a far cry from the rigid and regal portraits of earlier periods.

Jean-Honoré Fragonard (1732–1806) was the last of the great Rococo painters. *The Swing* (fig.17.11) captures the charming mood and playful essence of an era that was quickly waning. An unsuspecting elderly clergyman swings a young woman in a lovely pink dress while her suitor, hidden in the bushes below, gets a good look up her skirt as she swings by. His hat in his hand that gestures toward her, and her shoe, which she playfully kicks off, add to the eroticism of the scene as do the lush foliage and fluffy clouds. Classical imagery still has a part to play in the Rococo. We see cupids in two statues: Between the girl and the clergyman two cupids play with a dolphin, and above the young man another cupid puts his finger to his lips exhorting us to keep silent.

NEOCLASSICISM

By the time the French Revolution began in 1789 a new style had emerged that harked back to the styles and morals of ancient Greece and Rome. Just as the Rococo was a reaction against the Baroque style, so Neoclassicism reacted against the Rococo. In painting, gone were the frivolous scenes, pastel colors and painterly style of the Rococo, replaced by grand tales from history and mythology that spoke of heroism and

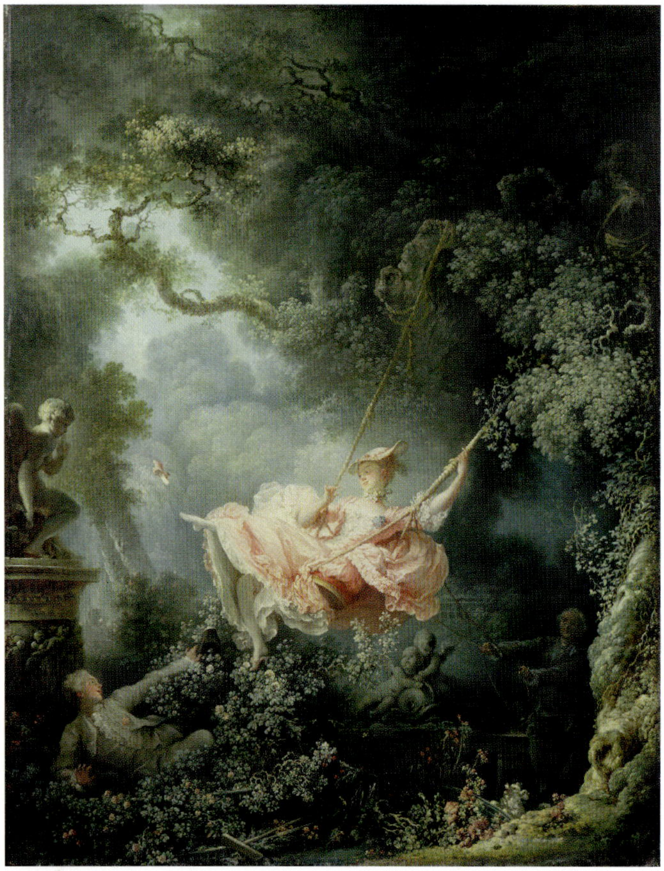

fig. 17.11 Jean-Honoré Fragonard, *The Swing,* 1766. Oil on canvas, 35 in. × 32 in. Wallace Collection, London.

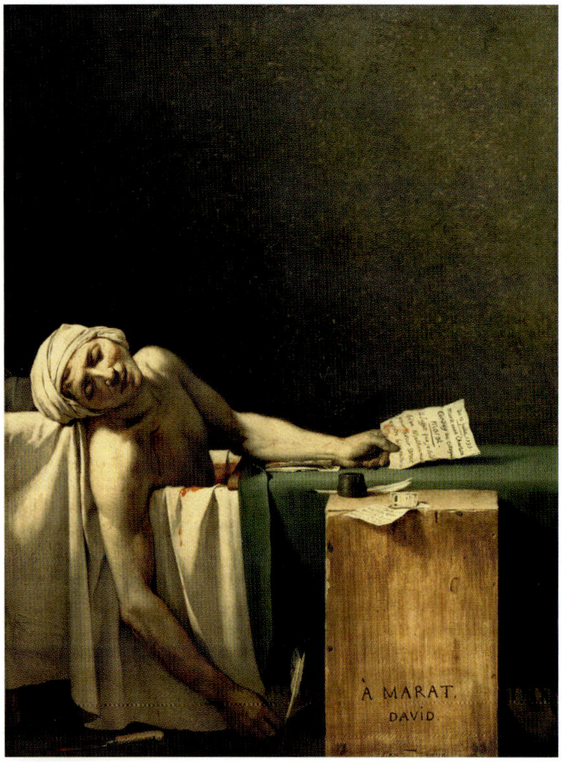

civic duty done in a hard-edged style with bolder colors and smooth brushwork. In architecture and interior design there was a return to the grander and more severe classical style. Archaeological discoveries at Pompeii and Herculaneum fueled the new style where well-preserved Roman buildings, paintings and sculpture came to light.

Neoclassicism also had a political component to it, especially in France. The works of **Jacques-Louis David** (1748–1825) best show this. *The Death of Marat* (fig. 17.12) is a marvel of political propaganda. A radical journalist and politician, Jean-Paul Marat often soaked and wrote in his bath because of a skin disease. It was there that Charlotte Corday, a member of a more conservative political party, stabbed him to death. David shows Marat slumped in death with his pen still in his right

fig. 17.12 Jacques-Louis David, *Death of Marat,* 1793. Oil on canvas, 5 ft. 5 in. × 4 ft. 2.5 in. Musées Royaux des Beaux-Arts de Belgique, Brussels. Charlotte Corday was arrested, tried and sent to the Guillotine four days after the murder.

hand. His left hand holds the letter of introduction that Charlotte Corday had used to gain an audience with him. Blood drips out of his chest wound, and the ivory-handled murder weapon lies on the floor. Marat's pose is strikingly similar to images of the dead Christ (see fig. 15.22), and this allusion is intentional on the part of David in order to make a martyr of Marat. The few objects in the scene are likened to holy **relics**.

The scene is highly **idealized**. It is doubtful Marat died in that pose, and there is very little blood for such a fatal wound. Furthermore, David ignored Marat's disease by giving him flawless skin. David depicts the scene as though it is a classical tableau by placing Marat close to the picture plane against a blank background that denies any distracting recession into space. David's masterpiece gives us the betrayal of a woman and the sacrifice of a hero in a grand style.

By the end of the eighteenth century a number of historical architectural styles revived in Europe and America, and there was a return to classicism that persisted well into the nineteenth century. America, once a backwater, now began to make itself known in the world of art and architecture. Thomas Jefferson (1743–1826) was an architect as well as a politician, and he designed a number of buildings in the Neoclassical style including his own home, Monticello (fig. 17.13). Monticello (which means "Little Mountain" in Italian) has a classical temple-like portico and dome that recall the Pantheon in Rome (figs. 11.10, 11.11 and 11.12). The house is deceiving from the outside. What appears to be a single-story home is actually three stories. The entablature and balustrade conceal a mezzanine and an attic floor. Jefferson incorporated many innovations into his home, including sliding doors, dumbwaiters and a "great clock."

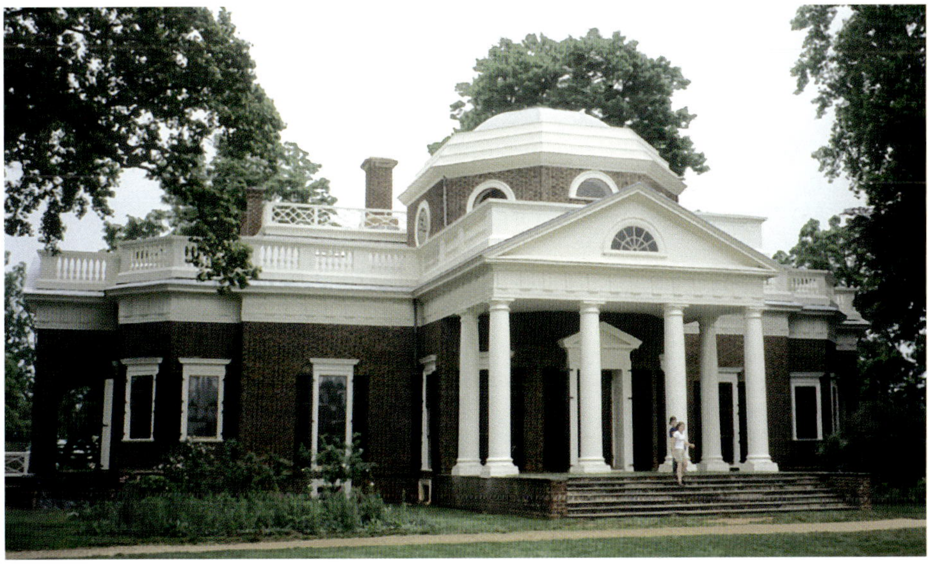

fig. 17.13 Thomas Jefferson, Monticello, 1770–1806. Charlottesville, Virginia.

SUMMARY

The Baroque style in seventeenth-century Europe is typically characterized by theatricality, dramatic lighting, curvilinear forms, movement, and immediacy, but there is no single style. Instead, the Baroque is a multiplicity of national and regional variations ranging from energetic melodrama to classical calm. Baroque artists rejected the artifice of Mannerist art and sought to involve the viewer more directly.

Major artists

Italy: GianLorenzo Bernini (*David*); Caravaggio (*Conversion of St. Paul*); Artemisia Gentileschi (*Judith Slaying Holofernes*); Borromini (San Carlo alle Quattro Fontane)

Flanders: Peter Paul Rubens (*Wolf and Fox Hunt*)

The Netherlands: Rembrandt (*Self Portrait*)

Spain: Diego Velázquez (Las Meninas)

France: Jule Hardouin-Mansart and Chalres Lebrun (Hall of Mirrors at the Palace of Versailles)

Rococo: An artistic style of the eighteenth century characterized by delicate curvilinear forms, pastel colors, and often frivolous subject matter. Examples: Watteau (*L'Indifferent*); Fragonard (*The Swing*).

Neoclassicism: A late eighteenth art movement that continued into the early nineteenth-century. Characterized by a revival of the classical style of ancient Greece and Rome. It was a reaction to the playful Rococo style. Examples: Jacques-Louis David (*Death of Marat*) and Thomas Jefferson's Monticello.

PRONUNCIATION GUIDE

Baroque (ba-**roke**)
Bernini, Gianlorenzo (ber-**nee**-nee, jahn-loh **ren** zoh)
Borromini (bore-oh-**mee**-nee)
Caravaggio (car-ah-**vah**-jyoh)
Chiaroscuro (kee-ar-oh-**skoor**-oh)
David, Jacques-Louis (dah-**veed, zhahk**-loo-**ee**)
Fragonard, Jean-Honoré (**fra**-goh-nar, zhon-oh-no-**ray**)
Gentileschi, Artemisia (jen-til-**es**-kee, ar-teh-**mee**-zhyuh)
Hardouin-Mansart, Jules (ar-**dwan**-man-**sar**, zhool)
Iconography (eye-kuh-**nog**-ruh-fee)
Monticello (mon-tih-**chel**-oh)
Rembrandt van Rijn (**rem**-brandt van **rine**)
Rococo (ruh-**koh**-koh)
Rubens (**roo**-bens)
Velázquez (veh-**lahs**-kez)
Versailles (vair-**sigh**)
Watteau (**wah**-toh)

GLOSSARY

Allegory. A story or image that refers to something else through symbolic imagery.

Baroque. A style in seventeenth-century Europe typically characterized by theatricality, dramatic lighting, curvilinear forms, movement, and immediacy.

Chiaroscuro. The gradations of light and dark in a painting or drawing used to create the illusion of three-dimensional form. Also called modeling.

Iconography. The analytic study of the symbolic, often religious meaning of objects, persons, or events depicted in works of arts.

Idealism. The representation of figures and forms that conforms to a concept of perfection rather than to reality.

Naturalism. A style of art that attempts to depict things as they actually appear in nature.

Neoclassicism. A late eighteenth and early nineteenth-century art movement characterized by a revival of the classical style of ancient Greece and Rome.

Relic. A body part, article of clothing, a piece of an instrument of martyrdom or other item associated with a saint. They are often thought to have special powers to heal the body and the soul.

Rococo. An artistic style of the eighteenth century characterized by delicate curvilinear forms, pastel colors, and often frivolous subject matter.

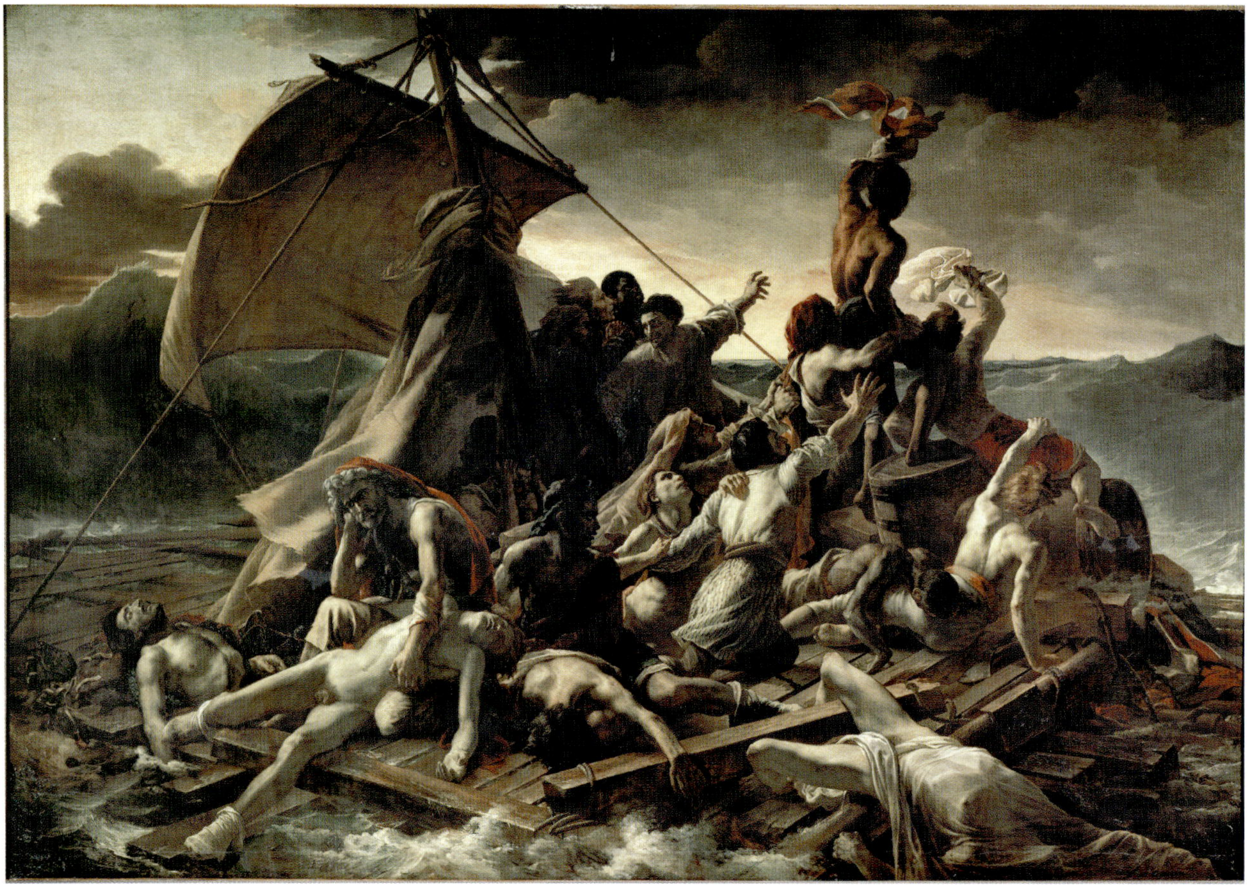

fig. 18.1 Théodore Géricault, *Raft of the Medusa,* 1819. Oil on canvas, 16 ft. 1 in. × 23 ft. 6 in. Louvre, Paris.
© Erich Lessing/Art Resource, NY.

18

THE 19TH CENTURY

The nineteenth century witnessed vast changes in society and art. The decline of Europe's monarchies that began with the French Revolution continued, and democracies arose in their place. Technology developed at an ever faster pace. The invention of the steam and combustible engines led to great changes in manufacturing and transportation. Mass production made more and cheaper goods available, but it also began the pollution of the planet. By mid century trains crisscrossed the European and American continents, and by the end of the century automobiles began replacing horses.

In art, changes occurred with the same rapidity. The development of chemical pigments improved the quality and range of hues, and the invention of the tin tube for paint let artists carry their paints with them. Stylistically, there were no longer long-lasting historical art periods like the Gothic or the Renaissance; instead there was a series of shorter art movements (whose various names end with the suffix "-ism"). The century began with two dominant (and somewhat opposing) art styles, Neoclassicism and Romanticism, and ended with the much more abstracted style of Post-Impressionism. This led to the nonrepresentational art (and more "isms") of the 20th century. France remained the most influential country in the visual arts until World War II.

ROMANTICISM

The Neoclassicism of the late eighteenth century (discussed at the end of the last chapter) continued into the nineteenth century and became an opposing trend to another artistic style: **Romanticism**. The term Romanticism derives from *romances,* stories from the Middle Ages written in the romance languages. In literature, macabre tales such as Mary Shelley's *Frankenstein* became popular. In art, Romanticism refers to a reaction against the strict and reasoned calm of the Neoclassical style. Instead, Romanticism deals with such themes as intense human emotions and struggles, the overwhelming power of nature and man's inhumanity to man. Political themes remained popular, especially when they related to human liberties or sufferings. Whereas David's *Death of Marat* (fig. 17.12) is the embodiment of a political statement painted in the Neoclassical style, **Théodore Géricault's** *Raft of the Medusa* (fig. 18.1) is one painted in the Romantic vein.

Géricault (1791–1824) depicted a contemporary scandal involving a government ship named the *Medusa* that was transporting a group of colonists to Senegal. Because of the ineptness of the captain (a political appointee) the ship sank off the coast of Africa. Taking the lifeboats for themselves, the captain and the crew towed a makeshift raft that held the 149 passengers. This proved cumbersome and slow so the captain ordered the towrope cut, and the passengers were set adrift to fend for themselves without food or water. When they were finally rescued twelve days later, only fifteen of the 149 were still alive; the rest had died of exposure or dehydration.

In order to depict an authentic scene, Géricault interviewed the survivors and learned the true horrors of their ordeal, which included madness and cannibalism. He painted the climactic moment when the few survivors on the sea-tossed raft see a ship on the horizon where there is a break in the stormy sky. The grouping of figures forms a lopsided pyramid with the bare-chested figure waving a piece of cloth at its apex. Everything guides our eyes to the upper right as the other figures gesture toward the ship. To balance the composition, the rudimentary mast and sail jut out in an opposing diagonal on the left side. The people are ragged, some are dead, and one poignant grouping shows a despondent father holding his dead son in a pose reminiscent of the Pietà, recalling the sufferings of Christ much as David had done with the pose of Marat.

When shown to the public, the huge painting (nearly 24 feet wide) caused shock and revulsion because it depicted a current event in all its horror, not something from the distant past. The human suffering, the injustice, the gruesome details and the exposure of appalling government incompetence made this painting a paragon of the Romantic Movement.

Like many Romantics, Géricault lived fast and dangerously, and he died young. **Eugène Delacroix** then inherited the mantle of Romanticism and is probably the one artist most associated with the movement. His *Death of Sardanapalus* (fig. 18.2) derives from a poem by the English Romantic poet, Lord Byron, which relates the tale of an Assyrian king who when confronted with military defeat, decided to destroy all his possessions and himself to spite the enemy. Like the *Raft of the Medusa,* this is a scene of motion and emotion. While Sardanapalas lies calmly on his elephant-head bed (as though in the eye of a storm), his servants kill his harem and his horses. The diagonal composition, the strong contrasts of light and dark and the rich blood-red colors emphasize the whirlwind of violence. The painterly style of broad thick brushstrokes (unlike the smooth brushwork of the Neoclassical artists) also adds to the dramatic effect.

The Spanish artist **Francisco Goya** (1746–1828), often classified as a Romantic artist, really deserves a category of his own because he went beyond Romanticism in content and style and became a truly modern painter. Like Géricault, Goya depicted man's inhumanity to man. His *Third of May, 1808* (fig. 18.3), shows an event from the Napoleonic Wars when France ruled Spain. On May 2, the day

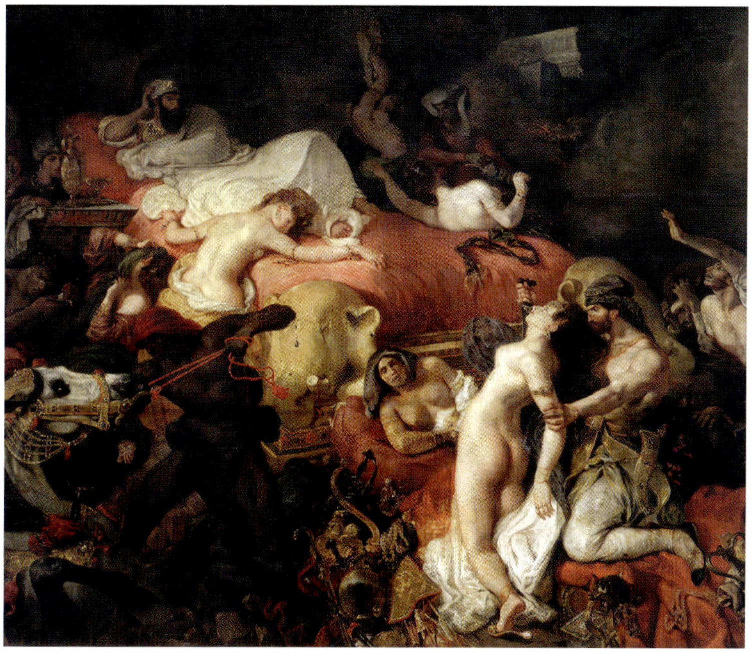

Roger-Viollet/The Image Works.

fig. 18.2 Eugène Delacroix, *Death of Sardanapalus,* 1827. Oil on canvas, 12 ft. 1.5 in. × 16 ft. 3 in. Louvre Paris.

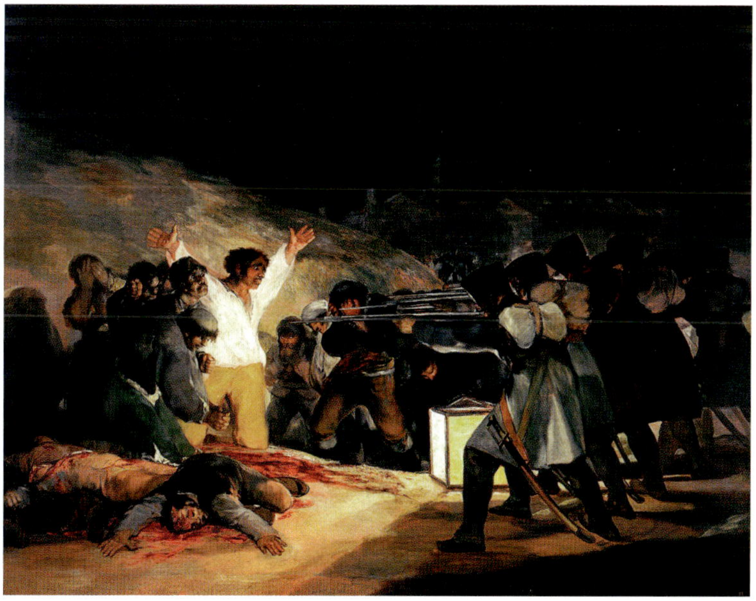

© V&W/the Image Works

fig. 18.3 Francisco Goya, *The Third of May, 1808,* 1814. Oil on canvas, 8 ft. 9 in. × 13 ft. 4 in. Prado, Madrid.

before, a few rabble-rousers in Madrid had attacked the French troops. As punishment, the French rounded up hundreds of men at random and had them summarily executed. On the right we see the French firing squad as a series of faceless figures that appear more as a killing machine devoid of any human emotion. Their pointed rifles lead our eye to the illuminated figure with outstretched arms about to be shot. Resigned to his fate, he, like the bloodied dead on the ground beside him or those waiting in line behind him, is a martyr, and his pose recalls the crucified Christ. A large lantern on the ground gives off an eerie light revealing only the essential details. Most of the scene remains in darkness, including the church in the distance, which symbolizes the dark side of human nature. This painting goes beyond depicting a specific horrific event to embodying human brutality.

J.M.W. Turner (1775–1851) epitomizes the Romantic Movement in England. *The Slave Ship* (fig. 18.4) illustrates yet another scene of human cruelty, but the subject is almost lost in the swirling loose brushwork. A ship carrying slaves (itself a cruelty) faces sinking in a storm. To lighten the load, the captain orders that the slaves be tossed overboard. In a

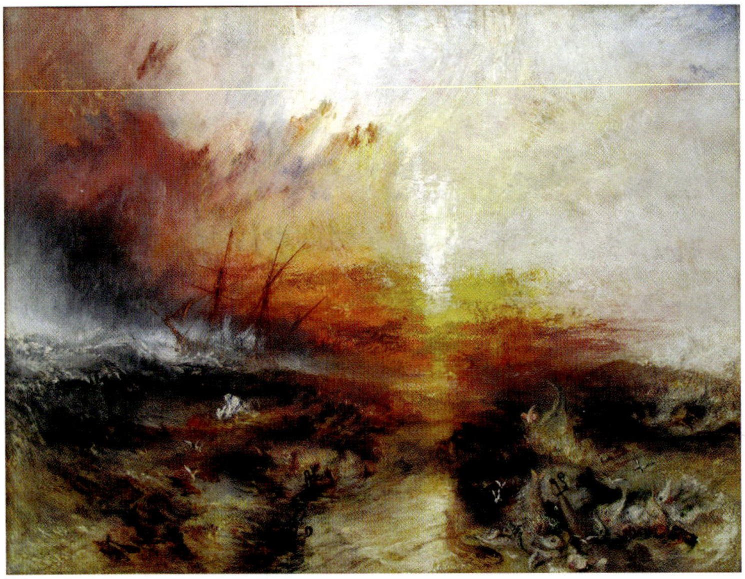

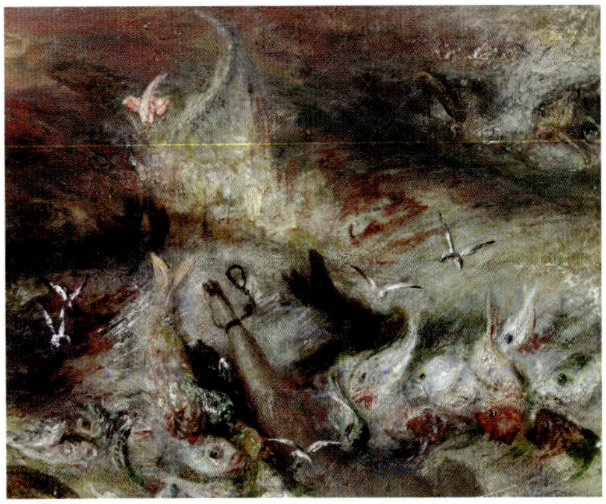

fig. 18.4 Joseph Mallord William Turner, *The Slave Ship*, 1840. Oil on canvas, 3 ft. × 4 ft. Museum of Fine Arts, Boston. Critics often ridiculed Turner's loose brushwork; in fact at one point he was accused of painting with a broom.

tumultuous sea we can pick out flailing arms of the hapless slaves and also the eyes of hungry sharks. Turner's dynamic compositions are unique, and his loose brushwork style prefigures Impressionism.

American Romanticism is more concerned with nature and the vast expanses of unspoiled wilderness in the still young nation. **Thomas Cole** (1801–1848) founded the Hudson River School, a group that painted Romantic landscapes. *The Oxbow* (fig. 18.5) is his most famous work. The panoramic view shows a forested hilltop (where we can see the artist painting) overlooking the river and a vast cultivated plain. Although bucolic, there are hints of industrialization with the wisps of smoke in the distance. The coming storm and the dead tree in the left foreground allude to the inevitable loss of simpler times.

REALISM

Realism as a movement that began mid century does not necessarily refer to the optically true representation developed in the Renaissance, but to the idea of portraying ordinary scenes without idealism, exoticism, sensationalism

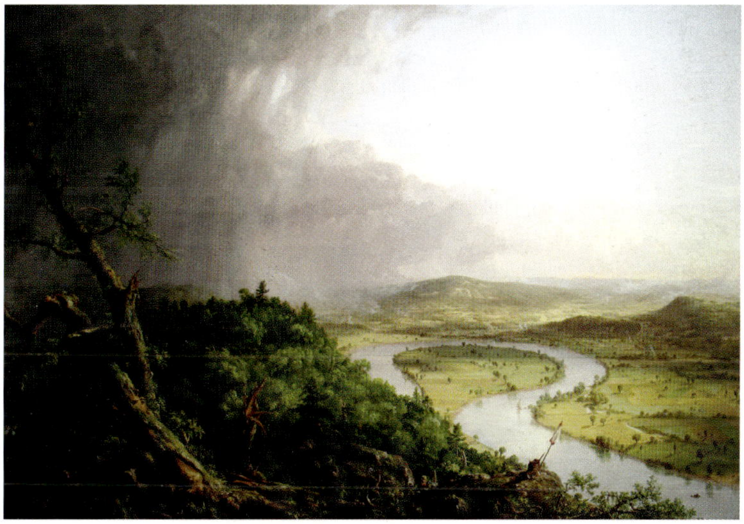

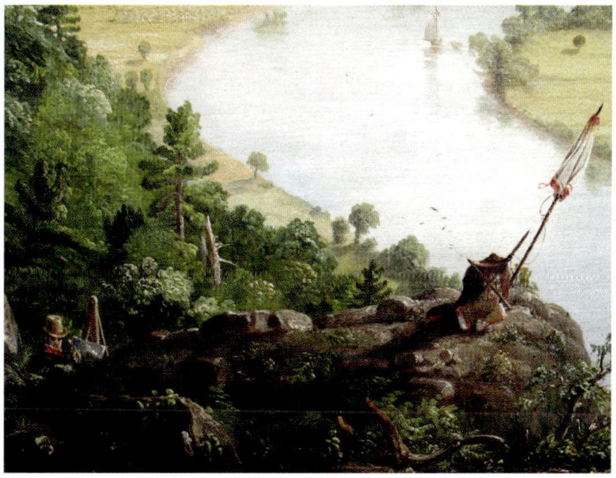

fig. 18.5 Thomas Cole, *The Oxbow,* 1836. Oil on canvas, 4 ft. 3.5 in. × 6 ft. 4 in. Metropolitan Museum of Art, New York.

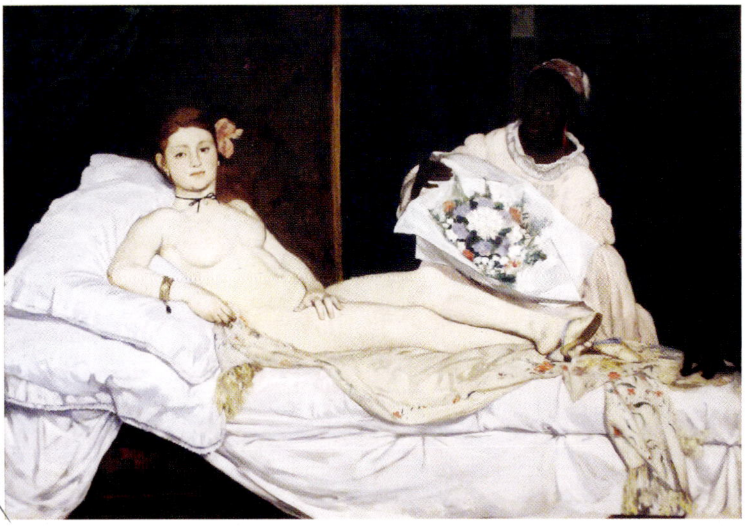

fig. 18.6 Édouard Manet, *Olympia,* 1863. Oil on canvas, 4 ft. 3 in. × 6 ft. 2 in. Musée d'Orsay, Paris.

or emotional overtones. Artists restricted themselves to what they could actually see and experience. They shunned mythological and religious figures so popular in previous centuries; instead peasants and ordinary citizens became common subjects in painting.

Art critics never fully understood **Édouard Manet** (1832–1883), a truly modern painter. His *Olympia* (fig. 18.6) shows a reclining female nude, a traditional subject seen since the Renaissance (compare Titian's *Venus of Urbino,* fig. 15.17) and whose ultimate source was the art of ancient Greece. This painting differed, however, in that the figure was not a goddess or some anonymous female, but a recognizable model in the guise of a prostitute directly confronting the viewer. The painting caused a scandal not only because of its subject, but also because of its style. Manet painted in large patches of flat color and avoided the traditional modeling techniques. For him the paint itself was as much the subject as the image. He forced the viewer to look at the painted surface. Manet's modernist approach made him an **avant-garde** artist who inspired the Impressionists.

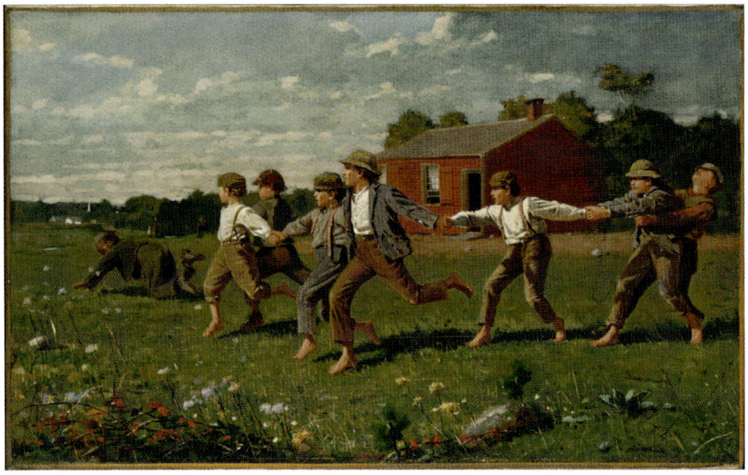

fig. 18.7 Winslow Homer, *Snap the Whip,* 1872. Oil on canvas, 12 in. × 20 in. Metropolitan Museum of Art, New York.

In America **Winslow Homer** (1836–1910) was admired for his realist scenes such as *Snap the Whip* (fig. 18.7), which portrays a common event in everyday life in rural America at the time—schoolboys playing a game at recess. Homer, a self-taught artist, was quoted as saying that he painted his subjects exactly as they appear.

In 1839 Louis Daguerre improved the photographic process invented in the 1820s. The medium quickly became popular with artists like **Nadar** (1820–1910), who became a noted portrait photographer in the 1850s in Paris. Nadar's dramatically posed and lit **photographs** of famous people turned a merely mechanical process into an artistic one. His portrait of Sarah Bernhardt (fig. 18.8), a leading actress known for her dramatic tragic roles, illustrates Nadar's genius. With lighting from the side and voluminous folds of drapery, Nadar recreates the chiaroscuro effect of master painters.

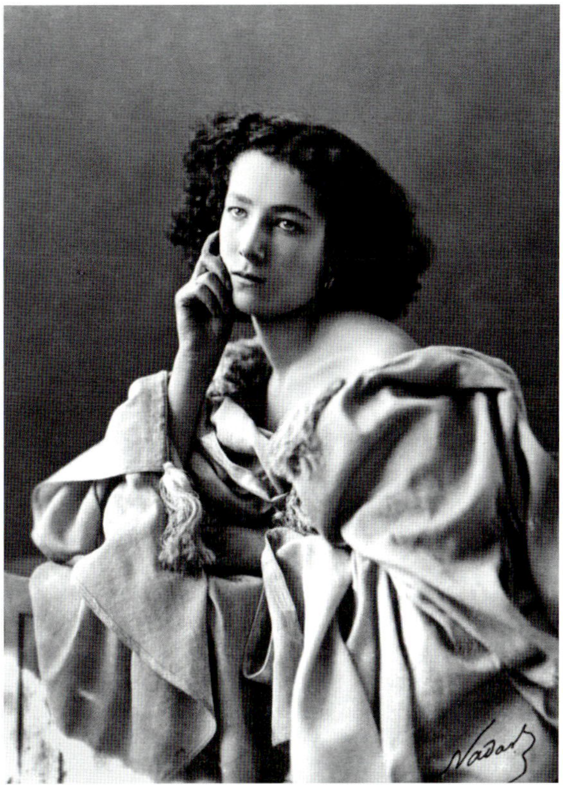

fig. 18.8 Nadar, *Sarah Bernhardt,* c. 1864. Photograph.

IMPRESSIONISM

Impressionism was a revolutionary movement that began around 1870 and profoundly affected later Western art. Influenced by the loose brushwork of earlier painters such as Turner and by recent discoveries in the physics of color perception, the Impressionists attempted to paint the fleeting atmospheric effects of light and color by painting outdoors directly from nature. Because they painted quickly to capture the moment, their paintings are sketchy. Small daubs of juxtaposed color coalesce from a distance to create vibrant shimmering forms. Get too close to the canvas and the forms dissolve into textures of brushstrokes.

The Impressionists truly observed nature and painted what they saw even if it seemed to contradict common sense. For instance, the shade cast by a tree with green leaves is not black—it has a green tint to it. Paradoxically, as imprecise (or impressionistic) as the Impressionists were, they were in one sense realists because they tried to show the actual **optical** effects of light and color as our brain interprets them.

The quintessential Impressionist (and longest lived) was **Claude Monet** (1840–1926). His small painting of 1872 entitled *Impression: Sunrise* gave the movement its name. *The Japanese Footbridge* (fig. 18.9) is one of many pond scenes Monet painted at his estate in Givenchy. It beautifully captures the ephemeral effects of light and color complicated by the water's reflections. Often he would set up a number of canvases and proceed from one to the next as the light changed. Monet continued painting in the Impressionist style until his death in 1926, long after many other art movements had come and gone.

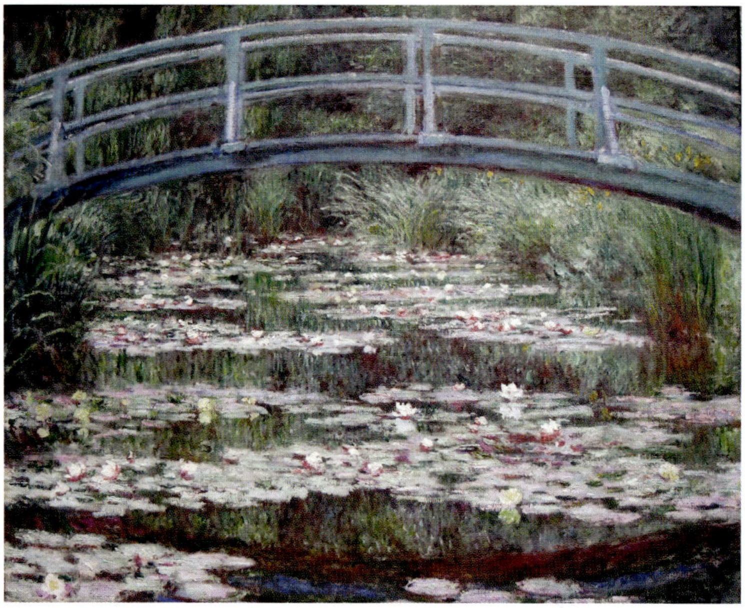

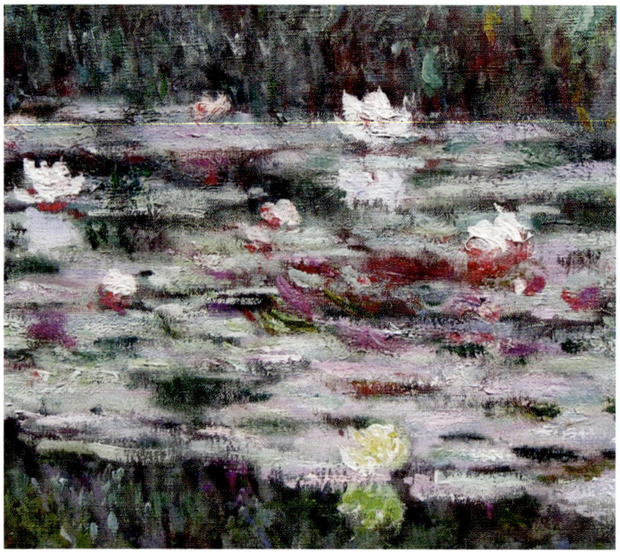

fig. 18.9 Claude Monet, *The Japanese Footbridge,* 1889. Oil on canvas, 39.75 in. × 47.5 in. National Gallery, Washington, D.C.

Whereas Monet concentrated on inanimate objects such as ponds, haystacks and church facades, another great Impressionist, **Pierre-Auguste Renoir** (1841–1919), painted people. *La Moulin de la Galette* (fig. 18.10) shows people dancing and chatting at a popular outdoor café on a Sunday afternoon. Small patches of light color speckle the canvas to indicate the sunlight filtering through the treetops. Renoir makes the event even more immediate to the viewer by arbitrarily cutting off the figures at the left and right edges, causing the scene to expand into our space.

As an official movement, Impressionism lasted until about 1886. The artists who followed are called Post-Impressionists for lack of a better term. Many artists felt restricted by the Impressionist style—for them it focused too much on the momentary and did not allow sufficient personal expression or substance. Using Impressionism as a departure point, artists such as Vincent van Gogh, Henri de Toulouse-Lautrec, Georges Seurat and Paul Cézanne developed new styles.

POST-IMPRESSIONISM

The Dutch artist **Vincent van Gogh** (1853–1890) is the most famous Post-Impressionist. Although he lived in poverty because he was unable to sell his works, by the end of the twentieth century they were being auctioned for tens of millions of dollars. In his mature works, Van Gogh employs the sketchy brushwork of the Impressionists, but he intensifies the color and the thickness of the paint. Like his Dutch predecessor Rembrandt, van Gogh painted many self portraits (fig. 18.11). The artist stares at the viewer apparently unembarrassed by his self mutilation for he makes no attempt to hide his bandaged ear. On the wall behind him hangs a Japanese **print**, an art form that heavily influenced his own art. Brilliant reds and greens fleck his skin that have nothing to do with optical reality—instead they reflect van Gogh's increasingly disturbed emotional state.

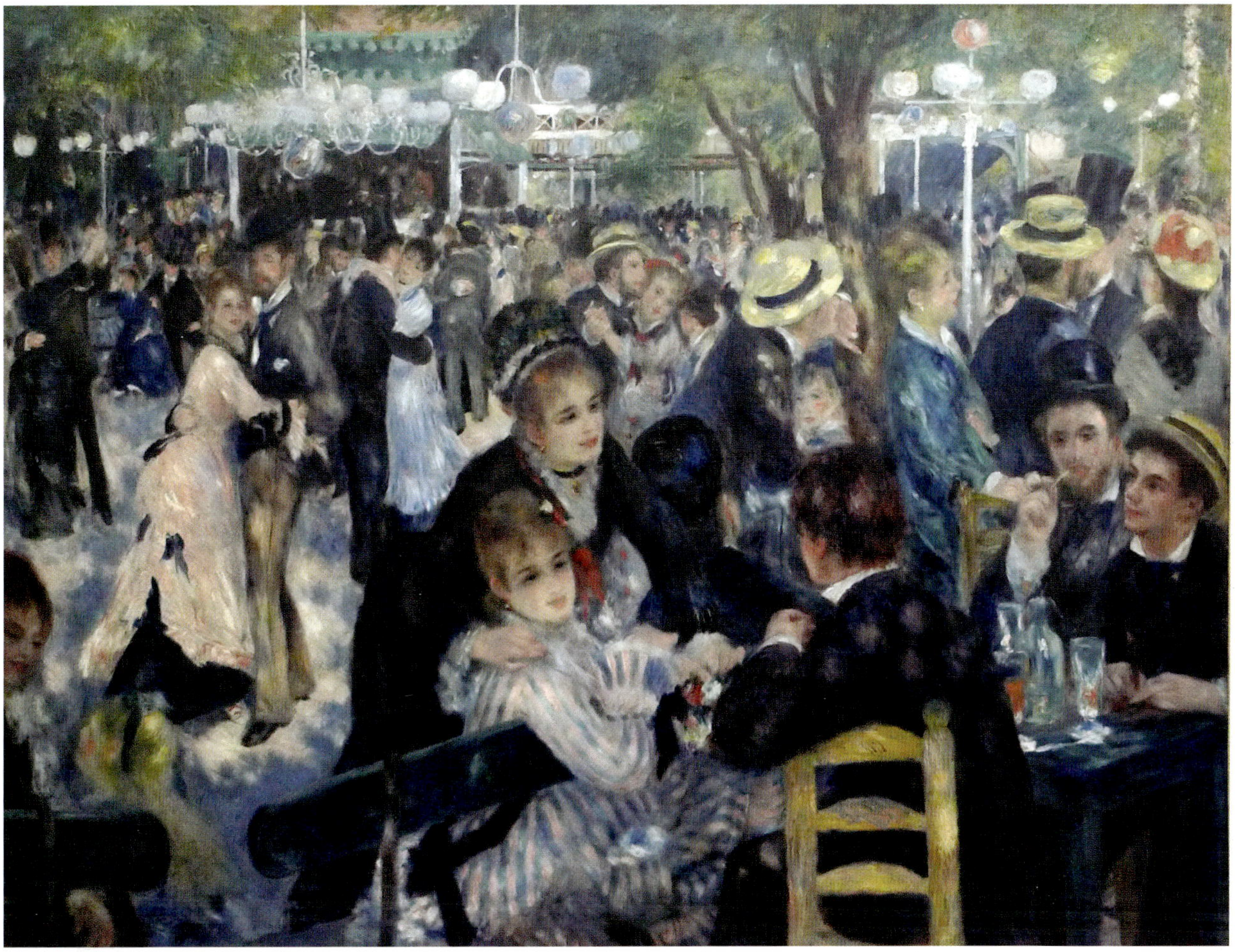

fig. 18.10 Pierre-Auguste Renoir, *Le Moulin de la Galette,* 1876. Oil on canvas, 4 ft. 3 in. × 5 ft. 8 in. Musée d'Orsay, Paris.

The same can be said for van Gogh's most famous painting, *Starry Night* (fig. 18.12), which is much reproduced and even has a song written about it (Don McLean's "Vincent"). The night sky above the sleepy village is alive with a radiant moon and swirling stars. In the foreground an earthbound cypress tree (a symbol of death and eternity) reaches toward the heavens. The brushwork is intense and thick. It is as though van Gogh painted his emotions on this canvas in a fevered frenzy with an attempt to unite himself with the cosmos. Although the work has the appearance of being painted rapidly, the composition is planned and balanced. The cypress tree anchors the work, echoes the church steeple in the distance and counterbalances the brightly lit moon on the opposite side of the canvas. As energetic as the scene is, it does not disintegrate into chaos.

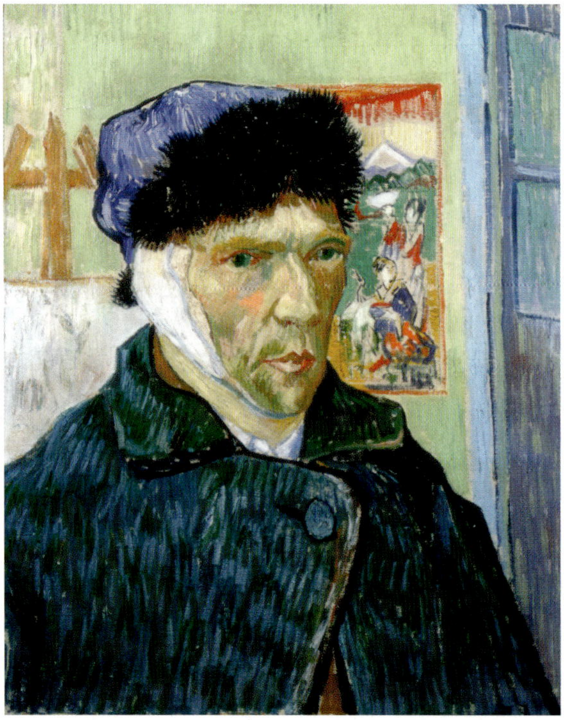

© Art Media/Heritage-Images/The Image Works

fig. 18.11 Vincent van Gogh, *Self Portrait,* 1889. Oil on canvas, 23.5 in. × 19 in. Courtauld Institute, London.

Henry de Toulouse-Lautrec (1864–1901) concentrated on the human figure, and his many posters advertising nightclub acts (fig. 18.13) elevated the poster to the level of art. Born into an old noble family, he broke both legs as a child. They stopped growing, giving his adult body a deformed appearance. As a result, he rejected high society and lived an alcoholic life among Paris's demimonde of bohemians and prostitutes. His posters capture the essence of the featured entertainer and make good use of the **lithographic** technique, which was perfect for the bold flat areas of color he desired.

Norwegian artist **Edvard Munch** (1863–1944) traveled to Paris and saw works by his contemporaries, including van Gogh and Lautrec. His work takes van Gogh's emotional qualities and intensifies them into a personal anguish unseen before in Western art. His famous work, *The Scream* (fig. 18.14), has become the poster painting for unrelenting anxiety in our modern age. It is also one of the most spoofed works of Western art (fig. 18.15). The skeletal-like figure on the bridge emits an anguished internal scream that is so powerful and full of despair that it radiates out to the very

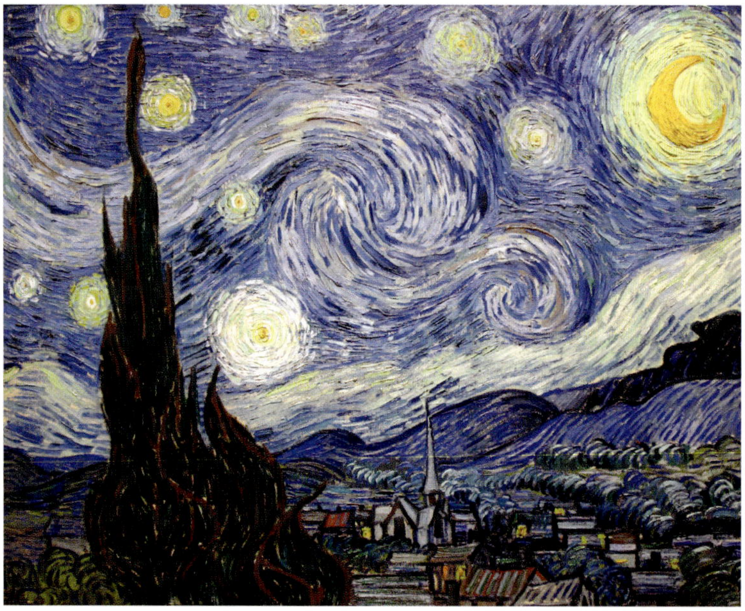

© The Museum of Modern Art/Licensed by SCALA/Art Resource, NY

fig. 18.12 Vincent van Gogh, *Starry Night,* 1889. Oil on canvas, 2 ft. 5 in. × 3 ft. Museum of Modern Art, New York.

environment beyond. The intense reds in the sky have an almost sickening tint to them, which heightens the inner torment of the figure.

Compared to the emotionalism of van Gogh and Munch, **Georges Seurat** (1859–1891) and **Paul Cézanne** (1839–1906) are disciplined and scientific. In a sense there are two trends in Post-Impressionism that continue the dichotomy of Neoclassicism and Romanticism. The works of Van Gogh and Munch fit into the Romantic trend with their emotional content while the works of Seurat and Cézanne embody the Neoclassical trend with their calm precision.

A Sunday on the Island of La Grande Jatte (figs. 18.16a and 18.16b) is Georges Seurat's enduring work, and it is often modified for use in advertising. There is even a Broadway musical based on this painting (Stephen Sondheim's "Sunday in the Park with George"). Seurat carefully studied emerging theories of color optics and invented a new technique he called **divisionism**; today it is called **pointillism**. Seurat applied small dots of unmixed color closely spaced on his canvases. He thought juxtaposed colors would fuse in the viewer's brain to create more intense colors than if he simply mixed the pigments. This does not actually happen because the dots of color remain visible, but the technique does produce a dazzling surface quality. Since discreet dots compose the forms, they are rigid and formal, yet that is their appeal.

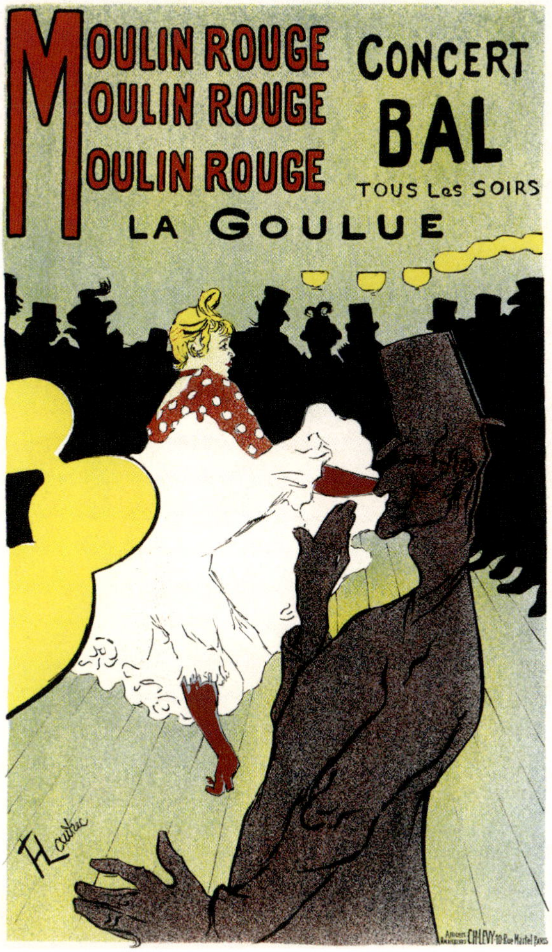

fig. 18.13 Henri de Toulouse-Lautrec, *La Goulue at the Moulin Rouge Concert Bal,* 1891. Lithograph, 6 ft. 3 in. × 3 ft. 10 in.

Paul Cézanne used patches of color to achieve three-dimensional form in his works. Concerned with underlying structure, he did not paint the apples in his *Still Life with Apples and Biscuits* (fig 18.17) with the traditional chiaroscuro technique. Instead, Cézanne defines the forms by varying intensity of hue, using advancing (**warm**) and receding (**cool**) colors, and juxtaposing **complementary colors**. He reduces forms to their basic structure and in the process breaks up traditional space. Cézanne, the painter's painter, was more important than any other nineteenth-century artist for the development of art in the twentieth century.

Although Impressionism and Post-Impressionism primarily apply to painting, the sculpture of **Auguste Rodin** (1840–1917) fits into the era well. Rodin studied the sculpture of Michelangelo, but he rejected classical idealism in favor of naturalism. What he took from Michelangelo was the

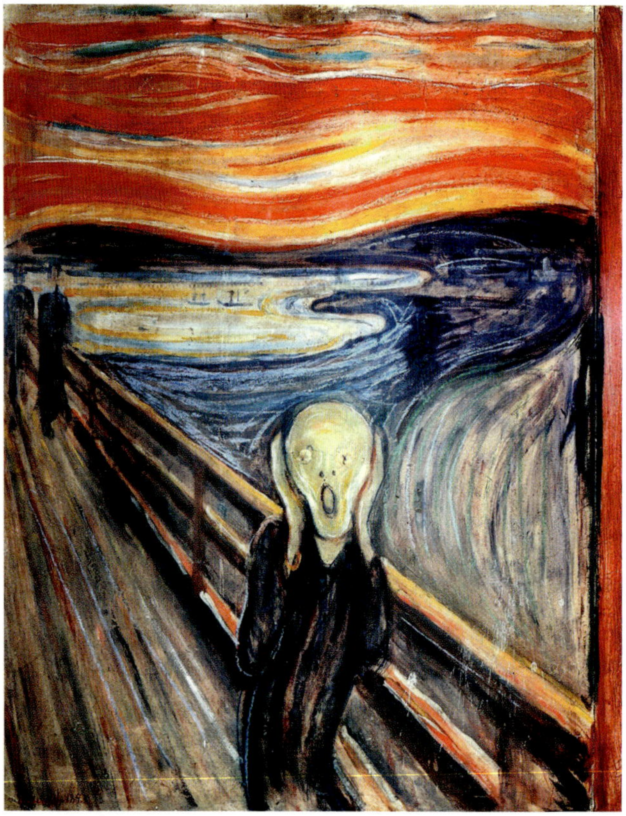

fig. 18.14 Edvard Munch, *The Scream,* 1893. Tempera and pastels on cardboard, 3 ft. × 2 ft. 5 in. National Gallery, Oslo.

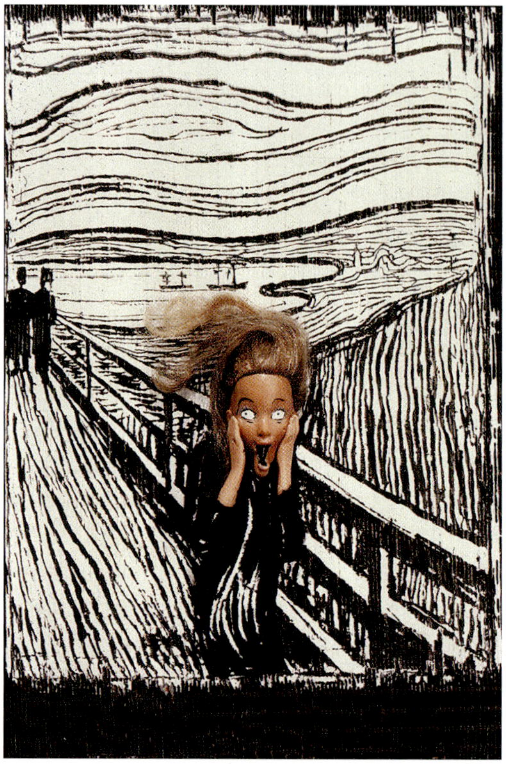

fig. 18.15 Spoof of *The Scream* with Barbie.

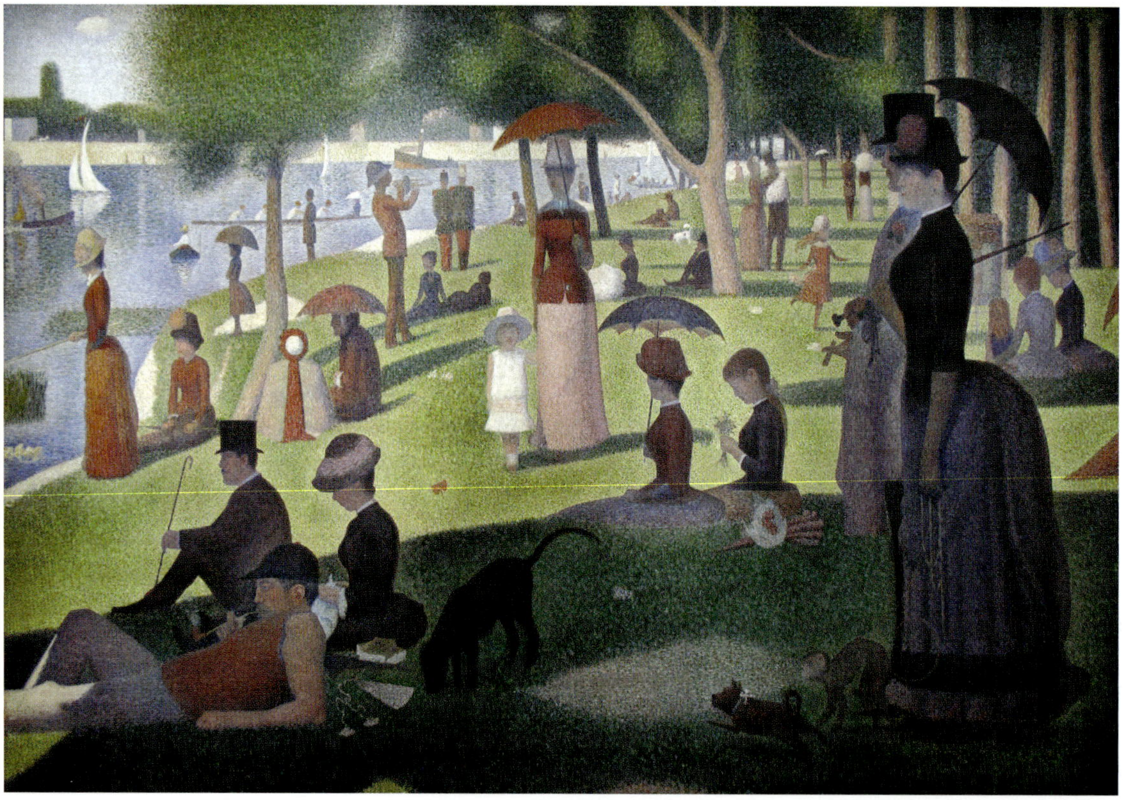

fig. 18.16a Georges Seurat, *A Sunday on La Grande Jatte,* 1884–86. Oil on canvas, 6 ft. 9 in. × 10 ft. Art Institute, Chicago.

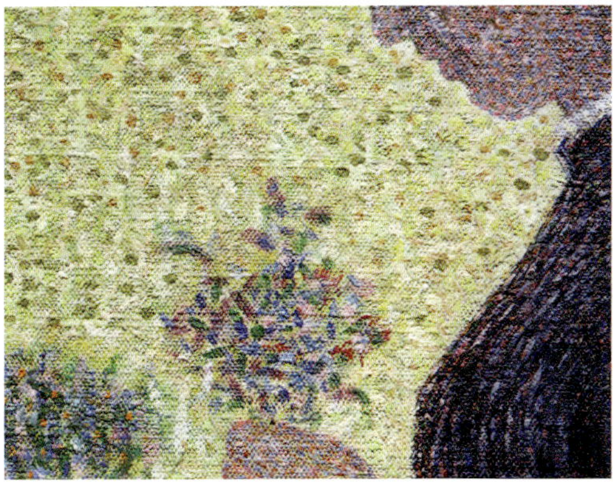

fig. 18.16b Detail.

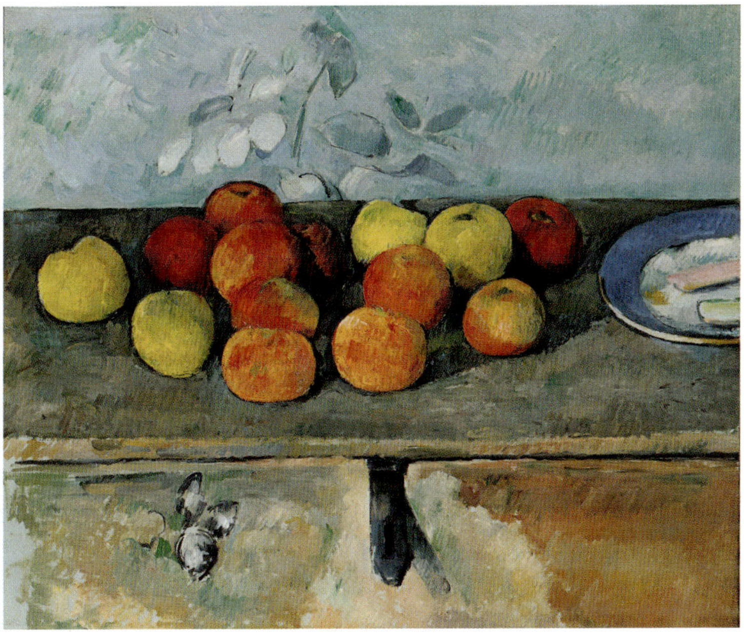

fig. 18.17 Cézanne, *Still Life with Apples and Biscuits,* c. 1880. Oil on canvas, 18 in. × 22 in. Musée de l'Orangerie, Paris.

commanding power of his figures. Because Rodin departed radically from the traditional **academic style**, he was highly criticized for much of his career, but by the twentieth century he was acclaimed as a great sculptor who had reinvigorated the medium. Rodin did not carve like Michelangelo; he modeled in clay and then had his pieces cast in bronze. Rodin also did not work with human models in stationary poses as was customary. He preferred to observe people in motion and quickly capture their essence in clay.

His largest commission was the *The Gates of Hell,* a monumental portal adorned with numerous figures and figure groups intended for a museum of decorative arts. He never finished it, but many of the figures were cast separately in multiple copies. *The Thinker* (fig. 18.18), his most famous work, was positioned at the top of the *The Gates of Hell.* The seated brooding nude figure ponders all that is below him. This is yet another iconic work that lends itself to being spoofed (fig. 18.19).

In architecture, **cast iron** created new possibilities for buildings (see page 140). One of the more spectacular structures built using this new

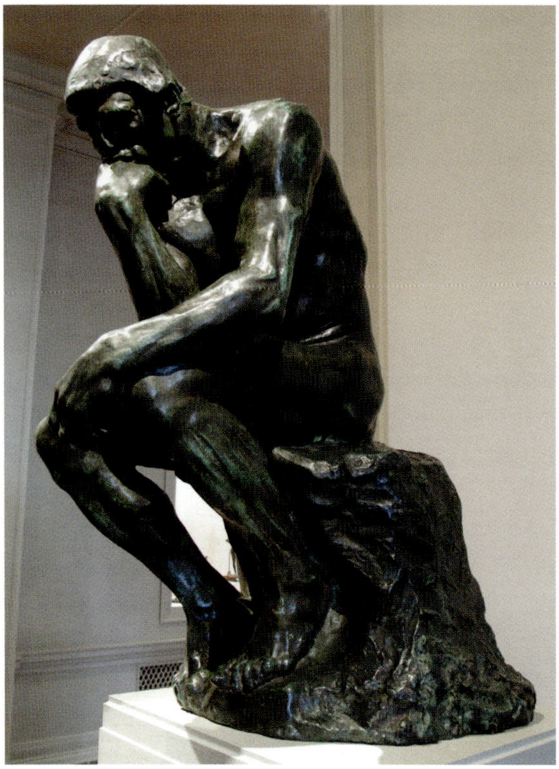

fig. 18.18 Auguste Rodin, *The Thinker,* model 1880, cast 1901. Bronze, 28 in high. National Gallery, Washington, D.C.

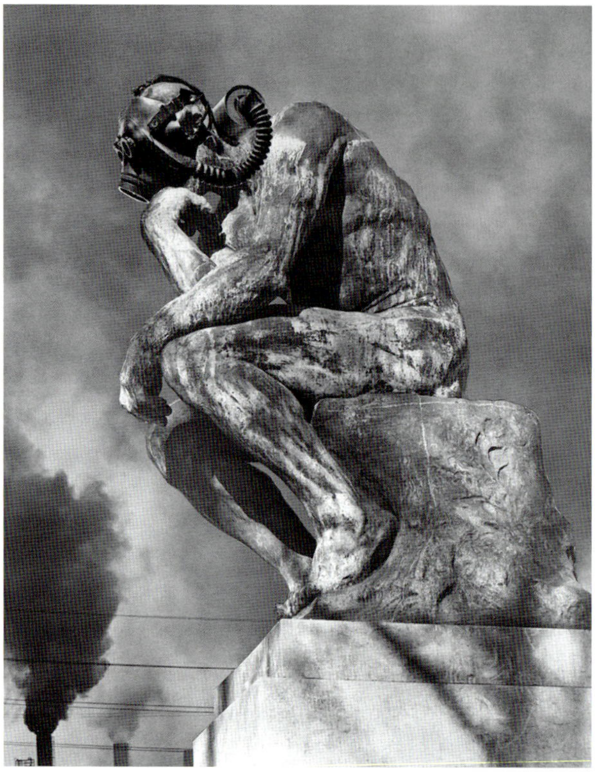

fig. 18.19 Spoof on Rodin's *The Thinker.*

medium was the Eiffel Tower in Paris (fig. 18.20). Designed by **Gustave Eiffel** for the 1889 Paris Exposition, it was the tallest man-made structure in the world at 984 feet. At the time, the public highly criticized it for towering over the rest of Paris and intended to dismantle it after twenty years. Instead, however, it became a symbol of the city (and a useful perch for radio and television antennas) and remains standing. Paris without the Eiffel Tower would be unthinkable today.

SUMMARY

The nineteenth century was one of "isms" in art. Many changes took place in society. The development of the steam and combustible engines led to trains and automobiles. Mass production of goods made them cheaper and more widely available. Chemical pigments improved the quality and range of colors, and the invention of the tin tube allowed painters to carry their paints with them outdoors.

Major movements of the 19th Century:

Neoclassicism: A late eighteenth art movement that continued into the early nineteenth-century. Characterized by a revival of the classical style of ancient Greece and Rome, it was a reaction to the playful Rococo style.

Romanticism: An art movement in the early nineteenth century characterized by dramatic, emotional content and rich painterly colors. It arose in reaction to Neoclassicism.

Major Romantic artists:
Théodore Géricault (*Raft of the Medusa*)
Eugène Delacroix (*Death of Sardanapalus*)
Francisco Goya (*The Third of May, 1808*)
Joseph Mallord William Turner (*The Slave Ship*)

Realism: A mid 19th-century movement in art characterized by everyday mundane subject matter.

Major Realist artists:
Édouard Manet (*Olympia*)
Winslow Homer (*Snap the Whip*)

Impressionism: A late 19th-century art movement that began in France and was characterized by capturing fleeting moments and the effects of light.

Major Impressionist artists:
Claude Monet (*White Water Lilies*)
Auguste Renoir (*Le Moulin de la Galette*)

Post-Impressionism: A variety of individualistic styles in the late 19th-century after Impressionism. Post-Impressionist artists expanded Impressionism by emphasizing geometric forms or distorting forms.

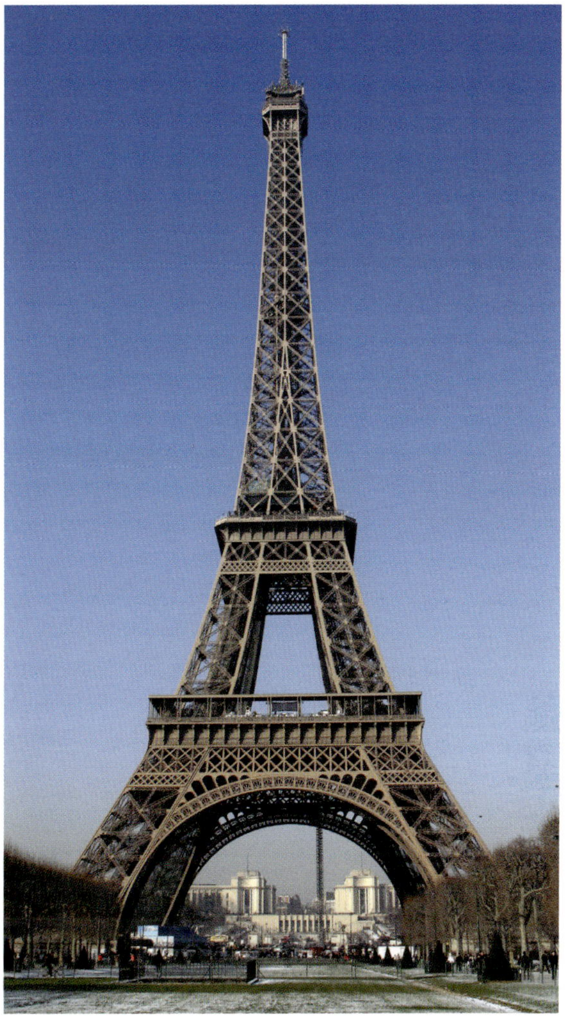

fig. 18.20 Alexandre-Gustave Eiffel, Eiffel Tower, 1889. Paris, France.

Major Post-Impressionist artists:
Vincent Van Gogh (*Starry Night*, many self-portraits)
Henri de Toulouse-Lautrec (*La Goulue at the Moulin Rouge Concert Bal*)
Edvard Munch (*The Scream*)
Georges Seurat (*A Sunday on La Grande Jatte*)
Paul Cézanne (*Still Life with Apples and Biscuits*)

Major early photographer: Nadar (*Portrait of Sarah Bernhardt*)
Major late 19th-century sculptor: August Rodin (*The Thinker*)
Major late 19th-century architect: Alexandre-Gustave Eiffel (*Eiffel Tower*)

PRONUNCIATION GUIDE

Avant-garde (uh-vahnt-**gard** or ah vahn **gard**)
Cézanne (say-**zahn**)
Daguerre, Louis (duh-**gair**, **Loo**-ee)
Delacroix, Eugène (deh-luh-**krwa**, oo-**zhen**)
Eiffel (**eye**-fuhl)
Géricault, Théodore (zhair-ee-**koh**, tey-oh-**dore**)
Goya (**goy**-uh)
Manet, Eduoard (ma-**nay**, ey-**dwahr**)
Marat (mah-**rah**)
Monet, Claude (moh-**nay**, klohd)
Munch, Edvard (moonk, **ed**-vard)
Nadar (nah-**dar**)
Plein air (**plane air**)
Pointillism (**point**-til-iz-um or **pwan**-til-iz-um)
Renoir, Pierre August (ren-**wahr**, pee-**err** oh-**goost**)
Rodin (roh-**dan**)
Sardanapalus (sar-duh-**nah**-puh-luhs)
Seurat, George (si-**rah**, zhorzh)
Toulouse-Lautrec, Henri de (too-**loos**-loh-**trek**, on-**ree** de)
Van Gogh (van **go**)

GLOSSARY

Academic style. A realistic style of painting that adhered to the rules of the French Academy in the nineteenth century.

Avant-garde. Innovators in a particular field. From the French for "advance guard" (in a platoon).

Cast iron. A hard but brittle alloy of iron and carbon produced in molds.

Complementary colors. Pairs of colors that are opposite each other on the color wheel (see fig. 2.18), such as red and green or blue and orange.

Cool color. A color such as blue or green that appears to be cool in temperature and to recede in space when contrasted with warm colors such as red and yellow.

Divisionism. See Pointillism.

Impressionism. A late nineteenth-century art movement that began in France and was characterized by capturing fleeting moments and the effects of light.

Lithograph. A print made from the lithography process in which involves drawing the image with a greasy material on a polished stone.

Local Color. An object's actual color in white light. (See also Optical color.)

Neoclassicism. A late eighteenth and early nineteenth-century art movement characterized by a revival of the classical style of ancient Greece and Rome.

Optical color. The perceived color of an object, which varies according to atmospheric and other light conditions. (See also Local color.)

Photography. The capturing of an image onto a light sensitive surface such as photographic film or a digital sensor.

Plein-air painting. Painting done outdoors on site.

Pointillism. A late nineteenth-century style of painting developed by the French artist George Seurat in which small dots of pure unmixed color are applied to the canvas and intended to fuse or mix in the mind's eye. Also called Divisionism.

Post Impressionism. A style of painting in the late nineteenth century that evolved from Impressionism. It is characterized by color and brushwork used for expressive (rather than decorative or factual) means.

Print. A work of art made by one of the printmaking processes such as engraving or etching. A print can also be a photograph made from a negative.

Realism. A mid nineteenth-century movement in art characterized by everyday mundane subject matter.

Romanticism. An art movement in the early nineteenth century characterized by dramatic, emotional content and rich painterly colors. It arose in reaction to Neoclassicism.

Steel. An alloy of mostly iron to which carbon and other elements have been added to make it stronger and less brittle.

Warm color. A color such as red or yellow that appears to be warm in temperature and to advance in space when contrasted with cool colors such as blue and green.

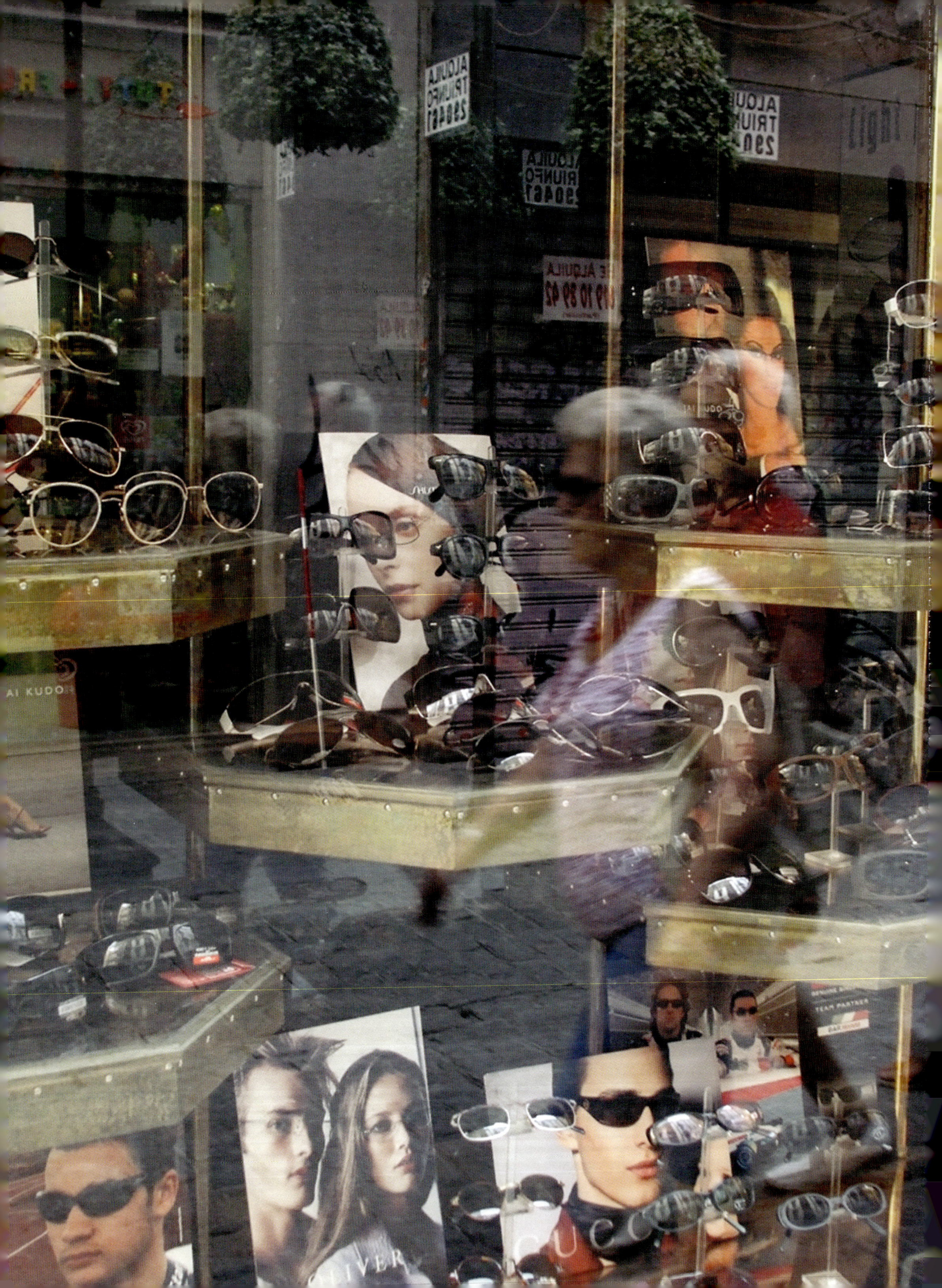

19 PHOTOGRAPHY

Photography is one of the most influential forces in art and in society in general. We are a visual culture, and much of the knowledge we acquire about the world we live in comes from photographs. Today almost all fields of human endeavor use some form of photography. We see it in advertising, fashion, medicine, nature, criminal justice, journalism, and astronomy, among many other fields. The word photography derives from the Greek words for light and writing because the image is in essence written or drawn on the film with light. The process was invented in the early nineteenth century, but its antecedents go back much further. A Muslim scientist named Ibn al-Haytham invented the *camera obscura* and pinhole camera (see "Camera Obscura, Pinhole Photography" box) in the tenth century, and Albert Magnus discovered silver nitrate, one of the chemicals used in traditional photographic development processes, in the thirteenth century.

Photography not only involves the particulars of the photographic equipment (camera, **lens**, and **film** or sensor) but also the many variables of composition (light, angle of view, distance, etc.) Using a camera can force us to see the world in a different way. Although the camera mimics the human eye, it is not nearly as versatile. When we look at a store window, we can focus on the street reflections in the glass or we can focus through the window at the items on display and totally ignore the reflections. The camera captures both, and the result can be unsatisfying (fig. 19.1)

There are two main types of photography: film and digital. Photographic film captures an image when light strikes the film. Processing with photographic chemicals develops the film, creating negatives from which the photographer makes positive prints with an enlarger, light-sensitive photographic paper, and an additional chemical process. In the case of color slides, the photographer develops a positive image that he can then project with a slide projector. Slides are more brilliant than prints because they transmit light rather than reflect it—just as a digital photograph looks more vibrant on your computer screen than when you print it out. Early film photography was black-and-white only, although the first color photography followed soon after in the mid-nineteenth century. Even after researchers fully developed color photography (Kodak introduced its color Kodachrome® film in the 1930s), people still often preferred black-and-white because of its tonal capabilities and traditional look.

Film photography is labor intensive and expensive because it requires a completely dark photographic lab with all the proper equipment and chemicals. Despite this, many artists still use film photography who have a personal preference for a more involved hands-on experience with subtle

fig. 19.1 Shop window.

Camera Obscura, Pinhole Photography

A *camera obscura* (meaning 'dark room') was a dark room with a small hole in one wall that allowed sunlight to pass through and project an inverted image of whatever was outside onto the opposite wall. Later its size was reduced to that of a portable dark box, making it more practical. Artists used it as an aid for drawing because they could trace the outlines of the projected image. The *camera obscura* forms the basis for the pinhole camera. Students in beginning photography classes often start out with pinhole photography because it teaches the basic principles of **aperture** size (the opening that lets in light) and exposure (how long light enters the opening). A pinhole camera does not have a lens. Like the *camera obscura* it has a very small hole (the pinhole) instead that light passes through, projecting an inverted image onto the opposite side. Simple pinhole cameras can be handmade using any type of thin lightproof box with a pinhole at one end (typically made with the tip of a sewing needle) and a piece of film or photographic paper at the other end. A flap of cardboard can act as the shutter to open and close the hole. The smaller the hole, the sharper the image, but the longer the exposure required. Exposure times can vary from a few seconds to several hours.

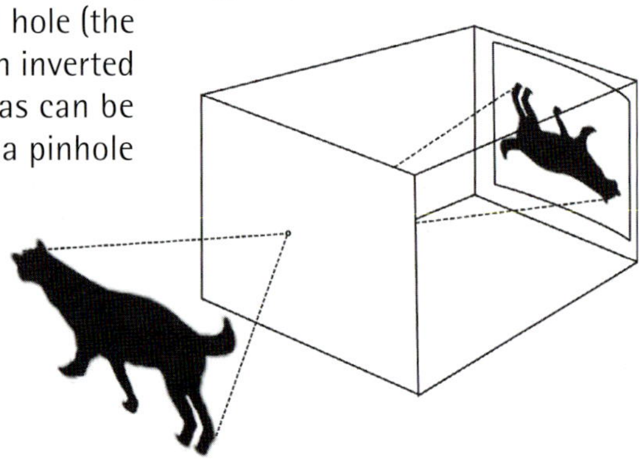

artistic manipulation possible at all stages of the process: shooting, developing, and printing. Film also records a greater dynamic range than digital photography, and different processing techniques and photographic papers permit varied effects. Jim Knipe's *Todi, Italy* (fig. 19.2) shows the afternoon sun entering a lonely curved street in the small Italian town. The great contrast between the foreground shadows and the intensely sunlit background is well transitioned and gives the scene a melancholy atmosphere. The photograph is as much a portrait of light as it is of an abandoned street. Such transitions of light and the accompanying tonal values would be more difficult to achieve with digital photography.

The advent of digital photography in the 1990s caused a radical change. In digital photography an image sensor records the image as a set of electronic data, eliminating the chemical processes of film. At first the resolution did not approach that of film, and then when it did the equipment was so expensive as to be out of reach for most people. Now high-resolution cameras are available at affordable prices. Even many point-and-shoot cameras have good resolution. Almost all commercial enterprises, from newspapers and magazines to portrait studios and most of the general public, have switched to digital photography. Some companies like Kodak, Canon and Nikon now make few or no film camera models. Kodak also ceased production of its slide projectors and Kodachrome® film. Furthermore, it is increasingly difficult to find commercial establishments that sell or develop film. Film photography remains mostly as an artist's medium.

Digital photography has many advantages. You can instantly review your photo and delete it if it isn't what you want; you can store hundreds of photos on a media card within the camera; and you can print your own photos with a computer and a color printer. Additionally, digital photography allows an almost infinite degree of manipulation using a computer and appropriate software. The photographer avoids the expense of equipping a photo lab, the exposure to chemicals and the time-consuming developing and printing processes, but there is a steep learning curve for acquiring the advanced skills of digital photo manipulation. Tom Pallante's digital photograph, *Flying Kites* (fig. 19.3), illustrates the differences with the digital method. Using layer masks, cutting and pasting, and color manipulation he is able to achieve effects not possible with film photography.

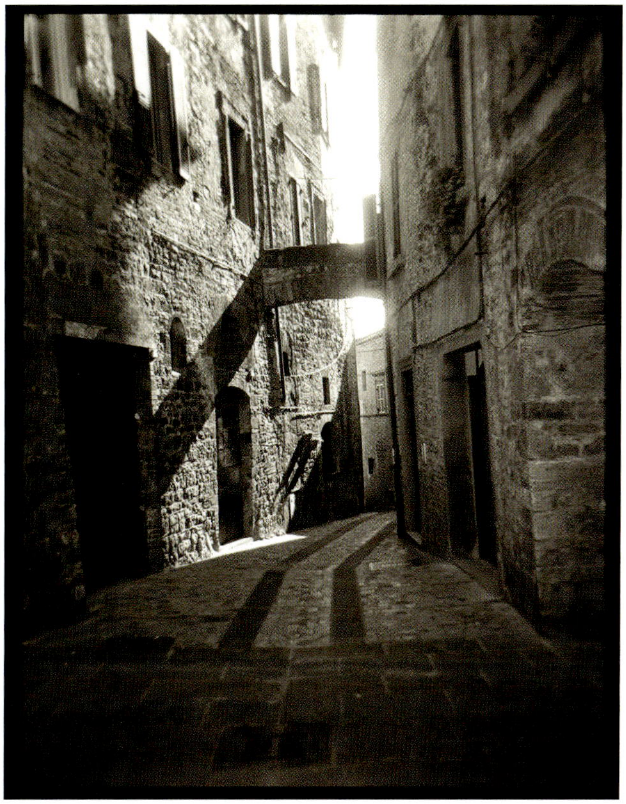

fig. 19.2 Jim Knipe, *Todi, Italy,* 2006. Gelatin silver print.

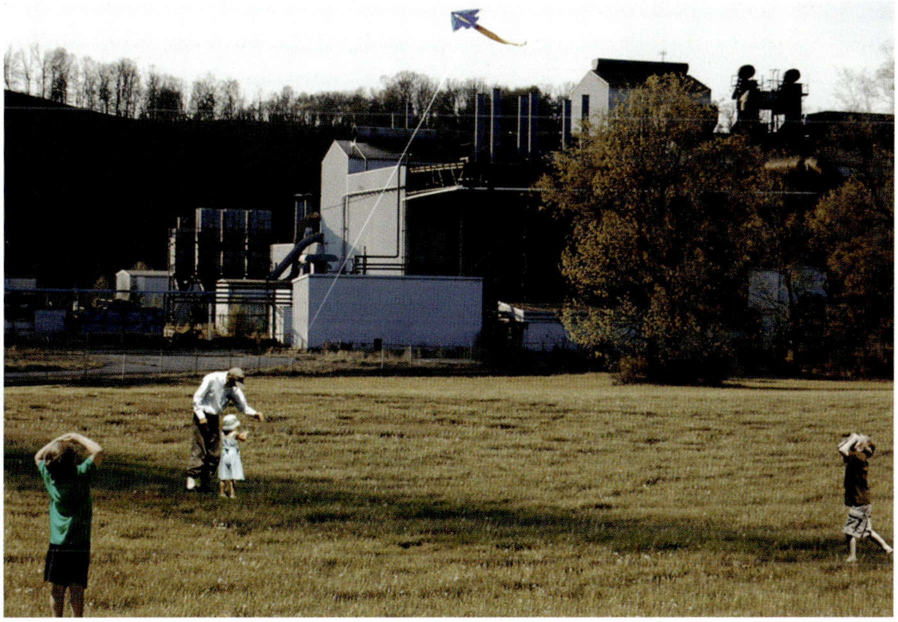

fig. 19.3 Tom Pallante, *Flying Kites,* 2008. Photo-composite of four photographs.

Digital photography has raised certain ethical issues because of its manipulative qualities. The old maxim, "The camera never lies," is no longer true, or at least it may no longer be true after the photographer subjects the digital image to editing software. Because of this, many courts of law will not accept digital images as evidence. We have all seen photos of highly improbable scenes, such as a man with a 200-pound cat on his lap or a gigantic shark leaping out of the water to attack a rescuer on the dangling ladder of a hovering helicopter.

PHOTOGRAPHY AS ART

The first use of photography was to document things, especially people. Photographic portraits democratized the art of portraiture. Many people who could not afford the traditional painted portrait could purchase a photographic portrait. Most people did not consider photography as art, however, but rather a mechanical duplication process. Even so, artists lamented what they thought would be the end of painting in favor of the photograph, just as moviemakers in the 1950s thought television would replace motion pictures. Neither came to pass. And even if many artists did not treat photography as an art, many made good use of it as an aid to painting. Rather than do a preliminary sketch, artists could photograph a scene and have an image to paint from that was more detailed and could better catch the nuances of light and shade.

The push to elevate photography to the level of an art began in earnest with such early twentieth photographers as Alfred Steiglitz, Edward Steichen and Edward Weston. They promoted photography as a fine art by creating painterly photographs such as Steichen's *Flatiron Building* (fig. 19.4), whose atmospheric effects give the photograph a dreamy artistic quality. Later photographers like Ansel Adams created sharply focused scenes to emphasize the photograph as photograph and not as something trying to imitate another medium (fig. 19.5). The efforts of these pioneering photographers paid off—photography has now attained the status of art. Most large museums have photography collections, and some photographs bring high prices at auction. In 2001 Andreas Gursky's large color photograph *99 cent II Diptychon* fetched several million dollars.

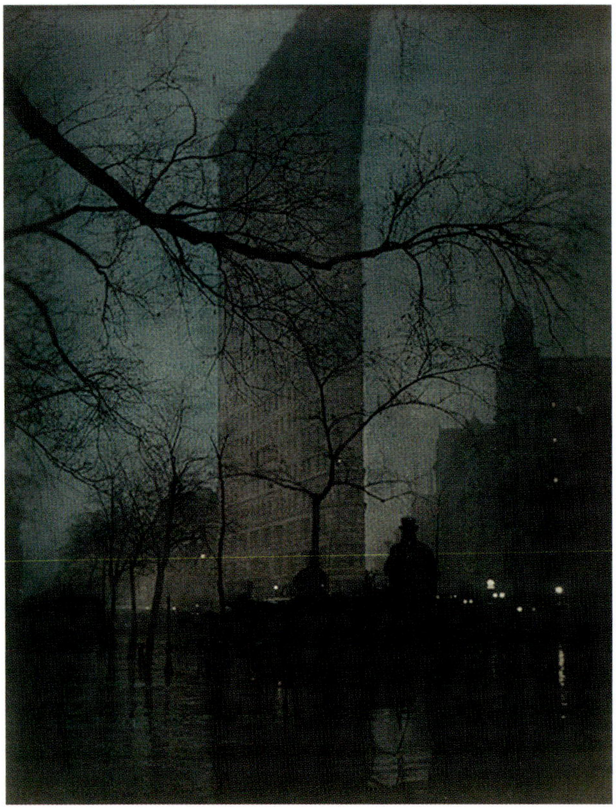

fig. 19.4 Edward Steichen, *Flatiron Building*, 1904. Photograph.

Camera Basics

Although many cameras are now fully automatic, it helps to understand a few basics about aperture, shutter speed and film speed, which apply to both film and digital cameras. The aperture size is how large the lens opening is when the shutter button is released; the shutter speed is how long the lens opening stays open; and the film speed refers to how sensitive the film or digital sensor is to light. Sufficient light is crucial for a successful photograph. The larger the aperture the more light enters through the lens. Aperture sizes are indicated by special numbers that typically range from 1.8 to 16 with 1.8 being the largest aperture and 16 being the smallest. The advantage of a large aperture is that you can take pictures in lower light situations. The disadvantage is a shallow depth of field—objects in front of or behind the main subject may be out of focus. Smaller apertures provide greater depth of field so more of the image will be in focus, but they require more light or a slower shutter speed. Usually a shutter speed slower than 1/30 of a second results in blurry pictures because a person cannot hold the camera steady. (Most digital cameras now have an anti-shake feature to help correct for this.) Although cameras have a built-in flash for low light situations, the flash range on a point-and-shoot camera is typically only about twelve feet. Higher film speed numbers (ISO) allow photography in lower light situations, but the higher the number, the more grainy (film) or pixilated (digital) the image will be.

Selecting a Point-and-Shoot Camera

Digital cameras are usually promoted by the number of **megapixels** (MP) they have. Generally, the more megapixels the greater the image resolution (how sharp the image is). But the quality of the lens and the sensor is more important. An 8MP camera with a good lens and sensor will give you better photos than a 12MP camera with a lesser quality lens and sensor. Unless you are going to be enlarging your photos to sizes greater than 8 × 10 inches, eight megapixels is sufficient. When purchasing a digital camera, do some research online to see which ones in your price range are highly rated. (Two good sites are *www.steves-digicams.com* and *www.dpreview.com/reviews.*) In addition to lens quality and number of megapixels, important features to consider are a large aperture (2.8 or larger), slow film speed equivalent (ISO) of 80 or lower and optical image stabilization (OIS).

Ansel Adams' *Monument in Cemetery* (fig. 19.5) is an example of documentary photography, which also achieved status as an art form in the twentieth century, especially if the photographs promoted social change. Adams documented the tragedy of the United States government placing American citizens of Japanese ancestry into camps during World War II. Dorothea Lange documented the equally tragic plight of people suffering through the economic devastation of the 1930s. Her *Migrant Worker* from 1936 unflinchingly documents the harsh reality of the Great Depression (fig. 19.6)

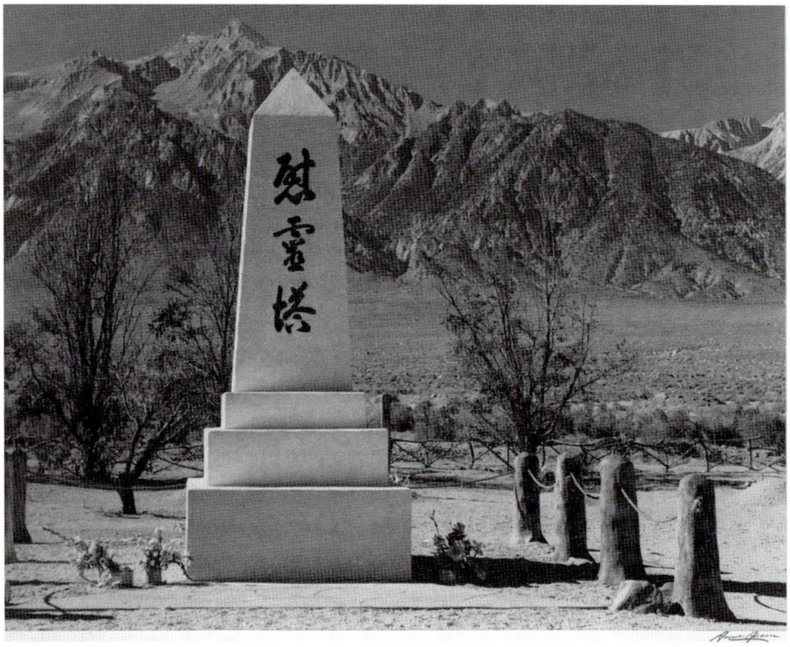

Library of Congress, Prints & Photographs Division, Ansel Adams, photographer

fig. 19.5 Ansel Adams, *Monument in Cemetery,* 1943. Gelatin silver print.

SUMMARY

Photography is ubiquitous in today's world as almost all fields of human endeavor make use of it. It has greatly influenced art since its invention in the nineteenth century. At first it was feared photography would replace painting, but this did not happen. Photography began to be viewed as art (versus mere documentation) in the early twentieth century, and today many noted museums maintain large photograph collections, and some photographs have sold for millions of dollars at auction.

There are two main types of photography: film and digital. Digital photography has largely replaced film photography because it is cheaper and simpler. There are no chemicals or time-intensive processes to deal with, and digital images are much easier to store. Furthermore, you get instant feedback on your photographs, and those you don't like can be immediately deleted. Although film photography is now less used for documentary purposes, it will probably survive as an art form because it is easier to achieve subtle artistic effects than with digital photography. Furthermore, film photography still maintains its reputation of revealing the true

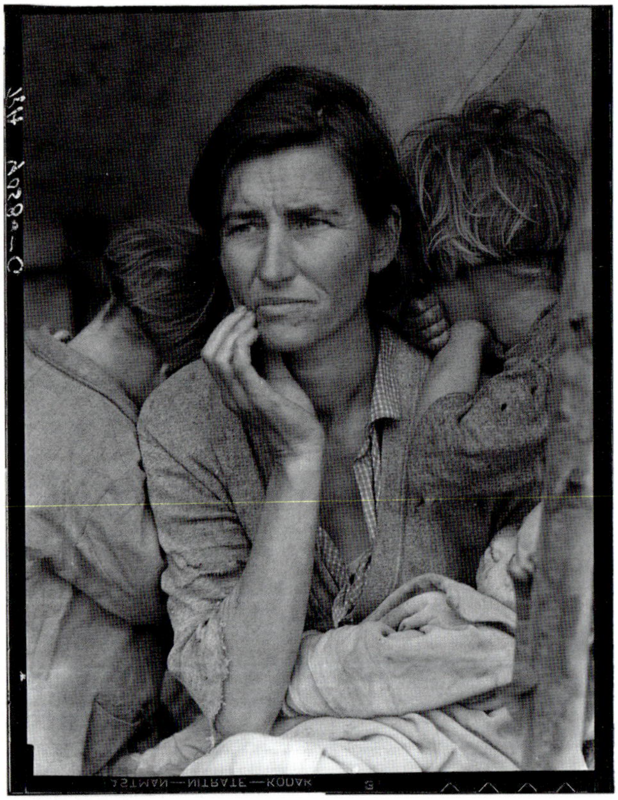

Library of Congress, Prints & Photographs Division, FSA/OWI Collection

fig. 19.6 Dorothea Lange, *Migrant Worker,* Nipomo, California, 1936. Gelatin silver print.

nature of the image photographed. Digital photography, on the other hand, has changed the way we perceive the truth of recorded images. Easily manipulated with software programs, digital photographs can lie and you can never be sure of the true nature of the subject photographed.

PRONUNCIATION GUIDE

Aperture (**ap**-er-cher)
Camera obscura (**kam**-er-uh ob-**skyoor**-ah)
Gelatin (**jel**-uh-tin)

GLOSSARY

Aperture. An opening. In photography, the camera lens opening.

Camera obscura. Latin for "dark room." A precursor to the modern camera. A tiny hole in the wall of an enclosed space allows light through to project an inverted image on the opposite wall.

Digital art. Art that is created with the assistance of a computer or other electronic instruments. It encompasses the fields of web design, graphic design, and digital photography, among others.

Film. A thin sheet of cellulose material coated with a photosensitive material.

Gelatin silver print. A photographic process used with black-and-white films and printing papers in which a suspension of silver salts in gelatin is coated onto acetate film or resin coated paper.

Lens. A transparent object with at least one curved surface that results in a convergence of light rays passing through it. The human eye and cameras have lenses that focus images.

Megapixel. One million pixels, used as a measure of resolution in digital cameras. (A pixel [short for "picture element] is a very small point of data.)

Photography. The capturing of an image onto a light sensitive surface such as photographic film or a digital sensor.

Print. A photograph made from a negative.

Shutter. In photography, the device for opening and closing the aperture to allow light onto the film or sensor.

Shutter speed. How long the shutter of a camera stays open.

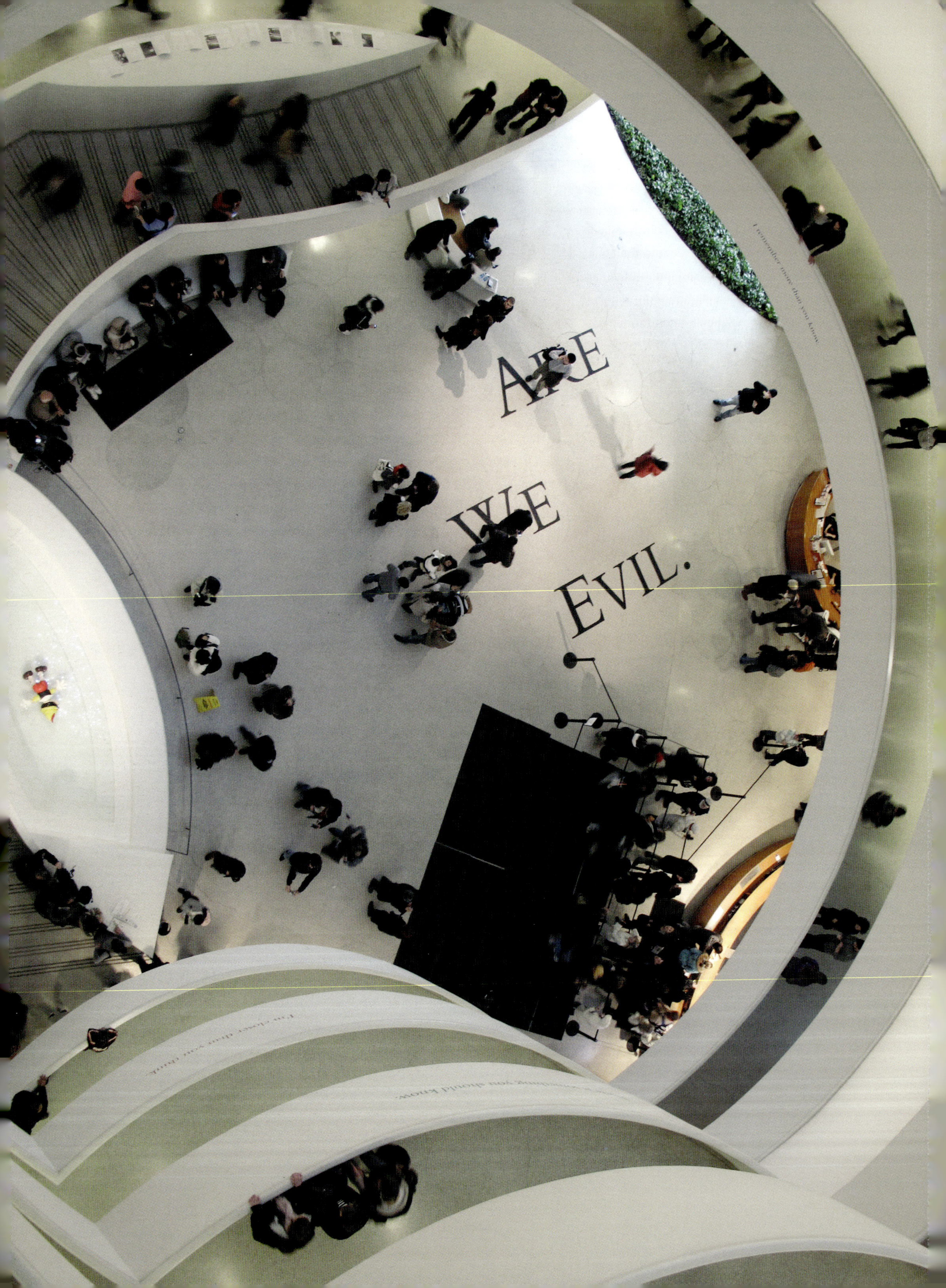
ARE
WE
EVIL.
I remember more than you know.
I'm closer than you think.
you should know.

20

20TH CENTURY ART

The twentieth century saw two major world wars (plus a host of smaller conflicts), the development of atomic energy and the end of colonial empires. Albert Einstein developed his Theory of Relativity giving us a new concept of the universe, and Sigmund Freud introduced psychoanalysis of the human mind. Technology evolved with ever greater rapidity as the century progressed. At the beginning of the century people still rode horses as a major form of transportation, and the telephone and electric light bulb were relatively new inventions. By the end of the century huge jets ferried people across the globe, missions into space were commonplace, and personal electronic items proliferated. It is now hard for us to conceive of a world without televisions, personal computers, cell phones and i-Pods.

In art, the artistic capital of Western art switched from Paris to New York, new styles evolved from the trends of the late nineteenth century, and new mediums developed. Like the nineteenth century, the twentieth century is a series of individual movements, but there are far more of them, and they evolve far more quickly. The liberation of form and color that began with the Impressionists and the Post Impressionists culminates in the twentieth century. This chapter briefly describes some of the major trends and artists of the century. It is by no means a complete survey, and it omits many important artists in the interest of space. Note also that the main emphasis is on painting.

FAUVISM

Fauvism comes from the French word *fauve,* which means "wild beast." The name was coined by an art critic who lambasted an exhibition of paintings in the new style by such French artists as Henri Matisse, André Derain, Georges Dufy and Georges Rouault. The use of color by Post Impressionists such as Van Gogh and art from non-Western cultures (which many of them collected) heavily influenced these artists. Bold and bright arbitrary color characterizes Fauve art. Yellow skies, green faces and blue grass shocked the public and critics alike.

Red Room (fig. 20.1) by **Henri Matisse** (1869–1954) shows us a traditional interior scene with a landscape view out the window, but tradition stops there. The walls and tablecloth are shockingly red with no modulation of color to indicate depth. The vine pattern of the wallpaper, which

fig. 20.31 Interior of Guggenheim Museum.

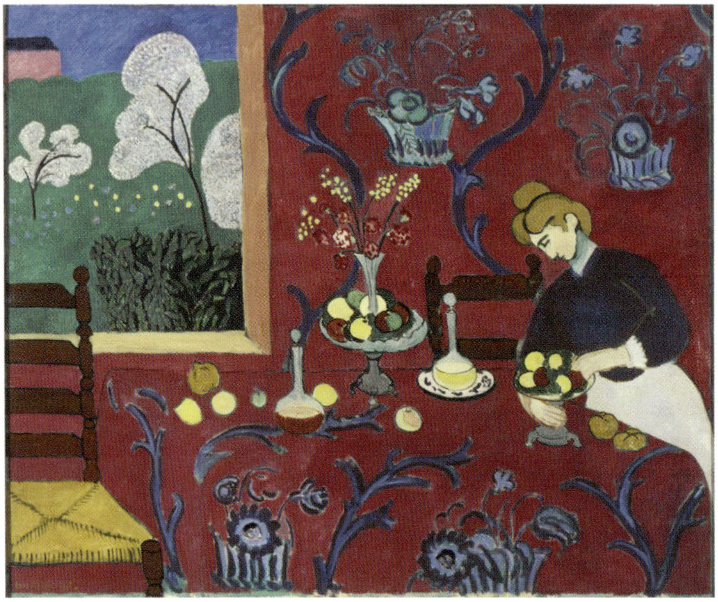

fig. 20.1 Henri Matisse, *Red Room* (*Harmony in Red*), 1908–1909. Oil on canvas, 5 ft. 11 in. × 8 ft. 1 in. State Hermitage Museum, St. Petersburg.

continues in the tablecloth design, further obscures depth. A single black horizontal line is our only indication of where the table ends and the wall begins. Composed of simplified forms, the single figure almost becomes part of the overall patterned design. Matisse omits details because he does not want to distract the viewer from the essence of the reality that he wants to impart to the viewer. What is important to Matisse is an overall feeling, and he reconstructs reality using flowing decorative lines and brilliant arbitrary color to communicate a sense of the joy of life (*joie de vivre*). Fauvism was a short-lived movement lasting only four or five years in the first decade of the century.

The French Fauvist movement led into two German Expressionist schools called "The Bridge" and "The Blue Rider." Russian painter **Wassily Kandinsky** (1866–1944) was a member of the latter group, and he was the first artist to paint a totally abstract (**nonrepresentational**) composition—that is, a painting with no discernible subject matter. *Improvisation No. 23* (fig. 20.2) is one of a series Kandinsky

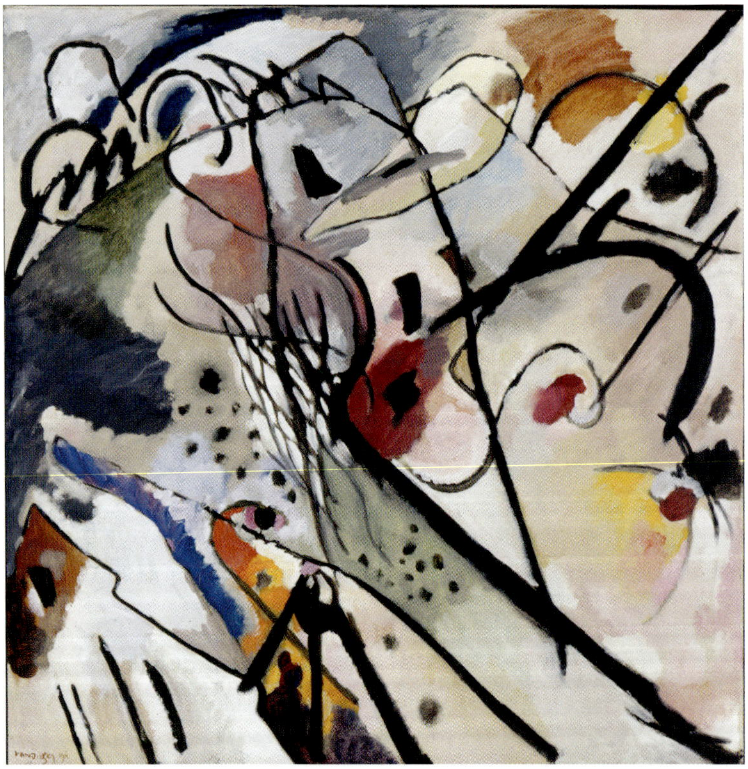

fig. 20.2 Wassily Kandinsky, *"Improvisation No. 23,"* 1911 Roethelyl no. 402 page 389. Oil on canvas, 43.25 in. × 43.2 in. Munson-Williams-Proctor Arts Institute, Utica, New York.

painted in a spontaneous mode. He did not consciously work out the composition—he simply painted. The work is a kaleidoscope of color applied in loose brushstrokes. For Kandinksy, the subject was the feeling the viewer experiences when contemplating the work.

An example of total abstraction in sculpture is *Bird in Space* (fig. 20.3) by Romanian sculptor **Constantin Brancusi** (1876–1957). Brancusi does not show us a realistic bird; instead he has reduced the concept of a bird and flight to its essence. The highly polished curved tapering form alludes to aspects of a bird such as a feather or a wing, and its aerodynamic form embodies the concept of flight.

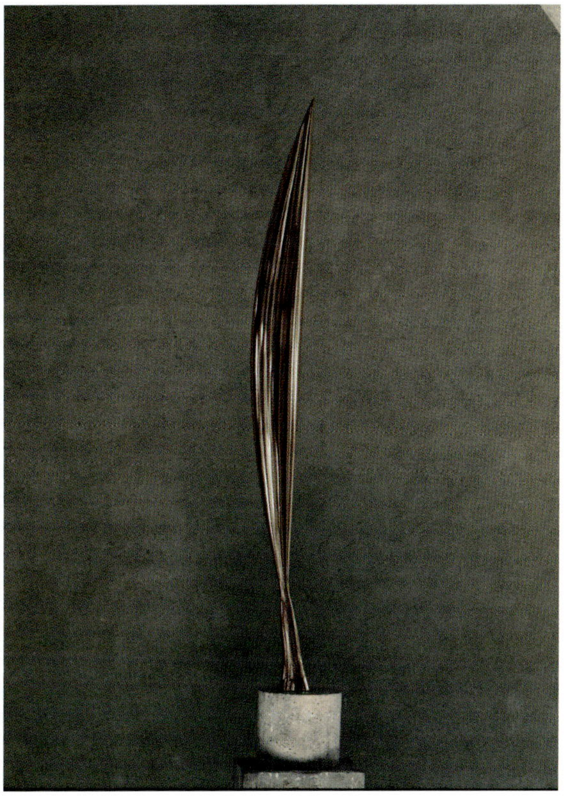

fig. 20.3 Constantin Brancusi, *Bird in Space,* 1924. Bronze, 4 ft. 2 in. high. Museum of Modern Art, New York. This work caused a stir at U.S. Customs when it was shipped to the United States for an exhibition. The customs inspector refused to classify it as art; therefore it could not enter the country duty free. The case went to court where a jury had to decide what is art and what isn't. The bird won.

CUBISM

Cubism is one of the major movements of the twentieth century, and its main proponent, **Pablo Picasso** (1881–1973) is one of the titans of modern art. Cézanne set the stage for the development of Cubism with his abstracted structural forms. Picasso developed cubism along with fellow artist Georges Braque around 1908. Cubism breaks up forms and shows them as faceted planes and cubes, often from multiple points of view. A portrait of a girl might show the front of her face and the side of her nose at the same time. In a way, the style fits in with Einstein's theories of space and time. Picasso's breakthrough painting, *Les Demoiselles d'Avignon* (fig. 20.4), illustrates the style before it became fully developed. Five female nudes pose in an interior space with a still life of fruit in the foreground. Avignon refers to a street in Barcelona known for its brothels, and the poses of the women, who appear to be displaying their wares, indicate they are prostitutes. Picasso breaks up the forms into sharp-edged facets with little indication of depth. The blue background looks like fragments of broken glass. The faces of the three outer figures clearly show the influence of African masks, which Picasso collected. This painting was shocking in its conception because it totally negated much of traditional Western art. Many considered the work simply ugly.

The monumental *Guernica* (fig. 20.5) illustrates Picasso's late cubist style. Created as a protest against the forces of General Franco and the Spanish Civil War (1936–1939), the work commemorates the total destruction of the Spanish town of Guernica. (It was the first time aerial bombing obliterated a town.) The huge canvas (more than 25 feet wide) is a powerful indictment against the brutality of war. The angular faceted forms fit appropriately with the anguished themes of terror, confusion, death and

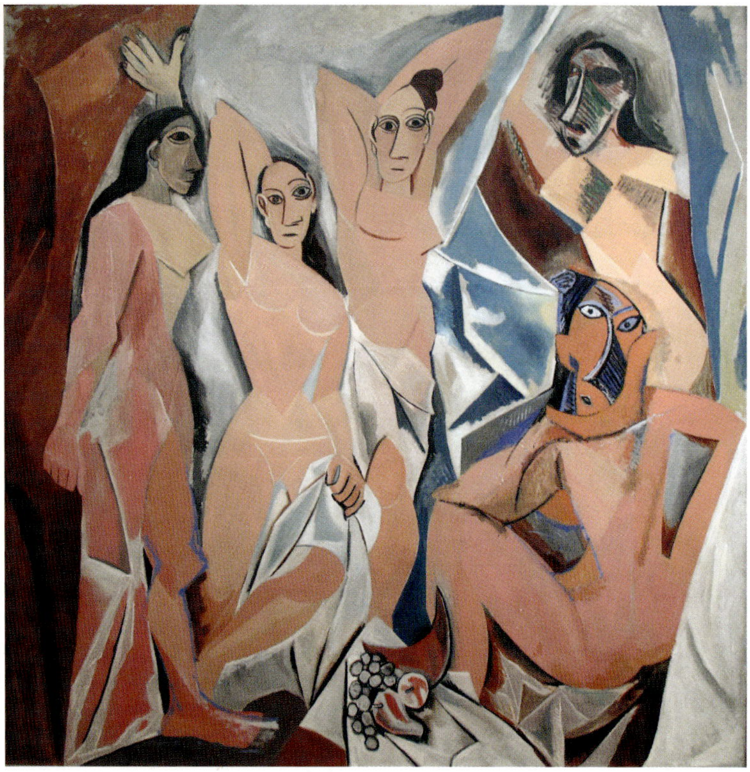

fig. 20.4 Pablo Picasso, *Demoiselles d'Avignon,* 1907. Oil on canvas, 8 ft. × 7 ft. 8 in. Museum of Modern Art, New York.

destruction and in fact reinforce them. In the center beneath an eye-shaped light (perhaps a symbol for the eye of God) a speared horse screams in agony as it dies. Below, a fallen man lies on the floor with a broken knife in his right hand. To the left, a speared bull (a symbol of Spain) looks out at the viewer while below him a mother wails over her dead baby in a pose that clearly recalls the Pietà (Mary holding the dead Christ in her lap). Picasso left his painting to Spain, but he stipulated that it was not to go there while Franco was still in power. *Guernica* did not arrive home until forty-four years after its completion.

Cubism profoundly influenced other artists. **Marcel Duchamp** (1987–1968) created a sensation at an exhibition in New York in 1913 with his *Nude Descending a Staircase* (fig. 20.6). Duchamp uses the faceted forms of Cubism and repeats the figure in overlapping layers to create a sense of movement. Although now considered a seminal work of the early twentieth century, it was ridiculed at the time. One critic referred to it as an explosion in a shingle factory.

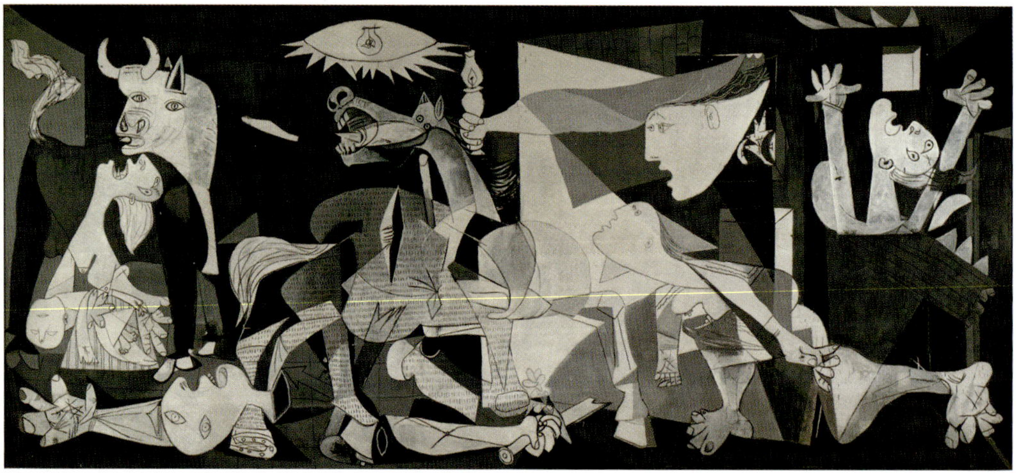

fig. 20.5 Pablo Picasso, *Guernica,* 1937. Oil on canvas, 11 ft. 6 in. × 25 ft. 6 in. Museo Nacional Centro de Arte Reina Sofia, Madrid.

FUTURISM

Futurism was essentially a movement of Italian artists (Giacomo Balla, Gino Severini, Carlo Carrà and Umberto Boccioni) who wanted to show the speed and motion of the twentieth century. Using the faceted and shifting planes of Cubism as their starting point, they created such works as *Unique Forms of Continuity in Space* (fig. 20.7) by **Umberto Boccioni.** This bronze sculpture of a striding man clearly evokes quick movement through space. The planar facets of his muscles are whipped back into points at his hips and calves as though being blown by the figure's swift passage through space, much as one's scarf would wave if walking quickly.

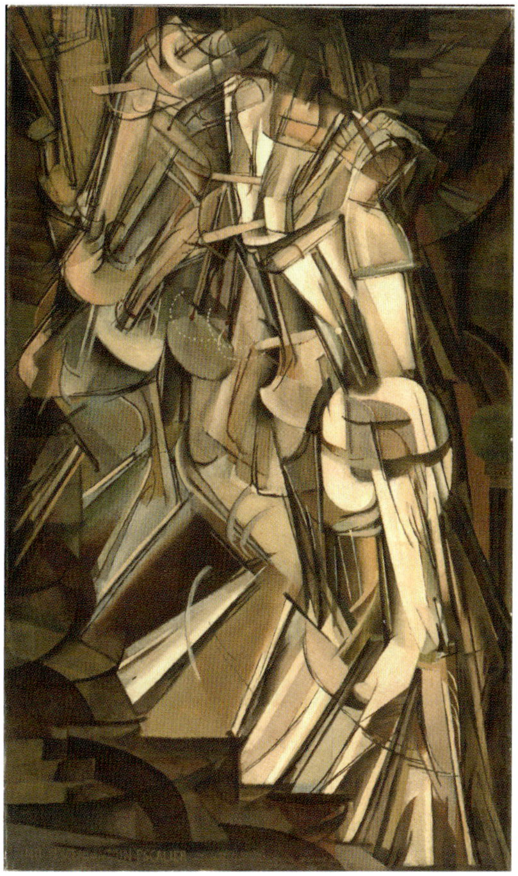

fig. 20.6 Marcel Duchamp, *Nude Descending a Staircase,* 1912. Oil on canvas, 4 ft. 10 in. × 2 ft. 11 in. Philadelphia Museum of Art, Philadelphia.

DADA

The horrors of World War I (1914–1918) negated the optimistic view of society promoted by the Futurists. Many artists became disillusioned, and one group created an anti-art movement called **Dada**. Dada is a nonsense word with no apparent meaning. Dada artists observed the lack of human reason in the world and responded with art that appeared to be as nonsensical but was in fact witty and imaginative. Duchamp was one of the principal Dada artists, and he often used already made objects in his art. He created *Fountain* (fig. 20.8) for exhibition in a gallery whose owners said they would accept anything submitted. To test them, he took a porcelain urinal, turned it on its side and then signed it "R. Mutt." The gallery owners rejected the work. Duchamp maintained that it did not matter if Mr. Mutt had actually made the fountain (the urinal); it was the fact that he created a new idea for the object that made it worthy of display.

Duchamp produced other "**readymades**" such as a bicycle wheel mounted on a stool, and other Dada artists also modified readymade objects and exhibited them. Artist Man Ray created a work he titled *The Gift,* which was an iron purchased from a housewares store whose ironing surface he then studded with sharp nails for a witty and confusing contradiction.

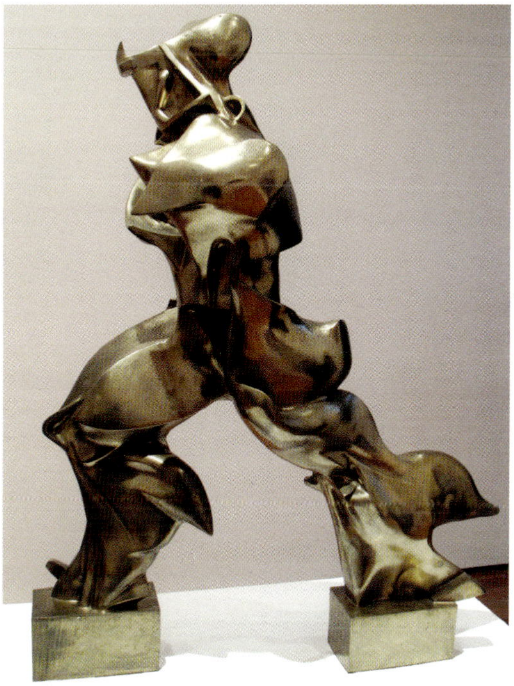

fig. 20.7 Umberto Boccioni, *Unique Forms of Continuity in Space,* 1913. Bronze, 3 ft. 8 in. high. Metropolitan Museum of Art, New York.

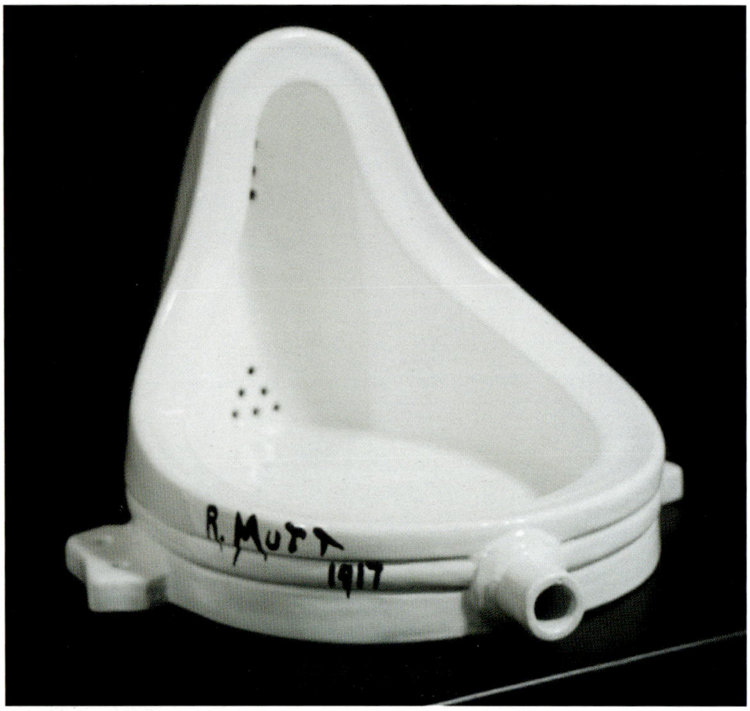

fig. 20.8 Marcel Duchamp, *Fountain* (second version), 1950 (original made in 1917). Readymade urinal with black paint, 24 in. high. Philadelphia Museum of Art, Philadelphia.

SURREALISM

Dada lasted only about six years (1916–1922), but its bizarre and contradictory associations led to one of the most popular movements of the twentieth century, **Surrealism**. Surrealism (which means "beyond realism") also embraced Sigmund Freud's ideas of free association and dream analysis. Surrealist artists wanted to depict the human subconscious. The movement is strongly associated with the Spanish painter **Salvador Dalí** (1904–1989). *The Persistence of Memory* (fig. 20.9) shows a seaside landscape with three limp pocket watches in the foreground. One watch (with a fly on its face) is draped over the corner of a wooden box, another is slung over the limb of a dead tree, and the third lies on top of a bizarre **biomorphic** form with a nose, tongue and closed eyelid with long lashes. A fourth stiff watch covered with ants rests on the box at the lower left. The imagery is incongruous. Watches are made of metal and are not supposed to be limp or be devoured by insects. Only in dreams would we see such odd things (and paradoxically, while dreaming they often seem perfectly normal). Sometimes the imagery is personal and not readily understood by the viewer. In this work the wilting watches attacked by insects associated with rot and decay may refer to the end of time. And the decomposing biological form could refer to the demise of humanity. The fact that Dalí paints in a highly realistic style adds to its super-real quality.

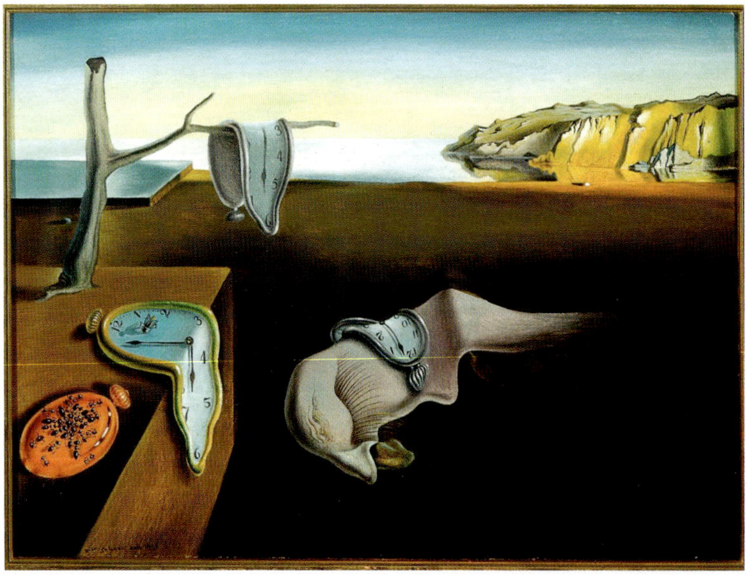

fig. 20.9 Salvador Dali, *The Persistence of Memory,* 1931. Oil on canvas, 9.5 in. × 13 in. Museum of Modern Art, New York.

AMERICAN REGIONALISM

American art still lagged behind European trends in the first part of the twentieth century, especially with its isolationist attitude, and many considered American art provincial. That began to change in the 1930s with American Regionalism, whose artists sought inspiration in uniquely American subjects. **Grant Wood** (1892–1942), a native of Iowa, painted in a style that was simple yet alluring. *American Gothic* (fig. 20.10) is one of the iconic images of American art.

A rural couple stands emotionless before their simple house with its neo-Gothic pointed window prominently shown between them. (The painting's title derives from this architectural detail.) Wood wanted to depict the "basically good and solid people" he knew as a child growing up in Iowa. (The models were in fact his sister and his dentist.) The detailed rendering shows the influence of northern Renaissance painters like Jan van Eyck (see pages 201-202), and the simplified forms recall American folk art. Grant carefully planned the seemingly simple composition. He elongated the heads of the two figures so that they would fit better with the long Gothic window, and the three-pronged pitch fork echoes the three points indicated by the two heads and the window.

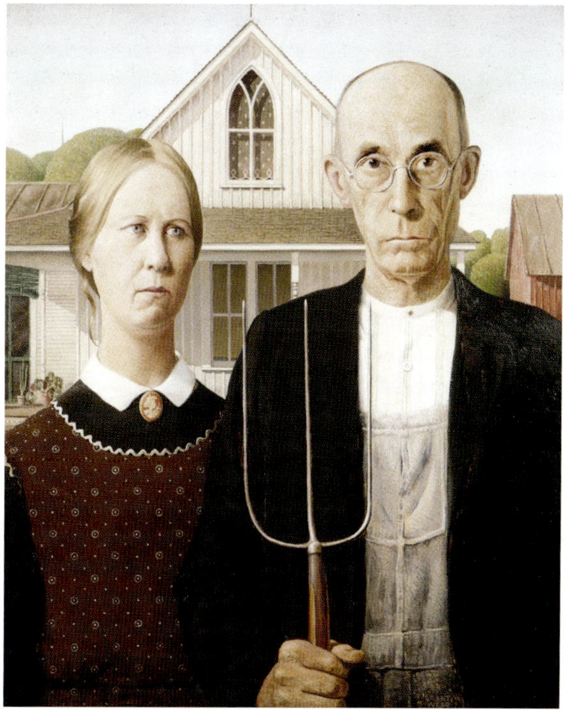

fig. 20.10 Grant Wood, *American Gothic,* 1930. Oil on canvas, 2 ft. 6 in. × 2 ft. 1 in. Art Institute of Chicago, Chicago.

Edward Hopper (1882–1967) also created his own unique style within the context of American Regionalism. Hopper dealt with human loneliness. His depictions of individuals in everyday locations such as hotel rooms, diners and gas stations exude a sad isolation. In *Nighthawks* (fig. 20.11) we see three customers at the counter

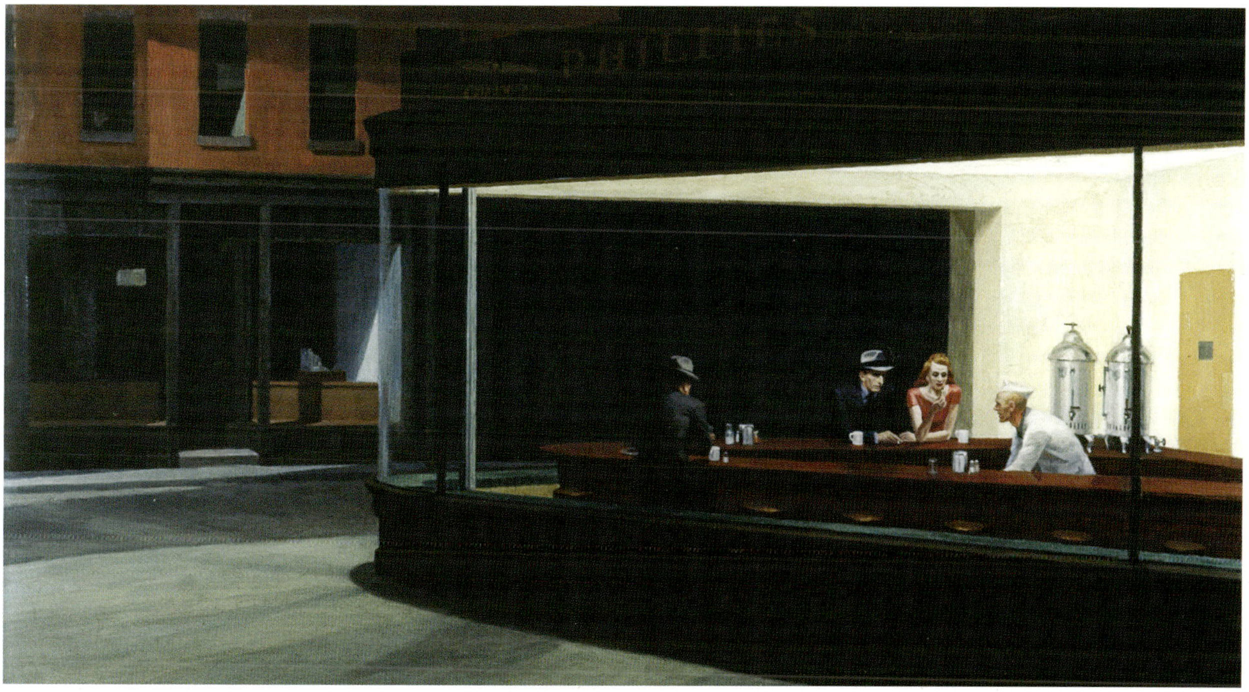

fig. 20.11 Edward Hopper, *Nighthawks,* 1942. Oil on canvas, 2 ft. 6 in. × 4 ft. 8.5 in. Art Institute of Chicago, Chicago.

of a diner late at night. All three seem self-absorbed with their inner thoughts and do not communicate with each other. Hopper achieves an eerie effect by carefully controlling light and shadow and by eliminating extraneous details.

DE STIJL

De Stijl is a movement synonymous with the Dutch artist **Piet Mondrian** (1872–1944). De Stijl is Dutch for "The Style," and it attempted to rid art of emotion. Mondrian is famous for his great number of paintings that consist of several rectangular forms in primary colors (red, yellow and blue) against a white ground divided into sections by black horizontal and vertical lines. He carefully planned each composition to achieve a perfect balance and harmony among the various forms and colors. He painted *Broadway Boogie Woogie* (fig. 20.12) near the end of his life when he lived in New York, a city whose excitement and vitality he loved. Still employing his characteristic rectangles in primary colors, Broadway Boogie Woogie gives the viewer an abstracted aerial view of central Manhattan with its pulsating rhythms and bright lights. One gets the sense of automobile headlamps swiftly traveling down straight streets.

ABSTRACT EXPRESSIONISM

World War II (1939–1945) disrupted the art scene in Europe, and after the war New York became the most important city for art in Western culture. American artists finally began to set artistic trends, rather than

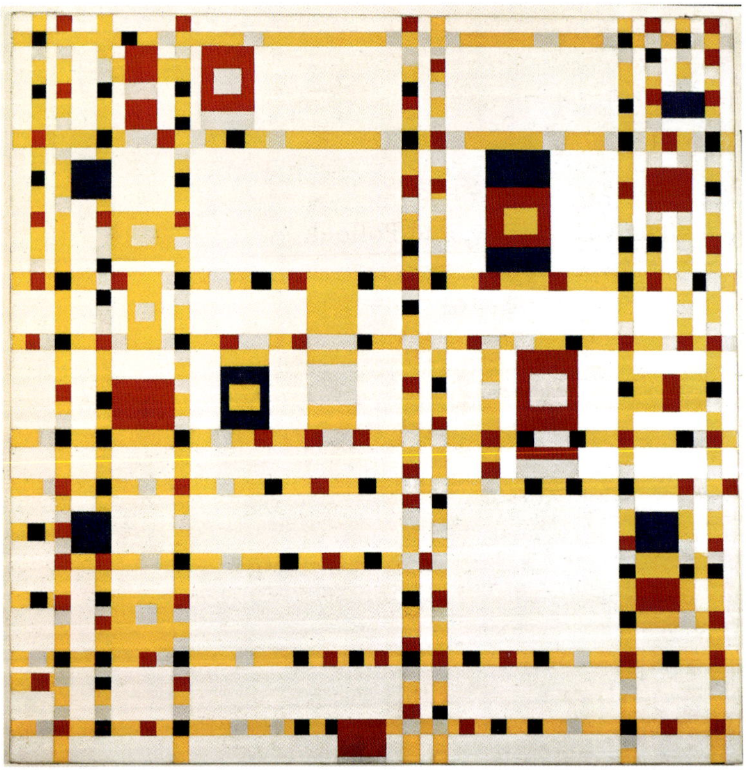

fig. 20.12 Piet Mondrian, *Broadway Boogie Woogie,* 1942–1943. Oil on canvas, 4 ft. 2 in. × 4 ft. 2 in. Museum of Modern Art, New York.

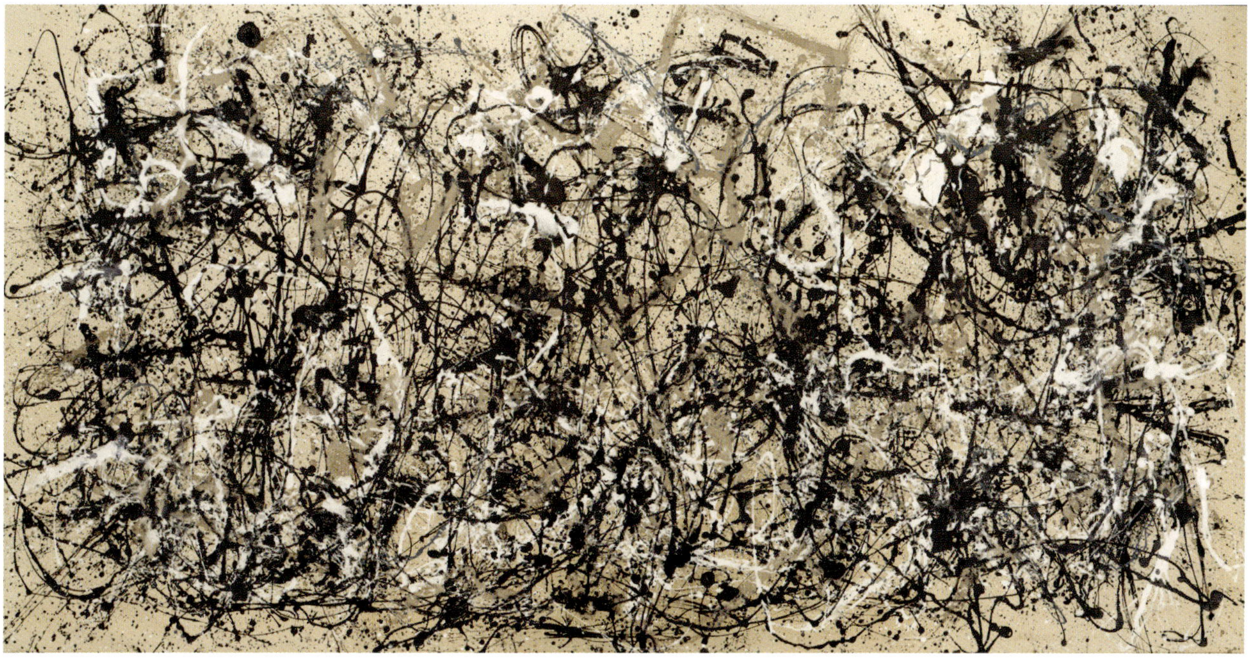

fig. 20.13 Jackson Pollock, *Autumn Rhythm,* 1950. Enamel on canvas 8 ft. 9 in. × 17 ft. 3 in. Metropolitan Museum of Art, New York.

looking to Europe to see what was current. **Abstract Expressionism** was the major artistic innovation in painting in the second half of the century, and **Jackson Pollock** (1912–1956) was its primary innovator. Pollock's paintings, such as *Autumn Rhythm* (fig. 20.13), were as much about the process of painting as anything else. Pollock spread his large canvases on the floor of his barn studio and then proceeded to drip, pour, spatter and fling the paint onto the canvas in a frenetic manner using various sized brushes or even pouring paint directly from the can. This method, called **Action Painting**, resulted in an intimate relationship with his paintings because he would actually stand on the canvas and almost become one with it. The resulting compositions were alive with energy, and Pollock became known as "Jack the Dripper." His method may at first seem haphazard and subject to the whims of chance, but Pollock was in command of his technique. He could control the thickness of the paint, its color and how he applied it. By expressing emotion through abstraction, Pollock and the other Abstract Expressionists made a huge contribution to art.

Pollock's neighbor on Long Island was fellow Abstract Expressionist **Willem de Kooning** (1904–1997), a Dutch-born artist who specialized in figural abstraction. That is, he did not eliminate the human figure from his works. *Woman I* (fig. 20.14) is one of a series portraying women painted with a slashing brushwork technique. They are big bosomed women, and De Kooning compared them to the Venus of Willendorf (see fig. 3.2). With large, shark-like eyes and barred teeth, this woman is frankly scary looking, and people accused De Kooning of being a misogynist with his woman paintings.

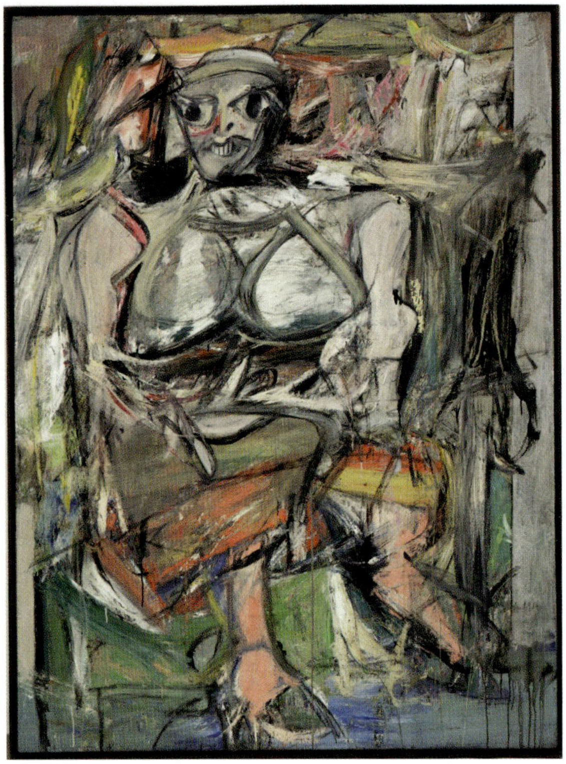

fig. 20.14 Willem De Kooning, *Woman I*, 1950–1952. Oil on canvas, 6 ft. 4 in. × 4 ft. 10 in. Museum of Modern Art, New York.

Color Field painting was an offshoot of Action Painting. Artists like **Mark Rothko** (1903–1970) painted large rectangular areas of modulated color against a different colored background (fig. 20.15). The edges of the rectangles are ill-defined, allowing the forms to hover over the background and induce a meditative effect. The large scale of Rothko's paintings draws the viewer into them. By varying the color combinations Rothko was able to elicit feelings ranging from joy to melancholy. His late works are done in darker colors and evoke a sadness that was autobiographical because he committed suicide.

Abstract Expressionism took hold quickly in the art scene, and before too long some artists reacted against it. In the 1950s two artists (who shared an apartment for several years) broke new ground with their use of recognizable imagery. Considered pre-Pop artists because their art looks forward to the Pop Art movement of the early 1960s, **Jasper Johns** (1930–) and **Robert Rauschenberg** (1925–2008) used elements of Dada and Surrealism in their art. Johns often depicted familiar items in his paintings so that the viewer could easily get beyond the subject matter. *Flag* (fig. 20.16) shows an American flag. The flag is a familiar and concrete object in American culture yet it represents abstract

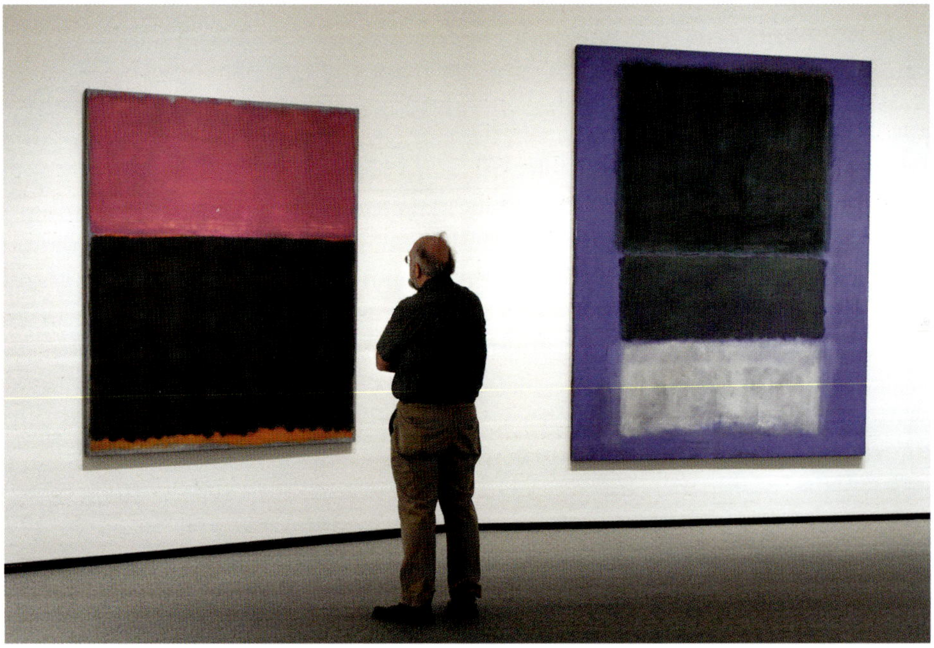

fig. 20.15 Mark Rothko, Man looking at two Rothko paintings.

concepts (freedom and democracy). Johns revived the ancient encaustic method of painting (pigment mixed with wax) to give his flag a luminous and textural surface. With this tactile technique, Johns forces the viewer to examine a common image in an artistic light.

Robert Rauschenberg's *Monogram* (fig. 20.17) is a **mixed media** installation of various materials and objects, including a goat with a rubber tire around it. Rauschenberg called works like these *combines* because they combine painting and sculpture. *Monogram* recalls the Dadaist use of found objects, and the resulting work combines disparate objects and painted images in the spirit of Surrealism. Like Duchamp, Rauschenberg wanted to show that any object is worthy of becoming art.

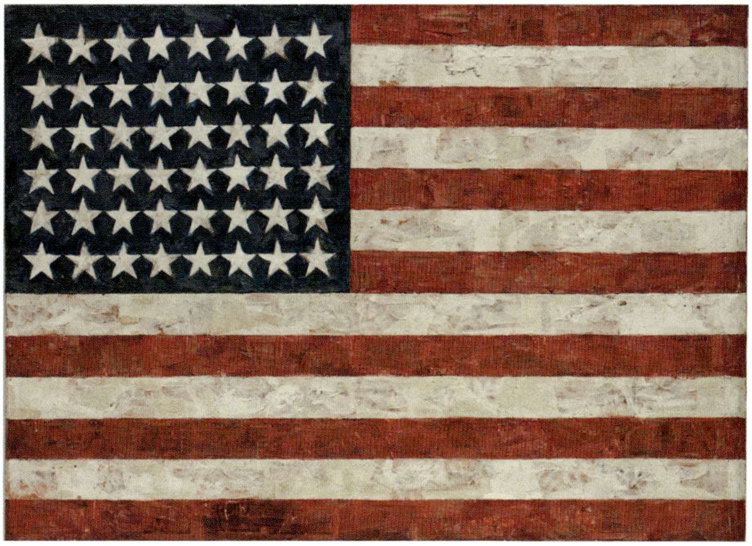

fig. 20.16 Jasper Johns, *Flag*, 1954. Encaustic, oil and collage on fabric mounted on plywood. Museum of Modern Art, New York.

POP ART

Pop Art hit the art scene in the late 1950s. Pop artists like Andy Warhol, Roy Liechtenstein and Claes Oldenburg used objects of popular culture (either the actual objects or reproductions of them) in their art, such as soup cans, movie star photos, cartoons or other everyday objects. **Andy Warhol** (1930–1987) is the artist most associated with the movement. His *Campbell's Soup Cans* (fig. 20.18) takes a well-known American commodity and repeats it over and over like an advertisement. He did the same with a variety of

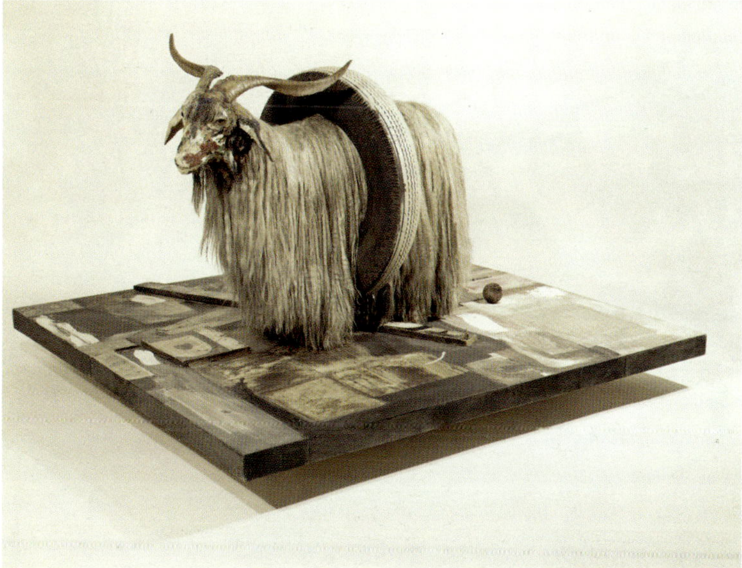

fig. 20.17 Robert Rauschenberg, *Monogram*, 1955–1959. Freestanding combine: oil, paper, fabric, printed paper, printed reproductions, metal, wood, rubber shoe heel and tennis ball on canvas, with oil on Angora goat and rubber tire, on wood platform mounted on four casters, 42 in. × 63 in. × 64.5 in. Moderna Museet, Stockholm.

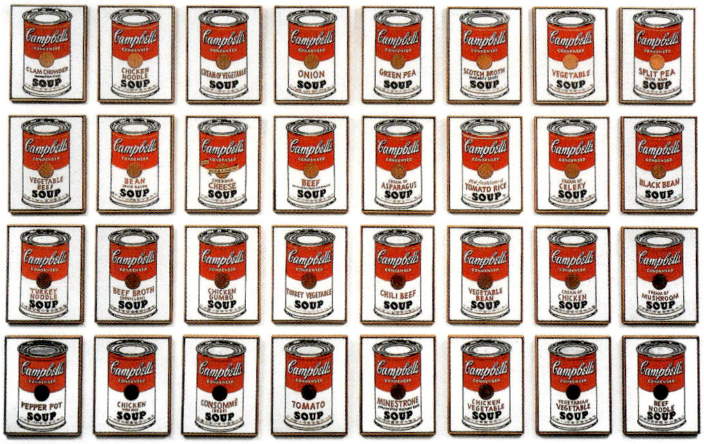

fig. 20.18 Andy Warhol, *Campbell's Soup Cans,* 1962. Synthetic polymer paint on 32 canvases, each 20 in. × 16 in. Museum of Modern Art, New York.

images from popular culture including coke bottles and portraits of famous people like Elvis Presley, Elizabeth Taylor and Marilyn Monroe. The repetition of the same thing eliminates any kind of emotion in Warhol's art. Warhol eventually turned the production of his art over to assistants and concentrated on his fame by always appearing at trendy parties and events. He soon became famous for being famous.

Comic books inspired **Roy Lichtenstein** (1923–1997) who created his own comic book images mimicking the mechanical printing process of small dots of colors. By painting on a huge scale the dots become readily visible to the viewer. Lichtenstein concentrated on melodramatic romance (sex) and battle images (violence), using them as critical comments on American values (fig. 20.19).

Claes Oldenburg (1929–) creates pop sculpture on a gigantic scale. His enlarged re-creations of everyday objects such as a clothespin, a shuttlecock, a trowel or a spoon (fig. 20.20) not only make us smile, they also make us aware of the power of size.

Like Rauschenberg, **Louise Nevelson** (1899–1988) scoured her New York neighborhood for found objects, but she restricted herself

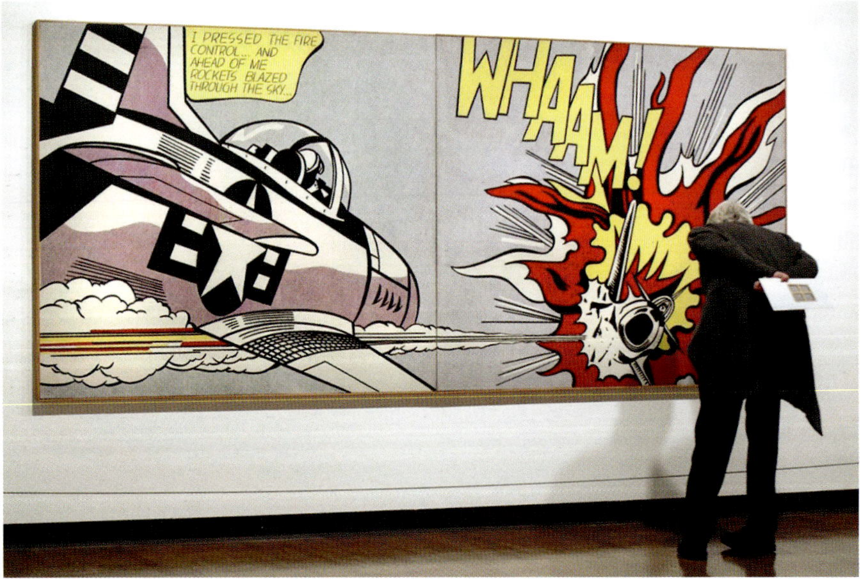

fig. 20.19 Roy Lichtenstein, *Whaam!* 1963. Magna acrylic on canvas, 68 in. × 106 in. (two canvases). Tate Gallery, London.

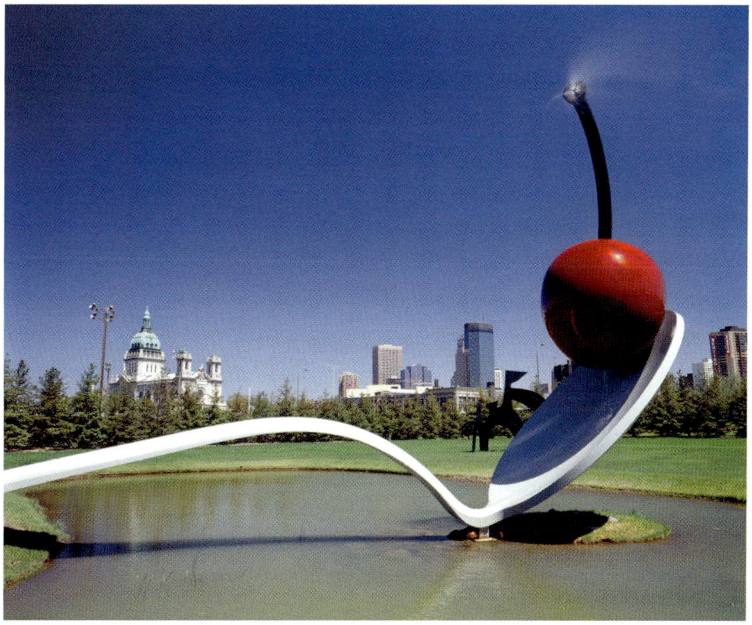

fig. 20.20 Claes Oldenburg, *Spoonbridge and Cherry,* 1985–1988. Aluminum, **stainless steel**, and paint, 51.5 ft. long. Minneapolis.

to wood. Arranging various pieces of abandoned boards, banisters and boxes into crate cubicles, she created altars of wood like *Sky Cathedral* (fig. 20.21). Nevelson had no real love for the grain or texture of wood itself because she always painted it, usually black. She took humanity's discards and assembled them into monumental works of contemplation.

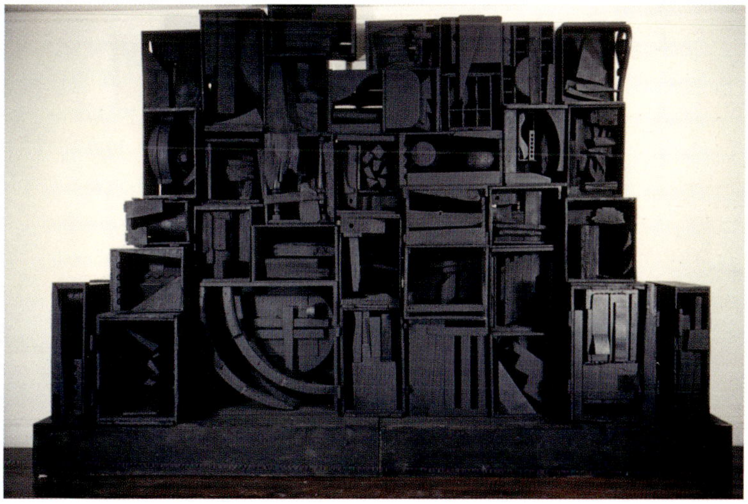

fig. 20.21 Louise Nevelson, *Sky Cathedral,* 1958. Painted wood, 11 ft. 4 in. × 10 ft. 8 in. Museum of Modern Art, New York.

Graffiti and Street Art

Graffiti is lettering or images drawn or painted on a surface such as a wall or the side of train car. The word comes from the Italian word *graffio* (a scratch). The imagery is usually in a public area and anonymous. Graffiti has existed throughout history as far back as ancient Egypt. Some consider graffiti an art form in its own right. Others think it is merely defacement and vandalism. Graffiti can express political and social messages or it can signal gang activity or gang territory. Spray paint and markers are the most common graffiti media.

Street art is art seen in on the streets in public areas (and could include performance art such as juggling and pantomime). Its origins go back to the illegal street art of Keith Haring and Jean-Michel Basquiat in the early 1980s before both artists became famous and exhibited in museums and galleries (see www.haring.com and http://basquiat.com). Street art images are more fully developed in the artistic sense than traditional graffiti, they use a wider range of media, and they don't necessarily carry the stigma of gang activity and/or vandalism that is often associated with graffiti. Street artists are more concerned with communicating socially important ideas to the general public in an aesthetic way. Also, street artists are often trained artists and their compositions tend to be more sophisticated than those of graffiti artists, who are usually self-taught. Some art critics define street art as all art on the street that is not graffiti. Street art is sometimes referred to as post-graffiti art.

There is a wide variety of street art, and a number of street artists have become famous, such as Bansky and Above (see www.banksy.co.uk and www.goabove.com), although they may use pseudonyms to conceal their true identities in order to avoid prosecution. An ongoing problem for city officials in their attempt to continually remove street art, some cities have established specific areas where street art is encouraged (and legal). In fact, street art has come into the mainstream with museum and gallery exhibitions and feature films such as *Bomb It* (2008), a documentary film about street art around the world.

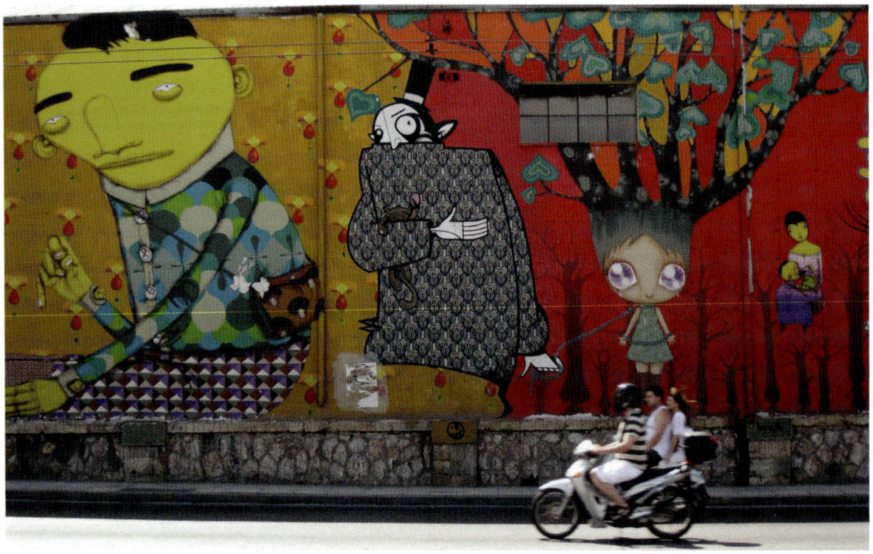

Street art in Athens, Greece

MINIMALISM

Minimalism was another reaction against Abstract Expressionism. In both sculpture and painting Minimalist artists kept the abstraction of Abstract Expressionism, but they removed the expressive quality by creating impersonal **hard-edged** geometric forms. **Ellsworth Kelly** (1923–) creates razor sharp edges to his smooth, simple shapes of pure color like those in *Orange Relief with Green* (fig. 20.22), yet it is not so much the edges that interest him as the interplay of the colored masses. Kelly eliminates narrative and feeling in the interest of pure form.

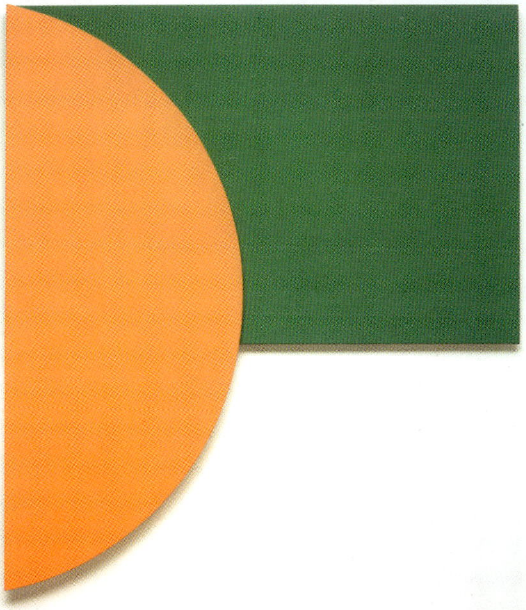

fig. 20.22 Ellsworth Kelly, *Orange Relief with Green,* 1991. Oil on canvas, 93.5 in × 85 in. Tate Gallery, London.

OP ART

Op Art concerns itself with optical perception. **Bridget Riley** (1931–) constructs images of closely spaced lines that give the illusion of oscillating movement as the spectator passes by the canvas (fig. 20.23). The effect is so profound that some people actually become nauseous looking at her works.

PHOTO REALISM

A complete break with abstraction came with **Photo Realism**, a style of art that used the photographic image as a starting point. Artists like **Richard Estes** (1936–) projected images taken with a camera onto canvas and used them as a guide for their compositions. With smooth precise

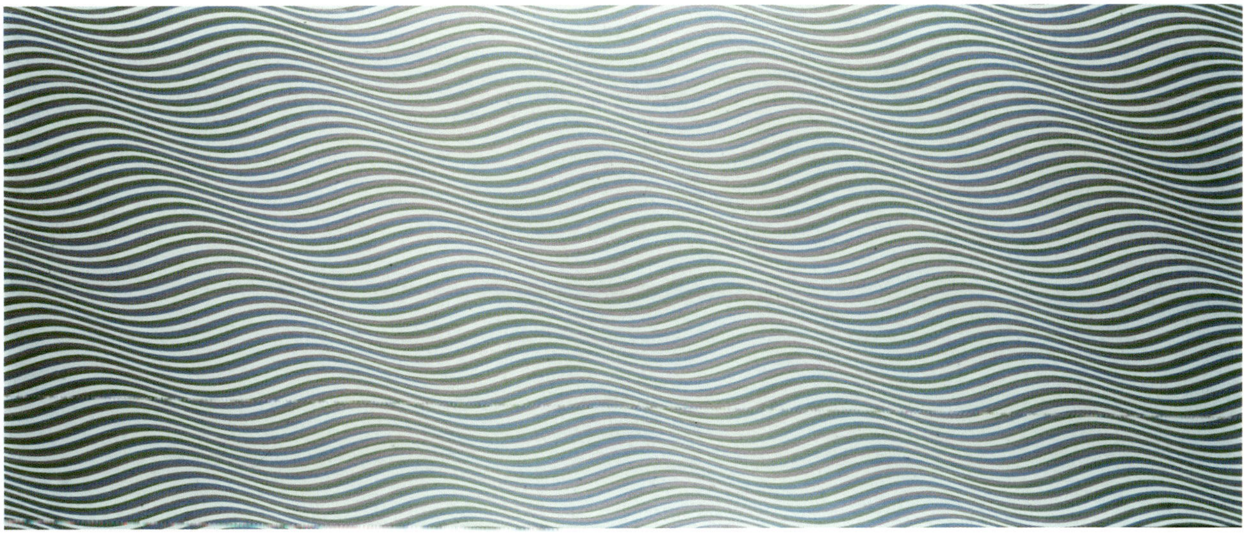

fig. 20.23 Bridget Riley, *Sheng-Tung,* 1974.

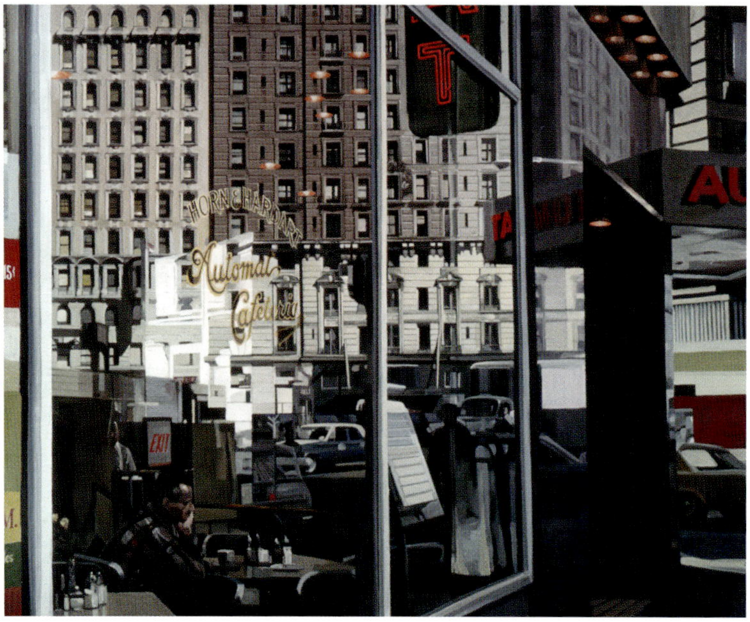

fig. 20.24 Richard Estes, *Horn and Hardart Automat,* 1967. Oil on masonite.

brushstrokes Estes painted an image so life-like that it resembled the photograph upon which it was based. Photo Realism forces us to see the complex optical effects in nature that we normally do not observe. For example, when looking at merchandise in a store window we focus on the items and filter out the reflections on the glass. Should we choose, we could focus on the reflections instead of the merchandise, but the camera captures everything in sharp focus, giving the image a super real quality as seen in Estes' *Horn and Hardart Automat* (fig. 20.24).

Duane Hanson (1925–1996) carried the photo realistic concept into sculpture by creating super real copies of ordinary people. By making plaster casts of willing volunteers and then dressing the finished life-sized sculptures with their own clothes and jewelry, Hanson created replicas so convincing that people often approach them in museums and begin to speak before realizing they are talking to a statue. Although *Man with Camera* (fig. 20.25) is made of bronze, most of Hanson's figures were made of polyester resin reinforced with fiberglass. Unfortunately, he did not take proper safety precautions and ultimately the noxious fumes from the process gave him terminal cancer.

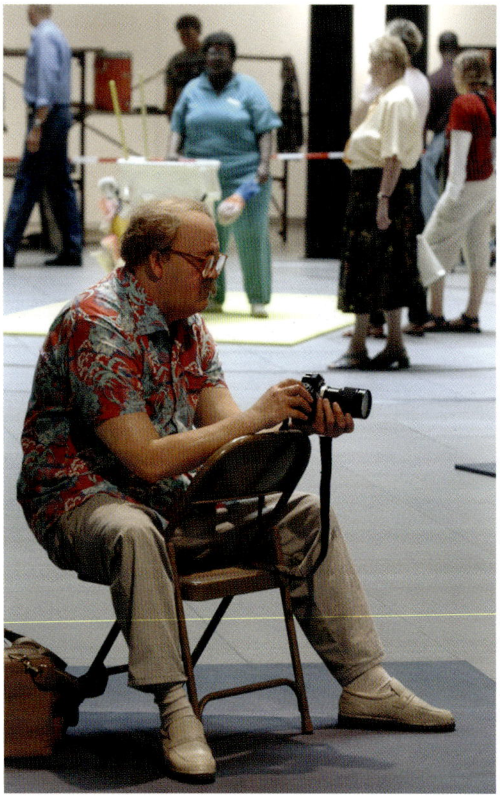

fig. 20.25 Duane Hanson, *Man with Camera,* 1991. Polychromed bronze with mixed media, life-size. Collection of Mrs. Duane Hanson.

ENVIRONMENTAL ART

The grandiose **installations** of **Christo** (1935–) **and Jeanne-Claude** (1935–2009) exemplify **Environmental Art** at its best and most sophisticated. They have encased large buildings with high-tech fabric, installed miles of running fences of cloth and even draped an island. The *Umbrellas* (fig. 20.26) was a project involving two countries on two continents. They installed 1,760 large yellow umbrellas over a stretch of 18 miles in a California valley. In a valley in Japan, they installed 1,340 blue umbrellas over 12 miles. They spaced the yellow umbrellas more widely than their blue Japanese counterparts because of the greater expanses of space in the United States, which is considerably larger than Japan. (Japan is about the size of California alone.) Furthermore, the yellow color coincided with the dry, parched California landscape whereas the blue paralleled the more lush

Japanese landscape. Like all of Christo and Jeanne-Claude's projects, they financed this multi-million dollar project by the sale of preparatory drawings, studies, scale models, collages and original lithographs. They accept no official sponsorship. Volunteers help with the installations (over 1,800 assisted with *The Umbrellas*).

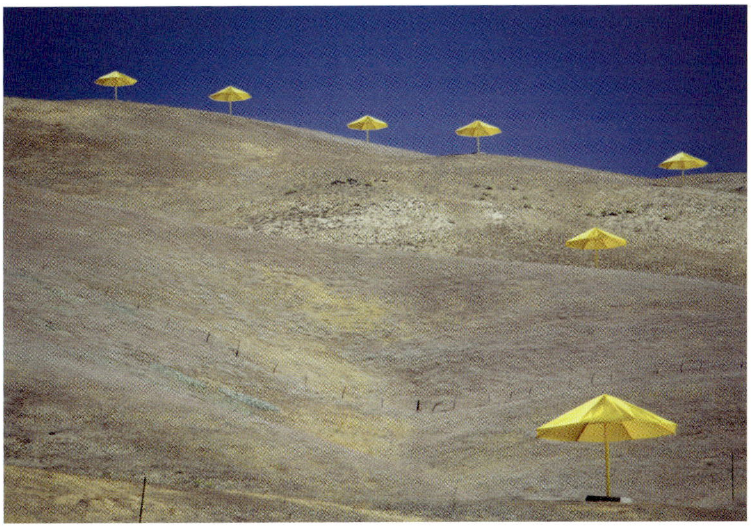

fig. 20.26 Christo and Jeanne-Claude, *The Umbrellas,* Japan-U.S.A, 1984–1991: Detail of the 1,760 yellow umbrellas in California. Nylon and aluminum.

Outdoor public art is a type of permanent installation art. The *Vietnam Veteran's Memorial* (fig. 20.27a and b), designed by **Maya Lin** (1959–), caused an uproar when her design was selected from over 1,400 entries. It was nothing like traditional war memorials; instead it consisted of two simple sloping walls set into the earth with the names of more than 58,000 fallen carved into their surfaces (in chronological order of death date). Many people, especially in the military, were furious—there were no images of brave soldiers, just two walls of names. Despite the intense criticism, the project went forth, and today many consider it one of the most emotionally moving memorials ever created. The appropriately black granite is highly polished so that viewers see reflections of their living selves when searching for names of the dead.

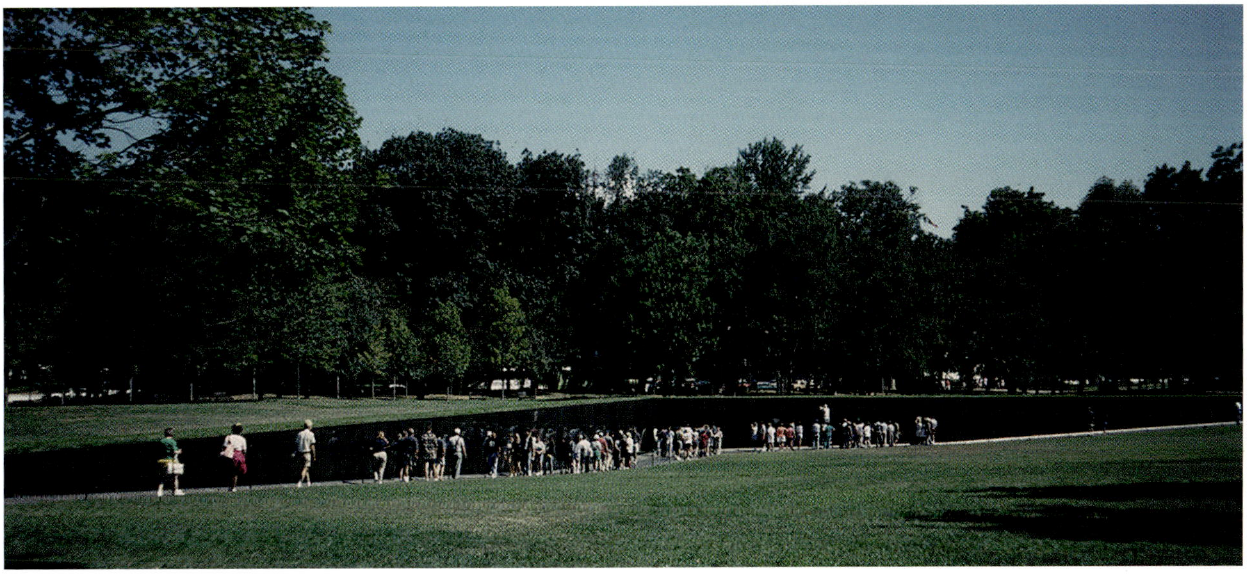

figs. 20.27a and b Maya Ying Lin, *Vietnam Veterans Memorial,* 1981–1983. Black granite, each wall 10 ft. 1 in. × 246 ft. 9 in. The Mall, Washington, D.C.

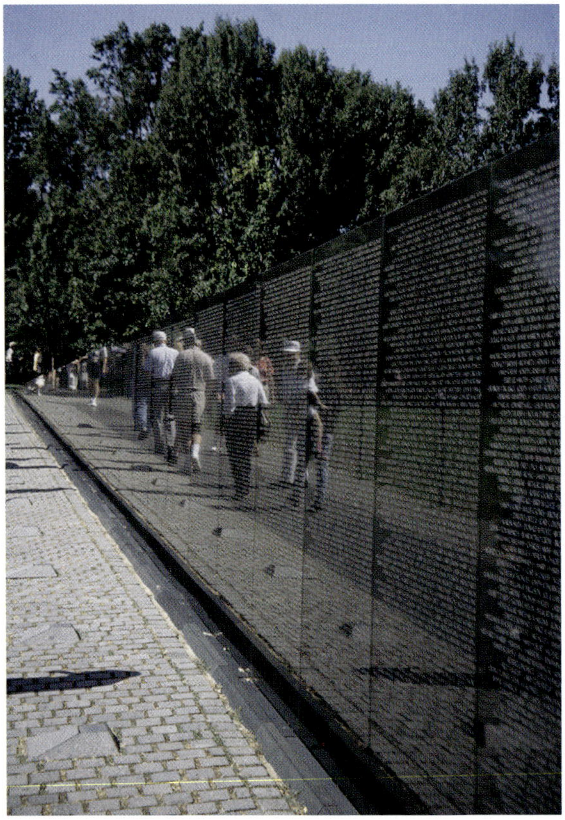

figs. 20.27b

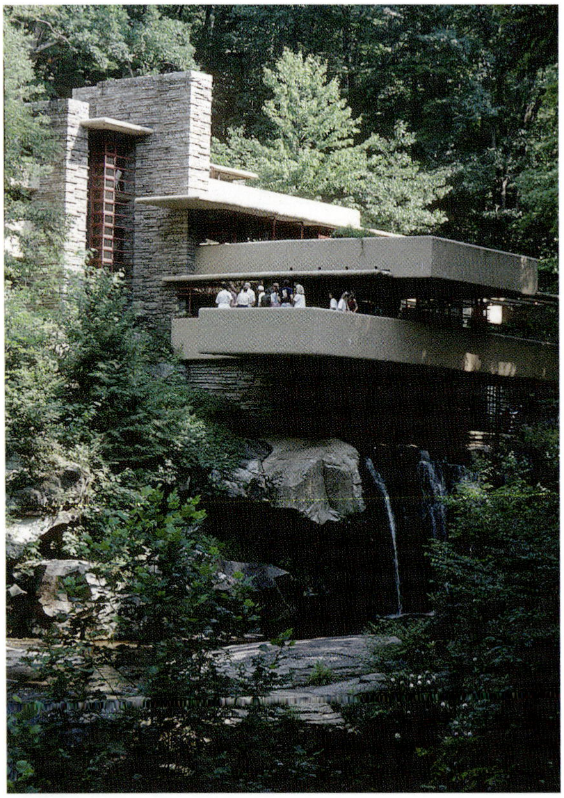

ARCHITECTURE

Architecture advanced rapidly in the twentieth century. Skyscrapers reached heights of more than a hundred stories, and new materials and techniques allowed forms going well beyond the traditional post-and-lintel system. **Frank Lloyd Wright** (1867–1959) was one of the pioneering architects of the century. His early domestic architecture, called the Prairie style because he designed the houses to fit into the Midwestern landscape, was revolutionary. He introduced cathedral ceilings, built-in furniture, indirect lighting, split-level structures, carports and the idea of one room flowing into another among other now traditional features. *Fallingwater,* a summer home built for the Kaufmann family of Pittsburgh (fig. 20.28), embodies the idea of a site-specific structure built in harmony with its natural surroundings. Using the new technology of **cantilevered reinforced concrete** slabs, Wright designed a house with walls of local stone over a stream so that it literally became one with nature. Vast expanses of windows ensure that nature is always present even from the inside. In many cases, where a structural element would normally appear at a corner, there is only glass (fig. 20.29).

Wright's later design for the Guggenheim Museum in New York was also ingenious (fig. 20.30). The circular building was unlike anything else built up to that time. The main gallery consists of a long curving ramp that begins at the top and spirals down to the bottom (fig. 20.31, page 260). Although innovative, Wright was not without his critics. Some complained of the low ceilings in many of his houses saying they made the rooms somewhat claustrophobic and unsuitable for warmer climates (where high ceilings allow the warmer air to rise). Others criticize the Guggenheim Museum because the floor (being a ramp) is slightly tilted and the spectator is not on level ground when looking at works of art.

In the latter part of the century, new engineering capabilities permitted even more radical designs than the Guggenheim. Danish architect **Jørn Utzon** (1918–2008) had to wait over a decade

fig. 20.28 Frank Lloyd Wright, Kaufmann House (Fallingwater), Bear Run, Pennsylvania, 1936–1939.

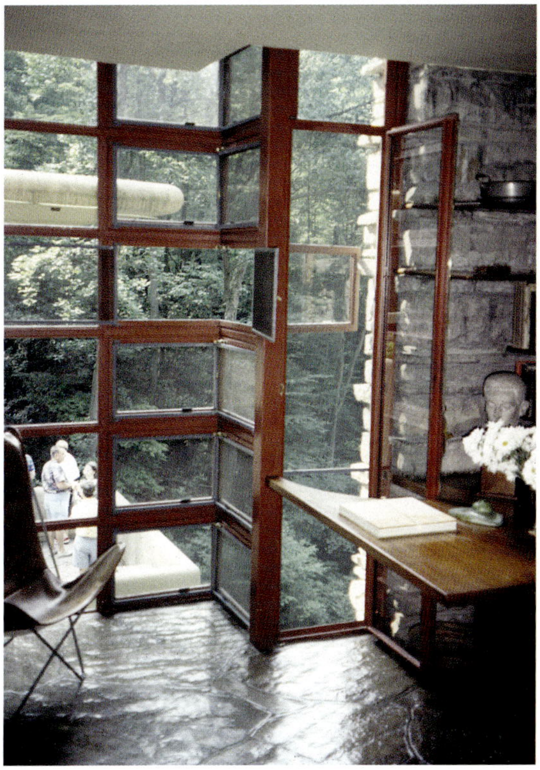

fig. 20.29 Bedroom, Fallingwater.

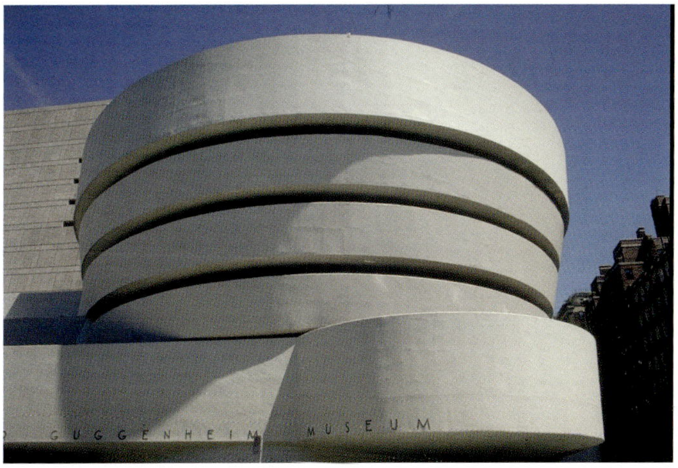

fig. 20.30 Frank Lloyd Wright, Solomon R. Guggenheim Museum, New York, 1943–1959.

before engineering technology caught up with his visually stunning design for the Sydney Opera House (fig. 20.32). Made to look like sails, it is an appropriate image for a building that sits in a harbor. With its asymmetrical design, the building's appearance changes dramatically depending on the point of view (fig. 20.33).

Traditional architectural forms reappear in the late twentieth century with post modern architecture (architecture that is imaginative and eclectic as opposed to the traditional modernist style) and in specific structures such as the entrance to the Louvre (fig. 20.34) by **I. M. Pei** (1917–). Pei's design reinvigorates the ancient architectural form of the pyramid to not only evoke the antiquities that lie inside the museum, but also to illuminate a vast new entry lobby below since the pyramid is made of glass. Being inside the museum beneath the pyramid is just as interesting as viewing the exterior (fig. 20.35).

Museum design reached new heights with a daring plan by **Frank Gehry** (1929–) for the Guggenheim Museum in Bilbao, Spain (fig. 20.36). The limestone and titanium-clad structure is an interleaving of large curved surfaces to create an organic form unlike any previous architecture. He referred to it as his "metallic flower." The interior has the same organic feel with its unusually shaped galleries and huge glass atrium (fig. 20.37). In addition to providing a unique museum for the display of art, Gehry's eccentric building had the further benefit of revitalizing an old and deteriorated part of Bilbao. The city now attracts many tourists who come to see the museum. The success of Gehry's design spawned

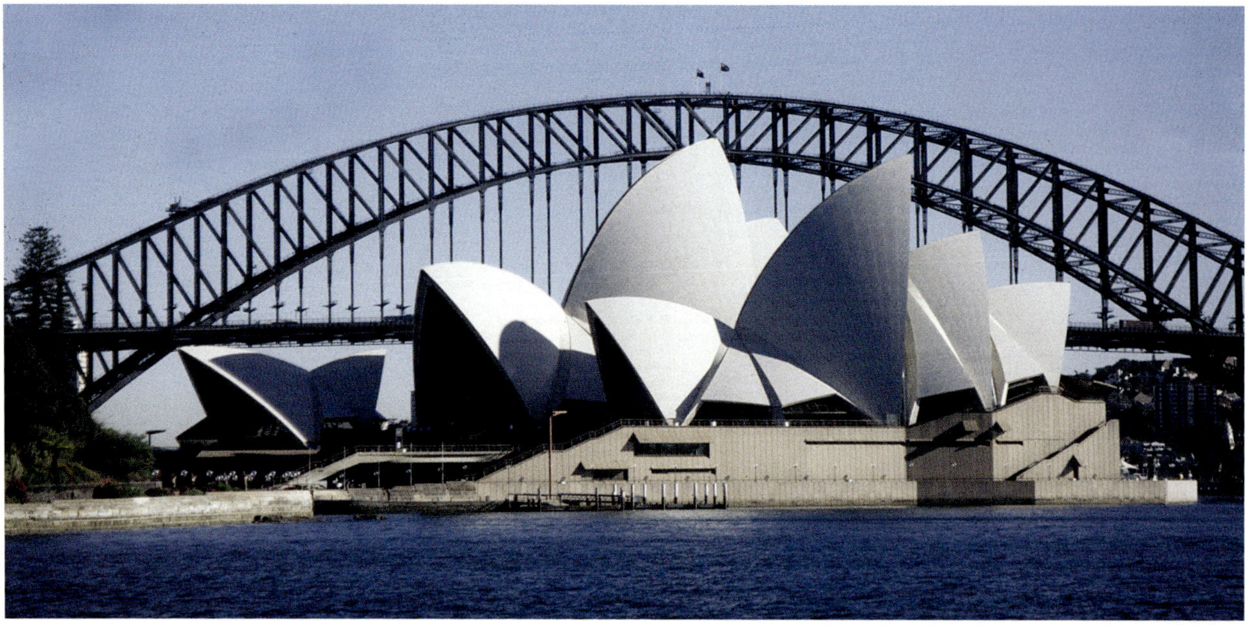

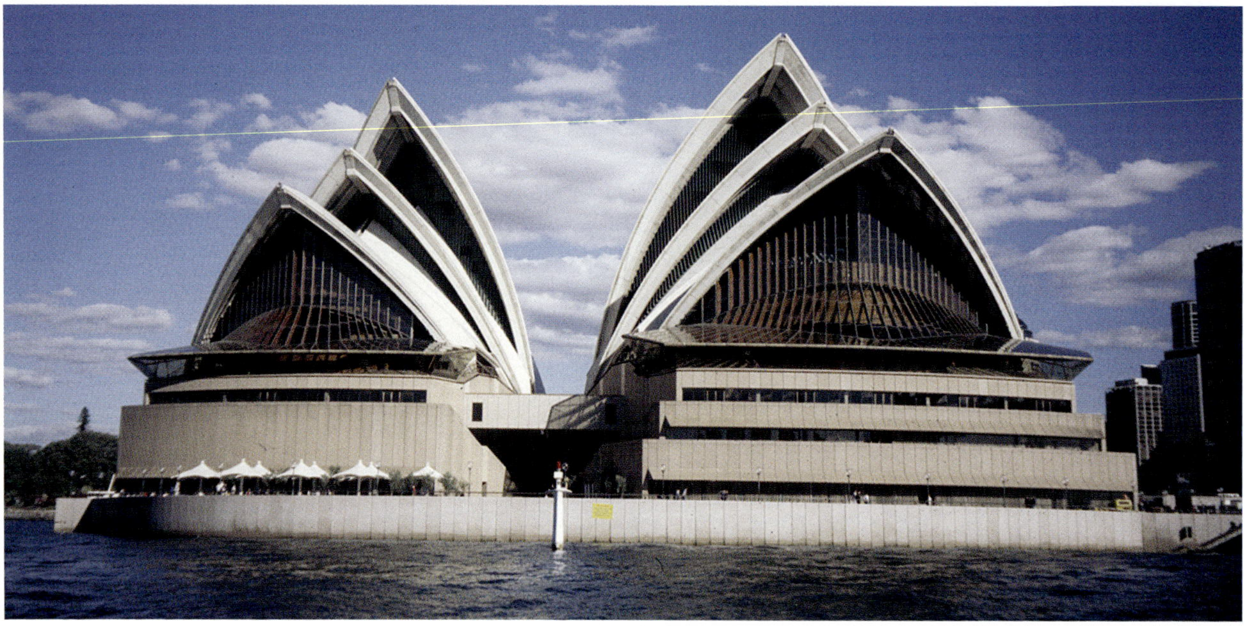

figs. 20.32 and 20.33 Jørn Utzon, Sydney Opera House, Sydney, Australia, 1959–1972.

derivative structures by his protégés and other admiring architects, such as the new art museum in Roanoke, Virginia (fig. 20.38).

At the end of the twentieth century artists were still able to shock the public. Andrés Serrano's *Piss Christ* (a crucifix suspended in the artist's urine) offended many people. And African artist Chris Ofili caused a stir in New York with his *The Holy Virgin Mary* because it incorporated elephant dung. Western critics neglected to consider the value dung has in many non-Western cultures.

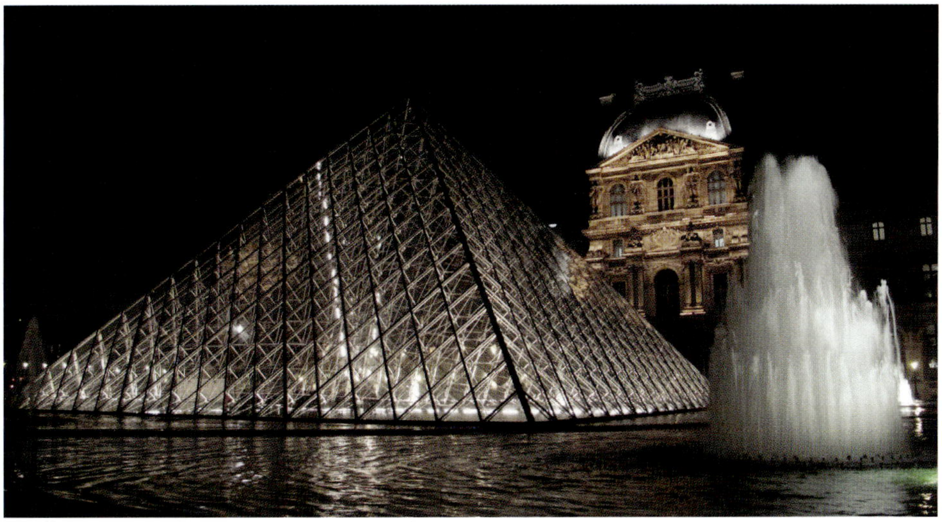

fig. 20.34 I.M. Pei, Louvre Pyramid, 1988. Paris.

Although many say art has reached its limit—what else can artists come up with?—new art forms still continue to arise. Ariana Page Russell creates art out of her body. She suffers from an immune condition called dermotographia, and her skin is extremely hypersensitive; hives and welts appear wherever she scratches her skin. Russell uses this phenomenon to create art by scratching designs and words on her skin, then photographing the result before it fades. (See *www.arianapagerussell.com/words.html.*)

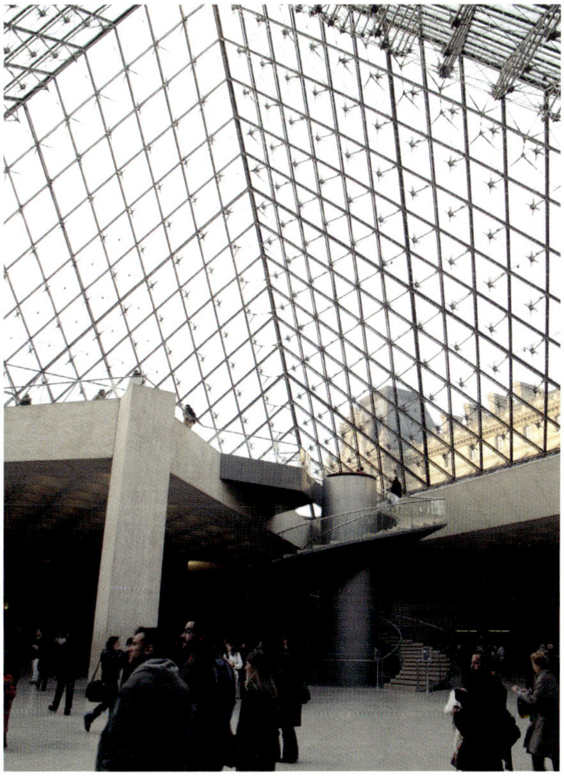

fig. 20.35 Beneath the Louvre Pyramid.

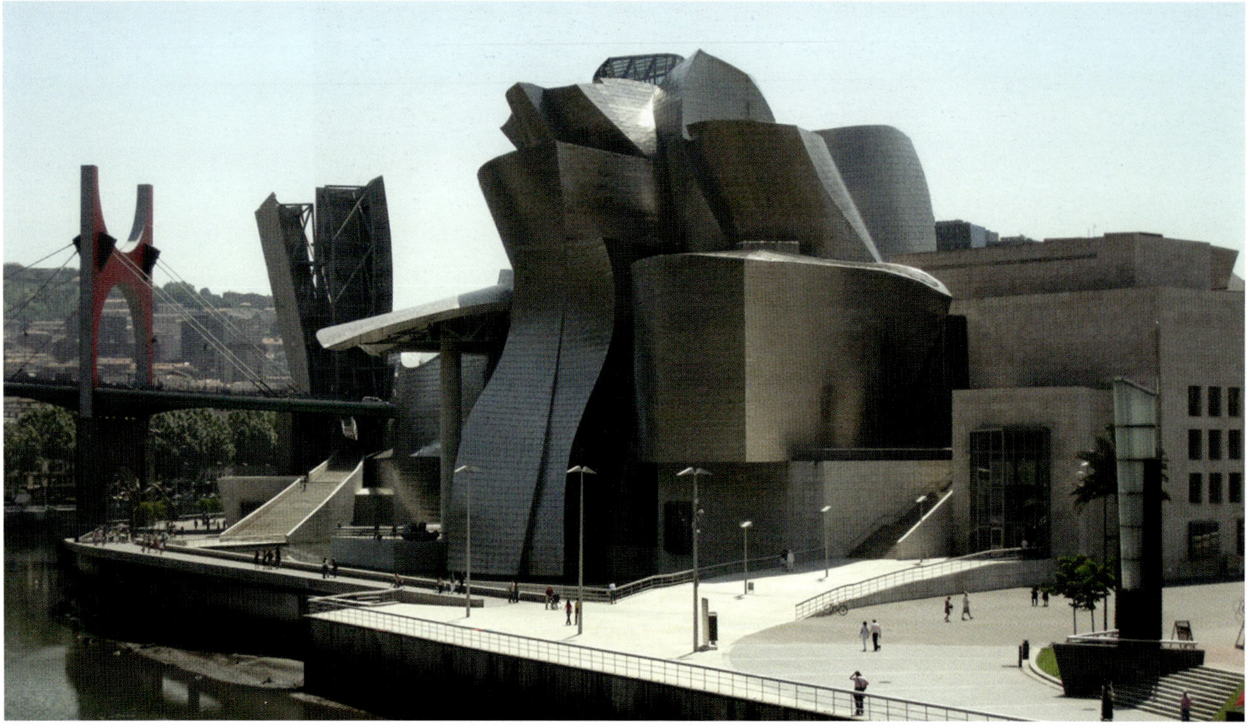

fig. 20.36 Frank Gehry, Guggenheim Museum Bilbao, 1993–1997. Bilbao, Spain.

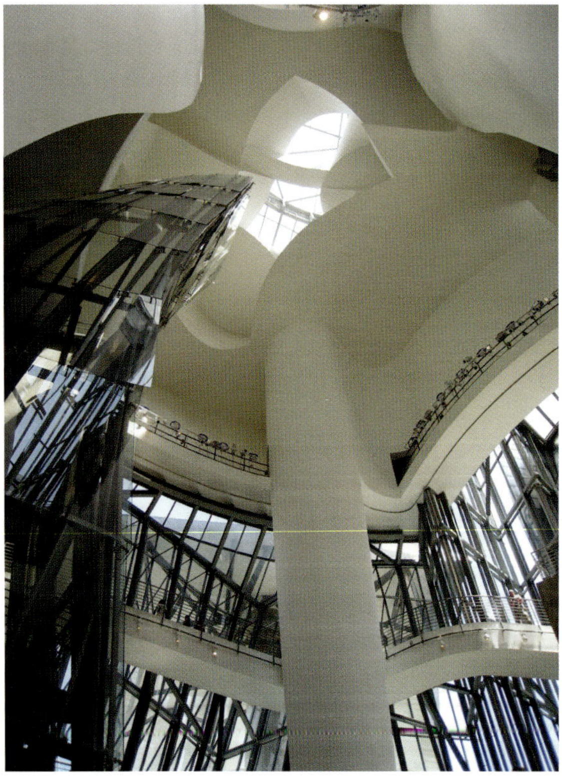

fig. 20.37 Atrium of Guggenheim Museum Bilbao.

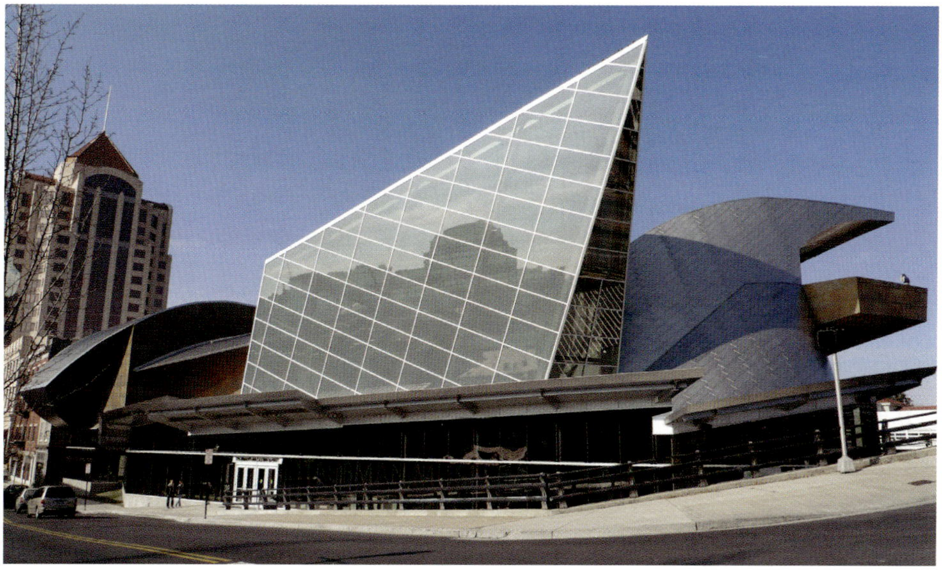

fig. 20.38a Randall Stout, Taubman Museum, completed 2008. Roanoke, Virginia.

Seven German artists with head lice put themselves on display in an Israeli museum where they actually moved in. The idea was that just as the museum hosted them, their heads hosted the lice. Although many considered this outrageous, the museum curator explained "Art is no longer a painting on the wall."

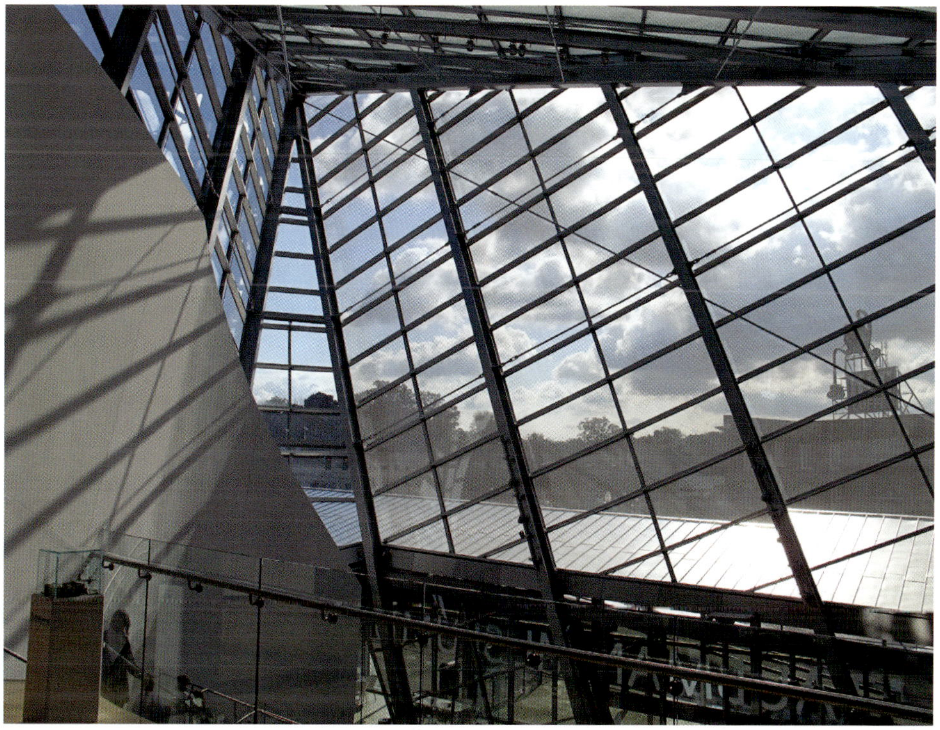

fig. 20.38b Interior.

Humorous Architecture

Architecture took on a humorous role in the latter part of the century with such structures as the McDonald's building (fig. 20.39) and the WonderWorks building (fig. 20.40), both in Orlando, Florida. In mock compliance with the architectural dictum "Form follows function," the McDonald's building looks like an order of French fries. WonderWorks (a tourist fun house) takes Classical architecture and turns it upside down, literally. The building appears to be a classically styled building (with Ionic columns supporting a triangular pediment) that has been uprooted and flipped over. Inside, the illusion continues as you look up at the grand staircase hovering upside down above you.

Conceptual artist Gregor Schneider (1969–) displayed sunbathers in a cage on the beach in Australia. Later he exhibited a starving dog in a Nicaraguan gallery—he tethered the dog just out of reach of food. Now he wants to display a terminally ill patient in a gallery.

Conceptual art such as this is meant to foster new conversations about art and the human condition, but some of it also brings forth serious moral concerns. In fact, gallery owners have refused to display a

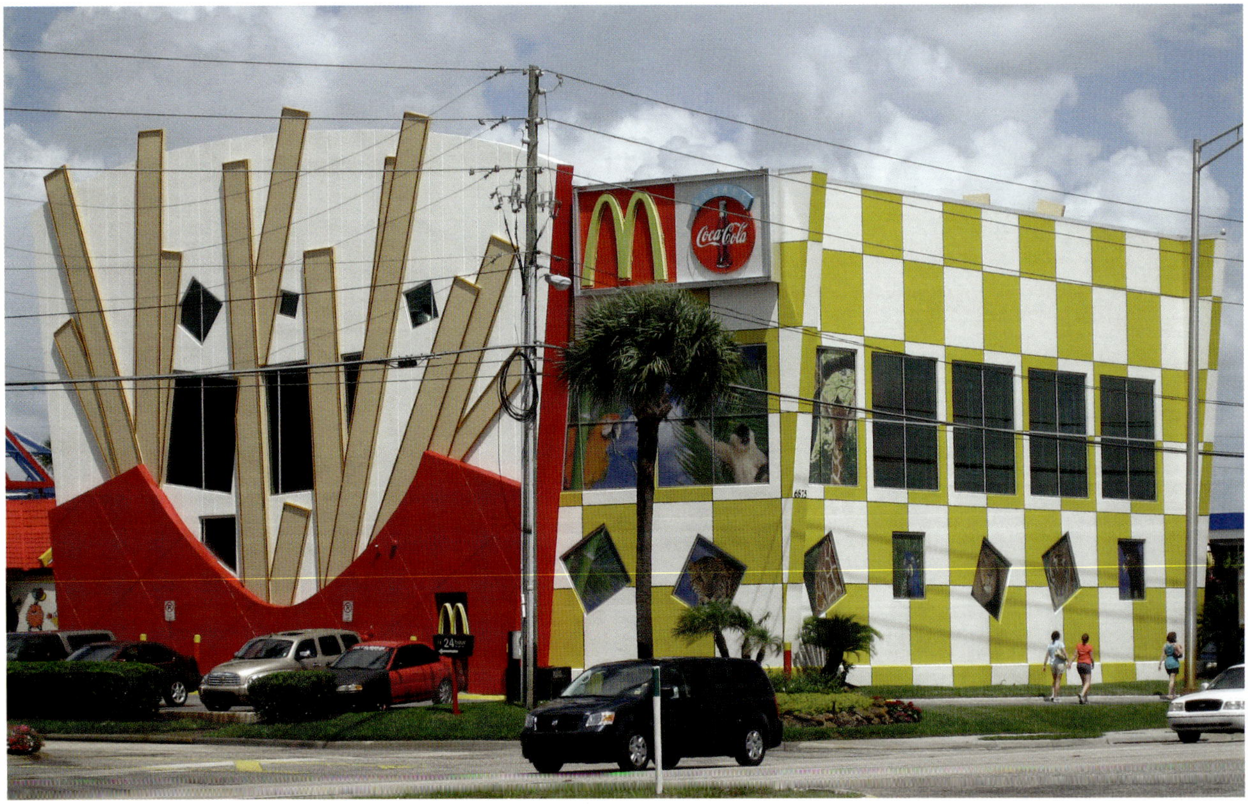

fig. 20.39 McDonald's, Orlando, Florida.

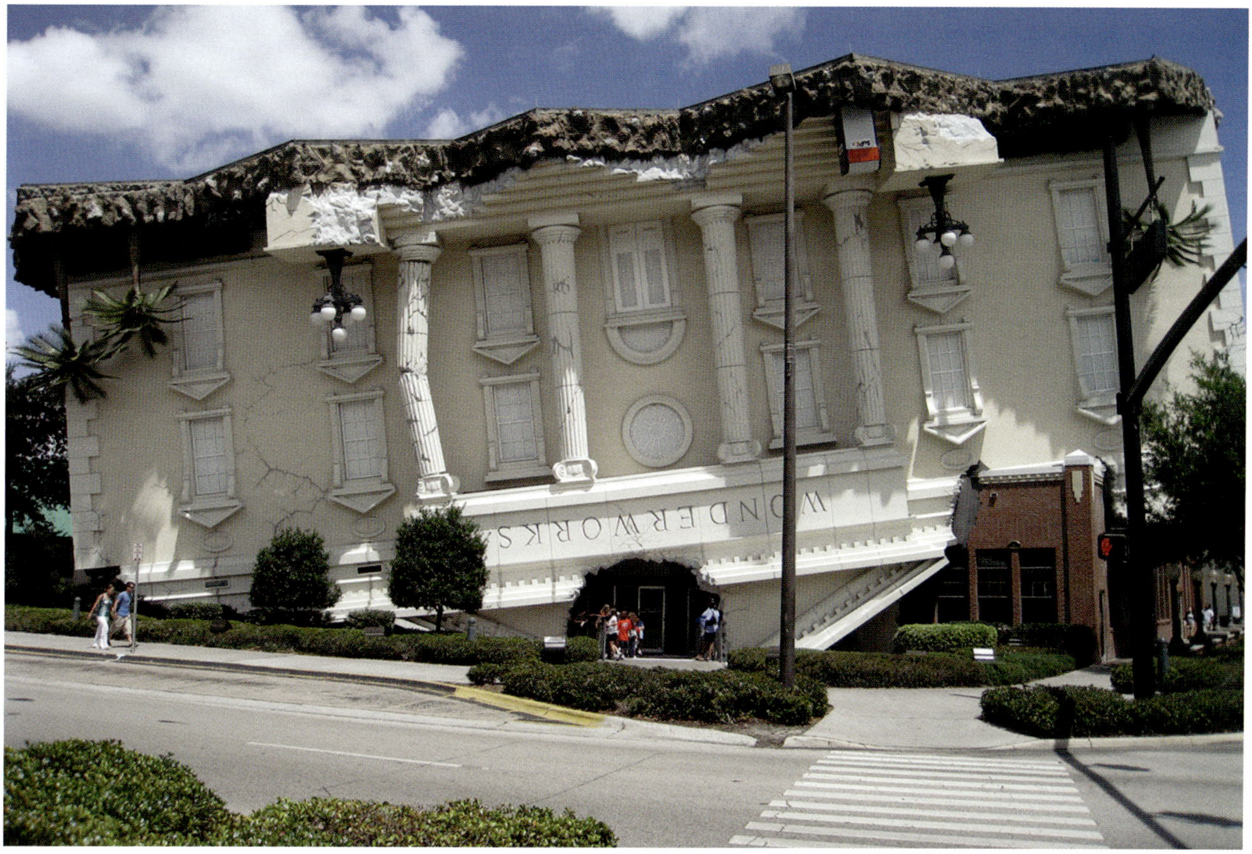

fig. 20.40 WonderWorks, Orlando, Florida.

terminally ill patient even if Scheider finds a willing volunteer. Some critics think that aspiring artists want to create something offensive simply so they can quickly achieve celebrity status when it is banned.

Art continues to evolve in the twenty-first century as it always has, and it will be interesting to see where it takes us.

SUMMARY

Two world wars, atomic energy, numerous scientific theories, psychoanalysis, space exploration, medical advances, and ever-evolving technologies made the 20th century one of the most diverse and fastest changing centuries in human history. The center of art in Western culture switched from Paris (where it had been for the last three centuries) to New York after World War II. Non-representational art came into being. The century is a steady stream of new art movements.

Major movements of the 20th Century

Fauvism: An early twentieth century art movement that had color as the dominant formal element, although the colors often did not represent the true colors of the objects in the painting. Example: Matisse (*Red Room*).

Nonrepresentational art: For the first time artists create works that are totally abstract. Examples: Wassily Kandinksy [Blue Rider School] (*Improvisation No. 23*); Constantin Brancusi (*Bird in Space*).

Cubism: A style of art, created by Pablo Picasso and Georges Braque around 1908, that rejected naturalistic depictions and instead used fragmented forms and multiple points of view. Example: Pablo Picasso (*Demoiselles d'Avignon* and *Guernica*).

Futurism: An early twentieth-century Italian art movement that emphasized the speed and movement of the modern industrial era. Examples: Umberto Boccioni (*Unique forms of Continuity in Space*); Marcel Duchamp (*Nude Descending a Staircase*). Note: Duchamp's work also exhibits cubist qualities.

Dada: An "anti-art" art movement that arose during World War I. It challenged conventional art and the absurdities of modern civilization, and was often whimsical and humorous. Example: Marcel Duchamp (*Fountain*).

Surrealism: An art movement that began in the 1920s characterized by dream imagery, bizarre juxtapositions, and chance occurrences. Example: Salvador Dali (*The Persistence of Memory*).

American Regionalism: Art by American artists in the 1930s that dealt with rural American subjects in a realistic manner. Example: Grant Wood (*American Gothic*).

De Stijl (The Style): A Dutch art movement founded in 1917 that expressed utopian ideals using simple geometric forms and primary colors. Example: Piet Mondrian (*Broadway Boogie Woogie*).

Abstract Expressionism: A style of art that developed in the late 1940s in which artists represented personal expression using abstracted forms. Example: Jackson Pollock (*Autumn Rhythm*); Willem de Kooning (*Woman I*); Mark Rothko.

Pop Art: A style of art in the late 1950s and 1960s that utilized commercial and popular imagery, such as soup cans or images of famous people. Example: Andy Warhol (*Campbell's Soup Cans*); Roy Lichtenstein (*Whaam!*); Claes Oldenburg (*Spoonbridge and Cherry*).

Minimalism: A nonrepresentational style of art in the 1960s characterized by few visual elements. Example: Ellsworth Kelly (*Orange Relief with Green*).

Op Art: A style of art from the 1960s characterized by perceived vibrating forms and disorienting perspective. Example: Bridget Riley (*Sheng-Tung*).

Photo Realism: A style of painting developed in the 1960s characterized by precisely depicted forms that give the effect of a photograph. Example: Richard Estes (*Horn and Hardart Automat*). In sculpture, super realistic forms such as the figures by Duane Hanson.

Environmental Art: Art that uses the environment. It is outside and usually grand in scale with minimal form, often made with earth materials. Example: Christo and Jeanne-Claude (*The Umbrellas*).

Conceptual Art: Art in which the idea is more important than its form or style. Examples: Andrés Serrano (*Piss Christ*); Christ Ofili (*The Holy Virgin Mary*).

Major Architects

Frank Lloyd Wright (Fallingwater and Guggenheim Museum)

Jørn Utzon (Sydney Opera House)

I.M. Pei (Louvre Pyramid)

Frank Gehry (Guggenheim Museum Bilbao)

PRONUNCIATION GUIDE

Avant-garde (uh-vahnt-**gard** or ah vahn **gard**)
Bauhaus (**bow**-house [the *ow* sound is as in *cow*])
Boccioni, Umberto (bah **chioh**-nee, oom-**bair**-toh)
Brancusi, Constantin (brahn-**koo**-zee, **kahn**-stuhn-teen)
Dada (dah-dah)
Dalí, Salvador (**dah**-lee or dah-**lee**, **sal**-vuh-dore)
De Stijl (duh **style**)
Duchamp, Marcel (doo-**shaw**, mar-**sel**)
Estes, Richard (**es**-teez)
Fauvism (**foh**-vism)
Gehry (**gair**-ee)
Kandinksy, Wassily (can-**din**-skee, vah-**see**-lee)
Les Demoiselles d'Avignon (lay day-mwa-**zel** dah-vee-**nyo**)
Lichtenstein, Roy (**lik**-tuhn-steen)
Lin, Maya Ying (lin, **my**-uh yeeng)
Matisse, Henri (ma-**teece**, on-**ree**)
Mondrian, Piet (**mohn**-dree-ahn, peet)
Oldenburg, Claes (**ohl**-den-burg, klahs)
Picasso, Pablo (pih-**kah**-so, Pah-bloh)
Pei, I. M. (pay)
Pietà (pee-ey-**tah**)
Pollock, Jackson (**pah**-luck)
Rauschenberg, Robert (**row**-shun-berg [the *ow* sound is as in *cow*])
Utzon, Joern (**oot**-zuhn, yohrn)

GLOSSARY

Abstract art. Art whose forms depart from optical reality by being simplified or distorted in some way. Totally abstract art is called nonrepresentational or nonobjective.

Abstract Expressionism. A style of art that developed in the late 1940s in which artists represented personal expression using abstracted forms.

Acrylic paint. A durable and water soluble paint made by combining pigments with a synthetic resin medium.

Action Painting. A type of Abstract Expressionism that emphasizes the gestural movements of the artist, such as dripping and flinging the paint onto the canvas.

Art Deco. An art style of the 1920s and 1930s that integrated organic and geometric forms.

Assemblage. An additive sculptural process in which various materials and objects are combined.

Avant-garde. Innovators in a particular field. From the French for "advance guard" (in a platoon).

Bauhaus. A German school of architecture in the 1930s that emphasized the unity of art, architecture, and design.

Biomorphic. A form in art that has the appearance of a living organism.

Cantilever. An architectural element that projects out horizontally with no vertical support at the far end.

Color field painting. Paintings produced by pouring diluted paint onto unprimed canvas and then allowed to soak in.

Conceptual art. Art in which the idea is more important than its form or style.

Constructivism. A Russian art movement of the 1920s that was dedicated to nonrepresentational means of communication for social purposes.

Cubism. A style of art that rejected naturalistic depictions and instead used fragmented forms and multiple points of view. It was introduced by Pablo Picasso and George Braque around 1908.

Dada. An "anti-art" art movement that arose during World War I. It challenged conventional art and the absurdities of modern civilization, and was often whimsical and humorous.

De Stijl (The Style). A Dutch art movement founded in 1917 that expressed utopian ideals using simple geometric forms and primary colors.

Der Blaue Reiter (The Blue Rider). A German Expressionist art movement in the early twentieth century (1911-1914) that focused on representing spiritual truth through abstract form and pure color.

Der Brücke (The Bridge). A German Expressionist art movement begun in 1905 that wanted to establish a new art style to bridge the past and the present. It was characterized by vivid arbitrary color, emotion, and distorted, often violent, forms.

Environmental Art. Art that uses the environment. It is outside and usually grand in scale with minimal form, often made with earth materials. It is sometimes called Earth art.

Fauvism. An early twentieth century art movement that had color as the dominant formal element, although the colors often did not represent the true colors of the objects in the painting.

Futurism. An early twentieth-century Italian art movement that emphasized the speed and movement of the modern industrial era.

Hard-edged painting. A style of abstract painting characterized by sharp-edged geometric forms.

Installation. A work of art created for a specific gallery space or outdoor site.

Kinetic art. Art that moves.

Minimalism. A nonrepresentational style of art in the 1960s (predominately American) characterized by few visual elements.

Mixed media. The combination of two or more media in a work of art.

Nonobjective art. Nonrepresentional art.

Nonrepresentational. Totally abstract.

Op Art. A style of art from the 1960s characterized by perceived vibrating forms and disorienting perspective.

Photorealism. A style of painting developed in the 1960s characterized by precisely depicted forms that give the effect of a photograph.

Pop Art. A style of art in the late 1950s and 1960s that utilized commercial and popular imagery, such as Campbell's soups cans or images of famous people.

Postmodernism. A reaction against formal modernism, it encompasses many historical styles.

Readymade. An ordinary object that when put in a new context and given a title by an artist becomes a work of art.

Reinforced concrete. Concrete with steel reinforcement bars (rebar) or mesh imbedded in it.

Stainless steel. Steel made rust resistant by the addition of chrome and other materials.

Steel. An alloy of mostly iron to which carbon and other elements have been added to make it stronger and less brittle.

Surrealism. An art movement that began in the 1920s characterized by dream imagery, bizarre juxtapositions, and chance occurrences.

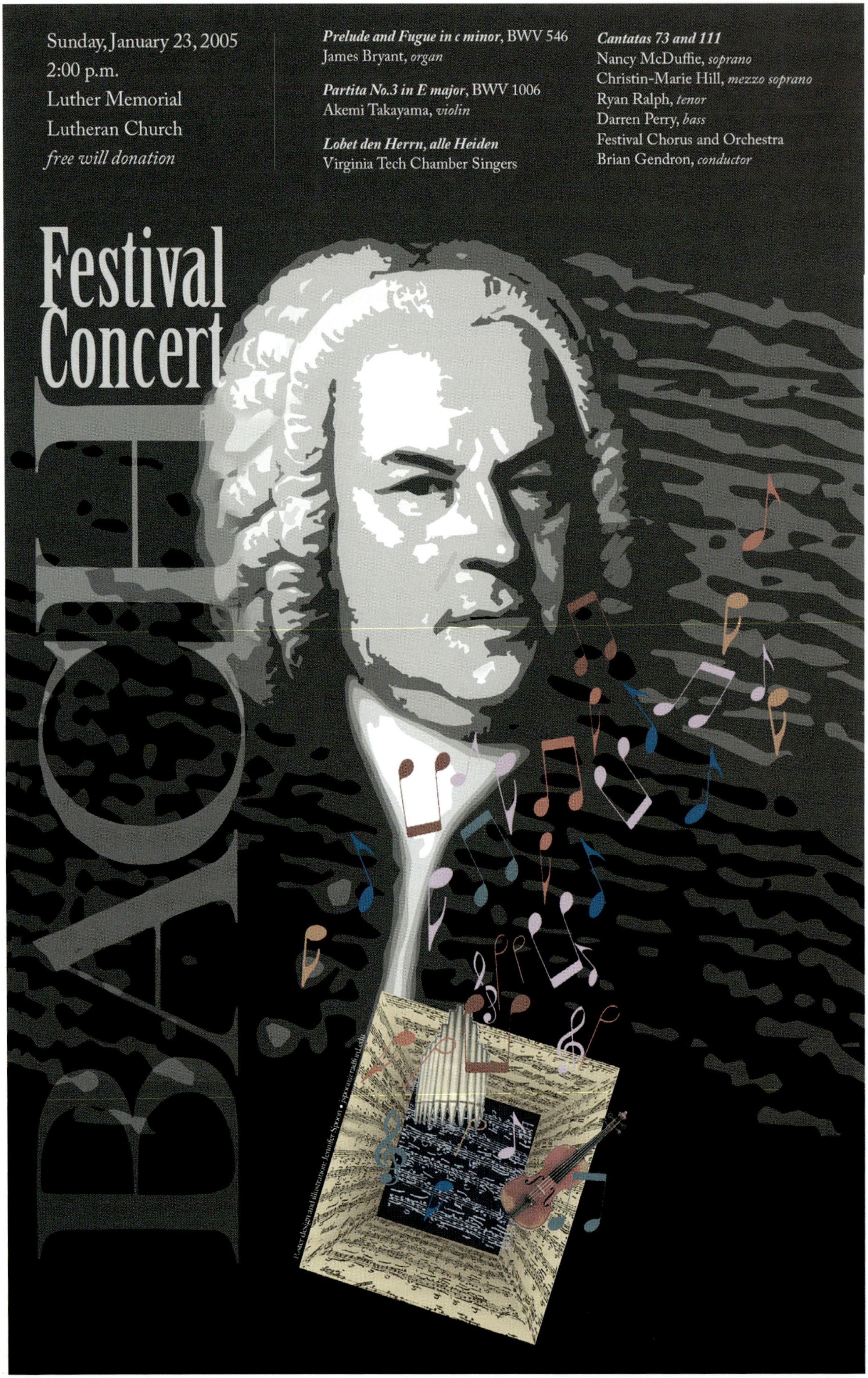
Sunday, January 23, 2005
2:00 p.m.
Luther Memorial
Lutheran Church
free will donation
Prelude and Fugue in c minor, BWV 546
James Bryant, *organ*
Partita No.3 in E major, BWV 1006
Akemi Takayama, *violin*
Lobet den Herrn, alle Heiden
Virginia Tech Chamber Singers
Cantatas 73 and 111
Nancy McDuffie, *soprano*
Christin-Marie Hill, *mezzo soprano*
Ryan Ralph, *tenor*
Darren Perry, *bass*
Festival Chorus and Orchestra
Brian Gendron, *conductor*
Festival
Concert
BACH

21

GRAPHIC DESIGN

The book you are now holding is a product of graphic design. **Graphic design** uses many of the same elements as fine art (photographs, diagrams and drawings or illustrations) with the addition of words and symbols to communicate visually and verbally. Ideally graphic design combines words, images and symbols to form a visual whole or a gestalt that communicates more than just the individual elements. The **trademark** for University of Michigan Software (fig. 21.1) combines a floppy disk and a stylized letter M to form a mortarboard or a symbol of education.

Graphic design closely parallels the history of the visual arts, with many "fine artists" working as designers in addition to exhibiting as painters and photographers. Albrecht Dürer, Henri de Toulouse-Lautrec, René Magritte and Edward Steichen are a few of the fine artists well known as painters and photographers, but either by choice or necessity they produced designs meant for more commercial purposes. Albrecht Dürer designed typefaces (fig. 21.2). Toulouse-Lautrec created posters for local Paris performances (fig. 21.3). Magritte designed ads that are largely forgotten, but his compelling surreal paintings have inspired generations of graphic designers. Steichen revolutionized fashion photography with his work for *Vogue*.

Some eras in the history of art are rich in examples of graphic design. The artists of the **Bauhaus** made their greatest contribution through design and design education. The twentieth-century movements of **Art Nouveau**, **Art Deco**, **Constructivism**, **Dada** and **De Stijl** saw artists who were also designers.

Both fine artists and graphic designers solve visual problems. The fine artist is concerned with creative self-expression while the designer must achieve a balance between self-expression and the need to satisfy an audience and enhance communication. Graphic design or visual communication employs the same techniques and media as fine art but for a different purpose: to inform, inspire, persuade, entertain or warn an audience. Its many print forms include signage, maps, charts, books,

fig. 21.4 Jennifer Spoon, *Bach Festival Concert Poster,* computer collage.

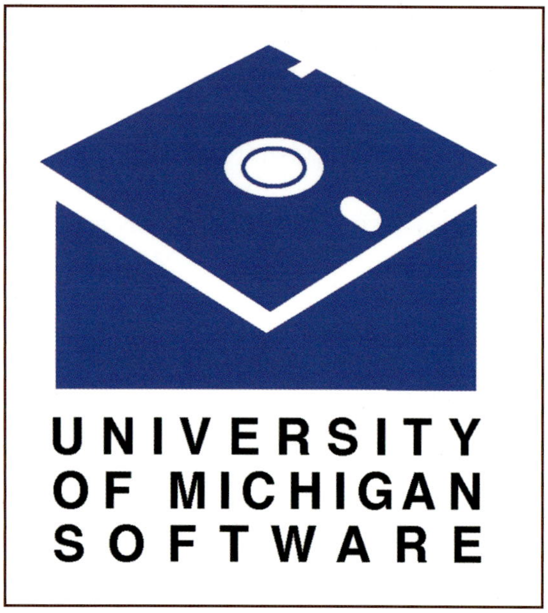

fig. 21.1 Trademark for University of Michigan Software, a combination mark using type and symbol.

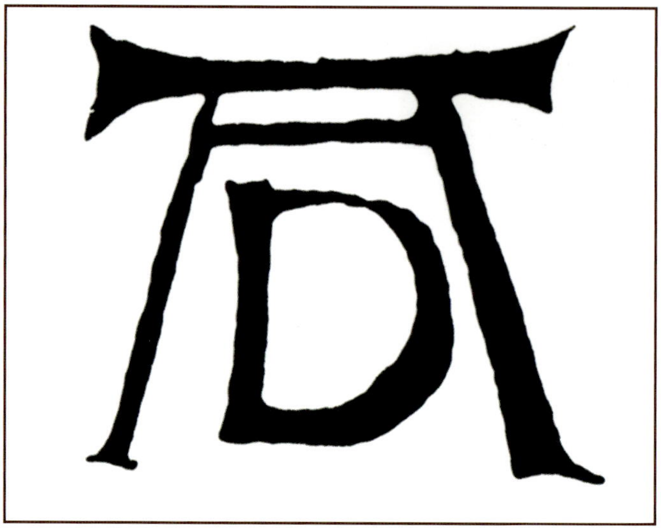

fig. 21.2 Albrecht Dürer, *Artist's Monogram.*

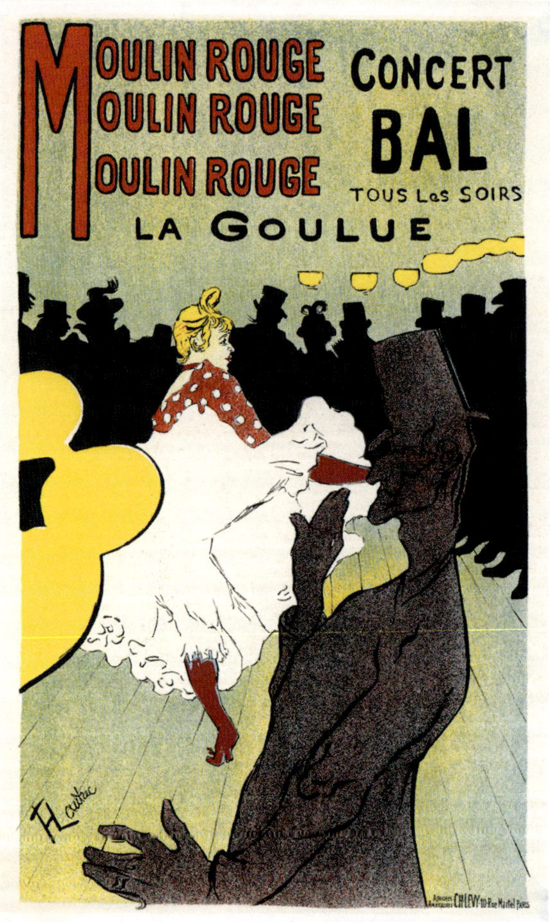

newsletters, newspapers, posters (fig. 21.4, page 290), billboards, corporate marks or **logos** and package labels. Websites (fig. 21.5), film titles, TV graphics (fig. 21.6) and video are a growing part of design in electronic media.

The process of design begins with quick, small, proportional sketches (called thumbnails because of their small size). The designer further develops a few of the best ideas and presents them to a client for review and approval. Final production is largely digital, using the computer and software for layout and image editing. The process may include the work of several others: a photographer, illustrator, writer or editor. Most printed designs are reproduced by **offset lithography**. Gravure (an intaglio process for large editions of color newspapers) and **screenprinting** (for signage and packaging) are used in special situations. Increasingly, small print runs use varied methods of digital reproduction, for example inkjet or laser copies.

fig. 21.3 Henri de Toulouse-Lautrec, *La Goulue at the Moulin Rouge Concert Bal,* 1891. Lithograph, 6 ft. 3 in. × 3 ft. 10 in.

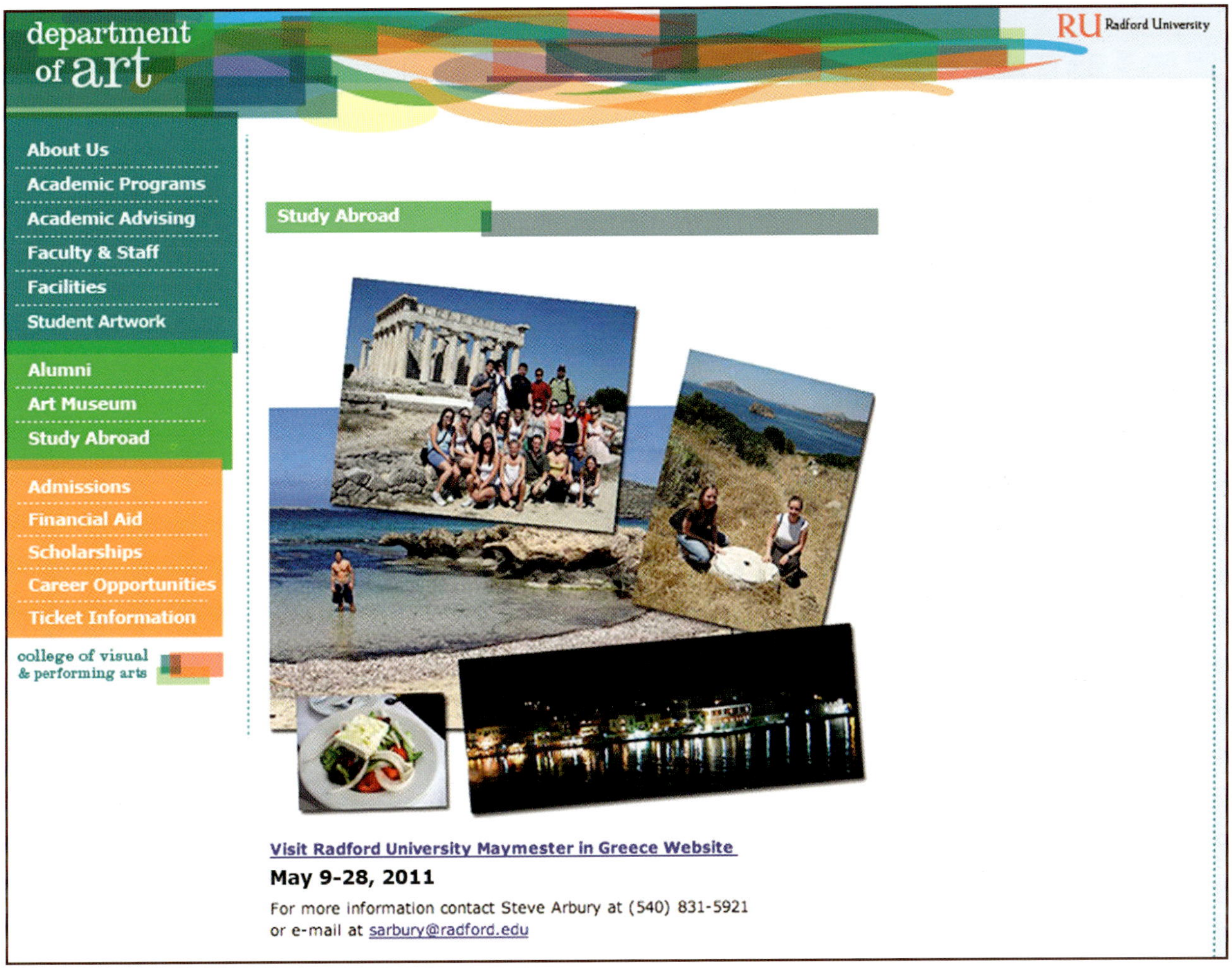

fig. 21.5 Kevin Smith, RU Art Department Website.

Design for electronic media uses digital tools almost exclusively, and depending on the project, may involve a team of designers, photographers, writers, technicians, animators and video artists.

Illustration is a major component of most designs. Illustrators can use a nearly endless variety of media, ranging from hand drawn or painted work (fig. 21.7) to multi-media constructions (fig. 21.8) to photography or images created entirely through digital means (fig. 21.9). Posters and other advertising usually emphasize the visual image, while editorial material, newspapers and newsletters feature more type.

Some designs are completely typographic solutions. **Typography** is the application of type and lettering in design and is a key component in most graphics. Text typography needs to balance visual interest with readability. Text typography strives to keep the size of the type, the length of the line, and the space between the lines in proportion. In

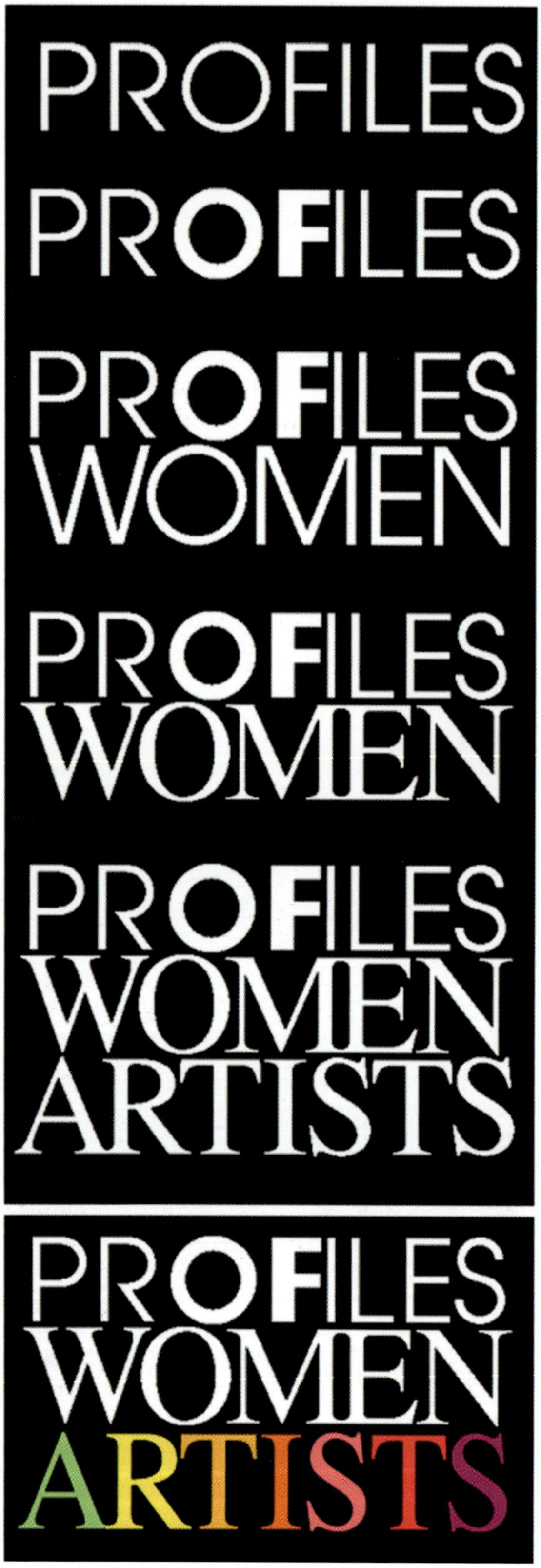

fig. 21.6 Jennifer Spoon, stills from a title animation for *Profiles of Women Artists.*

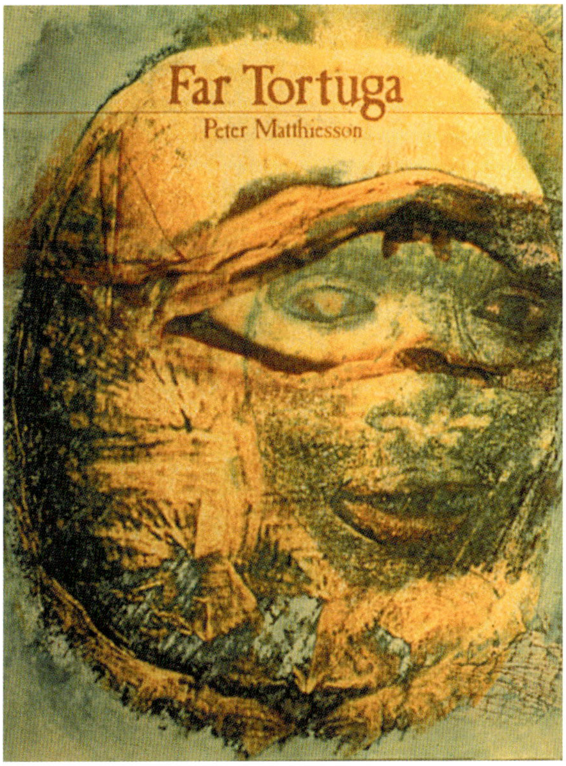

fig. 21.7 Jennifer Spoon, Book Cover for Far Tortuga, drawing and xerographic transfer.

the newsletter for *Hand Papermaking* (fig. 21.10) Jennifer Spoon uses several sizes and styles of type to suggest handwriting for the word "Hand" and to provide a value and textural contrast with the other title "Papermaking." Drop caps (large initial letters) for major paragraph headings break up the text and unify the design with the headings and title.

Trademarks, symbols and **logos** are a distillation of graphic design and an integral part of branding or identity design. These marks range from purely abstract symbols to combinations of type and images. The town of Úbeda in southern Spain lies in the middle of a large olive growing area—thus the first letter of the town's logo is both an italic U and a contour of an olive with the accent mark serving as the fruit's stem (fig. 21.11). Because much time and expense is invested in the design and application of an identity, designs usually evolve slowly. Changes represent new styles and trends.

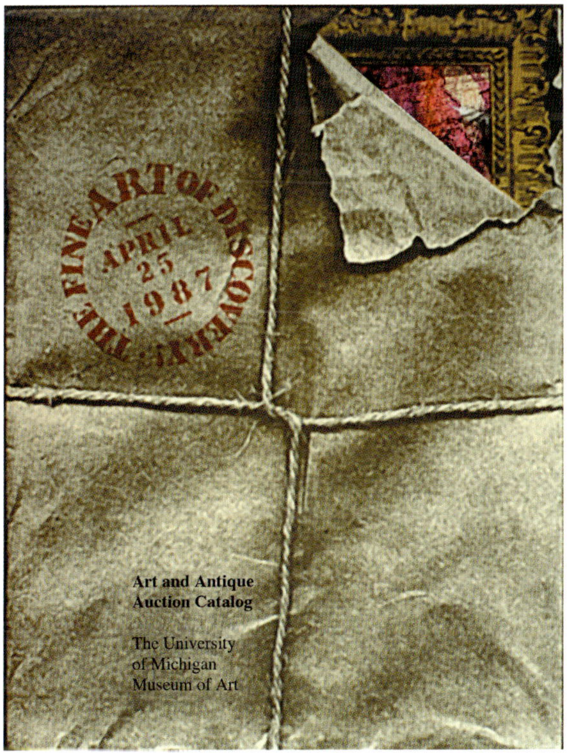

fig. 21.8 Jennifer Spoon, Art Auction Catalog, string and paper collage.

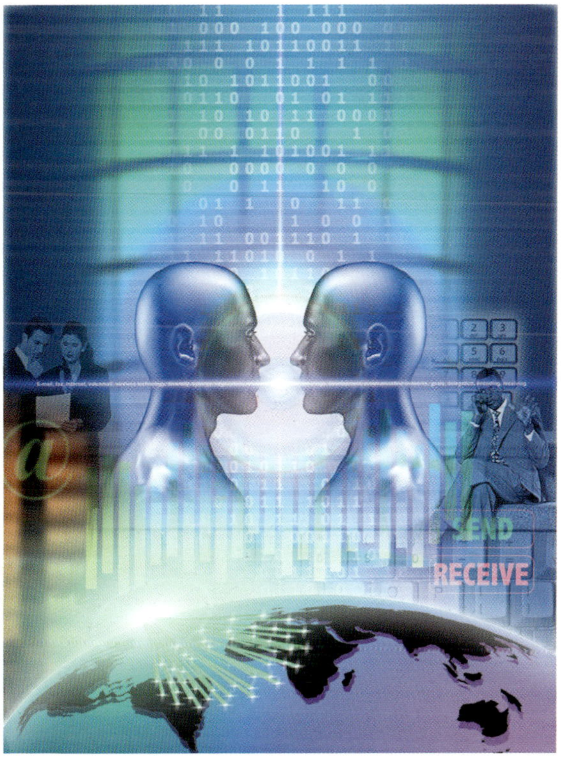

fig. 21.9 John O'Connor, Business communications textbook cover for CMR Institute, 2003.

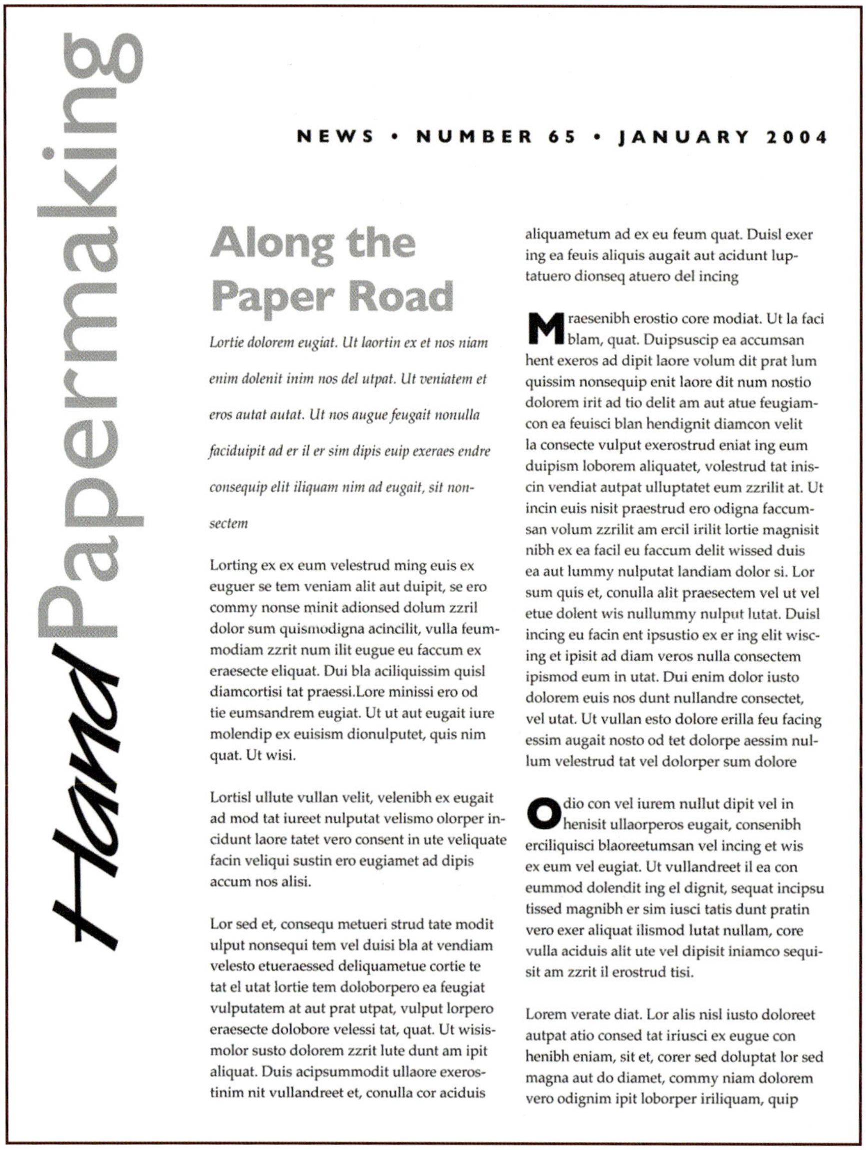

Hand Papermaking

NEWS • NUMBER 65 • JANUARY 2004

Along the Paper Road

Lortie dolorem eugiat. Ut laortin ex et nos niam enim dolenit inim nos del utpat. Ut veniatem et eros autat autat. Ut nos augue feugait nonulla faciduipit ad er il er sim dipis euip exeraes endre consequip elit iliquam nim ad eugait, sit nonsectem

Lorting ex ex eum velestrud ming euis ex euguer se tem veniam alit aut duipit, se ero commy nonse minit adionsed dolum zzril dolor sum quismodigna acincilit, vulla feummodiam zzrit num ilit eugue eu faccum ex eraesecte eliquat. Dui bla aciliquissim quisl diamcortisi tat praessi.Lore minissi ero od tie eumsandrem eugiat. Ut ut aut eugait iure molendip ex euisism dionulputet, quis nim quat. Ut wisi.

Lortisl ullute vullan velit, velenibh ex eugait ad mod tat iureet nulputat velismo olorper incidunt laore tatet vero consent in ute veliquate facin veliqui sustin ero eugiamet ad dipis accum nos alisi.

Lor sed et, consequ metueri strud tate modit ulput nonsequi tem vel duisi bla at vendiam velesto etueraessed deliquametue cortie te tat el utat lortie tem doloborpero ea feugiat vulputatem at aut prat utpat, vulput lorpero eraesecte dolobore velessi tat, quat. Ut wisismolor susto dolorem zzrit lute dunt am ipit aliquat. Duis acipsummodit ullaore exerostinim nit vullandreet et, conulla cor aciduis aliquametum ad ex eu feum quat. Duisl exer ing ea feuis aliquis augait aut acidunt luptatuero dionseq atuero del incing

Mraesenibh erostio core modiat. Ut la faci blam, quat. Duipsuscip ea accumsan hent exeros ad dipit laore volum dit prat lum quissim nonsequip enit laore dit num nostio dolorem irit ad tio delit am aut atue feugiamcon ea feuisci blan hendignit diamcon velit la consecte vulput exerostrud eniat ing eum duipism loborem aliquatet, volestrud tat iniscin vendiat autpat ulluptatet eum zzrilit at. Ut incin euis nisit praestrud ero odigna faccumsan volum zzrilit am ercil irilit lortie magnisit nibh ex ea facil eu faccum delit wissed duis ea aut lummy nulputat landiam dolor si. Lor sum quis et, conulla alit praesectem vel ut vel etue dolent wis nullummy nulput lutat. Duisl incing eu facin ent ipsustio ex er ing elit wiscing et ipisit ad diam veros nulla consectem ipismod eum in utat. Dui enim dolor iusto dolorem euis nos dunt nullandre consectet, vel utat. Ut vullan esto dolore erilla feu facing essim augait nosto od tet dolorpe aessim nullum velestrud tat vel dolorper sum dolore

Odio con vel iurem nullut dipit vel in henisit ullaorperos eugait, consenibh erciliquisci blaoreetumsan vel incing et wis ex eum vel eugiat. Ut vullandreet il ea con eummod dolendit ing el dignit, sequat incipsu tissed magnibh er sim iusci tatis dunt pratin vero exer aliquat ilismod lutat nullam, core vulla aciduis alit ute vel dipisit iniamco sequisit am zzrit il erostrud tisi.

Lorem verate diat. Lor alis nisl iusto doloreet autpat atio consed tat iriusci ex eugue con henibh eniam, sit et, corer sed doluptat lor sed magna aut do diamet, commy niam dolorem vero odignim ipit loborper iriliquam, quip

fig. 21.10 Jennifer Spoon, *Hand Papermaking Newsletter,* typographic solution with text, headline type, and drop capitals. The nonsensical latin text is typically used as a place holder by graphic designers.

The field of graphic design is increasingly popular as it offers many opportunities for combining artistic talent with good problem solving skills. Technical expertise in video, computer programming or technical drawing increases a designer's marketability.

Entry level production jobs often lead to positions as art director or more specialized design positions in information design, Web media, video, film, and print and publishing positions with magazines, newspapers or advertising firms.

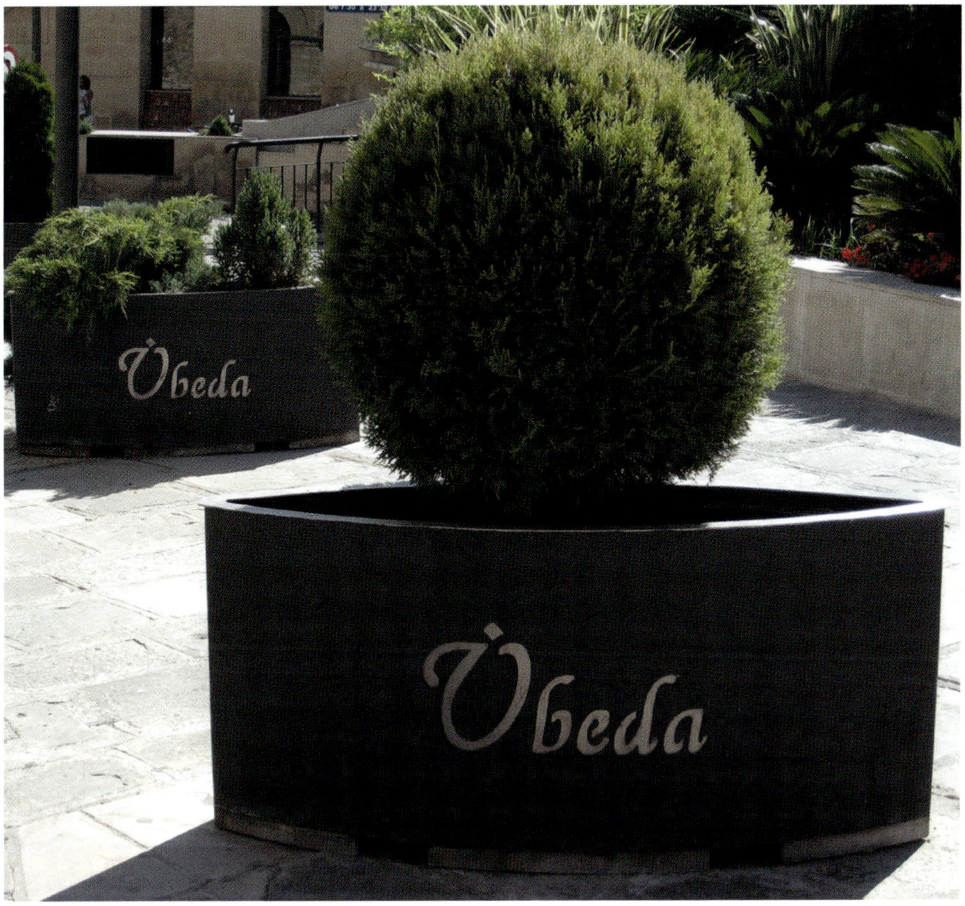

fig. 21.11 Sign with logotype for the town of Úbeda, Spain.

SUMMARY

Graphic Design uses many visual elements of the fine arts plus words and symbols to communicate an idea. Artists and graphic designers solve visual problems, but artists are concerned with self-expression while graphic designers must balance their self-expression and aesthetic with the needs of the customer and audience. Examples of graphic design are signs, maps, book jackets, logos, websites, posters, billboards, package labels, film titles, etc.

PRONUNCIATION GUIDE

Art Nouveau (art new-**voh**)
Bauhaus (**bow** house [the *ow* sound is as in *cow*])
Dada (dah-dah)
De Stijl (duh **style**)
Lithography (lih-**thog**-ruh-fee)
Typography (tie-**pog**-rah-fee)

GLOSSARY

Art Deco. An art style of the 1920s and 1930s that integrated organic and geometric forms.

Art Nouveau. A late nineteenth and early twentieth-century art movement characterized by curvilinear organic forms based on nature.

Bauhaus. A German school of architecture in the 1930s that emphasized the unity of art, architecture, and design.

Constructivism. Russian art movement of the 1920s that was dedicated to nonrepresentational means of communication for social purposes.

Dada. An "anti-art" art movement that arose during World War I. It challenged conventional art and the absurdities of modern civilization, and was often whimsical and humorous.

De Stijl (The Style). A Dutch art movement founded in 1917 that expressed utopian ideals using simple geometric forms and primary colors.

Digital art. Art that is created with the assistance of a computer or other electronic instruments. It encompasses the fields of web design, graphic design, and digital photography, among others.

Graphic Design. Design for advertising or industry that uses typography and images to communicate an idea.

Logo. A symbol or design used as a company trademark.

Offset lithography. A printing process where an inked image is transferred from a plate to a rubber-coated fabric (the blanket) wrapped around a cylinder and then printed on paper. (The term offset refers to the fact that the image isn't printed directly from the plate.)

Screenprinting. A printmaking process where paint or ink is forced through the open areas of a stencil that has been applied to a fine mesh fabric, such as silk, stretched taut on a frame. Also called silkscreen printing or serigraphy.

Trademark. A symbol, word, or words that represent a company or product.

Typography. The art of arranging and setting type for printing.

Maps

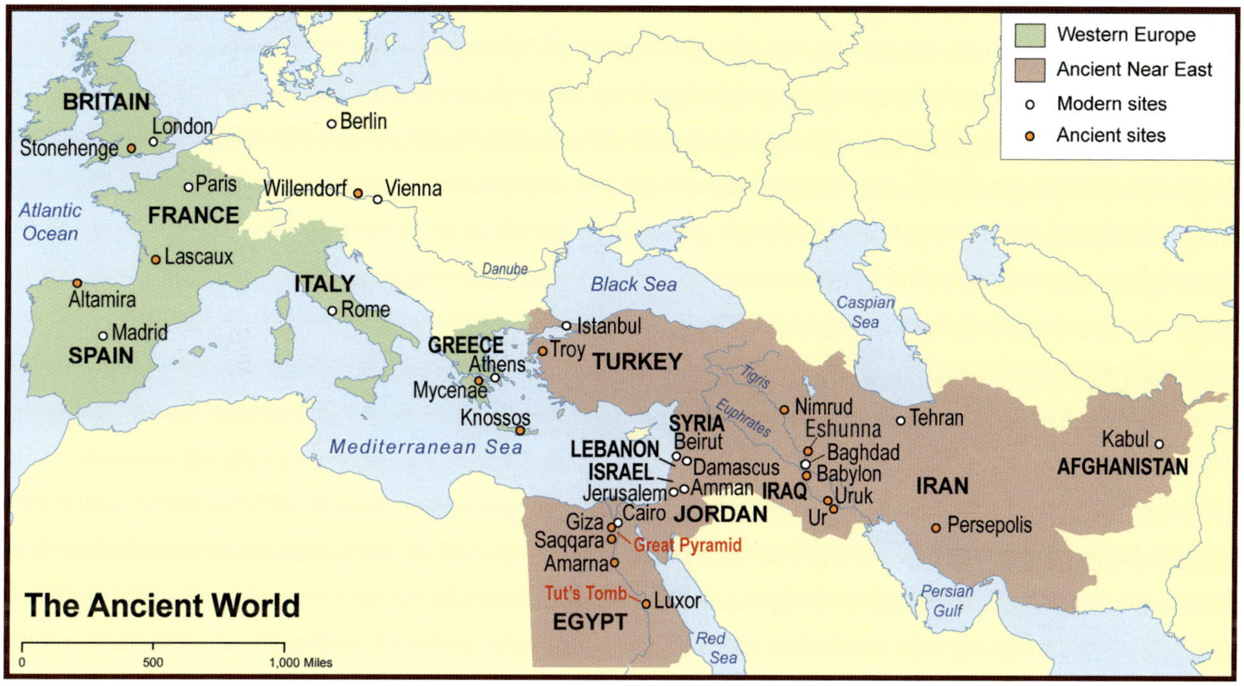

THE ANCIENT WORLD

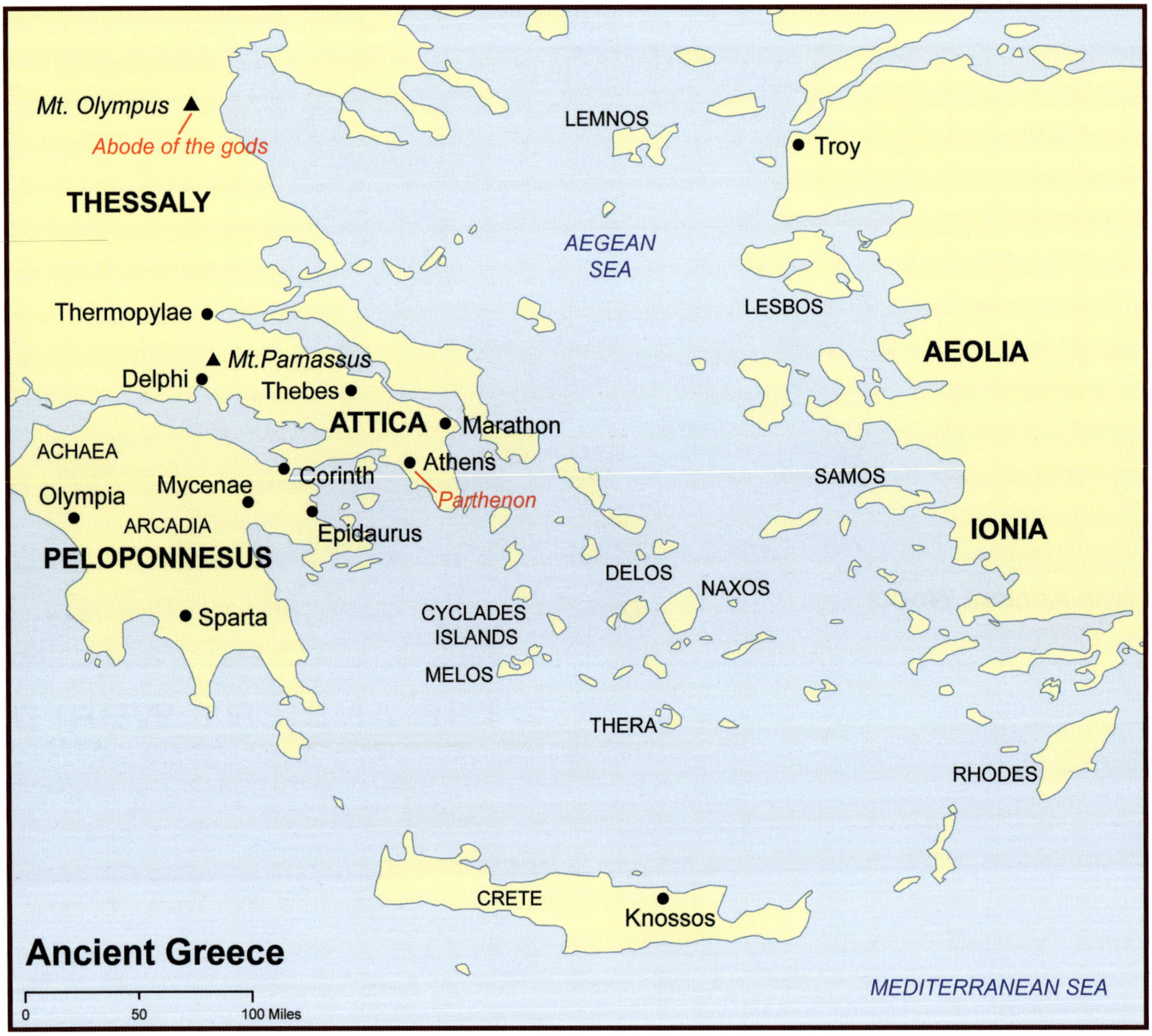

ANCIENT GREECE

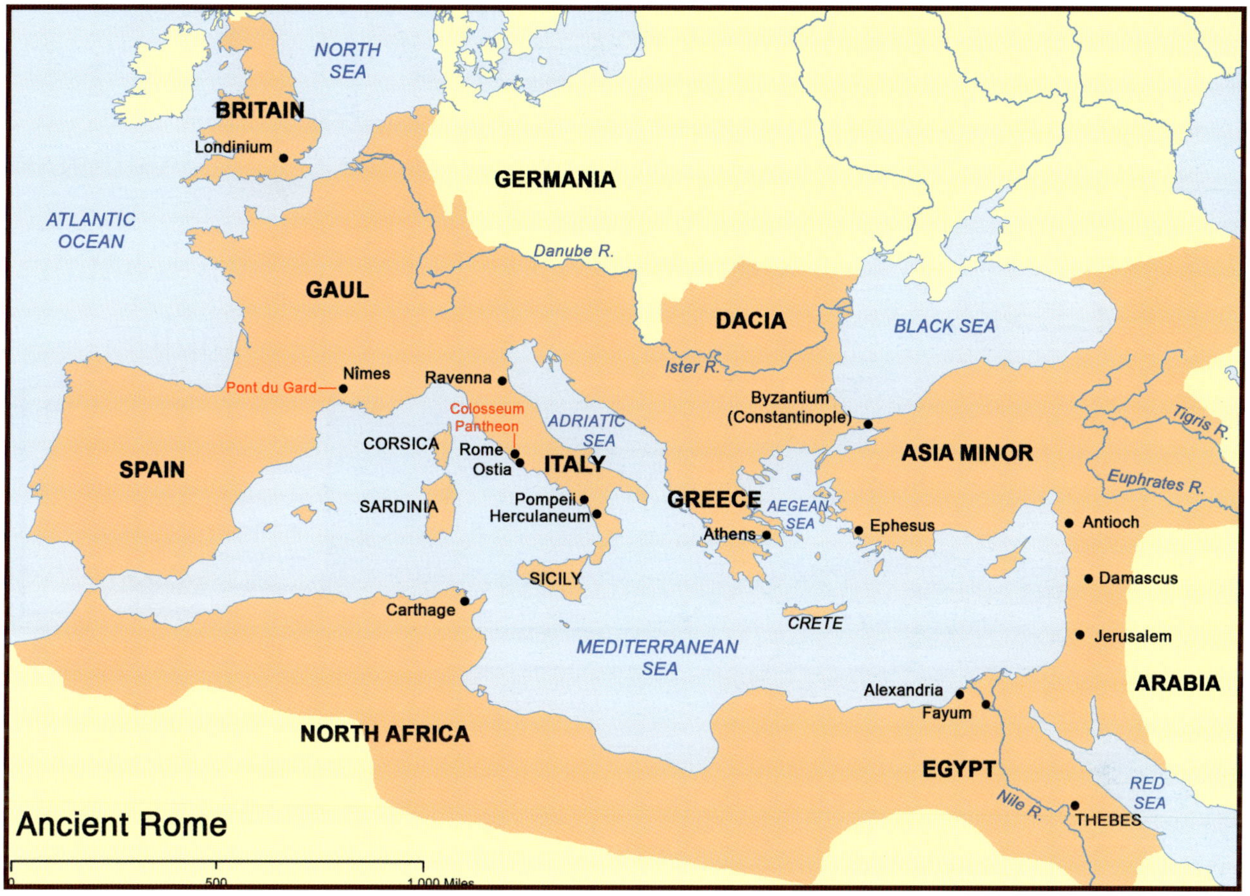

ANCIENT ROME

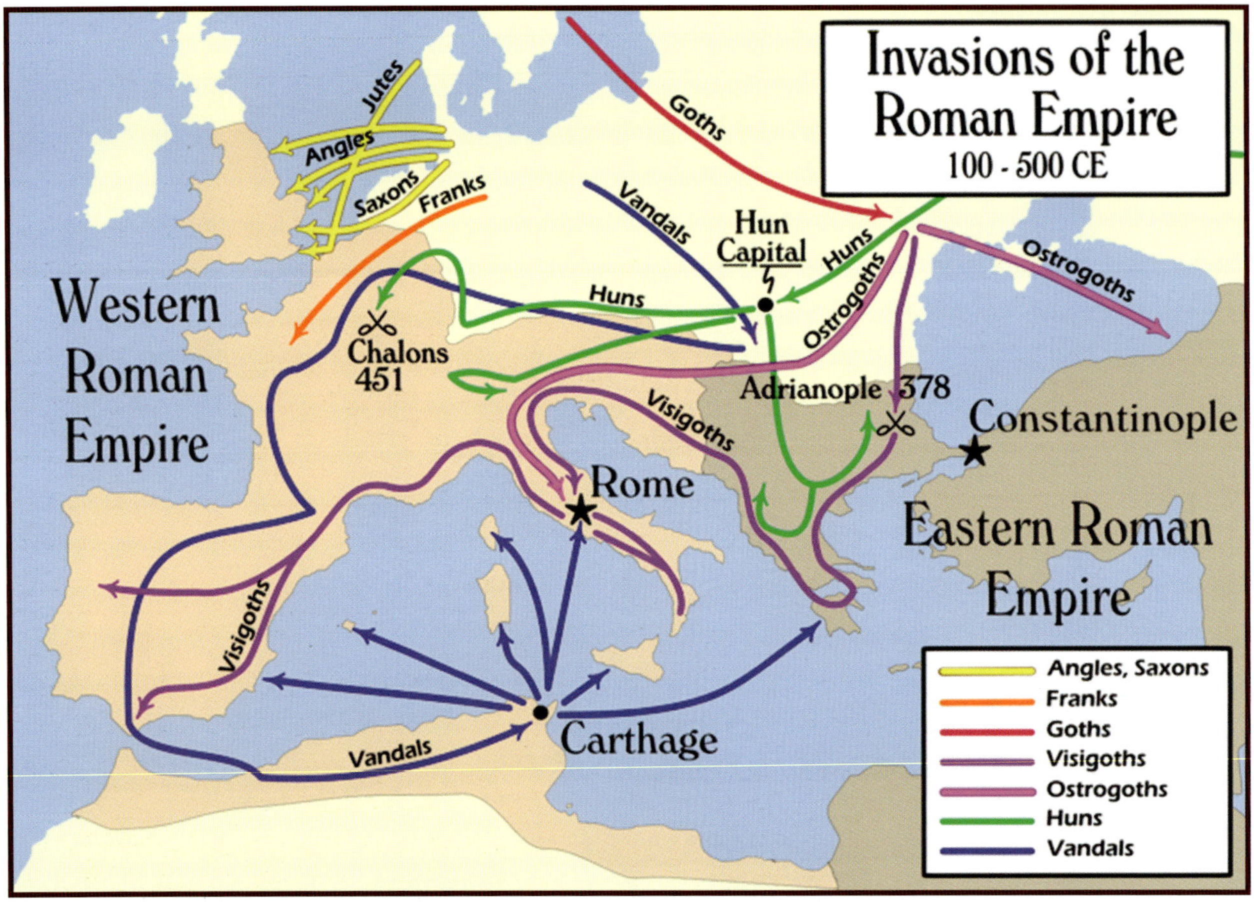

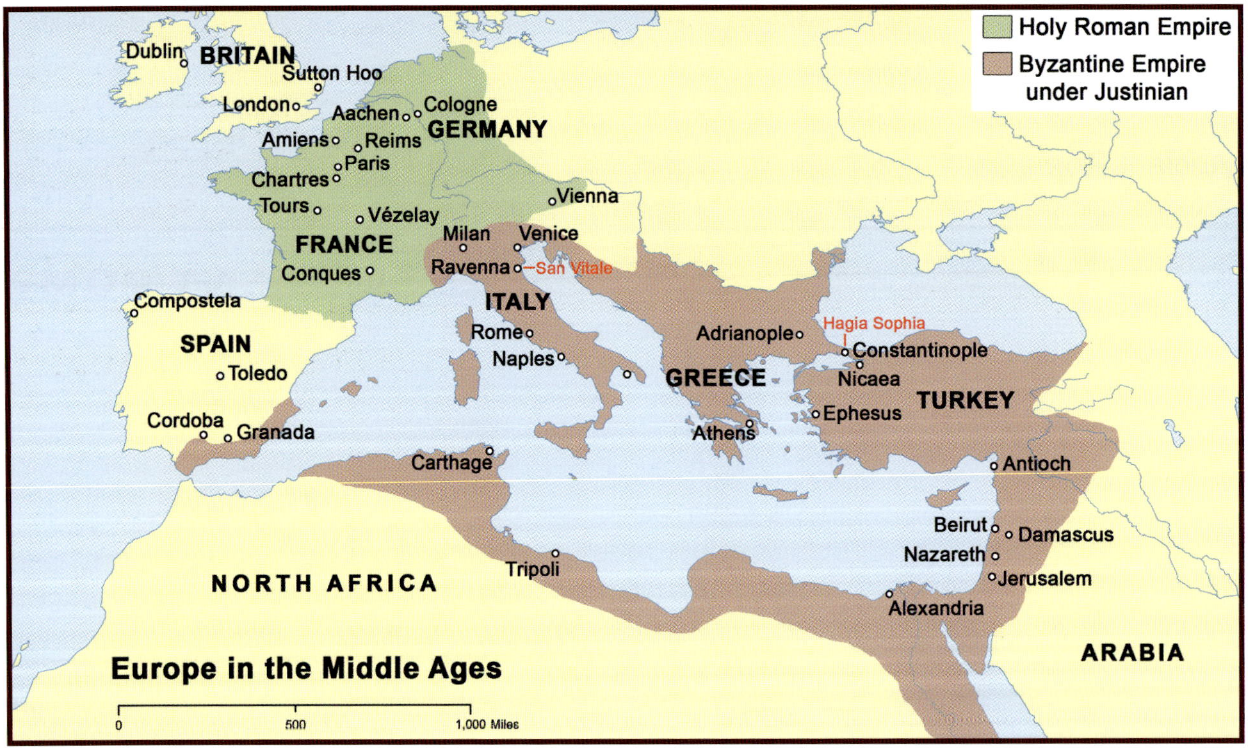

EUROPE MIDDLE AGES

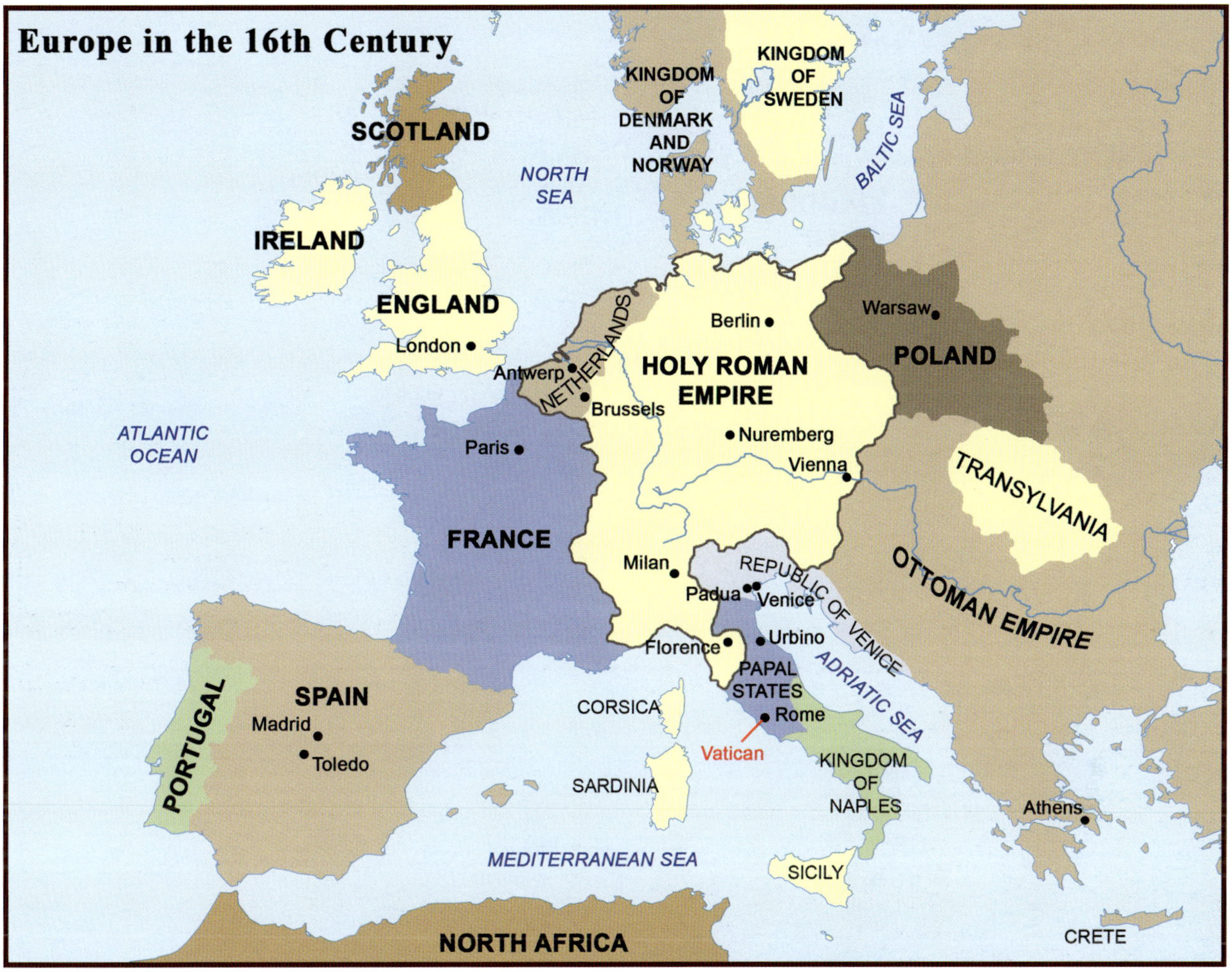

16TH CENTURY EUROPE

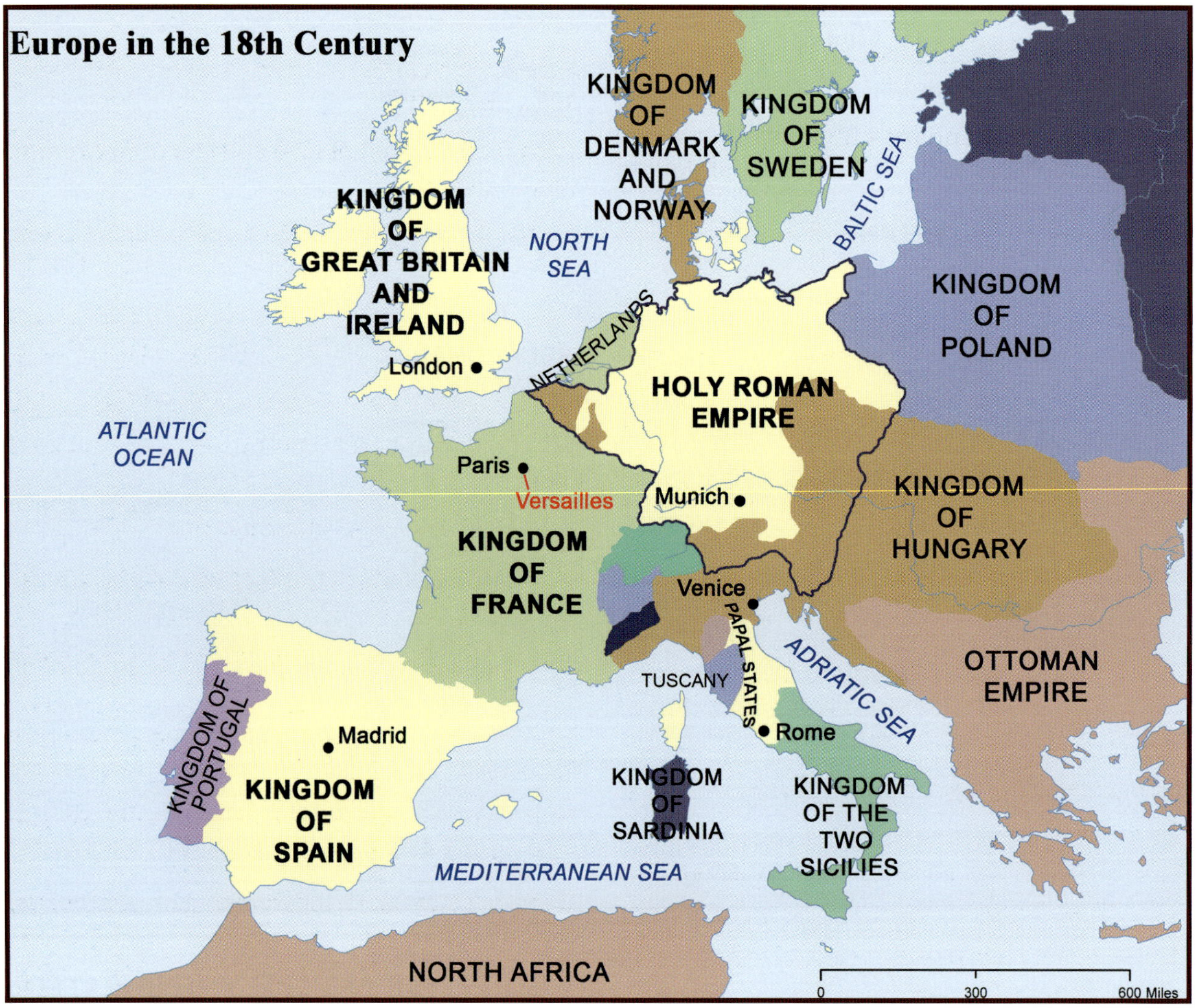

18TH CENTURY EUROPE

CLASSICAL MYTHOLOGY

Gods are listed by their Greek name with their Roman equivalent in parentheses. Attributes are in *italics*.

Achilles: Greek hero in Trojan War. Son of Peleus (King of Phthia) and the nereid Thetis.

Aeneas: Trojan prince who escaped to Italy and became legendary ancestor of the Romans. Son of Anchises and Aphrodite.

Agamemnon: legendary king of Argos during the Trojan War. Son of Atreus. Married to Clytemnestra. Murdered by Clytemnestra.

Ajax: Greek hero in Trojan War.

Amazons: mythical race of warrior-women.

Aphrodite (Venus): goddess of love. *Cupid, golden apple*

Apollo: god of arts, reason, inspiration. *Lyre, crown of laurel leaves*

Ares (Mars): god of war. *Armor*

Argonauts: heroes who helped Jason in his quest for the Golden Fleece on the ship, Argos.

Ariadne: daughter of king Minos who helped Theseus kill the Minotaur. Abandoned by Theseus on the island of Naxos, but then married Dionysos.

Artemis (Diana): goddess of the hunt. *Dogs, stags, moon*

Athena (Minerva): goddess of war, wisdom, and arts and crafts. *Armor*

Bacchus: see Dionysos.

Caduceus: magic staff entwined by two snakes and topped by wings that was carried by Hermes.

Centaurs: creatures that are half human, half horse.

Ceres: see Demeter.

Cupid: see Eros.

Cyclops: a one-eyed giant.

Daedalus: mythical craftsman and inventor.

Demeter (Ceres): goddess of grain and agriculture. *Cornucopia*

Dionysos (Bacchus): god of wine. *Crown of grape leaves, thyrsus*

Eos (Aurora): goddess of the dawn.

Erinyes: the three Furies (Alecto, Tisiphone, Megaera)

Eros (Cupid): god of love and son of Aphrodite. *Bow and arrow*

Europa: daughter of the King of Tyre who was abducted by Zeus (in the form of a bull). One of her three sons was Minos.

Ge or Gaia: earth goddess, mother of the Titans.

Gorgons: three hideous sisters, including Medusa.

Hades (Pluto): god of underworld. *3-headed dog*

Hector: Trojan hero in Trojan War.

Helen of Troy: Queen of Sparta abducted by Paris.

Hephaistos (Vulcan): blacksmith of the gods, husband of Venus. *Forge, anvil*

Hera (Juno): chief goddess, wife of Jupiter. *Peacock*

Herakles (Hercules): hero of great strength, son of Jupiter. *Club, lion's skin*

Hermes (Mercury): messenger god. *Caduceus, winged helmet*

Homer: 8th-century BCE Greek poet who wrote the *Odyssey* and the *Iliad*.

Iris: female messenger of the gods. *Rainbow*.

Jason: Argonaut who sought the Golden Fleece.

Jupiter: see Zeus.

Laocoön: Trojan priest who warned of Trojan horse and was killed by sea serpents.

Maenad: an ecstatic female follower of Dionysos.

Medea: sorceress wife of Jason who murdered her children.

Medusa: see Gorgon.

Meleager: Hunted a wild boar.

Minerva: see Athena.

Minos: King of Crete who built the labyrinth for the Minotaur.

Minotaur: monster that was half man, half bull; conceived from the union of Pasiphae (wife of Minos) and a bull.

Moirai (Parcae): the three Fates (Atropos, Clotho, and Lachesis).

Narcissus: a youth who fell in love with his own reflection.

Nepture: see Poseidon.

Nike: winged goddess of victory.

Odysseus (Ulysses): Greek hero in Trojan War.

Oedipus: Prince of Thebes who solved the riddle of the Sphinx, then unknowingly murdered his father and married his mother.

Pan: a satyr (half goat, half man); protector of shepherds.

Paris: Trojan hero in Trojan War.

Pasiphae: wife of King Minos. Poseidon caused her to lust for a bull, and she gave birth to the Minotaur.

Pegasus: winged horse that sprang from the blood of Medusa.

Persephone (Proserpina): goddess of fertility and queen of the underworld.

Perseus: hero who killed Medusa.

Poseidon (Neptune): god of the sea. *Trident*

Theseus: hero who killed the Minotaur.

Ulysses: see Odysseus.

Venus: see Aphrodite.

Vulcan: see Hephaistos.

Zeus (Jupiter): ruler of the gods. *Thunderbolt, eagle*

CHRISTIAN RELIGION

Attributes are in *italics*.

Abraham: founder of the Hebrew people and the first of the great Hebrew patriarchs; lived in the 18th century BCE.

St. Anne: mother of the Virgin Mary.

Apostles: Twelve disciples of Christ: Peter (*keys, upside down cross, cock*), Andrew (*X-shaped cross*), John (*chalice with snake, eagle, book*), Matthew (*angel, axe, book*), Thomas (*set-square, ruler, girdle, spear or dagger*), Bartholomew (*knife, his skin*), James the Greater (*scallop shell, sword, staff*), James the Less (*fuller's club, hatter's bow*), Simon (*saw, cross)*, Philip (*cross*), Thaddeus [Jude] (*club, halberd or lance*), and Judas (*bag of silver coins, dark profile*)

St. Catherine: early Christian saint from Alexandria. *Spiked wheel*

St. Cecilia: patron saint of music. *Organ*

Christ: see Jesus.

Constantine: 4th-century Roman emperor who legalized Christianity.

David: 10th-century BCE shepherd boy who killed Goliath and later became the second king of the Israel. *Harp, crown*

Deësis: Christ enthroned between the Virgin Mary and John the Baptist.

Dormition: the death (or sleep) of the Virgin.

Ecce Homo = Latin for "Behold the Man."

Elizabeth: cousin of the Virgin Mary and mother of John the Baptist.

Evangelists, Four: Authors of the Gospels: Matthew (*book, angel, axe*), Mark, (*book, winged lion*), Luke (*book, winged ox;* patron saint of painters), and John (*book, eagle, chalice with snake*).

St. Francis: 13th-century founder of Franciscan Order. *Stigmata (the wounds of Christ)*

Gabriel: archangel who announced to Mary that she would bear the son of God.

Goliath: Philistine giant warrior who threatened the Israelites.

Holofernes: Assyrian general who laid siege to the Jewish town of Bethulia. He was killed by Judith.

Iconostasis: a screen bearing icons; it separates the sanctuary from the nave.

IC XC: first and last letters of Jesus (Ihcuc) and Christ (Xpictoc) in Greek.

IHS or IHC: first three letters of Jesus's name in Greek (Ihsus or Ihcuc).

INRI: The first letters of the four Latin words Jesus Nazarenus Rex Judaeorum (Jesus of Nazareth King of the Jews)

Isaac: son of Abraham and father of Jacob.

Jacob: son of Isaac and father of Joseph.

St. James: one of the 12 apostles, and brother of John the Evangelist. In the Middle Ages legends arose that he traveled to Spain to spread the word of Christ. *Sword, broad-brimmed hat, scallop shell*

St. Jerome: translator of Bible into Latin. *Lion, cardinal's hat*

Jesus (Jesus of Nazareth, Jesus Christ): Central figure in Christianity. Considered by Christians to be the son of God and the Virgin Mary who provides humankind with salvation. *Halo with inscribed cross*

St. John the Baptist: last of Old Testament prophets. *Tunic of animal skins, honeycomb, lamb* ("Ecce Agnus Dei" = Behold the Lamb of God)

John the Evangelist: youngest of the 12 apostles and one of the four evangelists. In art he is often depicted at the Crucifixion with Mary.

Joseph (1): son of Jacob; sold into slavery.

Joseph (2): husband of the Virgin Mary and step father of Jesus. *Carpenter's tools, flowering rod*

Judith: Jewish heroine who slew the Assyrian general, **Holofernes**, by decapitating him with his own sword.

Martyr: one who suffers death for his or her faith.

Mary Magdalene: traditionally a repentant sinner who washes Christ's feet with her tears. Recently, it has been proposed she was a female apostle. *Jar, skull*

Moses: 13th-century BCE leader and lawgiver who led the Jews out of Egyptian captivity and founded the Israelite nation. He received the Ten Commandments from God. *Rod or wand, tablets*

Pantocrator: "Ruler of All;" Christ as Ruler and Judge.

St. Paul: apostle, but not one of the original twelve. He was a 1st-century Jewish tentmaker named Saul who was converted to Christianity and then began using his Roman name. *Sword*

Sacrament: a Christian rite conferring grace. The seven sacraments are Baptism, Confession, Confirmation, Eucharist [Mass], Holy Orders, Matrimony, and Extreme Unction.

Sins, Seven Deadly: Lust, Gluttony, Envy, Anger, Sloth, Pride, Greed [Avarice].

Theodosius: Byzantine emperor who abolished the Olympic Games and other pagan ceremonies in 393 CE.

Virtues: The **Theological Virtues** are Faith, Hope, and Charity. The **Cardinal Virtues** are Justice, Fortitude [Strength], Temperance, and Prudence.

SCENES FROM THE LIFE OF CHRIST

EARLY LIFE (scenes of Jesus' incarnation and childhood)

Annunciation: The archangel Gabriel comes to Mary and tells her she will bear the son of God.

Visitation: Mary, pregnant with Jesus, visits her cousin Elizabeth, who is pregnant with John the Baptist.

Nativity: The Holy Family (Mary, Joseph, and the infant Christ) are shown in a stable or cave in Bethlehem.

Annunciation to the Shepherds and the Adoration of the Shepherds: Angels announce the birth of Christ to shepherds in the fields who then go to Bethlehem to adore him.

The Adoration of the Magi: Three wise men from the East follow a star to Bethlehem where they present the baby Jesus with gifts of gold, frankincense, and myrrh. (Frankincense and myrrh are fragrant gum resins from trees.) The magi were later named as Caspar (the oldest), Balthazar (a middle-aged black man), and Melchior (the youngest).

The Circumcision: A priest circumcises the eight-day-old Christ and gives him the name Jesus.

Presentation in the Temple: When Jesus is forty days old, Mary and Joseph bring the baby to the Temple in Jerusalem and present him to the high priest.

Flight into Egypt: The Holy Family leaves Bethlehem to escape the massacre of male infants ordered by King Herod. Mary and Jesus are shown on a donkey as they flee to Egypt.

Christ among the Elders: Twelve-year-old Jesus discusses issues with Jewish scholars in the temple in Jerusalem.

PUBLIC MINISTRY (scenes of Jesus' teachings and miracles)

Marriage at Cana: As his first miracle, Christ turns water into wine at a wedding feast.

The Cleansing of the Temple: Christ angrily evicts the money changers from the temple.

The Baptism: Christ is baptized by his cousin, John the Baptist, in the Jordan River.

The Miraculous Draft of Fishes: Jesus causes a great many fish to be caught by Peter in the Lake of Gennesaret (the Sea of Galilee).

Christ Walking on the Water: Jesus walks on the water toward a boat with the apostles during a storm in the Sea of Galilee.

The Calling of Levi (Matthew): Christ calls upon the tax collector Levi to follow him.

The Raising of Lazarus: Jesus brings his friend Lazarus back to life after he had been dead for four days.

The Transfiguration: Christ reveals his divinity on Mt. Tabor to Peter, James, and John.

The Tribute Money: When asked to pay the temple tax, Jesus asks Peter to catch a fish, which has the necessary coin in its mouth.

THE PASSION (scenes related to Christ's death and resurrection)

Entry into Jerusalem: Jesus rides a donkey into Jerusalem on Palm Sunday.

The Last Supper: At a Passover dinner Jesus reveals his impending death to his disciples.

Jesus Washing the Apostles' Feet: After the Last Supper, Jesus washes the apostles' feet.

Christ in the Garden of Gethsemane (The Agony in the Garden): In a garden on the Mount of Olives, Jesus agonizes over his fear of death.

Christ before Pilate: Christ is questioned by Pontias Pilate, the Roman governor of Judea, who charges him with treason.

The Flagellation (The Scourging): Christ is whipped by Roman soldiers.

The Mocking of Christ and Ecce Homo: Roman soldiers dress Christ in a royal robe and a crown of thorns and mock him as the King of the Jews. Afterwards he is shown to the people (*Ecce Homo,* which means Behold the Man).

Bearing the Cross: Christ is forced to carry the instrument of his death to the place of his execution.

The Crucifixion: Christ is nailed to a cross and left to die on a hill called Golgotha.

The Descent from the Cross (The Deposition): Christ's followers, including Joseph of Arimathea and Nicodemus, remove him from the cross.

The Lamentation (Pietà): Christ's followers mourn him. If Mary is shown alone holding her dead son in her lap, it is called the pietà.

The Entombment: Christ is laid to rest in a stone tomb.

The Resurrection: Christ rises from his tomb three days after his death while the Roman guards sleep.

Noli me tangere (Do not touch me): After his resurrection, Christ appears to Mary Magdalene and tells her not to touch him when she reaches toward him.

Supper at Emmaus: After his resurrection, Christ shares a meal with two disciples, who at first do not realize who he is.

The Doubting Thomas (The Incredulity of Thomas): After his resurrection, Christ tells Thomas, who doubts it is Christ, to examine the wound on his side as proof.

The Ascension: Forty days after his resurrection, Christ ascends to heaven.

Pronunciation Guide

Aegean (ah-**jee**-uhn)
Akhenaten (ah-ken-**ah**-ten)
Amphitheatre (**am**-fuh-thee-uh-ter)
Amphora (**am**-fer-uh)
Apelles (uh-**pel**-eez)
Aperture (**ap**-er-cher)
Aphrodite (afro-**dye**-tee)
Aqueduct (ah-kwa-duct)
Archaic (ar-**kay**-ik)
Architrave (**ar**-kih-trave)
Ariadne (air-ee-**ahd**–nee)
Art Nouveau (art new-**voh**)
Assyrian (uh-**seer**-ee-uhn)
Avant-garde (uh-vahnt-**gard** OR ah vahn **gard**)
Axonometric (ak-suh-noh-**meh**-trik)
Baroque (ba-**roke**)
Bartholdi (bar-**thal**-dee)
Bas relief (bah-rih-**leef**)
Bauhaus (**bow**-house [the *ow* sound is as in *cow*])
Bayeux (bay-**yoo** OR bay-**yer**)
Bernini, Gianlorenzo (ber-**nee**-nee, jahn-loh **ren** zoh)
Boccioni, Umberto (bah **chioh**-nee, oom-**bair**-toh)
Borromini (bore-oh-**mee**-nee)
Bosch, Hieronymus (bosh, hir-**own**-uh-mus)
Boscoreale (bos-kor-ee-**ah**-lay)
Botticelli (bah-tih-**chel**-ee)
Brancusi, Constantin (brahn-**koo**-zee, **kahn**-stuhn-teen)
Bronzino (bron-**zee**-no)
Brunelleschi, Filippo (broon–el-**les**-kee, fih-**lee**-po)
Buon fresco (bwon **fres**-ko)
Byzantine (**biz**-uhn-teen)
Camera obscura (**kam**-er-uh ob-**skyoor**-ah)
Campanile (com-pah-**nee**-lay)
Caravaggio (car-ah-**vah**-jyoh)
Caricature (**care**-ih-kuh-cher)
Caryatid (care-ee-**at**-id)
Casein (**kay**-seen)
Cézanne (say-**zahn**)
Chiaroscuro (kee-ar-oh-**skoor**-oh)
Chihuly, Dale (chi-**hoo**-lee, Dale)
Chryselephantine (kris-el-uh-**fan**-tin)
Cire perdue (**seer** per-**doo**)
Cloisonné (kloy-za-**nay** OR klwa-zo-**nay**)
Colosseum (kahl-uh-**see**-um)
Constantinople (kon-stan-teh-**no**-pull)
Conté (**kawn**-tay)
Contrapposto (kohn-trah-**pah**-stoh)
Couch (Kooch)
Cuneiform (**kyoo**-nih-form OR **kyoo**-nee-uh-form)
Cycladic (sih-**kla**-dik)
Cyclopean (sigh-kluh-**pee**-uhn)
Dada (dah-dah)
Daguerre, Louis (duh-**gair**, **Loo**-ee)
Dalí, Salvador (**dah**-lee OR dah-**lee**, **sal**-vuh-dore)
David, Jacques-Louis (dah-**veed**, **zhahk**-loo-**ee**)
Dehn, Adolf (dane)
De Stijl (duh **style**)
Delacroix, Eugène (deh-luh-**krwa**, oo-**zhen**)
Dionysos (dye-uh-**nayh**-sus)
Donatello (don-ah-**tell**-oh)
Doryphoros (doe-**rif**-or-os)
Dürer, Albrecht (**dur**-er, awl-brecht)
Duchamp, Marcel (doo-**shaw**, mar-**sel**)
Eiffel (**eye**-fuhl)
Elgin (**el**-gin [the 'g' is hard like in gun] OR **el**-jin)
Entasis (**en**-tuh-sis)
Equestrian (eh-**kwes**-tree-uhn)
Estes, Richard (**es**-teez)
Etruscan (ih-**truss**-kun)
Exekias (eh-**zee**-kee-us)
Fabergé (fab-er-**zhey**)
Façade (fuh-**sahd**)
Fauvism (**foh**-vism)
Fragonard, Jean-Honoré (**fra**-goh-nar, zhon-oh-no-**ray**)
Gehry, Frank (**gair**-ee)

Gelatin (**jel**-uh-tin)
Genre (**zhahn**-ruh)
Gentileschi, Artemisia (jen-til-**es**-kee, ar-teh-**mee**-zhyuh)
Géricault, Théodore (zhair-ee-**koh**, tey-oh-**dore**)
Giclée (jee-**clay** OR zhee-**clay**)
Giotto (**jot**-toh OR joht-toh)
Giza (**gee**-zah [hard 'g' as in gun])
Goya (**goy**-uh)
Gouache (gwash)
Gravure (gruh-**vyoor**)
Guernica (**gwair**-nih-kuh)
Hagia Sophia (**hah**-gee-uh [hard 'g' as in gun] so-**fee**-uh, OR **hey**-jee-uh so-**fee**-ah)
Hammurabi (hah-moo-**rah**-bee)
Hardouin-Mansart, Jules (ar-**dwan**-man-**sar**, zhool)
Hierarchical (high-uh-**rahr**-kih-kuhl)
Hieratic (high-uh-**rat**-ik)
Hieroglyphics (high-roh-**glif**-iks OR high-er-uh-**glif**-iks)
Hokusai (hoh-ku-**sigh** OR **hoh**-kuh-sigh)
Huichol (**wee**-chole)
Hydria (**high**-dree-uh)
Hyksos (**hick**-sohs)
Iconography (eye-kuh-**nog**-ruh-fee)
Iktinos (ik-**tie**-nohs)
Intaglio (in-**tah**-lyoh)
Ionic (eye-**on**-ik)
Kallicrates (kuh-**lik**-rah-teez)
Kandinksy, Wassily (can-**din**-skee, vah-**see**-lee)
Khufu (**koo**-foo)
Knossos (**nos**-ohs OR kuh-**nos**-ohs)
Kore (**kor**-ey)
Kouros (**koor**-os)
Krater (**kray**-ter)
Kylix (**kayh**-liks)
Labyrinth (**lab**-uh-rinth)
Lamassu (la-**mah**-soo)
Laocoön (lay-**ahk**-oh-on)
Lascaux (lass-**koh**)
Leonardo da Vinci (lay-oh-**nar**-doh dah **vin**-chee)
Lekythos (**lek**-uh-thos)
Les Demoiselles d'Avignon (lay day-mwa-**zel** dah-vee-**nyo**)
Lichtenstein, Roy (**lik**-tuhn-steen)
Lin, Maya Ying (lin, **my**-uh yeeng)
Lithography (lih-**thog**-ruh-fee)
Louvre (loovre)
Manet, Eduoard (ma-**nay**, ey-**dwahr**)
Marat (mah-**rah**)
Marcus Aurelius (**mar**-kus oh-**ree**-lee-us)
Masaccio (ma-**sah**-chee-oh)
Matisse, Henri (ma-**teece**, on-**ree**)
Medici (**med**-ih-chee)
Megaron (**meg**-uh-ron)
Menes (**mee**-neez)
Menkaure (men-**cow**-ray)
Mesopotamia (mes-uh-puh-**tay**-mee-uh)
Metope (**met**-uh-pee)
Michelangelo Buonarroti (my-kuhl-**an**-juh-loh, bwan-nah-**roh**-tee)
Minoan (mih-**noh**-uhn)
Minotaur (**min**-oh-tore)
Mihrab (**mee**-rahb)
Mondrian, Piet (**mohn**-dree-ahn, peet)
Monet, Claude (moh-**nay**, klohd)
Monticello (mon-tih-**chel**-oh)
Mosque (mosk)
Munch, Edvard (moonk, **ed**-vard)
Mycenae (my-**see**-nee OR my-**see**-nayh)
Mycenaean (my-sih-**nee**-uhn)
Nadar (nah-**dar**)
Nebuchadnezzar (neh-boo-kahd-**nez**-zar)
Nefertiti (nef-er-**tee**-tee)
Niello (nee-**el**-oh)
Nîmes (neem)
Oculus (**ock**-yuh-luhs)
Oenochoe (ee-**nok**-oh-ee)
Oldenburg, Claes (**ohl**-den-burg, klahs)
Orthogonal (or-**thog**-uh-nal)
Papyrus (puh-**pie**-ruhs)
Parthenon (**par**-thuh-non)
Pastel (pa-**stel**)
Patina (puh-**tee**-nuh)
Pei, I. M. (pay)
Pendentive (pen-**den**-tiv)
Perikles (**pear**-ih-kleez)
Picasso, Pablo (pih-**kah**-so, Pah-bloh)
Pietà (pee-ey-**tah**)
Plein air (**plane air**)
Pointillism (**point**-til-iz-um OR **pwan**-til-iz-um)
Pollock, Jackson (**pah**-luck)
Polykleitos (polly-**klayh**-tus)
Pompeii (pom-**pay**)
Pont du Gard (pohn-dew-**gar**)
Pontormo, Jacopo da (pon-**tore**-moh, **yah**-kopo da)

Poseidon (poe-**sigh**-den)
Raphael (rahf-eye–**el**)
Rauschenberg, Robert (**row**-shun-berg [the *ow* sound is as in *cow*])
Reims (reems)
Reliquary (**rel**-ih-kwair-ee)
Rembrandt van Rijn (**rem**-brandt van **rine**)
Renaissance (**ren**-uh-sahnce)
Renoir, Pierre August (ren-**wahr**, pee-**err** oh-**goost**)
Repoussé (reh-poo-**say**)
Rococo (ruh-**koh**-koh)
Rodin (roh-**dan**)
Rubens (**roo**-bens)
San Vitale (sahn vih-**tah**-lee)
Sarcophagus (sar-**koff**-uh-gus)
Sardanapalus (sar-duh-**nah**-puh-luhs)
Serigraphy (sih-**rig**-ruh-fee)
Seurat, George (si-**rah**, zhorzh)
Sfumato (sfoo-**mah**-toh)
Steenwyck (**steen**-wick)
Steichen (**sty**-kun)
Stele (**stee**-lee)
Stieglitz (**steeg**-lits)
Sumer (**soo**-mer)
Tesserae (**tes**-uh-rye OR **tes**-uh-ree)
Titian (**tish**-uhn)
Toulouse-Lautrec, Henri de (too-**loos**-loh-**trek**, on-**ree** de)
Triptych (**trip**-tik)
Tusche (toosh)
Typography (tie-**pog**-rah-fee)
Tutankhamen (toot-ahng-**kah**-muhn)
Ur (er)
Utzon, Joern (**oot**-zuhn, yohrn)
Van Eyck, Jan (van **ike**, yahn)
Van Gogh (van **go**)
Vanitas (vahn-ee-tahs)
Velázquez (veh-**lahs**-kez)
Vermeer, Jan (vur-**meer**, yahn)
Versailles (vair-**sigh**)
Watteau (**wah**-toh)
Willendorf (**vil**-en-dorf)
Zeus (zoos)
Zeuxis (**zook**-is)
Ziggurat (**zig**-uh-rat)

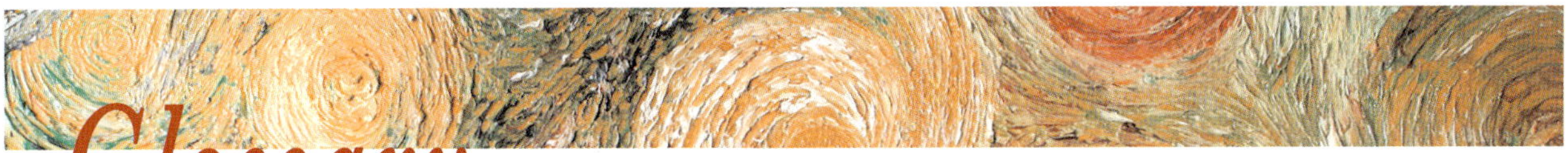

Glossary

The glossary can be viewed on the website.

Abstract art: Art whose forms depart from optical reality by being simplified or distorted in some way. Totally abstract art is called nonrepresentational or nonobjective.

Abstract Expressionism: A style of art that developed in the late 1940s in which artists represented personal expression using abstracted forms.

Academic style: A realistic style of painting that adhered to the rules of the French Academy in the nineteenth century.

Acrylic paint: A durable and water soluble paint made by combining **pigments** with a synthetic resin **medium**.

Action Painting: A type of Abstract Expressionism that emphasizes the gestural movements of the artist, such as dripping and flinging the paint onto the canvas.

Additive process: 1) In color, when the various colors of the visible light spectrum are added together the result is white light. 2) In sculpture, the creation of a form by construction, assemblage, or modeling.

Aerial perspective: See **Perspective**.

Allegory: A story or image that refers to something else through symbolic imagery.

Amazons: Mythical race of warrior-women.

Ambulatory: In a church, a continuation of the side aisles that become a passageway around the **apse**.

Amphitheatre: A circular or oval arena with tiered seating used for various spectacles and events. The Colosseum in Rome is an amphitheatre.

Amphora: A large vase for the transport and storage of liquids.

Aperture: An opening. In photography, the camera lens opening.

Apostles: The twelve disciples of Christ (attributes in parentheses): Peter (*keys, upside down cross, cock*), Andrew (*X-shaped cross*), John (*chalice with snake, eagle, book*), Matthew (*angel, axe, book*), Thomas (*set-square, ruler, girdle, spear or dagger*), Bartholomew (*knife, his skin*), James the Greater (*scallop shell, sword, staff*), James the Less (*fuller's club, hatter's bow*), Simon (*saw, cross*), Philip (*cross*), Thaddeus [Jude] (*club, halberd or lance*), and Judas (*bag of silver coins, dark profile*).

Apotropaic: Having the power to ward off evil influences.

Apse: A semicircular projection of a building, especially in a church.

Aquatint: An **intaglio** printmaking process that uses powdered particles of resin to give the print a granular appearance.

Aqueduct: A structure for transporting water from its source to a city or town.

Arcade: A series of arches on columns or piers.

Archaic period: The period of ancient Greek art (c. 600 – 480 BCE) before the Classical period.

Architrave (also called an epistyle): In classical architecture, the lower portion of the **entablature** that rests on the columns and supports the **frieze**.

Art Deco: An art style of the 1920s and 1930s that integrated organic and geometric forms.

Artist's proof: In printmaking, a trial print that the artist uses to see the progress of his/her work.

Art Nouveau: A late nineteenth and early twentieth-century art movement characterized by curvilinear organic forms based on nature.

Assemblage: An additive sculptural process in which various materials and objects are combined.

Atmospheric perspective: See **Perspective**.

Atrium: A courtyard, usually colonnaded, within a building or leading into a building.

Avant-garde: Innovators in a particular field. From the French for "advance guard" (in a platoon).

Axonometric view: An architectural drawing that shows a cutaway view of a building from an angle in a three-dimensional format to reveal the exterior and part of the interior.

Balance: Arranging forms to achieve equilibrium or harmony.

Baroque: A style in seventeenth-century Europe typically characterized by theatricality, dramatic lighting, curvilinear forms, movement, and immediacy.

Barrel vault: A semi cylindrical roof constructed on the arch principle. It is essentially a deep arch over an oblong space.

Basilica: A Roman hall of justice, later an early Christian church.

Bas relief: In sculpture, low relief in which the forms project only slightly from the background plane.

Bauhaus: A German school of architecture in the 1930s that emphasized the unity of art, architecture, and design.

Bema: Raised platform from which Greek orators spoke. Later the altar area in a church.

Biomorphic: A form in art that has the appearance of a living organism.

Binder: A substance that that holds **pigments** together and allows them to adhere to the **support**.

Bisque firing: In **ceramics**, a first firing that hardens the vessel.

Black-figure technique: A vase painting technique in which the painted figures end up black against a red background after a three-stage firing process.

Bronze: A metal alloy of copper and tin.

Burin: A sharp cutting tool used by engravers.

Burnish: To polish by rubbing.

Burr: In the **drypoint** printmaking process, the ridge of metal that results from the engraving tool being pulled across the printing plate.

Buttress: A mass of masonry against the wall of a building to help support a vault. In Gothic cathedrals, **flying buttresses** are external supports that counteract the forces of the vault above the level of the aisles.

Byzantine: The period from the time of the Roman emperor Constantine who moved the capital from Rome to Byzantium (now Istanbul) in the fourth century to 1453, when the Turks conquered the city.

Camera obscura: Latin for "dark room." A precursor to the modern camera. A tiny hole in the wall of an enclosed space allows light through to project an inverted image on the opposite wall.

Campanile: A church bell tower that is a separate structure.

Cantilever: An architectural element that projects out horizontally with no vertical support at the far end.

Capital: The topmost part of a **column**.

Caricature: A picture or description, often humorous, that distorts or exaggerates certain characteristics.

Cartoon: A full-size drawing often done in preparation for a **fresco** painting or a **tapestry**.

Caryatid: A column in the form of a female figure.

Carving: Cutting a figure or object out of a solid material such as wood or stone (as opposed to **modeling**).

Casein: A protein-based substance derived from milk. Used as a **binder** for **tempera** paint.

Casting: Making a sculpture by pouring molten material into a mold that has an impression of the sculpture.

Cast iron: A hard but brittle alloy of iron and carbon produced in molds.

Catacombs: An underground network of tunnels and chambers used for burials.

Cella: The sanctuary of a classical temple containing the cult statue of the god.

Centaur: A mythological creature that is half human, half horse.

Central plan: In architecture, a building with a central space surrounded by symmetrical areas.

Ceramics: Objects formed out of clay and then hardened by being baked (**fired**) in a very hot oven (**kiln**).

Centering: A wooden framework used to support an arch, vault, or dome during construction.

Chalk: A type of soft limestone that can be pulverized and formed into sticks for drawing.

Charcoal: A black carbon substance produced by partially burning organic material (such as wood) that can be used a drawing tool.

Chiaroscuro: The gradations of light and dark in a painting or drawing used to create the illusion of three-dimensional form. Also called modeling.

Chiton: A long woolen tunic worn in ancient Greece.

Chryselephantine: Made of gold and ivory.

Ciborium: a receptacle to house the Host.

Classical period: The period in ancient Greece from around 480 to 400 BCE.

Cloisonné: A metalwork technique wherein small compartments (made by soldering metal strips on the edges of a metal background) are filled with enamel or glass.

Coffer: A sunken panel in a ceiling or vault.

Coiling: A method of ceramic construction in which long ropelike pieces of clay are wound in a spiral formation, and then smoothed, to form the vessel.

Colonnade: A row of columns supporting a roof or arcade.

Color-field painting: Paintings produced by pouring diluted paint onto unprimed canvas and then allowed to soak in.

Column: A cylindrical supporting element in architecture that usually consists of a base (sometimes omitted), shaft, and **capital**. Stone columns can be monolithic (made of a single piece of stone) or composed of **drums**. An engaged column is a column embedded in a wall.

Complementary colors: Pairs of colors that are opposite each other on the color wheel (see fig. 2.18), such as red and green or blue and orange.

Composition: The way an artist organizes the visual elements in a work of art.

Conceptual art: Art in which the idea is more important than its form or style.

Concrete: A construction material made of gravel, sand, water, and cement.

Constructivism: A Russian art movement of the 1920s that was dedicated to **nonrepresentational** means of communication for social purposes.

Conté crayon: A crayon made of graphite and clay used for drawing.

Contour line: A line that defines the outer shape of an object.

Contrapposto: The natural stance of the human body in which one leg is relaxed while the other bears most of the weight, causing one hip to be slightly higher than the other.

Contrast: An abrupt change, such as that caused by juxtaposed light and dark areas.

Cool color: A color such as blue or green that appears to be cool in temperature and to recede in space when contrasted with warm colors such as red and yellow.

Coptic. Pertaining to Egyptian Christian culture, especially in the 5th–8th centuries.

Corinthian order: One of the orders of Greek architecture where the capitals of the columns have the form of acanthus leaves. It is more ornate than the **Doric** or **Ionic** orders.

Cornice: The uppermost part of the **entablature** that frames the **pediment**.

Couch. In papermaking, to transfer (a sheet of pulp) from the wire mesh or screen to a felt blanket or board.

Cross-hatching: Intersecting sets of closely spaced parallel lines that create **modeling** and the illusion of three-dimensional form on a two-dimensional surface.

Cubism: A style of art that rejected naturalistic depictions and instead used fragmented forms and multiple points of view. It was introduced by Pablo Picasso and George Braque around 1908.

Cuneiform: A system of writing consisting of wedge-shaped characters that was used in ancient Mesopotamia.

Cyclopean walls: Walls composed of large irregularly shaped blocks of stone, so called because later peoples thought only a Cyclops could have built them. They are associated with Mycenaean architecture.

Cyclops: In Greek mythology, a one-eyed giant.

Dada: An "anti-art" art movement that arose during World War I. It challenged conventional art and the absurdities of modern civilization, and was often whimsical and humorous.

Der Blaue Reiter (The Blue Rider): A German Expressionist art movement in the early twentieth century (1911–1914) that focused on representing spiritual truth through abstract form and pure color.

Der Brücke (The Bridge): A German Expressionist art movement begun in 1905 that wanted to establish a new art style to bridge the past and the present. It was characterized by vivid arbitrary color, emotion, and distorted, often violent, forms.

De Stijl (The Style): A Dutch art movement founded in 1917 that expressed utopian ideals using simple geometric forms and primary colors.

Digital art: Art that is created with the assistance of a computer or other electronic instruments. It encompasses the fields of web design, graphic design, and digital photography, among others.

Divisionism: See **Pointillism**.

Dome: A roof with a hemispherical shape.

Doodle: An informal drawing (n.), or to make informal drawings (v.).

Doric order: One of the orders in Greek architecture characterized by columns with sharp-edged **fluting,** no bases, and simple bowl-like **capitals;** and a **frieze** consisting of **triglyphs** and **metopes**.

Drawing: The art of moving an implement that leaves a mark across a surface, such as paper. Drawings are typically made with **pencil**, **charcoal**, pen & ink, etc., and include the finished drawing, **cartoon**, **sketch**, and **doodle**.

Drum: 1) A circular wall that supports a **dome**. 2) One of the cylindrical blocks of stone that are used to build a **column**.

Drypoint: An **intaglio** printmaking process in which the **burin** is pulled back across the surface of the printing plate leaving a **burr**.

Elevation: An architectural drawing that shows the exterior façade of a building.

Embroidery: The art of sewing colored threads (needlework) onto fabric to form a design or composition.

Encaustic: A painting medium in which the pigment is mixed with molten wax and applied to the surface while hot.

Engraving: 1) The process of incising an image on a hard surface, such as a copper plate. 2) A print made by this process.

Entablature: The portion of a Greek architectural **order** above the column **capital**. The entablature consists of and **architrave**, **frieze**, and **cornice**.

Entasis: Slight swelling in the shaft of Classical columns.

Environmental Art: Art that uses the environment. It is outside and usually grand in scale with minimal form, often made with earth materials. It is sometimes called Earth art.

Equestrian portrait: A depiction of a person on horseback.

Etching: 1) A printmaking process in which the image is etched, or eaten into the metal plate by acid. 2) A print made by this process.

Eucharist: The sacrament of Holy Communion to commemorate the Last Supper, or the bread and wine used for the sacrament.

Evangelists, The Four: Authors of the Gospels: Matthew, Mark, Luke, and John. They are often accompanied by their symbols: Angel (Matthew), lion (Mark), ox (Luke), and eagle (John). Luke is the patron saint of painters.

Ex-voto: An object offered in gratitude for a favor or in fulfillment of a vow.

Façade: The front of a building.

Faience: A glazed ware made of powdered quartz covered with an alkaline (glass-like) glaze.

Fauvism: An early twentieth century art movement that had color as the dominant formal element, although the colors often did not represent the true colors of the objects in the painting.

Figurative art: Art that represents human or other figures.

Figure-ground relationship: The relationship between the main figure or subject and the rest of the composition or background.

Figure-ground reversal: A shift in the viewer's perception causing the figure and the background to switch back and forth so that what was the figure becomes the background and what was the background becomes the figure. (See the Rubin Vase, fig. 2.5).

Filigree: Thin wires of silver or gold intertwined and interlaced.

Film: A thin sheet of cellulose material coated with a photosensitive material.

Firing: Baking a clay object in a very hot oven (**kiln**).

Fluting: Vertical grooves on a **column**. In the **Doric order** the edges of the flutes are sharp; in the **Ionic order** they are flat.

Flying buttress: See **Buttress**.

Focal point: The place in a composition that is the center of visual attention.

Foreshortening: The illusion of figures or objects extending back from the picture plane by diminishing the size of their parts.

Form: The shape and mass of an object or figure.

Freestanding sculpture: Sculpture that is carved fully in the round and not attached to a wall or slab.

Fresco: A painting on plaster. With true fresco (*buon fresco*) the paint is applied while the plaster is still wet and it chemically binds with the plaster. With dry fresco (*fresco secco*), the paint is applied to plaster that has already dried.

Frieze: The portion of the entablature between the **architrave** and the **cornice**. It often contains **relief sculpture**.

Futurism: An early twentieth-century Italian art movement that emphasized the speed and movement of the modern industrial era.

Gelatin silver print: A photographic process used with black-and-white films and printing papers in which a suspension of silver salts in gelatin is coated onto acetate film or resin-coated paper.

Genre scene: A depiction of everyday life.

Gesso: A plaster mixture applied to a **support** or canvas and used as a surface for painting.

Gestural drawing: A quick sketch of a live model.

Giclée: A fine art print made from a digital source using a high quality inkjet printer.

Gild: To apply thin sheets of gold leaf to a surface.

Glass: A transparent or translucent hard, brittle material made by fusing sand with soda and lime at a high temperature and then cooling it rapidly.

Glaze: 1) A thin layer of translucent paint. 2) In ceramics, a thin liquid mixture applied to pottery that when fired forms a glassy surface.

Gorgons: Three hideous monster sisters, including Medusa.

Gothic: An art historical period from about 1150 to 1500 in Europe (to 1400 in Italy). In architecture, it is characterized by pointed arches.

Goths: Germanic tribe that settled north of the Black Sea in the 3d century. They split into the Visigoths and the Ostrogoths; the latter conquered Italy in the 5th century. The term *Gothic* derives from their name.

Gouache: A type of **watercolor** that is opaque rather than transparent because the pigment particles are larger and the ratio of pigment to water is greater.

Graffiti: Writing or images painted (usually spray painted) on walls or other surfaces in public places.

Granulation: The soldering of tiny spheres of gold (or silver) to a flat gold (or silver) background.

Graver: A cutting tool used by engravers.

Griffin: A mythological creature with the body of a lion and the head and wings of an eagle.

Graphic Design: Design for advertising or industry that uses **typography** and images to communicate an idea.

Greek cross plan: An architectural plan in the form of a cross with four arms of equal length.

Groin vault: A **vault** formed by the intersection of two **barrel vaults**.

Ground: A coating applied to a canvas or printmaking plate to prepare it for painting or etching.

Ground plan: The floor plan of a building.

Gum: A sticky substance found in many plants that is used to bind **pigments**.

Gum Arabic: A specific **gum** from the African acacia plant.

Gymnasium: In ancient Greece, a building complex with facilities for athletics, intellectual education, and socializing.

Hard-edged painting: A style of abstract painting characterized by sharp-edged geometric forms.

Hatching: Closely spaced fine lines that create the effect of **shading** or **modeling**.

Hellenistic: The period in the ancient world between the death of Alexander the Great in 323 BCE and the death of Cleopatra in 30 BCE.

Hierarchical or hieratic scale: Depicting more important figures larger than less important ones.

Hieroglyphic: A system of writing in ancient Egypt that used images of objects as characters.

High relief: Sculpture in which the figures project prominently from the background to which they are attached.

Himation: A cloak worn in ancient Greece.

Horizon line: In scientific or linear **perspective**, the imaginary line (often where the sky and earth seem to meet) where lines converge.

Hue: Color.

Humanism: In the **Renaissance** a secular philosophy that stressed education and knowledge (especially knowledge of Classical antiquity), the importance of the individual and the ability for self-determination (free will), and civic duty. It emphasized humankind as the standard by which all things are measured.

Hydria: A vessel for water.

Iconography: The analytic study of the symbolic, often religious meaning of objects, persons, or events depicted in works of arts.

Idealism: The representation of figures and forms that conforms to a concept of perfection rather than to reality.

IHS or IHC: First three letters of Christ's name in Greek (*Ihsus* or *Ihcuc*).

Illumination: See **Manuscript**.

Impasto: A thick application of paint on the canvas or other **support**.

Implied line: A line that is completed in the mind of the viewer.

Impressionism: A late nineteenth-century art movement that began in France and was characterized by capturing fleeting moments and the effects of light.

INRI: Latin initials for *Jesus Nazarenus Rex Judaeorum* (Jesus of Nazareth King of the Jews).

Installation: A work of art created for a specific gallery space or outdoor site.

Intaglio: Any of several printmaking processes in which lines are incised into the printing plate. **Engraving**, **drypoint**, **etching**, **aquatint**, and **mezzotint** are all intaglio processes.

Intensity: See **Saturation**.

Ionic order: One of the orders in Greek architecture characterized by columns with flat-edged **fluting**, bases, and **capitals** in the shape of scrolls or **volutes**; and a continuous **frieze**.

Jamb: In architecture, a vertical element on either side of a doorway.

Kiln: An oven used to bake **ceramics** at very hot temperatures.

Kinetic art: Art that moves.

Kitsch: Art that is overly sentimental and commercial.

Kore: Greek for "maiden." A sculpture of a clothed female figure in **Archaic** Greek art.

Kouros: Greek for "male youth." A sculpture of a nude male figure in **Archaic** Greek art.

Krater: A large open vessel used for mixing wine with water.

Kufic: Relating to or being an angular form of the Arabic alphabet used by early Muslims to record the Qur'an.

Kylix: A type of drinking cup.

Labyrinth: A maze.

Lamassu: In ancient Assyrian art, a hybrid creature with a human head and the winged body of a lion or bull.

Lantern: A structure crowning a dome that lets in light.

Lapis lazuli: A semi-precious blue stone found mostly in Afghanistan. The polished stones are used in jewelry. It was ground to form the blue pigment known as ultramarine.

Latin cross plan: An architectural plan in the form of a cross that has one arm longer than the other three.

Lens: A transparent object with at least one curved surface that results in a convergence of light rays passing through it. The human eye and cameras have lenses that focus images.

Linear: A style of art in which lines are used to depict figures and forms with precise outlines.

Linear perspective: See **Perspective**.

Linocut: A form of relief printmaking in which the design is carved in a block of linoleum. The resulting print is also called a linocut.

Lintel: The upper horizontal portion of a doorway or opening.

Lithograph: A print made from the lithography process in which involves drawing the image with a greasy material on a polished stone.

Local Color: An object's actual color in white light. (See also **Optical color**.)

Logo: A symbol or design used as a company **trademark**.

Longitudinal plan: An architectural plan in which the parts of the building are organized around a central axis.

Lost wax technique (cire-perdue): A method of casting bronze (and other materials) in which a mold is made around an image modeled in wax. The wax is then melted out and replaced with bronze.

Magazine: Storeroom for food or munitions.

Mannerism: A style of art in the sixteenth century characterized by elongated forms, cramped compositions, and vivid colors.

Manuscript: A handwritten book made in the **Middle Ages** or **Renaissance**. If it has illustrations, it is called an illuminated manuscript.

Martyr: Someone who dies for their faith.

Mass: The bulk of a three-dimensional object, or the implied bulk of an object on a two dimensional surface.

Meander pattern: A zigzag key-like pattern.

Medium: 1) A material used to create a work of art. 2) In painting, a liquid added to **pigment** so that it can be applied to the **support**.

Megalith: A large stone used in prehistoric monuments.

Megapixel: One million pixels, used as a measure of resolution in digital cameras. (A pixel [short for "**picture element**] is a very small point of data).

Megaron: The principal hall of a Mycenaean palace with a hearth in the center.

Memento mori: A phrase or image, such as a skull, that is a reminder of death.

Metope: An architectural element consisting of a square area, often filled with relief sculpture, between two **triglyphs** on a **Doric** frieze.

Mezzotint: A type of print in which the plate is pitted with a special tool.

Middle Ages: The period in western history from the fall of the Roman empire in the late 5th century to the Renaissance in the 15th century.

Minimalism: A **nonrepresentational** style of art in the 1960s (predominately American) characterized by few visual elements.

Minotaur: A creature borne by Pasiphae (wife of King Minos of Crete) that was half human and half bull.

Mixed media: The combination of two or more media in a work of art.

Modeling: 1) The use of **hatching** or **chiaroscuro** to create the illusion of three-dimensional form on a two-dimensional surface. 2) Shaping a form in a pliable material such as clay or plaster.

Mosaic: A decoration composed of small pieces of colored glass, stone or other material.

Mosque: A place of prayer in the Islamic religion. The word derives from the Arabic for "place of prostration."

Mummification: The process of preserving the body, usually by means of desiccation.

Narthex: The lobby or entrance area to a church.

Naturalism: A style of art that attempts to depict things as they actually appear in nature.

Naumachia: A mock naval battle in the flooded arena of a theatre or amphitheatre.

Nave: The central aisle of a church that leads to the altar.

Neoclassicism: A late eighteenth and early nineteenth-century art movement characterized by a revival of the classical style of ancient Greece and Rome.

Niello: A process that darkens certain areas of silver objects.

Nonobjective art: Nonrepresentional art.

Nonrepresentational: Totally abstract.

Oculus: A round central opening in a dome.

Offset lithography: A printing process where an inked image is transferred from a plate to a rubber-coated fabric (the blanket) wrapped around a cylinder and then printed on paper. (The term offset refers to the fact that the image isn't printed directly from the plate).

Oinochoe: A wine pitcher or jug with a curved handle.

Oil paint: A slow drying and flexible paint made by mixing **pigments** with an oil medium.

Op Art: A style of art from the 1960s characterized by perceived vibrating forms and disorienting perspective.

Optical color: The perceived color of an object, which varies according to atmospheric and other light conditions. (See also **Local color**).

Order: One of the architectural systems (**Doric**, **Ionic**, and **Corinthian**) used by the ancient Greeks and Romans. An architectural order consists of three basic parts: a base or platform, a **colonnade**, and an **entablature**. Other orders, such as Tuscan and Composite, were later developed based on these three original orders.

Orthogonals: Perceived lines that converge at the **vanishing point** in scientific **perspective**.

Outsider art: Art created by self-taught artists living outside the mainstream of society.

Palaistra: In ancient Greece, a complex of rooms around a court, used for educational or athletic (especially boxing or wrestling) purposes; often attached to a gymnasium.

Panel painting: Painting on a wooden panel.

Papyrus: A type of paper in the ancient world made from the reeds of the papyrus plant.

Parchment: Treated animal skin prepared as a surface for painting or writing.

Pastel: 1) A drawing stick or crayon made of dry pigments, chalk, and gum. 2) A drawing made with pastels.

Patina: A fine crust that forms on bronze and copper as a result of oxidation. It is often greenish in color.

Pediment: The triangular area defined by the **cornice**.

Pendentive: A dome on pendentives is as though you cut off the top of a groin vault and place the dome on top. The triangular areas left are the pendentives.

Pencil: A drawing implement made of a rod of graphite encased in wood.

Peplos: A one-piece mantle worn by women in ancient Greece.

Peribolos: A wall or colonnade enclosing a sacred area. Also, the area itself.

Personification: An abstract idea or concept represented by a human figure.

Perspective: A method of showing depth on a two-dimensional surface. In scientific perspective (also called linear perspective), real or implied parallel lines (orthogonals) converge at one or more vanishing points to give the illusion of recession into space. Objects intended to be further away from the viewer are shown smaller. In atmospheric perspective (also called aerial perspective) forms in the distance are shown less distinct and bluish in color.

Photography: The capturing of an image onto a light sensitive surface such as photographic film or a digital sensor.

Photorealism: A style of painting developed in the 1960s characterized by precisely depicted forms that give the effect of a photograph.

Pier: In architecture, a rectangular supporting element.

Pigment: A powdered material used to give color to inks and paints.

Pilaster: A flat vertical element projecting from a wall. It usually does not have a supporting function.

Planographic printing: Any method of printing from a flat surface, such as **lithography**.

Plein-air painting: Painting done outdoors on site.

Pointillism: A late nineteenth-century style of painting developed by the French artist George Seurat in which small dots of pure unmixed color are applied to the canvas and intended to fuse or mix in the mind's eye. Also called **Divisionism**.

Pop Art: A style of art in the late 1950s and 1960s that utilized commercial and popular imagery, such as Campbell's soups cans or images of famous people.

Porcelain: A fine translucent **ceramic** made from white clay that is fired at a high temperature.

Post-and-lintel construction: A building technique in which two vertical elements (posts) support a horizontal element (lintel).

Post-canonical: Written after the Bible.

Post Impressionism: A style of painting in the late nineteenth century that evolved from **Impressionism**. It is characterized by color and brushwork used for expressive (rather than decorative or factual) means.

Postmodernism: A reaction against formal modernism, it encompasses many historical styles.

Potsherd (Potshard): A broken piece of pottery.

Pottery: Bowls, dishes, cups, etc., made of clay that have been hardened by heat.

Primary colors: Colors that cannot be created from a mixture of other colors and from which all other colors are made. With pigments, they are red, blue, and yellow.

Print: A work of art made by one of the printmaking processes such as **engraving** or **etching**. A print can also be a photograph made from a negative.

Proof: See **Artist's proof**.

Proportion: The relation of parts to the whole with regard to size. Compare **Scale**.

Propylaia: An entrance gateway to a sacred precinct.

Putto (plural putti): A cherub-like young boy.

Readymade: An ordinary object that when put in a new context and given a title by an artist becomes a work of art.

Realism: 1) Portraying objects as they actually are. 2) A mid nineteenth-century movement in art characterized by everyday mundane subject matter.

Red-figure technique: A vase painting technique in which the painted background ends up black after a three-stage firing process leaving the figures in the natural reddish color of the pottery.

Reinforced concrete: Concrete with steel reinforcement bars (rebar) or mesh imbedded in it.

Relic: A body part, article of clothing, a piece of an instrument of martyrdom or other item associated with a saint. They are often thought to have special powers to heal the body and the soul.

Reliquary: A receptacle to house a **relic**. They are often elaborate and made of precious materials.

Relief printing: Any printmaking process wherein any area of the plate not to be printed is carved away leaving the projecting areas to form the image.

Relief sculpture: Sculpture whose figures are only partially carved out so that they are still attached to the background. Relief sculpture can be high relief, low (bas) relief, or sunken relief where the figures are carved into the surface of the stone or other material.

Renaissance: The period of history that began in Italy around 1400 and lasted through the sixteenth century. It was characterized by a renewed interest in Classical antiquity.

Repousée: A metalworking technique in which a malleable metal is ornamented or shaped by hammering from the reverse side.

Rib: In architecture, a structural element that helps support a **groin vault**.

Rococo: An artistic style of the eighteenth century characterized by delicate curvilinear forms, pastel colors, and often frivolous subject matter.

Romanesque: An artistic style of the **Middle Ages** that preceded the **Gothic** style. In architecture it was characterized by round arches and barrel vaults.

Romanticism: An art movement in the early nineteenth century characterized by dramatic, emotional content and rich painterly colors. It arose in reaction to **Neoclassicism**.

Rose window: A large circular window decorated with stained glass in a petal-like pattern.

Rhythm: The effect created by repeating forms, colors, or other elements in a composition.

Sarcophagus: Literally, "consumer of flesh," it is a large coffin (usually stone), often decorated with relief sculpture.

Saturation: The degree of purity of a color. Also called intensity.

Scale: The relative size of an object compared to other objects. Compare **Proportion**.

Scientific perspective: See **Perspective**.

Screenprinting: A printmaking process where paint or ink is forced through the open areas of a stencil that has been applied to a fine mesh fabric, such as silk, stretched taut on a frame. Also called silkscreen printing or serigraphy.

Secondary color: A color formed by mixing two primary colors in equal amounts. With pigments, the secondary colors are orange, green, and violet.

Section: An architectural drawing that shows a building as though it has been sliced in two vertically to reveal the interior.

Serigraphy: See **Screenprinting**.

Sfumato: Literally, "vanished in smoke," it refers to the smoky, hazy atmosphere that softens outlines, typical of the paintings by Leonardo da Vinci.

Shade: A color modified by the addition of another color, usually black, resulting in a **hue** of lower value. For instance, the addition of black to red produces maroon. Compare **Tint**.

Shading: A gradual change from light to dark on a surface.

Shape: In a two-dimensional work, an area defined by a border.

Shutter: In photography, the device for opening and closing the **aperture** to allow light onto the film or sensor.

Shutter speed: How long the **shutter** of a camera stays open.

Sibyl: In ancient times a woman who foresaw the future.

Silkscreen: A print made by the silkscreen process. See **Screenprinting**.

Silverpoint: A method of drawing using a stylus made of silver to produce fine, but faint lines.

Simultaneous contrast: The juxtaposition of two **complementary colors**, which makes them seem brighter and more intense than when seen alone.

Sketch: A quickly executed drawing done to get an idea or an image down on paper.

Slip: A mixture of fine clay, water and sometimes **pigment** used to decorate pottery.

Spoof: A humorous imitation of something, such as a work of art.

Stained glass: Windows made of pieces of colored glass held in place with lead strips.

Stainless steel: Steel made rust resistant by the addition of chrome and other materials.

Steel: An alloy of mostly iron to which carbon and other elements have been added to make it stronger and less brittle.

Stele: An inscribed vertical stone slab that marks something such as a grave.

Stippling: The use of closely spaced dots to create a form or pattern.

Style: A typical manner of artistic expression that is characteristic of an individual or group of individuals, geographical region, or era; the way an artwork looks.

Stylized: When the depiction of a figure or form departs from optical reality to conform to artistic conventions or to emphasize certain characteristics.

Stylobate: The top step of the platform of a Greek temple. It supports the columns.

Subtractive process: 1) With color, when the various pigment colors are mixed together the result is a darker and duller color. The more colors added together, the closer to black the resulting color becomes because less light is reflected. 2) In sculpture, the carving process in which material is taken away to form the image. Compare **Additive process**.

Support: The two-dimensional surface on which an artist works, such as canvas, paper, a panel of wood, or a wall.

Surrealism: An art movement that began in the 1920s characterized by dream imagery, bizarre juxtapositions, and chance occurrences.

Symmetry: When two halves of a composition are aesthetically balanced in terms of size, shape, color, and/or the placement of forms.

Tapestry: A design woven into a thick fabric with colored yarns.

Tempera: A type of paint in which the binding medium is egg yolk or **casein**.

Tesserae: Small cubes of stone, glass, etc., used in mosaic work.

Texture: The visual (implied) or tactile (actual) surface quality of a form or object.

Tholos: A circular domed structure.

Tint: A color modified by the addition of another color, usually white, resulting in a **hue** of higher value. For instance, the addition of white to red produces pink. Compare **Shade**.

Trademark: A symbol, word, or words that represent a company or product.

Transept: The "arm" of a church that intersects the **nave** at a right angle.

Triglyph: An architectural element on a **Doric frieze** that alternates with the **metopes**. It consists of three vertical projections (glyphs) that recall the end of a wooden beam.

Triptych: A panel painting in three sections. Often the two outer sections (wings) are smaller and hinged so that they can close over the larger central panel.

Trompe l'oeil: French for "fools the eye." A type of super illusionistic painting that attempts to deceive viewers into believing they are seeing real objects rather than representations of them.

Tusche: A greasy material used for drawing on a **lithography** stone.

Tympanum: the semicircular area or lunette over the doorway of a church, defined by an arch above and a lintel below. It often contains sculpture.

Typography: The art of arranging and setting type for printing.

Unity: The oneness or wholeness of a work of art.

Value: The degree of lightness (high value) or darkness (low value) in a color.

Value contrast: The degrees of difference between **shades** of gray.

Vanishing point: In scientific or linear **perspective**, the point on the **horizon line** where parallel lines appear to converge.

Vanitas: A painting whose subject matter deals with the vanity, fragility, and transience of human life. Typical objects in a *vanitas* painting are skulls, timepieces, musical instruments, and wilting flowers. The term derives from Ecclesiastes 1:2 ("Vanity of vanities . . .").

Vault: An arched roof or ceiling usually made of stone, brick, or **concrete**. See also **Barrel vault** and **Groin vault**.

Vehicle: A liquid such as water or oil used to mix **pigments** for painting.

Vellum: A high quality parchment made from calfskin, kidskin, or lambskin.

Volume: The mass or bulk of a three-dimensional object, or the amount of space it contains.

Volute: A scroll-like architectural element typically found on **Ionic** capitals.

Warm color: A color such as red or yellow that appears to be warm in temperature and to advance in space when contrasted with cool colors such as blue and green.

Warp: The vertical threads of a loom or woven cloth.

Wash: A thin, watery layer of paint, especially **watercolor**.

Watercolor: A painting **medium** in which the **pigments** are suspended in a solution of water and **gum Arabic**.

Weaving: A way of making fabrics by interlacing horizontal and vertical threads or fibers.

Weft: The horizontal threads of a loom or woven cloth. Also called woof.

Weight shift: See **Contrapposto**.

Woodcut: 1) A relief printmaking process in which a wood block is carved so that those parts not intended to print are cut away, leaving the design raised. 2) A print made by this process.

Wood engraving: 1) A relief printmaking process in which fine lines are carved into a wood block using the harder end grain. 2) A print made by this process.

Woof: See **Weft**.

Ziggurat: A rectangular religious structure in ancient Mesopotamia composed of several stacked platforms of diminishing sizes.

Websites

WebMuseum: www.ibiblio.org/wm

Mother of All Art: www.umich.edu/~motherha

Timeline of art history: www.metmuseum.org/toah/

Art Dictionary: www.artlex.com

Art Cylcopedia: www.artcyclopedia.com

Color: http://www.colormatters.com

Bad art: www.museumofbadart.org

Ancient Rome: http://www.romereborn.virginia.edu

Lascaux cave, video tour: tp://www.lascaux.culture.fr/#/fr/00.xml

Optical Illusions: http://www.michaelbach.de/ot

Bronze casting: www.youtube.com/watch?v=gVe3VeQfyzw

Printmaking:

Color woodblock printing: http://www.youtube.com/watch?v=dliF74ojOho

Offset lithography: http://www.youtube.com/watch?v=ClbQL_Oso40

Giclée: http://www.youtube.com/watch?v=2LmtQti5QgE

Intaglio: www.youtube.com/watch?v=SNKn4PORGBI

Lithography: www.youtube.com/watch?v=JHw5_1Hopsc

Relief: www.youtube.com/watch?v=O0skLwaFpn0

Screenprinting: www.youtube.com/watch?v=wogKeYH2wEE

Japanese printmaking: www.fitzmuseum.cam.ac.uk/pharos/sections/making_art/index_japan.html

Street art and graffiti:

http://woostercollective.com

Banksy: www.banksy.co.uk

Above: www.goabove.com

Art of graffiti: graffiti.keusta.net

Worldwide graffiti gallery: puregraffiti.com/art

TIME collection of graffiti: www.time.com/time/archive/collections/0,21428,c_graffiti,00.shtml

Art Crimes: www.graffiti.org

Ancient graffiti in Saudi Arabia: www.splendidarabia.com/location/riyadh/graffiti/

Typography: http://www.rsub.com/typographic/

Vatican collections: http://mv.vatican.va/3_EN/pages/MV_Visite.html

Sistine Chapel: http://www.stumbleupon.com/su/1kpcQm/www.vatican.va/various/cappelle/sistina_vr/index.html

Index

C

N

Q

R

Y

Z